Against Throne and Altar

Modern republicanism – distinguished from its classical counterpart by its commercial character and jealous distrust of those in power, by its use of representative institutions, and by its employment of a separation of powers and a system of checks and balances – owes an immense debt to the republican experiment conducted in England between 1649, when Charles I was executed, and 1660, when Charles II was crowned. Though abortive, this experiment left a legacy in the political science articulated both by its champions, John Milton, Marchamont Nedham, and James Harrington, and by its sometime opponent and ultimate supporter, Thomas Hobbes. This volume examines these four thinkers, situates them with regard to the novel species of republicanism first championed in the early 1500s by Niccolò Machiavelli, and examines the debt that he and they owed the Epicurean tradition in philosophy and the political science crafted by the Arab philosophers Alfarabi, Avicenna, and Averroës.

Paul A. Rahe holds a B.A. from Yale University, an M.A. in *Litterae Humaniores* from University of Oxford, and a Ph.D. in ancient history from Yale University. He is the author, most recently, of *Soft Despotism, Democracy's Drift: Montesquieu, Rousseau, and Tocqueville on the Modern Prospect* (2009) and *Montesquieu and the Logic of Liberty: War, Religion, Commerce, Climate, Terrain, Technology, Uneasiness of Mind, the Spirit of Political Vigilance, and the Foundations of the Modern Republic* (2009). He has co-edited *Montesquieu's Political Science: Essays on the Spirit of Laws* and edited *Machiavelli's Liberal Republican Legacy*, and he has published a host of articles in journals and chapters in edited books. Professor Rahe is the Charles O. Lee and Louise K. Lee Chair in the Western Heritage and professor of History and Political Science at Hillsdale College.

Against Throne and Altar

*Machiavelli and Political Theory under
the English Republic*

PAUL A. RAHE

Hillsdale College

CAMBRIDGE
UNIVERSITY PRESS

CAMBRIDGE UNIVERSITY PRESS
Cambridge, New York, Melbourne, Madrid, Cape Town, Singapore,
São Paulo, Delhi, Dubai, Tokyo, Mexico City

Cambridge University Press
The Edinburgh Building, Cambridge CB2 8RU, UK

Published in the United States of America by Cambridge University Press, New York

www.cambridge.org
Information on this title: www.cambridge.org/9780521123952

First published 2008
First paperback edition 2009

A catalogue record for this publication is available from the British Library

Library of Congress Cataloguing in Publication Data

Rahe, Paul Anthony.
Against throne and altar : Machiavelli and political theory under the English Republic /
Paul A. Rahe.
p. cm.
Includes bibliographical references and index.
ISBN 978-0-521-88390-0 (hardback)
1. Machiavelli, Niccolò, 1469–1527 – Influence. 2. Republicanism – Great Britain – History –
17th century. 3. Great Britain – Politics and government – 1649–1660. 4. Great Britain –
History – Commonwealth and Protectorate, 1649–1660. I. Title.
JC143.M4R35 2008
320.092′ 241–dc22   2007031033

ISBN 978-0-521-88390-0 Hardback
ISBN 978-0-521-12395-2 Paperback

Antonia Marie Rahe

Contents

Acknowledgments

While working on this book, I piled up many debts. Over the years, I have learned a great deal from exchanges with James W. Muller, David Wootton, Blair Worden, Jonathan Scott, James Hankins, Charles Butterworth, Ralph Lerner, Harvey C. Mansfield, Cary J. Nederman, Antony Black, and William Connell. On two occasions, Lars Engle, chairman of the Department of English at the University of Tulsa, and I co-taught a seminar titled "The English Revolution: Politics and Literature," and in the course of our discussions in and out of class he taught me much. Lori Curtis, who was for some years director of Special Collections at McFarlin Library at the University of Tulsa, was assiduous in locating and securing pertinent materials, and Marc Carlson, Ann Blakely, Tamara Stansfield, and the staff at the interlibrary loan office at that library performed miracles. Charles Burnett at the Warburg Institute kindly responded to my inquiries regarding the reception of Averroism in the Christian West; Antony Black allowed me to see the pertinent chapters of his forthcoming book comparing political thought in Islam with that in the West; and, shortly before the publication of his fine book on John Milton, Andrew Marvell, and Marchamont Nedham, Blair Worden generously shared with me the page proofs, enabling me to add citations and make small adjustments in the copyedited manuscript of this work. Eldon Eisenach, who was my colleague many years ago at Cornell University and later at the University of Tulsa, read and commented on an early draft; Erik Midelfort read and commented on the first chapter; Charles Butterworth read and commented on the second and fourth chapters; Nicholas von Maltzahn, Martine Watson Brownley, Colleen Sheehan, Lars Engle, and Paulina Kewes read and commented on an early version of the third chapter; Paul Cantor read and commented on the third and fourth chapters; Timothy Fuller read and commented on the eighth through tenth chapters; and John Headley read and commented on the book in its entirety. My wife, Laura, more than once went over every word.

While on sabbatical in 2005–2006, I received generous support from the Research Office at the University of Tulsa and from Thomas Benediktson, dean of Henry Kendall College of Arts and Sciences at that institution. I also had the privilege of spending Michaelmas term in 2005 and Hilary term in 2006 in congenial company at All Souls College, Oxford – where, as a Visiting Fellow, I took ample advantage of library facilities unequalled anywhere else in the world and profited from conversations with Jeremy Butterfield, who suggested the title of this volume; with Noel Malcolm and Sir Keith Thomas, who were generous in sharing their encyclopedic knowledge of this period; and with Fergus Millar, John Robertson, Peter Ghosh, Ian Maclean, Eleanor Dickey, Robert Maltby, Patrick Finglass, Andrei Rossius, James Adams, Myles Burnyeat, Gerald Cohen, Wolfgang de Melo, Simon Green, Alison Brown, and Magnus Ryan, who went very far out of his way to be helpful to an itinerant scholar. I owe a particular debt to the generations of librarians responsible for the collection and safekeeping of the books lodged in the Bodleian Library, the Codrington Library, the Taylorian Institution, and the library at Balliol College. This book was finished late in March 2006 during my last week in residence at All Souls.

An earlier version of the prologue was published in *Machiavelli's Liberal Republican Legacy*, ed. Paul A. Rahe (New York: Cambridge University Press, 2006), and material drawn from it is reprinted with permission. Earlier versions of Chapters 1 and 3 appeared as Paul A. Rahe, "In the Shadow of Lucretius: The Epicurean Foundations of Machiavelli's Political Thought," *History of Political Thought* 28:1 (Spring 2007): 30–55, and "The Classical Republicanism of John Milton," *History of Political Thought* 25:2 (Summer 2004): 243–75, and material drawn from them is reprinted here with permission. Some of the material found in the preface to Part Three and in Chapters 5 through 7 was published in Paul A. Rahe, "An Inky Wretch: The Outrageous Genius of Marchamont Nedham," *The National Interest* 70 (Winter 2002–2003): 55–64, and in *Machiavelli's Liberal Republican Legacy*, ed. Paul A. Rahe (New York: Cambridge University Press, 2006), and is reprinted here in revised form with the permission of the editor of *The National Interest* and of Cambridge University Press. Chapter 11 is adapted from material published in *Republics Ancient and Modern: Classical Republicanism and the American Revolution* by Paul A. Rahe, Copyright © 1992 by the University of North Carolina Press, and republished in *Machiavelli's Liberal Republican Legacy*, ed. Paul A. Rahe (New York: Cambridge University Press, 2006), and is used here by permission of the two publishers.

Abbreviations and Brief Titles

In the notes, I have adopted the standard abbreviations for classical texts and inscriptions and for books of the Bible provided in *The Oxford Classical Dictionary*, third edition revised, ed. Simon Hornblower and Antony Spawforth (Oxford, UK: Oxford University Press, 2003), and in *The Chicago Manual of Style*, 15th edition (Chicago: University of Chicago Press, 2003), 15.50–3. Where possible, the ancient texts and medieval and modern works of similar stature are cited by the divisions and subdivisions employed by the author or introduced by subsequent editors (that is, by book, part, chapter, section number, paragraph, act, scene, line, Stephanus page, or by page and line number). In some cases, where further specification is needed to help the reader to locate a particular passage, I have included as the last element in a particular citation the page or pages of the pertinent volume of the edition used. For modern works frequently cited, the following abbreviations and short titles have been employed:

ABL   John Aubrey, *Aubrey's Brief Lives*, ed. Oliver Lawson Dick (London: Secker & Warburg, 1949).

CDPR   *The Constitutional Documents of the Puritan Revolution, 1625–1660*, third edition, ed. Samuel Rawson Gardiner (Oxford, UK: Clarendon Press, 1906).

CTH   *The Correspondence of Thomas Hobbes*, ed. Noel Malcolm (Oxford, UK: Clarendon Press, 1994).

Hobbes, *Behemoth*   Thomas Hobbes, *Behemoth, or The Long Parliament*, second edition, ed. Ferdinand Tönnies (New York: Cass, 1969).

———, *De cive*   Thomas Hobbes, *De Cive: The Latin Version*, ed. Howard Warrender (Oxford, UK: Clarendon Press, 1983).

———, *Elements of Law*   Thomas Hobbes, *The Elements of Law, Natural and Politic*, second edition, ed. Ferdinand Tönnies (London: Cass, 1969).

———, *EW*   Thomas Hobbes, *The English Works of Thomas Hobbes of Malmesbury*, ed. Sir William Molesworth (London: J. Bohn, 1839–1845).

———, *Leviathan*   Thomas Hobbes, *Leviathan*, ed. C. B. Macpherson (Harmondsworth, UK: Penguin, 1971), to which I have added, where appropriate, the paragraph numbers supplied in Thomas Hobbes, *Leviathan: With Selected Variants from the Latin Edition of 1688* [1651], ed. Edwin Curley (Indianapolis, IN: Hackett, 1994).

———, *LW Thomæ Hobbes Malmesburiensis opera philosophica quae Latine scripsit omnia in unum corpus*, ed. William Molesworth (London: J. Bohn, 1839–1845).

———, *Philosophicall Rudiments* Thomas Hobbes, *Philosophicall Rudiments Concerning Government and Society*, in Hobbes, *De Cive: The English Version*, ed. Howard Warrender (Oxford, UK: Clarendon Press, 1983).

JHO James Harrington's Oceana, ed. S. B. Liljegren (Heidelberg: C. Winter, 1924).

Machiavelli, *AG Niccolò Machiavelli, Dell'arte della guerra*, in Machiavelli, *Opere*, 301–89, to which, where appropriate, I have added the sentence numbers supplied in Niccolò Machiavelli, *Art of War*, ed. and tr. Christopher Lynch (Chicago: University of Chicago Press, 2003).

———, *Discorsi Niccolò Machiavelli, Discorsi sopra la prima deca di Tito Livio*, in Machiavelli, *Opere*, 75–254, to which, where appropriate, I have added the paragraph numbers supplied in Niccolò Machiavelli, *Discourses on Livy*, ed. and tr. Harvey C. Mansfield and Nathan Tarcov (Chicago: University of Chicago Press, 1996).

———, *Opere Niccolò Machiavelli, Tutte le opere*, ed. Mario Martelli (Florence: G. C. Sansoni, 1971).

Marsilius of Padua, *Defensor pacis Marsilius of Padua, The Defensor Pacis of Marsilius of Padua*, ed. C. W. Previté-Orton (Cambridge, UK: Cambridge University Press, 1928).

Milton, *CPW Complete Prose Works of John Milton*, ed. Don M. Wolfe (New Haven, CT: Yale University Press, 1953–1982).

———, *CW The Works of John Milton*, ed. Frank Allen Patterson (New York: Columbia University Press, 1931–1938).

MP Mercurius Politicus

Nedham, *CCES Marchamont Nedham, The Case of the Commonwealth of England, Stated* (1650), ed. Philip A. Knachel (Charlottesville: University Press of Virginia, 1969).

———, *EFS [Marchamont Nedham], The Excellencie of a Free State* (1656), ed. Richard Baron (London: A. Millar and T. Cadell, 1767).

———, *True State [Marchamont Nedham], A True State of the Case of the Commonwealth of England, Scotland, and Ireland* (London: Tho. Newcomb, 1654).

OFB The Oxford Francis Bacon, ed. Graham Rees and Lisa Jardine (Oxford, UK: Clarendon Press, 1996–).

PWoJH The Political Works of James Harrington, ed. J. G. A. Pocock (Cambridge, UK: Cambridge University Press, 1977).

WoFB The Works of Francis Bacon, ed. James Spedding, Robert Leslie Ellis, and Douglas Denon Heath (London: Longman, 1857–1874).

WoJH James Harrington, Works: The Oceana and Other Works of James Harrington, ed. John Toland (London: T. Becket, T. Cadell, and T. Evans, 1771).

WrSOC The Writings and Speeches of Oliver Cromwell, ed. Wilbur Cortez Abbott (Cambridge, MA: Harvard University Press, 1937–1947).

Introduction

This book is a sequel of sorts. Sixteen years ago, its author published a work entitled *Republics Ancient and Modern: Classical Republicanism and the American Revolution*. Although it was some twelve hundred pages in length, inevitably, it gave some figures short shrift, and others it neglected entirely. Niccolò Machiavelli was discussed and his importance was underlined, but his thinking was not treated in depth. John Milton and Marchamont Nedham were not mentioned at all. Thomas Hobbes was accorded a chapter, but little was said about the evolution of his thought; and, while James Harrington's significance was emphasized, the foundations of his thinking were not discussed at length.

What follows is an attempt to redress the balance – to do justice to Milton and Nedham, to explore in greater depth the thinking of Machiavelli and Hobbes, and to provide a setting within which to understand Harrington. Its purview is the political opening that took place in the period that began on 30 January 1649 – when the execution of a recalcitrant English king occasioned an abortive experiment in the construction of a republic in Britain – and that ended on 1 May 1660, when a Parliament more or less freely elected voted to recall to the throne that king's eldest son. Its subject is the republican speculation, of a sort hitherto unprecedented, to which this brief, abortive experiment gave rise. It is not my claim that a close study of Milton, Nedham, and Harrington – or, for that matter, Hobbes – is crucial for understanding the course of events in the period. Their thinking was, to a considerable degree, epiphenomenal. Initiative lay in the hands of the self-styled saints. I do wish to suggest, however, that the long-term impact of their speculative effort was considerable – that their thinking marked a turning point in the history of constitutional prudence, that one of the principal reasons the events of the period deserve close attention is that they inspired such thinking, and that what Milton, Nedham, and Harrington had to say can best be understood when considered as a response the thinking of Machiavelli and, in Harrington's case, to that of Hobbes as well.

I begin, therefore, with the author of *The Prince* and the *Discourses on Livy* – with an exploration of the reasons why his republicanism initially failed to catch fire, with a consideration of the circumstances that induced Englishmen to pay more attention to the latter work in and after 1649, and with a close examination of the character of his thinking not only as a republican but also as a critic of what one of his most ardent English admirers dubbed "Priest-craft." Readers should be warned that the Machiavelli whom they will encounter in these pages is not the unabashed admirer of classical antiquity commonly portrayed in late-twentieth-century literature on the subject. If I am correct, Machiavelli was a critic of classical republicanism, and he owed far more to Epicurus than to Aristotle, Herodotus, and Thucydides and far more to Lucretius than to Cicero, Sallust, and Livy. Moreover, I argue that, if he is to be properly understood, his political science must also be situated with regard to a conceptually powerful tradition of thought crafted in tenth-century Baghdad in response to the epochal political transformation that the emergence of universal, monotheistic religions equipped with clerical establishments had brought about. This tradition, which reached Europe by way of the Latin translation of works written by the Arab philosophers Alfarabi, Avicenna, and Averroës and by Averroës' fellow Cordoban Maimonides, provided Machiavelli with a point of departure. It is my contention that the new species of republicanism, which he fashioned in the intellectual netherworld dominated by Averroës and Lucretius, was grounded in an appropriation, critique, and break with the thinking of them both.

My treatment of Milton is no less unorthodox. Some readers will surely regard it as heretical. If I am correct, the poet who became Secretary of Foreign Tongues for the Commonwealth of England, Scotland, and Ireland was precisely what Machiavelli was not – a genuine classical republican, profoundly indebted to Plato and Aristotle, to Thucydides and Isocrates, to Cicero, Sallust, and Livy – and I try to show that he studied Machiavelli's *Discourses on Livy* with care and that he considered and in the end rejected its argument on rigorously classical republican grounds. If, I argue, he was nonetheless at odds with Aristotle and Cicero, with Herodotus, Thucydides, Livy, and Sallust, it was because, like Machiavelli, he lived in the epoch of revealed religion and had to cope with the consequences – which he tried to do, not in the fashion recommended by Lucretius (whom he read, appreciated, and recommended) nor by means of the Erastianism advocated by Paolo Sarpi, the Machiavellian state theologian of Venice (whose work he studied and admired), but in a manner faithful to the teaching of the Arab *falāsifa* and Maimonides: by becoming a practitioner of the art they called *kalām* – which is to say, by deploying his rhetorical and poetics gifts in an attempt to reconfigure the dominant superstition as a civil religion, favorable to political liberty and friendly to philosophy as well.

Milton's "particular friend" and "crony" Marchamont Nedham I treat, by way of contrast, as a genuine Machiavellian. If I am right, it was he who first Anglicized the Florentine's thought, exploiting certain bourgeois propensities inherent in Machiavelli's argument, restating as a critique of episcopalianism and presbyterianism alike his mentor's analysis of priestcraft, and refashioning the Florentine's novel account of republicanism in such a fashion as to make it not only compatible with the establishment of a free state on an extended territory but also supportive of the traditional English concern with rights, the security of property, and the rule of law. If Milton found the company of so notorious a libertine congenial, it was arguably because, though they differed in the measures they thought best suited to countering priestcraft and promoting republican liberty, the two men shared a common appreciation for the merits of philosophy and a common enemy.

In my judgment, James Harrington, the man who actually coined the term "Priest-craft," was not, as was in the last century so often supposed, a thoroughgoing Machiavellian. His thought, as I try to demonstrate, is rooted in Thomas Hobbes's appropriation, critique, and reorientation of the argument presented in *The Prince* and the *Discourses on Livy*. To fully understand Harrington, I argue, to situate him properly within his intellectual milieu, one must first trace Hobbes's trajectory – noting the Machiavellian and republican proclivities he displayed in his youth, exploring the manner in which he was led to a more positive appreciation of monarchy in the course of the 1620s as he worked on Thucydides and contemplated the struggle emerging between Parliament and King and attending to the profound debt he owed Sir Francis Bacon, Paolo Sarpi, the poet Lucretius, and their admirers among the French libertines. Then, one must consider the Machiavellian foundations of his argument; attend to the analysis of priestcraft that he shared with the Florentine and with Sarpi, Milton, and Nedham; and take note of the radically Erastian posture he adopted with regard to ecclesiastical polity. Above all, one must attend to the degree to which the Malmesbury philosopher's monarchism was at all times prudential, provisional, and subject to republican revision, and one must ponder whether, in publishing *Leviathan*, in returning to England, and taking the Engagement required by the Commonwealth, he was not just acquiescing in the Roundhead victory, as scholars generally assume, but actively lending support to the Rump and to its lord general, Oliver Cromwell, by offering them sage counsel and by attempting to guide public policy – especially with regard to ecclesiastical polity.

If, in the end, England's republican experiment failed, I contend, it was largely because of the inadequacy of its leaders. They were faced with grave difficulties, largely of their own making, to be sure; and, though impressive in a variety of ways, as statesmen they were found wanting in the end. If the theorists examined here also as statesmen fell short, if they failed to provide those who sought to direct events with the guidance required, it was in part because they were not in tune with the religious sentiments of those responsible for Pride's Purge, and in part because they were genuinely at odds with one another. What Oliver Cromwell reportedly said to his murmuring officers shortly after the establishment of the Protectorate could have been said with equal justice to nearly everyone involved in the project of republican construction: they knew not what they meant – or, rather, though they certainly knew what it was that they were rejecting, they could not agree on what to put in its place.

If the speculative efforts of Milton, Nedham, Hobbes, and Harrington were nonetheless of lasting significance, it is because of their legacy. They pioneered lines of thinking that others – such as Henry Neville, Algernon Sidney, John Locke, the contributors to the standing army controversy of the late 1690s, the third earl of Shaftesbury, the authors of *The Independent Whig* and *Cato's Letters*, David Hume, and the baron de Montesquieu – would recast in such a fashion as to enable statesmen, at the time of the American and the French Revolutions, to act on their schemes. This book's aim is to explore the earliest stages in the development of the various Whig understandings of the constitution of liberty.

Prologue

Machiavelli in the English Revolution

In mid-afternoon on the 30th of January, 1649, Charles Stuart, king of England, Scotland, and Ireland, stepped out of a window on the second floor of the Banqueting House in London onto a platform erected within the yard of the Palace of Westminster. He had spent the morning in prayer. Now he gave a brief speech to those in close attendance. He began by asserting his innocence, and he asked God's forgiveness for those responsible for his trial and condemnation. He attested his desire for the "liberty and freedom" of his countrymen, which consisted, he said, "in having of government, those laws by which their life and their goods may be most their own." He denied that the people had a rightful "share in government." That, he argued, "is nothing pertaining to them," for "a subject and a sovereign are clear different things." These remarks he concluded with a confession, confirming that he died a Christian according to the profession of the Church of England as he had found it left him by his father. "I go," he observed, "from a corruptible to an incorruptible Crown, where no disturbance can be, no disturbance in the world." Then, and only then, as a deep groan issued from the otherwise silent crowd below, did he surrender his head to the executioner's axe.[1]

This grave and unprecedented event shocked all of Christendom; and, though to all appearances it owed nothing at all to the reflections of the Florentine Niccolò Machiavelli, it nonetheless marked an epoch in the reception of his thinking. Prior to the clear, bitterly cold day on which the English beheaded their king, Machiavelli was generally known to the larger world as a counselor of princes, as an enemy to morality and the Christian religion, and as an inspiration to the advocates of *raison d'état*, who had glossed over his argument on behalf of personal aggrandizement, repackaged his harsh account of the dictates of political necessity, and rendered it more palatable to men of conscience by defending the occasional use of deceit and even injustice in domestic and foreign affairs as requisite for the good of each and every realm.[2] It was not until the

---

[1] For a detailed account, see C. V. Wedgwood, *A Coffin for King Charles: The Trial and Execution of Charles I* (New York: Book-of-the-Month Club, 1964), 191–223.

[2] Note Machiavelli, *Discorsi* 3.41, in *Opere*, 249, where the Florentine invites us to misread him as an impassioned patriot; and, for a survey of those who fell prey to the temptation to do so, see Giuseppe Toffanin, *Machiavelli e il "Tacitismo": la "politica storica" al tempo della Controriforma* (Padua: A. Draghi, 1921); Friedrich Meinecke, *Machiavellism: The Doctrine of Raison d'État and Its Place in Modern History*, tr. Douglas Scott (New Brunswick, NJ: Transaction, 1998), 1–204; George L. Mosse, *The Holy Pretence: A Study in Christianity and Reason of State*

decade that followed the execution of Charles I that Machiavelli would become almost equally famous also as an advocate for republican rule.

There is no great mystery in this. Machiavelli's *Prince* is, at least on the surface, a much more accessible book than his *Discourses on Livy*. It is shorter, pithier, and more vigorous, and it enjoyed a *grand succès de scandale* from the very first. In contrast, the *Discourses on Livy* is long, and it is quite obviously difficult to decipher – not, as some suppose,[3] because it is unfinished, fragmentary, provisional, and replete with confusion (though there is reason to think that Machiavelli may have been revising the work when he died),[4] but because it is exceedingly subtle, complex, and playful in a literary manner. In short, the work in which republicanism looms large is as unattractive to the casual reader as *The Prince* is alluring. Even today, the longer book is much more rarely read.

Of course, from the outset, there were those who argued that Machiavelli revealed his true opinions only in his *Discourses on Livy*. Within six years of the appearance of the Florentine's two great masterpieces in printed form, an inquisitive and well-connected English visitor to Florence named Reginald Pole was told by one or more of Machiavelli's compatriots that the author of the *Discourses on Livy* had written *The Prince* solely to trip up the Medici and bring about their demise. Machiavelli had purportedly acknowledged as much himself. Although Pole was not himself inclined to entertain this claim,[5] others

from William Perkins to John Winthrop (Oxford, UK: Blackwell, 1957); Rodolfo de Mattei, *Il problema della 'ragion di stato' nell'età della Controriforma* (Milan: Ricciardi, 1979); Peter S. Donaldson, *Machiavelli and Mystery of State* (Cambridge, UK: Cambridge University Press, 1988), 111–40; Peter Burke, "Tacitism, Scepticism and Reason of State," in *The Cambridge History of Political Thought, 1450–1700*, ed. J. H. Burns and Mark Goldie (Cambridge, UK: Cambridge University Press, 1991), 479–98; and Victoria Kahn, *Machiavellian Rhetoric: From the Counter-Reformation to Milton* (Princeton, NJ: Princeton University Press, 1994), 60–165. Machiavelli is accorded a less prominent role in Richard Tuck's discussion of Tacitism and reason of state: see *Philosophy and Government, 1572–1651* (Cambridge, UK: Cambridge University Press, 1993), 30–119.

3 Cf. Francesco Bausi, "Introduzione," in Niccolò Machiavelli, *Discorsi*, ed. Francesco Bausi (Rome: Salerno Editrice, 2001), I ix–xxxiii, and Bausi, *Machiavelli* (Rome: Salerno Editrice, 2005), 163–81, who is inclined to explain in these terms the contradictions that abound and Machiavelli's frequent misrepresentation of classical sources, with Harvey C. Mansfield, *Machiavelli's New Modes and Orders: A Study of the Discourses on Livy* (Ithaca, NY: Cornell University Press, 1979), who attempts to do justice to the Florentine's literary playfulness and to his rhetorical skill. For an earlier statement along similar lines, see Francesco Bausi, *I "Discorsi" di Niccolò Machiavelli: Genesi e strutture* (Florence: Sansoni, 1985).

4 See Cecil H. Clough, *Machiavelli Researches* (Naples: Istituto Universitario Orientale, 1967), 79–107, and Clough, "Father Walker's Presentation and Translation of Machiavelli's *Discourses* in Perspective," in *The Discourses of Machiavelli*, ed. and tr. Leslie J. Walker, second edition (London: Routledge & Kegan Paul, 1975), xv–xlviii (at xxii–xxxix).

5 See the report in his *Apologia ad Carolum Quintum* (1539), in *Epistolarum Reginaldi Poli S. R. E. Cardinalis et aliorum ad ipsum collectio*, ed. Angelo M. Quirini (Brescia: J. M. Rizzardi, 1744–1757), I 66–171 (esp. 151–52, which is cited in L. Arthur Burd, "Introduction," in Niccolò Machiavelli, *Il Principe*, ed. L. Arthur Burd [Oxford, UK: Clarendon Press, 1891], 36–38) – where Pole refers to a visit to Florence that took place in the winter of 1538. The full Latin text of Pole's discussion of Machiavelli has been reprinted as an appendix to Heinrich Lutz, *Ragione di stato und christliche Staatsethik im 16. Jahrhundert* (Münster in Westfalen: Aschendorffsche Verlagsbuchhandlung, 1961), 48–62. In this connection, see Donaldson, *Machiavelli and Mystery of State*, 1–35, 87–88, and Sydney Anglo, *Machiavelli – The First Century: Studies in Enthusiasm,*

who learned of the report were perfectly prepared to do so,[6] and the tendency for students of the subject to discount *The Prince* on one ground or another and to treat the *Discourses on Livy* as representative of Machiavelli's real thinking has had adherents ever since – especially in the English-speaking world, where in some quarters Machiavelli's apparent espousal of republicanism has long inspired admiration.[7]

Alberico Gentili is a case in point. In a scholarly volume on the conduct of embassies, which he dedicated to Sir Philip Sidney and published in 1585, not long before he was created Regius Professor of Civil Law at Oxford University, Gentili singled out as "precious" the *Discourses on Livy*, described their author as "*Democratiae laudator et assertor*," termed him "a very great enemy to tyranny," and claimed that he had written *The Prince* not "to instruct the tyrant but to expose openly his secret deeds and exhibit him naked and clearly recognizable to the wretched peoples" of the world. "It was," he explained, "the strategy of this most prudent of all men to educate the people on the pretext of educating the prince."[8]

Hostility, and Irrelevance (Oxford, UK: Oxford University Press, 2005), 115–42. It is by no means inconceivable that Machiavelli engaged in such special pleading when, toward the end of his life, the Medici were overthrown, the republic was for a brief time restored, and he sought to regain the office he had lost in 1512. Pole was closely acquainted with a number of figures who had known Machiavelli, and through them he no doubt met more: see Thomas F. Mayer, *Reginald Pole: Prince and Prophet* (Cambridge, UK: Cambridge University Press, 2000), 97–98.

[6] See, for example, Giovanni Matteo Toscano, *Peplus Italiae* (Paris: Morelli, 1578), 52, and André Rossant, *Les meurs, humeurs et comportemens de Henry de Valois* (Paris: P. Mercier, 1589), 11. Cf., however, Thomas Fitzherbert, *The First Part of a Treatise Concerning Policy and Religion* (Douai: L. Kellam, 1606), 412. Although Pole's *Apologia ad Carolum Quintum* was not published in printed form until the eighteenth century, what he said therein almost immediately found its way into diplomatic reports: see *Letters and Papers (Foreign and Domestic) of the Reign of Henry VIII*, ed. J. W. Brewer, James Gairdner, and R. H. Brodie (London: Longmans, 1862–1910), XIV:1, no. 200.

[7] For an analysis and critique of the most influential recent attempt to drive a wedge between *The Prince* and the *Discourses on Livy* and to justify giving precedence to the latter, see Paul A. Rahe, "Situating Machiavelli," in *Renaissance Civic Humanism: Reappraisals and Reflections*, ed. James Hankins (Cambridge, UK: Cambridge University Press, 2000), 270–308. For an otherwise informative example of this species of special pleading not treated in my essay, see Cecil H. Clough, "Niccolò Machiavelli's Political Assumptions and Objectives," *Bulletin of the John Rylands Library* 53:1 (Autumn 1970): 30–74.

[8] Alberico Gentili, *De legationibus libri tres* (London: Thomas Vautrollerius, 1585) 3.9 (Sig. oiii). The pertinent passage is quoted at length in Pierre Bayle, "Machiavel," in Bayle, *Dictionnaire historique et critique* (Basel: Brandmuller, 1741), III 246–49 (at 248, note O), and in Burd, "Introduction," 63–64. For an English translation, see Alberico Gentili, *De legationibus libri tres*, tr. Gordon J. Laing (New York: Oxford University Press, 1924), II 156. Cf. Diego Panizza, "Machiavelli e Alberico Gentili," *Il pensiero politico* 2:3 (1969): 476–83, with Donaldson, *Machiavelli and Mystery of State*, 86–110. Traiano Boccalini's satirical account of his contemporaries' response to Machiavelli points in the direction of Gentili's conclusions: see *De'ragguagli di Parnaso* (Venice: P. Farri, 1612–1615) 1.89. Parts of this work were translated into English in 1626 by William Vaughan and again in 1656 by Henry, earl of Monmouth. Spinoza and Rousseau advanced a quite similar claim: see Baruch Spinoza, *Tractatus politicus* 5.7, in *Benedicti de Spinoza opera, quotquot reperta sunt*, ed. J. van Vloten and J. P. N. Land (The Hague: Martinus Nijhoff, 1914), II 24, and Jean-Jacques Rousseau, *Du contrat social* 3.6 (with note a), in Rousseau, *Oeuvres complètes*, ed. Bernard Gagnebin and Marcel Raymond (Paris: Bibliothèque de la Pléiade, 1959–1995), III 409, 1480.

Some of the most enthusiastic seventeenth-century admirers of Machiavelli's republican reflections thought this sort of special pleading preposterous. Henry Neville was one such. After the Restoration, James Harrington's longtime friend and associate published an English translation of Machiavelli's works, to which he contributed a preface. Included in his preface was a letter purportedly by Machiavelli himself, describing *The Prince* as "both a Satyr against" tyrants "and a true Character of them." To this letter, which was to mislead unsuspecting readers from the late seventeenth well into the nineteenth century, Neville puckishly assigned the date 1 April 1537 – which was April Fool's Day, some ten years after its putative author's death.[9]

Neville's gentle mockery of those who could not stomach *The Prince* should serve as a warning to us all, for it makes no sense to suppose that work incompatible with his *Discourses on Livy*. After all, these two books were written concurrently,[10] and each presupposes and refers to the other.[11] Moreover, Machiavelli's republican book is by no means as unfriendly to principality as one might suppose. In fact, the author of the *Discourses on Livy* appears to have been no less willing than the author of *The Prince* to dispense his advice indiscriminately – not just to republics and their citizens, but to princes, to aspirants to one-man rule, and even to those whom he unashamedly singles out as tyrants.[12] In both works, the Florentine displays a marked interest in and a decided admiration for what he calls "the new prince." His *Discourses* are

---

[9] See *The Works of the Famous Nicholas Machiavel, Citizen and Secretary of Florence* (London: John Starkey, 1675) sig. (***3) v. On the letter and its authorship, see Felix Raab, *The English Face of Machiavelli: A Changing Interpretation, 1500–1700* (London: Routledge & Kegan Paul, 1964), 219–21, 267–72, and Anna Maria Crinò, "Un Amico Inglese del Granduca Cosimo III di Toscana: Sir Henry Neville," *English Miscellany* 3 (1962): 235–47.

[10] There are three reasons to suppose this true. *The Prince*, which reached its final form and began circulating in 1516, makes reference to the *Discourses on Livy*: see Machiavelli, *Il principe* 2, 8, in *Opere*, 258, 269. The *Discourses* makes no mention of any events subsequent to 1517. And Machiavelli makes no use of the first six books of Tacitus' *Annals*, which were first published in 1515, until well into the third book of the *Discourses*: cf. Machiavelli, *Discorsi* 3.19–23, in *Opere*, 225–30, with Tac. *Ann.* 3.52–55, and see Robert W. Ulery, Jr., "Cornelius Tacitus," in *Catalogus translationum et commentariorum: Mediaeval and Renaissance Latin Translations and Commentaries*, ed. Paul Oskar Kristeller, F. Edward Cranz, and Virginia Brown (Washington, DC: Catholic University of America Press, 1960–), VI 87–174 (esp. 92–97), VIII 334–35. He makes use of these books as well in his *Florentine Histories*, which were composed in the early 1520s: cf. Machiavelli, *Istorie fiorentine* 2.2, in *Opere*, 659–60, with Tac. *Ann.* 1.79. In this connection, see Kenneth C. Schellhase, "Tacitus in the Political Thought of Machiavelli," *Il pensiero politico* 4:3 (1971): 381–91, and Schellhase, *Tacitus in Renaissance Political Thought* (Chicago: University of Chicago Press, 1976), 3–30 (esp. 12–13), 66–84 (esp. 78–83).

[11] This is evident from the cross-references: see Machiavelli, *Il principe* 2, 8, and *Discorsi* 2.1.3, 20, 3.19, 42, in *Opere*, 147, 176, 225–26, 250, 258, 269. See Felix Gilbert, "The Composition and Structure of Machiavelli's *Discorsi*," reprinted in Gilbert, *History: Choice and Commitment* (Cambridge, MA: Harvard University Press, 1977), 115–33. Although there is much of value to be found in David Wootton, "Introduction," in Niccolò Machiavelli, *The Prince*, ed. and tr. David Wootton (Indianapolis, IN: Hackett, 1995), xi–xliv, I remain unpersuaded by his attempt to explain away the apparent references within *The Prince* to the *Discourses on Livy*.

[12] See Machiavelli, *Discorsi* 1.16.3–5, 19, 21, 25–27, 30, 32, 33.5, 40–43, 45.3, 51, 55.5, 2.12–14, 18.5, 20, 23.3, 24, 27–28, 31, 3.3–6, 8, 11, 15, 22–23, 26.2, 27, 29–30, 34.3, 38, 42–44, in *Opere*, 99–101, 104–6, 108–10, 112–16, 123–28, 133, 138, 161–64, 173, 176, 180–84, 186–88, 191–92, 198–213, 216–17, 221–22, 228–31, 233–37, 242, 246–47, 249–52.

addressed neither to the citizens of republics as such nor even to "those who are princes" already, but rather to "those who, for their infinite good parts, deserve to be" princes – for, in a republic, individual citizens may "by means of their *virtù* become princes," as happened, he expressly notes, in the case of Hiero of Syracuse.[13] It is no wonder that readers have nearly always tended to give priority to Machiavelli's counsel concerning the acquisition and retention of political power.

Bad timing no doubt contributed as well to the eclipse of Machiavelli's republican teaching. The Florentine composed *The Prince* and much, if not all of his *Discourses on Livy* in the second decade of the sixteenth century after the collapse of the Florentine republic and the reestablishment of Medici rule. *The Prince* circulated widely in manuscript for some time after it took final form in 1516, both in Florence and abroad. The *Discourses on Livy* is not known to have become available in manuscript until shortly after its author's death in 1527. But within five years both books were published in Rome, alongside the *Florentine Histories*, under the imprimatur of this last work's patron Clement VII, the second of the two Medici popes.[14] Machiavelli's *Discourses on Livy*

[13] See Machiavelli, *Discorsi* Ep. Ded., 2.2.3, in *Opere*, 75, 150, which should be read in light of *Il principe* 1, 6–14 (esp. 6 and 13), in *Opere*, 258, 264–80. The manner in which the ethos of *The Prince* periodically reappears in the pages of the *Discourses on Livy* is all too often ignored by partisans of the latter: see, for example, Quentin Skinner, *The Foundations of Modern Political Thought I: The Renaissance* (Cambridge, UK: Cambridge University Press, 1978), 180–86, and *Machiavelli* (New York: Hill and Wang, 1981), 48–77; and the work dedicated to him by his student Maurizio Viroli, *From Politics to Reason of State: The Acquisition and Transformation of the Language of Politics, 1250–1600* (Cambridge, UK: Cambridge University Press, 1992), 154–77. Whether one is intent on depicting Machiavelli as a civic humanist, as a classical republican, or as a radical populist who simply "resents, despises, and distrusts" the rich and well-born, one will be tempted to avert one's gaze from the evidence suggesting that it was his opinion that, even in republics, princes rule – and that they do so there with even greater prospects for success than in principalities: see, for example, John P. McCormick, "Machiavellian Democracy: Controlling Elites with Ferocious Populism," *American Political Science Review* 95:2 (June 2001): 297–313. For a far more interesting attempt – elaborate, ingenious, quite often penetrating, but, at crucial moments, fanciful and more than a little bit perverse – to get around the pertinent evidence for the purpose of representing Machiavelli as an enthusiast of positive liberty who celebrates the fleeting moment of revolutionary rupture when, we are told, the distinction between rulers and ruled dissolves and the democratic potential inherent in political *práxis* is fully realized, see Miguel E. Vatter, *Between Form and Event: Machiavelli's Theory of Political Freedom* (Dordrecht: Kluwer Academic, 2000). This work should be read in light of Hannah Arendt, *On Revolution* (New York: Viking Press, 1963), passim (esp. 139–285), which is itself grounded on a vulgar misreading of Martin Heidegger's *Being and Time* as a work of moral philosophy focused on political freedom. Much can also be learned from Mikael Hörnqvist's anything but fanciful attempt to subordinate *The Prince* to the *Discourses on Livy* by way of treating Machiavelli as a patriot – intent on promoting Florentine imperialism at all costs, and blind to the consequences of the larger forces that he is thereby unleashing: see Hörnqvist, *Machiavelli and Empire* (Cambridge, UK: Cambridge University Press, 2004).

[14] For the pre-publication and publication history of Machiavelli's works, see Adolph Gerber, *Niccolò Machiavelli: Die Handschriften, Ausgaben und Übersetzungen seiner Werke im 16. und 17. Jahrhundert* (Turin: Bottega d'Erasmo, 1962). Giovanni Gaddi appears to have played a role in editing for posthumous publication both the *Discourses on Livy* and the *Florentine Histories*: see Bernardo Giunta, "Dedicatory Letter to Giovanni Gaddi," 8 May 1532, reprinted in *Opere di Niccolò Machiavelli* (Turin: UTET, 1984–1999), I:1 407–9. For what is known and can perhaps

could not have appeared at a moment less favorable to the republican cause. In the century that followed, everything conspired to strengthen the executive power.

The military revolution, to which Machiavelli had contributed much, restored infantry to the supremacy that it had enjoyed in classical times,[15] but in the process it eliminated the usefulness of the feudal levy and thereby undermined the contractual foundations of limited kingship. The consequence was not a revival of the citizen militia along the lines that had sustained the republics of classical antiquity. Nor did this revolution eventuate in the arrangement Machiavelli had himself championed: the establishment of conscript armies drawn promiscuously from the various polities' citizen and subject populations.[16] The infantry's new-found primacy contributed, instead, to the predominance of professional armies, the traditional tool of absolute rulers. To make matters worse, in the very same years in which the military revolution began to reshape the conditions of political rule, the Reformation shattered the unity of Christendom and gave rise to civil strife and war in central and western Europe on a scale hitherto unknown. In this environment, almost without exception, civic republics became principalities,[17] and, in principalities, representative assemblies generally ceased to meet. The formalities associated with securing consent count for little when disorder looms and life becomes increasingly nasty, brutish, and short. In times of anarchy, for the sake of peace and protection, most men will sacrifice everything else.

Of course, England was to some extent an exception to the rule,[18] and Englishmen were acutely sensitive to this fact.[19] Prior to the 1640s, England

---

be surmised regarding the circumstances in which the *Discourses on Livy* were published, see Clough, *Machiavelli Researches*, 90–105.

[15] See Geoffrey Parker, *The Military Revolution: Military Innovation and the Rise of the West, 1500–1800* (Cambridge, UK: Cambridge University Press, 1988).

[16] Machiavelli did not, as is often suggested, link arms-bearing with citizenship per se: note Machiavelli, *Il principe* 12–13, 20, and *Discorsi* 1.21, 2.10, 12.4, 13.2, 20, 24, 30, 3.24, in *Opere*, 105–6, 159–60, 162–64, 176, 181–84, 190–91, 231, 275–78, 289–91, and see *AG* 1, in *Opere*, 305–13. Cf. J. G. A. Pocock, *The Machiavellian Moment: Florentine Political Thought and the Atlantic Republican Tradition* (Princeton, NJ: Princeton University Press, 1975), 194–218 (esp. 199–203, 208–14), 384–86, and "Historical Introduction," in *PWoJH*, 18–19, 43–44.

[17] In Italy, the exceptions were Venice, Genoa, and Lucca: see William J. Bouwsma, *Venice and the Defence of Republican Liberty Renaissance Values in the Age of the Counter Reformation* (Berkeley: University of California Press, 1968); Rodolfo Savelli, *la repubblica oligarchica: Legislazione, istituzioni, e ceti a Genova nel Cinquecento* (Milan: A. Giuffrè, 1981), Giorgio Doria and Rodolfo Savelli, "'Cittadini di governo' a Genova: Richezza e potere tra Cinque e Seicento," *Materiali per una storia della cultura giuridica* 10 (1980): 277–355; and Peter N. Miller, "Stoics Who Sing: Lessons in Citizenship from Early Modern Lucca," *The Historical Journal* 44:2 (June, 2001): 313–39. For the fate of republican theorizing in Italy in this period, see Vittor Ivo Comparato, "From the Crisis of Civil Culture to the Neapolitan Republic of 1647: Republicanism in Italy between the Sixteenth and Seventeenth Centuries," in *Republicanism: A Shared Heritage* I: *Republicanism and Constitutionalism in Early Modern Europe*, ed. Martin van Gelderen and Quentin Skinner (Cambridge, UK: Cambridge University Press, 2002), 169–93.

[18] For a recent attempt to situate England's experience within that of Europe's as a whole, see Jonathan Scott, *England's Troubles: Seventeenth-Century English Political Instability in European Context* (Cambridge, UK: Cambridge University Press, 2000).

[19] See William E. Klein, "Parliament, Liberty and the Continent in the Early Seventeenth Century: The Perception," *Parliamentary History* 6:2 (1987): 209–20, and Robert Zaller, "Parliament

managed to escape the sort of disorder that had paralyzed France in the late sixteenth century, and its parliament not only continued to meet throughout this period: it gained in strength, influence, and assertiveness,[20] while local self-government flourished in the parishes, boroughs, and shires.[21] This caused some of the English crown's subjects to think of themselves as citizens and even to conceive of England as a republic of sorts,[22] and it occasioned on the part of many of the better-educated a keen interest in the political institutions, practices, and ethos of the ancient commonwealths and a curiosity concerning the sources of Venice's undoubted success.[23] Playwrights, such as William Shakespeare and Ben Jonson, seized upon this fashion as an opportunity for the exploration of republican themes,[24] and translators and commentators used Tacitus' account

and the Crisis of European Liberty," in *Parliament and Liberty: From the Reign of Elizabeth to the English Civil War*, ed. J. H. Hexter (Stanford, CA: Stanford University Press, 1992), 201–24.

[20] Cf. Wallace Notestein, "The Winning of the Initiative by the House of Commons," *Proceedings of the British Academy* 11 (1924–25): 125–75, with G. R. Elton, "A High Road to Civil War?" in *From the Renaissance to the Counter-Reformation: Essays in Honor of Garrett Mattingly*, ed. Charles H. Carter (New York: Random House, 1965), 325–47, and see J. H. Hexter, "The Apology," in *For Veronica Wedgwood These: Studies in Seventeenth-Century History*, ed. Richard Ollard and Pamela Tudor-Craig (London: Collins, 1986), 13–44; then, cf. J. E. Neale, *The Elizabethan House of Commons* (London: J. Cape, 1949), *Elizabeth I and Her Parliaments, 1559–1581* (London: J. Cape, 1953), and *Elizabeth I and Her Parliaments, 1584–1601* (London: J. Cape, 1957), with G. R. Elton, *The Parliament of England, 1559–1581* (Cambridge, UK: Cambridge University Press, 1986), and see Patrick Collinson, "Puritans, Men of Business and Elizabethan Parliaments," in Collinson, *Elizabethan Essays* (London: The Hambledon Press, 1994), 59–86; then, consider J. H. Hexter, "Parliament, Liberty, and Freedom of Elections"; Johann P. Sommerville, "Parliament, Privilege, and the Liberties of the Subject"; David Harris Sacks, "Parliament, Liberty, and the Commonweal"; Clive Holmes, "Parliament, Liberty, Taxation, and Property"; Charles M. Gray, "Parliament, Liberty, and the Law"; and Thomas Cogswell, "War and the Liberties of the Subject," in *Parliament and Liberty*, 1–200, 225–51.

[21] See Mark Goldie, "The Unacknowledged Republic: Officeholding in Early Modern England," in *The Politics of the Excluded, ca. 1500–1850*, ed. Tim Harris (Houndsmills, UK: Palgrave, 2001), 153–94.

[22] See Patrick Collinson, "The Monarchical Republic of Queen Elizabeth I," *Bulletin of the John Rylands University Library of Manchester* 69:2 (Spring 1987): 394–424, reprinted in *Elizabethan Essays*, 31–57, and Markku Peltonen, "Citizenship and Republicanism in Elizabethan England," in *Republicanism: A Shared Heritage* I: *Republicanism and Constitutionalism in Early Modern Europe*, 85–106.

[23] Note Lisa Jardine and Anthony Grafton, "'Studied for Action': How Gabriel Harvey Read his Livy," *Past & Present* 129 (November 1990): 30–78, and see Markku Peltonen, *Classical Humanism and Republicanism in English Political Thought, 1570–1640* (Cambridge, UK: Cambridge University Press, 1995). In part because he fails to recognize the degree to which Machiavelli's *Discourses on Livy* embodies an attack on the actual presumptions of Renaissance humanism, Peltonen misconstrues as merely Ciceronian Sir Francis Bacon's quite radical critique of the contemplative life and as classical republican his interest in national greatness: cf. ibid., 136–45, 157, 169–70, 190–228, 254–57, 259–61, 265–66, with Paul A. Rahe, *Republics Ancient and Modern: Classical Republicanism and the American Revolution* (Chapel Hill: University of North Carolina Press, 1992), 80–104, 260–363, and see Robert K. Faulkner, *Francis Bacon and the Project of Progress* (Lanham, MD: Rowman and Littlefield, 1993).

[24] The larger political significance of their plays has attracted considerable attention in recent years: see Allan Bloom, "On Christian and Jew: *The Merchant of Venice*," "Cosmopolitan Man and the Political Community: *Othello*," and "The Morality of the Pagan Hero: *Julius Caesar*," in Allan Bloom with Harry V. Jaffa, *Shakespeare's Politics* (New York: Basics Books, 1964),

of the Julio–Claudian era as an interpretive guide to the character of the royal courts they encountered in their own day.[25] In England, a handful of would-be statesmen even turned to the *Discourses on Livy* for enlightenment concerning their country's aptitude for imperial grandeur.[26] By and large, however, interest in the ancients and in Machiavelli remained speculative: it did not, at that time, eventuate in the public advocacy of a concrete program of reform,[27] much less

13–112; Paul A. Cantor, *Shakespeare's Rome: Republic and Empire* (Ithaca, NY: Cornell University Press, 1976); Gail Kern Pastor, "To Starve with Feeding: The City in *Coriolanus*," *Shakespeare Studies* 11 (1978): 123–44; Michael Platt, *Rome and Romans According to Shakespeare*, revised edition (Lanham, MD: University Press of America, 1983); Jan H. Blits, *The End of the Ancient Republic: Shakespeare's Julius Caesar* (Lanham, MD: Rowman and Littlefield, 1993); Pamela K. Jensen, "'This is Venice': Politics in Shakespeare's *Othello*," in *Shakespeare's Political Pageant*, ed. Joseph Alulis and Vickie B. Sullivan (Lanham, MD: Rowman and Littlefield, 1996), 155–87; David Lowenthal, *Shakespeare and the Good Life: Ethics and Politics in Dramatic Form* (Lanham, MD: Rowman and Littlefield, 1997), 109–72; *Perspectives on Politics in Shakespeare*, ed. John A. Murley and Sean D. Sutton (Lanham, MD: Lexington Books, 2006); Blair Worden, "Shakespeare and Politics," *Shakespeare Survey* 44 (1991): 1–15, and "Ben Jonson among the Historians," in *Culture and Politics in Early Stuart England*, ed. Kevin Sharpe and Peter Lake (Stanford, CA: Stanford University Press, 1993), 67–90; and Martin Dzelzainis, "Shakespeare and Political Thought," in *A Companion to Shakespeare*, ed. David Scott Kastan (Oxford, UK: Blackwell, 1999), 100–16, as well as Andrew Hadfield, *Shakespeare and Renaissance Politics* (London: Thomson Learning, 2004), and *Shakespeare and Republicanism* (Cambridge, UK: Cambridge University Press, 2005). Note also Daniel Cliness Boughner, *The Devil's Disciple: Ben Jonson's Debt to Machiavelli* (New York: Philosophical Library, 1968); Anne Barton, "Livy, Machiavelli and Shakespeare's *Coriolanus*," in *Essays, Mainly Shakespearean* (Cambridge, UK: Cambridge University Press, 1994), 136–60; Robin Headlam Wells, "*Julius Caesar*, Machiavelli, and the Uses of History," *Shakespeare Survey* 55 (2002): 209–18; and Hugh Grady, *Shakespeare, Machiavelli, and Montaigne: Power and Subjectivity from Richard II to Hamlet* (Oxford, UK: Oxford University Press, 2002).

[25] See Alan T. Bradford, "Stuart Absolutism and the 'Utility' of Tacitus," *Huntington Library Quarterly* 46:2 (Spring 1983): 127–55; J. H. M. Salmon, "Stoicism and Roman Example: Seneca and Tacitus in Jacobean England," *Journal of the History of Ideas* 50:2 (April 1989): 199–225; David Womersley, "Sir Henry Savile's Translation of Tacitus and the Political Interpretation of Elizabethan Texts," *Review of English Studies* n. s. 42:167 (August 1991): 313–42; and Malcolm Smuts, "Court-Centred Politics and the Uses of Roman Historians, c. 1590–1630," in *Culture and Politics in Early Stuart England*, 21–43.

[26] Cf. Mario Praz, "Machiavelli and the Elizabethans," *Proceedings of the British Academy* 14 (1928): 49–97, and Christopher Morris, "Machiavelli's Reputation in Tudor England," *Il pensiero politico* 2:3 (1969): 416–33, with Sydney Anglo, "The Reception of Machiavelli in Tudor England: A Reassessment," *Il politico* 31:1 (March 1966): 127–38, and see Peltonen, *Classical Humanism and Republicanism in English Political Thought*, 73–102, 190–270, 302–4, 310–12. For particular examples, see Sydney Anglo, "A Machiavellian Solution to the Irish Problem: Richard Beacon's *Solon His Follie* (1594)," in *England and the Continental Renaissance: Essays in Honour of J. B. Trapp*, ed. Edward Chaney and Peter Mack (Woodbridge, UK: Boydell Press, 1990), 153–64; Markku Peltonen, "Classical Republicanism in England: The Case of Richard Beacon's *Solon His Follie*," *History of Political Thought* 15:4 (Winter 1994): 469–503; and Vincent Carey, "The Irish Face of Machiavelli: Richard Beacon's *Solon his Follie* and Republican Ideology in the Conquest of Ireland," in *Political Ideology in Ireland, 1534–1641*, ed. Hiram Morgan (Dublin: Four Courts, 1999), 83–109, as well as Anne Jacobson Shutte, "An Early Stuart Critique of Machiavelli as Historiographer: Thomas Jackson and the Discorsi," *Albion* 15:1 (Spring 1983): 1–18; and Michael Mendle, "A Machiavellian in the Long Parliament before the Civil War," *Parliamentary History* 8:1 (1989): 116–24.

[27] A potential exception to the rule was Thomas Starkey, who privately urged just such a program on Henry VIII in the 1530s – but to no avail: see Thomas F. Mayer, *Thomas Starkey and the*

in a political movement aimed at the establishment of a republic on English soil.

In the Elizabethan and Jacobean periods, most Englishmen took it for granted that their king governed by divine right.[28] Most also understood their rights and responsibilities in terms of prescription under the common law as a matter of tradition made rational by a process of trial and error, and sanctioned by time out of mind.[29] Some were inclined to think all government contractual, to treat the king's coronation oath as confirmation of this fact and even to envisage their monarchy as some sort of mixed regime,[30] but republicans in the strict sense they were not. Even in 1642, when the ancient constitution had ceased to function, when King and Parliament were mutually mistrustful and at daggers drawn, when civil war loomed on the horizon, and Henry Parker stepped forward to cut the Gordian knot by jettisoning divine right, tradition, and the common law and by justifying the absolute supremacy of Parliament on the basis of an appeal to popular sovereignty,[31] almost no one contemplated actually doing without a king; and it was not until the Long Parliament itself experienced paralysis in the face of a monarch defiant in defeat – who simply refused to knuckle under, abandon episcopalianism, and surrender his prerogative – that the Levellers emerged to redeploy against a parliament with no evident intention of holding new elections the radical populist doctrine that Parker had propagated.[32] Had anyone predicted in 1640 that, within a few

---

Commonweal: Humanist Politics and Religion in the Reign of Henry VIII (Cambridge, UK: Cambridge University Press, 1989).

[28] See Johann P. Sommerville, *Royalists and Patriots: Politics and Ideology in England, 1603–1640* (London: Longman, 1999), 9–54. This did not preclude their believing the king's prerogative limited in its scope: see Conrad Russell, "Divine Rights in the Early Seventeenth Century," in *Public Duty and Private Conscience in Seventeenth-Century England: Essays Presented to G. E. Aylmer*, ed. John Morrill, Paul Slack, and Daniel Woolf (Oxford, UK: Clarendon Press, 1993), 101–20.

[29] Cf. J. G. A. Pocock, *The Ancient Constitution and the Feudal Law: a Study of English Historical Thought in the Seventeenth Century: A Reissue with a Retrospect* (Cambridge, UK: Cambridge University Press, 1987), with Glenn Burgess, *The Politics of the Ancient Constitution: An Introduction to English Political Thought, 1603–1642* (University Park: Pennsylvania State University Press, 1993); Sommerville, *Royalists and Patriots*, 81–104; and John Phillip Reid, *Rule of Law: The Jurisprudence of Liberty in the Seventeenth and Eighteenth Centuries* (Dekalb: Northern Illinois University Press, 2004), and *The Ancient Constitution and the Origins of Anglo-American Liberty* (DeKalb: Northern Illinois University Press, 2005); then, see Alan D. T. Cromartie, "The Constitutionalist Revolution: The Transformation of Political Culture in Early Stuart England," *Past & Present* 163 (May, 1999): 76–120.

[30] See Sommerville, *Royalists and Patriots*, 55–80, and Peltonen, *Classical Humanism and Republicanism in English Political Thought*, 47–51, 91–98, 106–8, 112–13, 119–89, 229–70, 304, 309.

[31] Consider [Henry Parker] *Observations upon Some of His Majesties Late Answers and Expresses* (London: s.n., 1642), which is reprinted in photographic facsimile in *Tracts on Liberty in the Puritan Revolution, 1638–1647*, ed. William Haller (New York: Columbia University Press, 1934), II 167–213, in light of Michael Mendle, *Henry Parker and the English Civil War: The Political Thought of the Public's "Privado"* (Cambridge, UK: Cambridge University Press, 1995).

[32] See [Richard Overton and William Walwyn], *A Remonstrance of Many Thousand Citizens, and Other Freeborn People of England to Their Owne House of Commons* (London: s.n., 1646), which is reprinted in *The English Levellers*, ed. Andrew Sharp (Cambridge, UK: Cambridge

years, the nation would be bitterly divided over the question of ecclesiastical polity and that advocates of episcopacy, presbyterianism, and congregationalism under the supervision of godly magistrates, and nearly complete congregational autonomy would soon be at odds with Quakers who interrupted church services, with Fifth Monarchists intent on establishing by force the rule of the elect, and with one another, he would have been regarded as utterly daft.

When Thomas Hobbes blamed the outbreak of the English Civil War on the fact that so many of his countrymen were well read in the classics,[33] he greatly exaggerated the importance of the phenomenon.[34] Sir Philip Sidney came closer to the truth in his *Arcadia* when he treated the late Elizabethan enthusiasm for republicanism on the model of Athens, Sparta, and Rome as an academic concern, "a matter more in imagination than practice" appealing solely to "the discoursing sort of men."[35] If, in the Elizabethan and Jacobean periods, ordinary educated Englishmen took to heart anything from their reading of Herodotus, Thucydides, Xenophon, Isocrates, Plato, Aristotle, Demosthenes, Polybius, Cicero, Sallust, Livy, Tacitus, and Roman law, it was not a predilection for participatory self-government and political liberty on the ancient Greek or Roman model: it was an understanding of personal, individual freedom in contrast with chattel slavery that rendered them deeply suspicious of measures and practices on the part of the Crown tending in any way to subvert their independence and threatening thereby what they were pleased to call their status as "free subjects." Political liberty was not for them, as it had been for the ancients, an end in itself: it was an instrument requisite for the protection of their "lives, Liberties and Estates."[36] Edmund Burke hit the nail on the head

---

University Press, 1998), 33–53, and which the House of Commons had burned at the Old Exchange in London and in the New Palace Yard at Westminster on 22 May 1647.

[33] See Hobbes, *Leviathan* II.xxi.8–9. This was a recurring theme: see Hobbes, *Elements of Law* II.viii.10; *De cive* III.xii.3; and *Behemoth*, 158, as well as Thomas Hobbes, *Historia ecclesiastica* 365–84, in *LW*, V 359.

[34] See Blair Worden, "Republicanism, Regicide and Republic: The English Experience," in *Republicanism: A Shared Heritage* I: *Republicanism and Constitutionalism in Early Modern Europe*, 307–27. Cf. David Norbrook, *Writing the English Republic: Poetry, Rhetoric and Politics, 1627–1660* (Cambridge, UK: Cambridge University Press, 1999).

[35] Sir Philip Sidney, *The Countess of Pembroke's Arcadia (The Old Arcadia)*, ed. Jean Robertson (Oxford, UK: Clarendon Press, 1973), 320–21. See Blair Worden, *The Sound of Virtue: Philip Sidney's Arcadia and Elizabethan Politics* (New Haven, CT: Yale University Press, 1997), esp. 209–94, and consider Worden, "Classical Republicanism and the Puritan Revolution," in *History and Imagination: Essays in Honour of H. R. Trevor-Roper*, ed. Hugh Lloyd-Jones, Valerie Pearl, and Blair Worden (London: Duckworth, 1981), 182–200.

[36] Cf. Quentin Skinner, "Classical Liberty, Renaissance Translation, and the English Civil War," in *Visions of Politics* (Cambridge, UK: Cambridge University Press, 2002) II: *Renaissance Virtues*, 308–43, with Rahe, *Republics Ancient and Modern*, 17–229 (esp. 28–54); then, cf. Chaim Wirszubski, *Libertas as a Political Idea at Rome during the Late Republic and Early Principate* (Cambridge, UK: Cambridge University Press, 1950), with P. A. Brunt, "*Libertas* in the Republic," in *The Fall of the Roman Republic and Related Essays* (Oxford, UK: Clarendon Press, 1988), 281–350, and see Claude Nicolet, *The World of the Citizen in Republican Rome* (Berkeley: University of California Press, 1980). Here, as elsewhere, Skinner errs in failing to see that for the Romans (as for the Greeks), in contrast to nearly all of their English admirers at this time, non-domination was less an end in itself than an instrument providing access to a political participation which they took to be of greater dignity. The ancients understood what modern

when, in looking back on this period, he observed, "Abstract liberty, like other mere abstractions, is not to be found. Liberty inheres in some sensible object; and every nation has formed to itself some favorite point, which by way of eminence becomes the criterion of their happiness. It happened ... that the great contests for freedom in this country were from the earliest times chiefly upon the question of taxing. Most of the contests in the ancient commonwealths turned primarily on the right of election of magistrates, or on the balance among the several orders of the state. The question of money was not with them so immediate. But in England it was otherwise."[37]

It is no surprise, then, that, in England as well as on the continent, Machiavelli was at first valued almost solely for the advice that he gave to princes, their ministers, and aspirants to princely rule on matters of state.[38] In fact, given the unfavorable character of the circumstances in which his books became available to the larger world, the only real ground for astonishment is that the Florentine ever came to be widely appreciated for his republicanism at all. In England, it took a revolution to force a positive reassessment of the *Discourses on Livy*, and even then there were serious obstacles standing in the way.

After all, the trial and execution of Charles I were not a part of anyone's plan. When the Long Parliament was elected late in October 1640, its members were chosen for the purpose of achieving a redress of grievances. Apart, perhaps, from Henry Marten,[39] no one at the time was intent on overthrowing England's ancient constitution: their goal was to save it. Apart, perhaps, from Thomas Hobbes, who appears to have forecast the disaster as early as 1629,[40] no one else even imagined that their attempt at a redress of grievances would eventuate in civil war, the beheading of a king, the abolition of the monarchy and House of Lords, and the establishment of a republic on English soil. Had anyone even suggested the possibility, nearly all of those elected to the Long Parliament would have recoiled in horror.[41]

---

students of the subject tend to forget: that the notion of exercise central to the idea of positive liberty presupposes the opportunity inherent in negative liberty and that a way of life grounded on the former must embrace the latter as well. See Rahe, "Situating Machiavelli," 270–308.

[37] See Edmund Burke, Speech on Moving Resolutions for Conciliation with the Colonies, 22 March 1775, in *The Writings and Speeches of the Right Honourable Edmund Burke* (Boston: Little, Brown, 1901), II 120–21.

[38] See Raab, *The English Face of Machiavelli*, 30–117; Kahn, *Machiavellian Rhetoric*, 85–148; Peltonen, *Classical Humanism and Republicanism in English Political Thought*, 73–102, 190–270; and Anglo, *Machiavelli – The First Century*, passim.

[39] See Edward Hyde, earl of Clarendon, *The Life of Edward Earl of Clarendon* (Oxford, UK: Clarendon Press, 1857) 1.91. In this connection, see also Edward Hyde, earl of Clarendon, *The History of the Rebellion and Civil Wars in England*, ed. W. Dunn Macray (Oxford, UK: Clarendon Press, 1888) 5.280

[40] See Chapter Nine of this text.

[41] See Margaret Atwood Judson, *The Crisis of the Constitution: An Essay in Constitutional and Political Thought in England, 1603–1645* (New Brunswick, NJ: Rutgers University Press, 1949). Note also Hugh R. Trevor-Roper, "Oliver Cromwell and His Parliaments," *The Seventeenth Century: Religion Reformation, and Social Change* (New York: Harper & Row, 1968), 345–91 (esp. 345–55).

Of course, when the Civil War began in earnest, as it did late in 1642, a few bold speculators did think their way through the logic then unfolding;[42] and in Parliament, from that time on, Marten, Sir Peter Wentworth, and the handful of radicals under their sway exploited the conflict mercilessly, seizing on every opportunity to attack royal authority, to intensify the antagonisms occasioned by bloodshed, and to subvert the awe and reverence then still almost universally accorded the king.[43] Their efforts, however, were largely wasted, for all but a tiny minority of their colleagues did, in fact, recoil in horror in December 1648 and January 1649, when the erstwhile adherents of the parliamentary cause found themselves forced to choose between the unpalatable alternatives of regicide and a compromise with Charles that was tantamount to an abandonment of nearly everything for which they had fought.[44]

There can be little doubt as to the revulsion provoked by the trial and execution of the king. As everyone understood at the time, this was an unprecedented, revolutionary act.[45] On the day of Charles's beheading, a bold and enterprising printer named William Dugard published a royalist tract entitled *Eikon Basilikē: The Portraiture of His Sacred Majesty in His Solitudes and Sufferings*, which had been cleared for publication by as-yet-unpurged presbyterian licensers shocked by the coup d'état carried out by the New Model Army, enraged at the regicide, and intent on subverting what they regarded as a tyranny.[46] Within a year of its appearance, this remarkable work went through thirty-five editions in London and twenty-five more in Ireland and elsewhere.[47]

---

[42] See David Wootton, "From Rebellion to Revolution: The Crisis of the Winter of 1642/43 and the Origins of Civil War Radicalism," *English Historical Review* 105:416 (July 1990): 654–69.

[43] Begin with C. M. Williams, "Extremist Tactics in the Long Parliament, 1642–1643," *Historical Studies* 15:57 (October 1971): 136–50; then see Sarah Barber, *Regicide and Republicanism: Politics and Ethics in the English Revolution* (Edinburgh, UK: Edinburgh University Press, 1998), 1–146, and *A Revolutionary Rogue: Henry Marten and the English Republic* (Phoenix Mill, UK: Sutton, 2000), 1–24. On Marten more generally, see Williams, "The Anatomy of a Radical Gentleman: Henry Marten," in *Puritans and Revolutionaries: Essays in Seventeenth-Century History Presented to Christopher Hill*, ed. Donald Pennington and Keith Thomas (Oxford, UK: Clarendon Press, 1978), 118–38, and Sarah Barber, *A Revolutionary Rogue*, passim.

[44] See David Underdown, *Pride's Purge: Politics in the Puritan Revolution* (Oxford, UK: Clarendon Press, 1971), 7–256, and Barber, *Regicide and Republicanism*, 121–46. Those most intimately involved in the regicide displayed considerable reluctance as well: see John Adamson, "The Frighted Junto: Perceptions of Ireland, and the Last Attempts at Settlement with Charles I," in *The Regicides and the Execution of Charles I*, ed. Jason T. Peacey (Houndmills, UK: Palgrave, 2001), 36–70.

[45] See Underdown, *Pride's Purge*, 260–61, 297–335.

[46] See Jason T. Peacey, *Politicians and Pamphleteers: Propaganda during the English Civil Wars and Interregnum* (Aldershot, UK: Ashgate, 2004), 119, 132 62 (esp. 156–57).

[47] Note Francis F. Madan, *A New Bibliography of the Eikon Basilike of King Charles the First* (Oxford, UK: Oxford University Press, 1950), and see Hugh Trevor-Roper, "'Eikon Basilikē:' The Problem of the King's Book," *Historical Essays* (New York: Harper & Row, 1957), 211–20; Philip Knachel, "Introduction," *Eikon Basilike: The Portraiture of His Sacred Majesty in His Solitudes and Sufferings* (Ithaca, NY: Cornell University Press, 1966), xi–xxxii; Lois Potter, *Secret Rites and Secret Writing: Royalist Literature, 1641–1660* (Cambridge, UK: Cambridge University Press, 1989), 156–207; Thomas N. Corns, "Lovelace, Herrick and the *Eikon Basilike*," in Corns, *Uncloistered Virtue: English Political Literature, 1640–1660* (Oxford, UK:

By the dark deed that gave it birth, the English republic was arguably doomed from the start.[48]

The recognition of their isolation to a very considerable degree paralyzed the Rump that governed England after Colonel Thomas Pride's purge of the Long Parliament on 6 December 1648.[49] It was not until 19 May 1649, more than four months after the execution of the king, that this assembly even managed formally to declare England "a Commonwealth and Free State . . . henceforth to be governed . . . by the supreme authority of this nation, the representatives of the people in Parliament, . . . and that without any king or House of Lords."[50] The knowledge, however, that the regicide republicans were a small and insular minority did not deter the handful of men in Parliament who had already demonstrated, in the crisis of this time, the extraordinary resolution requisite if they were to follow through on the logic of what they had almost all so innocently and unheedingly begun more than eight years before. If anything, their sense of isolation made these men all the more resolute: all the more insistent on defending the propriety of all that they had done, all the more intent on asserting the dignity and legitimacy of the new regime, and all the more eager to prove it a success in its endeavors both at home and abroad.[51]

It was among this select group and the small proportion of those within the populace as a whole who admired their courage and determination that we find those who set out to rethink English politics from the ground up in light of the new species of republicanism championed by Niccolò Machiavelli. These were, however, exceedingly few in number, for most of their fellow republicans were Puritans,[52] and for understandable reasons, as we shall soon see, devout

Oxford University Press, 1992), 80–91; Kevin Sharpe, "The King's Writ: Royal Authors and Royal Authority in Early Modern England," in *Culture and Politics in Early Stuart England*, 117–38 (esp. 136–38); Steven Zwicker, "The King's Head and the Politics of Literary Property: The *Eikon Basilike* and *Eikonoklastes*," in Zwicker, *Lines of Authority: Politics and English Literary Culture, 1649–1689* (Ithaca, NY: Cornell University Press, 1993), 36–59; and Elizabeth Skerpan Wheeler, "*Eikon Basilike* and the Rhetoric of Self-Representation," in *The Royal Image: Representations of Charles I*, ed. Thomas N. Corns (Cambridge, UK: Cambridge University Press, 1999), 122–40. For the role played in this period by the royalist press, see Amos Tub, "Mixed Messages: Royalist Newsbook Reports of Charles I's Execution and of the Leveller Rising," *Huntington Library Quarterly* 67:1 (March 2004): 59–74.

[48] See Kevin Sharpe, "'An Image Doting Rabble': The Failure of Republican Culture in Seventeenth Century England," in *Refiguring Revolutions: Aesthetics and Politics from the English Revolution to the Romantic Revolution*, ed. Kevin Sharpe and Steven N. Zwicker (Berkeley: University of California Press, 1998), 25–56

[49] See Underdown, *Pride's Purge*, 258–96; Blair Worden, *The Rump Parliament, 1648–1653* (Cambridge, UK: Cambridge University Press, 1974); and Barber, *Regicide and Republicanism*, 147–201. See also Worden, "Republicanism, Regicide and Republic," 316–27.

[50] "An Act Declaring England to be a Commonwealth," 19 May 1649, in *CDPR*, 388.

[51] Cf. Barber, *Regicide and Republicanism*, 1–146, with ibid., 147–201, and see Sean Kelsey, *Inventing a Republic: The Political Culture of the English Commonwealth, 1649–1653* (Stanford, CA: Stanford University Press, 1997), and Norbrook, *Writing the English Republic*, 192–242.

[52] Scott, *England's Troubles*, passim, quite rightly emphasizes the centrality of the religious issue. See also Jonathan Scott, *Commonwealth Principles: Republican Writing of the English Revolution* (Cambridge, UK: Cambridge University Press, 2004), passim (esp. 41–62).

Christians tended to balk at the prospect of embracing a thinker who was thought to have given to the devil his English moniker "Old Nick."[53]

---

[53] See Samuel Butler, *Hudibras*, ed. John Wilders (Oxford, UK: Clarendon Press, 1967) 3.1.1313–16. For a later example, see [John Mackenzie], "A Letter to the People" (1769), in *The Letters of Freeman, etc.: Essays on the Nonimportation Movement in South Carolina, Collected by William Henry Drayton*, ed. Robert M. Weir (Columbia: University of South Carolina Press, 1977), 21. In 1771, while in self-imposed exile in London, Drayton gathered and published as a book this material, which had appeared two years before in the *South-Carolina Gazette*. Whether the devil's moniker is so derived is a matter of controversy: cf. Ernst Leisi, "On the Trail of Old Nick," in *The History and the Dialects of English: Festchrift for Eduard Kolb*, ed. Andreas Fischer (Heidelberg: Carl Winter, 1989), 53–57.

PART I

MACHIAVELLI'S NEW REPUBLICANISM

Preface

It is by no means fortuitous that, in seventeenth-century England, Machiavellianism was synonymous with evil. After all, Machiavelli's most famous book was designed to shock, and shock it did. To see why, one need only examine the fifteenth chapter of *The Prince*.

There its author takes up a question first examined by Aristotle in his *Nicomachean Ethics* and, then, subsequently revisited by Thomas Aquinas in his *Summa Theologiæ* – "the qualities for which human beings, and princes in particular, are generally praised or condemned." And just as Aristotle and Thomas, in the course of their discussion of these qualities, had produced a list of eleven moral virtues juxtaposed with their attendant vices, so in this context Machiavelli lists eleven pairs of apparently opposed qualities.[1]

Before doing so, however, Machiavelli insists that his account of the virtues and vices is somehow radically novel: that in his discussion of "the modes and government" proper for dealing "with subjects or with friends" he has departed "from the orders of others." As he puts it, his intention of writing "a thing useful for one who understands it" renders it "more profitable" for him "to go after the effectual truth of the matter (*andare drieto alla verità effettuale della cosa*) rather than its image (*che alla imaginazione di essa*)." The efforts of his "many" predecessors, who "have imagined republics and principalities which have never been seen or known to exist in truth," he dismisses as worthless. There is, he explains, so great "a distance between how one lives and how" one is taught, "one ought to live" that "he who abandons that which is done in favor of that which ought to be done learns rather his ruin than his preservation." He therefore concludes that "it is necessary for a prince, if he would maintain himself, to learn how not to be good," as this term is in all societies

---

[1] Cf. Arist. *Eth. Nic.* 1105b19–1109b26 (esp. 1105b28–1106a1) and Thomas Aquinas, *Summa Theologiæ* I 2, qq. 59–60 (esp. q.60.a.5.c) with Machiavelli, *Il principe* 15, in *Opere*, 280; note Leo Strauss, *Thoughts on Machiavelli* (Glencoe, IL: Free Press, 1958), 236 (with 338–39 n. 139); and see Clifford Orwin, "Machiavelli's Unchristian Charity," *American Political Science Review* 72:4 (December 1978): 1217–28, and Richard H. Cox, "Aristotle and Machiavelli on Liberality," in *The Crisis of Liberal Democracy: A Straussian Perspective*, ed. Kenneth L. Deutsch and Walter Soffer (Albany: State University of New York Press, 1987), 125–47. In this connection, note Deirdre N. McCloskey, *The Bourgeois Virtues* (Chicago: University of Chicago Press, 2006), 370–72 (with 201–2).

conventionally understood, "and to use this knowledge or not as necessity demands."[2]

The pronounced admiration that he displays for moral dexterity in this passage helps explain why there is no apparent order to Machiavelli's list of the qualities ordinarily praised and blamed, why it is so often unclear which he considers the virtue and which the vice, why he places a much greater emphasis on the reputation for virtue than on its practice, and why, in his enumeration, justice – the last and greatest of the moral virtues examined by Aristotle and Thomas – is never even mentioned at all. As the last sentence of his fifteenth chapter and the substance of the three chapters immediately succeeding it make abundantly clear, in the Florentine's view, fidelity and the other "qualities which are held to be good" and treachery and the other qualities which "appear" to be vices are not intrinsic qualities of soul: they are postures, which – in one's dealings not only with enemies but also with subjects and even with friends – one needs to assess, assume, and advertise solely with an eye to "one's own security and well-being." In short, the *virtù* that Machiavelli recommends to his "new prince" is a species of virtuosity practiced without regard to genuine moral evil and good.[3]

Of course, Machiavelli's rhetorical strategy in the *Discourses on Livy* was markedly different from that which he followed in *The Prince*. If he included passages intended to shock, there were nonetheless others designed to console, and for the purpose of persuasion he was perfectly prepared to resort to ordinary moral language of the sort that he elsewhere debunked. He deliberately invited thereby the misunderstanding to which that work has always given rise,[4] for he had a profound appreciation for the subversive uses to which contradiction and confusion can be put, and he recognized that he was most likely to attract disciples by enticing, titillating, reassuring, and then seducing his fellow Renaissance humanists: the less than fully devout, classically trained admirers of pagan Greece and Rome.

The Florentine begins his *Discourses on Livy* by administering to its readers a gratifying shock. In the opening sentence of its preface, a section of the book he composed with evident care,[5] he presents himself as a revolutionary innovator by comparing himself with Christopher Columbus of Genoa, with Amerigo

---

[2] See Machiavelli, *Il principe* 15, in *Opere*, 280. One can best make sense of Machiavelli's peculiar use of the term *imaginazione* in this passage by attending to Lucretius' use of the term *imago* in his account of vision (4.51–52): see John M. Najemy, *Between Friends: Discourses of Power and Desire in the Machiavelli-Vettori Letters of 1513–1515* (Princeton, NJ: Princeton University Press, 1993), 189–90 (with n. 23).

[3] Consider Machiavelli, *Il principe* 15–18, in *Opere*, 280–84, in light of the remarks it elicited in the Elizabethan period from the Oxford don John Case: see Charles B. Schmitt, *John Case and Aristotelianism in Renaissance England* (Kingston: McGill-Queen's University Press, 1983), 181–86.

[4] Consider, for example, Edward Hyde, Earl of Clarendon, *The History of the Rebellion and Civil Wars in England*, ed. W. Dunn Macray (Oxford, UK: Clarendon Press, 1888) 10.169, in light of Machiavelli, *Discorsi sopra la prima deca di Tito Livio* 1.26, in Machiavelli, *Opere*, 109.

[5] It is the only part of the book that survives as an autograph, and it shows evidence of careful redrafting: see Carlo Pincin, "Le prefazioni e la dedicatoria dei *Discorsi* di Machiavelli," *Giornale storico della letteratura italiana* 143:441 (First Trimester, 1966): 72–83.

Vespucci of Florence, and the like – men whose discoveries had all been quite recently made. It is, he argues, "no less perilous to discover new modes and orders (*modi ed ordini nuovi*) than to search unknown waters and lands," and he contends that the "new modes and orders" which he has discovered constitute "a path (*via*) as yet untrodden by anyone (*non essendo suta ancora da alcuno trita*)."[6] Then, a few sentences thereafter, he suddenly and unexpectedly reverses course, and to those inclined to regard radical innovation with suspicion, he offers a species of consolation by presenting himself as an advocate for a return to patterns of conduct abandoned long before.

In the latter passage, Machiavelli at first draws attention to the honor accorded in his day to classical antiquity – to the manner in which ancient art was then sought after and imitated, to the degree to which "the civil laws" and the "medicine" of his day were "nothing other than judgments (*sentenze*) handed down by ancient juriconsults" and "the experiments carried out by ancient physicians." Then, he laments the fact that "in ordering republics, in maintaining states, in governing kingdoms, in ordering the military and administering war, in judging subjects, and in increasing empire, neither prince nor republic is to be found that has recourse to the examples of the ancients." This failure he traces "not so much" to "the weakness (*debolezza*) into which the present religion has conducted the world" or to "the evil done many Christian provinces and cities" by the "ambitious idleness (*ambizioso ozio*)" of the clergy as to his contemporaries not possessing "a true knowledge of histories, through not drawing from reading them that sense (*senso*) nor from savoring them that taste that they have in themselves."[7]

In composing an extended commentary on the histories of the Roman writer Livy, Machiavelli would appear to be attempting to make available to his readers the crucial "knowledge" that they lack by teaching them to "read" not just Livy but "all the histories," including the Bible, "in a sensible and judicious fashion (*sensatamente*)" suited to "drawing from reading them that sense (*senso*)" and "from savoring them that taste that they have in themselves."[8] It soon becomes evident, however, that one's first impression is more nearly correct, that reading *sensatamente* has very little to do with gaining a genuine appreciation for what Livy, the authors of the Bible, and the other historians of antiquity actually had in mind, and that Machiavelli's antiquarianism is a red herring – designed to gull the credulous and to enable him to insinuate an understanding of republicanism that is no less novel and shocking than his teaching in *The Prince* concerning the posture that one should adopt with regard to one's friends. If we are ever to understand the thinking of those in England who advocated republicanism in the period stretching from 1649 to 1660, it is with an exploration of the new species of republicanism articulated by Machiavelli that we must begin.

---

[6] See Machiavelli, *Discorsi* 1 Proemio, in *Opere*, 76.

[7] See Machiavelli, *Discorsi* 1 Proemio, in *Opere*, 76.

[8] Consider Machiavelli, *Discorsi* 1 Proemio, in *Opere*, 76, in light of *Discorsi* 1.23.4, 3.30.1, in *Opere*, 107, 237.

I

Machiavelli's Populist Turn

Niccolò Machiavelli was no doubt many things, but a classical republican he was not.[1] The classical republican argument, familiar to all in antiquity but articulated most fully in the works of Aristotle and Cicero on the basis of their observation of Greek and Roman practice,[2] was grounded in the conviction that

[1] Elsewhere I have made a systematic attempt to correct this error: note its revival by J. H. Whitfield, *Machiavelli* (Oxford, UK: Basil Blackwell, 1947), and Zera S. Fink, *The Classical Republicans: An Essay in the Recovery of a Pattern of Thought in Seventeenth-Century England*, second edition (Evanston, IL: Northwestern University Press, 1962); then cf. Quentin Skinner, *The Foundations of Modern Political Thought I: The Renaissance* (Cambridge, UK: Cambridge University Press, 1978), 152–86; *Machiavelli* (New York: Hill and Wang, 1981), 21–77, 96; "Machiavelli on the Maintenance of Liberty," *Politics* 18:2 (November 1983): 3–15; "Ambrogio Lorenzetti: The Artist as Political Philosopher," *Proceedings of the British Academy* 72 (1986): 1–56; "Political Philosophy," in *The Cambridge History of Renaissance Philosophy*, ed. Charles B. Schmitt, Quentin Skinner, Eckhard Kessler, and Jill Kraye (Cambridge, UK: Cambridge University Press, 1988), 389–452 (esp. 430–41); "Machiavelli's *Discorsi* and the Pre-Humanist Origins of Republican Ideas" and "The Republican Ideal of Political Liberty," in *Machiavelli and Republicanism*, ed. Gisela Bock, Quentin Skinner, and Maurizio Viroli (Cambridge, UK: Cambridge University Press, 1990), 121–41, 293–309; and "The Vocabulary of Renaissance Republicanism: A Cultural *longue-durée*?" in *Language and Images of Renaissance Italy*, ed. Alison Brown (Oxford, UK: Clarendon Press, 1995), 87–110, with Paul A. Rahe, "Situating Machiavelli," in *Renaissance Civic Humanism: Reappraisals and Reflections*, ed. James Hankins (Cambridge, UK: Cambridge University Press, 2000), 270–308; and, finally, cf. J. G. A. Pocock, *The Machiavellian Moment: Florentine Political Thought and the Atlantic Republican Tradition* (Princeton, NJ: Princeton University Press, 1975), passim (esp. 156–218, 383–400), with Vickie B. Sullivan, "Machiavelli's Momentary 'Machiavellian Moment': A Reconsideration of Pocock's Treatment of the *Discourses*," *Political Theory* 20:2 (May 1992): 309–18, and see Paul A. Rahe, *Republics Ancient and Modern: Classical Republicanism and the American Revolution* (Chapel Hill: University of North Carolina Press, 1992), 15–541 (esp. 28–135, 260–67, 364–444). See also Friedrich Mehmel, "Machiavelli und die Antike," in *Antike und Abendland: Beiträge zum Verständnis der Griechen und Römer und ihres Nachlebens*, ed. Bruno Snell (Hamburg: Marion von Schröder Verlag, 1948), III 152–86; Claude LeFort, *Le Travail de l'oeuvre Machiavel* (Paris: Gallimard, 1972), and "Machiavel et la *verità effetuale*," in *Écrire: À l'Épreuve du politique* (Paris: Calmann-Lévy, 1992), 141–79; Vickie B. Sullivan, *Machiavelli's Three Romes: Religion, Human Liberty, and Politics Reformed* (DeKalb: Northern Illinois University Press, 1996), and *Machiavelli, Hobbes, and the Formation of a Liberal Republicanism in England* (Cambridge, UK: Cambridge University Press, 2004), 31–79; Marco Geuna, "La tradizione repubblicana e i suoi interpreti: famiglie teoriche e discontinuità concettuali," *Filosofia politica* 12:1 (April 1998): 101–32, and Miguel E. Vatter, *Between Form and Event: Machiavelli's Theory of Political Freedom* (Dordrecht: Kluwer Academic, 2000), passim (esp. 18–21).

[2] For a systematic attempt to make evident the manner in which Aristotelian theory is an elucidation of prior Greek political practice, see Rahe, *Republics Ancient and Modern*, 17–229.

the distinctive human feature is man's capacity for reasoned speech (*lógos*). By this, its exponents meant that, in contrast with the other animals, man possesses more than mere voice (*phōnē*) – that he can do more than communicate his feelings and appeal to the passions of his listeners. For Cicero, as for Aristotle, *lógos* is something more refined than the capacity to introduce private feelings and passions into the public arena: it enables the human being to perform as no other animal can; it makes it possible for him to perceive and make clear to others through reasoned discourse the difference between what is advantageous and what is harmful, between what is just and what is unjust, and between what is good and what is evil. It is the sharing of these things, they insist, which constitutes the household and the political community, each as a moral community (*koinōnia*).

This emphasis on man's capacity for moral and political rationality eventuated in an understanding of politics and the common good that transcended the simple pursuit of material interest. Politics may begin with the concern for mere life, as Aristotle insists, but it is sustained, he also contends, by the desire to live nobly and well. Public deliberation begins with the question of advantage but somehow can never escape the question of justice and the good. For politics to achieve what it can, however, the citizens must receive a moral and intellectual education: they must become virtuous. Their *paideía* in virtue, the development of their natural potential in this regard, is the first concern of the Aristotelian and Ciceronian lawgiver.[3]

This helps explain why Plato's Athenian stranger could intelligibly claim that politics is "the art whose task is caring for souls."[4] It makes comprehensible the fact that one ancient observer defined regime (*politeía*) as "the one way of life of a whole *pólis*," while Isocrates spoke of the community's *politeía* as "the city's soul."[5] It would, nonetheless, be a mistake to understand the regime analysis of the Romans and Greeks in a narrowly cultural sense. To be sure, in one passage of *The Politics*, Aristotle suggests that it is the provision of a common *paideía* – and nothing else – that turns a multitude (*plêthos*) into a unit and constitutes it as a *pólis*. Yet in another, he indicates that it is the constitution or regime – the *politeía* as determined by its *políteuma* or "ruling order" – that defines the *pólis* as such. Though apparently in contradiction, the two statements are in fact equivalent[6] – for Aristotle's conviction is that what really matters most with regard to political understanding is this: to decide who is to rule or what sorts of human beings are to share in rule and function as

---

[3] Cf. Cic. *Off.* 1.16.50–17.58; *Inv. Rh.* 1.1.1–2.3, 4.5, 5.6–7, 2.51.156–59.178; *De or.* 1.3.12, 6.20, 8.31–34, 15.68–69, 2.2.5–6, with Arist. *Pol.* 1252b27–1253a39, 1278b15–30, 1280a25–1281a10, 1283b42–1284a3; *Eth. Nic.* 1097a15–1098b8, 1169b16–18; and then see Cic. *Off.* 1.4.11–7.24, 2.5.16–17, 12.41–42, 3.5.21–6.27, 17.69; *Fin.* 2.14.45–47, 5.13–14.38, 23.65–66; *Rep.* 2.36.61, 3.2.3–4.7, 22.33, 25.37, 31.43–35.48, 5.4.6–6.8; *Leg.* 1.6.18–16.45, 22.58–24.63, 2.5.11–13. In this connection, see Paul A. Rahe, "The Primacy of Politics in Classical Greece," *American Historical Review* 89:2 (April 1984), 265–93; *Republics Ancient and Modern*, 15–229 (esp. 28–135); and "Situating Machiavelli," 270–308.

[4] Pl. *Leg.* 1.650b.

[5] See Schol. Pl. *Leg.* 1.625b and Isoc. 7.14

[6] Cf. Arist. *Pol.* 1263b36–37 with 1276a8–b15.

a community's *políteuma* is to determine which of the various and competing titles to rule is to be authoritative; in turn, this is to decide which qualities are to be admired and honored in the city, what is to be considered advantageous and just, and how happiness (*eudaimonía*) is to be pursued; and this decision – more than any other – determines the *paideía* that constitutes "the one way of life of a whole *pólis*." Put bluntly, it is the distribution and disposition of a polity's offices and honors (*táxis tōn archōn*), the act constituting its *políteuma* – that, more than anything else, shapes the *paideía* that makes of its citizens something more than a random collection of otherwise unassociated individuals.[7]

Differential Moral and Political Rationality

The classical republicans were persuaded that the quality that distinguishes man from the animals also distinguishes men from one another: they embraced a doctrine of differential moral and political rationality. Thus, in a manner reminiscent of the Greek orator and educator Isocrates, Cicero emphasizes the unequal distribution of reason among men and the significance of this distribution with regard to their capacity for political speech. The "wise man (*vir sapiens*)," whom he singles out in his rhetorical works and identifies there, in his *Tusculan Disputations*, and in *Pro Sestio* as the political community's founder, is nature's nobleman – able by the exercise of "reason and speech (*ratio et oratio*)" to render his "auditors merciful and mild" where they had always been quite "savage and wild"; able "to draw scattered mankind into a single place"; able "to lead them from a brutish and uncivilized life" to the "cultivation of citizenship and their humanity"; able "to prescribe within cities already established laws, judgments, and the sense of right"; able, in sum, to bring philosophy, virtue, and judgment to bear on human affairs and to form thereby a community of moral discourse accommodating and transcending mere material interest.[8] In both *De inventione* and in *De oratore*, Cicero stresses that, in developing his potential for *ratio et oratio*, such a *vir sapiens* can come to "surpass" other human beings in the very sphere in which they are most superior to the other animals.[9]

---

7 After reading Pl. *Resp.* 8.543c–9.592b and *Leg.* 3.689e–701b, 4.712b–715d, note *Leg.* 1.631d–632c, 3.696c–698a, 4.707a–d, 711b–d, and consider 6.752b–768e in light of 5.734e–735a, 6.751a–b, and 7.822d–824a (esp. 823a); then compare Arist. *Pol.* 1273a39–b1 and 1278b6–15 with 1295a40–b2; consider 1328b2–23 (esp. 13–14, 22–23 – where I am inclined to adopt the reading of Lambinus) in light of 1328a35–b1; and see Arist. *Rh.* 1365b21–1366a22. And finally, note Arist. *Pol.* 1264a24–1266b38, 1276b1–13, 1277a12–b32, 1283a3–42, 1288a6–b4, 1289a10–25, 1292b11–21, 1294a9–14, 1297a14–b34, 1311a8–20, 1317a40–b17, 1323a14–1342b34; and see Cic. *Leg.* 3.12.28–14.32.

8 Cf. Cic. *Inv. Rh.* 1.2.2–3 and *De or.* 1.8.33 with Xen. *Mem.* 4.3.11–12 and Isoc. 3.5–9, 15.253–56, and see Cic. *Sest.* 42.91–92, *Tusc.* 1.25.62, 5.2.5. Note also Cic. *Nat. D.* 2.59.148.

9 The pertinent passages (Cic. *Inv. Rh.* 1.4.5, *De or.* 1.8.32–33) need to be read in light of Cicero's insistence on subordinating *oratio* to *ratio* (*Off.* 1.16.50–17.58, *Inv. Rh.* 1.1.1–5.7, 2.51.156–59.178, *De Or.* 1.3.12, 6.20, 8.31, 34, 15.68–69, 2.2.5–6) and in light of his commitment to a notion of differential moral and political rationality: *Off.* 1.4.11–7.24, 2.5.16–17, 12.41–42, 3.5.21–6.27, 17.69; *Fin.* 2.14.45–47, 5.13–14.38, 23.65–66; *Rep.* 2.36.61, 3.2.3–4.7, 22.33, 25.37, 31.43–35.48, 5.4.6–6.8; *Leg.* 1.6.18–16.45, 22.58–24.63, 2.5.11–13.

This inventor of the *pólis* Aristotle singles out as the greatest benefactor of human kind.[10] Cicero's account of the origins of the political community is merely an elaboration of what Aristotle has to say in this regard.[11] There were, to be sure, other accounts, no less indebted to the peripatetic, in which oratory loomed less large. What the two sets of accounts had in common, nonetheless, what united them and made them distinct from alternative accounts, was a shared conviction that deliberation concerning common advantage inevitably leads on to a concern with the just and the good.[12]

On the question of differential moral and political rationality, Aristotle was, as we would expect, even more blunt than Cicero later would be. We exclude slaves from the political community, he explains, because some men are by nature lacking in the capacity for prudential deliberation (*tò bouleutikón*) regarding the advantageous, the just, and the good; we exclude women, though they possess this capacity, because it is without authority (*ákuros*) over them; and we exclude children because they possess it in incomplete form. There can be no doubt that Cicero agrees.[13]

In fact, in antiquity, nearly everyone agreed. An aristocratic presumption underlay not only the theory of classical republicanism, but its practice as well. As is amply evident in Pericles' Funeral Oration and in Vergil's famous encomium on Rome, the ancients resorted to the principle of differential rationality to justify not only the enslavement of men incapable of managing their own affairs, but also the subordination of peoples lacking in sufficient measure the virtues requisite for self-rule.[14] In short, when Alexis de Tocqueville spoke of the ancient republic as "an aristocracy of masters," he spoke the truth and nothing but the truth.[15] Had he wished to say more by way of an aside, the preeminent exponent of modern democracy might even have noted – on the authority of Aristotle and Cicero, no less – that it is perfectly consistent with the logic underpinning classical republican practice that the best regime

---

[10] Arist. *Pol.* 1252b27–1253a39.

[11] Cf. Cary J. Nederman, "Nature, Sin, and the Origins of Society: The Ciceronian Tradition in Medieval Political Thought," *Journal of the History of Ideas* 49:1 (January 1988): 3–26, who neglects Aristotle's brief allusion to the genesis of the political community and draws a sharp contrast between Cicero's account and that of the peripatetic. See also Nederman, "The Union of Wisdom and Eloquence before the Renaissance: The Ciceronian Orator in Medieval Thought," *The Journal of Medieval History* 18:1 (March 1992): 75–95, which quite rightly emphasizes that Cicero's *vir sapiens* is able to persuade human beings to join the political community precisely because, even in their brutish state, they already "possess a potential for sociability implicit in their common rational and linguistic nature."

[12] See, for example, Polyb. 6.3.5–10.14. Cf. Thomas Cole, *Democritus and the Sources of Greek Anthropology* (Atlanta, GA: Scholars Press, 1990), whose attempt to make of Polybius a disciple of Democritus rests on a failure to appreciate the role played by calculation concerning advantage in Aristotle's account of the genealogy of morals.

[13] Cf. Arist. *Pol.* 1260a4–13 with Cic. *Rep.* 3.25.37–38.

[14] Cf. Thuc. 2.34–46 with Verg. *Aen.* 6.847–53. Note, in this connection, Hans Dieter Meyer, *Cicero und das Reich* (Cologne: Photosetelle der Üniversität zu Köln, 1957), and P. A. Brunt, "*Laus Imperii,*" in *Imperialism in the Ancient World*, ed. P. D. A. Garnsey and C. R. Whittaker (Cambridge, UK: Cambridge University Press, 1978), 159–91.

[15] Alexis de Tocqueville, *De la Démocratie en Amérique*, 2.1.3, in *Oeuvres, papiers et correspondances*, ed. J.-P. Mayer (Paris: Gallimard, 1951-), I:2 22.

imaginable should be a monarchy in which one man, far superior to all the rest, would rule by virtue of his character and wisdom.[16]

The aristocratic and even monarchical bent evident in Aristotle's discussion of regimes and in Cicero's more narrowly political and philosophical works is merely the extreme expression of a principle inherent in all genuine classical republicanism. Whether public deliberation is desirable depends on the character of the citizens – on their natural gifts; on the *paideía* to which they have been subjected; on whether, by inclination and an education in virtue, they have been sufficiently liberated from the dominion of the passions to be able to enter upon "the middle ground (*tò méson*)" constituted by *lógos*, wherein they can reason together in public concerning the transcendent common good.[17] Otherwise, where reason remains enslaved to the passions and genuine virtue is unattainable, the most that one can hope for from the citizen is a shrewd calculation of individual self-interest and its fierce, resolute pursuit. In the absence of a citizenry educated in moral virtue for freedom, or in those circumstances in which a community is endowed with an individual or with a handful of men who are decisively superior to their compatriots in virtue and wisdom, it is entirely appropriate that a monarchy or aristocracy be established. The classical republican outlook that Aristotle and Cicero shared with Herodotus, Thucydides, Xenophon, Isocrates, Sallust, Livy, Suetonius, Tacitus, and Seneca and passed on to the scholastics of the late Middle Ages and the humanists of the Renaissance was not an ideology blindly dictating partisan regime preferences;

[16] Cf. Arist. *Pol.* 1252b27–1253a39, 1278b15–30, and 1280a25–1281a10 with 1283b20–84b33, and see Paul A. Vander Waerdt, "Kingship and Philosophy in Aristotle's Best Regime," *Phronesis* 30:3 (1985): 249–73, and W. R. Newell, "Superlative Virtue: The Problem of Monarchy in Aristotle's 'Politics'," *Western Political Quarterly* 40:1 (March 1987): 159–78; then consider Cic. *Rep.* 1.25.39–45.70, 3.2.3–4.7, 22.33, 25.37, 31.43–35.48, 5.4.6–6.8, in light of *Off.* 1.4.11–7.24, 2.5.16–17, 12.41–42, 3.5.21–6.27, 17.69; *Fin.* 2.14.45–47, 5.13–14.38, 23.65–66; *Rep.* 2.36.61; *Leg.* 1.6.18–16.45, 22.58–24.63, 2.5.11–13.

[17] For the relationship between *tò méson* and *lógos*, see Theog. 495; Solon F10.2 (West); Hdt. 1.206.3, 3.80.2, 83.1, 4.97.5, 6.129.2, 130.1, 7.8.δ 2, 8.74.2; Eur. *Supp.* 438–41; Dem. 18.139. Note, in this connection, Pl. *Pol.* 284e, where *tò méson* is regarded as the sphere within which it is proper to weigh and determine what is measured, fitting, timely, needful, and the like. From *tò méson*, rightful authority was also thought to emanate: cf. Hdt. 1.170.3 with Plut. *Sol.* 14.6, and see Ar. *Av.* 992–1009 (esp. 1004–9), Pl. *Ti.* 34a–c, and *Leg.* 10.886c–910d (esp. 893b–894a, 898a–b). Consider Alc. F129 (Lobel-Page) in light of Louis Robert, "Recherches épigraphiques. v: inscriptions de Lesbos," *Revue des études anciennes* 62:3–4 (July–December 1960): 285–315 (at 300–311), and see Victor Ehrenberg, *RE*, XV:1 (1931), 1103–4. Thus, to deny that Delphi is the world's navel (*omphalós*), lying at the center (*mésos*) of both land and sea, is to question the oracle's authority: Epimenides *Vorsokr.*[6] 3 B11. The term comes to be identified with the political community as such: cf. Hdt. 3.142.3, 4.161.3, 7.164.1 with Archil. F91.30 and Theog. 678 (West), and see *IG*, XII:5872.27, 31, 38. Thus, what is placed *es méson* becomes community property to be held in common or parceled out (Hdt. 7.152; Eur. *Cyc.* 547; Plut. *Mor.* 483c–e; Lucian *Cronosolon* 19), and one might describe Aristophanes' *Congresswomen* as a comic exploration of the boundary between what is by nature private and what can, in fact, be placed *es méson*: note, especially, Ar. *Eccl.* 602–3. Compare the use of *tò koinón* and its cognates: note Aesch. *Supp.* 366, and cf. Hdt. 1.67.5, 5.85.1, 109.3, 6.14.3, 8.135.2, 9.117 with 3.82.3–4, 84.2; with 3.156.2, 5.109.3; and with 6.50.2, 9.87.2. Note what happens when men employ a *koinòs lógos*: 1.166.1, 2.30.3. See also 8.58.1, and note that *tò koinón* can be used to refer to the public treasury: 6.58.1, 7.144.1, 9.87.2. See Eur. *Ion* 1284.

it was a way of thinking about human association that left ample room for and even demanded the exercise of political prudence.[18]

Res Publica

Within the classical republic, everything turned on *lógos*. In the time of Caesar's dictatorship, for example, when Cicero remarked to his brother that there was no longer at Rome a *res publica*, and when, after Caesar's assassination, he spoke in *De officiis* of the *res publica* as having fallen and as being utterly lost, he was using the pertinent term polemically, in a new and perhaps unprecedented fashion, to lament the complete disappearance of "the middle ground" opened up by the practice of *lógos* in political deliberation, and he was suggesting that the dictatorship of Caesar was indistinguishable from tyranny and incompatible with the *consensus iuris* that bound the city together. At Rome, Cicero contended, "only the walls of the city's buildings stand and remain." At Rome, he pointedly insisted, "eloquence" is at an end. At Rome, there is no genuinely public business (*negotium*), no space for political contention, no opportunity for a man to display his abilities in public debate concerning the advantageous, the just, and the good. On a city, wherein for centuries *oratio* had arisen from a competitive exercise of *ratio* on the part of the leading citizens, an ominous and seemingly permanent silence has fallen. The *res publica* is no more; it has been overturned. Such was the conclusion that he had reached.[19]

In similar fashion, when Tacitus later asked in plaintive tone how many there were still alive at the time of Augustus' death who had actually laid eyes on the *res publica*, and when he described Tiberius as initially conducting himself at the time of his accession "as if the old *res publica* were in existence," he was condemning the principate as a tyranny wholly incompatible with the public deliberation purportedly still taking place. This was also the conviction that he intended to convey when he had Galba sadly observe in the wake of Nero's death that, "if the immense body of the empire really could be sustained without a single ruler (*rector*)," he would himself be a worthy man (*dignus*), indeed, were the *res publica* to have its inception from him. And it was the

[18] In this connection, see James Hankins, "Humanism and the Origins of Modern Political Thought," in *The Cambridge Companion to Renaissance Humanism*, ed. Jill Kraye (Cambridge, UK: Cambridge University Press, 1996), 118–41, and Hankins, "De Republica: Civic Humanism in Renaissance Milan (and Other Renaissance Signories)," in *I Decembrio e la tradizione della Repubblica di Platone tra Medioevo e Umanesimo*, ed. Mario Vegetti and Paolo Pissavino (Naples: Bibliopolis, 2005), 485–508. See also Chapter Three, this volume.

[19] Consider Cic. *Q. Fr.* 3.5.4 and *Off.* 2.8.27–29, 13.45, in light of Cic. *Fam.* 4.4.4 and *Off.* 2.1.2–4, 19.65–67, 3.1.2–4, and see Cic. *Rep.* 3.31.43–33.45; then, peruse Rahe, "The Primacy of Politics in Classical Greece," 265–93, and *Republics Ancient and Modern*, 28–54. For further evidence of the connection between public deliberation and the *res publica*, see Livy 2.28.3. There was no precise Greek counterpart for the term *res publica*. In its absence, those responsible for the Greek translation of the *Res Gestae Divi Augusti*, a work of propaganda celebrating Augustus' putative restoration of the *res publica*, tended, tellingly, to use phrases including the word *prágmata*, a cognate of *práxis* (the word denoting political activity) that would ordinarily be translated into Latin as *negotium*: see Clifford Ando, "Was Rome a Polis?" *Classical Antiquity* 18:1 (April 1999): 5–34.

import of the historian's report that, at the time of Galba's death, it was the general opinion that, while the Roman *imperium* actually had survived the victories of Julius and Augustus Caesar, the *res publica* had not – though it certainly "would have survived under Pompey and Brutus."[20] By the same token, when Suetonius remarked that "Augustus twice thought of giving the *res publica* back" to the Senate and Roman people but balked at the prospect of handing Rome over for supervision to more than one man (*plurium arbitrio*), he was repeating the charge brought by Tacitus, and he was providing further evidence when he reported that Drusus had once sent a letter to his older brother Tiberius, proposing that they join forces to compel Augustus to restore liberty (*ad restituendam libertatem*) to Rome.[21]

With these telling words, the two historians repudiated as bald-faced lies the preposterous claims that Augustus had made on his own behalf – that early in his career he had "restored (*vindicavi*) to liberty a *res publica* oppressed by the domination of a faction"; that he had subsequently been elected a triumvir for the purpose of reconstituting the *res publica* (*rei publicae constituendae*); and that, after the civil wars, he had graciously "transferred the *res publica*" from his own "power (*ex mea potestate*) to supervision by the Senate and Roman People (*in senatu populique Romani arbitrium*)." And with the same words, the two made a mockery of the wish Augustus had expressed in writing that he "be allowed to situate the *res publica* in its proper seat, safe and sound," and that "the foundations" that he had laid "for the *res publica* should remain in the place marked out."[22] The putative savior of the *res publica* had been its destroyer. So they implied. But they did not in the process repudiate monarchy as such.

Nor did anyone else. According to Cicero, Sallust, and Livy, silence had not been the rule under Rome's early kings: as they represented it, the *res publica* predated the election of the first consuls in 509 B.C. by centuries, for the monarchy, seconded by a senate from the start, had been the crucible within which the *res publica* had taken shape.[23] Monarchy came to be inconsistent with the health and safety of the *res publica* only when Tarquinius Superbus, ruling without the approval of the people and the sanction of the Senate, began judging capital cases on his own without consultation and started administering public business in accord with counsel furnished solely by the members of his own household.[24] On this matter, the Roman understanding was indistinguishable

---

[20] See Tac. *Ann.* 1.1–7, *Hist.* 1.16, 50, and consider Tac. *Dial.* passim in light of Arlene W. Saxonhouse, "Tacitus' Dialogue on Oratory: Political Activity under a Tyrant," *Political Theory* 3:1 (February 1975): 53–68, and James Chart Leake, "Tacitus' Teaching and the Decline of Liberty at Rome," *Interpretation* 15:1 (January 1987): 55–96 (esp. 58–80), 15:2/3 (May and September 1987): 195–308 (esp. 240–97).

[21] See Suet. *Aug.* 28.1, *Tib.* 50.

[22] See *Res Gestae Divi Augusti* 1.1–4, 7.1, 34.1–2, in *Res Gestae Divi Augusti: The Achievements of the Divine Augustus*, ed. and tr. P. A. Brunt and John Michael Moore (Oxford, UK: Oxford University Press, 1967), 18, 20, 34, and Suet. *Aug.* 28.2.

[23] Consider Livy 1.30.2, 35.6, 49.7, in light of 2.1–2, and see Cic. *Rep.* 1.25.39–46.70 and Sall. *Cat.* 6.6–7. Note also Livy's use of the phrase *res Romana*: 1.9.1, 9, 12.10, 23.5, 31.1, 33.1, and consider the implications of Cic. *ad Brut.* 5.1.

[24] See Livy 1.49.1–8. With Livy's opinion in this regard, Machiavelli was fully familiar: see Machiavelli, *Discorsi* 3.5, in *Opere*, 199–200.

from that of the Greeks: the *res publica* would cease to exist only when it was wholly subsumed within the *res privata*.

Of course, for the classical republican conception to make sense, for there to be a genuine *res publica* distinct in character from the *res privata*, for there to be a political community distinct from a household, one thing is requisite: there really must be a "middle ground" within which to deliberate concerning the transcendent common good. There must be a foundation in nature for right and for wrong; it must be meaningful to speak of the genuinely advantageous, the just, and the good. For our purposes here, it matters little whether one refers to natural right, as Aristotle does, or to natural law in the manner of the Stoics, of Cicero, or Thomas Aquinas.[25] If moral reason is to be the foundation for republicanism, there must be something in the way of a noble and a good to reason about. It is, Cicero implies, only when men become aware of "the common utility (*utilitas communis*)" that the *res publica* is born.[26]

In short, if the discursive republicanism of the ancients – centered, as it is, on reasoned speech (*lógos*) within the public assembly – is not to descend into idle chatter and mere rhetorical manipulation, if there is to be a genuine link between *oratio* and *ratio*, if eloquence and wisdom are to be united in the manner that Cicero thought necessary and proper, it must in principle be feasible to sketch out what it means to achieve that combination of success and happiness that Aristotle in his *Nicomachean Ethics* calls *eudaimonía*. This, in his *Discourses on Livy*, Machiavelli manifestly refuses to do,[27] and his refusal in this regard lays the foundations not only for the sharp distinction between republics and principalities that came to characterize modern political discourse,[28] but also

[25] The distinction does, of course, matter a great deal when one's focus is other than it is here: see Leo Strauss, *Natural Right and History* (Chicago: University of Chicago Press, 1974), 81–164 (esp. 144–64). Cf. Gisela Striker, "Origins of the Concept of Natural Law," in Striker, *Essays on Hellenistic Epistemology and Ethics* (Cambridge, UK: Cambridge University Press, 1996), 209–20, who takes a slightly different tack.

[26] Cic. *Sest.* 42.91.

[27] As one exceedingly sympathetic, recent interpreter intimates, to fully accept the Florentine's teaching, one must be prepared to embrace moral and political anarchy and even nihilism as a recurring, even primordial state: see Vatter, *Between Form and Event*, passim (esp. 11–16, 51–97). Cf. John P. McCormick, "Addressing the Political Exception: Machiavelli's 'Accidents' and the Mixed Regime," *American Political Science Review* 87:4 (December 1993): 888–900, who recognizes Machiavelli's starting point for what it is and, then, by interpreting the discord embraced by the Florentine as a species of political blending along Aristotelian lines, tries to evade the conclusion that "the unrestricted nature of political phenomena" requires at least one "unrestricted political actor," if not, as Vatter insists, many more.

[28] For the *locus classicus*, see Machiavelli, *Il principe* 1, in *Opere*, 258. In this connection, see Wolfgang Mager, "Republik," in *Geschichtliche Grundbegriffe: Historisches Lexikon zur politisch-sozialen Sprache in Deutschland*, ed. Otto Brunner, Werner Conze, and Reinhardt Koselleck (Stuttgart: E. Klett, 1972–97), V 549–651; Hankins, "De Republica: Civic Humanism in Renaissance Milan (and Other Renaissance Signories)," 488–99; and David Wootton, "The True Origins of Republicanism, or *de vera respublica*," in *Il repubblicanesimo moderno. L'idea di repubblica nella riflessione storica di Franco Venturi*, ed. Manuela Albertone (Naples: Bibliopolis, 2006), 271–304, who traces the distinction from Machiavelli through Girolamo Savonarola and Bartolomeo Scala to its apparent source: Ptolemy of Lucca. In ancient Rome, the *populares*, who looked back to the Gracchi, were partisan in much the same fashion as Ptolemy, Savonarola, and Scala. For a summary of their argument, see Cic. *Rep.* 1.32.48–33.50. Machiavelli's populist partisanship was of a radically different sort, as we shall soon see.

for a denial to this distinction of any moral significance, a denial implicit in the reduction of republics and principalities alike to the status of mere "states" – constituted by what Max Weber later called a *"monopoly of the legitimate use of physical force* within a given territory."[29]

Machiavellian Republicanism

Machiavelli's republicanism is grounded on the conviction that all talk of natural human ends is nonsense: he mentions neither natural right nor natural law, and his account of republican virtue is strictly instrumental. In contrast with Herodotus, Thucydides, Xenophon, Isocrates, Aristotle, and Polybius, in manifest opposition to Cicero, Livy, Sallust, Suetonius, Tacitus, and Seneca, he disdains moral virtue, and he judges political regimes with an eye to their capacity to project power and not in light of the quality of the human beings that they tend to produce.[30] For Machiavelli, character is never more than an ancillary concern – and quite rarely that.

It is, after all, Sallust, not Machiavelli, who condemns monarchy on the ground that "the good are more suspect to kings than the bad," lamenting that "the virtue of another is always formidable to these."[31] And it is Tacitus and

---

[29] See Max Weber, "Politics as a Vocation," *From Max Weber: Essays in Sociology*, tr. and ed. H. H. Gerth and C. Wright Mills (New York: Oxford University Press, 1946), 78. The term was introduced by Machiavelli, who used *lo stato* to allude to "command over men," and it reached its full development in the political science of Thomas Hobbes, whose account inspired Weber's definition. See J. H. Hexter, "The Predatory Vision: Niccolò Machiavelli. *Il Principe* and *lo stato*," in *The Vision of Politics on the Eve of the Reformation: More, Machiavelli, and Seyssel* (New York: Basic Books, 1973), 150–78, and Harvey C. Mansfield, "On the Impersonality of the Modern State: A Comment on Machiavelli's Use of *Stato*," *American Political Science Review* 77:4 (December 1983): 849–57, which is reprinted as Mansfield, "Machiavelli's *Stato* and the Impersonal Modern State," in Mansfield, *Machiavelli's Virtue* (Chicago: University of Chicago Press, 1996), 281–94; then, consider Quentin Skinner, "The State," in *Political Innovation and Conceptual Change*, ed. Terence Ball, James Farr, and Russell L. Hanson (Cambridge, UK: Cambridge University Press, 1989), 90–131. See also Quentin Skinner, "Hobbes and the Purely Artificial Person of the State," in Skinner, *Visions of Politics* (Cambridge, UK: Cambridge University Press, 2002) *III: Hobbes and Civil Science*, 177–208. The state is an abstract entity constituted by power; and to the extent that it has a tangible existence, it is indistinguishable from the arms by which that power is exerted – the police forces, the standing army, and the bureaucracy that make up the permanent government in every modern polity. The state is never synonymous with the body politic, and it is never itself a true community. This is evident enough from the manner in which it is consistently coupled with and distinguished from the individual, the church, and society. In this connection, one would do well to ponder Nietzsche's observation that "State is the name of the coldest of all the cold monsters. Coldly as well does it lie; and this lie creeps out of its mouth: 'I, the State, am the People.'" As Nietzsche goes on to suggest, it is "a Faith and a Love," not the State, that constitute a People. See Friedrich Nietzsche, *Also Sprach Zarathustra* 1, "Vom neuen Götzen," in *Werke in Drei Bände*, ed. Karl Schlecta (Munich: Carl Hanser Verlag, 1966), II 313.

[30] For a penetrating discussion, see William J. Connell, "Machiavelli on Growth as an End," in *Historians and Ideologues: Essays in Honor of Donald R. Kelley*, ed. Anthony T. Grafton and J. H. M. Salmon (Rochester, NY: University of Rochester Press, 2001), 259–77. See also Mikael Hörnqvist, *Machiavelli and Empire* (Cambridge, UK: Cambridge University Press, 2004).

[31] Sall. *Cat.* 7.2. Early in *The Art of War*, when Machiavelli's interlocutor Fabrizio Colonna is still trying to pass himself off as a civic humanist, he says much the same thing: consider

Suetonius, not Machiavelli, who relentlessly expose the manner in which princely rule corrupts the Roman nobility and so debases Rome's ruling house morally that, in its depravity, the family of Augustus and Livia almost literally devours itself.[32] It is by no means fortuitous that Thomas Hobbes describes Aristotle as someone "whom Cicero and Seneca, Tacitus and thousands have followed."[33] As the Malmesbury philosopher understood, no one had done a better job of articulating the principles underpinning ancient republican practice.

In *The Prince*, the Florentine signals his own peculiar preference for republican government by observing that "in republics there is greater life, greater hatred, more desire for revenge" than in principalities and by then arguing that, since "the memory of ancient liberty does not and cannot leave them in repose," republics are extremely hard for a prince to subdue.[34] In his *Discourses on Livy*, when he comes to explain why he thinks Rome superior to Sparta and Venice, he emphasizes the more populist state's inclination for and capacity to achieve imperial expansion.[35] In one passage, he later remarks, "A city that lives in freedom has two ends: the first is to acquire, the other is to maintain its independence (*libertà*)."[36] In another, he observes that submission to a republic is "the harshest" of "all the harsh servitudes" not only because it is "more durable" but also because "the end of the republic is to enervate and weaken for the purpose of its own body's growth all other bodies."[37] That Machiavelli's standard for judgment is a polity's propensity for aggrandizement and not its mode of governance there can be no doubt.[38] For Athens and its radical democracy, he has hardly a good word.[39]

If there was any classical author to whom Machiavelli was profoundly beholden, it cannot, then, have been Herodotus, Thucydides, Xenophon, Plato, Isocrates, Aristotle, or Polybius. Nor can it have been Cicero, Sallust, Seneca,

---

Machiavelli, *AG* 2.293, in *Opere*, 332, in light of Christopher Lynch, "Interpretive Essay," in Niccolò Machiavelli, *Art of War*, ed. and tr. Christopher Lynch (Chicago: University of Chicago Press, 2003), 179–226 (esp. 200–26).

[32] This should be perfectly evident to anyone who reads through Tacitus' *Annals* or Suetonius' lives of *Augustus, Tiberius, Caligula, Claudius*, and *Nero*.

[33] See Hobbes, *Historia ecclesiastica* 370–71, in *LW*, V 359.

[34] See Machiavelli, *Il principe* 5, in *Opere*, 263–64.

[35] See Machiavelli, *Discorsi* 1.5–6, in *Opere*, 83–87.

[36] See Machiavelli, *Discorsi* 1.29.3, in *Opere*, 111–12.

[37] See Machiavelli, *Discorsi* 2.2.4, in *Opere*, 150.

[38] In this connection, see Nicolai Rubinstein, "*Florentina Libertas*," *Rinascimento* n. s. 26 (1986): 3–26. The more fervent admirers of Machiavelli's populism are inclined to discount, dismiss, or ignore this evidence and to read their own predilections – political moderation and a profound longing for stability and prosperity, an admiration for equality under the law, a seething resentment of the rich and well-born, an enthusiasm for the moment of revolutionary rupture when the distinction between ruler and ruled purportedly dissolves – into the Florentine: cf. Whitfield, *Machiavelli*, passim (esp. 106–57); LeFort, *Le Travail de l'oeuvre Machiavel*, 451–690, and "Machiavel et la *verità effetuale*," 168–79; John P. McCormick, "Machiavellian Democracy: Controlling Elites with Ferocious Populism," *American Political Science Review* 95:2 (June 2001): 297–313; and Vatter, *Between Form and Event*, passim.

[39] The exceptional word of praise proves the rule: see Machiavelli, *Discorsi* 1.58.3, 59, 2.2.1, in *Opere*, 141–43, 148. Cf. Machiavelli, *Discorsi* 1.2.6, 28, 53.4–5, 2.3, 4.1, 10.3, 24.4, 3.16.1–2, in *Opere*, 80–81, 110, 135–36, 151–53, 160, 184, 222–23.

Tacitus, Suetonius, or even Titus Livy – for, though the Florentine read and profited from them all, he rejected the premise of differential moral and political rationality on which their thinking was grounded, and he drew conclusions concerning the ends of government diametrically opposed to theirs.[40]

If there was any classical author to whom Machiavelli was quite deeply in debt, it must, then, have been a critic of the primacy accorded political life in ancient Greece and Rome. It must have been someone who anticipated the Florentine in debunking the high-minded pretensions that underpinned classical republican aspirations. There is one obvious candidate – the poet Lucretius, author of *De rerum natura* – and his influence deserves careful attention. For, in 1576, within fifty years of the Florentine's death, Innocent Gentillet argued that it was "from" the "school" of Epicurus that "Machiavelli and the Machiavellians emerged (*sont sortis*)."[41] It is to the question that his testimony raises – whether Epicureanism really was the Florentine's point of departure – that we must now turn.

In the Shadow of Lucretius

Niccolò Machiavelli came of age in a Florence ruled by Lorenzo de' Medici and shaped ideologically, at least in some measure,[42] by the loosely organized Platonic academy that had formed around Marsilio Ficino in the years after he had gained support for his philosophical project from Lorenzo's grandfather Cosimo.[43] He witnessed the anti-Platonic reaction that foreshadowed the

[40] It is in this light that one must consider the "truncated Aristotelianism" that Janet Coleman, *A History of Political Thought from the Middle Ages to the Renaissance* (Oxford, UK: Blackwell, 2000), 199–276 (esp. 241–71), traces in Machiavelli's *Prince* and in his *Discourses on Livy*. Once one has abandoned the outlook articulated in the *Nicomachean Ethics* and in the first three books of *The Politics*, one can pillage the fourth and fifth books of the latter work and *The Rhetoric* for practical insights.

[41] See Innocent Gentillet, *Discours contre Machiavel*, ed. Antonio D'Andrea and Pamela D. Stewart (Florence: Casalini Libri, 1974) II.ii.108–20. With regard to Gentillet as an interpreter of Machiavelli and his influence, see Sydney Anglo, *Machiavelli – The First Century: Studies in Enthusiasm, Hostility, and Irrelevance* (Oxford, UK: Oxford University Press, 2005), 229–433.

[42] In the past, scholars have tended to follow Ficino in exaggerating the local impact of his activity and the degree to which the Medici lent him support: see James Hankins, "Cosimo de' Medici and the 'Platonic Academy,'" *Journal of the Warburg and Courtauld Institutes* 53 (1990): 144–62; "Lorenzo de' Medici as Patron of Philosophy," *Rinascimento* n. s. 34 (1994): 15–53, "The Myth of the Platonic Academy of Florence," *Renaissance Quarterly* 44:3 (Autumn 1991): 429–75, and "The Invention of the Platonic Academy of Florence," *Rinascimento*, n. s. 41 (2001): 3–37 – all now reprinted, along with "Lorenzo de' Medici as a Student of Ficino: The *De summo bono*," in Hankins, *Humanism and Platonism in the Italian Renaissance* (Rome: Edizioni di Storia e Letteratura, 2003–4) II: *Platonism*, 185–395 – who is right to point out that the Medici patronized Aristotelians, Thomists, and Averroists as well. In this connection, see also Jill Kraye, "Lorenzo and the Philosophers," in *Lorenzo the Magnificent: Culture and Politics*, ed. Michael Mallett and Nicholas Mann (London: Warburg Institute, 1996), 151–66.

[43] In this connection, see Arthur Field, *The Origins of the Platonic Academy of Florence* (Princeton, NJ: Princeton University Press, 1988), and "The Platonic Academy of Florence," in *Marsilio Ficino: His Theology, His Philosophy, His Legacy*, ed. Michael J. B. Allen, Valery Rees, and Martin Davies (Leiden: Brill, 2002), 369–76, along with Alison Brown, "The Humanist Portrait of Cosimo de' Medici, *Pater Patriae*," in Brown, *The Medici in Florence: The Exercise and*

expulsion of the Medici in 1494, two years after Lorenzo's death, and set in with a vengeance in the aftermath of that upheaval.[44] He was admirably well-positioned to profit from Poggio Bracciolini's unearthing of the manuscript of *De rerum natura* in Germany in 1417, from the circulation of copies in manuscript in and after the 1450s, and from the work's eventual publication in Brescia in 1473,[45] some four years after his birth – and he evidently shared in the growing interest in Lucretius exhibited by his father's close friend Bartolomeo Scala, by other members of Scala's generation among the Florentine humanists, and by younger Florentines such as Machiavelli's putative teacher Marcello Virgilio Adriani, who succeeded Angelo Poliziano as chaired professor at the Florentine Studio in 1494 and then Scala himself as secretary of the First Chancery of the Florentine republic in mid-February 1498, just four months before Machiavelli was himself named secretary of the Second Chancery.[46]

Language of Power (Florence: L. S. Olschki, 1992), 3–52; then consider Mario Martelli, "La cultura letteraria nell'età di Lorenzo," in *Lorenzo il Magnifico e il suo tempo*, ed. Gian Carlo Garfagnini (Florence: L. S. Olschki, 1992), 39–84, and see Alison Brown, "Platonism in Fifteenth-Century Florence," in *The Medici in Florence*, 215–45. More generally, see James Hankins, *Plato in the Italian Renaissance* (Leiden: E. J. Brill, 1991).

[44] This revolution was occasioned by the French invasion of 1494, but the groundwork was laid in Florence well before: see Alison Brown, "Pierfrancesco de' Medici, 1430–1476: A Radical Alternative to Elder Medicean Supremacy?" in *The Medici in Florence*, 73–102, and "The Revolution of 1494 in Florence and its Aftermath: A Reassessment," in *Italy in Crisis, 1494*, ed. Jane Everson and Diego Zancani (Oxford, UK: Leganda, 2000), 13–40. In this connection, see also *The French Descent into Renaissance Italy, 1494–95: Antecedents and Effects*, ed. David Abulafia (Aldershot, UK: Variorum Press, 1995). Note, in particular, David Laven, "Machiavelli, *Italianità*, and the French Invasion of 1494," in ibid., 355–69.

[45] See Wolfgang Bernard Fleischmann, "Titus Lucretius Carus," in *Catalogus translationum et commentariorum: Mediaeval and Renaissance Latin Translations and Commentaries*, ed. Paul Oskar Kristeller, F. Edward Cranz, and Virginia Brown (Washington, DC: Catholic University of America Press, 1960–), II 349–65; Michael D. Reeve, "The Italian Tradition of Lucretius," *Italia medioevale e umanistica* 23 (1980): 27–48; and Leighton Durham Reynolds, "Lucretius," in *Texts and Transmission: A Survey of the Latin Classics*, ed. Leighton Durham Reynolds (Oxford, UK: Clarendon Press, 1983), 218–22. For a list of the printed editions and a discussion of the work's publishing history, see Cosmo Alexander Gordon, *A Bibliography of Lucretius* (Winchester, UK: St. Paul's Bibliographies, 1985), passim (esp. 49–53).

[46] See Sergio Bertelli, "Noterelle Machiavelliane: Ancora su Lucrezio e Machiavelli," *Rivista storica italiana* 76:3 (September 1964): 774–92; note Charles Dempsey, *The Portrayal of Love: Botticelli's Primavera and Humanist Culture at the Time of Lorenzo the Magnificent* (Princeton, NJ: Princeton University Press, 1992), and see Alison Brown, "Lucretius and the Epicureans in the Social and Political Context of Renaissance Florence," *I Tatti Studies: Essays in the Renaissance* 9 (2001): 11–62, and "Reinterpreting Renaissance Humanism: Marcello Adriani and the Recovery of Lucretius," in *Interpretations of Renaissance Humanism*, ed. Angelo Mazzocco (Leiden: Brill, 2006), 267–91. In this connection, note also F. La Brasca, "'Hinc mel, hinc venenum': l'Édition commentée du *De rerum natura* par Giovanni Nardi (1647)," in *Présence de Lucrèce*, ed. Rémy Poignault (Tours: Centre de Recherches A. Piganiol, 1999), 381–98; and Ubaldo Pizzani, "Lucrezio nell'umanesimo italiano e nei giudizi dei primi commentatori d'Oltralpe," in *Rapporti e scambi tra umanesimo italiano ed umanesimo europeo: "l'Europa è uno stato d'animo,"* ed Luisa Rotondi Secchi Tarugi (Milan: Nuovi Orizzonti, 2001), 515–38. Regarding Scala, see Alison Brown, *Bartolomeo Scala, 1430–1497, Chancellor of Florence: The Humanist as Bureaucrat* (Princeton, NJ: Princeton University Press, 1979). Machiavelli's father is the chief interlocutor in a dialogue composed by Scala: see Bartolomeo Scala, "De legibus et iudiciis dialogus" (February–March 1483), in Scala, *Humanistic and Political Writings*, ed. Alison Brown

We know that Machiavelli read Lucretius' philosophical poem with very great care. In fact, he thought the work of sufficient significance that, at some point in the mid-to-late 1490s, when Girolamo Savonarola was riding high and the poem's Florentine expositors had come under attack from the Dominican's pulpit, he went to the trouble of copying by hand in its entirety the 1495 Venetian edition and of incorporating within his copy the as-yet-unpublished emendations proposed by that work's devotee, Scala's new son-in-law, the scholarly Greek soldier-poet Michele Marullo Tarcaniota.[47]

There is reason to suppose that by the time he began writing his two main political works, Machiavelli had also read that other great source of Epicurean lore, the tenth book of Diogenes Laertius' *Lives of the Eminent Philosophers*. The manuscript of the lives arrived in Florence from Constantinople in 1416. Seventeen years later, Ambrogio Traversari presented Cosimo de' Medici with a Latin translation, and his translation found its way into print by the early 1470s. In the three decades that followed, the volume was frequently republished,[48] and in due course Machiavelli read considerable parts of it, and probably the whole, with attention and care. From the sixth book, he borrowed an anecdote that he deployed in his *Art of War*,[49] which was published in 1521, and from the biographies of Aristippus, Bion, Aristotle, and the cynic Diogenes he lifted nearly all of the witty remarks and clever rejoinders that he attributed to Castruccio Castracani in the semifictional biography of that figure that he

(Tempe, AZ: Medieval & Renaissance Texts & Studies, 1997), 338–64. For a translation, see Bartolomeo Scala, "Dialogue on Laws and Legal Judgements," tr. David Marsh, in *Cambridge Translations of Renaissance Philosophical Texts*, ed. Jill Kraye (Cambridge, UK: Cambridge University Press, 1997), II 173–99.

47 The manuscript was discovered almost half a century ago in the Vatican library (Ross. 884): see Sergio Bertelli and Franco Gaeta, "Noterelle Machiavelliane: Un codice di Lucrezio e di Terenzio," *Rivista storica italiana* 73:3 (September 1961): 544–57 (at 544–53). For the precise date and context in which the poem was transcribed, see Bertelli, "Noterelle Machiavelliane: Ancora su Lucrezio e Machiavelli," 774–90 (esp. 774, n. 3), whose observations need adjustment in light of Mario Martelli, "L'altro Niccolò di Bernardo Machiavelli," *Rinascimento* n.s. 14 (1974): 39–100 (at 93–95); Reeve, "The Italian Tradition of Lucretius," 44–48; and Peter Godman, *From Poliziano to Machiavelli: Florentine Humanism in the High Renaissance* (Princeton, NJ: Princeton University Press, 1998), 149, n. 105. See also Brown, "Lucretius and the Epicureans in the Social and Political Context of Renaissance Florence," 11–61 (esp. 56–62). On Marullo, who married Alessandra Scala in 1496, see Benedetto Croce, *Michelle Marullo Tarcaniota: Le elegie per la patria perduta ed altri suoi carmi: Biografia, testi e traduzioni con due ritratti del Marullo* (Bari: Laterza & Sons, 1938), and Carol Kidwell, *Marullus: Soldier Poet of the Renaissance* (London: Duckworth, 1989). Marullo's emendations were incorporated into the 1512–1513 Giuntine edition a dozen years after he drowned while fording a stream: see Gordon, *A Bibliography of Lucretius*, 51–53.

48 Note James Hankins, "Cosimo de' Medici as a Patron of Humanistic Literature," in *Cosimo 'il Vecchio' de' Medici, 1389–1464*, ed. Francis Ames-Lewis (Oxford, UK: Clarendon Press, 1992), 69–94 (esp. 71–73), which is reprinted in Hankins, *Humanism and Platonism in the Italian Renaissance* I: *Humanism*, 427–55, and see A. C. de la Mare, "Cosimo and His Books," in *Cosimo 'il Vecchio' de' Medici*, 115–56 (esp. 127–33, 147); Maria Rita Pagnoni, "Prime note sulla tradizione medioevale ed umanistica di Epicuro," *Annali della Scuola Normale Superiore di Pisa* ser. 3, 4 (1974): 1143–77 (esp. 1457–60); and Agostino Sottile, "Il Laerzio latino e greco e altri autografi di Ambrogio Traversari," in *Vestigia: Studi in onore di Giuseppe Billanovich*, ed. Rino Avesani et al. (Rome: Edizioni di storia e letteratura, 1984), 699–745.

49 Cf. Machiavelli, *AG* 1.25, in *Opere*, 304, with Diog. Laert. 6.2.23.

penned at about the same time.[50] Given his interests, it is difficult to believe that the Florentine ignored Diogenes Laertius' *Life of Epicurus*.

Even, however, if he did so, even if, for some reason unknown, he resolutely averted his gaze from that author's tenth book, it would not matter – for what can be affirmed is twofold: that *De rerum natura* is an exceedingly faithful and comprehensive account of Epicurean doctrine,[51] and that its argument remained on the Florentine's mind in the years in which he worked on his *Discourses on Livy*.[52] In fact, circa 1517, when he paused from his labors on that work to pen a satire of the human condition for inclusion in his poem *The Ass*, he took as his starting point and model the critique that Lucretius had articulated in *De rerum natura* against the very possibility of Providence. In this work, when Machiavelli's asinine protagonist confronts a great hog who has in the past undergone the transformation from man to beast that he has more recently suffered himself, he discovers to his surprise that his interlocutor has not the slightest interest in having the metamorphosis reversed. "To nature we [animals] are much greater friends," the latter explains, "and to us she more freely dispenses her *virtù* – while making you [men] beggars for her every good." The eagle, he observes, is superior in vision; the dog, in smell and taste. If men nonetheless excel in their sensitivity to touch, this putative advantage does them no honor and results in their subjection to a venereal "appetite" that gives them "greater trouble and bother." The animals are born fully "clothed." "Only man is born denuded of every defense, possessing no hide, spines, feathers, fleece, bristles, or scales to make a shield." Of course, the hog concedes, "nature did give you hands and speech, but with them she gave you ambition also and avarice, which cancel whatever good these have conferred." Seconded by lust, these passions produce scabs for men to pick at – and nothing more. "Nature subjects you to so many infirmities, and then fortune! How many goods it promises you without any effect!" In sum, he concludes, "No other animal finds that it has a life more fragile. None has a greater desire for life. None is more confounded by fear. None is possessed by a greater frenzy."[53]

As this critique of nature's provision suggests, by 1517 or so, if not well before, Machiavelli had made Lucretius' repudiation of religion and his

---

[50] Cf. Machiavelli, *La vita di Castruccio Castracani da Lucca*, in *Opere*, 613–28 (at 626–28), which was composed in 1520, with Diog. Laert. 2.8.66–79, 4.7.49–51, 5.1.20, 6.2.29–32, 39–40, 44, 54, 57, 61, 68, and see Leo Strauss, *Thoughts on Machiavelli* (Glencoe, IL: Free Press, 1958), 223–25.

[51] One might even describe it as a defense of Epicurean orthodoxy: see David Sedley, *Lucretius and the Transformation of Greek Wisdom* (Cambridge, UK: Cambridge University Press, 1998).

[52] For a sober assessment of the evidence pertinent to dating its composition, see Cecil H. Clough, "Father Walker's Presentation and Translation of Machiavelli's *Discourses* in Perspective," in *The Discourses of Machiavelli*, ed. and tr. Leslie J. Walker, second edition (London: Routledge & Kegan Paul, 1975), xv–xlviii (at xxii–xxxix, xli–xlv).

[53] Cf. Machiavelli, *L'Asino* 7.115–8.151 (esp. 8.106–51), in *Opere*, 972–76, with Lucr. 5.195–234 (esp. 223–27), 5.953–57, 990–91, and see Gennaro Sasso, "*Ambizione*, 1–60," in Sasso, *Machiavelli e gli antichi e altri saggi* (Milan: Riccardo Ricciardi, 1987–1997), IV 3–37 (esp. 6–17, 33–35). In this connection, see also Gennaro Sasso, "L'*Asino*: Una satira antidantesca," in *Machiavelli e gli antichi e altri saggi*, IV 39–128, and Stelio Zeppi, "Il pessimo antropologico nel Machiavelli del periodo anteriore ai *Discorsi*," *Filosofia politica* 6:2 (August 1992): 193–242 (esp. 216–24). With regard to the date that can be assigned these lines, see Francesco Bausi, *Machiavelli* (Rome: Salerno Editrice, 2005), 143–52.

rejection of natural teleology his own.[54] Among his associates, he was notorious as a scoffer. He so rarely attended mass that it was a subject of comment, and he is said by a friend never to have given thought to the well-being of his soul or to the fate reserved for it: he conducted his life in accord with what Francesco Guicciardini pointedly identified as "a contrary profession" of faith. Sending him to find a preacher, as the Wool Guild had done, Guicciardini wrote in May 1521, was like sending a well-known pederast to choose for his friend a beautiful and elegant wife.[55] Some six years after his death, Machiavelli was remembered by Luigi Guicciardini as "someone who found it difficult to believe the things that had to be believed, not to mention those that are risible,"[56] and when the latter Guicciardini penned a dialogue on the question of free will, he depicted his old friend as a thoroughgoing skeptic, inclined to raise powerful objections against Christian doctrine of a sort consonant with the ultimate logic, if not the actual argument, of *De rerum natura*.[57]

We should not, then, be surprised that the account of the origins of human society and the treatment of the political psychology of religion found in Machiavelli's *Discourses on Livy* should owe a great deal to the anthropology articulated in *De rerum natura*.[58] Nor should we be shocked to find him in that same work marshalling a defense for the controversial notion – asserted in one way by Aristotle and Averroës, restated in another by Epicurus and Lucretius, but wholly incompatible with revelation as propagated by Moses, Jesus, and Muhammad – that the universe is eternal.[59] We should not be startled that the

---

[54] Consider Lucr. 1.62–158, 921–50, 2.40–60, 167–82, 598–660, 1090–1104, 3.31–1094, 4.1–25, 823–57, 1233–87, 5.1–234, 380–431, 6.1–91, 379–422, 738–68, 1276–86 (esp. 4.823–57 and 5.195–234) in light of 5.1161–1240; note Leo Strauss, "Notes on Lucretius," in Leo Strauss, *Liberalism Ancient and Modern* (New York: Basic Books, 1968), 76–139, and James H. Nichols, Jr., *Epicurean Political Philosophy: The De rerum natura of Lucretius* (Ithaca, NY: Cornell University Press, 1976), 13–178; and see Alberto Tenenti, "La religione di Machiavelli," *Studi storici* 10:4 (October–December 1969): 709–48, which is reprinted in Tenenti, *Credenze, ideologie, libertinismi: Tra Medioevo ed età moderna* (Bologna: Il Mulino, 1978), 175–219; Emanuele Cutinelli-Rèndina, *Chiesa e religione in Machiavelli* (Pisa: Instituti Editoriali e Poligrafici Internationali, 1998); Agnès Cugno, "L'Idée de Dieu chez Machiavel," in *Les Athéismes philosophiques*, ed. Emmanuel Chubilleau and Eric Puisais (Paris: Kimé, 2001), 29–43; and Jérémie Barthas, "Au Fondement intellectuel de l'irréligion machiavélienne, Lucrèce? Controverses, notes et considérations," in *Sources antiques de l'irréligion moderne: Le Relais italien, XVIᵉ–XVIIᵉ siècles*, ed. Jean-Pierre Cavaillé and Didier Foucault (Toulouse: Presses Universitaires du Mirail, 2001), 68–90.

[55] See Letters from Francesco Vettori on 23 November 1513 and Francesco Guicciardini on 17 May 1521, in Machiavelli, *Opere*, 1157–58, 1202–3.

[56] See Letter from Luigi Guicciardini to Francesco Guicciardini on 30 May 1533, in Francesco Guicciardini, *Opere inedite*, ed. Piero Guicciardini and Luigi Guicciardini (Florence: Barbèra, Bianchi e Comp., 1857–1867), IX 267–68.

[57] The manuscript survives in Florence's Biblioteca Nazionale (Magl. VIII, Codex 1422, fols. 59r–68v) among the papers of Luigi Guicciardini: see Felix Gilbert, "Machiavelli in an Unknown Contemporary Dialogue," *Journal of the Warburg Institute* 1:2 (October 1937): 163–66.

[58] See Strauss, *Thoughts on Machiavelli*, 201–3, 279–80, 291–92, and Gennaro Sasso, "Machiavelli e i detrattori, antichi e nuovi, di Roma," in *Machiavelli e gli antichi e altri saggi*, I 401–536 (at 467–79); then note John M. Najemy, "Papirius and the Chickens, or Machiavelli on the Necessity of Interpreting in Religion," *Journal of the History of Ideas* 60:4 (October 1999): 659–81 (esp. 667).

[59] Consider Machiavelli, *Discorsi* 2.5, in *Opere*, 154–55, in light of Strauss, *Thoughts on Machiavelli*, 142–44, 201–23; Sasso, "De aeternitate mundi (*Discorsi*, II 5)," in *Machiavelli e gli antichi*

Florentine should follow the ancient atomists in giving to touch as sensation epistemological priority over sight, hearing, taste, and smell.[60] Nor should it seem in any way odd that, in the Epicurean manner,[61] he should presume that generation and dissolution characterize "mixed" as opposed to "simple bodies."[62] Least of all should we be puzzled by the fact that in describing human nature in general in his *Discourses on Livy* Machiavelli should resort to language of the sort used in *De rerum natura* to depict matter in flux and to draw a contrast between the disposition of the *vulgus* – the common crowd of men beset by superstition and care – and the temper of the blessed handful who have not only liberated themselves from anxiety by acknowledging the absence

e altri saggi, I 167–399 (esp. 202–16); and Cutinelli-Rèndina, *Chiesa e religione in Machiavelli*, 235–41, and see Lucr. 2.1048–1174, 5.55–109, 187–94, 235–836, 6.601–7 (along with 1.54–61, 215–64, 311–28, 482–502, 528–634, 950–51, 1102–13, 2.294–311, 569–80, 751–54, 1002–12), who denies that our world (*mundus*) lasts forever but asserts that the atoms (*primordia*) that make up the universe (*summa rerum*) are eternal. Machiavelli appears to be responding not only to Aristotle and Averroës but to Lucr. 5.324–44 as well. Note, in this connection, Marie-Dominique Couzinet, "Sources antiques de l'irréligion moderne chez Machiavel: Crise religieuse et imitation des Anciens," in *Sources antiques de l'irréligion moderne*, 47–67.

[60] Cf. Machiavelli, *Il principe* 18 and *Mandragola* 5.2, in *Opere*, 284, 888–89, with Lucr. 1.298–304, 2.398–477, 680–85, 730–990. Consider the connection that Aristotle (*Eth. Nic.* 1117b24–1119b18) makes between touch, self-indulgence (*akolasía*), a general lack of moderation (*sōphrosúnē*), and those faculties which link man most closely with the other animals, and note Machiavelli's suggestion that our sensitivity to touch is linked with venereal appetite: see *L'Asino* 8.112–16, in *Opere*, 975. Note also *Averroes on Plato's Republic*, ed. and tr. Ralph Lerner (Ithaca, NY: Cornell University Press, 1974) 65.29–66.5, and Maimonides, *Guide of the Perplexed*, tr. Shlomo Pines (Chicago: University of Chicago Press, 1963), II 36 (371), 40 (384), III 8 (432–33), 49 (608). Cf. ibid. I 2, 46 (101). Throughout Plato's *Republic*, seeing is taken to be a more adequate test of truth than hearing and is therefore used as a metaphor for philosophical understanding: cf. 2.357b–c with 367c in light of 5.475d–e, 6.484c–d, 488a–489a, 500b–c, 507b–7.533d, and see *Ti.* 46e–47c. And though Aristotle is inclined to link intelligence with tactile sensitivity, to compare the soul with a hand, to speak of thought as a form of apprehension or grasping, and even to consider taste, hearing, and vision as species of touch, he, too, insists on according primacy to sight: cf. *De an.* 421a7–25, 429a10–b9 (esp. 429a15–21), 431a1–432a14 (esp. 432a1–6), 433b31–435b25, *Metaph.* 1072b20–23 with 980a21–28, and note *De an.* 428b30–429a4. It is by no means fortuitous that our word for abstract thinking should be derived from *theōría* – the term used by the Greeks to describe a voyage undertaken to attend a religious festival such as the Olympic games and look on: cf. Cic. *Tusc.* 5.3.8–10 with Arist. F58 (Rose), and note the manner in which one form of *theōría* gives way to another in Plato's *Republic*: consider 1.327a–328b in light of the remainder of the book. Note the fashion in which Aristotle differentiates theoretical insight from the practical know-how one gains from what is now sometimes called hands-on experience: F52 (Rose). See Kenneth C. Blanchard, Jr., "Being, Seeing, and Touching: Machiavelli's Modification of Platonic Epistemology," *Review of Metaphysics* 49:3 (March 1996): 577–607.

[61] See Lucr. 2.1048–1174, 5.55–109, 187–94, 235–836, 6.601–7 (along with 1.54–61, 215–64, 311–28, 482–502, 528–634, 950–51, 1102–13, 2.294–311, 569–80, 751–54, 1002–12), who denies that mixed bodies, such as our world (*mundus*) and the things within it, last forever but asserts that the simple bodies or atoms (*primordia*) that make up the universe (*summa rerum*) are eternal.

[62] See Machiavelli, *Discorsi* 2.5.1, in *Opere*, 154, and *Discorsi* 3.1, in *Opere*, 195–96, and note Strauss, *Thoughts on Machiavelli*, 142–44, 168–73, 201–3, 221–23; Sasso, "De aeternitate mundi (*Discorsi*, II 5)," 167–399; Eugenio Garin, "Aspetti del pensiero di Machiavelli," in Garin, *Dal Rinascimento all'Illuminismo: Studi e ricerche* (Pisa: Nistri-Lischi, 1970), 43–77 (esp. 56–67); and Harvey C. Mansfield, *Machiavelli's New Modes and Orders: A Study of the Discourses on Livy* (Ithaca, NY: Cornell University Press, 1979), 202–6. In this connection, see Couzinet, "Sources antiques de l'irréligion moderne chez Machiavel," 60–67.

of Providence and embracing the finality of death but have also withdrawn from the world and jettisoned all of the attendant troubles for the purpose of achieving philosophical enlightenment, a moderation of the passions, and the freedom from troubles and anxieties (*tarachē*) that Epicurus had called *ataraxía* or tranquility of soul.[63] Although the Florentine ultimately reserved judgment, acknowledging that "we do not have knowledge (*notizia*) regarding things natural and supernatural,"[64] he nonetheless adopted as his working hypothesis an Epicureanism of sorts.

Machiavelli was, we must never forget, a deeply learned and profoundly playful man. He was thoroughly familiar with Christian theology and the pagan classics, and he was steeped as well in the judicial astrology that, in the Middle Ages and the Renaissance, so often went hand in hand with Aristotelianism as interpreted by the Arab *falāsifa*.[65] In addressing his contemporaries, he was more than capable of deploying the tropes and metaphors generated within each of these traditions, and, when it suited his rhetorical purpose, he was by no means reluctant to do so.[66] In this vein, when alluding to the dependence of nations and individuals on circumstances utterly beyond their control, he repeatedly spoke of the judgment of heaven, the dictates of *fortuna*, and the influence of the stars, but it would be an error to conclude from this manner

[63] Note Gisela Striker, "*Ataraxia*: Happiness as Tranquillity," in *Essays on Hellenistic Epistemology and Ethics*, 183–95, and cf. Machiavelli, *Discorsi* 1.37.1, 2 Proemio 2–3, in *Opere*, 119, 145, with Lucr. 1.265–92, 329–98, 418–920, 951–1113, 2.62–164, 4.26–28, 5.55–109, 186–94, 235–836, 6.601–7, and then see 2.1–61, 3.1–93, 288–322, 830–1094 (esp. 978–1023), 4.1–25, 5.1–52, 1105–1349, 1409–35, 6.1–91, which should be read in light of 2.348–70 and 5.1052–53.

[64] See Machiavelli, *Discorsi* 1.56, in *Opere*, 139.

[65] See Garin, "Aspetti del pensiero di Machiavelli," 56–63, and Marco Bertozzi, "Il fatale ritmo della storia: La teoria delle grandi congiunzioni astrali tra XV e XVI secolo," *I Castelli di Yale* 1 (1996): 29–49 (esp. 40–44). Note Richard Joseph Lemay, *Abu Ma'shar and Latin Aristotelianism in the Twelfth Century: The Recovery of Aristotle's Natural Philosophy Through Arabic Astrology* (Beirut: American University of Beirut, 1962), and then see Lynn Thorndike, *A History of Magic and Experimental Science* (New York: Columbia University Press, 1923–1958), II 66–93, 246–78, 874–947 (esp. 897–98), V 94–110 (esp. 98–99, 107–9), and "Franciscus Florentinus, or Paduanus, an Inquisitor of the Fifteenth Century, and His Treatise on Astrology and Divination, Magic and Popular Superstition," in *Mélanges Mandonnet: Études d'histoire littéraire et doctrinale du Moyen Age* (Paris: Librairie Philosophique J. Vrin, 1930), II 353–69 (esp. 357–60), along with Bruno Nardi, "La teoria dell'anima e la generazione delle forme secondo Pietro d'Abano" and "Intorno alle dottrine filosofiche di Pietro d'Abano," in Nardi, *Saggi sull'aristotelismo padovano dal secolo XIV al XVI* (Florence: G. C. Sansoni, 1958), 1–74. For an overview, see Eugenio Garin, *Astrology in the Renaissance: The Zodiac of Life*, tr. Carolyn Jackson, June Allen, and Clare Robertson (London: Arkana, 1990), and John D. North, "Celestial Influence – The Major Premiss of Astrology," in *'Astrologi hallucinati': Stars and the End of the World in Luther's Time*, ed. Paola Zambelli (Berlin: Walter de Gruyter, 1986), 45–100, which should be read in conjunction with Richard Lemay, "Acquis de la traduction scientifique grecque confrontés aux realités des civilisations médiévales: Cas particulier de l'astrologie-cosmologie," in *Perspectives arabes et médiévales sur la tradition scientifique et philosophique grecque*, ed. Ahmad Hasnawi, Abdelali Elamrani-Jamal, and Maroun Aouad (Leuven-Paris: Peeters, 1997), 137–71.

[66] For a brief work in which the Florentine displays his mastery of Christian theology, see Niccolò Machiavelli, *Exortazione alla penitenza*, in *Opere*, 932–34. Note also Niccolò Machiavelli, *Elocuzione fatta ad un magistro* and *Capitolo dell'ambizione* 16–30, in *Opere*, 36–37, 983–84.

of speaking that he actually depended on Ptolemy, Al-Kindi, Abu Mash'ar, or the like for the cosmology underpinning his political science,[67] for one can no more imagine the author of *The Prince* and the *Discourses on Livy* advising a statesman to have his horoscope cast than one can imagine him urging such a man to examine his conscience, repent, seek out a priest, confess his sins, and confine his future conduct to the narrow and straight.

The reason for our instinctive reluctance in this regard is not a failure of imagination on our part. Although ordinary readers have rarely, if ever, penetrated to the roots of the Florentine's argument, they have always quite sensibly been disinclined to attribute to him a consoling cosmology consistent with the presumption that human affairs are orderly and predictable,[68] and this was no less true in the epoch when astrology was a genuine intellectual temptation than it is in our own time. As Gentillet observed in 1576, when this occult science was still regarded by most men of letters with profound respect, it was Machiavelli's judgment "that the course of the sun, moon, and stars; the distinctions between the seasons of spring, summer, autumn, and winter; the political government of man; the produce of the earth, fruit, plants, animals – that all of this comes about by accident and chance (*à l'aventure et par rencontre*)," for he followed "the doctrine of Epicurus . . . who judged that all things take place and happen by fortuitous circumstance and an accidental encounter of atoms (*par cas fortuit et rencontre des atomes*)."[69] When Machiavelli speaks of fortune, when he appeals to necessity, he evokes a universe hard to distinguish from the one depicted in *De rerum natura*.[70]

The Paradox of a Political Epicureanism

Machiavelli did not openly advertise his debt to anyone – apart, that is, from Titus Livy. But he was perfectly prepared to intimate that which he owed Lucretius. In the opening lines of his *Discourses on Livy*, he not only did so, he did so with his customary playfulness, discretion, and panache, and he did so in such a manner as to confirm what those already in the know had discerned on their own, for he modeled the claim to originality that he advanced in these lines on a similar claim put forward by the poet. Where Lucretius proudly averred that, in composing *De rerum natura*, he "is wandering through pathless (*avia*) haunts of the Muses of Pieria, hitherto untrodden by anyone's foot (*nullius ante trita solo*)," Machiavelli asserted, as we have seen,[71] that he had discovered "a path (*via*) as yet untrodden by anyone (*non essendo suta ancora*

[67] Although Giovanni di Napoli, "Niccolò Machiavelli e l'Aristotelismo del Rinascimento," *Giornale di metafisica* 25 (1970): 215–64, and Anthony J. Parel, *The Machiavellian Cosmos* (New Haven, CT: Yale University Press, 1992), are unpersuasive in arguing for such a conclusion, their work is nonetheless indispensable for understanding Machiavelli's rhetoric.

[68] For a thoughtful exploration of Machiavelli's rhetoric in this regard, see Strauss, *Thoughts on Machiavelli*, 17–19, 47–48, 201–23.

[69] See Gentillet, *Discours contre Machiavel* II.i.12–24.

[70] In this connection, see Garin, "Aspetti del pensiero di Machiavelli," 53–56.

[71] See the Preface to Part One, this volume.

da alcuno trita)."[72] In doing so, Machiavelli tacitly acknowledged – as had
Lucretius before him when he deployed what was already in his day a well-
worn trope[73] – that his dramatic claim to originality should be taken with a
grain of salt. Such was the Florentine's capacity for self-mockery.

If, despite this oblique acknowledgment of debt, Machiavelli nonetheless
broke with Lucretius in preferring the world of political action to the garden
of Epicurus,[74] if with full knowledge and evident zest he embraced all of the
troubles and anxieties attendant on the former, if he harbored disdain for those
who preferred leisure and idleness (*ozio*) and sought *ataraxía* through the contemplative life,[75] and if he refused to espouse philosophical resignation and
advocated, instead, a bold rebellion against fortune's rule,[76] it was not because
he entertained hopeful expectations of the sort that Lucretius had attacked as
illusions. When the Florentine warned his prospective prince that "in the world
there is no one but the common crowd (*vulgo*), and [that] the few have no
place (*luogo*) when the common crowd has somewhere something sufficient on
which to lean,"[77] he was restating the convictions of the Epicurean poet. As
Lucretius makes clear in the sustained critique he levels against the political
life,[78] he regards the high-minded presumptions of the classical republicans as
preposterous. In nearly all respects, he anticipated Machiavelli's harsh, unspar-
ing depiction of the world of political action.

---

[72] Cf. the language that Machiavelli deploys in *Discorsi* 1 Proemio, in *Opere*, 76 (esp. the participle
trita), with Lucr. 1.926–27, 4.1–2, and see Felix Gilbert, *Machiavelli and Guicciardini: Politics
and History in Sixteenth-Century Florence* (Princeton, NJ: Princeton University Press, 1965),
158, n. 19, and John M. Najemy, *Between Friends: Discourses of Power and Desire in the
Machiavelli-Vettori Letters of 1513–1515* (Princeton, NJ: Princeton University Press, 1993), 337–
38.

[73] Cf. Lucr. 1.926–27, 4.1–2 with Callim. *Aet.* 1: F1.25–28 (Massimilla), and note the non-
metaphorical usage of the trope at Ennius *Ann.* 43 (Skutsch). Note also Dion. Hal. *Thuc.* 9.4,
who may be following Callimachus, and Varro *Ling.* 5.5, Verg. *G.* 3.289–93, Plin. *NH* Praef. 14,
Nemes. *Cyn.* 8–11, who borrow the trope from Lucretius. For a brief discussion of its history,
see Giulio Massimilla's commentary on Callimachus' *Aetia*, in Callimachus, *Aitia: Libri primo
e secondo*, ed. and tr. Giulio Massimilla (Pisa: Giardini, 1996), 219, 221.

[74] It is with this in mind that one should consider the dramatic context within which Machiavelli's
dialogue *The Art of War* takes place and the pointed introductory remarks of Fabrizio Colonna,
his chief interlocutor: see Machiavelli, *AG* 1.8–31, in *Opere*, 302–4.

[75] Where Cicero consoled himself with the thought that it was possible to combine *otium* with
dignitas (*Sest.* 98, *De or.* 1.1), Machiavelli was dismissive: note *Il principe* 14, in *Opere*, 280,
and see *Discorsi* 1 Proemio, 1.4, 6.4, 10.1, 30.1, 55.3–5, 2.2.2, 19.2–20.1, 25.1, 3.1.4, 10.1, in
Opere, 76–78, 86–87, 91–92, 112–13, 137–39, 149–50, 175–76, 185, 196–97, 214; *AG* Proemio
10, 2.290–304, 7.236, 240, 243, in *Opere*, 302, 332, 388–89; and *Istorie fiorentine* 5.1, in *Opere*,
738–39.

[76] See Machiavelli, *Il principe* 25, in *Opere*, 295–96. This is a subject to which Machiavelli frequently returned: note Letter to Giovan Battista Soderini on 13–21 September 1506 and *Capitolo
di fortuna*, in *Opere*, 976–79, 1082–83, and cf. *Discorsi* 2.29 with 2.30.5, and see 3.1, 8–9, in
Opere, 188–91, 195–97, 211–14.

[77] See Machiavelli, *Il principe* 18, in *Opere*, 284.

[78] One should consider the pertinent passages (Lucr. 2.1–61, 3.995–1010, 5.43–51, 1105–59, 1281–
1349, 6.1–91) in light of Lucretius' analysis of the moral and political consequences of the fear
of death: 3.41–93, 830–1094. Note that his putative aim in the poem is to draw Memmius away
from a concern with the common safety (*communis salus*): 1.29–43.

Machiavelli's critique of ancient Epicureanism is entirely internal. For inspiration, he may have looked to Cicero's report that the Stoic Posidonius had dismissed as incoherent Epicurus' account of the gods and had suggested that the Athenian philosopher's theology was mere window-dressing, fabricated for the purpose of sidestepping ill will (*invidia*) and avoiding accusation (*crimen*).[79] Machiavelli's silence in this regard suggests on his part an awareness that Lucretius had not made an even remotely plausible case for the existence of immortal gods, indifferent to man and free from all care, as well as a recognition on the Florentine's part that it is hard to see how, in an infinite universe constituted solely by atoms in motion and the void, anything at all could be exempt from dissolution – apart, of course, from the atoms themselves.[80] The fact that Machiavelli is similarly silent on the famous Epicurean swerve – the *clinamen* or *declinatio* – suggests that, like Cicero in *De fato* and *De finibus*,[81] he regarded Epicurus' attempt to reconcile the physics of Democritus with human freedom as little more than a dodge. "Improvised and fanciful (*commenticia*)," Cicero had called it, and not just "invented out of whole cloth (*ficta*)," but fabricated "in a manner arbitrary (*ad libidem*)" and "childish (*pueriliter*)."[82]

Machiavelli initiates his own breach with Lucretius by applying to the Roman poet's defense of moderation and to his entrancing vision of the good life purportedly open to those liberated from illusion by philosophy – the very arguments that the latter had directed against political idealism. Early in the *Discourses on Livy*, Machiavelli prepares his ground by exploring the case for political moderation. He asks his readers to consider whether someone wishing to "order a republic anew" would be well advised to establish a polity on the model of Sparta or Venice that will seek to "remain quiet" – or whether such a lawgiver should imitate Rome, instead, and design his republic for expansion

---

[79] See Cic. *Nat. D.* 1.44.123, 3.1.3.

[80] Consider Lucr. 1.44–49, 2.644–51, 1093–1104, 3.18–24, 5.82, 146–85, 6.68–79 (esp. the promise made at 5.155 but never redeemed) in light of the warning to the reader implicit in 1.933–50, 4.8–25, and the account given of the origins of the idea of gods at 5.1161–1240.

[81] These were familiar texts long before Machiavelli's day: see Richard H. Rouse, "*Academica posteriora* and *De finibus bonorum et malorum*" and "*De natura deorum, De divinatione, Timaeus, De fato, Topica, Paradoxa Stoicorum, Academica priora, De legibus*," in *Texts and Transmission*, 112–15, 124–28, and note Leighton Durham Reynolds, "The Transmission of the *De finibus*," *Italia medoevale e umanistica* 35 (1992): 1–30. For the numerous printed editions available prior to the time in which Machiavelli is thought to have begun work on *The Prince* and his *Discourses on Livy*, see Remo Giomini, "Conspecto editionum quae in apparatu critico laudantur," in M. Tulli Ciceronis, *Scripta quae manserunt omnia* XIV: *De divinatione, De fato, Timaeus*, ed. Remo Giomini (Leipzig: Teubner, 1975), xxxvi–xxxvii, and Leighton Durham Reynolds, "Index editorum et virorum doctorum qui infra laudantur," in M. Tulli Ciceronis, *De finibus bonorum et malorum libri quinque*, ed. Leighton Durham Reynolds (Oxford, UK: Clarendon Press, 1998), xxix–xxxiv (at xxix).

[82] Cf. Lucr. 2.216–93 with Cic. *Fat.* 10.21–11.26 and *Fin.* 1.6.17–21. For a comic exploration of the difficulties vis-à-vis human freedom that any cosmology rejecting natural teleology is bound to confront, see Pl. *Phd.* 97b7–99d2. The motives that induced Imannuel Kant to write his *Kritik der reinen Vernunft* appear to have been similar to those that inspired Epicurus to posit the swerve, for the former's aim was to accommodate Newtonian physics, with its bleak vision of a world constituted by nothing but matter in motion, epistemologically in such a manner as to leave ample space for human freedom.

in dominion and power. Initially, in a manner designed to placate his humanist readership, Machiavelli pretends to follow Plato, Aristotle, and Augustine in preferring peace to war and rest to political motion. If it were possible to render the republic difficult to capture and to make its lack of ambition obvious to all so that attack would be deterred and in no way provoked, "if it were possible to hold the thing balanced in this mode," he asserts, "it would be the true political way of life (*vivere politico*) and the true quiet of a city." Having offered the bait, however, he quickly makes the switch, arguing that such a balancing act cannot indefinitely be sustained and that a lawgiver should fortify his city against the worst – and he phrases his argument in such a fashion that it has an unmistakable Epicurean ring: "All the things of men are in motion," he warns, "and they cannot remain fixed; they must either rise or fall; and to many things that reason does not lead you, necessity leads you."[83] With the thrust of this last argument, Lucretius would have been in accord.

A bit later, however, Machiavelli plays the same game of bait and switch with those who looked for guidance to *De rerum natura* and to the tenth book of Diogenes Laertius' *Lives of the Eminent Philosophers*. In the middle of the first book of his *Discourses on Livy*, he restates the case made by the ancient Epicureans (and others both before and after) on behalf of a withdrawal from the public sphere, and he does so with a vigor and gusto they never excelled. He not only denies that within the political sphere constituted by the "new prince" a "middle course (*via del mezzo*)" can be found; he depicts the horrid consequences of its absence in vivid terms; and he suggests that rather than descend to "modes cruel, enemies to every way of life, not only Christian but human," of the sort that an engagement in politics requires, a "man should take to flight and wish very much to live in private."[84] Then, having made his case, after a hiatus of seventy chapters, more than sufficient to throw unsuspecting readers off the scent,[85] he returns to the question and demolishes his own argument. If the Epicurean critique of the political life really is correct, he argues, if political tranquility is an oxymoron, then political involvement is, in fact, indispensable – for within such a world there can be no place for a life of moderation confined to the private realm. In Machiavelli's view, the garden of Epicurus is no less illusory than are the republics and principalities imagined by Plato, Aristotle, Augustine, Thomas, and their humanist successors: for within a world like the one depicted by Lucretius "a man notable for his quality" is destined to "live in constant peril." "It is not sufficient to say," Machiavelli concludes, "'I do not care for anything. I desire neither honors nor things of use. I wish to live quietly and without trouble (*briga*).' For these excuses are listened to and not accepted. Nor is it possible for men who possess quality to elect to stand aside even when they elect such a course truly and without

---

[83] Note Pl. *Leg.* 1.625c–632e, 2.660e–664a, 666e–667a, 3.688a–d; Arist. *Pol.* 1267a21–36, 1323a14–1337a6, and August. *De civ. D.* 19.12, and see Machiavelli, *Discorsi* 1.6.3–4, in *Opere*, 85–87. Note also *Discorsi* 2.19, *Istorie fiorentine* 5.1, and *L'Asino* 3.79–128, in *Opere*, 173–75, 738–39, 960–62.

[84] See Machiavelli, *Discorsi* 1.26, in *Opere*, 109.

[85] For one such reader, see Isaiah Berlin, "The Originality of Machiavelli," in *Studies on Machiavelli*, ed. Myron P. Gilmore (Florence: Sansoni, 1972), 147–206 (esp. 194–96).

ambition, for they are not believed: so if they wish to stand aside, they are not allowed by others to do so."[86]

This same point Machiavelli made in another and even more devastating fashion by demonstrating that *ataraxía* is a pipe dream incompatible with the Epicurean understanding of the universe. The foundation of his teaching concerning politics and morals is, as we have seen, his claim that the human world is consonant with the natural world depicted in *De rerum natura* – which is what one would expect if nothing were to exist apart from matter in motion. This being the case, he concludes, the human world can afford man no stability, for everything within it must also be in flux. Such is implied in the Florentine's assertion that "all the things of men are in motion, and they cannot remain fixed." By this Machiavelli meant to convey something closely akin to what Thomas Hobbes and David Hume would later have in mind when they asserted that reason is the slave of the passions, for the turmoil that he had in mind was not just political: it was fundamental to human psychology. As he put it by way of explanation, "the human appetites" are "insatiable"; "by nature" human beings "desire everything" while "by fortune they are allowed to secure little"; and since "nature has created men in such a fashion" that they are "able to desire everything" but not "to secure everything," their "desire is always greater than the power of acquisition (*la potenza dello acquistare*)."[87]

From this premise, Machiavelli draws two conclusions. In *The Prince*, he remarks, "In truth, to acquire is a thing quite natural and ordinary, and always, when men do it who can, they will be praised and not blamed."[88] And in the *Discourses on Livy*, he adds that "whenever engaging in combat out of necessity is taken from men, they engage in combat out of ambition, which is so powerful in human breasts that, to whatever rank they ascend, it abandons them never."[89]

In accepting this doctrine, in denying that man can ever be at rest, Machiavelli dismissed as utopian not only the political teachings advanced by his classical and Christian predecessors but their moral teachings as well; and under its guidance, he rejected as illusory both the Aristotelian doctrine of the mean and the Epicurean quest for a moderation of the passions and tranquility of soul. The pursuit of moderation he treated as a species of folly, and he contended that in a world in constant flux there simply is not and cannot be "a middle course

---

[86] See Machiavelli, *Discorsi* 3.2, in *Opere*, 197–98.

[87] Cf. Machiavelli, *Discorsi* 1.6.4, 37.1, 2 Proemio 2–3, 3.1, and *L'Asino* 5.28–127 (esp. 34–75), in *Opere*, 86–87, 119, 145, 966–67, with Hobbes, *Leviathan* I.iii.3–5, viii.14–16, and with David Hume, *A Treatise of Human Nature*, ed. L. A. Selby-Bigge (Oxford, UK: Clarendon Press, 1888) II.iii, and see Machiavelli, *Il principe* 24 and *Discorsi* 1.32, in *Opere*, 114, 294–95. In this connection, see Markus Fischer, "Machiavelli's Political Psychology," *The Review of Politics* 59:4 (Fall 1997): 789–829; *Well-Ordered License: On the Unity of Machiavelli's Thought* (Lanham, MD: Lexington Books, 2000); and "Machiavelli's Rapacious Republicanism," in *Machiavelli's Liberal Republican Legacy*, ed. Paul A. Rahe (Cambridge, UK: Cambridge University Press, 2006), xxxi–lxii. See also Christian Lazzeri, "Les Racines de la volonté de puissance: Le 'Passage' de Machiavel à Hobbes," in *Thomas Hobbes: Philosophie première, théorie de la science et politique*, ed. Yves Charles Zarka and Jean Bernhardt (Paris: Presses Universitaires de France, 1990), 225–46 (esp. 225–36).

[88] See Machiavelli, *Il principe* 3, in *Opere*, 261.

[89] See Machiavelli, *Discorsi* 1.37.1, in *Opere*, 119.

(*via del mezzo*)" of any kind. In the absence of war, he argued, if there were no external constraints and "leisure and idleness (*ozio*)" really were to become the norm, republics would not prosper: they would become "effeminate or divided." Lawgivers should, therefore, "think of" what he tellingly describes as "the more honorable part," and they should take their bearings from the worst conceivable case.[90] They should make a virtue of necessity: they should foster acquisitiveness and promote acquisition.

So he insisted, and he evidently thought that every argument that he made concerning cities applied with equal force to individuals acting on their own. To the best of their ability, human beings should construct dikes and dams to contain fortune's flood, and when confronted with a crisis that renders such preparations nugatory, they should be defiant, impetuous, and ferocious. Fortune they should command with sheer audacity. So he writes in *The Prince*.[91]

In that work, as a consequence of his analysis of the passions, Machiavelli anticipates Hobbes's scandalous assertion that in political affairs "[t]he Passion to be reckoned upon, is Fear," arguing that ordinarily "it is safer to be feared than to be loved" and justifying his claim on the grounds that men are "ingrates." They are, he tells us, "inconstant." They are "feigners and dissemblers, fugitives from danger, desirers of gain," and they are far more likely to calculate their interests and ruminate on their prospects for survival than to be governed by a sense of obligation. "Friendships," he observes, "which are acquired at a price and not with greatness and nobility of spirit, are earned but not owned – and when the time comes they cannot be employed." The cause of this is self-evident: "men have less hesitation (*respetto*) to offend one who makes them love than one who makes them fear, for love is held fast by a chain of obligation – which, because men are a sad, bad lot (*tristi*), they break for their own utility at every opportunity (*occasione*) – but fear is held fast by a dread of punishment that abandons you never."[92]

It is on the basis of these and similar observations that the Florentine concludes in his *Discourses on Livy* that one must take one's political bearings from a fact putatively admitted by "all who reason concerning civic life (*vivere civile*)" but, in reality, nowhere baldly asserted in this particular fashion by anyone prior to Machiavelli himself: that a lawgiver intent on setting up a republic and ordaining its laws must "presuppose that all men are wicked (*rei*) and that they will make use of the malignity of their spirit whenever they are free and have occasion to do so."[93] This revolutionary claim – that one could combine a vision of pristine human nature akin to Augustine's account of man's character

---

[90] See Machiavelli, *Discorsi* 1.6.4, in *Opere*, 86–87. Note also Machiavelli, *L'Asino* 5.94–96, in *Opere*, 967. With regard to the *via del mezzo*, note Machiavelli, *Del modo di trattare i popoli della Valdichiana ribellati*, in *Opere*, 13–16; see Machiavelli, *Discorsi* 1.26–27, 2.23.3–4, 3.2–3, 21, 40.2, and *AG* 3.155–60 (at 159), in *Opere*, 109–10, 179–81, 197–99, 226–28, 249, 342–43; and consider Hörnqvist, *Machiavelli and Empire*, 76–112.

[91] See Machiavelli, *Il principe* 25, in *Opere*, 295–96. Cf. Parel, *The Machiavellian Cosmos*, 63–100.

[92] Cf. Machiavelli, *Il principe* 17, in *Opere*, 282, with Hobbes, *Leviathan* I.xiv.31. Note also Machiavelli, *Il principe* 9 (at the end), in *Opere*, 272.

[93] See Machiavelli, *Discorsi* 1.3.1, in *Opere*, 81. Although one could easily imagine an Augustinian agreeing with such sentiments, to the best of my knowledge, no Augustinian in the period prior

after the Fall with something like political idealism and with a towering, trans-
formative legislative ambition – provides the foundation for a new species of
republicanism: a republicanism consistent with Lucretius' vision of nature as
nothing more than matter in motion through an endless void, in accord with
the Roman poet's account of man's tenuous place within a universe indifferent
to his very existence, in harmony with the critique that the Epicureans had
articulated against the classical republicanism regnant in ancient Greece and
Rome – and yet, as we have seen, fiercely opposed to philosophical resignation
in the face of fortune of the sort that Epicurus, Lucretius, and their followers
had espoused.[94]

Virtue, Corruption, and Fear

Machiavelli's depiction of the human condition is grim, indeed. But he does
offer some consolation to the run-of-the-mill moralist. He speaks incessantly
of virtue and corruption, and he does so in a familiar and reassuring manner.[95]
He attributes great importance to "good examples," and he even contends that
these "arise from good education."[96] It would be easy to latch on to these
statements. It would be easy to give them great weight and to build upon them
a towering edifice. It would be easy to suppose that they provide license for
discounting the Florentine's more shocking claims.[97]

   All of this is, however, a snare and a delusion designed to dupe the inattentive
humanist – for though he affects to admire antiquity, Machiavelli nowhere
advocates a reliance on moral or political virtue. In fact, as we have seen, he
thinks it prudent that one regard all men as vicious. In his estimation, the presumption that men are educable and capable of moral improvement is not
a proper starting point for political reflection. It is far better, he insists, that
one begin with a sober appreciation for human defects and a determination
to put them to the best possible use. In his judgment, one must start off by
acknowledging "the effectual truth of the matter."

---

   to Machiavelli concerned himself with the foundation of a republic. Ptolemy of Lucca and his
   heirs were Aristotelians indebted for their theology to Thomas Aquinas.

[94] When one recognizes the importance of *De rerum natura* for Machiavelli, the observations of
   Sheldon S. Wolin, "Machiavelli: Politics and the Economy of Violence," in Wolin, *Politics and
   Vision: Continuity and Innovation in Western Political Thought*, second edition (Princeton, NJ:
   Princeton University Press, 2004), 173–213 (esp. 187–95), seem especially prescient.

[95] See, for example, Machiavelli, *Discorsi* Ep. Ded., 1 Proemio 2, 1.4, 2.3, 9.2, 10, 11.3, 16–18,
   20, 23.4, 29–30, 31.1, 33.2, 35, 37.1, 40.4, 42–43, 46, 49, 52.1, 55, and 2 Proemio 1–2, 2.1,
   16.1, 17, 18.3–4, 19, 22.1, 24, 27.4, 29.1, 3.1.2–3, 6.19, 8, 10.1, 11, 16–17, 21.3, 22, 27.3, 28,
   30, 33.1, 34, 42–43, 49.4, in *Opere*, 76–80, 90–94, 99–107, 110–15, 117–19, 124, 126, 131–33,
   137, 144–48, 166–75, 178, 181–84, 187–89, 195–96, 209–10, 211–17, 222–24, 227–30, 234–
   37, 240–43, 249–51, 254. In this connection, note Alfredo Bonadeo, *Corruption, Conflict, and
   Power in the Works and Times of Niccolò Machiavelli* (Berkeley: University of California Press,
   1973), 1–34, and read with care Riccardo Breschi, "Il concetto di 'corruzione' nei *Discorsi*,"
   Studi storici 29:3 (July–September 1988): 707–35.

[96] Machiavelli, *Discorsi* 1.4.1, in *Opere*, 82.

[97] More than one such edifice has been built: see the secondary literature cited in note 1, this
   chapter.

It is with regard to the "effectual truth" that Machiavelli rejects as untenable the regime typology of the ancients.[98] In human affairs, he argues, corruption and license are the norm – so much so, in fact, that within a generation of the foundation of a simple polity, it inevitably goes awry. As soon as the salutary fear that had originally inspired the establishment of a new form of government has waned, the ruling element becomes abusive and begins to take unfair advantage: kingship collapses into tyranny, aristocracy into oligarchy, and well-ordered popular government into the regime variously called democracy, anarchy, or mob rule. In short, as one would expect in a universe constituted solely by matter in motion, chaos is natural and the norm, and order is as fragile as it is artificial.

If the mixed regime established by the Romans has any advantage, Machiavelli adds, it derives not from a combination of the virtues of its constituent parts: it is due solely to the fact that "the one" part "guards the other" and that reciprocal "fear" serves as a restraint on all.[99] The same can be said for the dictatorship, which would have been a danger to Rome had its term of office not been short and had the Senate, the consuls, and the tribunes not retained sufficient "authority" to serve as "a guard."[100] It even helps if there is a foreign threat to keep the citizens alert, vigilant, and, in the selection of magistrates, carefully attentive to the public need.[101]

There is more, however, to Machiavelli's argument than the suggestion – advanced in antiquity by Polybius and Sallust on the basis of an observation made by Aristotle – that, in the absence of a salutary fear, moral virtue and political solidarity can in any regime easily give way.[102] The Florentine's doctrine

---

[98] For this regime typology, cf. Polyb. 6.3.5–10.14 with Xen. *Mem.* 4.6.12, *Oec.* 21.9–12; Pl. *Pol.* 291d–303b, *Leg.* 3.689e–702d, 4.712c–715d, 8.832b–d; Arist. *Eth. Nic.* 1160a31–1161b10, *Pol.* 1278b30–1280a5, 1284b35–1285b33, 1295a7–24, *Rh.* 1365b21–1366a22; and see Pl. *Leg.* 6.756e–758a, Arist. *Pol.* 1281b22–38 (esp. 28–31), 1295a25–1297a12 (esp. 1296b14–16), 1297b1–27, 1329a2–17, 1332b12–41. Note, in this connection, Pind. *Pyth.* 2.86–88, Hdt. 3.80–83, and Thuc. 8.97.2. In Machiavelli's day, with the exception of a few fragments, the pertinent passages of Cicero's *Republic* (1.20.33–2.44.70, 3.13.23, 25.37–35.48) were as yet undiscovered.

[99] Cf. Machiavelli, *Discorsi* 1.2.2–3.1, in *Opere*, 79–82, with Polyb. 6.3.5–10.14, and see Gennaro Sasso, *Niccolò Machiavelli: Storia del suo pensiero politico* (Bologna: Società Editrice il Mulino, 1980), 441–47, along with Gennaro Sasso, "Machiavelli e la teoria dell'*anacyclosis*" and "Machiavelli e Polibio: Constituzione, potenza, conquista," in *Machiavelli e gli antichi e altri saggi*, I 3–118, and Harvey C. Mansfield, "Necessity in the Beginning of Cities," in *The Political Calculus: Essays in Machiavelli's Philosophy*, ed. Anthony J. Parel (Toronto: University of Toronto Press, 1972), 101–26, which is reprinted in Mansfield, *Machiavelli's Virtue*, 57–78, along with Mansfield, *Machiavelli's New Modes and Orders*, 28–42. Note also Machiavelli, *Discorsi* 1.40.7, 49.3, and AG 1.78–81, in *Opere*, 125, 131–32, 307.

[100] See Machiavelli, *Discorsi* 1.34–35, in *Opere*, 116–18.

[101] See Machiavelli, *Discorsi* 1.18.3, in *Opere*, 103, in conjunction with *Discorsi* 1.6.4, 2.25.1, 3.16, in *Opere*, 86, 185, 222–23.

[102] Consider Polyb. 6.3–10, 18, 44, 57, and Sall. *Cat.* 10–13, *Iug.* 41.1–5, *Hist.* 1.8–13 (McGushin) in light of Arist. *Pol.* 1308a24–30, and see Neal Wood, "Sallust's Theorem: A Comment on 'Fear' in Western Political Thought," *History of Political Thought* 16:2 (Summer 1995): 174–89, who errs solely in reading into Thucydides, Polybius, and Sallust a doctrine of necessity – "that men act well only under compulsion" – which, though quite visible in Machiavelli and Hobbes, is foreign to the moral outlook and the nuanced understanding of political psychology that guided these ancient historians.

is much more radical, for, in his opinion, it did not suffice that one remark on virtue's fragility. Machiavelli does not argue that republican *virtù* can more easily be sustained with the help of external supports. In accord with the conviction that he shares with Thomas Hobbes that the passion to be reckoned on is fear, he contends, instead, that such *virtù* is founded in and sustained by terror and terror alone – and he asserts, as a consequence, that, if a well-ordered republic is to endure, at frequent intervals, perhaps even on a daily basis, the primordial fear that animates it must be renewed. Such is what he has in mind when he speaks of a "return to first principles."[103]

The thoroughgoing dependence of popular, republican *virtù* on fear is nicely illustrated by Machiavelli's discussion of the early Roman Republic. Although the Florentine repeatedly denies that the early republic was corrupt, he acknowledges that, after the establishment of a junta called the Decemvirate for more than a year with power unchecked, Rome drifted rapidly in that direction. "It does not help," he observes, "that the matter (*materia*) is not corrupt – since an absolute authority corrupts the matter in a very short time and makes for itself friends and partisans." In kingdoms and republics, the Florentine concludes, "lawgivers" must be "quite ready to bridle human appetites," and they should make it a point "to eliminate every hope of being able with impunity to go astray."[104]

By the same token, if Machiavelli tends to associate equality with popular (as opposed to princely) virtue, if he identifies radical inequality with the wholesale corruption of a people,[105] and if he argues that in republics the public should be rich and private individuals poor,[106] it is because he firmly believes that republican virtue cannot withstand temptation. Where property is unequally distributed and some are rich and others poor, where influence and authority are confined to a few, where magistracies and commands are held for extended periods – in short, wherever patronage is on offer – citizens will readily sacrifice autonomy for advantage and seek private remedies for public wrongs. Parties will then grow up, along with sects more enduring and susceptible to repeated resurrection, and the common utility will be sacrificed for partisan and sectarian advantage.[107] In the bitterness of the struggle that then ensues, individuals and

[103] See Machiavelli, *Discorsi* 3.1, 49, in *Opere*, 195–97, 253–54, which should be read in light of Lucr. 2.1173–74, 5.92–96, 306–15. Cf. Machiavelli, *Discorsi* 3.22.3 with 3.17, in *Opere*, 223, 228–29.

[104] See Machiavelli, *Discorsi* 1.35, 40–42, in *Opere*, 117–18, 123–26. Note, in this connection, *Discorsi* 1.17.1, 3.22.4–5, 24, in *Opere*, 101, 229–31.

[105] See Machiavelli, *Discorsi* 1.17, 37.1, 55, 3.16, in *Opere*, 101–2, 119, 136–39. Note also *Discorsi* 1.2.3, 6.2, 11.3, 3.3.1, in *Opere*, 79–80, 85, 94, 198–99, 222–23, and see *Discorsi* 3.25 and *AG* 1.33, in *Opere*, 231–32, 304.

[106] See Machiavelli, *Discorsi* 1.37.1, 2.6, 19.1, 3.16.2, 25, in *Opere*, 119, 155–56, 173–74, 222–23, 231–32. In this connection, note *Discorsi* 1.34.2, in *Opere*, 116.

[107] Consider Machiavelli, *Discorsi* 1.17.1, 35, 37, 40–42, 49.2, in *Opere*, 101, 119–20, 124–25, 131, in light of *Discorsi* 1.46 and 3.28, and *Istorie fiorentine* 7.1, in *Opere*, 117–18, 123–26, 128–29, 234–35, 792–93. Consider also *Discorsi* 1.8, 24, 58, 3.1.3, in *Opere*, 88–90, 107–8, 140–42, 195–96, in light of *Discorsi* 3.8, in *Opere*, 211–13, and note what we are told about Cosimo de' Medici: see *Discorsi* 1.33 and *Istorie fiorentine* 4.27, in *Opere*, 114–16, 731–33. In this connection, see Bonadeo, *Corruption, Conflict and Power in the Works and Times of Niccolò Machiavelli*, 35–71, and Gisela Bock, "Civil Discord in Machiavelli's *Istorie*

groups will be ready to call in foreigners to support their cause,[108] and out of fear and ambition they will opt for tyranny.[109]

As Machiavelli uses the terms, "virtue" and "corruption" are not, as they are in Sallust, qualities of soul.[110] To bring this home to his readers, in *The Prince* and in the *Discourses on Livy*, he takes great care never even to mention the soul. Moreover, in Machiavelli's republican discourse, these evaluative terms are rarely used to describe character as such. Most often, they indicate the absence or presence of clientitial relations, and they identify the opposed patterns of behavior to which their presence and absence give rise.[111]

As one would then expect, the "education" said by Machiavelli to be productive of "good examples" is neither Greek nor Roman, neither Aristotelian nor Ciceronian: it is not a product of moral training and habituation; it is in no way aimed at liberating men from the dominion of their passions; and intellectual virtue is not its completion. Its goal is, rather, to shape, direct, and fortify the spirited passions.

Thus, when Machiavelli suggests that "good examples arise from good education," the Florentine immediately adds that "good education [arises] from good laws," and in this context he says nothing at all concerning religious

Fiorentine," in *Machiavelli and Republicanism*, 181–201, which needs to be amended in light of Harvey C. Mansfield, "Party and Sect in Machiavelli's *Florentine Histories*," in *Machiavelli and the Nature of Political Thought*, ed. Martin Fleisher (Princeton, NJ: Princeton University Press, 1972), 209–66, which is reprinted in Mansfield, *Machiavelli's Virtue*, 137–75.

[108] See Machiavelli, *Discorsi* 1.7, 59, 2.2.1, 15.2, 25.1, 3.14.1, 24, 27, in *Opere*, 87–88, 142–43, 148–49, 165–66, 184–85, 220, 231, 233–34.

[109] Consider Machiavelli, *Discorsi* 1.10.3, 6, 17.1, 29.3, 37, 40.5–7, 52.3, 3.8, 22, 24, in *Opere*, 92–93, 101, 111–12, 119–20, 124–25, 134, 211–13, 228–31, in light of *Discorsi* 1.16.3, in *Opere*, 99–100. In its very nature, tyranny is partisan: see *Il principe* 9 and *Discorsi* 1.40.5–7, in *Opere*, 124–25, 271–72.

[110] Cf. Sall. *Cat.* 1–13, *Iug.* 1–4, 41, who grounds his argument on Stoic principles and on the political psychology articulated in Plato's *Republic*: see S. Pantzerhielm Thomas, "The Prologues of Sallust," *Symbolae osloenses* 15/16 (1936): 140–62, and Bruce D. MacQueen, *Plato's Republic in the Monographs of Sallust* (Chicago: Bolchazy-Carducci, 1981). That Machiavelli read and exploited Sallust is now generally well understood: note Quentin Skinner, "Machiavelli's *Discorsi* and the Pre-Humanist Origins of Republican Ideas," in *Machiavelli and Republicanism*, 121–41, and see Patricia J. Osmond, "Sallust and Machiavelli: From Civic Humanism to Political Prudence," *Journal of Medieval and Renaissance Studies* 23:3 (Fall 1993): 407–38, and Benedetto Fontana, "Sallust and the Politics of Machiavelli," *History of Political Thought* 24:1 (Spring 2003): 86–108, who draw attention to the debt Machiavelli owed Sallust but misconceive its character. The degree to which the two thinkers were profoundly at odds needs closer attention than it has received. One's starting point should be Gennaro Sasso, "Machiavelli e i detrattori, antichi e nuovi, di Roma," in *Machiavelli e gli antichi e altri saggi*, I 401–536 (at 441–60). See also Sasso, *Niccolò Machiavelli: Storia del suo pensiero politico*, 485–94. Sallust's importance for the development of civic humanism stems in part from the fact that his works were available from the Carolingian period onward and were read in the universities. On his fortunes and influence, see Patricia J. Osmond and Robert W. Ulery, Jr., "Gaius Sallustius Crispus," in *Catalogus translationum et commentariorum*, VIII 183–326.

[111] The fact that Machiavelli recognizes that human beings tend to get into ruts and that very few, if any, are capable of the flexibility that he thinks requisite for princes does not justify the assertion that his account of human moral psychology is akin to that of Aristotle: cf. Carey J. Nederman, "Machiavelli and Moral Character: Principality, Republic, and the Psychology of *Virtù*," *History of Political Thought* 21:3 (Autumn 2000): 349–64.

indoctrination, the humanist project, or the forms of civic *paideía* known to antiquity. Moreover, he implies that these "good laws" have their origins neither in the wisdom of an outstanding statesman nor in the prudence that public deliberation was generally thought to promote. They arise, instead, we are told, from an unexpected source: "the tumults (*tumulti*) that many so inconsiderately condemn." And then, by way of explanation, Machiavelli drew from his premise that the founder of a republic must operate on the presumption that all men are wicked a series of conclusions that astonished his contemporaries and that would have surprised the ancients even more – arguing, as we have already seen, that commonwealths aiming at expansion, as Rome did, are far more viable than commonwealths, such as Sparta and Venice, which aim only at preserving what they already have, and also contending that Roman liberty was rooted in a salutary political turbulence and that in a republic the people are safer and better guardians of liberty than the nobles.[112] It is to these last two assertions that we now must turn.

A Question of Appetite

Although he was profoundly hostile to formed parties and to ideological, sectarian politics, Machiavelli was not a proponent of consensus and political harmony. Instead, he was persuaded that, in the absence of corruption and partisanship, class strife, when properly channeled and restrained, is salutary in the extreme. To convey what he meant by political health, he resorted – as had Plato and Aristotle, Thomas Aquinas, and Girolamo Savonarola before him – to language borrowed from Hippocratic medicine, which explained disease and health in terms of an imbalance and a salutary balance in what it called "the humors." But, as was his wont, Machiavelli broke with Plato, Aristotle, Thomas Aquinas, and Girolamo Savonarola and used this familiar language in a manner unprecedented, severing the relationship posited in pre-modern thought between humoral balance within the polity and the virtue of justice, treating humor itself in light of his reorientation of Epicureanism solely as a function of human appetite, and embracing political conflict well managed as a positive good.[113] Those who are inclined to denounce political turmoil and to argue for social and political harmony "have not," he argued, "considered how it is that in every republic there are two diverse humors – that of the people, and that of the great ones (*grandi*) – and that all the laws that are made in favor of liberty are born from this disunion." To those who think this last claim preposterous, he replies that "every city ought to have modes by which

---

[112] Machiavelli, *Discorsi* 1.4–6, in *Opere*, 82–87. Note, in this connection, Machiavelli, *Il principe* 12, in *Opere*, 275–77.

[113] Though extremely useful, the one systematic attempt to make sense of humor as a category of political analysis in Machiavelli has this defect: it confuses the Florentine's appropriation of the traditional term with an acceptance on his part of pre-modern political psychology, and it thereby fails to do full justice to the radical novelty of his understanding of the political import of class tensions: cf. Parel, *The Machiavellian Cosmos*, 89, 101–52, with Gérald Sfez, "Machiavel: La raison des humeurs," *Rue Descartes* 12–13 (May 1995): 11–37, who provides a corrective.

the people can vent their ambition," arguing that "the demands of a free people are seldom pernicious and rarely endanger their liberty: they arise from
oppression or from the suspicions that they entertain that they are about to be
oppressed."[114]

It is in this context – while denouncing the well-known hostility to political
discord of authorities such as Aristotle, Cicero, Sallust, and Livy, and of the
ancients more generally;[115] while jettisoning the commitment to civic consensus and harmony displayed by the civic humanists of his own time;[116] and while
calling for there to be modes through which the people can express and display
their ambition – that Machiavelli defends popular participation in public deliberation, and to this end he cites Cicero and hints by way of context at a crucial
and telling qualifier, which points to the critical feature that distinguishes his
republicanism from the classical account embraced by the greatest orator of
ancient Rome. When "the opinions of the people are false," Machiavelli tells
us with regard to a situation in which what is at stake is the existence or likelihood of oppression, "there is a remedy in the public assemblies where a good
man can stand up and, in speaking, demonstrate to the people that they are in
error."[117] As Machiavelli's depiction of this situation suggests, in rejecting natural law, natural right, and with them the classical notion of moral and political
rationality, the Florentine reduces public reason to multitudinous private calculations concerning material self-interest. It is this great shift that underpins
and explains the peculiar character of Machiavelli's populist turn.

The crucial fact that one has to keep always in mind, Machiavelli insists,
is that the people "have less of an appetite for usurpation" than the *grandi*. If
one ponders the ends which "the nobles" pursue and those pursued by "the
ignoble," one will recognize that the former's purposes arise from "a grand

---

[114] See Machiavelli, *Discorsi* 1.4.1, in *Opere*, 82–83.

[115] See Rahe, *Republics Ancient and Modern*, 55–135.

[116] It was by means of his fascination with intestine conflict that Machiavelli distinguished himself
as an historian from classical republicans such as Leonardo Bruni: *Istorie fiorentine* Proemio,
in *Opere*, 632–33. Note, in this connection, Francis Bacon, *The Advancement of Learning*, ed.
Michael Kiernan, II.xxii.6, in *OFB*, IV 150. If Skinner, *The Foundations of Modern Political
Thought* I: *The Renaissance*, 180–86, errs in supposing that, apart from Machiavelli's belief
that Christianity and *virtù* are incompatible, his invention of this species of corporate, institutional analysis is the only element that distinguishes his understanding of political affairs from
that of his predecessors and contemporaries, he is, nonetheless, correct in stressing the latter's
significance. To think through what the Florentine's institutional political science presupposes
is to discover just how radical a break he made with all previous political philosophy and
science. A genuine admirer of classical republicanism could easily share Machiavelli's disdain
for Christianity, but he could hardly accept the notion that *stásis* is the true source of political
well-being: note, for example, Francesco Guicciardini, *Ricordi*, ed. Ettore Barelli (Milan: Biblioteca Universale Rizzoli, 1977) C para. 123, B paras. 14, 95, 124; then, consider Francesco
Guicciardini "Considerazioni sui Discorsi del Machiavelli," in Guicciardini, *Opere inedite*, I
12–14. On the latter work, note Mark Phillips, *Francesco Guicciardini: The Historian's Craft*
(Toronto: University of Toronto Press, 1977), 81–93.

[117] Cf. Machiavelli, *Discorsi* 1.4.1, in *Opere*, 82–83, with Cic. *Amic.* 25.95. Note, in this connection, *Il principe* 9, in *Opere*, 271–72; *Discorsi* 1.17.3, in *Opere*, 102; and *Istorie fiorentine* 3.1,
4.1, 7.1, in *Opere*, 690–91, 715–16, 792–93; and see Sasso, "Machiavelli e i detrattori, antichi
e nuovi, di Roma," 401–536.

desire for domination" and the latter's "solely from a desire not to be dominated" – that the former "desire to acquire" while the latter "fear to lose what
they have acquired."[118] If, then, the people are better guardians of liberty than
the nobility, it is not because they possess any natural inclination for justice
but because a defect in "appetite" renders them more timid and less likely to
exploit the opportunities presented to them. Machiavelli makes much of "the
popular desire . . . to be free," but he insists that only "a very small part" of the
people "desire to be free in order to command; all the others, who are infinite
in number, desire liberty in order to live securely."[119]

In reading these claims, one must take great care – for, immediately after
introducing the pertinent class distinctions, Machiavelli subverts and qualifies
them, as is his wont – first, by intimating that most of those conventionally
thought to be *grandi* actually belong by nature to the *popolo*,[120] and later by
enabling his readers to see that those who emerge as leaders of the *popolo*
rarely lack the "appetite" that inspires on the part of the *grandi* so powerful
a "desire for domination."[121] In general, he observes, men "hold possessions
(*roba*) in higher regard than honors," and the Roman nobility was, he insists, no
exception: its members were always quite willing to concede honors to the *plebs*
but they were fiercely obstinate in defending their possessions. Thus, those who
"desire to be free in order to command all the others" are as few in number
as they are great in weight, and "the common utility" that ordinary men –
whether born rich or poor – draw "from a free way of life (*vivere libero*)" is
extremely prosaic, even bourgeois: "being able to possess one's things freely
without any suspicion, not having grounds for doubting the honor of women
and of children, not fearing for oneself." Men of such a humor, "when they are
governed well, neither seek nor want any other freedom."[122]

---

[118] Cf. Machiavelli, *Discorsi* 1.5.2, in *Opere*, 83–84, which should be read in conjunction with
Il principe Ep. Ded., 9, *Discorsi* 1.4.1, and *Istorie fiorentine* 3.1, 4.1, in *Opere*, 82–83, 257,
271–72, 690–91, 715–16, with Sallust's report concerning the diatribe of the *popularis* tribune
Gaius Memmius (*Iug.* 31.23), from which the Florentine borrowed this description of the two
classes, and see Osmond, "Sallust and Machiavelli," 415–17.

[119] See Machiavelli, *Discorsi* 1.16.5, in *Opere*, 100.

[120] See Machiavelli, *Discorsi* 1.5.4, in *Opere*, 84.

[121] Consider what Machiavelli has to say about the behavior of the *plebs* once it has secured what it
has acquired: *Discorsi* 1.37, in *Opere*, 119–20. The uncharacteristic ambition that the plebeians
then display would appear to stem from that of the natural aristocrats in their number: *Discorsi*
1.16.5, in *Opere*, 100–1.

[122] Consider Machiavelli, *Discorsi* 1.16.3–5, 37.3, 3.5, in *Opere*, 100–1, 121, 200, which should
be read in light of *Discorsi* Ep. Ded., 2.2.3, in *Opere*, 75, 150. Vatter, *Between Form and
Event*, passim, would not have felt so great a need to elevate the people's pedestrian "desire
not to be dominated" into a metaphysical principle, and he would not have been required
to do such violence to the plain meaning of Machiavelli's text had he reflected adequately
on the role played at Rome by the "very small part" of the *popolo* who "desire to be free
in order to command" and on that played by the no less meager proportion of the so-called
grandi governed by something more magnificent than a fear of losing what they have already
acquired – which is to say, had he attended sufficiently to that handful of men within the two
orders who thrilled at the prospect that, within a republic such as Rome, "those who, for
their infinite good parts, deserve to be" princes "can by means of their *virtù* become" just
that.

This analysis of the circumscribed character of "the popular desire...to be free" may owe something to the mercantile character of the Florence within which Machiavelli lived and wrote. After all, he did not reside in a Greek *pólis* or in the Roman *civitas*, and he knew it. His immediate audience was not composed of farmers and warriors. It was made up of merchants, bankers, tradesmen, and craftsmen – "men," as he put it, "who draw their nourishment from the exchange of merchandise (*uomini nutricati nella mercanzia*)."[123] Mindful of the condition of those for whom they wrote, Italian humanists in and before his time – men such as Leon Battista Alberti, Leonardo Bruni, Poggio Bracciolini, Vespasiano da Bisticci, Francesco Guicciardini, and the like – consistently failed, when speaking in a civic vein, to display toward men of commerce the haughty disdain evidenced by classical republicans in antiquity.[124] The course that these humanists adopted as a consequence of rhetorical necessity, Machiavelli appears to have embraced out of conviction.

The mercantile ethos of Florence may also go a long way toward explaining why Machiavelli thinks it so important that a prince "encourage his citizens so that they can quietly engage in their occupations, both in commerce and in agriculture and in every other occupation pursued by men," by seeing to it "that one man is not afraid to improve on his properties for fear that they will be taken from him, and another is not afraid to open a business (*uno traffico*) for fear of taxes."[125] It was not for nothing that Peter Laslett, some years ago, suggested that John Locke be considered "Machiavelli's philosopher."[126] One takes a giant step from Machiavelli's position toward that of liberal individualism and one severs the last tenuous link connecting the Florentine's understanding of the purpose of liberty with that of the ancients when one follows through on the logic of Machiavelli's populism and grounds the polity exclusively on the desire of the *popolo* for security while subordinating to that desire quite systematically the vain aspirations of the *grandi* for honor, glory, conquest, and command.[127]

---

[123] See Machiavelli, *Istorie fiorentine* 1.39, in *Opere*, 658.

[124] Consider Mark Jurdjevic, "Virtue, Commerce, and the Enduring Florentine Republican Moment: Reintegrating Italy into the Atlantic Republican Debate," *Journal of the History of Ideas* 62:4 (October 2001): 721–43, in light of Rahe, *Republics Ancient and Modern*, 55–104.

[125] See Machiavelli, *Il principe* 21, in *Opere*, 292.

[126] It may seem odd, but this dimension of Locke's argument has been more closely attended to in Chicago than in Cambridge: cf. Peter Laslett, "Introduction," in John Locke, *Two Treatises of Government*, second edition, ed. Peter Laslett (Cambridge, UK: Cambridge University Press, 1967), 86–87, with Nathan Tarcov, "Locke's *Second Treatise* and 'The Best Fence against Rebellion,'" *The Review of Politics* 43:2 (April 1981): 198–217 (esp. 211–17); Thomas L. Pangle, "Executive Energy and Popular Spirit in Lockean Constitutionalism," *Presidential Studies Quarterly* 17:2 (Spring 1987): 253–65 (esp. 259–64); Harvey C. Mansfield, *Taming the Prince: The Ambivalence of Modern Executive Power* (New York: Free Press, 1989), 121–211; and Margaret Michelle Barnes Smith, "The Philosophy of Liberty: Locke's Machiavellian Teaching," in *Machiavelli's Liberal Republican Legacy*, 36–57. One might wish to begin by considering the significance of the fact that Locke chose as the epigraph for his *Two Treatises of Government* a fiery passage from Livy (9.1.10) repeatedly cited by Machiavelli in his most populist moments: cf. Machiavelli, *Discorsi* 3.12.2, *Il principe* 26, and *Istorie fiorentine* 5.8, in *Opere*, 218, 297, 743–44, with Locke, *Two Treatises of Government*, 154.

[127] When Machiavelli rejects the classical notion that the quest for honor and glory points beyond itself to the pursuit of virtue and human excellence or, indeed, to anything higher than fame

Machiavelli's Modern Populism

Later in the *Discourses on Livy*, when Machiavelli once again sounds his populist theme, he underlines even more emphatically the elements within his argument that mark his break with the ancients, and he signals this theme's novelty, its radicalism, and its significance for his teaching as a whole by directly attacking his authority Livy. This time, he explicitly debunks the classical presumption that the wise and virtuous few are superior to the foolish and vicious many. In doing so, he points to the fact that if a legislator really must presuppose that "all men are wicked and that they will make use of the malignity of their spirit whenever they are free and have occasion to do so," there is no place for the classical republican principle of differential moral and political rationality. Not just Livy, he contends, but "all the other historians" and, indeed, "all the writers" are profoundly mistaken. In fact, all are in error who have preceded Machiavelli and who have therefore been unable to profit from his discovery of the "new modes and orders" that constitute "a path as yet untrodden by anyone" – for they all denounce "the multitude" as "vain and inconstant." Livy in particular is wrong when he claims that "the nature of the multitude" is such that "it either serves humbly or dominates proudly." The truth is that "all men in particular and princes especially can be accused of the defect" that these writers attribute to the people, "for everyone who is not regulated by the laws would make the same errors as the multitude unshackled (*sciolta*)." Indeed, "all" are "equally" apt to "go astray when all can go astray without" what he calls "*rispetto*" – that is, without the hesitation that arises from "looking back" in shame or in fear. In any case, Machiavelli adds, it makes no sense to compare such a multitude with kings who are subject to the law: to such kings one should compare "a multitude in the same fashion regulated by laws" – such as "the Roman people who, while the republic remained uncorrupt, never served humbly or dominated proudly."

In practice, Machiavelli informs us, "a prince unshackled from the laws will be more ungrateful, various, and imprudent than the people." This is not due to the "diverse nature" of the prince and the people but to the relative timidity of the latter – to "their having more or less respect (*rispetto*) for the laws under which the one and the other live." If, when "the one and the other are unshackled, one sees fewer errors in the people than in the prince," and their errors are less severe and more easily remedied, it is evidently because the people are defective in appetite and, when lacking genuine leaders as "heads," hopelessly irresolute: "to a licentious and tumultuous people a good man can speak, and they can easily be returned to the good way." Thus, if one wishes to "cure the malady of the people, words are sufficient," but "to cure that of the prince requires iron." The real danger that arises when "a people is completely unshackled" stems not from what the people might do on their own hook but

itself, he not only eliminates the ground for distinguishing the wise and virtuous few from the foolish and vicious many; as he knows all too well, he prepares the way for the collapse of his own distinction between the *grandi* and the *popolo*: consider Pind. F215 (Bowra) and Theog. 1104a–1106 (West) in light of Arist. *Eth. Nic.* 1123b35–1124a2; then, ponder *Il principe* 18 (at the end), in *Opere*, 284, and see *Machiavelli's Liberal Republican Legacy*, passim.

from the opportunity that this offers to those of their "heads" who are only nominally "ignoble," possessing, as they do, the appetite for command that distinguishes "those who, for their infinite good parts, deserve to be" princes not only from the *popolo* but also from those among the *grandi* who share its plebeian tastes. "In so much confusion," we are told, "a tyrant can be born."[128]

Machiavelli insists that Livy, "all the other historians," and "all the writers" in general are united in embracing the classical republican principle of differential moral and political rationality, and he puts considerable effort into defending the *popolo* against the charge that arises from what he takes to be a false presumption. He does, however, concede the superiority of princes in one highly significant particular – "in ordaining laws, forming civil life, ordaining new statutes and orders." The people are superior, he tells us, only in "maintaining things" already "ordained." Because of its defect in appetite, the populace seems unable to initiate. In fact, it needs guidance from "someone" of sufficient appetite "in whom it has faith" – for, often, "deceived by a false image of the good, the people desire their own ruin." Fortunately, in judging between orators of "equal *virtù*," the populace tends to "the better opinion." Rarely, says Machiavelli, are the people "incapable" of discerning "the truth that they hear." It is as if they are in possession of "an occult virtue" enabling them to "foresee their own ill and their good." To exercise that virtue, however, they must be turned away from false images of the good and liberated from all abstract notions and from every glittering moral and political "generality." "By finding a mode in which they have to descend to particulars," he tells us, "one can make the people open their eyes."[129]

Of course, in defending populism, Machiavelli is inclined to speak not just of "virtue" and "corruption," but of "the common good" – and to do so in a manner that unsuspecting admirers of the ancients tend to find morally appealing. For example, when considering the "unshackled," he observes that "the cruelty of the multitude" is deployed only "against those who, they fear, will lay hold of the common good" while that of the prince is deployed "against those who, he fears, will lay hold of his own good."[130] The contrast might be taken as an indication that peoples and princes somehow differ in character, but, as we have seen, this is not Machiavelli's view: he never budges from his position that a legislator must presume all men wicked. In any case, his common good is not really held in common: to be enjoyed, it must be allocated to individuals, if only for a time, or it must be divided and distributed; it cannot truly be shared. In Machiavelli's republic, the individual citizen is no more interested in a good not privately his own than is the prince: it simply happens to be the case that the material interests of the common people in the aggregate coincide more or less with the material interests of the community as a whole; and if a minority loses out, this is a matter of no concern. Machiavelli traces the popular "affection

---

[128] Note Livy 6.7, 14, 24.25, and consider Machiavelli, *Discorsi* 1.58, in light of 1.2.3, 44, 54, and 57, in *Opere*, 79–80, 126–27, 136, 139–42, with an eye to *Discorsi* Ep. Ded., 1.5.2, 16.3–5, in *Opere*, 75, 83–84, 100–101.

[129] Machiavelli, *Discorsi* 1.47, 53.1, 54, 58.3, in *Opere*, 129–30, 134, 136, 141–42.

[130] Machiavelli, *Discorsi* 1.58.4, in *Opere*, 142.

for living in liberty (*vivere libero*)" not to any high-minded notion of honor, glory, nobility, or virtue nor to any appreciation on the part of the people of the intrinsic dignity of political liberty itself, but to their recognition of the simple fact that "cities have not grown either in dominion or riches when not in a condition of liberty." It is in this context that he observes that "the end of the republic is to enervate and weaken for the purpose of its own body's growth all other bodies." Machiavelli is the martial ancestor of the modern entrepreneur: he has conquest and tribute, profit and acquisitions, and nothing nobler in mind when he writes, "It is not the particular good but the common good which makes cities great, and without a doubt this common good is not observed if not in republics."[131]

What this means is that Machiavelli's populism is thoroughly modern. It rests not on any conviction that man is by nature a political animal endowed with moral and political rationality, nor on any judgment as to the human capacity to transcend private interest in pursuit of a transcendent common good, nor on any belief that the human potential for *ratio et oratio* points toward justice, equity, and even the good. There is for this reason nothing in Machiavelli's own account of the origins of civil society comparable to the references in Isocrates, Aristotle, and Cicero to nature's provision to man of a capacity for reason and speech.[132] Machiavelli's populism rests, then, solely on his common-sense recognition that while ordinary human beings may not be as skilled as some among them in searching out the consequences of various courses of action, they are perfectly capable, when presented with the arguments by two orators of equal ability, of judging what they have to say – at least when induced to descend to the particulars of their own lives and made to weigh these arguments as they pertain to their own material interests. No one, Machiavelli implies, is as good a judge in calculating his own self-interest thus narrowly understood as is the individual concerned.

---

[131] See Machiavelli, *Discorsi* 2.2, in *Opere*, 148–51, who restates a theme sounded by Sallust (*Cat.* 7) while dropping all reference to friendship (*Cat.* 6.1–5), to the absence of discord, and to justice (*Cat.* 8–9): cf. Osmond, "Sallust and Machiavelli," 413–14, with Markus Fischer, "Machiavelli's Rapacious Republicanism," xxix–lx (esp. xxix–xxxvi). The qualification added at the very end of the last of Machiavelli's sentences quoted deserves particular attention.

[132] Consider *Discorsi* 1.1–2 (esp. 2.3), in *Opere*, 77–81, in light of Mansfield, *Machiavelli's New Modes and Orders*, 28–41, and see Mansfield, "Necessity in the Beginning of Cities," 101–26.

2

The Ravages of an Ambitious Idleness

There is more to Machiavelli's argument than a mere description of what he termed "the effectual truth of the matter."[1] Behind the description lies an elaborate program. In the well-polished preface to the first book of his *Discourses on Livy*,[2] as we have seen,[3] the Florentine presents himself as an intrepid explorer of a political continent hitherto unknown, contending that it is "no less perilous to discover new modes and orders (*modi ed ordini nuovi*) than to search unknown waters and lands," and claiming that the "new modes and orders" which he has discovered constitute "a path as yet untrodden by anyone."[4] It is this path that he is inviting his readers to follow.

The phrase that Machiavelli deploys, *modi ed ordini nuovi*, is pregnant with meaning. When he speaks of orders, Machiavelli means magistracies and other institutions; in mentioning modes, he refers to the practices governing the operation of these magistracies and institutions.[5] But there is far more to the significance of the Florentine's choice of words than this, for he has borrowed the pertinent expression from Thomas Aquinas, who used *modus ed ordo* in his commentary on Aristotle's *Politics* where that work's author had alluded to "the distribution and disposition of offices and honors (*táxis tōn archōn*)" that constituted a polity's ruling order (*políteuma*) and thereby defined its political regime (*politeía*).[6] Moreover, in *The Prince*, Machiavelli had already associated the introduction of "new orders and modes (*nuovi ordini e modi*) with the work of "new princes," such as "Moses, Cyrus, Romulus, Theseus, and the like," whom he also described as "innovators."[7] When the Florentine describes himself as having discovered "new modes and orders," he is presenting himself as a new prince of sorts and as a political innovator. His aim in publishing *The Prince* and his *Discourses on Livy* is the establishment of a species of *politeía* hitherto unknown.

[1] See Machiavelli, *Il principe* 15, in *Opere*, 280.
[2] See Carlo Pincin, "Le prefazioni e la dedicatoria dei *Discorsi* di Machiavelli," *Giornale storico della letteratura italiana* 143:441 (First Trimester, 1966): 72–83.
[3] See the Preface to Part One, this volume.
[4] See Machiavelli, *Discorsi* 1 Proemio, in *Opere*, 76.
[5] See Machiavelli, *Discorsi* 1.18.2, in *Opere*, 102–3.
[6] Consider Thomas Aquinas, in Aristotle, *Politics* 1289a2–6, liber IV, lectio 1, in light of Leo Strauss, "Walker's Machiavelli," *Review of Metaphysics* 6:3 (March 1953): 437–46 (at 440).
[7] See Machiavelli, *Il principe* 6, in *Opere*, 264–65, where he attributes to "Moses, Cyrus, Romulus, Theseus, and the like" the introduction of "new orders and modes."

To this achievement, in Machiavelli's estimation, there was one great obstacle. In the preface to the first book of his *Discourses*, he alludes to "the weakness into which the present religion has conducted the world" and to "the evil done many Christian provinces and cities" by the "ambitious idleness (*ambizioso ozio*)" of the clergy. There, however, he places his greatest emphasis on the absence of "a true knowledge of histories," contending that his contemporaries do not get "from reading them that sense nor from savoring them that taste that they have in themselves." This happens, we are told, because Machiavelli's contemporaries take pleasure in "hearing of the variety of incidents they contain without otherwise thinking of imitating them, judging imitation not only difficult but impossible – as if heaven, the sun, the elements, men have varied in motion, in order, and in power from what they were in antiquity." Machiavelli's task in the *Discorsi* is "to draw men from this error." What this means, however, only becomes evident later when Machiavelli traces "the weakness of present-day men" to "their weak education and their slight information concerning things" and then hints that what causes them to "judge ancient judgments in part inhuman, in part impossible" are "certain ... opinions" peculiar to the post-pagan age. These "modern opinions" may not have to do with a variation in the motion, order, and power of heaven, the sun, and the elements, but they do pertain to just such a transformation – one putatively worked by divine grace in the situation of men. For his part, Machiavelli insists that "men ... have and have had always the same passions" and that, if "their works are more virtuous in this province at present than in that, and in that more than in this," it is "in accord with the form of education from which those people have derived their mode of living."[8]

Like Aristotle, Machiavelli appears to have had a double-edged understanding of regime. To effect a profound transformation in the "distribution and disposition of offices and honors," to introduce "new modes and orders," to replace one *politeía* with another, one would have to do more than rearrange institutions. One would also have to overthrow the existing *políteuma* and replace, or at least eliminate, the *paideía* that sustains the old ruling order.

Machiavelli's thinking about this question was shaped to a considerable degree by a figure no less significant for him than was Lucretius.[9] Tommaso Campanella once described "the Averroist Aristotle" as "the workshop (*officina*) of Machiavellianism," and he intimated that Averroës, his

---

[8] Cf. Machiavelli, *Discorsi* 1 Proemio with 2 Proemio 2–3, 3.27.2, 43, in *Opere*, 76, 144–46, 233–34, 250, and see Marie-Dominique Couzinet, "Sources antiques de l'irréligion moderne chez Machiavel: Crise religieuse et imitation des Anciens," in *Sources antiques de l'irréligion moderne: Le Relais italien, XVIe–XVIIe siècles*, ed. Jean-Pierre Cavaillé and Didier Foucault (Toulouse: Presses Universitaires du Mirail, 2001), 47–67.

[9] Note Leo Strauss, "What Is Political Philosophy?" in Strauss, *What Is Political Philosophy? and Other Studies* (Glencoe, IL: Free Press, 1959), 9–55 (at 47), who, at one point in the mid-1950s, suggested with regard to Machiavelli that the "theoretical basis of his teaching was a kind of decayed Aristotelianism." In using this phrase, I presume, Strauss had in mind the *Defensor pacis* of Marsilius of Padua, which embraces Aristotle but nonetheless abandons virtuous republicanism for a republicanism oriented toward self-preservation alone: see the secondary works cited in note 78, in this chapter.

predecessors, and, by implication, their Latin successors were privately dismissive of all religious belief.[10] On both questions, the wayward Dominican had grounds for his convictions.[11] Certainly, no one since has possessed a better instinctive grasp of the intellectual atmosphere of Renaissance Italy with all of its various undercurrents, and Campanella's book *Atheism Conquered* – composed in the vernacular in a Neapolitan prison and finished in 1607;[12] translated into Latin some years later, expanded, and put briefly into print in Rome in 1631; and finally published in Paris in 1636 for all who could read Latin to peruse[13] – was almost universally regarded at the time, among Catholics, Protestants, and clandestine atheists alike, as a thinly disguised, more fully elaborated restatement of Machiavelli's attack on religion, designed to tease out and make explicit what the Florentine had left implicit.[14]

[10] See Tommaso Campanella, *Apologia pro Galileo*, ed. Tobias Adami (Frankfurt: Godfried Tambach, 1622), 23, 33. On Campanella's *Auseinandersetzung* with Aristotle and Machiavelli, see John M. Headley, *Tommaso Campanella and the Transformation of the World* (Princeton, NJ: Princeton University Press, 1997), 145–96. Note, in this connection, Giuliano Procacci, "Machiavelli Aristotelico," in Procacci, *Studi sulla fortuna del Machiavelli* (Rome: Instituto Storico Italiano, 1965), 45–75 (esp. 70–75); Salvatore Femiano, "L'Antiaristotelismo essenziale di Tommaso Campanella," *Sapienza* 22:1–2 (June 1969): 137–59; Giovanni di Napoli, "Niccolò Machiavelli e l'Aristotelismo del Rinascimento," in Napoli, *Studi sul Rinascimento* (Naples: Giannini, 1973), 161–244; and Germana Ernst, *Religione, ragione et natura: Ricerche su Tommaso Campanella e il tardo Rinascimento* (Milan: Franco Angeli, 1991), 73–104.

[11] For a systematic attempt to prove the first of these two propositions true, see Giovanni di Napoli, "Niccolò Machiavelli e l'Aristotelismo del Rinascimento," *Giornale di metafisica* 25 (1970): 215–64.

[12] The original manuscript was recently rediscovered and has been published in a critical edition with an anastatic reproduction of the original: see Tommaso Campanella, *L'Ateismo trionfato, overo Riconoscimento filosofico della religione universale contra l'antichristianesmo Machiavellesco*, ed. Germana Ernst (Pisa: Scuola Normale Superiore, 2004). For a discussion of what can be ascertained concerning its composition, transmission, and translation, see Germana Ernst, "Introduzione," in ibid., vii–lv (esp. vii–xxv).

[13] Consider Tommaso Campanella, *Atheismus Triumphatus, seu Reductio ad religionem per scientiarum veritates . . . contra antichristianismum Achitophellisticum sexti tomi pars prima* (Rome: Bartholomew Zannetti, 1631), and *Atheismus Triumphatus, seu Reductio ad religionem per scientiarum veritates . . . contra antichristianismum Achitophellisticum* (Paris: Toussaint du Bray, 1636), to which in each case the appendix, consisting in chapters eighteen and nineteen, is an addition not present in the Italian manuscript, in light of Ernst, "Introduzione," xxxvii–lv.

[14] See Andrzej Nowicki, "Gli incontri tra Vanini e Campanella," in *Tommaso Campanella (1568–1639): Miscellanea di studi nel 4° centenario della sua nascita* (Naples: Fausto Fiorentino, 1969), 473–85; note Tullio Gregory, *Theophrastus redivivus: Erudizione e ateismo nel Seicento* (Naples: Morano, 1979), 102–4, 155–56, 166–67, 201, 210–11 (with the attendant notes); and ponder the implications of *Theophrastus redivivus*, ed. Guido Canziani and Gianni Paganini (Florence: La Nuova Italia, 1981), I 153, 212–13. II 352, 355–58, 379, 394, 439, 451, 486, 490–91, 517–18, 525–26 (with the attendant notes, esp. 355–57, n. 15). Then see Giorgio Spini, *Ricerca dei libertini: La teoria dell'impostura delle religioni nel Seicento Italia*, second edition (Florence: La Nuova Italia, 1983), 83–124; Gianni Paganini, "La critica della 'civiltà' nel *Theophrastus redivivus* I: Natura e cultura," in *Ricerche su letteratura libertina e letteratura clandestina nel Seicento*, ed. Tullio Gregory et al. (Florence: La Nuova Italia, 1981), 49–82 (esp. 56, 75–80); Germana Ernst, "Campanella 'Libertino?'" in ibid., 231–41, "La Ruse et la nature: Remarques sur le rapport Campanella/Machiavel en marge de la *Monarchie d'Espagne*," *Revue des sciences, philosophiques et theologiques* 72:2 (April 1988): 252–62, and "Introduzione," vii–viii, xxv–xxxvii; and, most interesting of all, Headley, *Tommaso Campanella and the Transformation of*

The Theologico-Political Doctrine of Averroës

In the Latin West, the proximate source for the controversial doctrine singled out by Campanella was Abū al-Walīd Muhammad ibn Rushd of Cordoba in Spain.[15] Although this doctrine bears his name, the man known
throughout Western Christendom as Averroës was no more its progenitor than
was Lucretius, the author of Epicureanism. As Campanella appears to have
known,[16] Averroës was an intermediary. The man who first fashioned the Averroist argument was a tenth-century philosopher named Abū Nasr Muhammad ibn al-Tarkhān al-Fārābī, who taught and wrote in Baghdad, and who
came to be regarded in Arab philosophical circles as a thinker inferior in wisdom to Aristotle alone. It is only in the last few decades – as scholars such
as Muhsin Mahdi have unearthed manuscripts once thought lost and have
edited, published, translated, and commented on them – that we have begun
to have something approaching a full appreciation for the accomplishments of
the philosopher whom the Arabs called "the second teacher."

Although Alfarabi relied on Aristotle for guidance in philosophy more generally, he nonetheless fashioned his political doctrine on the basis of a careful
consideration of the political teaching laid out by Plato in his *Republic* and
Laws. He and his disciples took as their starting point the fact that, in the former work, Socrates had denied that "the multitude" can ever become "devoted
to wisdom" and had insisted that "the many" are by their very nature hostile to

<hr />

the World, 132–33, 180–96, whose argument against the propriety of the judgment handed down
by Campanella's early readers, in fact, provides grounds for accepting that very judgment – once
one takes seriously the possibility that Machiavelli is acutely sensitive to the power exercised by
unarmed prophets and that he has a sneaking admiration for the ecclesiastical principality and a
desire to appropriate its techniques. After reading Headley's brilliant analysis of Campanella, one
should compare what Machiavelli emphatically denies in *Il principe* 6, in *Opere*, 264–65, with
what he cryptically asserts in *Il principe* 11, in *Opere*, 273–74, and then ponder the Florentine's
suggestion as to how Christianity might be reconfigured in *Discorsi* 2.2.2, in *Opere*, 149–50,
before considering the possibility explored in Vickie B. Sullivan, *Machiavelli's Three Romes:
Religion, Human Liberty, and Politics Reformed* (DeKalb: Northern Illinois University Press,
1996), passim (esp. 119–90). In this connection, see Vittorio Frajese, "*Atheismus Triumphatus*
come romanzo filosofico di formazione," *Bruniana & Campanelliana* 4:2 (1998): 313–42, and
Profezia e machiavellismo: Il giovane Campanella (Rome: Carocci, 2002).

[15] For an overview, see Ernest Renan, *Averroès et l'averroisme: Essai historique*, third edition
(Paris: Michel Lévy Frères, 1866), who pioneered the study of this subject; Léon Gauthier, *Ibn
Rochd (Averroès)* (Paris: Presses Universitaires de France, 1948); and Miguel Cruz Hernan-
dez, *Abū-L-Walīd Ibn Rušd: Vida, Obra, Pensamiento, Influencia* (Córdoba: Publicaciones del
Monte de Piedad y Caja de Ahorros de Cordoba, 1986), along with Joseph Puig, "Materials on
Averroes's Circle," *Journal of Near Eastern Studies* 51:4 (October 1992): 241–60. See also Mario
Grignaschi, "Indagine sui passi del *Commento* suscettibili di avere promosso la formazione di
un Averroismo politico," in *L'Averroismo in Italia* (Rome: Accademia Nazionale dei Lincei,
1979), 237–78, who is more reliable in surveying the pertinent texts available in the Latin West
in the thirteenth and fourteenth centuries, in discussing the accuracy of the translations, and
in charting the use to which Averroës' arguments were put than in discerning the lineaments
of his theologico-political doctrine and assessing the relationship between Marsilius of Padua's
Averroism and the political teaching he articulated in *Defensor pacis*. On this last question, see
the material collected in note 78, this chapter.

[16] See Campanella, *Apologia pro Galileo*, 23, who mentions, among others, Alfarabi and Avicenna.

the philosophical enterprise.[17] They recognized that, if true, these assumptions have profound implications for the comportment of philosophers within the political community.[18] And they were no less impressed by what Plato in his

---

[17] Note Pl. *Resp.* 6.487a–501a (esp. 494a), 7.520a–b, 9.581c–592b, *Phd.* 64b, *Grg.* 485d–486d, 521d–522c, *Ep.* 7.324c–345a (esp. 328e, 331c–d, 332d–e, 338b–345a), *Ti.* 51e, *Phlb.* 52b; consider Xen. *Ap.* 2–9 and *Mem.* 4.8.4–10 in light of *Cyr.* 3.1.13–40; and see Arist. *Eth. Nic.* 1179b4–19; Cic. *Tusc.* 2.1.1–4 ; Strabo 1.2.8; Sen. *Ep.* 5.2; *Alfarabi's Philosophy of Plato and Aristotle*, second edition, ed. and tr. Muhsin Mahdi (Ithaca, NY: Cornell University Press 1969) 1.2.34–36, 3.40, 4.50–62, 2.3.7, 5.14–6.25, 7.29, 10.38, 3.1.2, 12–13, 15–16; *Averroes on Plato's Republic*, ed. and tr. Ralph Lerner (Ithaca, NY: Cornell University Press, 1974) 23.6–9, 24.6–9, 25.13–32, 48.19–29, 61.20–72.33 (esp. 62.7–64.2), 74.14–29, 78.26–79.9, 103.25–104.10; Pietro Pomponazzi, *Tractatus de immortalitate animae* (Haverford, PA: Haverford College, 1938), xxiv–xxxiii (esp. xxiv–xxvii, xxix, xxxii–xxxiii), which can be read in translation in *The Renaissance Philosophy of Man*, ed. Ernst Cassirer, Paul Oskar Kristeller, and John Hermann Randall, Jr. (Chicago: University of Chicago Press, 1948), 350–77 (esp. 350–57, 363–65, 373–75). One should interpret Maimonides, *Guide of the Perplexed*, tr. Shlomo Pines (Chicago: University of Chicago Press, 1963) II 36 (371–72) in light of 40 (381–82) and I Introduction, 14, 31, 33–34, III 8, 27 (510), 51, 54. Note the prudent fashion in which Marsilius of Padua, *Defensor pacis* 1.13.1–8, skirts the issue playfully raised by the dramatic confrontation at Pl. *Resp.* 1.327a–328b.

[18] In this light, one should consider Pl. *Phd.* 62b, 89c–90d, *Phlb.* 15d–17a, *Phdr.* 274b–278c, *Tht.* 155e–156a, 180c–d, *Ep.* 2.312d, 313c, 314a–c; Arist. *Eth. Nic.* 1124b26–30; Cic. *Tusc.* 5.4.10–11, *De or.* 2.67.270; Strabo 1.2.8; Sen. *Ep.* 5.1–3, 14.14; Diog. Laert. 4.2; Clem. Al. *Strom.* 5.9.56–59; Origen *c. Cels.* 4.39; August. *De civ. D.* 8.4 (with *De vera religione* 1.1–2.2, 5.8), *De doctrina christiana* 4.9.23, *De ordine* 2.10.28–29 (Migne, *PL* 32.1008–9), *Ep.* 1.1, 118.17–33; Paul Kraus, "Raziana I. La conduite du philosophe: Traité d'éthique d'Abū Muhammad b. Zakariyyā Al-Rāzī," *Orientalia* 4:3/4 (1935): 300–334 (at 322–34) – translated into English by Charles E. Butterworth, "Al-Rāzī: The Book of the Philosophic Life," *Interpretation* 20:3 (Spring 1993): 227–36; *Alfarabi's Philosophy of Plato and Aristotle* 1.4.60–61, 2.10.36–38; Alfarabi, *Plato's Laws* Introduction 1–3, in *Medieval Political Philosophy*, ed. Ralph Lerner and Muhsin Mahdi (Glencoe, IL: Free Press, 1963), 83–85; Alfarabi, *Paraphrase of Aristotle's Topics* (MS, Bratislava, no. 231, TE 40, fol. 203), in *Al-Mantiqiyyat li-al-Farabi*, ed. M. T. Danesh-Pajuh (Qum: Maktabat Ayay Allah al-Uzma al-Marashi al-Najafi, 1987), I 382.1–6, and translated by Muhsin Mahdi, "Man and His Universe in Medieval Arabic Philosophy," in *L'Homme et son univers au moyen âge*, ed. Christian Wenin (Louvain-la-neuve: Editions de l'Institut supérieur de philosophie, 1986), I 102–13 (at 112–13); *Averroes on Plato's Republic* 77.12–29; Maimonides, *Guide of the Perplexed* I Introduction, 17, 31–35, 59, 68–69, II 29 (346–48), III Introduction. Note Cic. *Acad.* F21 (Müller) with August. *Conf.* 5.10.19 and *Acad.* 2.13.29, 3.7.14, 17.37–20.43, and see Cic. *Nat. D.* 1.5.10–6.14, 7.17, 21.57, 22.60, 2.1.2–3. Cf. Pl. *Phd.* 69c–d and *Symp.* 209e–212c, 215a–222b with Ar. *Nub.* 140–44, 250–509 (esp. 250–60, 497–99); then, see *II Vita Aristotelis Arabica* (Al-Mubashir) 37 with Cic. *Fin.* 5.4.10–5.14, Aul. Gell. *NA* 20.5, Plut. *Alex.* 7, Gal. *De substantia facultatum naturalium fragmentum* IV.757–58 (Kühn), Themistius *Or.* 26.385 (Dindorf), and the other material collected in Ingemar Düring, *Aristotle in the Ancient Biographical Tradition* (Göteborg: Elanders, 1957), 426–43. To think these passages revealing, one need not suppose that the ancient political philosophers and their successors privately espoused "secret doctrines" that they never even intimated in their published works. Cf. Pl. *Phdr.* 275e–278c and *Ep.* 7.340b–341e with *Leg.* 12.968d–e, and see *Resp.* 7.518b–519b with Maimonides, *Guide of the Perplexed* I Introduction (17–20), 17, 33–34, III Introduction; then, see George Boas, "Ancient Testimony to Secret Doctrines," *Philosophical Review* 62:1 (January 1953): 79–92; note Thomas More's allusion to the philosophy of the schools and his contention that there is "another, more politic philosophy (*alia philosophia civilior*)," which seeks to achieve its goals within the public sphere by an "indirect" or even "devious approach (*obliquo ductu*)": *The Complete Works of Thomas More* IV: *Utopia*, ed. Edward Surtz, S. J., and J. H. Hexter (New Haven, CT: Yale University Press, 1965), 86–102 (esp. 98–100); and consider Clem. Al. *Strom.* 1.1.7, 9–10 (with 6.7.61, 15.131), 11, 14–16, 18, 2.20, 12.53 (with 6.1.2, 7.18.110–11),

Republic and *Laws* and Aristotle in his *Metaphysics* had intimated with regard to the manner in which religious myths and other noble and medicinal lies can be deployed to help educate the common folk in civic virtues they could not otherwise attain.[19]

55, 4.2.4–5, 7.8.50, 9.53, in light of Ernest L. Fortin, "Clement of Alexandria and the Esoteric Tradition," in *Studia patristica* IX:3, ed. F. L. Cross (Berlin: Akademie Verlag, 1966), 41–56.

[19] After attending to Pl. *Ap.* 36b–38b (esp. 38a), consider *Alfarabi's Book of Letters (Kitāb al-Hurūf)*, ed. Muhsin Mahdi (Beirut: Dār al-Mashriq, 1970) §§ 108–57, in *Medieval Islamic Philosophical Writings*, ed. and tr. Muhammad Ali Khalidi (Cambridge, UK: Cambridge University Press, 2005), 1–27; Alfarabi, *Book of Religion*, in Alfarabi, *The Political Writings: Selected Aphorisms and Other Texts*, tr. Charles E. Butterworth (Ithaca, NY: Cornell University Press, 2001), 93–113; *Alfarabi's Philosophy of Plato and Aristotle* 1.2.34–36, 3.40, 4.50–2.1.3, 6.19–22, 25, 7.29–30, 3.1.1–3, 9, 12–13, 2.15–16, 13.90–19.99; and Alfarabi, *Plato's Laws*, tr. Muhsin Mahdi, in *Medieval Political Philosophy*, 83–94, in light of Muhsin S. Mahdi, *Alfarabi and the Foundation of Islamic Philosophy* (Chicago: University of Chicago Press, 2001). See also Miriam Galston, *Politics and Excellence: The Political Philosophy of Alfarabi* (Princeton, NJ: Princeton University Press, 1990), and Joshua Parens, *Metaphysics as Politics: Alfarabi's Summary of Plato's Laws* (Albany: State University of New York Press, 1995), and *An Islamic Philosophy of Virtuous Religions: Introducing Alfarabi* (Albany: State University of New York Press, 2006), along with Charles E. Butterworth, "Medieval Islamic Philosophy and the Virtue of Ethics," *Arabica* 34:2 (1987): 221–50, and "Socrates' Islamic Conversion," *Arab Studies Journal* 4:1 (Spring 1996): 4–11. Then, after considering the material collected in note 21, this chapter, ponder the decidedly inegalitarian implications of Pl. *Ap.* 24d–25b and 29c–32a in conjunction with *Tht.* 173c–176a; consider *Resp.* 5.473c–9.592b in light of 2.357a–368a, note 10.617d–621b, and see Arist. *Metaph.* 1074b1–7. See also Arist. F55, 61 (Rose), *Eth. Nic.* 1172a19–1178b31; Cic. *Fin.* 5.4.11; Cic. *Hortensius* ap. August. *De trin.* 14.9.12; *Averroes on Plato's Republic* 25.13–32, 29.9–33.5, 39.27–42.1, 60.26–61.1, 65.29–67.8, 77.12–29; and Maimonides, *Guide of the Perplexed* I Introduction, 1–2, 14, 31, 33–34, 50, II 36, 38, 40, III 8, 17–18, 27, 51, 54. Note as well Marsilius of Padua, *Defensor pacis* 1.1.6, 4.1, 16.23, in light of 2.30.4 (at the end). The same concerns account for the difference between what the *falāsifa* say in their public works concerning the afterlife and the doctrine they teach elsewhere: cf. Alfarabi, *The Principles of the Opinions of the People of the Virtuous City* 5.16.2–11 (esp. 8), in *Al-Farabi on the Perfect State: Abū Naṣr al-Fārābī's Mabādi' Ārā' Ahl Al-Madīna Al-Fāḍila*, ed. and tr. Richard Walzer (Oxford, UK: Clarendon Press, 1985), 260–77 (esp. 272–75), which should be read in light of Muhsin S. Mahdi, "Al-Fārābī's Imperfect State," *Journal of the American Oriental Society* 110:4 (October–December 1990): 691–726, and Charles Butterworth, "Alfarabi's Introductory Sections to the *Virtuous City*," forthcoming in *Adaptations and Innovations: Studies on the Interaction between Jewish and Islamic Thought and Literature from the Early Middle Ages to the Late Twentieth Century, Dedicated to Professor Joel L. Kraemer*, ed. Y. T. Langermann and Josef Stern (Leuven: Peeters, 2008), with Alfarabi, *The Political Regime* 51–53, in *Medieval Political Philosophy*, 37–39, and consider *The Harmonization of the Two Opinions of the Two Sages: Plato the Divine and Aristotle*, in Alfarabi, *The Political Writings*, 125–67, in light of Miriam Galston, "A Re-examination of Al-Fārābī's Neoplatonism," *Journal of the History of Philosophy* 15:1 (January 1977): 13–32, and in light of her response in Galston, *Politics and Excellence*, 9 n. 27, to Thérèse Druart, "Al-Farabi and Emanationism," in *Studies in Medieval Philosophy*, ed. John F. Wippel (Washington, DC: Catholic University of America Press, 1987), 23–43, before ruminating on the various reports regarding the claims Alfarabi advanced in his commentary on Aristotle's *Nicomachean Ethics*: see Ibn Tufayl, *Hayy the Son of Yaqzan* 13–14, in *Medieval Political Philosophy*, 140; Moritz Steinschneider, *Al-Farabi (Alpharabius) des arabischen Philosophen Leben und Schriften* (St. Petersburg: Buchdruckerie der kaiserlichen Akademie der Wissenschaften, 1869), 94, 102, 106; and Ibn Bajja MS Bodleian Library, Pococke 206, fol. 126b, in Shlomo Pines, "The Limitations of Human Knowledge According to al-Farabi, ibn Bajja, and Maimonides," in *Studies in Medieval Jewish History and Literature*, ed. Isadore Twersky (Cambridge, MA: Harvard University Press, 1979–2000), I 82–109 (at 82–84), which is

If, for the most part, in articulating his analysis of political affairs, Alfarabi chose to follow Plato rather than Aristotle, it appears not to have been, as was once supposed, because he had no access at all to the argument advanced in the latter's *Politics*.[20] He seems, instead, to have made the particular choice he made because he recognized that the cultural hegemony accorded revealed religion in his own day had radically transformed the political arena. Just as the pagan *ekklēsía* had in many lands given way to the Christian *ecclesia*, so it had been supplanted among Muslims by the mosque – and this had had profound consequences, as Alfarabi knew. Although the Greek *pólis* had disappeared and the Roman *civitas* was no more, that which the Greeks had called "the middle ground (*tò méson*)" and that which the Romans had spoken of as the *res publica* lived on in a new form, for *lógos* was now deployed by way of jurisprudence within Judaism and Islam and by way of apologetic, dialectical theology (*kalām*) among Christians, Jews, and Muslims alike, and public attempts were made at regular intervals in sermons delivered in the churches, synagogues, and mosques to reconcile *oratio* with a species of *ratio*. To political philosophers operating within Christendom and the House of Islam – to men intent on making sense of a political world radically reconfigured by a belief in prophecy and divine revelation, by monotheism and theology, by systematic religious indoctrination, proselytizing, and an aspiration to universal monarchy conceived of as theocracy – Plato's *Republic*, with its vision of direct rule by a man wise, virtuous, and skilled in the selective propagation of salutary lies concerning this world and the next, had much more to offer than Aristotle's *Politics*, with its near-total silence concerning religion, its presumption as to the self-sufficiency of political life, and its anachronistic focus on citizenship in the abstract and on its articulation within particular political regimes which promote the application of *lógos* to political *práxis* by way of public deliberation. Moreover, to

reprinted in *Maimonides: A Collection of Critical Essays*, ed. Joseph A. Buijs (Notre Dame, IN: Notre Dame University Press, 1988), 91–121 (at 91–93), and in *The Collected Works of Shlomo Pines* (Jerusalem: Magnes Press, 1979–1997), V: *Studies in the History of Jewish Thought*, ed. Warren Zev Harvey and Moshe Idel, 404–31 (at 404–6). If, in assessing this evidence, one resolutely ignores the distinction between the public, exoteric and the private, esoteric works of the *falāsifa*, one will indeed become confused: see, for example, Dimitri Gutas, "The Study of Arabic Philosophy in the Twentieth Century: An Essay in the Historiography of Arabic Philosophy," *British Journal of Middle Eastern Studies* 29:1 (May 2002): 5–25 (at 19–25), and David C. Reisman, "Al-Fārābī and the Philosophical Curriculum," in *The Cambridge Companion to Arabic Philosophy*, ed. Peter Adamson and Richard Taylor (Cambridge, UK: Cambridge University Press, 2005), 52–71. For a useful overview, see Patricia Crone, *God's Rule – Government and Islam: Six Centuries of Medieval Political Thought* (New York: Columbia University Press, 2004), passim (esp. 165–96).

[20] See Shlomo Pines, "Aristotle's *Politics* in Arab Philosophy," *Israel Oriental Studies* 5 (1975): 150–60, which is reprinted in *The Collected Works of Shlomo Pines* II: *Studies in Arabic Versions of Greek Texts and in Mediaeval Science*, 146–56, and in ibid., III: *Studies in the History of Arabic Philosophy*, ed. Sarah Stroumsa, 251–61. Cf., however, Rémi Brague, "Notes sur la traduction arabe de la *Politique*, derechef, qu'elle n'existe pas," in *Aristote politique: Études sur la Politique de Aristote*, ed. Pierre Aubenque (Paris: Presses Universitaires de France, 1993), 423–33. In part, no doubt, because of the lack of interest displayed by Alfarabi, Averroës and others in Andalusia and the Maghreb later had no access to *The Politics* in any form: see *Averroes on Plato's Republic* 22.3–5.

those operating within Islam, with its all-comprehending religious law, Plato's
Laws, with its depiction of rule by a rational law thought to have been revealed
to a lawgiver by a god, was thought to be of inestimable value as well.[21] When
Avicenna described this work as a book about prophecy and holy law,[22] he
spoke for all of the *falāsifa*.

Alfarabi was no less keenly aware that he lived in a new historical epoch
than were those Christians who appropriated the late Latin term *moderni* to
distinguish themselves from the country folk or *pagani*, who adhered to the
superstitions regnant in the pre-Christian age among those whom they dubbed

---

[21] The first to suggest such an analysis was Leo Strauss: see Strauss, *Philosophie und Gesetz:
Beiträge zum Verständnis Maimunis und seine Vorläufer* (Berlin: Schocken, 1935), 68–122, which
is available in English translation as *Philosophy and Law: Contributions to the Understanding
of Maimonides and his Predecessors*, tr. Eve Adler (Albany: State University of New York Press,
1995), 81–133; "Quelques remarques sur la science politique de Maïmonide et de Fârâbî," *Revue
des études juives* 100 *bis*:199–200 (January–June 1936): 1–37 (esp. 2–6), which is available in
English translation as "Some Remarks on the Political Science of Maimonides and Farabi,"
tr. Robert Bartlett, *Interpretation* 18 (1990): 3–30 (esp. 4–7); "On Abravanel's Philosophical
Tendency and Political Teaching," in *Isaac Abravanel: Six Lectures*, ed. John Brande Trend and
Herbert Martin James Loewe (Cambridge, UK: Cambridge University Press, 1937), 95–129 (at
95–99); "Farabi's Plato," in *Louis Ginzberg Jubilee Volume* (New York: American Academy
for Jewish Research, 1945), I 357–93, much of which can be found in Strauss, "Introduction,"
Persecution and the Art of Writing (Glencoe, IL: Free Press, 1952), 7–21; and "How Fārābī
Read Plato's *Laws*," in *Mélanges Louis Massignon* (Damascus: Institut francais de Damas, 1956–
1957), III 319–44, which is reprinted in *What Is Political Philosophy?*, 134–54. This hypothesis
was subsequently taken up by Shlomo Pines, "La Loi naturelle et la société: La Doctrine politico-
théologique d'Ibn Zur'a, philosophe chrétien de Bagdad," *Scripta Hierosolymitana* 9 (1961):
154–90 (at 188 n. 82), which is reprinted in *The Collected Works of Shlomo Pines*, III 156–92
(at 190 n. 82), and by Georges Vajda, "La Pensée religieuse de Maïmonide: Unité ou dualité,"
Cahiers de civilisation médiévale 9:1 (January–March 1966): 29–49 (at 40). The evidence available to Strauss was slender but highly suggestive; thanks largely to the efforts of Muhsin S.
Mahdi, much more is now known, and the case is now compelling: consider *Alfarabi's Book of
Letters (Kitāb al-Hurūf)* §§ 108–57, in *Medieval Islamic Philosophical Writings*, 1–27, in which
"the second teacher" articulates something very much like a philosophy of history, in light of
what Muhsin S. Mahdi, "Language and Logic in Classical Islam," in *Logic in Classical Islamic
Culture*, ed. G. E. Grunebaum (Wisbaden: Otto Harrassowitz, 1970), 51–83, reveals about the
context within which Alfarabi was writing, and see Muhsin S. Mahdi, "Alfarabi on Philosophy
and Religion," *Philosophical Forum* 4:1 (Fall 1972): 5–25, and Rémi Brague, "*Eorum praeclara
ingenia*: Conscience de la nouveauté et prétension à la continuité chez Fārābī et Maïmonide,"
Bulletin d'études orientales 48 (1996): 89–102 (esp. 89–95); then consider Alfarabi, *Book of
Religion*, in Alfarabi, *The Political Writings*, 93–113, in light of Muhsin S. Mahdi, "Remarks
on Alfarabi's *Book of Religion*," in *Perspectives arabes et médiévales sur la tradition scientifique
et philosophie grecque*, ed. Ahmad Hasnawi, Abdelali Elamrani-Jamal, and Maroun Aouad
(Leuven–Paris: Peeters, 1997), 583–608, and see Jeffrey Macy, "The Rule of Law and the Rule
of Wisdom in Plato, al-Farabi, and Maimonides," in *Studies in Islamic and Judaic Traditions*,
ed. William M. Brinner and Stephen D. Ricks (Atlanta, GA: Scholars Press, 1986), I 205–32
(esp. 205–11), and "Prophecy in al-Farabi and Maimonides: The Imaginative and Rational Faculties," in *Maimonides and Philosophy: Papers Presented at the Sixth Jerusalem Philosophical
Encounter, May 1985*, ed. Shlomo Pines and Yirmiyahu Yovel (Dordrecht: Martinus Nijhoff,
1986), 185–201 (esp. 185–92), along with Muhsin S. Mahdi, "Philosophy and Political Thought:
Reflections and Comparisons," *Arabic Sciences and Philosophy* 1:1 (March 1991): 9–29.

[22] See Avicenna, *On the Divisions of the Rational Sciences* 108, in *Medieval Political Philosophy*,
97.

by way of contrast the *antiqui*.[23] It was the Arab philosopher's conviction that the modern age was distinguished from antiquity by the establishment of a new *politeía*, of a sort entirely unknown in ancient Greece and Rome, encompassing all who adhered to a particular religious faith. Firmly ensconced within the *políteuma* of this novel *politeía* was, he recognized, a new class made up of jurists and of religious apologists and dialectical theologians (*mutakallimūn*) who were inclined to quarrel among themselves and to regard philosophy with profound suspicion, if not hostility.[24] It was this awareness of historical change and of the political significance of the new religious intelligentsia within both Christendom and Islam that provided the underpinnings for the philosophical posture that Alfarabi adopted and passed on to Avicenna, Averroës, and all those who called themselves in Arabic the *falāsifa*.[25]

Among the writings that Alfarabi's disciple Averroës dedicated to clarifying the relationship among religion, politics, and philosophy was *The Incoherence of the Incoherence*, an exoteric work aimed at literate Muslims but designed to instruct students of philosophy as well,[26] which consisted in sixteen disputations concerning metaphysics and four concerning physics and constituted a point-by-point reply to the fierce denunciation of Alfarabi, Avicenna, and the

---

[23] The distinction between the ancients and the moderns took other forms as well: note *Thesaurus linguae latinae* (Leipzig: D. B. Teubner, 1900–) s. v. *modernus*, and see M.-D. Chenu, "*Antiqui, Moderni*," *Revue des sciences philosophiques et théologiques* 17:1 (January 1928): 82–94; Walter Freund, *Modernus und andere Zeitbegriffe des Mittelalters* (Cologne: Böhlau Verlag, 1957); and Elisabeth Gössmann, *Antiqui und Moderni im Mittelalter: Eine geschichtliche Standortsbestimmung* (Munich: Ferdinand Schöningh, 1974). Note also Wilfried Hartman, "*Modernus* und *Antiquus*: Zur Verbreitung und Bedeutung dieser Bezeichnungen in der wissenschaftlichen Literatur vom 9. bis zur 12. Jahrhundert," and Elisabeth Gössmann, "*Antiqui* und *Moderni* im 12. Jahrhundert," in *Antiqui und Moderni: Traditionsbewusstsein und Fortschrittsbewusstsein im späten Mittelalter*, ed. Albert Zimmerman (Berlin: Walter de Gruyter, 1974), 21–57.

[24] Alfarabi and his successors regarded *kalām* as a Christian invention inadvertently inflicted on Judaism and Islam: begin with H.-D. Saffrey, "Le Chrétien Jean Philopon et la survivance de l'École d'Alexandrie au VIᵉ siècle," *Revue des études grecques* 67:316–18 (July–December 1954): 396–410; consider Shlomo Pines, "A Note on an Early Meaning of the Term *Mutakallim*," *Israel Oriental Studies* 1 (1971): 224–50, and "Some Traits of Christian Theological Writing in Relation to Moslem *Kalām* and to Jewish Thought," *Proceedings of the Israel Academy of Sciences and Humanities* 5 (1976): 105–25, which are reprinted in *The Collected Works of Shlomo Pines*, III 62–99, and Muhsin S. Mahdi, "The Arabic Text of Alfarabi's *Against John the Grammarian*," in *Medieval and Middle Eastern Studies in Honor of Aziz Suryal Atiya*, ed. Sami A. Hanna (Leiden: E. J. Brill, 1972), 268–84; and see Mahdi, "Alfarabi against Philoponus," *Journal of Near East Studies* 26:4 (October 1967): 233–60; then, after reading Steinschneider, *Al-Farabi (Alpharabius) des arabischen Philosophen Leben und Schriften*, 211–13 (with 85–89), consider Max Meyerhof, *Von Alexandrien nach Bagdad: ein Beitrag zur Geschichte des philosophischen und medizinischen Unterrichts bei den Arabern* (Berlin: Walter de Gruyter, 1930), note Moses Maimonides, *The Guide of the Perplexed*, tr. Shlomo Pines (Chicago: University of Chicago Press, 1963) I 71, and see Sarah Stroumsa, "Al-Fārābī and Maimonides on the Christian Philosophical Tradition: A Reevaluation," *Der Islam* 68:2 (1991): 263–87.

[25] In Andalusia, Alfarabi was a name to be conjured with long before Averroës came on the scene: see Abdelali Elamrani-Jamal, "Ibn al-Sïd al-Baṭalyūsī et l'enseignement d'al-Fārābī," *Bulletin d'études orientales* 48 (1996): 155–64.

[26] On its literary character, see Barry S. Kogan, *Averroes and the Metaphysics of Causation* (Albany: State University of New York Press, 1985), 17–25.

falāsifa more generally as atheists that had been set forth by the distinguished Muslim theologian Abū Hamid Muhammad ibn Muhammad al-Ghazāli.[27] In the concluding section of his book, the fourth *disputatio in physicis*, which the editors of the great Giunta edition of Averroës' commentaries on Aristotle would later identify as "the speech concerning the laws (*sermo de legibus*),"[28] Averroës contends that philosophers place a greater emphasis on the afterlife than anyone else. They do so, he explains, because they are persuaded of three things: that there is something "praiseworthy" among the "principles of action and the Traditions posited in each religion," that this praiseworthy element is constituted by that within each which "most incites the multitude to virtuous actions," and that nothing is more effectual in this regard than the doctrine of the afterlife – which is, in fact, essential for the firm establishment of "the moral virtues." Philosophy may provide direction with regard to "happiness," he explains, but this direction is available only to "a few intelligent people."

Moreover, Averroës argued, given that popular enlightenment is impossible, philosophy is insufficient for political purposes. As a supplement, it requires religious rhetoric expounding not only what the Greeks had called *nómos* but also what the Arabs called *sharī'a*. Philosophy's political inadequacy is, moreover, a serious matter, for "the select sort," constituted by "one in a thousand," cannot exist apart from "the common sort," and this gives the philosophers a genuine stake in the religion predominant, for "teaching the multitude in general" is a task that nothing but revealed religion can manage. In this regard, then, if in no other, the "common education" provided by an all-encompassing religious law is as "necessary for the existence of the select sort and for its life both in the moment of its youth and its growing up" as it is for the unenlightened multitude. It is, therefore, incumbent on the philosopher "not [to] make light of what he has grown up with," and it is crucial that he "interpret" his religious tradition "in the fairest way." If a philosopher were openly and explicitly to declare "a doubt about the Law-based principles in which he has grown up," if he were to propagate "an interpretation contradicting the prophets . . . and turning away from their path," then, above all others, he would deserve execution – unless, of course, he had intervened in favor of a genuinely superior religious law.

This last proviso is crucial – for, as Averroës goes on to explain, it is "obligatory" that the philosopher favor the religion "in his time" most conducive to virtue: "He is to believe that the most virtuous one will be abrogated by one more virtuous." This explains, he adds, why "the wise men who were teaching the people of Alexandria became Muslim when the Law of Islam reached them" and why "the wise men who were in the cities of Byzantium became Christian when the Law of Jesus . . . reached them."[29] In the end, if Averroës is

[27] For a bilingual Arabic–English edition of the work against which Averroës directed his attack, see al-Ghazāli, *The Incoherence of the Philosophers*, tr. Michael E. Marmura (Provo, UT: Brigham Young University Press, 2000), passim (esp. 1–5, 10–11).

[28] See the marginal note in Averroës, *Destructio destructionum*, in *Aristotelis Stagiritae omnia quae extant opera . . . Averrois Cordubensis in ea opera omnes qui ad nos pervenere commentarii* (Venice: Giunta, 1550–1552), IX 8ra–63vb (at 62vb–63vb).

[29] Consider Averroës, *The Incoherence of the Incoherence* 580.1–588.6, in Averroës, *The Decisive Treatise and Epistle Dedicatory*, ed. and tr. Charles E. Butterworth (Provo, UT: Brigham

correct, philosophy must be religion's judge, and, if the need arises, as it evidently did when al-Ghazāli launched his assault on the *falāsifa*, it is incumbent on the philosopher to shunt aside the jurists and the *mutakallimūn* and practice *kalām* in the latter's stead. In extreme circumstances, it is even his duty to promote a religious revolution. Indeed, if he possesses the requisite poetic gifts, it is right and proper, as Alfarabi had argued,[30] that the philosopher assume the mantle of a prophet himself and found a new theologico-political community. As a glance at the last book of the fourth and final part of Avicenna's great *Shifā'* confirms,[31] such was the public teaching of the *falāsifa* concerning the relationship between philosophy and religion.[32]

Young University Press, 2001), 43–46, which is a better translation than the one provided in Averroës, *Tahafut al-tahafut (The Incoherence of the Incoherence)*, tr. Simon van den Bergh (London: Luzac, 1954), in light of Richard Walzer, *Galen on Jews and Christians* (Oxford, UK: Oxford University Press, 1949), esp. 15–16, 56–74, 87–98, and note Synesius of Cyrene *Ep.* 105 (Hercher, *Epist. Gr.*). See also *Ep.* 96, 143. For the Latin version of Averroës' text likely to have been read after 1527, see *Averroes' Destructio Destructionum Philosophiae Algazelis in the Latin Version of Calo Calonymos*, ed. Beatrice H. Zedler (Milwaukee, WI: Marquette University Press, 1961), 452–56. There is other pertinent material at Averroës, *Tahafut al-tahafut* 194.10–195.5, 207.3–210.9, 255.15–257.2, 351.15–363.3, 396.2–397.3, 409.1–410.9, 427.9–430.8, 453.8–454.9, 463.9–464.1, 480.6–481.15, 503.6–13, 516.1–528.5. With this material in mind and that cited below, in notes 30–31, one should compare the classic statement on this subject published by Renan, *Averroès et l'averroisme*, 162–72, with the more nuanced restatement by Léon Gauthier, *La théorie d'Ibn Rochd (Averroès) sur les rapports de la religion et de la philosophie* (Paris: Ernest Leroux, 1909), which is grounded on a close reading of *The Book of the Decisive Treatise Determining the Connection between Law and Wisdom*, an exoteric work now available in a careful English translation by Charles E. Butterworth in Averroës, *The Decisive Treatise and Epistle Dedicatory*, 1–36. For recent secondary literature on this work, see Chapter Four, note 78, this volume.

[30] Consider Alfarabi, *The Principles of the Opinions of the People of the Virtuous City* 4.14.1–11 (esp. 7–9), 5.17.1–6 (esp. 2–4), in *Al-Farabi on the Perfect State*, 210–27 (esp. 218–25), 276–85 (esp. 278–83), in light of Richard Walzer's commentary thereon (ibid., 413–23, 471–81); then, see Walzer, "Al-Fārābī's Theory of Prophecy and Divination," in Walzer, *Greek into Arabic: Essays on Islamic Philosophy* (Oxford, UK: B. Cassirer, 1962), 206–19, whose observations overall need adjustment in light of Mahdi, "Al-Fārābī's Imperfect State," 691–726; Macy, "The Rule of Law and the Rule of Wisdom in Plato, al-Farabi, and Maimonides," I 205–11, and "Prophecy in al-Farabi and Maimonides," 185–92; and Butterworth, "Alfarabi's Introductory Sections to the *Virtuous City*." In this connection, see Shlomo Pines, "The Arabic Recension of *Parva Naturalia* and the Philosophical Doctrine Concerning Veridical Dreams According to al-Risāla al-Manāmiyya and Other Sources," *Israel Oriental Studies* 4 (1974): 104–53, which is reprinted in *The Collected Works of Shlomo Pines*, II 96–145.

[31] Consider Avicenna, *Shifā'* 4.10.2–5, in Avicenna, *al-Shifā': al-Ilāhiyyāt*, ed. Georges C. Anawati et al. (Cairo: al-Hay'ah al-'Ammah li-Shu'un al-Matabi' al-Amiriyah, 1960), II 441–55, in light of James W. Morris, "The Philosopher–Prophet in Avicenna's Political Philosophy," in *The Political Aspects of Islamic Philosophy: Essays in Honor of Muhsin S. Mahdi*, ed. Charles E. Butterworth (Cambridge, MA: Harvard University Press, 1992), 152–98. For an English translation of the pertinent chapters, see *Medieval Political Philosophy*, 99–110. There is now a bilingual, Arabic–English edition of the entire fourth part: see Avicenna, *The Metaphysics of the Healing*, tr. Michael E. Marmura (Provo, UT: Brigham Young University, 2004). There is also a recent French translation, see Avicenne, *La Métaphysique du Shifā'*, tr. Georges C. Anawati (Paris: Librairie Philosophique J. Vrin, 1978–1985), II 175–89.

[32] See Fazlur Rahman, *Prophecy in Islam: Philosophy and Orthodoxy* (London: George Allen & Unwin, 1958).

Averroës' *Incoherence of the Incoherence* survives in the original Arabic.[33] In Machiavelli's Italy, it was available in manuscript in multiple copies in a Latin translation produced in 1328 by Calonymos ben Calonymos ben Meir of Arles. Calonymos' handiwork is far from perfect, however, as we can now see. His Latin is awkward, and for no apparent reason he left out the sixteenth *disputatio in metaphysicis*. Here and there, moreover, his rendering of the original is inaccurate, and on occasion he introduced interpolations contrary to the thrust of the Arab philosopher's argument and favorable to the Judaism to which he himself adhered.[34] Nonetheless, Calonymos ben Calonymos succeeded in conveying the substance of Averroës' argument, and, in 1497, a truncated version – which omitted all four of the *disputationes in physicis* and the tenth, as well as the sixteenth, *disputatio in metaphysicis* – was published in Venice by Agostino Nifo.[35] The last of the *disputationes in physicis*, the *sermo legum*, which summarized the argument of the book as a whole, was not, in fact, available in print in Latin until the year in which Machiavelli died.[36] The delay in its publication mattered little, however. For, in the late fifteenth and early sixteenth centuries, scholars, including Nifo,[37] had access to manuscripts of Calonymos' translation, which included the *disputationes in physicis* that Nifo had chosen not to publish,[38] and the substance of the shocking argument that Averroës had advanced therein was widely known.

Moreover, the outlook of the Arab philosopher could easily be pieced together from the sections of his book that Nifo had, in fact, ushered into print.[39] Among these could be found a crucial passage from the sixth of the

[33] For the *editio princeps*, see Averroès, *Tahafot at-Tahafot*, ed. Maurice Bouyges (Beirut: Imprimerie Catholique, 1930).

[34] In this connection, see Grignaschi, "Indagine sui passi del *Commento* suscettibili di avere promosso la formazione di un Averroismo politico," 238 (esp. n. 7), 244–49, who raises the possibility that Calonymos was working from another version of the Arab text: see ibid., 268.

[35] See *Destructiones destructionum Averrois cum Augustini Niphi de Suessa expositione* (Venice: Octavianus Scotus, 1497).

[36] The truncated version was reprinted in 1508, 1517, 1529, and 1542. In time, a more accurate translation was made of the work in its entirety by Calo Calonymos: it was published in 1527 and then reprinted in 1550, 1560, 1573, and 1961: see Beatrice H. Zedler, "Appendix A: Chart of the Latin Editions of *Destructio Destructionum*," in *Averroes' Destructio Destructionum Philosophiae Algazelis in the Latin Version of Calo Calonymos*, 55–56.

[37] See *Destructiones destructionum Averrois cum Augustini Niphi de Suessa expositione*, 123rb–vb.

[38] Cf. Beatrice H. Zedler, "Introduction," in *Averroes' Destructio Destructionum Philosophiae Algazelis in the Latin Version of Calo Calonymos*, 1–53, who – though aware that Nifo had access in Latin to the *disputationes in physicis* (ibid., 45) – nonetheless takes it for granted that he published Calonymos' translation in its entirety, with Grignaschi, "Indagine sui passi del *Commento* suscettibili di avere promosso la formazione di un Averroismo politico," 244–49, who quotes from a fourteenth-century manuscript (MS Vatican. Lat. 2434), which is virtually identical with the fifteenth-century manuscript (MS Zanetti 251) preserved in the Biblioteca Marciana in Venice (ibid., 238 n. 7, 268), various passages of the *sermo legum* in that very translation. Grignaschi (ibid., 238 n. 7) mentions also but does not describe in detail an early sixteenth-century manuscript (MS 117), which survives in the Biblioteca Ricciardiana in Florence.

[39] See Averroës, *Tahafut al-tahafut* 194.10–195.5, 207.3–210.9, 255.15–257.2, 351.15–363.3, 396.2–397.3, 409.1–410.9, 427.9–430.8, 453.8–454.9, 463.9–464.1, 480.6–481.15.

disputationes in metaphysicis in which, according to Calonymos, Averroës had juxtaposed "the path taken by philosophers (*philosophorum via*)" with "the path taken by those who establish laws (*via leges ponentium*)." To clarify the difference between these two paths, as the translation made clear, the Arab philosopher had restated Plato's discussion of medicinal lies, intimating that religion is a drug, which philosophical statesmen administer to the common sort, who are for all practical purposes mentally ill, and specifying that philosophical truth, which is nourishment for the select sort, would be for the multitude a deadly poison.[40] That the implications of this passage were fully understood is clear from Nifo's commentary thereon.[41]

The interpretive difficulties faced by Nifo and by his predecessors among the Latin Averroists were eased also by the availability in Latin of important works by Alfarabi and Avicenna. They did not possess *The Principles of the Opinions of the People of the Virtuous City*, the popular work in which the former spelled out in detail his doctrine of prophecy.[42] Nor did they possess its esoteric counterpart, *The Political Regime*.[43] They did not have ready to hand the panoramic vision of human history elaborated in Alfarabi's *Book of Letters*,[44] and his *Book of Religion* was then unavailable as well.[45] But, from the late twelfth century on, scholars in Western Christendom were in a position to consult Alfarabi's *Enumeration of the Sciences*,[46] and there, in its

[40] See *Destructiones destructionum Averrois cum Augustini Niphi de Suessa expositione*, 79rb–80ra, and note the degree to which the Latin translation of Calonymos ben Calonymos departs from what Averroës appears to have written in the sixth of his *disputationes in metaphysicis* (*Tahafut al-tahafut* 351.15–363.3) but nonetheless elaborates knowledgeably on its significance.

[41] See *Destructiones destructionum Averrois cum Augustini Niphi de Suessa expositione*, 80ra–82ra.

[42] For a bilingual Arabic–English edition, see *Al-Farabi on the Perfect State*, 37–329, which should be read in light of the introductory sections of the work, omitted by Walzer and now translated in Butterworth, "Alfarabi's Introductory Sections to the *Virtuous City*."

[43] For a translation of the most important parts, see *Medieval Political Philosophy*, 32–56.

[44] The crucial passages (§§ 108–57) from *Alfarabi's Book of Letters (Kitāb al-Hurūf)*, which was published in 1970 in a critical edition by Muhsin Mahdi, can be found in translation in *Medieval Islamic Philosophical Writings*, 1–27.

[45] For an English translation see Alfarabi, *The Political Writings*, 93–113.

[46] For an edition of the Latin translation produced in 1175 by Gerard of Cremona, see Alfarabi, *Catálogo de las ciencias*, second edition, ed. and tr. Angel González Palencia (Madrid: Consejo Superior de Investigaciones Científicas, Patronato Menéndez y Pelayo, Instituto Miguel Asín, 1953), 117–76, where one can also find a Spanish translation (ibid., 1–78) and the Arabic original (ibid., 177–282). There was a second, truncated translation of the work by Domingo Gundisalvo, which eventually appeared in *Alpharabii vetustissimi Aristotelis interpretis, Opera omnia, quae Latina linguâ conscripta reperiri potuerunt*, ed. William Chalmers (Paris: Denys Moreau, 1638), and, in that form, it has been reprinted: see Alfarabi, *Catálogo de las ciencias*, 83–115. For a critical edition, see Domingo Gundisalvo, *De scientiis: Compilación a base principalmente de la Maqālah fī ihsā' al-'ulūm de Al-Fārābī*, ed. Manuel Alonso Alonso (Madrid: Escuelas de Estudios Arabes de Madrid y Granada, 1954). For a fourteenth-century Hebrew translation of the Arabic original, note also Mauro Zonta, *La "Classificazione della scienze" di Al-Fārābī nella tradizione ebraica: Edizione critica e traduzione annotata della versione ebraica di Qalonymos ben Qalonymos ben Me'ir* (Turin: Zamorani, 1992). From the outset, in the Latin West, the work's impact was considerable: see Charles Burnett, "The Coherence of the Arabic–Latin Translation Programme in Toledo in the Twelfth Century," *Science in Context* 14 (2001): 249–88.

fifth and final chapter, they could find a terse statement spelling out the scope of legislation, alluding to the manner in which one man's poison is another man's nourishment, and specifying the subordination of jurisprudence and theology (*kalām*) to political science.[47]

More significant yet was the fact that Avicenna's *Shifā'* was translated into Latin in its entirety at about the same time,[48] for in this form it circulated throughout Europe in a great many copies in and after the thirteenth century, and it was not only widely read by scholars but also frequently cited and commented on. The crucial fourth part, which dealt with metaphysics, politics, and prophecy, was published in printed form in 1495 and then reprinted thirteen years later in a revised edition.[49] In its concluding chapters, as we have just now had occasion to note, Avicenna restates the theologico-political doctrine of the *falāsifa*, starting with a rearticulation of Aristotle's account of man's need for the political community and his character as a political animal, and goes on to specify, in the manner of Alfarabi, the dependence of the political community for its well-being on a species of moral virtue which cannot be sustained in the absence of a firm belief in the justice of an omniscient God who metes out rewards and punishments in the life to come.

Thus, when Nifo's predecessors first read Averroës, quite often they were familiar with such arguments already.[50] Moreover, they had already come to

---

[47] Consider Alfarabi, *Catálogo de las ciencias*, 167–76, in light of Muhsin Mahdi, "Science, Philosophy, and Religion in Alfarabi's *Enumeration of the Sciences*," in *The Cultural Context of Medieval Learning*, ed. John Emery Murdoch and Edith Dudley Sylla (Dordrecht: Reidel, 1975), 113–47. The discussion of *kalām* was omitted from the translation made by Domingo Gundisalvo: see Alfarabi, *Catálogo de las ciencias*, 112–14, and Gundisalvo, *De scientiis*, 133–40. For an English translation of the Arabic original, see Alfarabi, *The Enumeration of the Sciences* 5, in Alfarabi, *The Political Writings*, 76–84.

[48] There is a three-volume critical edition of the Latin translation of its fourth part: see Avicenna Latinus, *Liber de philosophia prima: sive, scientia divina*, ed. Simone van Riet (Louvain: E. Peeters, 1977–1983). The translation is variously attributed to the two men who translated Alfarabi's *Enumeration of the Sciences*, Gerard of Cremona and Domingo Gundisalvo. In this connection, see Jules Janssens, "L'Avicenne Latin: Particularités d'une traduction," in *Avicenna and His Heritage*, ed. Jules Janssens and Daniel de Smet (Louvain: Leuven University Press, 2002), 113–29.

[49] On this, see Simone van Riet, "Traduction Latin et principes d'édition," in Avicenna Latinus, *Liber de philosophia prima I–V*, 123*–38*, and Georges C. Anawati, "Introduction," in Avicenne, *La Métaphysique du Shifā'*, I 11–79 (at 56–79). Avicenna's influence is especially visible in the work of Roger Bacon: see *Medieval Political Philosophy*, 357–89. In this connection, see also Amélie Marie Goichon, *La Philosophie d'Avicenne et son influence en Europe médiévale*, second edition, revised and corrected (Paris: Adrien–Maisonneuve, 1951), 89–133, along with Amos Bertolacci, "Albert the Great and the Preface of Avicenna's *Kitāb al-Šifā'*," Roland Teske, "William of Auvergne's Debt to Avicenna," Carlos Steel, "Avicenna and Thomas Aquinas on Evil," Jos Decorte, "Avicenna's Ontology of Relation: A Source of Inspiration to Henry of Ghent," Jean-Michel Counet, "Avicenne et son influence sur la pensée de Jean Duns Scot," Thérèse-Anne Druart, "Avicenna's Influence on Duns Scotus' Proof for the Existence of God in the *Lectura*," Mauro Zonta, "Avicenna in Medieval Jewish Philosophy," and Idit Dobbs-Weinstein, "Maimonides' Reticence towards Ibn Sīnā," in *Avicenna and His Heritage*, 131–296. Note also Nancy G. Sirasi, *Avicenna in Renaissance Italy: The Canon and Medical Teaching in Italian Universities after 1500* (Princeton, NJ: Princeton University Press, 1987).

[50] See Grignaschi, "Indagine sui passi del *Commento* suscettibili di avere promosso la formazione di un Averroismo politico," 263–64.

grips with Avicenna's analysis of the crucial role played by rituals and other forms of observance in sustaining religious belief; they had worked their way through his exploration of the dangers to the community attendant on an undisciplined and impolitic practice of *kalām* by the *mutakallimūn*; and they had considered his argument for prophecy's proper dependence on and subordination to philosophical wisdom.[51]

Moreover, from the thirteenth century on, an argument similar to that advanced by Averroës could be found as well in Latin translations of *The Guide of the Perplexed* by those – and they were legion – who cared to look.[52] For, like his fellow Cordoban, whose commentaries on Aristotle he greatly admired,[53] Moses Maimonides had read Alfarabi with considerable care, and the posture

---

[51] See Avicenna Latinus, *Liber de philosophia prima V–X*, 531–53. For an English translation of the Arabic original, see *Medieval Political Philosophy*, 99–110.

[52] This is a subject begging for a thorough investigation: note Wolfgang Kluxen, "Literargeschichtliches zum lateinischen Moses Maimonides," *Recherches de théologie ancienne et médiévale* 21 (1954): 23–50, and see Jacob Guttmann, "Der Einfluss der maimonidischen Philosophie auf das christliche Abendland," in *Moses ben Maimon: Sein Leben, seine Werke und sein Einfluss*, ed. Wilhelm Bacher et al. (Leipzig: Gustav Fock, 1908–1914), I 135–230; Wolfgang Kluxen, "Maimonides und die Hochscholastik," *Philosophisches Jahrbuch* 63 (1955): 151–65, "Die Geschichte des Maimonides im lateinischen Abendland als Beispiel einer christlich-jüdischen Begegnung," in *Judentum im Mittelalter: Beiträge zum christlich–jüdischen Gespräch*, ed. Paul Wilpert (Berlin: Walter de Gruyter, 1966), 146–66, and "Maimonides and Latin Scholasticism," in *Maimonides and Philosophy*, 224–32; Hermann Greive, "Die Maimonidische Kontroverse und die Auseinandersetzungen in der lateinischen Scholastik," in *Die Auseinandersetzungen an der Pariser Universität im XIII. Jahrhundert*, ed. Albert Zimmerman (Berlin: Walter de Gruyter, 1976), 170–80; Shlomo Pines, "Maimonide et la philosophie latine," in *Actas del V. Congresso Internacional de Filosofia Medieval* (Madrid: Editora Nacional, 1979), I 219–29, which is reprinted in *The Collected Works of Shlomo Pines*, V 393–403; and, in Hebrew, Yossef Schwartz, *"To Thee Is Silence Praise": Meister Eckhart's Reading in Maimonides' Guide of the Perplexed* (Tel-Aviv: 'Alma 'Am 'oved, 2002). For the manner in which Maimonides was initially read within the Jewish community, see Aviezer Ravitzky, "Samuel ibn Tibbon and the Esoteric Character of *The Guide of the Perplexed*," *Association for Jewish Studies Review* 6 (1981): 87–123, which is reprinted in Ravitzky, *History and Faith: Studies in Jewish Philosophy* (Amsterdam: J. C. Gieben, 1996), 205–45. With regard to his legacy, note Daniel J. Lasker, "Averroistic Trends in Jewish–Christian Polemics in the Late Middle Ages," *Speculum* 55:2 (April 1980): 294–304, and see Steven Harvey, "Did Maimonides' Letter to Samuel ibn Tibbon Determine Which Philosophers Would Be Studied by Later Jewish Thinkers?" *Jewish Quarterly Review* 83:1–2 (July 1992): 51–70, and Menachem Lorberbaum, "Medieval Jewish Political Thought," Gregg Stern, "Philosophy in Southern France: Controversy over Philosophic Study and the Influence of Averroes upon Jewish Thought," and Seymour Feldman, "The End and Aftereffects of Medieval Jewish Philosophy," in *The Cambridge Companion to Medieval Jewish Philosophy*, ed. Daniel H. Frank and Oliver Leaman (Cambridge, UK: Cambridge University Press, 2003), 176–200, 281–303, 414–45.

[53] This Maimonides made clear in a well-known letter to Samuel ibn Tibbon. For the pertinent paragraph in the Hebrew translation, see Alexander Marx, "Texts by and about Maimonides," *Jewish Quarterly Review* 25:4 (April 1935): 371–428 (at 374–81). For a critical edition of the letter as a whole, see Moses Maimonides, *Igrot ha-Rambam: Letters and Essays of Moses Maimonides*, ed. Isaac Shailat (Jerusalem: Maaliyot Press of Yeshivat Birkat Moshe, 1987–1988), II 530–54. For a translation of the pertinent paragraph, see Shlomo Pines, "The Philosophical Sources of *The Guide of the Perplexed*," in Maimonides, *The Guide of the Perplexed*, lvii–cxxiv (at lix–lx). For a recent discussion, see Harvey, "Did Maimonides' Letter to Samuel ibn Tibbon Determine Which Philosophers Would Be Studied by Later Jewish Thinkers?" 51–70.

adopted by the *falāsifa* with regard to the relationship between philosophy, prophecy, religion, law, custom, moral virtue, and the welfare of civil society he had made his own.[54] Moreover, in his *Guide*,[55] and in other works as well,[56] he had systematically applied this mode of analysis to the religion of his fellow Jews in the manner reserved for a philosophical practitioner of *kalām*.

It was also the case that a number of Averroës' middle and long commentaries on the works of Aristotle had been available to scholars since the middle of the thirteenth century.[57] Here, too, the Latin translations were awkward, imprecise,

[54] Consider Maimonides, *Guide of the Perplexed* II 32–48, in light of Leo Strauss, "Der Ort der Vorsehungslehre nach der Ansicht Maimunis," *Monatsschrift für Geschichte und Wissenschaft des Judentums* 81 (1937): 93–105 (esp. 101–2); and, after reading Leo Strauss, "The Literary Character of the *Guide for the Perplexed*," in *Essays on Maimonides*, ed. Salo Wittmayer Baron (New York: Columbia University Press, 1941), 37–91, which was reprinted in Strauss, *Persecution and the Art of Writing*, 38–94, and "How to Begin to Study *The Guide of the Perplexed*," in Maimonides, *The Guide of the Perplexed*, xi–lvi, which was reprinted in Strauss, *Liberalism Ancient and Modern* (New York: Basic Books, 1968), 140–84; Pines, "The Philosophical Sources of *The Guide of the Perplexed*," lvii–cxxiv; and Strauss, "Maimonides' Statement on Political Science," *Proceedings of the American Academy for Jewish Research* 22 (1953): 115–30, which was reprinted in *What Is Political Philosophy?*, 155–69, note Lawrence V. Berman, "The Political Interpretation of the Maxim: The Purpose of Philosophy Is the Imitation of God," *Studia Islamica* 15 (1961): 53–61, and see Berman, "Maimonides, the Disciple of Alfārābī," *Israel Oriental Studies* 4 (1974): 154–78, and Miriam Galston, "The Purpose of the Law According to Maimonides," *Jewish Quarterly Review* 69:1 (July 1978): 27–51, which were reprinted in *Maimonides*, 195–233; Alexander Altmann, "Maimonides and Thomas Aquinas: Natural or Divine Prophecy?" *Association for Jewish Studies Review* 3 (1978): 1–19; Joel L. Kraemer, "Alfarabi's *Opinions of the Virtuous City* and Maimonides' *Foundations of the Law*," in *Studia Orientalia Memoriae D. H. Baneth Dedicata* (Jerusalem: Magnes Press, 1979), 107–53; Jeffrey Macy, "The Theological–Political Teaching of *Shemonah Peraqim*: A Reappraisal of the Text and Its Arabic Sources," in *Proceedings of the Eighth World Congress of Jewish Studies, 1981* (Jerusalem: World Union of Jewish Studies, 1982) Division C: *Talmud and Midrash, Philosophy and Mysticism, Hebrew and Yiddish Literature*, 31–40, "The Rule of Law and the Rule of Wisdom in Plato, al-Farabi, and Maimonides," I 205–32 (esp. 211–20), and "Prophecy in al-Farabi and Maimonides," 185–201 (esp. 192–201); Brague, "*Eorum praeclara ingenia*," 87–102; Maurice Kriegel, "Réflexion philosophique et appartenance identitaire chez les penseurs juifs médiévaux," *Revue de métaphysique et de morale* 4 (October–December 1998): 529–49; and Steven Harvey, "Islamic Philosophy and Jewish Philosophy," in *The Cambridge Companion to Arabic Philosophy*, 349–69.

[55] It is, for example, in this light that one should consider Maimonides' account of the claim that man is made in "the image and likeness of God" and his bold reinterpretation of the Fall (*Guide of the Perplexed* I 1–2), his insistence on God's incorporeality and on his creation of the universe (I 35, II 13–31), his enigmatic defense of providence and his unorthodox reading of the story of Job (III 17–18, 22–23, 51), his depiction of the peculiar status of Moses as a prophet (II 33–36, 39, 45), his discussion of the aims of Holy Law (III 27), and his frank treatment of the doctrine of divine retribution for injustice simply and solely as a "belief . . . necessary for the sake of political welfare": cf. III 28 with I 26, 47, 50–54.

[56] See Ralph Lerner, *Maimonides' Empire of Light: Popular Enlightenment in an Age of Belief* (Chicago: University of Chicago Press, 2001).

[57] The precise route of transmission is in some respects disputed, but the fact of transmission at this time is not: see Charles Burnett, "Arabic into Latin: The Reception of Arabic Philosophy into Western Europe," in *The Cambridge Companion to Arabic Philosophy*, 370–404, which should be read in conjunction with René Antoine Gauthier, "Notes sur les débuts (1225–40) du premier 'averroïsme,'" *Revue des sciences philosophiques et théologiques* 66:3 (July 1982): 321–74; Steven Harvey, "Arabic into Hebrew: The Hebrew Translation Movement and the Influence

and, on relatively rare occasions, wrong-headed, and interpretive glosses sometimes found their way into the text.[58] But scholars were aware of these defects,
they were not an insuperable obstacle to understanding, and students of Aristotle read the commentaries with caution and care – for, in these, as they knew,
the philosopher from Cordoba had addressed the theologico-political question
from an angle more revealing yet.

In his commentaries, Averroës regards religious doctrine from a perspective more narrowly philosophical, and there, precisely where one would expect
him to comment in detail on the immortality of the individual soul and on the
afterlife, he is utterly, strikingly, ostentatiously silent[59] – as if to imply that,
while religious doctrine in this regard may be salutary, it is contrary to reason.[60] Moreover, there also, where, he supposes, none but initiates into the
mysteries of philosophy would ever be likely to rest their eyes, he intimates

of Averroes upon Medieval Jewish Thought," in *The Cambridge Companion to Medieval Jewish Philosophy*, 258–80. In this connection, note Fernand van Steenberghen, "Le Problème de
l'entrée d'Averroès en Occident," in *L'Averroismo in Italia*, 81–89, and see Charles Burnett,
"The 'Sons of Averroes with the Emperor Frederick' and the Transmission of the Philosophical Works by Ibn Rushd," in *Averroes and the Aristotelian Tradition: Sources, Constitution
and Reception of the Philosophy of Ibn Rushd (1126–1198)*, ed. Gerhard Endress and Jan A.
Aertsen (Leiden: Brill, 1999), 259–99. Much can also be learned from Moritz Steinchneider,
Die hebräischen Übersetzungen des Mittelalters und die Juden als Dolmetscher (Berlin: Kom-
missionsverlag des Bibliographischen Bureaus, 1893), and Mauro Zonta, *La filosofia antica nel
medioevo ebraico: Le traduzioni ebraiche medievali dei testi filosofici antichi* (Brescia: Paideia,
1996). For the dissemination of manuscripts, see Giuliano Tamani and Mauro Zonta, *Aris-
toteles Hebraicus: Versioni, commenti et compendi del Corpus Aristotelicum nei manoscritti
ebraici delle biblioteche italiane* (Venice: Supernova, 1966), and Harald Kischlat, *Studien zur
Verbreitung von Übersetzungen Arabischer philosophischer Werke in Westeuropa, 1150–1400:
Das Zeugnis der Bibliotheken* (Münster: Aschendorff, 2000).

[58] See Grignaschi, "Indagine sui passi del *Commento* suscettibili di avere promosso la formazione
di un Averroismo politico," 237–44, 248–78 (esp. 268–69).

[59] See Charles E. Butterworth, "New Light on the Political Philosophy of Averroës," in *Essays
on Islamic Philosophy and Science*, ed. George F. Hourani (Albany: State University of New
York Press, 1975), 118–27; Michael E. Marmura, "Some Remarks on Averroës's Statements
on the Soul," in *Averroës and the Enlightenment*, ed. Mourad Wahba and Mona Abousenna
(Amherst, NY: Prometheus Books, 1996), 263–91; and Richard C. Taylor, "Personal Immortality in Averroes' Mature Philosophical Psychology," *Documenti e studi sulla tradizione filosofica
medievale* 9 (1998): 87–110, and "Averroes' Philosophical Analysis of Religious Propositions,"
in *Was ist Philosophie im Mittelalter?* ed. Jan A. Aertsen and Andreas Speer (Berlin: Walter de
Gruyter, 1998), 888–94. See also Steven Harvey, "Averroes' Use of Examples in His *Middle
Commentary on the Prior Analytics* and Some Remarks on His Role as Commentator," *Arabic Sciences and Philosophy* 7:1 (March 1997): 91–113. For what appears to be a comparable
example from an earlier time, see Shlomo Pines, "A Tenth Century Philosophical Correspondence," *Proceedings of the American Academy for Jewish Research* 24 (1955): 103–36, which is
reprinted in *The Collected Works of Shlomo Pines*, V 177–210. The case of Avicenna deserves
attention as well: consider Avicenna, *Epistola sulla vita futura*, ed. Francesca Lucchetta (Padua:
Antenore, 1969), in light of M. M. Anawati, "Un Cas typique de l'ésotéricisme avicennien: Sa
Doctrine de la résurrection des corps," *Revue du Caire* 27:141 (June 1951): 68–94, and see Tariq
Jaffer, "Bodies, Souls and Resurrection in Avicenna's *ar-Risāla al-Aḍhawīya fī amr al-maʿād*,"
in *Before and After Avicenna*, ed. David C. Reisman (Leiden: Brill, 2003), 163–74.

[60] In one of his exoteric works, Averroës asserts that anyone who believes this is an infidel: see
Averroës, *The Book of the Decisive Treatise Determining the Connection Between Law and
Wisdom* 28, in Averroës, *The Decisive Treatise and Epistle Dedicatory*, 19.

that the harmony between religion and philosophy is, of necessity, incomplete. For example, in a brief set of remarks that appear in his commentary on a passage at the end of the second book of Aristotle's *Metaphysics*, which was frequently discussed in a similar fashion in philosophical circles both before and after,[61] Averroës is quite forthcoming. There is, he suggests, a deep, impassable divide between the two ways of interpreting the world, for religion is, in fact, a "very powerful (*fortissimum*)" impediment to philosophy. Human beings are not, he acknowledges, self-sufficient: "they do not achieve completion (*complementum*) except through associations (*per congregationes*)," and "association" both fosters and is fostered by "moral well-being (*bonitas*)." "It is," he says, "necessary that [human beings] be good but it is not necessary that they know the truth." The requisite *bonitas* is nourished by the laws (*leges*), which – being fundamentally religious – have as their "roots (*radices*)" certain "opinions." These opinions are in turn fostered by the laws but "not for the purpose of knowing." They are fostered, instead, "for the purpose of acquiring *bonitas*," and in the course of one's youth (*pueritia*) they give rise to a species of "habituation or custom (*consuetudo*)" – one might even say, "ethos," as Aristotle had in the passage commented on – that is binding and nearly impossible to escape. It is because of the *consuetudo* fostered by religious law that men "deny the existence of nature and even truth, deny that necessity exists, and assert that all things are possible."[62]

The doctrine of creation, which contradicts what Aristotle reveals concerning the eternity of the universe, is taught, Averroës elsewhere explains, by the *mutakallimūn* of all three of the religious traditions that claim to be based on prophecy and revelation. Such is the position of the religious apologists and dialectical theologians "who speak in defense of our law (*Loquentes nostrae legis, Loquentes in nostra lege*)," he reports. It is the position of "those who speak in defense of the Christian law (*Loquentes in ... lege Christiano*)." It is the position of "those who speak in defense of the three religions – those, at any rate, which exist today (*Loquentes trium legum, quae hodie quidem sunt*)." Such is, in fact, "the way of the *mutakallimūn* (*via loquentium*)" generally, for they "deny" what is demonstrably true: "that it is impossible that something can emerge from nothing (*negabant impossibile esse aliquid de nihilo*)."

---

[61] Note Pines, "A Tenth Century Philosophical Correspondence," 119–20, n. 71, which is reprinted in *The Collected Works of Shlomo Pines*, V 193–94, n. 71, and Shlomo Pines and Michael Schwarz, "Yaḥyā ibn ʿAdī's Refutation of the Doctrine of Acquisition: Edition, Translation, and Notes on Some of his Other Treatises," in *Studia Orientalia Memoriae D. H. Baneth Dedicata*, 49–94 (at 54–56); then, see Grignaschi, "Indagine sui passi del *Commento* suscettibili di avere promosso la formazione di un Averroismo politico," 248–57, and Brague, "*Eorum praeclara ingenia*," 89–102 (esp. 97–101).

[62] See Comment II.14 on Aristotle's *Metaphysics* II.3 (995a1–6), in *Aristotelis Stagiritae omnia quae extant opera ... Averrois Cordubensis in ea opera omnes qui ad nos pervenere commentarii*, VIII 17ra, which should be read in conjunction with what he has to say about the *Moderni* in Comment IX.7 on Aristotle's *Metaphysics* IX.3 (1047a11–b1), in ibid., VIII 109ra. For an English translation of the Arabic original, which treats what is here called *consuetudo* as a product of the study of *kalām*, and a commentary, see the appendix to Pines, "The Limitations of Human Knowledge According to Al-Farabi, Ibn Bajja, and *Maimonides*," I 102–3, which is reprinted in *Maimonides*, 113–15, and in *The Collected Works of Shlomo Pines*, V 424–25.

In embracing such a stance, they put themselves at odds not only with "the peripatetics," but with "the ancients" more generally.[63]

Elsewhere Averroës outlines the dilemma faced by the philosophers in a fashion even more blunt. In the prologue to his long commentary on Aristotle's *Physics*, in the prologue to his commentary on that work's eighth book, and again in his long commentary on Aristotle's *De anima*, he draws a sharp distinction between philosophers and the multitude, suggesting that to speak of the members of both classes as men is to equivocate.[64] In the prologue to his long commentary on the third book of *The Physics*, he then goes on to explain what it is that separates those who are fully human from those who are not, and he does so with an eye to the difference opened up between the ancients (*Antiqui*) and the moderns (*Moderni*) by the advent, propagation, and ultimate prevalence of revealed religion. The *mutakallimūn*, he begins, "the modern masters of rhetoric (*Moderni loquentes*)," those who speak in defense of the laws, quite rightly "say that he who in the beginning becomes imbued with and adept at (*adiscit*) philosophy cannot later become imbued with and adept at the laws, and that he who first becomes imbued with and adept at the laws" by studying *kalām* finds that "the other sciences are hidden from him." In the end, everything is a function of habit. The man in whom *consuetudo* is associated with "a comprehension of the truth" encounters no "impediment" standing in the way of his access to "truth," he explains, but this man "is forever impeded" instead from "falsehood, or in any case from those studies in which neither truth nor falsehood is to be found, such as the laws." But the "one who has contracted the *consuetudo* of accepting falsehood is apt to be

---

[63] See Comments II.22 and VIII.4 and 15 on Aristotle's *Physics* II.2 (194a18–27), VIII.1 (251a8–16 and 252a10–b6), and Comments II.14–16, IV.3, VII.31, and XII.18 on Aristotle's *Metaphysics* II.3 (995a1–20), IV.2 (1002b23–1004a2), VII.9 (1034a30–1034b8), and XII.3 (1070a27–30), in *Aristotelis Stagiritae omnia quae extant opera ... Averrois Cordubensis in ea opera omnes qui ad nos pervenere commentarii*, IV 27rb, 155ra–va, 158vb–160rb, VIII 17ra–va, 32ra–b, 85ra–vb, 142vb–143vb. The use of the term *loquentes* to translate *mutakallimūn* goes back at least to Gerard of Cremona who translated *kalām* as *ars elocutionis* and referred to the *mutakallim* as a *loquax*: see Alfarabi, *Catálogo de las ciencias*, 172.

[64] See Prologue to the Commentary on Aristotle's *Physics*, in *Aristotelis Stagiritae omnia quae extant opera ... Averrois Cordubensis in ea opera omnes qui ad nos pervenere commentarii*, IV 2ra–3vb (at 2ra–b), which should be read in light of Steven Harvey, "The Hebrew Translation of Averroes' Prooemium to his *Long Commentary on Aristotle's Physics*," *Proceedings of the American Academy for Jewish Research* 52 (1985): 55–84, and Averroës, Comment III.36 on Aristotle's *De anima* 431b16–19, in *Averrois Cordubensis commentarium magnum in Aristotelis De anima Libros*, ed. F. Stuart Crawford (Cambridge, MA: Medieval Academy of America, 1953), 495. Averroës' Prologue to the Commentary on Book VIII of Aristotle's *Physics* was excised by the editors of the Giunta edition from *Aristotelis Stagiritae omnia quae extant opera ... Averrois Cordubensis in ea opera omnes qui ad nos pervenere commentarii*, IV 153vb, where it should have appeared, on wrong-headed advice from Paul the Israelite, who thought it a later accretion, as the note on the pertinent page indicates. For a detailed discussion of the manuscript tradition, see Horst Schmieja, "Drei Prologe im grossen Physikkommentar des Averroes?" in *Aristotelisches Erbe im Arabisch–Lateinischen Mittelalter: Übersetzungen, Kommentare, Interpretationen*, ed. Albert Zimmerman (Walter de Gruyter: Berlin, 1986), 175–89 (esp. 184–89 – where Schmieja prints the missing prologue). In this connection, note also Grignaschi, "Indagine sui passi del *Commento* suscettibili di avere promosso la formazione di un Averroismo politico," 257–63.

impeded from approaching the truth." It is by way of *consuetudo* that "the tales propagated by the cities (*Apologi propositi civitatum*) corrupt" would-be philosophers, preventing them from understanding "many of the principles of nature." Moreover, "the degree of conviction displayed by the vulgar (*fides vulgi*) is much greater (*potentior*) than the *fides* displayed by the philosophers, since the vulgar are not accustomed (*assuevit*) to hear anything other" than what the laws teach, "while the philosophers hear many things." But, on the same principle, "when disputation and consideration are common to all," as they would be in a community of philosophers, "the *fides* of the vulgar is corrupted," and so in some places "the laws prohibit disputation," for where "opinion, which men have acquired through habituation and custom (*ex assuetudine*), is corrupted," serious political trouble is bound to arise: "among these the laws are for the most part destroyed."[65]

The Influence of Averroës

By the late fifteenth and early sixteenth centuries, as Campanella recognized, the theologico-political doctrine advanced by the *falāsifa* was, to say the least, well known. From the start, moreover, Averroës' suggestion that only the philosophers can truly be called men occasioned controversy,[66] and his treatment of religion as a species of politically salutary mythology was thought scandalous.

In the early thirteenth century, the Holy Roman Emperor Frederick II was a man renowned for his fascination with Arab learning. At his side, as an adviser, he kept a philosopher from the Levant – a man expert in the thinking of Alfarabi, Avicenna, and Averroës, who shared their conviction concerning the close connection that ought to subsist between philosophical wisdom and

[65] See Comment I.60 on *Physics* I.7 (190a13–31), in *Aristotelis Stagiritae omnia quae extant opera . . . Averrois Cordubensis in ea opera omnes qui ad nos pervenere commentarii*, IV 17vb–18ra, which should be read with an eye to the marginal note on the initial page, to the entry at the very bottom of ibid., IV 40rb, and to Horst Schmieja's detailed discussion of the manuscript tradition: see Schmieja, "Drei Prologe im grossen Physikkommentar des Averroes?" 175–89 (esp. 177–78, where he provides a critical edition of this particular prologue). In this connection, note also Grignaschi, "Indagine sui passi del *Commento* suscettibili di avere promosso la formazione di un Averroismo politico," 257–63. On the larger question raised in this and the preceding paragraph, see *Averroes on Plato's Republic* 37.8–38.18 (esp. 37.29–38.2), 61.20–72.33 (esp. 61.22–62.15, 65.30–67.5, 68.1–72.33), 74.14–29, 78.26–79.9, 80.16–105.4 (with special attention to the emphasis Averroës lays on the predominance of "unexamined opinion" in all the ignorant cities: 81.25–82.4, 12–19, 84.5–10, 88.11–17, 93.15–20, 31, 94.3), which should be read in conjunction with Muhsin S. Mahdi, "Alfarabi et Averroès: Remarques sur le commentaire d'Averroès sur la *République* de Platon," in *Multiple Averroès*, ed. Jean Jolivet (Paris: Les Belles Lettres, 1978), 91–101; Charles E. Butterworth, *Philosophy, Ethics, and Virtuous Rule: A Study of Averroes' Commentary on Plato's Republic* (Cairo: American University in Cairo Press, 1986); and Rémi Brague, "Averroès et la *République*," in *Images de Platon et lectures de ses œuvres: Les Interprétations de Platon à travers les siècles*, ed. Ada Neschke-Hentschke (Louvain-la-neuve: Peeters, 1997), 99–114. See also Averroës, *Tahafut al-tahafut* 356.7–358.12, 361.11–362.3, 427.9–430.8, 463.9–464.1.

[66] See Luca Bianchi, "Filosofi, uomini e bruti: Note per la storia di un'antropologia 'averroista,'" *Rinascimento* n. s. 32 (1992): 185–201, which is reprinted in Bianchi, *Studi sull'aristotelismo del Rinascimento* (Padua: Il Poligrafo, 2003), 41–61.

political rule, and who was not afraid to speak his mind.[67] This same Frederick freely addressed questions to philosophers in the Arab world, he sponsored the translation of Averroës' commentaries, and he was even said to have hosted the Andalusian Arab philosopher's sons.[68] Frederick was also accused of having concluded on the basis of his familiarity with the outlines of Aristotelian natural science that only "dolts (*fatui*)" could believe in the Virgin birth. "The entire world has been deceived," he reportedly claimed, "by three impostors (*barattoribus*) – I mean, of course, Christ Jesus, Moses, and Mohammed."[69]

This charge, which was laid by Frederick's enemy Pope Gregory IX, may have been false,[70] to be sure. But the fact that such an accusation was ready to hand is nonetheless telling, for, later in the same century, the theologico-political doctrine of Averroës helped occasion a great uproar at the University of Paris,[71] where, in reasserting the ancillary status accorded philosophy by the

[67] See Charles Burnett, "Master Theodore, Frederick II's Philosopher," in *Federico II e le nuove culture* (Spoleto: Centro Italiano di Studi sull'Alto Medioevo, 1995), 225–85. For the world from which Theodore came, see Charles Burnett, "Antioch as a Link between Arabic and Latin Culture in the Twelfth and Thirteenth Centuries," in *Occident et Proche-Orient: Contacts scientifiques au temps des croisades*, ed. Isabelle Draelants, Anne Tihon, and Badouin van den Abeele ([Turnhout]: Brepols, 2000), 1–78.

[68] See Charles Burnett, "Michael Scot and the Transmission of Scientific Culture from Toledo to Bologna via the Court of Frederick II Hohenstaufen," *Micrologus* 2 (1994): 101–26, and "The 'Sons of Averroes with the Emperor Frederick' and the Transmission of the Philosophical Works by Ibn Rushd," 259–99.

[69] Consider Letter from Pope Gregory IX to Henry, archbishop of Remini, ca. 20 April 1239, in *Epistolarum saeculi XIII e regestis Pontificum Romanorum selectæ*, ed. Georg Heinrich Pertz, No. 750, in *Monumenta Germaniæ Historica*, ed. Carl Rodenberg (Berlin: Wiedman, 1883–1894), I 645–54 (at 653), in light of the antecedents of this argument from within the House of Islam: see Louis Massignon, "La Legende De tribus impostoribus et ses origines Islamiques," *Revue d'histoire des religions* 82 (1920): 74–78, and the secondary literature cited in Chapter Four, note 42, this volume. The thesis purportedly argued by Frederick had a considerable afterlife as well: see Chapter Ten, note 40, this volume.

[70] See David Abulafia, *Frederick II: A Medieval Emperor* (London: Pimlico, 2000), 251–89 (esp. 254), who is quick – perhaps too quick – in dismissing the papal claim.

[71] In this connection, see Pierre Félix Mandonnet, *Siger de Brabant et l'averroïsme latin au XII-Ime siècle* (Louvain: Institut Superieur de Philosophie de l'Université, 1908–1911), which needs correction in light of Fernand van Steenberghen, *Siger de Brabant d'après ses oeuvres inédites* (Louvain: Éditions de l'Institut Supérieur de Philosophie, 1931–1942), *Les Œuvres et la doctrine de Siger de Brabant* (Brussels: Palais des Académies, 1938), and *Maître Siger de Brabant* (Louvain: Publications Universitaires, 1977); John F. Wippel, "The Condemnations of 1270 and 1277 at Paris," *Journal of Medieval and Renaissance Studies* 7:2 (Fall 1977): 169–201, and *Medieval Reactions to the Encounter between Faith and Reason* (Milwaukee, WI: Marquette University Press, 1995); and Roland Hissette, *Enquête sur les 219 articles condamnés à Paris le 7 mars 1277* (Louvain: Publications Universitaires, 1977), "Etienne Tempier et ses condamnations," *Recherche de théologie ancienne et médiévale* 47 (1980): 231–70, and "Note sur la réaction 'antimoderniste' d'Etienne Tempier," *Bulletin de philosophie médiévale* 22 (1980): 88–97, as well as Luca Bianchi, *Censure et liberté intellectuelle à l'université de Paris, XIIIᵉ–XIVᵉ siècles* (Paris: Belles Lettres, 1999), *La Condamnation parisienne de 1277: Nouvelle édition du texte latin, traduction, introduction et commentaire*, ed. David Piché (Paris: J. Vrin, 1999), and *Nach der Verurteilung von 1277: Philosophie und Theologie an der Universität von Paris im letzten Viertel des 13. Jahrhunderts: Studien und Texte*, ed. Jan A. Aertsen, Kieth Emery, Jr., and Andreas Speer (Berlin: Walter de Gruyter, 2001).

Church Fathers,[72] Bishop Etienne Tempier deployed against those who joined Aristotle and Averroës in believing in the autonomy of unassisted reason Saint Paul's famous injunction that one should "hold the intellect in captivity out of a reverence for Christ (*captivare intellectum in obsequium Christi*)."[73]

Shortly before this event, these doctrines had attracted the ire of Giles of Rome, who singled out for attack the passages from Averroës' commentaries cited above;[74] and these same passages loomed large in subsequent years in a widely circulated *florilegium*, composed by Marsilius of Padua, which epitomized the doctrine of Aristotle and that of the Arab philosopher known simply as the Commentator.[75] In similar fashion, in the early fourteenth century, when John of Jandun wrote his influential *Commentary on the Metaphysics of Aristotle* at the University of Paris, he grounded his account of the relationship between religion and philosophy on the crucial passage from Averroës' commentary on the same work that has been discussed here,[76] and his friend and colleague Marsilius did the same in his *Questiones supre metaphysice libros I–VI*.[77] It was on the teaching of Averroës, and perhaps Alfarabi as well, that Marsilius subsequently grounded the defense of Caesaro-Papism that he advanced in *Defensor pacis*,[78] and Dante appears to have been inspired by the

---

[72] See Paul A. Rahe, *Republics Ancient and Modern: Classical Republicanism and the American Revolution* (Chapel Hill: University of North Carolina Press, 1992), 219–29.

[73] Note II Cor. 10:5, in *Biblia sacra iuxta vulgatam versionem*, 4th edition, ed. B. Fischer et al. (Stuttgart: Deutsche Bibelgesellschaft, 1994), 1798 (*et in captivitatem redigentes omnem intellectum in obsequium Christi*), and consider *La Condamnation parisienne de 1277*, 84–85 (no. 18 [216]), in light of Luca Bianchi, "'Captivare Intellectum in Obsequium Christi,'" *Rivista critica di storia della filosofia* 38:1 (January–March 1983): 81–87.

[74] See Giles of Rome, *Errores philosophorum*, ed. Joseph Koch, tr. John O. Riedl (Milwaukee, WI: Marquette University Press, 1944), 14–25.

[75] See, for example, *Les Auctoritates Aristotelis: Un Florilège médiéval: Étude historique et édition critique*, ed. Jacqueline Hamesse (Louvain: Publications Universitaires, 1974), 120 (*Metaphysics* no. 67), 143 (*Physics* nos. 38–39), 149 (*Physics* nos. 113–16), 159 (*Physics* no. 229), which should be read in light of Jacqueline Hamesse, "Les Sources manuscrites," in ibid., 1–43; "Marsile de Padoue peut-il être considéré comme l'*auteur* des *Parvi flores*," *Medioevo* 6 (1980): 491–99; and "La Diffusion des florilèges aristotéliciens en Italie du XIVe au XVIe siècle," in *Platonismo e aristotelismo nel mezzogiorno d'Italia (secc. XIV–XVI)*, ed. Giuseppe Roccaro (Palermo: Officina di studi medievali, 1989), 41–55.

[76] See Mario Grignaschi, "Il pensiero politico e religioso di Giovanni di Janduno," *Bollettino dell'Instituto storico italiano per il Medio Evo e Archivio Muratoriano* 70 (1958): 425–96.

[77] Note Ludwig Schmugge, *Johannes von Jandun (1288/89–1328): Untersuchungen zur Biographie und Sozialtheorie eines Lateinischen Averroisten* (Stuttgart: Anton Hiersemann, 1966), 96–107, and see Jeannine Quillet, "Brèves remarques sur les *Questiones super metaphysice libros I–VI* (Codex Fesulano 161 f° 1ra–41va) et leurs relations avec l'Aristotélisme hétérodoxe," in *Die Auseinandersetzungen an der Pariser Universität im XIII. Jahrhundert*, 361–85, and "L'Aristotélisme de Marsile de Padoue et ses rapports avec l'Averroïsme," *Medioevo* 5 (1979): 81–142 (esp. 124–42, where an extensive part of the pertinent manuscript is printed).

[78] In passages artfully scattered through his book, Marsilius of Padua acknowledges the necessity that there be a civil theology, asserts that no one but the temporal ruler is empowered to suppress heretical speech, and suggests that he rightly does so only when that speech contravenes "human law," which turns out to be restricted to promoting man's welfare in this world: consider *Defensor pacis* 1.4.3, 5.2, 10, 12–14 (esp. 14), 9.2, 2.4.6, 30.4, in light of 1.4.4, 5.11, 10.3, and see 1.5.4, 7, 2.2.4, 8.5, 9.11, 10.4, 9, 17.8. One can, I think, make sense of the above only in light of the last sentence of 1.1.7. See Leo Strauss, "Marsilius of Padua,"

same authority when he penned *De monarchia*.[79] Whether, in turn, reading Averroës, learning of the charges lodged against Frederick II by Pope Gregory IX, or a familiarity with the tale's Arabic antecedents induced Giovanni Boccaccio to address the rivalry of the three *leges* by penning the allegorical "parable of the three rings" we do not know.[80]

Of course, Campanella may not have had full command of the pertinent bibliography. He may have been unaware of the careful, almost literal Latin translations of a number of Averroës' commentaries on Aristotle that Elijah del Medigo had made in Padua and in Machiavelli's Florence between 1481 and 1488 for Giovanni Pico della Mirandola and for Girolamo Donato, Domenico Grimani, and Antonio Pizzamanto,[81] and he probably knew nothing of del

in *Liberalism Ancient and Modern*, 185–202, and Charles E. Butterworth, "What Is Political Averroism?" in *Averroismus im Mittelalter und in der Renaissance*, ed. Friedrich Niewöhner and Loris Sturlese (Zurich: Spur Verlag, 1994), 239–50, and consider Shlomo Pines, "La Philosophie dans l'économie du genre humain selon Averroès: Une Réponse à al-Farabi?" in *Multiple Averroès*, 189–207, which is reprinted in *The Collected Works of Shlomo Pines*, III 357–75, along with Quillet, "Brèves remarques sur les *Questiones super metaphysice libros I–VI* (Codex Fesulano 161 f° 1 ra – 41 va) et leurs relations avec l'Aristotélisme hétérodoxe," 361–85, and "L'Aristotélisme de Marsile de Padoue et ses rapports avec l'Averroïsme," 81–142, and Antony Black, *The West and Islam: Religion and Political Thought in World History* (Oxford: Oxford University Press, 2008), 51–57 (with 156), who argue that Marsilius may have had access in Latin to Alfarabi's *Commentary on the Nicomachean Ethics of Aristotle*, which is now lost, and to a Hebrew translation of Averroës' *Commentary on Plato's Republic*. Whether Marsilius influenced Machiavelli remains a matter of dispute: see Antonio Toscano, *Marsilio da Padova e Niccolò Machiavelli* (Ravenna: Longo, 1981), and Thomas Itzbicki, "The Reception of Marsilius in the 15th and 16th Centuries," forthcoming in *A Companion to Marsilius of Padua*, ed. Gerson Moreno-Riaño and Cary J. Nederman (Leiden: Brill, 2008). In this connection, note also Conal Condren, "Marsilius and Machiavelli," in *Comparing Political Thinkers*, ed. Ross Fitzgerald (Sydney: Pergamon Press, 1980), 94–115.

79 Consider Dante Alighieri, *Monarchia*, ed. Prue Shaw (Cambridge, UK: Cambridge University Press, 1995), in light of Raffaello Morghen, "Dante e Averroè," in *L'Averroismo in Italia*, 49–62.

80 See Giovanni Boccaccio, *Decameron* I.3, in Boccaccio, *Decameron: Edizione diplomatico-interpretativa dell'autografo Hamilton 90*, ed. Charles S. Singleton (Baltimore: Johns Hopkins University Press, 1974), 37–39, and note Mario Penna, *La parabola dei tre anelli e la tolleranza nel medio evo* (Turin: Rosenberg, 1953), and Iris Shagrir, "The Parable of the Three Rings: A Revision of Its History," *Journal of Medieval History* 23:2 (June 1997): 163–77.

81 Note Umberto Cassuto, *Gli ebrei a Firenze nell'età del Rinascimento* (Florence: Tipografia Galletti e Cocci, 1918), 282–326 (esp. 282–301), and see Pietro Ragnisco, "Documenti inediti e rari intorno alla vita ed agli scritti di Nicoletto Vernia e di Elia del Medigo," *Atti e memorie della R. Accademia di scienze, lettere ed arti di Padova* n. s. 7 (1890–1891): 275–302; Bohdan Kieszkowski, "Les Rapports entre Elia del Medigo e Pic de la Mirandole," *Rinascimento* n. s. 4 (1964): 41–91; and Alberto Bartòla, "Eliyhau del Medigo e Giovanni Pico della Mirandola: La testimonianza dei codici vaticani," *Rinascimento* n. s. 33 (1993): 253–78, along with G. Dell'Acqua and L. Münster, "I rapporti di Giovanni Pico della Mirandola con alcuni filosofi ebrei," in *L'opera ed il pensiero di Giovanni Pico della Mirandola nella storia dell'umanesimo* (Florence: Instituto Nazionale di Studi sul Rinascimento, 1965), II 149–68; Kalman P. Bland, "Elijah del Medigo's Averroist Response to the Kabbalahs of Fifteenth-Century Jewry and Pico della Mirandola," *The Journal of Jewish Thought and Philosophy* 1:1 (1991): 23–53 (which is especially valuable); and Edward P. Mahoney, "Giovanni Pico della Mirandola and Elia del Medigo, Nicoletto Vernia and Agostino Nifo," in *Giovanni Pico della Mirandola: Convegno internazionale di studi nel cinquecentesimo anniversario della morte, 1494–1994*, ed. Gian Carlo Garfagnini (Florence: L. S. Oschki, 1997), I 127–56 (esp. 128–38). See also M. David Geffen, "Insights into the Life and Thought of Elijah del Medigo, Based upon His Published and Unpublished Works," *Proceedings of the American Academy for Jewish Research* 41–42 (1973–74):

Medigo's splendid translation of Averroës' *Commentary on Plato's Republic* –
for, though this last-mentioned work appears to have circulated in manuscript,[82]
more than five centuries were to pass before it was to find its way into print.[83]
Campanella may have not have been aware that in 1495, Antonio Fracanzano
and Francesco Macerata had published in Venice the fourth part of Avicenna's
Shifā' and that the monks at San Giovanni in Verdara in Padua had included
a revised edition of that part of the work in the collection of Avicenna's writings that they published 1508.[84] Campanella may have been oblivious to the

69–86 (esp. 85–86, where he provides a list of the translations, treatises, and supercommentaries produced by del Medigo). From 1488, Pico was associated as well with an admirer of
the Jewish kaballah, who was no less thoroughly steeped in Arab philosophy: consider B. C.
Novak, "Giovanni Pico della Mirandola and Jochanan Alemanno," *Journal of the Warburg and
Courtauld Institutes* 45 (1985): 125–47; Moshe Idel, "The Magical and Neoplatonic Interpretations of the Kabbalah in the Renaissance," and "Major Currents in Italian Kabbalah between
1560 and 1660," in *Essential Papers on Jewish Culture in Renaissance and Baroque Italy*, ed.
David B. Ruderman (New York: New York University Press, 1992), 107–69, 345–68; and Fab-
rizio Lelli, "Yohanan Alemanno, Giovanni Pico della Mirandola e la cultura ebraica italiana del
XV secolo," in *Giovanni Pico della Mirandola*, I 303–25, and "*Prisca Philosophia* and *Docta
Religio*: The Foundations of Rational Knowledge in Jewish and Christian Humanist Thought,"
Jewish Quarterly Review 91:1–2 (July–October 2000): 53–99, and see Bruno Nardi, "La mist-
ica averroistica e Pico della Mirandola," in Nardi, *Saggi sull'aristotelismo padovano dal secolo
XIV al XVI* (Florence: G. C. Sansoni, 1958), 127–46. In this connection, see Alfred L. Ivry,
"Remnants of Jewish Averroism in the Renaissance," in *Jewish Thought in the Sixteenth Century*, ed. Bernard Dov Cooperman (Cambridge, MA: Harvard University Press, 1983), 243–65
(esp. 250–61); Aryeh L. Motzkin, "Elia del Medigo, Averroes and Averroism," *Italia* 6 (1987):
7–19; Joseph Puig Montada, "Continuidad medieval en el Renascimento: El caso de Elia del
Medigo," *La Ciudad de Dios* 206 (1993): 47–64; Kalman P. Bland, "Elijah del Medigo, Unicity
of the Intellect, and Immortality of the Soul," *Proceedings of the American Academy for Jewish Research* 61 (1995): 1–22; and Joseph Puig Montada, "Elia del Medigo and His Physical
Quaestiones," in *Was ist Philosophie in Mittelater?*, 929–36.

82 Although the original is lost, a manuscript copy, made at Rome for Pietro Negroni by Raimondo
di Saleta and completed on 26 April 1491, survives in Siena: see "Expositio Comentatoris
Averois in librum *Politicorum Platonis*," MS Siena, Biblioteca Comunale degli Intronati, G VII
32, fols. 158r–188r, and note Paul Oskar Kristeller, *Iter Italicum: A Finding List of Uncatalogued
or Incompletely Catalogued Humanistic Manuscripts of the Renaissance in Italian and Other
Libraries* (London: Warburg Institute, 1963–1996), II 152.

83 See Averroës, *Parafrasi della Repubblica nella traduzione latine d'Elia del Medigo*, ed. Annalisa
Coviello and Paolo Edoardo Fornaciari (Florence: L. S. Olschki, 1992). For a thorough discus-
sion of the circumstances in which this translation was produced and of its high quality, see
Annalisa Coviello and Paolo Edoardo Fornaciari, "Introduzione," in ibid., v–xxvi, who com-
pare it favorably with the version subsequently produced by Jacob Mantino, *Auerois paraphrasis
super libros de Republica Platonis, nunc primùm latinitate donata, I. Mantino interprete* (Rome:
M. Valerium Doric. et Ludouicum Fratres Brixianos, 1539), which was included in *Francisci
Philelphi De morali disciplina libri quinque. Averrois Paraphrasis in libros De Repub. Platonis.
Francisci Robortelli in libros politicos Aristotelis disputatio* (Venice: Gualterum Scottum, 1552),
89–166, and reprinted in *Aristotelis Stagiritae omnia quae extant opera . . . Averrois Cordubensis
in ea opera omnes qui ad nos pervenere commentarii*, III 174va–191vb, and again in the great
edition of Averroës' commentaries on Aristotle published in 1562–1574 by Giunta in Venice.

84 See *Metaphysica Avicen[n]e sive eius prima philosophia*, ed. Franciscus de Macerata and Antonius Fracantianus (Venice: Bernardino dei Vitali, 1495), and *Auice[n]ne perhypatetici philosophi:
ac medicorum facile primi Opera in luce[m] redacta: ac nuper quantum ars niti potuit per canon-
icos emendata: Logyca. Sufficientia. De celo & mundo. De anima. De animalibus. De intelligentijs. Alpharabius De intelligentijs. Philosophia prima*, ed. Cecilio da Fabriano et al. (Venice:
Octavianus Scotus, 1508).

fact that, in 1497, Agostino Nifo had not only published from Averroës' *Incoherence of the Incoherence* fourteen of the *disputationes in metaphysicis* but had commented on these at length.[85] He may not have been able to specify what was missing from the series of Averroës' commentaries on the works of Aristotle that Nifo and his predecessors at the University of Padua – Lorenzo Canozio, Nicoletto Vernia, and Benardino de Tridino – had published in the period stretching from 1472 to 1495.[86] He may also have been unaware that in the time of Lorenzo the Magnificent, when Machiavelli was growing up, Averroists such as Joannes Argyropoulos, Antonius de Cittadinis, Alessandro Sermoneta, Antonio da Sulmona, and Albertino da Cremona had taught at the Florentine Studio; that, in the late 1470s, the students at that institution had agitated for the appointment of a prominent Averroist to the faculty who would provide instruction in what they tellingly called "the common doctrine of the philosophers (*doctrina communis philosophorum*)"; and that in 1481 Lorenzo had responded by making a concerted effort to lure Nicoletto Vernia from Padua to Florence.[87] He may not have known that the Averroist Bernardo Torni taught at Pisa from 1473 to 1497, that he played a prominent role in Florentine intellectual life, and that his student Galgano da Siena, who was no less keenly interested in the doctrines articulated by the Arab philosopher, taught at the Florentine Studio throughout the 1490s as well as in the early years of the sixteenth century.[88] And had he noticed Machiavelli's enthusiastic

---

[85] See *Destructiones destructionum Averrois cum Augustini Niphi de Suessa expositione*, passim. Note, in this connection, Paola Zambelli, "Problemi metodologici del necromante Agostino Nifo," *Medioevo* 1 (1975): 129–71, and Heinrich C. Kuhn, "Die Verwandlung der Zerstörung der Zerstörung: Bemerkungen zu Augustinus Niphus' Kommentar zur *Destruction destructionum* des Averroes," in *Averroismus im Mittelalter und in der Renaissance*, 291–308.

[86] The details can be gleaned from Paul Oskar Kristeller, "Paduan Averroism and Alexandrism in Light of Recent Studies," in *Aristotelismo Padovano e Filosofia Aristotelica* (Florence: Sansoni, 1960), 147–55; Harry Austryn Wolfson, "The Twice-Revealed Averroes," *Speculum* 36:3 (July 1961): 373–92, and "Revised Plan for the Publication of a *Corpus Commentariorum Averrois in Aristotelem*," *Speculum* 38:1 (January 1963): 88–104, which are reprinted in Wolfson, *Studies in the History of Philosophy and Religion* (Cambridge, MA: Harvard University Press, 1973–1977), I 371–401, 430–54; F. Edward Cranz, "Editions of the Latin Aristotle Accompanied by the Commentaries of Averroes," in *Philosophy and Humanism: Renaissance Essays in Honor of Paul Oskar Kristeller*, ed. E. P. Mahoney (Leiden: E. J. Brill, 1976), 116–28; Charles B. Schmitt, "Renaissance Averroism Studied through the Venetian Editions of Aristotle–Averroes," in *L'Averroismo in Italia*, 121–42; and Charles Burnett, "The Second Revelation of Arabic Philosophy and Science: 1492–1562," in *Islam and the Italian Renaissance*, ed. Charles Burnett and Anna Contadini (London: Warburg Institute, 1999), 185–98.

[87] Note Armando Felice Verde, *Lo studio fiorentino, 1473–1503: Ricerche e documenti* (Florence: Istituto Nazionale di Studi sul Rinascimento, 1973–1994), II 14–17, 32–34, 316–20, 510–11, IV:1 105–19, 171–97, 178, 273–74, 378–79, 386, 397–98, 405–11, IV:2 491, 929–30, IV:3 1059, and see James Hankins, "Lorenzo de' Medici as Patron of Philosophy," *Rinascimento* n. s. 34 (1994): 15–53 (at 26–32), which is reprinted in Hankins, *Humanism and Platonism in the Italian Renaissance* (Rome: Edizioni di Storia e Letteratura, 2003–2004), II: *Platonism*, 273–316 (at 285–91).

[88] Consider Verde, *Lo studio fiorentino*, II 126–40, 270–72, IV:2 485–90, 583–86, 833–35, 937–42, 982–1016, in light of Jill Kraye, "Lorenzo and the Philosophers," in *Lorenzo the Magnificent: Culture and Politics*, ed. Michael Mallett and Nicholas Mann (London: Warburg Institute, 1996), 151–66 (esp. 159–63).

description of Giovanni Pico della Mirandola, a devotee of Averroism who was a frequent visitor to Florence in the late 1480s and early 1490s,[89] as "a man almost divine (*uomo quasi che divino*),"[90] and had he known that in 1523 Agostino Nifo had published a Latin treatise for the most part plagiarized from Machiavelli's *Prince*,[91] Campanella would no doubt have cited these facts as evidence for the connection that he was attempting to establish.

But these are comparatively trivial details, for what Campanella possessed is the very thing that we lack – a proper appreciation of the significance of the Averroist revival that was underway in Machiavelli's day.[92] He may not have had access to any of the lecture notes taken on Averroës' theologico-political doctrine by the students of Pietro Pomponazzi at the University of Bologna in 1514, as we do now.[93] But he knew perfectly well that it was primarily from Padua – where, in the fifteenth century, not only Vernia, Nifo, and Pomponazzi, but also their distinguished predecessors, Paul of Venice and Cajetan of Thiene, had studied and taught[94] – that this controversial doctrine was

---

[89] Pico's impact on Florentine intellectual life in this period was considerable: see Verde, *Lo studio fiorentino*, IV:1 464, IV:2 547, 604–5, 640–42, 700–704, 846–50, 910–11, 963–65, IV:3 1092–93, 1135–37.

[90] See Machiavelli, *Istorie fiorentine* 8.36, in *Opere*, 843.

[91] See Giuliano Procacci, "*De regnandi peritia* di Agostino Nifo," in *Studi sulla fortuna del Machiavelli*, 3–26; note Sergio Bertelli, "Machiavelli riproposto in tutte le opere," *Archivio storico italiano* 157:4 (October–December 1999): 789–800 (esp. 792–93), who thinks that Machiavelli may have been party to Nifo's pious, conventional repackaging of the better part of his most controversial work; and consider Sydney Anglo, *Machiavelli – The First Century: Studies in Enthusiasm, Hostility, and Irrelevance* (Oxford, UK: Oxford University Press, 2005), 42–84, who attempts to analyze what Nifo was up to. For a facsimile reprint of the original text, with a French translation, see *Une Réécriture du "Prince" de Machiavel: Le "De regnandi peritia" de Agostino Nifo*, ed. Paul Larivaille, tr. Simone Pernet-Beau (Paris: University Paris X–Nanterre, 1987).

[92] For an overview, see M. M. Gorce, "Averroisme," *Dictionnaire d'histoire et de géographie ecclésiastiques*, ed. Alfred Baudrillart et al. (Paris: Letouzey et Ané, 1912–), V 1032–92 (esp. 1076–90), and Cruz Hernandez, *Abū-L-Walīd Ibn Rušd*, 249–307.

[93] The surviving *reportationes* show Pomponazzi focusing on the two crucial passages drawn from Averroës' commentaries on Aristotle cited at the beginning of note 62, this chapter: see Bruno Nardi, "Filosofia e religione," *Giornale critico della filosofia italiana* 30:3 (July–September 1951): 363–81, which is reprinted in Nardi, *Studi su Pietro Pomponazzi* (Florence: Felice Le Monnier, 1965), 122–48. In this connection, see also Nardi, "I corsi manoscritti di lezioni e il ritratto di Pietro Pomponazzi" and "Corsi inediti di lezioni di Pietro Pomponazzi," in ibid., 3–87.

[94] See Felice Momigliano, *Paolo Veneto e le correnti del pensiero religioso e filosofico nel suo tempo* (Udine: Tipografia Gio. Batt. Doretti, 1907); Bruno Nardi, "Paolo Veneto e l'averroismo padovano," in Nardi, *Saggi sull'aristotelismo padovano*, 75–93; Francis Ruello, "Paul de Venise: Théologien 'Averroiste?'" in *Multiple Averroès*, 257–72; and Alessandro D. Conti, *Esistenza e verità: Forme e strutture del reale in Paolo Veneto e nel pensiero filosofico del tardo Medioevo* (Rome: Istituto storico italiano per il Medioevo, 1996), along with Alan R. Perreiah, *Paul of Venice: A Bibliographical Guide* (Bowling Green, OH: Philosophy Documentation Center, 1986); then, see A. D. Sartori, "Gaetano de'Thiene, filosofo averroista nello Studio di Padova," *Atti della Società italiana per il progresso delle scienze, Riunione* 26 (Venice, 1937) III (1938): 340–70, and Silvestro da Valsanzibio, *Vita e dottrina di Gaetano di Thiene, filosofo dello studio di Padova, 1387–1465*, second edition (Padua: Studio filosofico dei FF. MM. Cappuccini, 1949); and consider Pietro Ragnisco, *Nicoletto Vernia: Studi storici sulla filosofia Padovana nella seconda metà del secolo decimoquinto* (Venice: Tipografia Antonelli, 1891); Bruno Nardi

propagated.[95] He did not have to read Gaspar Contarini to know that in the 1490s, when that future cardinal was a student in Padua, then "the most celebrated institution of higher learning (*gymnasium*) in all of Italy, the name and authority of Averroës the Commentator held the greatest sway (*plurimum poterat*), and all expressed their assent to the positions of this author and received them as oracles of a sort."[96]

Above all else, Campanella understood a brute fact forgotten by subsequent generations – that, given the intellectual fashions of the age, no well-informed humanist resident in one of the communes of northern Italy in this period could have escaped familiarity with the rough outlines of what the students of Florence had so tellingly called the *doctrina communis philosophorum* – and to the actual impact on Machiavelli of this doctrine, this Calabrian friar was admirably sensitive as well.[97] He was alert to the manner in which the Florentine had made use of the embryonic sociology of religion articulated by the Averroist Aristotelians of Padua,[98] and he noticed the shocking fashion in which the author of *The Prince* had imitated Alfarabi, Avicenna, Averroës, and Maimonides in blurring the distinction between the sacred and the secular in such a way as to indicate his awareness that in modern times the political community is constituted by religion, while its ruling order is to a considerable degree drawn from the intelligentsia responsible for propagating the doctrine authorized.[99] Campanella was even cognizant of the fact that Machiavelli and the Epicureans shared a great deal.[100]

"La miscredenza e il carattere morale di Nicoletto Vernia," *Giornale critico della filosofia italiana* 30:1 (January–March 1951): 103–18, and "Ancora qualche notizia e aneddoto su Nicoletto Vernia," *Giornale critico della filosofia italiana* 34: 4 (October–December 1955): 496–503, which are reprinted in Nardi, *Saggi sull'aristotelismo padovano*, 95–126; Eckhard Kessler, "Nicoletto Vernia oder die Rettung eines Averroisten," in *Averroismus im Mittelalter und in der Renaissance*, 269–90; and Edward P. Mahoney, *Two Aristotelians of the Italian Renaissance: Nicoletto Vernia and Augostino Nifo* (Aldershot, UK: Ashgate, 2000). Note, in this connection, John Monfasani, "Aristotelians, Platonists, and the Missing Ockhamists: Philosophical Liberty in Pre-Reformation Italy," *Renaissance Quarterly* 46:2 (Summer 1993): 247–76.

95 In this connection, see Erminio Troilo, *Averroism e aristotelismo padovano* (Padua: A. Milani, 1939), and Antonino Poppi, *Introduzione all'aristotelismo padovano* (Padua: Antenore, 1991). Note also John Herman Randall, Jr., *The School of Padua and the Emergence of Modern Science* (Padua: Antenore, 1961).

96 See Gaspar Cardinal Contarini, *De immortalitate animae* I (1518), in *Gasparis Contareni Cardinalis opera*, ed. Alvise Contareni (Paris: Sebastianum Niuellium, 1571), 179.

97 Note Campanella, *Ateismo trionfato*, 5–7, 11–12, 14–27, 125–31, 134, 152–55, 158–60, 165–66, 170 (with n. 16), 181–94, 223–24, and *De Gentilismo non retinendo* (Paris: Toussaint du Bray, 1636), 6–9, 16–17, 20–22, 40, 45–48, 50, as well as the considerable material along these lines that was added to the Latin translation of the former work: see, for example, *Atheismus Triumphatus* (1631), Praef., 5–15, 47–48, 154, 158–59, and *Atheismus Triumphatus* (1636), Praef., 7–12, 68–70, 216, 222.

98 See Machiavelli, *Discorsi* 1.10–15, and *L'Asino* 5.106–27, in *Opere*, 91–99, 967; note Headley, *Tommaso Campanella and the Transformation of the World*, 185–86; and consider the material collected in note 148, this chapter. Moreover, like the Averroists, Machiavelli was willing, as we shall soon see, to suppose the universe eternal and religions transitory.

99 See Machiavelli, *Il principe* 6, 11, in *Opere*, 264–65, 273–74, which I discuss later in this chapter.

100 See Campanella, *Ateismo trionfato*, 27, 40, 224; *Atheismus Triumphatus* (1631), 47, 159; *Atheismus Triumphatus* (1636), 68, 222; and *De gentilismo non retinendo*, 7–8, 47–48.

But if the renegade Dominican was astute and generally well informed, if he was sensitive to context and exceedingly alert, if he was intrepid and remarkably clever, in one particular he fell dismally short. In assessing Machiavelli's debt to Aristotle and to his admirers among the Arab *falāsifa*, Campanella failed to reflect on the significance of the Florentine's repudiation of moral virtue,[101] and for this reason he neglected to comment on the manner in which Renaissance Averroism was but a forerunner, paving the way for the absorption of a far more radical political doctrine – built upon an emphatic rejection of Aristotelian cosmology,[102] and constructed upon a no less firm repudiation of the central political premise embraced by Averroës. For Epicurus was disdainful of the emphasis that Plato, Aristotle, and their disciples placed on political prudence. As a consequence, Epicureans refused to contemplate the notion that philosophers have an interest in seeing that the multitude is provided with a moral education reinforced by fear of punishment in the afterlife, and they were open and public in their hostility to religion as such.[103] When Machiavelli reworked the argument of Averroës, contending that the religion of ancient Rome was politically salutary and asserting that Christianity was anything but,[104] Campanella failed to comment on the Florentine's reversal of the Averroist perspective regarding the salutary effects attendant on its doctrine of the afterlife. And when, thereafter, Machiavelli abruptly reversed course, abandoned his defense of paganism, and intimated that religion's contribution to political well-being is, at best, inconsequential,[105] the renegade Dominican seems not to have noticed at all, for he failed to recognize that Averroism was for Machiavelli what Epicureanism had been – a point of departure and nothing more.

The Ecclesiastical Principality

What bothered Machiavelli was what had most concerned Alfarabi, Avicenna, Averroës, and Maimonides: the cultural hegemony of revealed religion. Of

---

[101] Consider Machiavelli, *Il principe* 15–18, in *Opere*, 280–84, in light of the Preface to Part One, this volume.

[102] See Leo Strauss, *Thoughts on Machiavelli* (Glencoe, IL: Free Press, 1958), 17–19, 47–48, 201–23.

[103] Campanella's failure to comment on this divide may be due to the fact that he thought the Epicureans for all practical purposes indistinguishable from the peripatetics: see Campanella, *L'ateismo trionfato*, 114, *Atheismus Triumphatus* (1631), Praef., and *Atheismus Triumphatus* (1636), Praef. Though unjustified (especially with regard to political philosophy), this presumption is not entirely without grounds: consider Christopher A. Colmo, *Breaking with Athens: Alfarabi as Founder* (Lanham, MD: Lexington Books, 2005), in conjunction with Shlomo Pines, "La Philosophie dans l'économie du genre humain selon Averroès," 189–207, which is reprinted in *The Collected Works of Shlomo Pines*, III 357–75, which should be read in light of Pines, "The Limitations of Human Knowledge According to al-Farabi, ibn Bajja, and Maimonides," I 82–109, which is reprinted in *Maimonides*, 91–121, and in *The Collected Works of Shlomo Pines*, V 404–31, and Shlomo Pines, "Les Limites de la métaphysique selon al-Fārābī, Ibn Bājja, et Maïmonide: Sources et anthithèses de ces doctrines chez Alexandre d'Aphrodise et chez Themistius," *Sprache und Erkenntnis im Mittelalter*, ed. Jan B. Beckmann et al. (Berlin: Walter de Gruyter, 1981), I 211–25, which is reprinted in *The Collected Works of Shlomo Pines*, V 432–46.

[104] Consider Machiavelli, *Discorsi* 1.10–15, in *Opere*, 91–99, in light of *Discorsi* 2.2.2, in *Opere*, 149–50.

[105] See Machiavelli, *Discorsi* 1.19, in *Opere*, 104–5.

course, Christianity is not, like Islam, a religion of holy law; and, within Christendom, jurisprudence and religious jurists did not loom large. Understandably, then, Machiavelli had little, if anything, to say in this regard, but he did share the profound discomfort evidenced by his predecessors regarding the authority that revealed religion conferred on the religious apologists and dialectical theologians whom the Arabs called *mutakallimūn* and whom Averroës' early translators referred to in their rendering of one memorable passage as the *Loquentes trium legum, quae hodie quidem sunt*.[106] He differed from the *falāsifa* only in doubting that revealed religion was nonetheless a political good. In every one of his principal works, the Florentine decries, in one fashion or another, what he takes to be the damage done Christendom by the Christian faith.

Jean-Jacques Rousseau, who shared Machiavelli's opinion,[107] knew what he was talking about when he wrote of *The Prince*, "The Court of Rome has banned this book with great severity, and I can easily believe that it would; in it he depicts that Court with the greatest clarity."[108] In a crucial chapter in that work, which is sometimes dismissed and even more often ignored,[109] Machiavelli does just that, singling out for consideration ecclesiastical principalities, which are, we are soon made to see, a mystery quite deep, a puzzle profound. "With regard to these," Machiavelli observes,

all the difficulties arise before one takes possession, since they are acquired either through virtue or through fortune and maintained without either, for they are sustained by orders that have become ancient by means of religion – which have been so powerful and of such a quality that they hold their princes in state no matter how they proceed and no matter how they live. These alone possess states and do not defend them, and they possess subjects and do not them govern – and the states, though undefended, are not taken away, and the subjects, though ungoverned, do not care. Neither do they think of turning against (*alienarsi*) their princes nor are they able to do so. Only, then, these principalities are secure and happy (*felici*).

---

[106] See Comment XII.18 on Aristotle's *Metaphysics* XII.3 (1070a27–30), in *Aristotelis Stagiritae omnia quae extant opera... Averrois Cordubensis in ea opera omnes qui ad nos pervenere commentarii*, VIII 142vb–143vb.

[107] See Jean-Jacques Rousseau, *Du Contrat social; ou, Principes du droit politique* 4.8, in *Œuvres complètes de Jean-Jacques Rousseau*, ed. Bernard Gagnebin and Marcel Raymond (Paris: Bibliothèque de la Pléiade, 1959–1995), III 460–69.

[108] This remark is taken from a note found in manuscript, which was added in 1782 to the posthumous edition of *Du Contrat social; ou, Principes du droit politique* 3.6. See *Œuvres complètes de Jean-Jacques Rousseau*, III 1480.

[109] Cf., for example, Sheldon S. Wolin, "Machiavelli: Politics and the Economy of Violence," in Wolin, *Politics and Vision: Continuity and Innovation in Western Political Thought*, second edition (Princeton, NJ: Princeton University Press, 2004), 173–213 (at 198–99), who reads Machiavelli as contending "that ecclesiastical governments were irrelevant to the proper concerns" of his new political science and as thinking that they were "not politic enough to warrant the attention of political thought," and Quentin Skinner, *Machiavelli* (New York: Hill and Wang, 1981), who mentions Machiavelli's discussion of the ecclesiastical polity not at all. There are, of course, scholars who have attended to the chapter: see, for example, Strauss, *Thoughts on Machiavelli*, 32 (with n. 34), and Leo Paul de Alvarez, *The Machiavellian Enterprise: A Commentary on The Prince* (Dekalb: Northern Illinois University Press, 1999), 10–11, 48–52.

To his readers' dismay, after alerting them to the existence and significance of this puzzle, Machiavelli ostentatiously refuses further guidance. "But since," he writes, "these principalities are kept upright by superior cause, which the human mind cannot grasp, I will leave off speaking of them; and since they are exalted and maintained by God, to discourse on them would be the office of a man both presumptuous and rash."[110]

Of course, immediately thereafter, Machiavelli proceeds – by discoursing on the temporal power exercised in Italy by the church and its *mutakallimūn* – to make a mockery of this pious disclaimer and to flaunt the presumption and the recklessness that conferred on his book so great a *succès de scandale*, for it was his principle that "it is good to reason concerning everything." When confronted with the claims of tradition and faith, Machiavelli may write that "one should not reason" about a given subject, such as the accomplishments of Moses in his guise as a "new prince" – but in the aftermath he always does so, for his ultimate posture is one of resolute defiance. "I do not," he asserts, "judge it a defect to defend any opinion with reasons nor shall I ever judge it so" – and in this spirit he renounces all appeal to "either authority or force."[111] It is quite easy to see why later advocates of Enlightenment came to regard him as a forebear, for when Christopher Marlowe put on the English stage his *Machevill* and had him say, "I count Religion but a childish Toy,/And hold there is no sinne but Ignorance," he hit the nail on the head.[112]

In discussing the role played in Italy by the Papacy, however, Machiavelli does nothing to throw further light on the character of the ecclesiastical principality as such. Instead, after inducing his readers to think of the church as a principality that one could acquire and even lose, and after suggesting to them that no other principalities can be as happy and secure, he leaves them in the lurch.

The Florentine's silence in this regard is rendered all the more perplexing by the fact that, in an earlier chapter of *The Prince* dedicated to the study of "new principalities that are acquired through one's own arms and virtue," he had not only described "new princes" who establish "new orders and modes (*nuovi ordini e modi*)" in the familiar Averroist fashion as "prophets." He had also asserted that all of "the armed prophets were victorious" while all "the unarmed prophets came to ruin." If political "innovators" of this sort are to succeed in the face of "the incredulity of men, who do not, in truth, believe in new things," he had contended, if they are to come to grips with the ineluctable fact that their own partisans tend to be "lukewarm (*tepidi*)," they must take as a model Moses, Cyrus, Theseus, Romulus, and the like, rather than Girolamo Savonarola. After all, Machiavelli had explained, "the nature of peoples is changeable (*varia*)," and though they may be "easy to persuade," it is "difficult

---

[110] See Machiavelli, *Il principe* 11, in *Opere*, 273–74. In this connection, note *Istorie fiorentine* 8.17, in *Opere*, 829.

[111] Consider Machiavelli, *Il principe* 6 and 11, in *Opere*, 264–65, 274, in light of *Discorsi* 1.18.1, 58.1, in *Opere*, 102, 140.

[112] See Christopher Marlow, *The Jew of Malta* Prologue 5–15, in *The Complete Works of Christopher Marlow*, ed. Fredson Bowers (Cambridge, UK: Cambridge University Press, 1973), I 263, which should be read in light of David Riggs, *The World of Christopher Marlowe* (New York: Henry Holt, 2004).

to hold them firm in that persuasion – so that things ought to be ordered in such a manner that, when they no longer believe, one can make them believe through force."[113]

How, then, the attentive reader is induced to ask, did Jesus Christ, a prophet unarmed if ever there was one, manage to found a principality that was "so powerful and of such a quality" that it could hold its "princes in state no matter how they proceed and no matter how they live?" How, without the benefit of force, was the Prince of Peace able to conquer the known world? How did he overcome "the incredulity of men" and their "tendency to be lukewarm (*tepidezza*)"? How did he "make them believe"? Or did he possess and deploy arms of a new and unprecedented kind? Did Muhammad, the armed prophet par excellence, in any way outdo Christ? Did the founder of Islam not have to acquire arms of this new sort as well? And could another "new prince" come to possess such arms in his wake?

Such were the questions elicited from Girolamo Cardano, from Tommaso Campanella, from Giulio Cesare Vanini, and from other early readers of *The Prince* by its canny author.[114] As a writer, Niccolò Machiavelli aimed at sparking the curiosity of those who came across his book and at inviting their interest. In consequence, he seems rarely to have done much to satisfy the appetite he so powerfully whetted. It was all a great tease.

Satisfied and Stupefied

Or so it must seem – to the unsuspecting glance. For, later in the book, Machiavelli will convey an additional piece of information – that "the Christian pontificate" is, in one apparently crucial particular, similar to the polity established in Mameluk Egypt, for neither can be called "an hereditary or a new principality." After all, the sons of the old prince are not his heirs. Instead, "the one who is elected to that rank by those who have the authority" succeeds to the office, and though "the prince is new, the orders of that state are old and ordered to receive him as if he were their hereditary lord."[115]

What seems like an aside may be of much greater significance, for it comes at the end of a lengthy discussion in which Machiavelli singles out late imperial Rome, Ottoman Turkey, and Mameluk Egypt for comparison, and one of the features these principalities evidently have in common is the absence of a reliable hereditary succession. Moreover, closely connected with this feature is the new prince's dependence on those who have conferred on him the office. Unlike other dominions, republics and principalities alike, these three hybrid polities found their power neither on the *popolo* nor on the *grandi*. Nor do they strike a balance between the two. Each depends, instead, on a third "humor," a standing, professional army – analogous to the Muslim jurists and *mutakallimūn*

---

[113] Cf. Machiavelli, *Il principe* 6, in *Opere*, 264–65, with Machiavelli, *Discorsi* I Proemio, in *Opere*, 76.
[114] See Giuliano Procacci, "Machiavelli e Cardano," in *Studi sulla fortuna del Machiavelli*, 77–106 (esp. 82–83).
[115] See Machiavelli, *Il principe* 19, in *Opere*, 288–89.

and the clergy deployed by the Christian church – and these Roman emperors, Turkish caliphs, and Mameluk sultans tend to be "extremely cruel and rapacious," for, to survive, they must "satisfy the soldiers" and they cannot do so if they refrain from "any species of injury that they can commit against the peoples" they rule.[116]

Of course, the principality that existed in late imperial Rome was in no way happy and secure. Most of its rulers came to "a sad, bad end," as Machiavelli readily concedes. In fact, in the period singled out for consideration, the only emperor to die in his bed was Septimius Severus, who is elsewhere described as a "villain (*scelerato*)" endowed with "fortune and *virtù* on a very grand scale." In him, we are told, "there was so much virtue" that "at all times" he was "able to reign happily (*felicemente*)." Indeed, "from the perspective of the soldiers and the peoples" whom this man ruled, he was "so admirable" that, throughout his reign, "the latter remained in a certain fashion astonished and stupefied (*stupidi*) while these others were reverent (*reverenti*) and satisfied (*satisfatti*)."[117]

Elsewhere, in one of the central chapters of his *Discourses on Livy*, Machiavelli enables us to see that Severus is merely applying to his army the technique that had enabled republican Rome to subjugate the world. "Government (*uno governo*)," he explains, "is nothing other than laying hold of subjects in such a way that they are unable to offend you or [at least] should not do so: this is accomplished either by completely securing yourself against them, depriving them in every way of the capacity to harm you, or by benefiting them in such a way that it would not be reasonable that they should desire a change of fortune." To illustrate what he means, Machiavelli abbreviates a speech that Livy puts in the mouth of Marcus Furius Camillus, who urges that the Latins just vanquished be admitted to Roman citizenship forthwith. Such an expedient "for an augmentation of Rome" is sanctioned, he insists, "by the example of your ancestors: matter is ready to hand for growth by way of the greatest glory." "Therefore," he admonishes the Senate, "it is incumbent on you to take possession of the spirits of these by means of punishment or benefaction while they are stupefied with apprehension (*dum expectatione stupent*)." Such, we are led to believe, was the habitual policy of the Romans, who persistently avoided "the middle way."[118]

That the rulers of Western Christendom's ecclesiastical polity were unlike Marcus Furius Camillus and Septimius Severus – that ordinarily they lacked princely *virtù* and that they had no need for fortune – readers of *The Prince* are told early on. Somehow, in the absence of both, they must nonetheless have managed to take possession of the spirits of the converts whom they absorbed within their community. Somehow they must have managed to keep the people

---

[116] Consider Machiavelli, *Il principe* 19, in light of 9, in *Opere*, 271–72, 284–89; see *Discorsi* 1.2–8, in *Opere*, 78–90, and *Istorie fiorentine* 3.1, 4.1, in *Opere*, 690–91, 715–16; and consider *Discorsi* 3.24 and AG 1.64–93, 243–58, in *Opere*, 231, 306–8, 315–16.

[117] Consider Machiavelli, *Il principe* 19, in *Opere*, 284–89, in light of *Discorsi* 1.10.4, in *Opere*, 92.

[118] Consider Machiavelli, *Discorsi* 2.23, in *Opere*, 179–80, in light of Livy 8.11–14.

astonished and stupefied while rendering their clerical army, the shock troops of the Church Militant, Christianity's *mutakallimūn*, not just satisfied but reverent as well. Otherwise, it is hard to see how their principality can have been both happy and secure.

It is, of course, easy to see how someone of Machiavelli's disposition might suppose that the wealth and honors extracted by the church from the people would secure the loyalty of the clergy. After all, when he denounces as a threat to republics and to the political life (*vivere politico*) those whom he calls gentlemen (*gentiluomini*), when he speaks of this class of men as "entirely hostile to every species of civility (*ogni civilità*)," when he describes as "pernicious in every republic and every province" those "who live in idleness (*oziosi*) and abundance on the returns from their possessions, without having any care either for cultivation or for some other labor necessary to life," and when he contends that even "more pernicious are those who, apart from the riches (*fortune*) already mentioned, command from castles and have subjects who are obedient to them," Machiavelli has in mind a class much larger than the gentry and nobility of Europe, for he specifies that idlers of this sort fill not only the kingdom of Naples, the Romagna, and Lombardy, but also "the town (*Terra*) of Rome."[119]

It is, however, a bit more difficult to imagine what it was that left ordinary people so astonished and so stupefied that they were content to be subjected to men who bothered not at all with their governance – although, in an earlier chapter, Machiavelli does, in fact, proffer a clue. There, he tells the story of Remirro de Orco, "a man cruel and expeditious," whom Cesare Borgia sent to Romagna to "reduce" that disordered province to a condition "peaceful and united." When the dreadful deed was done, and "so excessive an authority" was no longer "necessary," Borgia, suspecting that this authority would become "odious," set up a court for the province, presided over by an able man. Then, "to purge the spirits of the peoples and secure them wholly for himself," he arranged for Remirro de Orco to be discovered "one morning in the piazza at Cesena in two pieces with a piece of wood and a bloody knife by his side." "The ferocity of this spectacle," we are told, "left these peoples at once satisfied and stupefied (*satisfatti e stupidi*)."[120]

Machiavelli was acutely sensitive to the impact that spectacles of this sort have on the *popolo*. It is no accident that, in one of the central chapters of the central book of his *Discourses on Livy*, he discusses Titus Manlius Torquatus' execution of his own son and cites the practice of *devotio* – by which Publius Decius Mus and his like-named son sought expiation, with the sacrifice of their own lives, for any offenses that their compatriots may have committed against the Roman gods. Nor is it fortuitous that the Florentine repeatedly returns to these events – in the chapter he devotes to the need for a frequent return to first

[119] See Machiavelli, *Discorsi* 1.55.3–5, in *Opere*, 137–39. Note, in this connection, *Istorie fiorentine* 5.27, in *Opere*, 757–58, and *Discursus florentinarum rerum post mortem iunioris Laurentii Medices*, in Machiavelli, *Opere*, 26–27.

[120] See Machiavelli, *Il principe* 7, in *Opere*, 267.

principles, and elsewhere as well.[121] If Machiavelli feels no need to mention the crucifixion and explain its significance for the peculiar political psychology regnant among both citizens and subjects in the modern age, if he is similarly silent on the role played by martyrdom in propagating Christianity and in renewing and sustaining its moral and political authority, it is because, in these passages, he has in other ways made it abundantly clear that, if one's purpose is to astonish and stupefy, to satisfy and elicit reverence, there is no spectacle even remotely as effective as the deliberate sacrifice of a human life. It is this that in large part explains the astonishing victory of a prophet unarmed.

The Subtle Art of Suggestion

In antiquity, it was recognized that moral and political persuasion is not unlike seduction. Accordingly, it was one of the principles of ancient rhetoric that one must by indirection make one's listener a participant in the process of achieving conviction. As Theophrastus put it,

It is not necessary to speak at length and with precision on everything, but some things should be left also for the listener – to be understood and sorted out by himself – so that, in coming to understand that which has been left by you for him, he will become not just your listener but also your witness, and a witness quite well disposed as well. For he will think himself a man of understanding because you have afforded him an occasion for showing his capacity for understanding. By the same token, whoever tells his listener everything accuses him of being mindless (*anóetos*).[122]

Machiavelli was steeped in classical rhetoric; he appreciated the force of Theophrastus' argument, and in its light he devised the strategy that he persistently and consciously pursued. He whets the appetite at every opportunity, and he always leaves his reader wanting more.

Nowhere is this more evident than in the Florentine's treatment of Giovampagolo Baglioni in his *Discourses on Livy*. In 1505, when Pope Julius II set off to wrest Bologna from the Bentivogli, the pontiff paused at Perugia en route for the purpose of ousting from that city the "tyrant" Baglioni; and driven by "fury" as was his wont, he entered the city "unarmed." According to Machiavelli, who was present in the papal entourage, "the prudent men" accompanying Julius were surprised not only by "the recklessness (*temerità*) of the pope" but even more so by "the cravenness (*viltà*) of Giovampagolo." These prudent men were at a loss as to why the latter had not, to his perpetual fame, crushed his enemy at one stroke and enriched himself with booty, since with the pope were all the cardinals with all their delights. Nor were these observers able to believe that Giovampagolo had held himself back out of goodness or because conscience acted as a restraint. For into the heart of a such a ruffian (*uomo facinosoro*), who had taken for himself his own sister, who had put to death his cousins

---

[121] Note Livy 8.7, 9–10, 10.26–29; consider Machiavelli, *Discorsi* 2.16.1, 3.22, 34.2, 45, in light of 3.1 as a whole, in *Opere*, 166, 194–97, 228–30, 241–42, 252, and see *PW*, V:1 277–80 (s.v. *devotio*).

[122] Theophr. F696 (Fortenbaugh).

and nephews in order to reign, no pious respect (*pietoso rispetto*) could have descended. But they concluded that his failure to act arose from the fact that men do not know how to be honorably wicked or perfectly good; and when malice has in itself greatness (*grandezza*) or is in any part generous, men do not know how to enter into it.

At the time, Machiavelli was evidently appalled, and he wants his readers to share in his dismay. After all, this Giovampagolo was a man "who did not think being incestuous or a public parricide a matter of concern." And, to make matters worse, "he had just occasion (*occasione*) to accomplish an enterprise (*impresa*) where everyone would have admired his spirit, an enterprise that would have left an eternal memory, for he would have been the first to show the prelates how little esteemed are those who live and reign as they do, and he would have accomplished something whose greatness would have overcome every disgrace (*infamia*), every danger that could have been its result." Yet, when confronted with an authority that derived from the sacrifice of Christ, Giovampagolo was no less astonished and no less stupefied than those evidently restrained by "pious respect." When placed in a position to seize an *occasione* wondrous beyond most men's wildest dreams, "he did not know how or, to say it better, he did not dare."[123]

That with practice and effort one could become "honorably wicked" and learn "to dare" Machiavelli had not the slightest doubt. In his *Florentine Histories*, he speaks in passing of one Stefano Porcari, "a Roman citizen, noble by blood and education (*dottrina*) but much more so by excellence in spirit," who "desired, according to the custom of men with an appetite for glory, to do, or at least attempt, something worthy of memory," and who tried "to see whether he could pull his fatherland from the hands of prelates and restore it to its ancient way of life (*ridurla nello antico vivere*)." Offended by "the wicked customs of the prelates," encouraged by "the discontent of the barons and the Roman people," inspired by a canzone of Petrarch prophesying achievements on the part of a Roman knight, and persuaded of his own superiority "to every other Roman in eloquence, education, favor (*grazia*), and friends," Porcari resolved to be "the executor of so glorious an enterprise (*impresa*)" in the hope that he would be remembered as "the new founder and second father" of Rome. But if his "intention" was worthy of praise, Machiavelli avers, if Rome really does require a "new founder and second father," Porcari's "judgment" nonetheless deserved blame "since enterprises like his (*simili imprese*) – if they have in themselves, in thinking of them, any shadow of glory – have in the execution almost always a certitude of harm (*certissimo danno*)." On the eve of the coup d'état they planned, Porcari and his friends were arrested, and soon thereafter

---

[123] Consider Machiavelli, *Discorsi* 1.27, in *Opere*, 109–10, in light of *Discorsi* 1.26, 30.1, in *Opere*, 109, 112–13, and see *AG* 1.50–62, in *Opere*, 305–6. At the end of *Il principe* 7, in *Opere*, 268, Machavelli makes a cryptic statement in which he seems to intimate that Cesare Borgia could and perhaps should have "prevented anyone from becoming Pope." See John T. Scott and Vickie B. Sullivan, "Patricide and the Plot of *The Prince*: Cesare Borgia and Machiavelli's Italy," *American Political Science Review* 88:4 (December 1994): 887–900.

they lost their lives.[124] This transpired, we are forced to conclude, not because Stefano Porcari failed to dare but simply because he did not know how.

Had Machiavelli not been steeped in classical rhetoric, in discussing these two cases, he might have rehearsed Lucretius' notorious analysis of the malign influence exercised over most men by powerful fears, religious in character, generated by their irrational anxiety with regard to death,[125] and he might have interpreted Giovampagolo Baglioni's loss of nerve and Stefano Porcari's resolute conduct variously – with an eye to the roots of religious awe, and to the latter's deployment of the antidote thereof. But from doing so the Florentine ostentatiously refrains. Instead, he illustrates by example the systematic exploitation of these fears in post-pagan times by princes of an entirely new species, who by this means "possess" states, which, "though undefended, are not taken away," and subjects, who, "though ungoverned, do not care," and he draws attention to a man who liberated himself from an intellectual captivity grounded in a reverence for Christ. His more astute readers he thereby invites to follow the path opened up by Alfarabi and the *falāsifa* by reflecting on the foundations of priestly hegemony. And he induces the same individuals to trace this peculiar species of exploitation to its ultimate source on their own hook. Lest, however, they fail to grasp the overall consequences of the cultural hegemony exercised by the ecclesiastical principality, these he spells out in fine detail.

Sinister Opinions, Sinister Decision

The Prince circulated in manuscript during Machiavelli's lifetime; his *Discourses on Livy* and *Florentine Histories* he left among his effects, to be published after his death.[126] His dialogue, *Of the Art of War*, was the only substantial work in prose that he published in his own lifetime. Not surprisingly, in it, Machiavelli was cautious to a greater degree than elsewhere.[127] In the preface, for example, writing in his own name, Machiavelli laments the discrepancy that exists between "the civil" and "the military life." That which "of necessity the ancient orders" brought together, he explains, modern orders persistently put asunder, and "sinister opinions (*sinistre opinioni*)" have arisen "which cause men to hate the military profession (*la milizia*) and to flee conversation with those engaged in it." If Machiavelli nonetheless writes "concerning the art of war (*della arte della guerra*)," he explains, it is "for the satisfaction of those

---

[124] See Machiavelli, *Istorie fiorentine* 6.29, in *Opere*, 785–86. Note the manner in which, upon close inspection, the high-minded distinction that Machiavelli draws between destroyers and founders dissolves: see *Discorsi* 1.10.1, in *Opere*, 91–92.

[125] See Lucr. 1.62–158, 2.1–61, 3.1–93, 830–1094, 4.1–25, 5.1194–1240.

[126] For the pre-publication and publication history of Machiavelli's works, see Adolph Gerber, *Niccolò Machiavelli: Die Handschriften, Ausgaben und Übersetzungen seiner Werke im 16. und 17. Jahrhundert* (Turin: Bottega d'Erasmo, 1962).

[127] See Harvey C. Mansfield, "An Introduction to Machiavelli's *Art of War*," in Mansfield, *Machiavelli's Virtue* (Chicago: University of Chicago Press, 1996), 191–218, and Christopher Lynch, "Introduction" and "Intepretive Essay," in Niccolò Machiavelli, *Art of War*, ed. and tr. Christopher Lynch (Chicago: University of Chicago Press, 2003), xiii–xxxiv, 179–226.

who are lovers of the ancient actions" and because he thinks it "not impossible to return the military profession (*ridurre*) to the ancient modes and give to it something of the form of *virtù* past." But the Florentine does not specify the character of the "sinister opinions" that stand in his way. Nor does he trace them to their source. And he does not tell us whether these opinions are responsible for the fact that, in his day, the "customs" of those who pursue "the civil life" are "effeminate."[128] Once again he leaves his readers in the lurch.

Only later, near the end of the second book, are we given a clue. There Machiavelli's protagonist, the mercenary captain Fabrizio Colonna, tries to explain why the martial *virtù* once possessed by the Romans was "not renewed" after the fall of imperial Rome. This he traces in part to the natural difficulty involved in restoring "orders when they have been spoiled." Then he mentions a second, no less salient, cause: "the fact that the mode of living today, as a consequence of the Christian religion, does not impose the necessity for self-defense that existed in ancient times." In antiquity, he explains,

men conquered in war were either massacred or were consigned to perpetual enslavement where they led their lives in misery. Then, the towns conquered were either destroyed or the inhabitants were driven out, their goods seized; and, after being sent out, they were dispersed throughout the world. And so those overcome in war suffered every last misery. Frightened at this prospect, men kept military training alive and honored those who were excellent in it. But today this fear is for the most part lost. Of the conquered, few are massacred; none are held for long in prison since they are easily freed. Cities, even if they have rebelled a thousand times, are not eliminated; men are left with their goods so that most of the time what is feared is a ransom. In consequence, men do not want to subject themselves to military orders.[129]

What is represented in the dialogue as ancient virtue can be instilled if and only if there is a profound change in "today's mode of living," and this is not likely to occur, we are led to conclude, unless "sinister opinions" cease to hold sway and the Christian religion is radically reinterpreted or simply replaced.

Machiavelli addresses the same theme in his *Florentine Histories*, which was written on commission from Pope Leo X (Giovanni de' Medici) on the recommendation of Giulio Cardinal de' Medici, who ascended himself to the papal throne as Pope Clement VII in 1523, two years before the work was completed. As one would then expect, in this book, Machiavelli was even more cautious than in his *Art of War*. In a letter penned to Francesco Guicciardini, he fretted that he might "offend too much either with enhancing or with diminishing things."[130] To his young friend Donato Giannotti, on more than one occasion, he remarked,

---

[128] Cf. Machiavelli, *AG* Proemio with *Discorsi* 2.2.2, in *Opere*, 149–50, 301–2. The phrase, "sinister opinions," appears only once in the *Discourses on Livy*: see Machiavelli, *Discorsi* 1.8.1, in *Opere*, 88. Consider the reference to "sinister modes" at *Istorie fiorentine* 4.3, in *Opere*, 716, in light of *Istorie fiorentine* 1.15, 2.2, in *Opere*, 643–44, 659–60.

[129] See Machiavelli, *AG* 2.305–9, in *Opere*, 332–33. Fabrizio's observations in this regard did not pass unnoticed: see Paul A. Rahe, "The Book That Never Was: Montesquieu's *Considerations on the Romans* in Historical Context," *History of Political Thought* 26:1 (Spring 2005): 43–89.

[130] See Letter to Francesco Guicciardini on 30 August 1524, in Machiavelli, *Opere*, 1212.

I cannot write this history from the time when Cosimo took the state until Lorenzo's death as I would write it if I were free from all hesitations (*da tutti i respetti*). The actions will be true, and I shall not omit anything; only I will not relate (*lascierò indrieto il discorrere*) the general causes (*le cause universali*) of things; for example, I will speak of the events that took place and the accidents that transpired when Cosimo took the state, but I will not relate (*lascierò indrieto il discorrere*) in what mode and by what means and trickery (*astutie*) one arrives at so great a height.

To see through the pretenses of Cosimo de' Medici, to unmask the man and discover the stratagems he devised, the book's reader must, he added, "note very well what I will make his adversaries say, because that which I will not want to say myself, as coming from me, I will make his adversaries say."[131] In dealing with other subjects, where it would have been highly imprudent to offend, Machiavelli also though it expedient to convey his meaning by methods no less indirect.

Early on, for example, when he depicts the misery that afflicted Italy and the other districts overrun by the barbarians at the time of the collapse of the Roman empire in the West, Machiavelli places great emphasis on the fact that a revolution followed – not just in government, but in laws, customs, mode of living, religion, language, and mode of dress, as well as in the names conferred on places and men. It was a time of profound uncertainty, for "the greater part" of those then alive knew not "to which God they should have recourse, and they died in a pitiful fashion, deprived of all help and of all hope." There is barely a hint in the passage to suggest regret on the author's part concerning the long-term consequences of the revolution itself, but it is telling, if one pauses to reflect on Machiavelli's predilections, that, after noting the new names conferred on rivers and districts, he remarks that "men also" have received new names: "from Caesars and Pompeys they have become Peters, Johns, and Matthews."[132]

There is, however, a later passage where Machiavelli is more forthcoming – but here, as at the beginning of the *Art of War*, he is cryptic in the extreme. In the first chapter of the fifth book of his *Florentine Histories*, Machiavelli pauses, in the manner of the *falāsifa*, to contemplate the strange course history took at the end of classical antiquity. "Usually," he writes,

most of the time, in the variations they undergo, provinces move from order to disorder and then cross over again from disorder to order, for nature does not allow the things of the world (*le mondane cose*) to come to a halt. When they arrive at their ultimate perfection, not having anywhere to climb, it comes about that they descend; and similarly, when they have descended and through disorders reached the ultimate debasement (*bassezza*), of necessity, being unable to descend further, it comes about that they climb. And so always from good they descend to bad and from bad they climb to good. For *virtù* gives birth to quiet, quiet to idleness (*ozio*), idleness to disorder, disorder to ruin; and similarly from ruin is born order, from order *virtù*, from this glory and good fortune.

---

[131] See Letter from Donato Giannotti to Antonio Michieli on 30 June 1533, in Luigi. A. Ferrai, "Lettere inedite di Donato Giannotti," *Atti del R. Instituto Veneto di Scienze, Lettere ed Arti*, ser. 6, 3 (1884–85): 1567–89 (at 1582).
[132] See Machiavelli, *Istorie fiorentine* 1.5, in *Opere*, 637.

Usually, Machiavelli insists, history is in this fashion cyclical – usually, but not always. It can, in fact, happen that men do not "become wise from the thrashings" to which they have been subjected. It can happen, he concedes, that they do not, "as has been suggested, return to order" – when, for example, "they are left suffocated by an extraordinary force (*una forza estraordinaria*)."

Such, Machiavelli asserts, has been the fate of Italy in the modern epoch. In antiquity, it was "at times happy, at times pitiful." But, thereafter, "on the Roman ruins nothing was built" that could bring Italy back from devastation "so that it might have been able to conduct itself (*operare*) in a glorious manner under a virtuous principality." There was sufficient *virtù* for the establishment of "new cities and new dominions (*imperii*)," to be sure, and these were able to liberate Italy from the barbarians and, for a time, sustain its defense. But, in the best of circumstances, he observes, there was still much amiss. "From the *virtù* of these new principalities" there did not emerge "times that were rendered quiet by a long peace." Nor did there emerge times "dangerous as a consequence of the bitterness of war." Italy knew neither: it hovered in between.

> For peace one cannot call a situation where the principalities with arms quite often assault one another; nor, again, can one call that war in which men are not butchered, cities are not sacked, principalities are not destroyed, for these wars eventuated in such weakness (*debolezza*) that they began in the absence of fear, were conducted without danger, and came to a conclusion without loss. In consequence, that *virtù*, which is usually snuffed out in other provinces through a long peace, was snuffed out in Italy by the baseness (*la viltà*) of these wars.... whence it will be seen how, in the end, the way was opened anew for barbarians and how Italy placed itself in servitude to them.

For centuries, then, Machiavelli asserts, history had stood more or less still: Italy had been "suffocated by an extraordinary force," and the results were clear for everyone to see.[133]

It no doubt takes imagination to recognize in the "extraordinary force" of the *Florentine Histories* the Christian faith – but, if one has read the *Art of War* with any care, it does not take a great deal.[134] Moreover, if one compares Machiavelli's *Prince* with his *Discourses on Livy* and then reads with even minimal care the narrative that Machiavelli provides in his *Florentine Histories*, one discovers that Italy is "enslaved and disgraced," divided and at odds with herself, vulnerable to barbarian invasion, and inclined to conduct war in a manner disgraceful and base largely, if not entirely because of its proximity to the papal court. If there are "frequent tumults and frequent changes" in Italy, Machiavelli observes, it is because it is the policy of the popes to "bring down" anyone in Italy whose "power has become great," and in the process of eliminating one threat, they nearly always inadvertently create another.[135] Moreover,

---

[133] See Machiavelli, *Istorie fiorentine* 5.1, in *Opere*, 738–39, which should be read in conjunction with *Discorsi* 2 Proemio, *Istorie fiorentine* 6.1, and *L'Asino* 5, in *Opere*, 144–46, 765–66, 967.

[134] Scholarly sophistication can, of course, be an insuperable obstacle to understanding: after noting Harvey C. Mansfield, Jr., "Party and Sect in Machiavelli's *Florentine Histories*," in *Machiavelli and the Nature of Political Thought*, ed. Martin Fleisher (Princeton, NJ: Princeton University Press, 1972), 209–66, which is reprinted in Mansfield, *Machiavelli's Virtue*, 137–75, consider Mark Phillips' deployment of his expertise in Renaissance historiography: see Phillips, "Commentary," in *Machiavelli and the Nature of Political Thought*, 267–75.

[135] See Machiavelli, *Istorie fiorentine* 2.10, in *Opere*, 665.

when Pepin, his son Charlemagne, and their successors in France, Germany, and Spain intervened in Italy, as from time to time they did, we are told that it was nearly always at the behest of a beleaguered or ambitious pope.[136]

The partisan divisions that afflict Italy have the same source. When Pope Gregory VII forced Henry IV, the Holy Roman Emperor, to kneel barefoot in the snow at Canossa begging forgiveness for his transgressions against the church, Machiavelli informs us, he sowed the "seeds" from which "the Guelf and Ghibelline humors" grew. As a consequence, he adds, when "Italy lacked barbarian inundations," she "has been torn apart by intestine wars."[137] And, of course, it was the Church that taught Italy's princes and citizens a fatal reliance on arms not their own – for, in its principled refusal to allow priests, prelates, and monks to take up arms, it set an example that no serious Christian could easily ignore.[138] A reliance on mercenaries was "the sinister decision (*partito sinistro*)," Machiavelli tells us in his *Art of War*, "that cut off the legs" of the Venetians and "prevented them from climbing to heaven," from "becoming more ample," and from achieving in the manner of the ancient Romans "a new monarchy of the world."[139] And this reliance goes a considerable distance toward explaining the vile fashion in which the Italians conducted war in Machiavelli's day, for mercenaries have a far greater interest in being paid and in preserving their lives than in risking death to achieve a victory that they will not themselves enjoy, and for this reason the mercenary captains in Italy came to an understanding with one another that enabled them to collect their salaries while minimizing their risks.[140] If Machiavelli persistently restrains himself, if he tantalizes his readers, if he never quite fully explains why "all the Christian armies" of his day can so "easily lose" and why "every middling *virtù* can take from them victory,"[141] it is because he is interested in addressing none but "the one who understands."[142]

The Honor of the World

In his *Discourses on Livy*, Machiavelli addresses the same set of issues, and though he is considerably less cautious therein, he is no less elusive and no

---

[136] See Machiavelli, *Discorsi* 1.12.2, *Istorie fiorentine* 1.9–11, 23, 25, in *Opere*, 95–96, 640–42, 648–50. Early on, this was a frequent occurrence: note *Istorie fiorentine* 1.9–30, in *Opere*, 640–53.

[137] See Machiavelli, *Istorie fiorentine* 1.15, in *Opere*, 643–44. Note also *Istorie fiorentine* 2.2, in *Opere*, 659–60, and consider what Machiavelli has in mind when he speaks of the "sinister modes (*sinistri modi*)" by which certain Florentine nobles renewed "the hatred" directed at "the generality (*lo universale*)" at *Istorie fiorentine* 4.3, in *Opere*, 716.

[138] Consider Machiavelli, *Il principe* 12–13, in *Opere*, 275–78, in light of *Il principe* 11 and *Istorie fiorentine* 1.39, in *Opere*, 273–74, 657–58.

[139] See Machiavelli, *AG* 1.172–83, in *Opere*, 312.

[140] Consider Machiavelli, *Istorie fiorentine* 5.1–2, 33–34, 6.1, in *Opere*, 738–40, 762–66, in light of *Discorsi* 1.43 and *Istorie fiorentine* 1.39, in *Opere*, 126, 657–58. Note *Discorsi* 2.18.3, *AG* 2.78, and *Istorie fiorentine* 1.34, in *Opere*, 172–73, 321, 655, and see *Discorsi* 2.30, in *Opere*, 190–91.

[141] See Machiavelli, *Discorsi* 2.16.2, in *Opere*, 167–68.

[142] See, for example, Machiavelli, *Discorsi* 2 Proemio 2–3 (esp. the last sentence), in *Opere*, 144–46, and then note *Il principe* 15, in *Opere*, 280, and see the Preface to Part One, this volume.

less coy. As "a form of education," Machiavelli explains, the Christian religion "makes us esteem less the honor of the world." In this regard, he goes on, it is inferior to that of the ancient Romans, which esteemed this honor "very much" and "lodged in it the greatest good." Thereby the latter religion rendered its adherents "in their actions more ferocious" than their modern counterparts.

> This can be assessed from a consideration of many of their institutions, starting with the magnificence of their sacrifices in contrast with the humility of ours, where there is a certain pomp more delicate than magnificent but no ferocious or spirited action. Here there was no lack of pomp or magnificence of ceremony, but there was added the action of the sacrifice, full of blood and ferocity, with a multitude of animals suffering butchery. This sight, being terrible, rendered men similar to itself. Besides, the ancient religion did not beatify men if they were not full of worldly glory, as were captains of armies and princes of republics. Our religion has conferred more glory on men who are humble and contemplative than on those who are active. It has then lodged the greatest good in humility, abjectness, and contempt for human things; the other lodged it in greatness of spirit, strength of body, and all other things suited to making men very strong. And if our religion requests that you have in yourself strength, it wishes you to be apt more to suffer than to do something strong. This mode of living, then, seems to have rendered the world weak and to have given it in prey to wicked men, who can manage it securely, seeing that the collectivity (*università*) of men, in order to go to paradise, think more of enduring their thrashings than of avenging them.

In concluding this diatribe against what an English republican admirer would later dub "Priest-craft," Machiavelli raises the possibility that Christianity only "appears" to have rendered "the world...effeminate and heaven disarmed," and he invites future theologians to recast it as a more worldly doctrine, suggesting, with malice aforethought, that the troubles which he identifies arise less from Christianity itself than "from the cowardice of those who have interpreted our religion according to leisure and idleness (*ozio*) and not according to *virtù*."[143]

This last passage has, on occasion, been taken as an indication that Machiavelli was a genuine believer profoundly upset – as many, in fact, were – at the moral corruption besetting the Renaissance church.[144] It is easy to see why. Machiavelli invites such a reading when he prefaces his critique of priestcraft with the remark that "our religion shows forth the truth and the true way."[145] Indeed, if one thought it possible for Christianity to dispense with the idea of divine Providence, with the notion of the fall, with an awareness of sin as sin, with a conviction of the possibility of repentance, and a faith in God's

---

[143] See Machiavelli, *Discorsi* 2.2.2, in *Opere*, 149–50; note James Harrington, *Pian Piano or, Intercourse between H. Ferne, Dr. in Divinity and J. Harrington, Esq. Upon Occasion of the Doctors Censure of the Common-wealth of Oceana* (London: Nath. Brook, 1656), 8, 60; and see Mark Goldie, "The Civil Religion of James Harrington," in *The Languages of Political Theory in Early-Modern Europe*, ed. Anthony Pagden (Cambridge, UK: Cambridge University Press, 1987), 197–222.

[144] See, for example, Sebastian de Grazia, *Machiavelli in Hell* (Princeton, NJ: Princeton University Press, 1989); Marcia L. Colish, "Republicanism, Religion, and Machiavelli's Savonarolan Moment," *Journal of the History of Ideas* 60:4 (October 1999): 597–616; and Carey J. Nederman, "Amazing Grace: Fortune, God, and Free Will in Machiavelli's Thought," ibid., 617–38.

[145] See Machiavelli, *Discorsi* 2.2.2, in *Opere*, 149.

provision of grace, one might take the emphasis that the Florentine places on human wickedness as a sign that he was a disciple of Augustine.[146]

After all, early in the *Discourses*, Machiavelli goes to considerable lengths to present himself as a friend and admirer of the Christian religion. After praising the religion of ancient Rome, he piously declaims, "If such religion (*la quale religione*) had been maintained by the princes of the Christian republic (*la republica cristiana*), as was, in fact, ordained by its giver, the Christian states and republics would be more united and much happier than they are." Here, however, he is being coy. For in the Italian his phrasing suggests what he knows to be false – that, as originally established by its founder, Christianity was of the same character (*la quale*) as the religion of pagan Rome – and, in the same chapter, with this preposterous claim as his premise, he gleefully invites his readers to join him in "conjecturing" with regard to the church's "decline"; he asks them to "consider its foundations and see how much present usage diverges from these"; and he expresses confidence that those who join in these ruminations "will judge, without a doubt, that either its ruin or its scourging is near."[147]

What Machiavelli means by "scourging" and what he intends by "ruin," he makes abundantly clear in a later chapter in which, in a fashion sanctioned by the Latin Averroists[148] and in language suggesting, as we have

---

[146] And, of course, some have done so: see, for example, T. S. Eliot, *For Lancelot Andrewes: Essays on Style and Order* (Garden City, NY: Doubleday, Doran, 1929), 62, 65; Giuseppe Prezzolini, "The Christian Roots of Machiavelli's Moral Pessimism," *Review of National Literatures* 1:1 (Spring 1970): 26–37; and Bjorn Quiller, "The Machiavellian Cosmos," *History of Political Thought* 17:3 (Autumn 1996): 326–53.

[147] See Machiavelli, *Discorsi* 1.12.1, in *Opere*, 95 – where the allusion to Christ is parenthetical and the antecedent to *la quale* must be the religion maintained by Camillus and the other "princes" of pagan Rome.

[148] See, in particular, the work by Machiavelli's older contemporary Pietro Pomponazzi, *De naturalium effectuum causis, sive de incantionibus* (1520) 10, 12, in Pomponazzi, *Opera*, ed. Guglielmo Grataroli (Basel: Henricpetrina, 1567), 110–208, 219–97 (esp. 282–97), who interprets the growth and degeneration of the various religions as a natural phenomenon reflecting the astral cycle and then suggests that Christianity's demise may be approaching. For a French translation of the pertinent passages, see Pietro Pomponazzi, *Les Causes des merveilles de la nature, ou, Les enchantements*, tr. Henry Busson (Paris: Rieder, 1930), 172–217, 222–63 (esp. 250–63). On this work, which circulated widely in manuscript before it was published, see Henry Busson, "Introduction," in ibid., 9–105; Giancarlo Zanier, *Ricerche sulla diffusione e fortuna del "De incantionibus" di Pietro Pomponazzi* (Florence: La Nuova Italia, 1975), and Eugenio Garin, *Astrology in the Renaissance: The Zodiac of Life*, tr. Carolyn Jackson, June Allen, and Clare Robertson (London: Arkana, 1990), 96–105 (with the attendant notes), who draws attention (ibid., 134, n. 13) to discrepancies between the manuscript, dated to 1520, in Arezzo (Biblioteca della Fraternità dei Laici, MS 390 [389]) and the printed version and complains about the "small but insidious interpolations of Gratarol." Pomponazzi was by no means the first in the Christian West to follow Ptolemy, the Arab Aristotelian Al-Kindi, and his disciple Abu Ma'shar in suggesting that some sort of natural process underlay the *legum mutatio*: note Richard Joseph Lemay, *Abu Ma'shar and Latin Aristotelianism in the Twelfth Century: The Recovery of Aristotle's Natural Philosophy through Arabic Astrology* (Beirut: American University of Beirut, 1962), which can now be read in conjunction with Abu Ma'shar, *On Historical Astrology: The Book of Religions and Dynasties (on the Great Conjunctions)*, ed. Keiji Yamamoto and Charles Burnett (Leiden: Brill, 2000), and then see Lynn Thorndike, *A History of Magic and Experimental Science* (New York: Columbia University Press, 1923–1958), II

seen,[149] a predilection on his part for Epicurean physics, he treats the generation and demise of religions as a wholly natural phenomenon typical of "mixed" as opposed to "simple bodies," observing that religious "sects change two or three times in five or six thousand years" – which, if true, would suggest that the demise of what he pointedly calls "the Christian sect" might take place as early as 1666,[150] a date fraught, as Machiavelli no doubt knew, with apocalyptic significance.[151] In denouncing the *ambizioso ozio* of the clergy and in calling for a reinterpretation of "our religion" aimed at bringing it into accord with the dictates of *virtù*, the Florentine has in mind a transformation far more radical than Christian renewal.

The depths of Machiavelli's radicalism are especially evident in his subsequent discussion of the "return to first principles" achieved within Christendom by Saint Francis and Saint Dominic, who,

by means of poverty and the example of Christ, brought back into the minds of men that which was already burnt out: their new orders were so powerful that they are the cause that the dishonesty of the prelates and that of the heads of the religion do not bring it to ruin. Living in poverty still and having so much credit with the people through confessions and preaching, they give them to think that it is evil to say evil of evil and that it is good to live in obedience to these prelates and heads and, if these make an error,

66–93, 246–78, 874–947 (esp. 897–98), V 94–110 (esp. 98–99, 107–9), and "Franciscus Florentinus, or Paduanus, an Inquisitor of the Fifteenth Century, and his Treatise on Astrology and Divination, Magic and Popular Superstition," in *Mélanges Mandonnet: Études d'histoire littéraire et doctrinale du Moyen Age* (Paris: Librairie Philosophique J. Vrin, 1930), II 353–69 (esp. 357–60), along with Bruno Nardi, "La teoria dell'anima e la generazione delle forme secondo Pietro d'Abano" and "Intorno alle dottrine filosofiche di Pietro d'Abano," in Nardi, *Saggi sull'aristotelismo padovano*, 1–74. For an overview, see Garin, *Astrology in the Renaissance*, passim (esp. 16–28, 56–61); John D. North, "Celestial Influence – The Major Premiss of Astrology," in *'Astrologi hullucinati': Stars and the End of the World in Luther's Time*, ed. Paola Zambelli (Berlin: Walter de Gruyter, 1986), 45–100; and Marco Bertozzi, "Il fatale ritmo della storia: La teoria delle grandi congiunzioni astrali tra XV e XVI secolo," *I Castelli di Yale* 1 (1996): 29–49 (esp. 40–44). With regard to judicial astrology, note Averroës, *Tahafut al-tahafut* 491.15–492.15, 496.1–501.12, 510.1–511.15, 514.9–516.11. Pomponazzi was also by no means the last to address the *legum mutatio* in this fashion: see Girolamo Cardano, *Claudii Ptolemai Pelsiensis libri quattuor: De astrorum iudiciis* II Praef., in Cardano, *Opera omnia*, ed. Charles Spon (Lyons: Ioannis Antonii Huguetan and Marci Antonii Ravaud, 1663), V 220–21, which should be read in light of Anthony Grafton, *Cardano's Cosmos: The Worlds and Works of a Renaissance Astrologer* (Cambridge, MA: Harvard University Press, 1999), and consider Tullio Gregory, *Theophrastus redivivus: Erudizione e ateismo nel Seicento* (Naples: A. Morano, 1979), 123–54.

[149] See Chapter 1, this volume.

[150] Consider Machiavelli, *Discorsi* 2.5.1, in *Opere*, 154, and *Discorsi* 3.1, in *Opere*, 195–96, in light of Strauss, *Thoughts on Machiavelli*, 142–44, 168–73, 201–3, 221–23; Gennaro Sasso, "De aeternitate mundi (*Discorsi*, II 5)," in Sasso, *Machiavelli e gli antichi e altri saggi*, (Milan: Riccardo Ricciardi, 1987–1997), I 167–399; Eugenio Garin, "Aspetti del pensiero di Machiavelli," in Garin, *Dal Rinascimento all'Illuminismo: Studi e ricerche* (Pisa: Nistri–Lischi, 1970), 43–77 (esp. 56–67); and Harvey C. Mansfield, *Machiavelli's New Modes and Orders: A Study of the Discourses on Livy* (Ithaca, NY: Cornell University Press, 1979), 202–6. In this connection, see also Couzinet, "Sources antiques de l'irréligion moderne chez Machiavel," 47–67 (esp. 60–67).

[151] See Robin Bruce Barnes, *Prophecy and Gnosis: Apocalypticism in the Wake of the Lutheran Reformation* (Stanford, CA: Stanford University Press, 1988), 187–202 (esp. 188, 200).

to leave their chastisement to God. And so these do the worst that they can because they do not fear this punishment, which they neither foresee nor believe. It is this renewal, then, that has maintained and still maintains this religion.

The Florentine's message is crystal clear. Further renewal along genuinely Christian lines, as defined by the Sermon on the Mount, would serve only to intensify the catastrophe effected within Europe by the propagation of the Christian faith and the establishment of the ecclesiastical principality, for the decadence of the *moderni* has its foundation in the influence exercised by what he pointedly identifies as "the example of Christ."[152] In Machiavelli's opinion, the proper inspiration for theologians and the only plausible antidote for the disease that afflicts Europe is the "true knowledge" that he himself imparts by teaching men to "read" Livy and "all the histories," especially the Bible, *sensatamente* so that they can draw "from reading them that sense" and "from savoring them that taste that they have in themselves."[153]

The import of what Machiavelli had to say with regard to Christianity was by no means lost on his early readers. It was on the basis of the passages examined here that Tommaso Campanella observed that the Florentine had "given men to believe that religion is a clever contrivance (*astutia*) on the part of preachers and monks for dominating the people" and that the renegade Carmelite monk Giulio Cesare Vanini dubbed him "prince of the atheists,"[154] and there is good reason to suppose that they knew whereof they spoke, for the former was learned, and the latter had a keen interest in the subject. Indeed, soon after publishing his observations, Vanini was burned at the stake on orders from the Parlement of Toulouse for teaching the non-existence of God.[155]

---

[152] Cf. Machiavelli, *Discorsi* 3.1.4, in *Opere*, 196–97, with Matt. 5:1–7:28 (esp. 5:3-11, 21-26, 38-48, 6:19-21, 24-34, 7:1-5) and Luke 6:17-46 (esp. 20-42). Note also Rom. 12:17, 1 Thess. 5:15, Titus 3:1, James 4:11, 1 Pet. 2:1, 3:9. In this connection, see Vickie B. Sullivan, *Machiavelli's Three Romes: Religion, Human Liberty, and Politics Reformed* (DeKalb: Northern Illinois University Press, 1996), passim (esp. 15–59, 119–90); Emanuele Cutinelli-Rèndina, *Chiesa e religione in Machiavelli* (Pisa: Instituti Editorialie e Poligrafici Internationali, 1998), passim (esp. 93–314); Benedetto Fontana, 'Love of Country and Love of God: The Political Uses of Religion in Machiavelli," *Journal of the History of Ideas* 60:4 (October 1999): 639–58: and John Najemy, "Papirius and the Chickens, or Machiavelli on the Necessity of Interpreting in Religion," *Journal of the History of Ideas* 60:4 (October 1999): 659–81.

[153] Consider Machiavelli, *Discorsi* 1 Proemio, in *Opere*, 76, in light of *Discorsi* 1.23.4, 3.30.1, in *Opere*, 107, 237.

[154] Consider Campanella, *L'Ateismo trionfato*, 5–6, 9, 12, and Giulio Cesare Vanini, *Amphitheatrum aeternae providentiae* (1615) Exercitationes 6, 8, in *Le opere di Giulio Cesare Vanini*, ed. Luigi Corvaglia (Milan: Società Anonima Editrice Dante Alighieri, 1933–1934), I 23, 32–33, with an eye to the allusions therein to Machiavelli, *Il principe* 6, 11, and *Discorsi* 1.10–15, 2.2, 3.1, in *Opere*, 91–99, 148–51, 151, 264–65, 273–74; then, see Headley, *Tommaso Campanella and the Transformation of the World*, 180–96, and Jean-Pierre Cavaillé, "Le *Prince des athées*, Vanini et Machiavel," in *L'Enjeu Machiavel*, ed. Gérald Sfez and Michel Senellart (Paris: Presses Universitaires de France, 2001), 59–74.

[155] Vanini soon came to be regarded as a martyr in the cause of atheism: see *Patiniana, ou les bons mots de Mr. Patin*, 51–53, in *Naudæana et Patiniana, ou Singularitez Remarquables, prises des Conversations de Mess. Naudé et Patin*, second edition (Amsterdam: François vander Plaats, 1703), which should be read in light of René Pintard, *Le Mothe le Vayer – Gassendi – Guy Patin: Études de bibliographie et di critique suivies de textes inédit de Guy Patin* (Paris: Boivin

All of this should give one pause. As became evident in the last chapter, Machiavelli's political doctrine is mercenary in the extreme, and, as now should be abundantly clear, his account of Christianity – and, by implication, of Judaism and Islam – is decidedly unfriendly. That, upon reflection, serious Christians of any sort should find such a teaching unappetizing is relatively easy to understand. It is especially telling, however, that a man such as John Milton, though evidently tempted for a brief time, was also in the end quite reluctant to follow Machiavelli's lead – at least, in the political sphere.

et Cie, [1943]), 47–61. With regard to Vanini's remarkable trajectory, one should begin with Spini, *Ricerca dei libertini*, 125–43, and Emile Narner, *La Vie et l'oeuvre de J. C. Vanini, Prince des Libertins, mort à Toulouse sur le bûcher en 1619* (Paris: Vrin, 1980), and then turn to C. F. Senning, "Vanini and the Diplomats, 1612–1614: Religion, Politics, and Defection in the Counter-Reformation Era," *Historical Magazine of the Protestant Episcopal Church* 54:3 (1985): 219–39; Francesco de Paola, *Giulio Cesare Vanini da Taurisano, filosofo europeo* (Fasano: Schena, 1998); *Giulio Cesare Vanini e il libertinismo*, ed. Francesco Paolo Raimondi (Galatina: Congedo, 2000); Jean-Pierre Cavaillé, *Dis/simulations: Jules-César Vanini, François La Mothe le Vayer, Gabriel Naudé, Louis Machon et Torquatto Accetto: Religion, morale et politique au XVIIe siècle* (Paris: Champion, 2002), 39–140; Didier Foucault, *Giulio Cesare Vanini, 1585–1619: Un Philosophe libertin dans l'Europe baroque* (Paris: Champion, 2003); and Nicholas S. Davidson, "'Le plus beau et le plus meschant esprit que ie aye cogneu': Science and Religion in the Writings of Giulio Cesare Vanini, 1585–1619," in *Heterodoxy in Early Modern Science and Religion*, ed. John Brooke and Ian Maclean (Oxford, UK: Oxford University Press, 2005), 59–79.

PART II

REVOLUTIONARY ARISTOTELIANISM

Preface

It is impossible to slot John Milton into a pigeonhole. As one would expect from his spirited defense of intellectual liberty and from his trenchant critique of prior restraint of the press, the author of *Areopagitica* was nothing if not an independent mind. He was, to all appearances, a Puritan, and he professed to accept Scripture as his unerring guide. That he was a genuine believer few twentieth-century readers of *Paradise Lost* and *Paradise Regained* were inclined to doubt. But in an earlier and less credulous age, the poet Percy Bysshe Shelley argued that the first of these two poems "contains within itself a philosophical refutation of that system, of which, by a strange and natural antithesis, it has been a chief popular support,"[1] and there are reasons to wonder whether Milton's fidelity to revelation was not, in fact, feigned.[2] For all his apparent piety, Milton did not share the disdain for music, the theater, and the pagan classics evidenced by the more radical and austere among his fellow Puritans, and he championed divorce, looked favorably on polygamy, argued on biblical grounds against the doctrine of the Trinity, depicted Christ as God's adoptive son, endorsed a free-will doctrine similar to that of Arminius, embraced materialism, rejected creation *ex nihilo*, affirmed the indissoluble union of body and soul, and advocated a complete separation of church and state. By virtually any standard but his own, he must be judged a heretic.[3] The fact that so strange a Puritan, so heterodox a Christian, so discerning a classicist, so dedicated a friend to liberty, and so devoted a republican should nonetheless hesitate when confronting Machiavelli's republicanism suggests that it was by no means accidental that genuine Puritans of a more conventional turn of mind also shied away from embracing the nefarious Florentine.

---

[1] See Percy Bysshe Shelley, "A Defence of Poetry," in *The Complete Works of Percy Bysshe Shelley*, ed. Roger Ingpen and Walter E. Peck (New York: C. Scribner's Sons, 1926–1930), VII 109–40 (at 129–31). Note, in this connection, William Empson, *Milton's God*, revised edition (London: Chatto & Windus, 1965).

[2] See Paul M. Dowling, *Polite Wisdom: Heathen Rhetoric in Milton's Areopagitica* (Lanham, MD: Rowman & Littlefield, 1995). In this connection, one might consider what it would mean to take seriously the argument of Richard Strier, "Milton's Fetters, or, Why Eden is Better than Heaven," *Milton Studies* 38 (2000): 169–97.

[3] The recent challenge to Milton's authorship of *De doctrina christiana*, though ultimately unpersuasive, has stirred a renewed interest in his theology: see *Milton and Heresy*, ed. Stephen B. Dobranski and John P. Rumrich (Cambridge, UK: Cambridge University Press, 1998).

John Milton may have been the best-read Englishman of his generation.[4] From an early age, the man who would be named in March 1649 the English commonwealth's Secretary for Foreign Tongues had devoted his life to study: he was more than thirty years old before he finally allowed the political crisis gripping his country to interrupt his quest. By the time that he felt fully ready to turn away from what he later termed "a fugitive and cloister'd vertue, unexercis'd & unbreath'd, that never sallies out and sees her adversary,"[5] he had imbibed and digested not only the Bible, the classics, and the writings of the Church Fathers but many a modern work.

Within this mix, Machiavelli does not seem to have loomed especially large. There is good reason to suspect that Milton had read *The Prince* prior to the outbreak of the Civil War,[6] but nowhere does he see fit to cite or even mention the work. On the eve of the first civil war or at its beginning, he appears to have read Machiavelli's *Art of War* and to have paid particular attention to the passages within it favorable to republicanism and limited monarchy.[7] At that time or earlier, he may also have perused the Florentine's *Discourses on Livy*, but it was not until well after the beheading of Charles I that there is any evidence that he took the time to study this last-mentioned work with any particular care.

Late in 1651, however, and early in 1652, after the final defeat of the royalist forces at the battle of Worcester on 3 September 1651 – at a time when there was an expectation in republican circles that the Rump would soon impose a general settlement on England, at a time when Milton himself appears to have been puzzling over the political trajectory of ancient Rome with an eye to the situation and needs of his own country[8] – the commonwealth's Secretary for Foreign Tongues turned to Machiavelli's republican book, read it, or had it

---

4 John Selden, whom Milton quite rightly identified as "the chief of learned men reputed in this Land" and who matched and arguably surpassed him in erudition, was born a generation earlier in 1584. See *Areopagitica* (November 1644), in *CPW*, II 513.

5 *Areopagitica* (November 1644), in *CPW*, II 515.

6 As will become clear, he had *The Prince* in mind when he published his first tract *Of Reformation* (May 1641): see *CPW*, I 571–73. Note the dismissive manner in which Milton soon thereafter refers to "*Machiavell* . . . or any *Machiavillian* Priest" in *An Apology Against a Pamphlet* (April 1642): see *CPW*, I 908. See also the derogatory reference to a "politick law" as "one of *Matchiavel's*" in *The Doctrine and Discipline of Divorce* (1 August 1643), in *CPW*, II 321.

7 See "Milton's Commonplace Book," in *CW*, XVIII 164, 177. For another translation of the pertinent passages and for a discussion of the timing of their transcription, see "Milton's Commonplace Book," tr. Ruth Mohl, in *CPW*, I 421, 443. That Milton favored parliamentary supremacy from the outset seems highly likely: see Janel Mueller, "Contextualizing Milton's Nascent Republicanism," in *Of Poetry and Politics: New Essays on Milton and his World*, ed. P. G. Stanwood (Binghamton, NY: Center for Medieval and Renaissance Texts and Studies, 1995), 263–82. That he was then an out-and-out republican seems unlikely: see Blair Worden, *Literature and Politics in Cromwellian England: John Milton, Andrew Marvell, Marchamont Nedham* (Oxford, UK: Oxford University Press, 2007), 154–79.

8 Such would appear to have been the subject of his conversation in early January 1652 with the representative of a petty German principality: see Lee Miller, *John Milton and the Oldenburg Safeguard: New Light on Milton and His Friends in the Commonwealth from the Diaries and Letters of Hermann Mylius, Agonist in the Early History of Modern Diplomacy* (New York: Lowewenthal, 1985), 128.

read to him, and arranged to have his secretaries extract from its pages and transcribe in his *Commonplace Book* some fifteen discrete passages pertinent to the task of republican construction seemingly then at hand. He wanted to reflect at leisure on Machiavelli's denial that money is the sinews of war, on his assertion that against a bad monarch there is no remedy but the sword, on his discussion of the corruption in monarchies attendant on the hereditary principle, on his contention that no one is accorded greater honor than the founder of a religion, on the praise he lavishes on princes who leave opinion free, on his preference for republican forms, on his contention that republics must frequently be returned to their first principles, on his denial that fortresses are worth the cost, on his contention that offense is superior to defense, on his argument that infantry is superior to cavalry, on his discussion of the political preconditions for the successful practice of imperialism, on his claim that in alliances republics are more faithful than princes, and on the connection that he draws between periodic public disorder and the maintenance of republican liberty.[9] It would be fair to say that in these months John Milton came to know the *Discourses on Livy* exceedingly well – but it would be, as we shall soon see, a great mistake to suppose that he ever embraced the novel republican teaching that he found therein.

---

[9] See "Milton's Commonplace Book," in *CW*, XVIII 160, 183, 196–200, 210–12, 215–17. For a somewhat better English translation and extensive notes, see "Milton's Commonplace Book," tr. Ruth Mohl, in *CPW*, I 414–15, 456, 475–77, 495–96, 498–99, 504–5. For the period in which the pertinent passages were transcribed, see James Holly Hanford, "The Chronology of Milton's Private Studies," *Publications of the Modern Language Association of America* 36:2 (June 1921): 251–314 (at 281–83), and Maurice Kelley, "Milton and Machiavelli's *Discorsi*," *Studies in Bibliography* 4 (1951–1952): 123–27. See also Joseph Allen Bryant, "A Note on Milton's Use of Machiavelli's *Discorsi*," *Modern Philology* 47:4 (May 1950): 217–21, and Felix Raab, *The English Face of Machiavelli: A Changing Interpretation, 1500–1700* (London: Routledge & Kegan Paul, 1964), 175–81.

3

The Classical Republicanism of John Milton

At no time did John Milton allow the thinking of Niccolò Machiavelli to shape in any fundamental way the manner in which he wrote about, defended, and surreptitiously tried to guide the nascent English republic in strictly political affairs.[1] To be sure, in 1651–1652, when he worked his way through the *Discourses on Livy*, he at first found attractive the fierce populism of the Florentine, and in his Commonplace Book he pointed with approbation to the crucial chapter in which Machiavelli distinguishes his republicanism from that of the ancients by attacking Livy, "all the other historians," and "all the writers" of earlier times for their presumption that moral and political virtue are difficult but nonetheless possible to attain and that more is, therefore, to be expected from the educated and accomplished few than from the vulgar crowd.[2] But Milton soon changed his mind – and, even at this time, he was inclined to shy away from the Florentine's contention that republics devoted to imperial expansion are far more likely to be viable than those satisfied with what they already have.[3] Moreover, at no time did he embrace the fundamental premise on which the Florentine grounded this rejection of the classical republican principle of differential moral and political rationality. Nowhere did he echo the dictum that a

[1] Cf. Victoria Kahn, *Machiavellian Rhetoric: From the Counter-Reformation to Milton* (Princeton, NJ: Princeton University Press, 1994), 167–235. In general, it can be said that those who join J. G. A. Pocock in thinking Machiavelli a civic humanist are bound to be confused in their interpretations of the leading figures of seventeenth-century English thought: after reading Chapter 1, this volume, cf. Blair Worden, "Milton's Republicanism and the Tyranny of Heaven," in *Machiavelli and Republicanism*, ed. Gisela Bock, Quentin Skinner, and Maurizio Viroli (Cambridge, UK: Cambridge University Press, 1990), 225–45 (esp. 225–35); Steve Pincus, "Neither Machiavellian Moment nor Possessive Individualism: Commercial Society and the Defenders of the English Commonwealth," *American Historical Review* 103:3 (June 1998): 705–36; and Barbara Riebling, "Milton on Machiavelli: Representations of the State in *Paradise Lost*," *Renaissance Quarterly* 49:3 (Autumn 1996): 573–97. For an exception to the rule, see Chapter 5, note 27, this volume.

[2] Note Machiavelli, *Discorsi* 1.58, in *Opere*, 140–42, and see "Milton's Commonplace Book," in *CW*, XVIII 199, where Milton also singles out Machiavelli, *Discorsi* 3.34, in *Opere*, 241–43.

[3] See "Milton's Commonplace Book," in *CW*, XVIII 212, where Milton ignores Machiavelli, *Discorsi* 1.6, in *Opere*, 84–87, and seems to mistake the significance of the argument presented in Machiavelli, *Discorsi* 2.19, in *Opere*, 173–75. In this connection, see David Armitage, "John Milton: Poet against Empire," in *Milton and Republicanism*, ed. David Armitage, Armand Himy, and Quentin Skinner (Cambridge, UK: Cambridge University Press, 1995), 206–25, who at times seems not to recognize the significance for his own argument of Machiavelli's contention that republics which remain quiet ultimately cannot survive.

legislator must presuppose that "all men are wicked and that they will make use of the malignity of their spirit whenever they are free and have occasion to do so." Nowhere did he draw the conclusion that in a republic their weakness and lack of ambition makes the people safer and better guardians of liberty than the nobles. Nowhere did he adopt the novel and counter-intuitive doctrine, altogether unknown prior to its propagation in Machiavelli's *Discourses on Livy*, that Roman liberty was rooted in a salutary political turbulence.[4] And, in the end, upon reflection, he repudiated in no uncertain terms Machiavelli's modern populism, rejecting as "by experience found false" the Florentine's contention that "popular assemblies are to be trusted with the peoples libertie, rather than a Senat of principal men, because great men will be still endeavoring to inlarge thir power, but the common sort will be contented to maintain thir own libertie."[5]

It is not difficult to explain Milton's initial reticence concerning Machiavellian republicanism nor his ultimate rejection of it. As one would expect from reading the argument that he presents in *Areopagitica* concerning reason and truth, Milton was that rarity of rarities in mid-seventeenth-century England: a genuine, fully conscious classical republican.[6] In his isolation in this regard, he

---

[4] Of course, he did not object to God's shaking "a Kingdome with strong and healthfull commotions to a generall reforming," as was evidently happening in his own country, but this is not the same thing as suggesting that class conflict should be institutionalized: see *Areopagitica* (November 1644), in *CPW*, II 566.

[5] Cf. *The Readie and Easie Way to Establish a Free Commonwealth*, second edition (1–10 April 1660), in *CPW*, VII 437–40, with Machiavelli, *Discorsi* 1.5, in *Opere*, 83–84, and see Andrew Barnaby, "Machiavellian Hypotheses: Republican Settlement and the Question of Empire in Milton's *Readie and Easie Way*," *Clio* 19:3 (1990): 251–70 (esp. 265–66). Because he is at one with J. G. A. Pocock in presuming Machiavelli a moralist in the Aristotelian tradition, Barnaby fails to grasp the significance of Milton's rejection of Machiavelli's populism and misinterprets it as indicative of a disagreement concerning tactics and not ends. For a more nuanced treatment, see Jonathan Scott, *Commonwealth Principles: Republican Writing of the English Revolution* (Cambridge, UK: Cambridge University Press, 2004), 113–15, 136, 145–46, 153–55, 159–62, 170–77, 193–94, 201–2, 214–20, 233–41, 253–54, 262–64, 276–78, 311–14, 318–20 (with 37, 47–50, 52–58, 96, 135, 216–18, 294, 315).

[6] Cf. Zera S. Fink, *The Classical Republicans: An Essay in the Recovery of a Pattern of thought in Seventeenth-Century England*, second edition (Evanston, IL: Northwestern University Press, 1962), 90–122, with Martin Dzelzainis, "Milton's Classical Republicanism," in *Milton and Republicanism*, 3–24, and see Pincus, "Neither Machiavellian Moment nor Possessive Individualism," 713–15, 725–28; then, cf. Quentin Skinner, "John Milton and the Politics of Slavery," in *Visions of Politics* (Cambridge, UK: Cambridge University Press, 2002) II: *Renaissance Virtues*, 286–307 and Martin Dzelzainis, "Republicanism," in *A Companion to Milton*, ed. Thomas N. Corns (Oxford, UK: Blackwell, 2001), 294–308, with Paul A. Rahe, *Republics Ancient and Modern: Classical Republicanism and the American Revolution* (Chapel Hill: University of North Carolina Press, 1992), 15–229 (esp. 28–54). As will become clear, I believe that Skinner's discussion of Milton and of those in the Stuart parliaments whose thinking foreshadowed his in certain respects is grounded in a systematic confusion as to what it was that distinguished the thinking of the Romans regarding liberty. To focus, as he and Dzelzainis do, on the passages in the *Digest* and the *Code of Justinian* pertaining to slavery is to take the part for the whole; to focus on what the Greeks, the Romans, and the subsequent inhabitants of western Europe more generally took for granted; and to abstract from the understanding of liberty that distinguished the ancients, the civic humanists of the Renaissance, and figures such as Milton from those among his compatriots who were the forerunners of the Whig mainstream. As I have argued elsewhere

was a forerunner of the third earl of Shaftesbury.[7] And like his spiritual heir, Milton was not only steeped in the pagan classics, he professed to think it perfectly possible to reconcile the vision of politics found in Herodotus, Thucydides, Xenophon, Isocrates, Aristotle, Polybius, Sallust, Cicero, Seneca, Suetonius, and Tacitus with the demands of a Christianity fully and properly reformed,[8] and in both his poetry and his prose he consciously modeled himself on the *vir sapiens* of Cicero's rhetorical works.

In a Latin oration that he delivered while he was a student at Christ's College, Cambridge, Milton restated Cicero's theme,[9] arguing that the arts and sciences were responsible for the establishment of cities – that they had lured men hardly better than beasts within the city's walls. A quarter of a century later, in his *Defense of the English People*, he returned to the same theme, remarking that "at one time men lived scattered about, dispersed and inclined to stray," and that it took "someone both eloquent and wise" to "conduct them into civic life

with regard to Skinner's treatment of Machiavelli, he is inclined to lump where he should split: see Paul A. Rahe, "Situating Machiavelli," in *Renaissance Civic Humanism: Reappraisals and Reflections*, ed. James Hankins (Cambridge, UK: Cambridge University Press, 2000), 270–308.

[7] Cf. Jonathan Scott, "Classical Republicanism in Seventeenth-Century England and the Netherlands," in *Republicanism: A Shared European Heritage*, ed. Martin van Gelderen and Quentin Skinner (Cambridge, UK: Cambridge University Press, 2002) I: *Republicanism and Constitutionalism in Early Modern Europe*, 61–81 (at 65), who errs in attributing to me the view "that there was no classical republicanism in sixteenth- and seventeenth-century Europe," with Rahe, *Republics Ancient and Modern*, 433, 485–87, 495, where I discuss Richard Hooker, Gottfried Wilhelm von Leibniz, and the third earl of Shaftesbury. My claim was merely that the mainstream of what became Whig political thought presupposed a rejection of the republicanism embraced in ancient Greece and Rome. That there were outliers I never denied. On the continent, as it happens, outside Italy, political Aristotelianism appears to have remained for a considerable time the norm: consider Wyger R. E. Velema, "'That a Republic Is Better than a Monarchy': Anti-Monarchism in Early Modern Dutch Political Thought"; Anna Grześkowiak-Krwawicz, "Anti-Monarchism in Polish Republicanism in the Seventeenth and Eighteenth Centuries"; Karin Tilmans, "Republican Citizenship and Civic Humanism in the Burgundian-Hapsburg Netherlands (1477–1566)"; Robert von Friedeburg, "Civic Humanism and Republican Citizenship in Early Modern Germany"; Edward Opaliński, "Civic Humanism and Republican Citizenship in the Polish Renaissance"; Vittor Ivo Comparato, "From the Crisis of Civil Culture to the Neapolitan Republic of 1647: Republicanism in Italy between the Sixteenth and Seventeenth Centuries"; Martin van Gelderen, "Aristotelians, Monarchomachs and Republicans: Sovereignty and *Respublica Mixta* in Dutch and German Political Thought, 1580–1650"; Hans Erich Bödeker, "Debating the *Respublica Mixta*: German and Dutch Political Discourses around 1700"; Lea Campos Boralevi, "Classical Foundation Myths of European Republicanism: The Jewish Commonwealth"; Xavier Gil, "Republican Politics in Early Modern Spain: The Castilian and Catalano-Aragonese Traditions"; and Vittorio Conti, "The Mechanisation of Virtue: Republican Rituals in Italian Political Thought in the Sixteenth and Seventeenth Centuries," in *Republicanism: A Shared European Heritage I: Republicanism and Constitutionalism in Early Modern Europe*, 9–25, 43–59, 107–288, and II: *The Values of Republicanism in Early Modern Europe*, 73–83, in conjunction with my review of these two volumes, in *History of Political Thought* 25:3 (Autumn 2004): 558–64.

[8] Note the manner in which Milton deploys the classics in defense of the Commonwealth in the fifth chapter of his *Pro Populo Anglicano Defensio* (24 February 1651) V: see CW, VII 266–347. For a recent translation of the pertinent chapter, see *A Defence of the People of England* (24 February 1651) V, tr. Donald C. Mackenzie, in CPW, IV:1 422–53. In this connection, see Hugh Trevor-Roper, "Milton in Politics," in *Catholics, Anglicans and Puritans: Seventeenth Century Essays* (Chicago: University of Chicago Press, 1988), 231–82 (esp. 236–44).

[9] See Chapter 1, this volume.

(*vita civilis*)." Milton never doubted the conviction, which he had formed as a student, that, in the right circumstances, "a single man possessed of art and wisdom . . . could be sufficient to lead an entire commonwealth to excellence and virtue (*ad bonam frugem*)."[10] Nor did he ever doubt that he was himself that man. The establishment of the English republic merely provided an occasion for his revival of an "Eloquence" that, in "*Athens*" and "free *Rome*," had "Flourished/since mute."[11]

Thus, where Demosthenes and Cicero had nobly failed in freedom's defense, John Milton aimed to succeed in its recovery[12] – by prompting the men of his own "age to quit their cloggs/By the known rules of antient libertie."[13] By the sheer force of his eloquence in defense of the English commonwealth, he proposed, "after an extended intervall, to lead liberty, so long ago expelled, so long an exile, back to its home among the nations everywhere." It was his self-chosen task "to disseminate throughout the cities, kingdoms, and nations" occupying the territory once governed by imperial Rome "a renewed cultivation of citizenship and the free life."[14] It makes perfect sense that so fervent a believer in the power of *ratio et oratio* to create and shape a community of moral discourse accommodating and transcending mere material interest should enthusiastically embrace the classical republican principle of differential moral and political rationality.

Of course, a cursory reading of his treatise *The Tenure of Kings and Magistrates* might lead one to suppose the opposite: that Milton, the propagandist for liberty, was the very model of a modern populist. For in this work, written during the trial of Charles I, published within two weeks of his execution,[15] and designed to justify on abstract grounds the right of the people to sit in

---

[10] He was certainly aware of the pertinent passages in Cicero: consider *Prolusiones Quædam Oratoriæ* (1625–32) VII and *Pro Populo Anglicano Defensio* (24 February 1651) VII, in *CW*, I 258–59, 270–73, VII 394–97, in light of Cic. *Inv. Rh.* 1.2.2–3, *De or.* 1.8.33. For a recent translation of the passages from Milton, see *Prolusions* (1625–32) VII and *A Defence of the People of England* (24 February 1651) VII, tr. Donald C. Mackenzie, in *CPW*, I 292–93, 299, IV:1 473.

[11] See *Paradise Lost* 9.670–76, in *CW*, II:2 284.

[12] One must keep in mind the fact that Milton's *Pro Populo Anglicano Defensio* was modeled on Cicero's *Philippics*, which were modeled, in turn, on the *Philippics* of Demosthenes. In this connection, note *Pro Populo Anglicano Defensio* (24 February 1651) XII, in *CW*, VII 556–57. For a recent translation of this revealing passage, see *A Defence of the People of England* (24 February 1651) XII, tr. Donald C. Mackenzie, in *CPW*, IV:1 536–37. For a brief but highly suggestive discussion of Milton's debt to Cicero, see Martin Dzelzainis, "Introduction," in John Milton, *Political Writings*, ed. Martin Dzelzainis (Cambridge, UK: Cambridge University Press, 1991), ix–xxv (esp. xix–xx). Note also *Areopagitica* (November 1644), in *CPW*, II 539.

[13] "Sonnet XII" (1646), in *CW*, I:1 62.

[14] See *Pro Populo Anglicano Defensio Secunda* (30 May 1654), in *CW*, VIII 8–15. For a recent translation, see *A Second Defence of the English People* (30 May 1654), tr. Helen North, in *CPW*, IV:1 552–56. For further evidence of Milton's intentions, see Joseph Anthony Wittreich, Jr., "'The Crown of Eloquence': The Figure of the Orator in Milton's Prose Works," in *Achievements of the Left Hand: Essays on the Prose of John Milton*, ed. Michael Lieb and John T. Shawcross (Amherst: University of Massachusetts Press, 1974), 3–54.

[15] See John T. Shawcross, "Milton's 'Tenure of Kings and Magistrates': Date of Composition, Editions, and Issues," *The Papers of the Bibliographical Society of America* 60:1 (First Quarter, 1966): 1–8.

judgment on their rulers, Milton deploys an argument owing a great deal to Henry Parker's celebrated defense of the Long Parliament and even more to the Levellers' development of the radical potential implicit in Parker's argument[16] – which seems to foreshadow much of what is truly significant in John Locke's *Two Treatises of Government.*[17]

Milton's premise is that "all men naturally were borne free, being the image and resemblance of God himself," and that they are, therefore, "by privilege above all the creatures, born to command and not to obey." The establishment of "Citties, Townes and Common-wealths" he traces to "*Adams* transgression," which caused men to fall "among themselves to doe wrong and violence." Recognizing "that such courses must needs tend to the destruction of them all, they agreed by common league to bind each other from mutual injury, and joyntly to defend themselves against any that gave disturbance or opposition to such agreement." Then,

because no faith in all was found sufficiently binding, they saw it needfull to ordaine som authoritie, that might restrain by force and punishment what was violated against peace and common right. This authoritie and power of self-defence and preservation being originally and naturally in every one of them, and unitedly in them all, for ease, for order, and least each man should be his own partial Judge, they communicated and deriv'd either to one, whom for the eminence of his wisdom and integritie they chose above the rest, or to more then one whom they thought of equal deserving: the first was call'd a King; the other Magistrates.

These kings and magistrates were not, however, chosen to be "thir Lords and Maisters" – for they were "thir Deputies and Commissioners," selected "to execute, by vertue of thir intrusted power, that justice which else every man by the bond of nature and of Cov'nant must have executed for himself, and for one another." In Milton's opinion, there could be "no other end or reason . . . imaginable" why, "among free Persons, one man by civil right should beare autority and jurisdiction over another." In consequence, he concluded, those who hold power "in trust from the People" could and should be held accountable by the people "in whom the power yet remaines fundamentally," for it "cannot

---

16 Cf. [Henry Parker] *Observations upon Some of His Majesties Late Answers and Expresses* (London: s.n., 1642), which is reprinted in photographic facsimile in *Tracts on Liberty in the Puritan Revolution, 1638–1647,* ed. William Haller (New York: Columbia University Press, 1934), II 167–213, and which should be read in light of Michael Mendle, *Henry Parker and the English Civil War: The Political Thought of the Public's "Privado"* (Cambridge, UK: Cambridge University Press, 1995), with [Richard Overton and William Walwyn], *A Remonstrance of Many Thousand Citizens, and Other Freeborn People of England to Their Owne House of Commons* (London: s.n., 1646), which is reprinted in *The English Levellers,* ed. Andrew Sharp (Cambridge, UK: Cambridge University Press, 1998), 33–53, and which the House of Commons had burned at the Old Exchange in London and in the New Palace Yard at Westminster on 22 May 1647.
17 Cf. Nicholas von Maltzahn, "The Whig Milton, 1667–1700," in *Milton and Republicanism,* 229–53 (esp. 236–38) and Annabel Patterson, "The Good Old Cause," in *Reading between the Lines* (Madison: University of Wisconsin Press, 1993), 210–75, and *Early Modern Liberalism* (Cambridge, UK: Cambridge University Press, 1997), who seems unable, or unwilling, to distinguish commitment to a common program of reform in a particular setting from agreement on matters of fundamental principle. The crucial difference between the two stems from the fact that Locke's populism was Machiavellian: see Rahe, *Republics Ancient and Modern,* 445–520.

be tak'n from them, without a violation of thir natural birthright." In fact, he asserts, from this argument "it follows" that the people may "as oft as they shall judge it for the best, either choose him or reject him, retaine him or depose him though no Tyrant, meerly by the liberty and right of free born Men, to be govern'd as seems to them best."[18] On the face of it, the author of *The Tenure of Kings and Magistrates* would appear to be much more fully a populist than the Whig theorist John Locke.[19]

In the end, however, Milton robs his own account of the origins and nature of political authority of its democratic potential by reasserting the aristocratic principle of differential moral and political rationality that had underpinned both theory and practice in ancient Greece and Rome.[20] As the royalist writer Sir Robert Filmer was quick to point out, when Milton spoke of "the people," he quite often had in mind a much smaller and more select body of men.[21] In the first edition *The Tenure of Kings and Magistrates*, Milton insisted on distinguishing "those Worthies which are the soule of" the republican "enterprize" from "the throng ... of Vulgar and irrational men" who stood in their way; and the decision as to "who in particular is a Tyrant," he left to the "Magistrates, at least to the uprighter sort of them," reserving it not for "the people" as a whole nor even for the representatives they chose for themselves, but for that select group, "though in number less by many, in whom faction least hath prevaild above the Law of nature and right reason, to judge as they find cause." For "most men," even then, Milton had little political use. They are, he wrote, "apt anough to civill Wars and commotions as a noveltie, and for a flash hot and active; but through sloth or inconstancie, and weakness of spirit either fainting, ere thir own pretences, though never so just, be half attain'd, or through an

---

[18] *The Tenure of Kings and Magistrates* (13 February 1649), in *CPW*, III 198–206.

[19] Cf. Michael Zuckert, *Natural Rights and the New Republicanism* (Princeton, NJ: Princeton University Press, 1994), 77–93, who errs as well in terming Milton an exponent of political theology. As Martin Dzelzainis points out, Milton's treatise marks a genuine break with, not just a profound radicalization of, the Calvinist resistance theory found in the *Vindiciae Contra Tyrannos* and in other monarchomach tracts, and it effects this break by making nature, as opposed to revelation, the standard by which the legitimacy of a political regime and of resistance to it is to be judged. As such, though it gestures in the direction of political theology, it is resolutely secular in the argument on which it bases its conclusions. Milton owes more to Aristotle and Cicero than he does to the Bible. See Dzelzainis, "Introduction," ix–xxv (esp. ix–xix). That Milton's perspective was widely shared among the Puritan supporters of the regicide, Dzelzainis asserts but has not yet established: see Martin Dzelzainis, "Anti-Monarchism in English Republicanism," in *Republicanism: A Shared Heritage* I: *Republicanism and Constitutionalism in Early Modern Europe*, 27–41.

[20] It is this that explains the features in Milton's thinking that initially disappointed and later intrigued Perez Zagorin: cf. *A History of Political Thought in the English Revolution* (London: Routledge and Paul, 1954), 106–20, with *Milton, Aristocrat and Rebel* (Rochester, NY: D. S. Brewer, 1992). For a less sympathetic account, see Trevor-Roper, "Milton in Politics," 231–82.

[21] See Robert Filmer, *Observations Concerning the Originall of Government* (1652) I, in Filmer, *Patriarcha and Other Writings*, ed. Johann P. Sommerville (Cambridge, UK: Cambridge University Press, 1991), 198–99. In this connection, see Michael Fixler, *Milton and the Kingdoms of God* (Evanston, IL: Northwestern University Press, 1964), 133–71, and John Sanderson, *"But the People's Creatures": The Philosophical Basis of the English Civil War* (Manchester, UK: Manchester University Press, 1989), 128–41.

inbred falshood and wickednes, betray oft times to destruction with themselves, men of noblest temper joyn'd with them for causes, whereof they in their rash undertakings were not capable."[22]

Two years later, when, in his capacity as the English commonwealth's Secretary for Foreign Tongues,[23] Milton published in Latin his celebrated *Defense of the English People*, he insisted that "the true power of the people resided" at the time of Charles I's execution in "the better qualified, that is the more reasonable, part of the legislature (*Senatûs pars potior, id est sanior*)." In his opinion, "only the few, namely the wise and magnanimous, wish to take up liberty or are able to put it to use; the majority prefer" submission to "just lords" – to "lords who are," as he puts it, "nonetheless just."[24] There is, he would argue to the same end in his *Second Defense of the English People* in 1654, "nothing more in accord with nature, nothing more just, nothing more useful or better for human kind than that the lesser give way to the greater, not the lesser to the greater number but those lesser in virtue to those greater, those lesser in counsel to those greater. Those who are superior in prudence, in experience, in industry, and virtue, these, in my judgment, however few, shall everywhere be more numerous (*plures*) and better qualified (*potiores*) for exercising the suffrage than any mere number, however great."[25]

Rule by the *Sanior, Valentior Pars*

Of course, to make his case on behalf of the army and the Rump, Milton had to resort to some such argument. On no other grounds could he explain what it was that conferred on an assembly which was the product of a military coup the right to speak and act on the English people's behalf.[26] Thus, when he

---

[22] *The Tenure of Kings and Magistrates* (13 February 1649), in *CPW*, III 192, 197. The presence of these passages in the original edition of this book disproves the claim, recently advanced by Go Togashi, "Milton and the Presbyterian Opposition, 1649–1650: The Engagement Controversy and *The Tenure of Kings and Magistrates*, Second Edition (1649)," *Milton Quarterly* 39:2 (May 2005): 59–81, that it was only in the second edition of the work that Milton abandoned radical populism.

[23] For Milton's government service, see Robert Thomas Fallon, *Milton in Government* (University Park: Pennsylvania State University Press, 1993).

[24] Cf. *Pro Populo Anglicano Defensio* (24 February 1651) II, VI, in *CW*, VII 74, 356, with Sall. *Ep. Mithr.* 18. Note the emphasis that Milton places on the fact that the republic possesses the *sanae et integrae tantùm partis rationem*; note his insistence that the Long Parliament's *pars...sanior* called in the army; and note the special role he accords the *pars populi major vel potior*: ibid. Praefatio, I, VII, in *CW*, VII 28–30, 54, 388. For a recent English translation of the various passages cited, see *A Defence of the People of England* (24 February 1651) Preface, I–II, VI–VII, tr. Donald C. Mackenzie, in *CPW*, IV:1 316–17, 332, 343, 457, 470.

[25] *Pro Populo Anglicano Defensio Secunda* (30 May 1654), in *CW*, VIII 152–54. For a recent translation, see *A Second Defence of the English People* (30 May 1654), tr. Helen North, in *CPW*, IV:1 636. See David Norbrook, *Writing the English Republic: Poetry, Rhetoric and Politics, 1627–1660* (Cambridge, UK: Cambridge University Press, 1999), 331–37; Hugh Jenkins, "*Quid Nomine Populi Intelligi Velimus*: Defining the 'People' in *The Second Defense*," *Milton Studies* 46 (2007): 191–209; and Blair Worden, *Literature and Politics in Cromwellian England: John Milton, Andrew Marvell, Marchamont Nedham* (Oxford: Oxford University Press, 2007), 255–97, which should be read with an eye to ibid., 326–34.

[26] In this connection, see Ernest Sirluck, "Milton's Political Thought: The First Cycle," *Modern Philology* 61:3 (February 1964): 209–24, which should be read in conjunction with his discussion

was commissioned by the English commonwealth to pen his *Eikonoklastēs* in response to the *Eikon Basilikē* said to have been written by Charles I, he was not at all hesitant to pour scorn on the great mass of his fellow countrymen, for, as he knew only too well, they were deeply moved by that brilliant royalist tract. If he called them "the blockish vulgar" and "the mad multitude," if he denounced them as "an inconstant, irrational, and Image-doting rabble," and as "a credulous and hapless herd, begott'n to servility," it was because he really had no other choice. If his compatriots were not for the most part "exorbitant and excessive in all thir motions" and "prone ofttimes not to a religious onely, but to a civil kinde of Idolatry in idolizing thir Kings," if they were not guilty of "a besotted and degenerate baseness of spirit" and a "low dejection and debasement of mind," how could John Milton explain the profound revival of royalist sentiment then besettting his beloved England?[27]

There was, however, more to Milton's argument than a surrender to rhetorical necessity. He was also flattering, reassuring, and encouraging of those inclined to side with the regicides.[28] Moreover, he had respectable Protestant precedent for the aristocratic turn that he gave to an otherwise democratic argument.[29] The idea that, in certain circumstances, inferior magistrates are empowered to do what ordinary men are prohibited from doing – that they are, in fact, duty-bound to provide correction to a ruler who endeavors "by armes to defend transgressors, to subvert those things which are taught in the word of God" – originated in the middle of the sixteenth century with Luther's associate Martin Bucer. John Calvin had himself acknowledged that, in certain circumstances, not unlike those in which the Long Parliament was thought to have acted, inferior magistrates are authorized to mount resistance to their superiors,[30] and Huguenots such as Theodore Beza and the anonymous author of the *Vindiciae Contra Tyrannos* had further elaborated and extended this argument in the course of the French wars of religion,[31] as had John Knox

---

of Milton's divorce tracts and his other early prose writings: see Ernest Sirluck, "Introduction," in *CPW*, II 1–216 (esp. 12–52, 130–36, 145–58, 181–83).

[27] Note Milton, *Eikonoklastēs* (6 October 1649), in *CPW*, III 339, 343–45, 601, and see Steven Zwicker, "The King's Head and the Politics of Literary Property: The *Eikon Basilike* and *Eikonoklastes*," in Zwicker, *Lines of Authority: Politics and English Literary Culture, 1649–1689* (Ithaca, NY: Cornell University Press, 1993), 36–59, and Kevin Sharpe, "'An Image Doting Rabble': The Failure of Republican Culture in Seventeenth Century England," in *Refiguring Revolutions: Aesthetics and Politics from the English Revolution to the Romantic Revolution*, ed. Kevin Sharpe and Steven N. Zicker (Berkeley: University of California Press, 1998), 25–56.

[28] See Daniel Shore, "'Fit Though Few': *Eikonoklastes* and the Rhetoric of Audience," *Milton Studies* 45 (2006): 129–48.

[29] For a helpful survey of this line of thought, see Quentin Skinner, *The Foundations of Modern Political Thought II: The Age of Reformation* (Cambridge, UK: Cambridge University Press, 1978), 189–358

[30] John Calvin, *Institutes of the Christian Religion*, ed. John T. McNeill, tr. Ford Lewis Battles (Philadelphia: Westminster Press, 1960) 4.20.4–32 (esp., 23–32)

[31] See Theodore Beza, *De jura magistratum* (1574), in *Constitutionalism and Resistance in the Sixteenth Century: Three Treatises by Hotman, Beza, and Mornay*, tr. and ed. Julian H. Franklin (New York: Pegasus, 1969), 101–35, and *Vindiciae Contra Tyrannos*, ed. and tr. George Garnett (Cambridge, UK: Cambridge University Press, 1994). As Garnett, "Editor's Introduction," in ibid., lv–lxxvi, makes clear, even now, we are not in a position to determine whether the latter work, which was first published in 1579, was written by Hubert Languet, by Philippe du

and John Goodman in the British isles. Although throughout it remained the ostensible purpose of his tract to prove "That it is Lawfull, and hath been held so through all Ages, for any, who have the Power, to call to account a Tyrant, or wicked KING, and after due conviction, to depose, and put him to death; if the ordinary MAGISTRATE have neglected, or deny'd to doe it," in the second edition of his *Tenure of Kings and Magistrates*, Milton cited Bucer and his heirs, each and every one.[32]

Even more to the point, Milton could turn to one exceedingly influential strand within the Aristotelianism of the later Middle Ages.[33] As we have already had occasion to note,[34] the circulation of Averroës' commentaries on the works of Aristotle had occasioned on the part of some late medieval thinkers, such as Marsilius of Padua, a reassessment of the relationship between the secular and the spiritual authorities.[35] In 1324, in the course of laying out, in his *Defensor pacis*, an apology for the secular power against the divine-right claims of the papal monarchy, Marsilius had launched an appeal to the principle of popular

---

Plessis-Mornay, or by the two in collaboration. Note, in this connection, François Hotman, *Francogallia*, ed. Ralph Giesey, tr. J. H. M. Salmon (Cambridge, UK: Cambridge University Press, 1972), which was first published in 1573. The events in sixteenth-century France loomed large in English eyes: see J. H. M. Salmon, *The French Religious Wars in English Political Thought* (Oxford, UK: Oxford University Press, 1959).

[32] Note the subtitle of *The Tenure of Kings and Magistrates* (13 February 1649), in *CPW*, III 189; then, see ibid., 243–51, which was added to the second edition, published at some point thereafter in 1649 and then reissued on or shortly before 15 February 1650: see Shawcross, "Milton's 'Tenure of Kings and Magistrates': Date of Composition, Editions, and Issues," 6–8. Consider also *Pro Populo Anglicano Defensio Secunda* (30 May 1654), in *CW*, VIII 198. For a recent translation of the latter passage, see *A Second Defence of the English People* (30 May 1654), tr. Helen North, in *CPW*, IV:1 659.

[33] Cf. Dzelzainis, "Introduction," ix–xxv, who recognizes Milton's debt to medieval Aristotelianism but who nonetheless emphasizes Milton's populism to the virtual exclusion of his reassertion therein of the aristocratic principle of differential moral and political rationality.

[34] See Chapter 2, this volume.

[35] In this connection, see Leo Strauss, "Marsilius of Padua," in *Liberalism Ancient and Modern* (New York: Basic Books, 1968), 185–202, and Charles Butterworth, "What Is Political Averroism?" in *Averroismus im Mittelalter und in der Renaissance*, ed. Friedrich Niewöhner and Loris Sturlese (Zurich: Spur Verlag, 1994), 239–50, and consider Shlomo Pines, "La Philosophie dans l'économie du genre humain selon Averroès: Une Réponse à al-Farabi?" in *Multiple Averroès*, ed. Jean Jolivet (Paris: Les Belles Lettres, 1978), 189–207, which is reprinted in *The Collected Works of Shlomo Pines* (Jerusalem: Magnes Press, 1979–1997), III: *Studies in the History of Arabic Philosophy*, ed. Sarah Stroumsa, 357–75, and Jeannine Quillet, "L'Aristotélisme de Marsile de Padoue et ses rapports avec l'Averroïsme," *Medioevo* 5 (1979): 81–142. Note also Alan Gewirth, *Marsilius of Padua and Medieval Political Philosophy* (New York: Columbia University Press, 1951); Quentin Skinner, *The Foundations of Modern Political Thought I: The Renaissance* (Cambridge, UK: Cambridge University Press, 1978), 18–22, 60–65; Conal Condren, "Marsilius of Padua's Argument from Authority: A Study of its Significance in the *Defensor Pacis*," *Political Theory* 5:2 (May 1977): 205–18; Cary J. Nederman, *Community and Consent: The Secular Political Theory of Marsiglio of Padua's Defensor Pacis* (Lanham, MD: Rowman & Littlefield, 1995); and *The World of Marsilius of Padua*, ed. Gerson Moreno-Riaño (Turnhout: Brepols, 2006). Cf. George Garnett, *Marsilius of Padua and 'the Truth of History'* (Oxford: Oxford University Press, 2006), who makes no mention of Averroës at all, and who fails to distinguish between Marsilius' stance as a political theorist and the posture he is forced to assume as a statesman and an enlightened practitioner of *kalām*.

consent not unlike Milton's own,[36] and he, too, had circumscribed its democratic potential by conferring on the people's *"valentior pars"* – their sturdier, healthier, more vigorous, more resourceful, and weightier part – a right to legislate on behalf of the whole.[37] In later times, conciliarists, such as Nicholas of Cusa, would find Marsilius's discussion of the origins and nature of political authority attractive,[38] as would Protestants intent on asserting the legitimacy of secular governance over the church within a specific locality.[39] It is by no

[36] Consider Marsilius of Padua, *Defensor pacis* I.viii.2–4, ix.4–5, xii.1–xv.14, in light of I.i.1–7, iv.4, v.7, 10–14, xvii.1–13, xix.3–13, II.viii.5–9, xxviii.29, xxx.1–5.

[37] Consider Marsilius of Padua, *Defensor pacis* I. xii.3–xiii.8, II.xxvi.5, in light of Gewirth, *Marsilius of Padua and Medieval Political Philosophy*, 182–99, and see Georges de Lagarde, *Le Defensor Pacis* (Louvain: Nauwelaerts, 1970), 144–45 (with n. 163), 151–55; Jeannine Quillet, *Le Philosophie politique de Marsile de Padoue* (Paris: J. Vrin, 1970), 93–99; Michael Wilks, "Corporation and Representation in the *Defensor Pacis*," *Studia Gratiana* 15 (1972): 279–87; Conal Condren, "Democracy and the *Defensor Pacis*," *Il pensiero politico* 13:3 (1980): 301–16; James Blythe, *Ideal Government and the Mixed Constitution in the Middle Ages* (Princeton, NJ: Princeton University Press, 1992), 193–202; and Vasileios Syros, "The Sovereignty of the Multitude in the Works of Marsilius of Padua, Peter of Auvergne, and Some Other Aristotelian Commentators," in *The World of Marsilius of Padua*, 227–48. As Gewirth points out, the pertinent Latin phrase was first used in William of Moerbeke's translation of Arist. *Pol.* 1296b13–35, which should be read in light of Peter L. Phillips Simpson, *A Philosophical Commentary on the Politics of Aristotle* (Chapel Hill: University of North Carolina Press, 1998), 335–36. Note also J. H. Burns, "Majorities: An Exploration," *History of Political Thought* 24:1 (Spring 2003): 66–85 (esp. 66–73), who draws attention to the use in canon law, well before the recovery of Aristotle, of the phrase *maior et sanior pars* to make sense of the role played by authority in determining the decisions of monastic communities and cathedral chapters. This mode of thinking, in turn, had its roots in Roman law.

[38] Take note of Nicolaus de Cusa, *De concordantia Catholica libri tres*, ed. Gerhard Kallen (Hamburg: Felix Meiner, 1963) II.xxxiv.256, 265; see II.xiv.127, xvi.138–39, xxi.191–93, and then consider III.Proemio.275–79, 281–86, in light of 269–71 (esp. 270) – where, as Paul E. Sigmund, "The Unacknowledged Influence of Marsilius on XVth Century Conciliarism," *Journal of the History of Ideas* 23:3 (July 1962): 392–402, has shown, all of the classical citations are lifted from Marsilius. See also Sigmund, *Nicholas of Cusa and Medieval Political Thought* (Cambridge, MA: Harvard University Press, 1963); Jeannine Quillet, "Le *Defensor Pacis* de Marsile de Padoue et le *De Concordantia Catholica* de Nicolas de Cues," in *Nicolò Cusano agli inizi del mondo moderno. Atti del Congresso internazionale in occasione del V centenario della morte di Nicolò Cusano. Bressanone, 6–10 September 1964* (Florence: Sansoni, 1970), 485–506; and Blythe, *Ideal Government and the Mixed Constitution in the Middle Ages*, 203–59. Nicholas of Cusa was by no means peculiar in displaying such an interest: see Jeanine Quillet, *La Philosophie politique du Songe du vergier (1378): Sources doctrinales* (Paris: Vrin, 1977), 51–60, 139–66, and Cary J. Nederman, "A Heretic Hiding in Plain Sight: The Secret History of Marsiglio of Padua's *Defensor Pacis* in the Thought of Nicole Oresme," in *Heresy in Transition: Transforming Ideas of Heresy in Medieval and Early Modern Europe* (Aldershot, UK: Ashgate, 2005), 71–88.

[39] See Gregorio Piaia, *Marsilio da Padua nella Riforma e nella Controriforma: Fortuna ed interpretazione* (Padua: Antenore, 1977), along with Jean Céard, "L'Influence de Marsile de Padoue sur la pensée calviniste française de la fin du XVIᵉ siècle: Du Plessis-Mornay, lecteur du *Defensor Pacis*," *Medioevo* 6 (1980): 577–94. As Gewirth documents, *Marsilius of Padua and Medieval Political Philosophy*, 303 n. 5, it was common for defenders of the Papacy to charge that Luther had lifted his account of political authority from Marsilius. That publishers in Protestant Germany displayed an enthusiasm for the book is, moreover, perfectly clear: see Thomas Itzbicki, "The Reception of Marsilius in the 15th and 16th Centuries," forthcoming in *A Companion to Marsilius of Padua*, ed. Gerson Moreno-Riaño and Cary J. Nederman (Leiden: Brill, 2008).

means fortuitous that Thomas Cromwell, the minister who engineered Henry VIII's break with Rome, sponsored the first English translation of the *Defensor pacis*.[40] To justify the king's authority to initiate such a breach, Cromwell's protégé Thomas Starkey quite naturally turned to Marsilius;[41] and the Anglican divine Richard Hooker subsequently drew on the Paduan's arguments when he set out to defend the Elizabethan settlement of the English church.[42] Moreover, in Germany, on the Dutch border, Johannes Althusius cited *Defensor pacis* with a similar end in mind.[43] By Milton's day, Marsilius' argument was the common property of educated Protestants everywhere, and many of his countrymen thought it perfectly plausible. In 1660, for example, when the partisan of Parliament George Lawson published his *Politica sacra et civilis*, he, too, would speak of the role reserved for England's *sanior* and *valentior pars*.[44]

As we have had occasion to notice, the logic of the classical republican position requires that one be ready to embrace monarchy if the people in a polity are unfit to rule and an individual is, in fact, the polity's *valentior* and *sanior pars* – and this, at least in principle, John Milton was perfectly prepared to do.[45] In defending the execution of Charles I as justifiable tyrannicide,[46] he conceded that the Romans of the late republic had no longer been fit to be free, and he implied that on the Ides of March the assassins Brutus and Cassius had

---

[40] See G. R. Elton, "The Political Creed of Thomas Cromwell," in *Studies in Tudor and Stuart Politics and Government II: Parliament/Political Thought* (Cambridge, UK: Cambridge University Press, 1974), 215–35, and Harry S. Stout, "Marsilius of Padua and the Henrician Reformation," *Church History* 43:3 (September 1973): 308–18.

[41] Cf. Franklin L. Baumer, "Thomas Starkey and Marsilius of Padua," *Politica* 2 (1936): 188–205, with Thomas F. Mayer, *Thomas Starkey and the Commonweal: Humanist Politics and Religion in the Reign of Henry VIII* (Cambridge: Cambridge University Press, 1989), 139–46; then, see ibid., 215. Note also G. R. Elton, "Reform by Statute: Thomas Starkey's *Dialogue* and Thomas Cromwell's Policy," *Proceedings of the British Academy* 54 (1968): 165–88.

[42] Consider Marsilius of Padua, *Defensor pacis* I.viii.2–4, ix.4–5, xii.1–xv.14, in light of I.i.1–7, iv.4, v.7, 10–14, xvii.1–13, xix.3–13, II.viii.5–9, xxviii.29, xxx.1–5 ; then, note Richard Hooker, *Of the Laws of Ecclesiastical Polity*, ed. Georges Edelen, W. Speed Hill, and P. G. Stanwood (Cambridge, MA: Havard University Press, 1977–1981) VII.xi.8, and see I.x.3–14 (esp. 4, 8), VIII.i.4, iii.1–5. Cf., however, W. D. J. Cargill Thompson, "The Source of Hooker's Knowledge of Marsilius of Padua," *Journal of Ecclesiastical History* 25:1 (January 1974): 75–81.

[43] Johannes Althusius, *Politica Methodice Digesta*, ed. Carl J. Friedrich (Cambridge, MA: Harvard University Press, 1932) xxviii.32.

[44] See George Lawson, *Politica sacra et civilis*, second edition (London: T. Goodwin, 1689), 371, 383, which should be read with Conal Condren, "George Lawson and the *Defensor Pacis*: On the Use of Marsilius in Seventeenth-Century England," *Medioevo* 6 (1980): 595–617. Cf. Julian H. Franklin, *John Locke and the Theory of Sovereignty: Mixed Monarchy and the Right of Resistance in the Political Thought of the English Revolution* (Cambridge, UK: Cambridge University Press, 1978), 53–126, 131–35, with Condren, "Resistance and Sovereignty in Lawson's *Politica*: An Examination of a Part of Professor Franklin, His Chimera," *Historical Journal* 24:3 (September 1981): 673–81, and see Condren, *George Lawson's Politica and the English Revolution* (Cambridge, UK: Cambridge University Press, 1989), esp. 69, 87–93, 103–4, 174.

[45] See William Walker, "*Paradise Lost* and the Forms of Government," *History of Political Thought* 22:2 (Summer 2001): 270–99 (at 282–99), who errs only in lumping Milton together with Machiavelli.

[46] For a recent discussion of the grounds for Milton's profound hostility to Charles I, see Sharon Achinstein, "Milton and King Charles," in *The Royal Image: Representations of Charles I*, ed. Thomas N. Corns (Cambridge, UK: Cambridge University Press, 1999), 141–61. Note also Worden, *Literature and Politics in Cromwellian England*, 154–94.

only made matters worse, acknowledging that Julius Caesar, despite his resort to force, may have been "quite worthy of kingship (*regno ... dignissimus*)."[47] Milton was not, he insisted, an enemy to kingship per se: he merely thought it proper to extol monarchy "only if he who rules alone is the best of men and," like Caesar, "*regno dignissimus*."[48] It is, he argued, in good Aristotelian fashion, "neither fitting nor proper that there be a king unless he be far superior to all the rest," and "where many are equal, as in every political community (*civitas*) a great many are, ... they should exercise dominion equally (*imperium ex aequo*) and in turn."[49]

In general, Milton argued that the question which form of government was "most appropriate and advantageous" for a particular "people" was a matter for "the wisest men to ascertain." It is clear, he observed, "that the same form of government is not suited to every people nor is it at all times suited to any given people, but to this one now and to that one at another time as the virtue and industry of the citizens waxes and wanes."[50] For the most part, of course, he was extremely reluctant to admit that in his own day his own country was ripe for one-man rule,[51] and on one occasion he openly wondered whether anyone, apart from the son of God, could be "worthy to hold a power on earth similar to that of the deity."[52] There was, however, a time, which he would later bitterly regret, when Milton was willing to argue, at least in his official capacity as Secretary for Foreign Tongues, that in England the "virtue" of Oliver Cromwell was "not to be surpassed (*insuperabilis*)" and when he was also ready to assert that "there is nothing in human society more pleasing to God, or more agreeable to reason, nothing in the political community more equitable, nothing of greater use, than that the man most worthy manage affairs."[53] If Milton was personally horrified when Cromwell ousted the Rump

[47] Cf. *Pro Populo Anglicano Defensio* (24 February 1651) V, in *CW*, VII 336, with "Milton's Commonplace Book," in *CW*, XVIII 163. For a recent translation of the passage quoted, see *A Defence of the People of England* (24 February 1651) V, tr. Donald C. Mackenzie, in *CPW*, IV:1 449.

[48] *Pro Populo Anglicano Defensio* (24 February 1651) V and *Pro Populo Anglicano Defensio Secunda* (30 May 1654), in *CW*, VII 278, VIII 24. For a recent English translation of the pertinent passages, see *A Defence of the People of England* (24 February 1651) V, tr. Donald C. Mackenzie, and *A Second Defence of the English People* (30 May 1654), tr. Helen North, in *CPW*, IV:1 427, 561.

[49] Cf. *Pro Populo Anglicano Defensio* (24 February 1651) II, in *CW*, VII 126, with Arist. *Pol.* 1283b20–84b33. For a recent English translation of the pertinent passages, see *A Defence of the People of England* (24 February 1651) II, tr. Donald C. Mackenzie, in *CPW*, IV:1 366–67.

[50] *Pro Populo Anglicano Defensio* (24 February 1651) III, in *CW*, VII 190–93. For a recent English translation of the pertinent passages, see *A Defence of the English People* (24 February 1651) III, tr. Donald C. Mackenzie, in *CPW*, IV:1 392.

[51] His compatriots' capacity for self-rule is the subject of his *Areopagitica* (November 1644), in *CPW*, II 486–570. See Sharon Achinstein, *Milton and the Revolutionary Reader* (Princeton, NJ: Princeton University Press, 1994), 58–70.

[52] *Pro Populo Anglicano Defensio* (24 February 1651) V, in *CW*, VII 278. For a recent translation, see *A Defence of the People of England* (24 February 1651) V, tr. Donald C. Mackenzie, in *CPW*, IV:1 427–28.

[53] *Pro Populo Anglicano Defensio Secunda* (30 May 1654), in *CW*, VIII 222. For a recent English translation of the pertinent passages, see *A Second Defence of the English People* (30 May 1654), tr. Helen North, in *CPW*, IV:1 671–72. Cf. *Of Reformation* (May 1641), in *CPW*, I 571–73, 582–83.

on 20 April 1653, if he was appalled when the Lord General summoned the Nominated Parliament and then connived in its collapse on 12 December 1653, if he regarded Cromwell's subsequent assumption of the executive power and establishment of the Protectorate as a betrayal of the republican cause,[54] at the time he firmly bit his tongue.[55] It was not until August 1659, when Cromwell was safely dead, the Protectorate had been overthrown, and the Rump had been recalled that, writing in his own name, Milton contemptuously dismissed the period of Cromwellian rule, stretching from 20 April 1653 to 7 May 1659, as "a short but scandalous night of interruption."[56]

Then, of course, in February 1660 – after the Rump had been once again dismissed and once again recalled; when the Long Parliament had been reconstituted and was preparing to dissolve itself and call new elections; and a restoration of the monarchy seemed a foregone conclusion[57] – Milton, in a vain and courageous, even foolhardy, attempt to stave off the inevitable, actually expressed grave doubt as to whether any individual could possess the superiority requisite for monarchical rule, wondering "how any man who hath the true

54 For the sequence of events, see Austin H. Woolrych, *Commonwealth to Protectorate* (Oxford, UK: Clarendon Press, 1982).

55 That Milton was suspicious of Cromwell from the outset and that his misgivings quickly grew seem highly likely: consider Blair Worden, "John Milton and Oliver Cromwell," in *Soldiers, Writers and Statesmen of the English Revolution*, ed. Ian Gentles, John Morrill, and Blair Worden (Cambridge, UK: Cambridge University Press, 1998), 243–64, which should be read in light of Worden, "Toleration and the Cromwellian Protectorate," *Studies in Church History* 21 (1984): 199–233, and see Worden, *Literature and Politics in Cromwellian England*, 195–201, 221–22, 241–334, who argues that Milton welcomed Cromwell's ouster of the Rump and the collapse of the Nominated Parliament and became fully disillusioned only when, as Lord Protector, Cromwell assumed the trappings of regality and imposed on the Commonwealth a religious settlement falling well short of a complete liberty of conscience. Milton was no admirer of the Rump, as we shall soon see, and at the time he may well have regarded its demise as richly deserved. I doubt, however, that he viewed in similar fashion the dissolution of the Nominated Parliament, which was intent on passing a program of legislation that he strongly favored. The criticism that he directed at the latter assembly in his *Second Defense of the English People* was no doubt a prerequisite for that work's publication under the Protectorate in May 1654, but it is tepid in tone, to say the least. Note also Christopher Hill, *Milton and the English Revolution* (London: Faber and Faber, 1977), 193–94. Cf., however, Robert Thomas Fallon, "A Second Defence: Milton's Critique of Cromwell?" *Milton Studies* 39 (2000): 167–83.

56 One should read *Considerations Touching the Likeliest Means to Remove Hirelings* (August 1659), in *CPW*, VII 274–321 (at 274), in light of Austin H. Woolrych, "Milton and Cromwell: 'A Short but Scandalous Night of Interruption'?" in *Achievements of the Left Hand*, 185–218; "Historical Introduction (1659–1660)," in *CPW*, VII 1–228; and "Political Theory and Political Practice," in *The Age of Milton: Backgrounds to Seventeenth-Century Literature*, ed. C. A. Patrides and Raymond B. Waddington (Manchester, UK: Manchester University Press, 1980), 34–71, and then consider Worden, *Literature and Politics in Cromwellian England*, 42–44, 326–57, who suspects that Milton may have collaborated with Marchamont Nedham in producing the anonymous tract *A Publick Plea Opposed to a Private Proposal*, which appears to have been published in mid-May. Cf., however, Fallon, *Milton in Government*, 123–26, 181–85.

57 For the tangled course of events, see C. H. Firth, *The Last Years of the Protectorate, 1656–1658* (New York: Russell & Russell, 1964), and Godfrey Davies, *The Restoration of Charles II, 1658–1660* (San Marino, CA: Huntington Library, 1955). See also Austin H. Woolrych, "The Good Old Cause and the Fall of the Protectorate," *Cambridge Historical Journal* 13:2 (1957): 133–61, and "Historical Introduction (1659–1660)," in *CPW*, VII 1–228; and Ronald Hutton, *The Restoration: A Political and Religious History of England and Wales, 1659–1667* (Oxford, UK: Clarendon Press, 1985), 3–123.

principles of justice and religion in him, can presume or take upon him to be a king and lord over his brethren, whom he cannot but know, whether as men or Christians, to be for the most part every way equal or superiour to himself." Moreover, in this same tract, Milton acknowledged a failure of statesmanship on the part of the Rump. "When the monarchie was dissolvd," he confessed, "the form of a Commonwealth should have forthwith bin fram'd; and the practice therof immediatly begun; that the people might have soon bin satisfi'd and delighted with the decent order, ease and benefit therof: we had bin then by this time firmly rooted past fear of commotions or mutations, & now flourishing: this care of timely setling a new government instead of ye old, too much neglected, hath bin our mischief."

Yet the cause therof may be ascrib'd with most reason to the frequent disturbances, interruptions and dissolutions which the Parlament hath had partly from the impatient or disaffected people, partly from som ambitious leaders in the Armie; much contrarie, I beleeve, to the mind and approbation of the Armie it self and thir other Commanders, once undeceivd, or in thir own power. Which never Parlament was more free to do; being now call'd, not as heretofore, by the summons of a king, but by the voice of libertie: and if the people, laying aside prejudice and impatience, will seriously and calmly now consider thir own good both religious and civil, thir own libertie and the only means thereof, as shall be heer laid before them, and will elect thir Knights and Burgesses able men, and according to the just and necessarie qualifications (which for aught I hear, remain yet in force unrepeald, as they were formerly decreed in Parlament) men not addicted to a single person or house of lords, the work is don; at least the foundation firmly laid of a free Commonwealth, and good part also erected of the main structure. For the ground and basis of every just and free government (since men have smarted so oft for commiting all to one person) is a general council of ablest men, chosen by the people to consult of public affairs from time to time for the common good.

Now, Milton then insisted, at long last – with the death of Oliver Cromwell, the forced resignation of his son Richard, the collapse of the Protectorate, the return of the Long Parliament, and the calling of new elections – it ought to be possible to set everything right. "Now is the opportunitie," he wrote, "now the very season wherein we may obtain a free Commonwealth and establish it for ever in the land, without difficulty or much delay. Writs are sent out for elections, and which is worth observing in the name, not of any king, but of the keepers of our libertie, to summon a free Parlament: which then only will indeed be free, and deserve the true honor of that supreme title, if they preserve us a free people."[58] But, though Milton had once been an advocate of frequent parliamentary elections, on this occasion he called neither for the establishment of a democracy nor for "the conceit of successive Parlaments" elected at regular intervals on the basis of universal male suffrage. Instead, he spoke up for rule in England by a "Grand or General Councel" of the "ablest men" elected for life to "sit perpetual."[59]

[58] See *The Readie & Easie Way to Establish a Free Commonwealth*, first edition (23–29 February 1660), in *CPW*, VII 364, 430–32.

[59] Cf. *The Readie & Easie Way to Establish a Free Commonwealth*, first edition (23–29 February 1660), in *CPW*, VII 367–74, with *Eikonoklastēs* (6 October 1649), in *CPW*, III 398–400. Milton had been pondering such an idea for some time: see *A Letter to a Friend, Concerning the Ruptures of the Commonwealth* (20 October 1659), *Proposalls of Certaine Expedients for the Preventing*

Whatever John Milton may have been, he was not a modern populist. If he remained free from the delusion, deliberately courted by Machiavelli and regnant in many scholarly circles today, that the species of republicanism advocated in the *Discourses on Livy* is genuinely classical in character, it was because of his deep knowledge and appreciation of Aristotle and the classics in general and because of his familiarity with the manner in which the Aristotelian Marsilius had sought to reconcile popular consent with the rule of the wise and learned few over the ignorant and vulgar many.

A Republic of Moral Virtue

Milton very much regretted the influence that Machiavelli exercised over his compatriots. He deplored the fact that, in accord with "the usuall method of teaching Arts," young Englishmen were inclined to "betake them to State affairs, with souls so unprincipl'd in vertue, and true generous breeding, that flattery, and court shifts and tyrannous aphorismes" of the sort first propagated by the author of *The Prince* "appear to them the highest points of wisdom." From quite early on, he was inclined to argue that the true "end . . . of learning" was something altogether different: that it aimed at repairing "the ruins of our first parents by regaining to know God aright, and out of that knowledge to love him, to imitate him, to be like him, as we may the neerest by possessing our souls of true vertue, which being united to the heavenly grace of faith, makes up the highest perfection."[60]

Like the ancient Romans and Greeks,[61] Milton thought of political regimes in educational terms as well. The "education of children" he persisted in regarding as a matter of supreme political importance. There is, he argued, "nothing of greater weight with regard to the proper governance of a commonwealth, nothing as conducive to its long survival." And he knew of "nothing" with comparable staying power "for impressing on the minds of men the virtue whence arises true, interior liberty."[62] If in *Areopagitica* he rejected tutelage and the "licencing of books" as unlikely to "mend our condition," it was only to embrace "those unwritt'n, or at least unconstraining laws of vertuous education, religious and civill nurture, which *Plato*" singles out in his *Laws* "as the bonds and ligaments of the Commonwealth."[63] When he first entered the lists in 1641 with the publication of his tract *Of Reformation Touching Church-Discipline in England*, Milton sounded a theme that would run through and

---

of a Civill War Now Feard, & The Settling of a Firme Government (Fall 1659), and *The Present Means, and Brief Delineation of a Free Commonwealth, Easy to be Put in Practice, and without Delay. In a Letter to General Monk* (February/March 1660), in *CPW*, VII 324–33 (esp. 329–31), 336–39, 392–95. As Zagorin, *John Milton*, 113–14, points out, similar proposals were put forward by Edmund Ludlow, Sir Henry Vane, and Henry Stubbe.

[60] *Of Education* (June 1644), in *CPW*, II 366–67, 374–76.

[61] See Rahe, *Republics Ancient and Modern*, 15–27.

[62] See *Pro Populo Anglicano Defensio Secunda* (30 May 1654), in *CW*, VIII 132–33. For a recent translation of the particular passage quoted, see *A Second Defence of the English People* (30 May 1654), tr. Helen North, in *CPW*, IV:1 625.

[63] See *Areopagitica* (November 1644), in *CPW*, II 526.

underpin all of his subsequent contributions to the public debates: "that to govern well is to train up a Nation in true wisdom and vertue, and that which springs from thence magnanimity, . . . and that which is our beginning, regeneration, and happiest end, likenes to *God*, which in one word we call *godlines*." This, he insisted, and nothing else "is the true florishing of a Land."

Even then, he regretted that "the art of policie," though of the "greatest importance to the life of man," had "bin more canker'd in her principles, more soyl'd, and slubber'd with aphorisming pedantry" than any other art, and this misfortune he traced to those, inspired by Machiavelli, who solemnly preached "reason of state." Under the tutelage of these, he lamented, it had come to be considered "the masterpiece of a modern politician" to understand

how to qualifie, and mould the sufferance and subjection of the people to the length of that foot that is to tread on their necks, how rapine may serve it selfe with the fair, and honourable pretences of publick good, how the puny Law may be brought under the wardship, and controul of lust, and will; in which attempt if they fall short, then must a superficial colour of reputation by all means direct or indirect be gotten to wash over the unsightly bruse of honor.

Milton had no doubt that "the *Bible* is shut against" the practitioners and proponents of "reason of state," and he was similarly "certaine that neither *Plato*, nor *Aristotle* is for their turnes."[64]

Politics and Morality

Milton was himself a political moralist of the sort most abhorrent to Machiavelli: whatever doubts he may privately have entertained, to the public, he presented himself as a Christian Aristotelian who believed not only that Christian virtue and the moral virtues prized in pagan times could be made compatible, but that together they provided the only proper foundation for the political virtue required in a republic.[65] Long before he read with any care the *Discourses on Livy*, he had argued that "a Commonwelth ought to be but as one huge Christian personage, one mighty growth, and stature of an honest man, as big, and compact in vertue as in body." Consider, he wrote, "what the grounds, and causes are of single happines to one man," for "the same yee shall find them to a whole state, as *Aristotle* both in his ethicks, and politiks, from the principles of reason layes down."[66]

In contrast, therefore, with Machiavelli, Milton denied the primacy of foreign policy and urged his countrymen to concentrate their attention on domestic affairs. In the spring of 1654, when the power of the English commonwealth was nearing its height, he issued a warning to his compatriots. "Unless," he

---

[64] *Of Reformation* (May 1641), in *CPW*, I 571–73.

[65] In this connection, see David Hawkes, "The Politics of Character in John Milton's Divorce Tracts," *Journal of the History of Ideas* 62:1 (January 2001): 141–60. Whether the two species of virtue can, in fact, be reconciled is, to say the least, problematic: see Richard Strier, "Milton against Humility," in *Religion and Culture in Renaissance England*, ed. Claire McEachern and Debora Shuger (Cambridge, UK: Cambridge University Press, 1997), 258–86.

[66] *Of Reformation* (May 1641), in *CPW*, I 572.

told them, "you expel avarice, ambition, luxury from your minds and, indeed, extravagance (*luxu*s) from your families as well, that tyranny which you thought was to be sought out abroad and in the field of the sword you will experience at home, you will experience within – and it will be more burdensome (*durior*)."

Yes, indeed, many tyrants, impossible to bear, will daily sprout within your hearts. Conquer these first. This is the warfare of peace: these are its victories, difficult, to be sure, but bloodless, more beautiful by far than victories in war and gore. Unless here also you shall be victorious, that enemy and tyrant whom you conquered lately in the field you have conquered either not at all or to no end. For if you judge that, in a commonwealth, figuring out the most effective schemes (*rationes calidissimae*) enabling you to put a very large sum of money into the treasury, to fit out forces readily for land and sea, to negotiate circumspectly with embassies from abroad, and to put together with skill alliances and draw up treaties is something grander, of greater use, and wiser than rendering to the people judgments unspoiled by corruption, than coming to the aid of the oppressed and those who have suffered injury, than rendering promptly to every man that which is rightfully his, too late will you discover just how much you have been ruined by error – when unexpectedly these great affairs have proven to be a snare and a delusion, and these matters that now in your judgment seem paltry and that you have neglected shall have turned against you and become your destruction.

In the absence of justice, he explains, armies and adherents fall by the wayside. "Riches and honors, which most men pursue, quite easily change their masters: where virtue, where industry and a readiness for labor the more fully flourish, there they flee. The spiritless (*ignavi*) they desert. Thus, nation presses on nation and the sounder part (*sanior pars*) drives out that which is more corrupt." Such was the fate of the royalists, he adds, and such could easily be the fate reserved for their erstwhile adversaries. "If you sink into the same vices, if you imitate them, follow the same paths, chase after the same vanities, you will in effect become royalists yourselves"; and as they succumbed, Milton warns, so also will you.[67] Politics was for John Milton what it had been for the Athenian Stranger in Plato's *Laws*: "the art whose task is caring for souls."[68]

Milton never budged from this conviction. In *The Tenure of Kings and Magistrates*, he returned to this theme, emphasizing from the outset that man's capacity for self-government depends on his possession of the moral virtues that Machiavelli had thought an insuperable obstacle to the deployment of princely *virtù*. "If men within themselves would be govern'd by reason, and not generally give up thir understanding to a double tyrannie, of Custom from without, and blind affections within," he wrote, "they would discerne better, what it is to favour and uphold the Tyrant of a Nation. But being slaves within doors, no wonder that they strive so much to have the public State conformably govern'd

---

[67] See *Pro Populo Anglicano Defensio Secunda* (30 May 1654), in CW, VIII 240–445. For a recent translation, see *A Second Defence of the English People* (30 May 1654), tr. Helen North, in CPW, IV:1 680–84.

[68] Note Pl. *Leg.* 1.650b, and see *Areopagitica* (November 1644), in CPW, II 522–27. In this connection, see Cedric C. Brown, "Great Senates and Godly Education: Politics and Cultural Renewal in some Pre- and Post-Revolutionary Texts of Milton," in *Milton and Republicanism*, 43–60.

to the inward vitious rule, by which they govern themselves. For indeed none can love freedom heartilie, but good men; the rest love not freedom, but license; which never hath more scope or more indulgence then under Tyrants."[69] From Milton's perspective, the most powerful indictment that could be leveled at a king was that his rule relied upon and fostered moral corruption and degeneracy on the part of his subjects. The epigraph from Sallust's *Catiline*, with which he prefaced *Eikonoklastēs*, says it all: "The good are more suspect to kings than the bad; the virtue of another is always formidable to these."[70]

The real question that bedeviled Milton throughout was whether his compatriots were up to the challenge they faced. Had he paused to reflect on Aristotle's claim that, if a *pólis* is to function properly, it must be "easily surveyed" so that the citizens might know one another's characters, had he ruminated on the fact that a legislator can educate a multitude by fostering within a community a powerful ethos of shame only where such a community is exceedingly small, he might have pondered the obstacle to his ambitions posed by the immense geographical expanse encompassed by the revolutionary Commonwealth and the sheer magnitude of its population, and then, perhaps, he would have given up in despair.[71] But this, characteristically, he did not do.

In 1654, after Oliver Cromwell had become Lord Protector, Milton interrupted the peroration in praise of the Commonwealth and its supporters that graced his *Second Defense of the English People* with a warning to his fellow "citizens" that owed much to Sallust's famous description of the moral underpinnings of the rise and decline of the Roman republic.[72] Their "acquisition" and "retention of liberty" depended, he told them, first and foremost on "what sort of men" they turned out to be. In fact, he wrote, no doubt already then with Cromwell in mind, "unless your liberty is of such a kind as can neither be gained nor lost by arms, but is of that species only which, born from piety, justice, temperance, in short, true virtue, shall have taken deep and inmost root in your souls, there will not be lacking one who will in short order wrench from

---

[69] Cf. *The Tenure of Kings and Magistrates* (13 February 1649), in *CPW*, III 190, with Machiavelli, *Il principe* 15–18 and *Discorsi* 1.26–27, 41, in *Opere*, 109–10, 125–26, 280–84. For an earlier statement along these lines, see "Sonnet XII" (1646), in *CW*, I:1 62–63.

[70] Cf. *Eikonoklastēs* (1650), in *CPW*, III 336 (on the title page opposite), with Sallust *Cat.* 7.2. There is reason to suspect that in 1658 – when Milton ushered into print a collection of aphorisms put together late in the Elizabethan period, which presented itself as an advice book for princes and was largely drawn from Machiavelli's *Prince*, his *Discourses on Livy*, and subsequent works penned by the proponents of raison d'état – he intended its publication as an oblique critique of the Cromwellian regime, which, in his capacity as Secretary for Foreign Tongues, he also then served: see Martin Dzelzainis, "Milton and the Protectorate in 1658," in *Milton and Republicanism*, 181–205. Cf. Paul Stevens, "Milton's 'Renunciation' of Cromwell: The Problem of Raleigh's *Cabinet-Council*," *Modern Philology* 98:3 (February 2001): 363–92, and note Worden, *Literature and Politics in Cromwellian England*, 323–25.

[71] Consider Arist. *Pol.* 1326a5–b25 in light of Peter Laslett, "The Face to Face Society," in *Philosophy, Politics, and Society*, ed. Peter Laslett (Oxford, UK: Oxford University Press, 1956), 157–84, and see Rahe, *Republics Ancient and Modern*, 91–121 (esp. 105–9). See also Pl. *Resp.* 4.423a; 5.460a; *Leg.* 5.738d–e, 742d. Note also Thuc. 8.66.3, Isoc. 6.81, 15.171–72.

[72] Sallust *Cat.* 5.9–13.5. Milton preferred Sallust to all other historians: see Nicholas von Maltzahn, *Milton's History of Britain: Republican Historiography in the English Revolution* (Oxford, UK: Clarendon Press, 1991), 75–79.

you, even without arms, that liberty which you boast of having sought by force of arms."[73] This was for Milton, as we shall see, a persistent theme.

In the second edition of *The Readie and Easie Way to Establish a Free Commonwealth*, which Milton published as a last-ditch defense of "*the good Old Cause*" in early April 1660, just as the English republic issued its last gasp, the blind poet summed up his republican creed, arguing that "of all governments," that of the "Commonwealth aims most to make the people flourishing, vertuous, noble and high spirited," which "monarchs will never permitt," since their "aim is to make the people, wealthie indeed perhaps and well fleec't, for thir own shearing and the supplie of regal prodigalitie; but otherwise softest, basest, vitiousest, servilest, easiest to be kept under; and not only in fleece, but in minde also sheepishest." By then, he professedly had no doubt that no "government coms neerer to" the political precept

of Christ, then a free Commonwealth; wherin they who are greatest, are perpetual servants and drudges to the public at thir own cost and charges, neglect thir own affairs; yet are not elevated above thir brethren; live soberly in their families, walk the streets as other men, may be spoken to freely, familiarly, friendly, without adoration. Wheras a king must be ador'd like a Demigod, with a dissolute and haughtie court about him, of vast expence and luxurie, masks and revels, to the debaushing of our prime gentry both male and female.

In his judgment, "the happiness of a nation must needs be firmest and certainest in a full and free Councel of thir own electing, where no single person, but reason only swaies." This is what his compatriots had set out to build: "a tower.... to overshaddow kings, and be another *Rome* in the west." But he was forced to acknowledge that "this goodly tower of a Commonwealth," of which the English had once boasted, had fallen "into a wors confusion, not of tongues, but of factions, then those at the tower of *Babel*," and that his generation – "a strange degenerate contagion suddenly spread among us fitted and prepar'd for new slaverie" – was likely to leave "no memorial of thir work behinde them remaining, but in the common laughter of *Europ*."[74]

A few days later, in response to a sermon delivered and published by a vengeful Cavalier, Milton ushered into print his last prose contribution to the political debates of the interregnum. In what he termed *Brief Notes upon a Late Sermon*, he seemed almost entirely resigned. "Free Commonwealths," he wrote,

---

73 Consider *Pro Populo Anglicano Defensio Secunda* (30 May 1654), in CW, VIII 238–51 (esp. 238–41), in light of Worden, "John Milton and Oliver Cromwell," 243–64, and *Literature and Politics in Cromwellian England*, 195–201, 221–22, 241–334. For a recent translation of the particular passage quoted, see *A Second Defence of the English People* (30 May 1654), tr. Helen North, in *CPW*, IV:1 680.

74 *The Readie and Easie Way to Establish a Free Commonwealth*, second edition (1–10 April 1660), in *CPW*, VII 422–23, 425, 427, 460, 462. For the response that this work, in its two editions, provoked, see Nicholas von Maltzahn, "From Pillar to Post: Milton and the Attack on Republican Humanism at the Restoration," in *Soldiers, Writers and Statesmen of the English Revolution*, 265–85. Note, in this connection, Woolrych, "The Good Old Cause and the Fall of the Protectorate," 133–61, and Worden, *Literature and Politics in Cromwellian England*, 326–57.

have bin ever counted fittest and properest for civil, vertuous and industrious Nations, abounding with prudent men worthie to govern: monarchie fittest to curb degenerate, corrupt, idle, proud, luxurious people. If we desire to be of the former, nothing better for us, nothing nobler then a free Commonwealth: if we still needs condemn our selves to be of the latter, desparing of our own vertue, industrie and the number of our able men, we may then, conscious of our own unworthiness to be governed better, sadly betake us to our fitting thraldom.

Milton qualified this willingness to surrender so much of what he had once held dear in only one particular, specifying that the supporters of the Good Old Cause should as their monarch choose "out of our own number one who hath best aided the people, and best merited against tyrannie." That "a victorious people should give up themselves again to the vanquishd" he could hardly imagine. It was, he said, "never yet heard of; seems rather void of all reason and good policie, and will in all probabilitie subject the subduers to the subdu'd, will expose to revenge, to beggarie, to ruin and perpetual bondage the victors under the vanquishd: then which what can be more unworthie?"[75]

Milton's Misgivings

These worries, as to whether his compatriots really were suited to republican rule, Milton had long in private entertained. In a sonnet, left unpublished, that he had composed in August 1648 in praise of Thomas Lord Fairfax, commander of the Roundhead forces, he had intimated that something was very much amiss with the Long Parliament and that it would take much more than victory on the battlefield to set things right. "For what can Warr," he had asked, "but endless warr still breed,/Till Truth, & Right from Violence be freed,/And Public Faith cleard from the shamefull brand/Of Public Fraud. In vain doth Valour bleed/While Avarice, & Rapine share the land."[76]

Subsequently, in a digression initially intended for inclusion in his *History of Britain* but eventually cut, which he appears to have drafted in the weeks intervening between Charles I's execution on 30 January 1649 and his own selection by the Rump as Secretary for Foreign Tongues on 15 March but may have composed or redrafted at a considerably later date,[77] Milton analyzed in

---

[75] See *Brief Notes upon a Late Sermon* (10–15 April 1660), in *CPW*, VII 481–82.

[76] "Sonnet XV" (August 1648?), in *CW*, I:1 64.

[77] In the debate concerning the digression's date, I believe Nicholas von Maltzahn's argument more plausible than those advanced by Austin Woolrych and Blair Worden: cf. Woolrych, "The Date of the Digression in Milton's *History of Britain*," in *For Veronica Wedgwood These: Studies in Seventeenth-Century History*, ed. Richard Ollard and Pamela Tudor-Craig (London: Collins, 1986), 217–46, with Maltzahn, *Milton's History of Britain*, 1–48; then, cf. Woolrych, "Dating Milton's *History of Britain*," *Historical Journal* 36:4 (December 1993): 929–43, with Maltzahn, "Dating the Digression in Milton's *History of Britain*," *Historical Journal* 36:4 (December 1993): 945–56, and see Worden, *Literature and Politics in Cromwellian England*, 410–26, who believes that the digression was composed or substantially redrafted after the Restoration but acknowledges (ibid., 168–72) what is crucial for my argument here: that the digression reflects conclusions that Milton had reached by 1648, when he wrote his sonnet in praise of Fairfax. For a brief discussion of the themes linking this sonnet with the digression, see Norbrook, *Writing the English Republic*, 182–91.

considerable depth the moral and intellectual defects that had resulted in the Long Parliament's failure to take advantage of the "smooth occasion" offered them by their struggle with the king. He had once regarded that assembly's members as the "publick benefactors of their country." In 1642, he had celebrated "their noble deeds, the unfinishing whereof already surpasses what others before them have left enacted with their utmost performance through many ages." He had then ascribed to them "mature wisedome, deliberat vertue, and deere affection to the publick good." They are, he then wrote, "unmov'd with the baits of preferment, and undaunted for any discouragement and terror." He even compared them favorably with "those ancient worthies [who] deliver'd men from such tyrants as were content to inforce only an outward obedience, letting the minde be as free as it could," contending that the members of the Long Parliament "have freed us from a doctrine of tyranny that offer'd violence and corruption even to the inward persuasion," a doctrine that gave to tyranny a "second life...guarded with superstition[,] which hath no small power to captivate the minds of men otherwise most wise." The members of this Parliament, he insisted, "neither were taken with" the "miter'd hypocrisie" of this new, quintessentially modern species of tyranny, "nor terrifi'd with the push of her bestiall hornes, but breaking them immediately forc'd her to unbend the pontificall brow, and recoile."

That, for the purposes of exhortation and encouragement, he was indulging in hyperbole and overstating his case – "praising great designes before the utmost event" – Milton readily conceded at the time.[78] But there can be no doubt that his hopes had then been genuine and his expectations exceedingly high, and the disappointment and bitterness that gripped him late in 1648 and in early 1649 were proportionate. "They had armies, leaders and successes to thir wish," he then observed, "but to make use of so great advantages was not thir skill."

To other causes therefore and not to want of force, or warlike manhood in the Brittans..., wee must impu[te] the ill husbanding of those faire opportunities, which migh[t] seeme to have put libertie, so long desir'd, like a brid[le] into thir hands.... For a parlament being calld and as was thought many things to redress, the people with great courage & expectation to be now eas'd of what discontented them chose to thir behooff in parlament such as they thought best affected to the public good, & some indeed men of wisdome and integritie. The rest, and to be sure the greatest part whom wealth and ample possessions or bold and active ambition rather then merit had commended to the same place, when onc[e] the superficial zeale and popular fumes that acted thir new magistracie were cool'd and spent in them, straite every one betooke himself, setting the common-wealth behinde and his private ends before, to doe as his owne profit or ambition led him. Then was justice delai'd & soone after deny'd, spite and favour determin'd all: hence faction, then treacherie both at home & in the field, ev'ry where wrong & oppression, foule and dishonest things commited daylie, or maintain'd in secret or in op'n. Some who had bin calld from shops & warehouses without other merit to sit in supreme councel[s] & committies, as thir breeding was, fell to hucster the common-wealth; others did thereafter as men could sooth and humour them best.... Thir votes and ordinances which men look'd should have contain'd the repealing of bad laws & the immediate constitution of better, resounded with nothing els but new impositions, taxes, excises, yearlie, monthlie, weeklie[,] not to reck'n the offices, gifts, and preferments

---

[78] See *An Apology against a Pamphlet* (April 1642), in *CPW*, I 922–28.

bestow'd and shar'd among themselves.... There were of thir owne nu[m]ber [some] who secretly contriv'd and fomented those troubles and combustions in the land which openly they sate to remedy, & would continually finde such worke, as should keepe them from ever being brought to the terrible stand of laying downe thir authoriti[e] for lack of new buisness.

"Thus," Milton observed, "they who but of late were extolld so great deliverers, and had a people wholy at thir devotion, by so discharging thir trust as wee see, did not onely weak'n and unfitt themselves to be dispencers of what libertie they pretended, but unfitted also the people, now growne worse & more disordinate, to receave or to digest any libertie at all." Here, as elsewhere, Milton turned to antiquity for a moral, remarking, once again no doubt with Brutus and Cassius in mind, that "libertie sought out of season in a corrupt and degenerate age brought Rome it self into further slaverie."

To make full sense of the Long Parliament's failure, Milton suggested that his countrymen reflect on the fact that, while Britain may be "a land fruitful enough of men stout and couragious in warr" it is "naturallie not over fertil of men able to govern justlie & prudently in peace." In fact, "trusting onelie on thir Mother-witt, as most doo," the leading men within the British isles "consider not that civilitie, prudence, love of the public more then of money or vaine honour are to this soile in a manner outlandish," that these "grow not here but in minds well implanted with solid & elaborate breeding," and that, as a consequence, the British are "too impolitic els and too crude, if not headstrong and intractable to the industrie and vertue either of executing or understanding true civil government." They are "valiant indeed and prosperous to winn a field," he acknowledged, "but to know the end and reason of winning, unjudicious and unwise, in good or bad success alike unteachable." In Milton's judgment, the only remedy for this malady was a proper political education of the sort afforded the commonwealth's Secretary for Foreign Tongues by his study of the classics: "as wine and oyle are imported to us from abroad, so must ripe understanding and many civil vertues bee imported into our minds from forren writings & examples of best ages: wee shall else miscarry still and com short in the attempt of any great enterprise." In a republic, he concluded, all would be hopeless "unless men more then vulgar, bred up, as few of them were, in the knowledge of Antient and illustrious deeds, invincible against money, and vaine titles, impartial to friendships and relations ... conducted thir affaires."[79]

That Milton eventually came to think the Rump no better than its predecessor, there can be no doubt.[80] There is, in fact, reason to think that he had

---

[79] See "The Digression," in *CPW*, V:1 441, 443, 445, 447, 449, 451. I cite the surviving seventeenth-century manuscript (Harvard MS Eng. 901) of the former work rather than the version extracted from the manuscript of Milton's *History of Britain*, edited, and published by the Tory propagandist Roger L'Estrange in 1681 under the title *Mr. John Miltons Character of the Long Parliament and Assembly of Divines in MDCXLI*. The latter can be found on the even-numbered pages corresponding to those cited earlier. In this connection, note Worden, *Literature and Politics in Cromwellian England*, 392–98

[80] Consider *Pro Populo Anglicano Defensio Secunda* (30 May 1654), in *CW*, VIII 244–49, in light of the digression penned for inclusion in his *History of Britain*, which is quoted at length earlier in this chapter; then see *Pro Populo Anglicano Defensio Secunda* (30 May 1654), in *CW*, VIII 220–21, which suggests that what is presented as an exhortation against misbehavior is

reached this conclusion by February 1652, if not before.[81] To a visiting diplomat whom he had befriended, he remarked that the difficulties which the man had experienced in his dealings with the Council of State had arisen not just from "the lack of expertise (*imperitia*)," but from "the malice of those" within the government "who enjoy the majority of the votes." Those who formed "the stronger party within the commonwealth (*potior pars Reipublicae*)" he dismissed with contempt as "the offspring of Mars and Mercury." They were "artisans (*mechanici*), soldiers, householders (*domestici*)" unfamiliar with the larger world. Of the forty members who served on the Council of State, he observed, only three or four had ever even set foot outside England. Such men might be "sufficiently courageous and fierce" on the field of battle, but they were "extremely inexperienced in political matters and public affairs." As for those who were "more prudent," they were not even permitted to convey what they had in mind. There was no point, therefore, in blaming "the *saniores*" – England's more reasonable, sounder, saner men.[82]

After the Fall

John Milton was steadfast in good times and bad.[83] From the analysis of the defects of his country's political leaders – foreshadowed in the hyperbolic praise he conferred on the Long Parliament in 1642 and spelled out in the digression to his *History of Britain*, intimated in his sonnets, hinted at in the various tracts he wrote in his official capacity as Secretary of Foreign Tongues, and restated with vigor and clarity in *The Readie & Easie Way to Establish a Free Commonwealth* – he never deviated one jot. On his overall outlook, the Restoration had little, if any effect.

Milton's masterpiece, *Paradise Lost*, which he appears to have begun writing during the Protectorate, about a decade before its publication in 1667, is a meditation on matters of greater grandeur than England's failed republican experiment: it presents itself as a theodicy designed to "assert Eternal Providence, and justifie the wayes of God to men."[84] And yet one cannot help noticing what early readers of the poem did notice, in fact: that, in this cosmic

a description of what transpired. For a recent translation of the two passages, see *A Second Defence of the English People* (30 May 1654), tr. Helen North, in *CPW*, IV:1 671, 682–83.

[81] From the outset, as Worden, *Literature and Politics in Cromwellian England*, 174–94, demonstrates in detail, Milton evidenced more confidence in the army than that had conducted Pride's Purge than in the Rump. Then, in November 1651, the radical faction that he favored lost the considerable leverage that it had hitherto exercised within the Council of State, and Milton found himself at odds with his new masters: see ibid., 195–201, 241–49.

[82] See the citations from the diary of Hermann Mylius reprinted in Lee Miller, *John Milton and the Oldenburg Safeguard: New Light on Milton and His Friends in the Commonwealth from the Diaries and Letters of Hermann Mylius, Agonist in the Early History of Modern Diplomacy* (New York: Loewenthal, 1985), 171–72. Cf. Sean Kelsey, *Inventing a Republic: The Political Culture of the English Commonwealth, 1649–1653* (Stanford, CA: Stanford University Press, 1997), 68.

[83] See Barbara Lewalski, "Milton: Political Beliefs and Polemical Methods," *PMLA* 74:3 (June 1959): 191–202.

[84] *Paradise Lost* 1.25–26, in *CW*, II:1 9. See Dennis Danielson, "The Fall of Man and Milton's Theodicy," in *The Cambridge Companion to Milton*, ed. Dennis Danielson (Cambridge, UK: Cambridge University Press, 1989), 113–29.

drama, Satan depicts himself as a republican in rebellion against a tyrant god and that his rhetoric owes a considerable debt to the political tracts of Milton himself.[85] It would, however, be an error to conclude from this that William Blake was right in asserting that the author of *Paradise Lost* was "of the Devils party without knowing it,"[86] and it would for similar reasons be a mistake to take this as a sign that Milton ever consciously repented or lost heart and abandoned as a snare and delusion the cause of ancient liberty.[87]

Like Goethe, Milton regarded poetry as the supreme form of rhetoric. He did not explicitly say, as in due course the German poet would, that "the soul" of a great dramatic poet's plays can become "the soul of the people," but early on he did argue that "to imbreed and cherish in a great people the seeds of vertu and publick civility" is one of poetry's chief aims,[88] and he had great faith in poetry's power.[89] As a young student at Cambridge, Milton had speculated that if "holy Song," such as that produced by the "Crystall sphears," were to "Once bless our humane ears" and "Enwrap our fancy long," the human condition would be utterly transformed:

> Time will run back, and fetch the age of gold,
> And speckl'd vanity
> Will sicken soon and die

[85] See *Vindiciae Carolinae or, A Defence of Eikon basilike, the Portraicture of His Sacred Majesty in his Solitudes and Sufferings: in Reply to a Book Intituled Eikonoklastes, Written by Mr. Milton, and Lately Re-printed at Amsterdam* (London: Luke Meredith, 1692), 3, and John Dryden, *The Works of Virgil* (London: Jacob Tonson, 1697), 154. Nicholas von Maltzahn, "Laureate, Republican, Calvinist: An Early Response to Milton and *Paradise Lost* (1667)," *Milton Studies* 29 (1992): 181–98 (at 197 n. 32), who draws attention to these passages, suggests on the basis of Oxford, Bodleian Library, Tanner MS 26, f. 15, that the anonymous author of the former tract may have been the nonjuring bishop William Lloyd.

[86] Note "The Marriage of Heaven and Hell," in *The Complete Poetry and Prose of William Blake*, ed. David V. Erdman, newly revised edition (Berkeley: University of California Press, 1982), 33–44 (at 34–35). Then, cf. C. S. Lewis, *A Preface to Paradise Lost* (London: Oxford University Press, 1942), with William Empson, *Milton's God*, revised edition (London: Chatto & Windus, 1965), and see Stanley Eugene Fish, *Suprised by Sin: The Reader in Paradise Lost* (London: MacMillan, 1967).

[87] Cf. Trevor-Roper, "Milton in Politics," 279–82, and Worden, "Milton's Republicanism and the Tyranny of Heaven," 235–45, with Zagorin, *John Milton*, 121–48, and see Mary Ann Radzinowicz, "The Politics of *Paradise Lost*," in *Politics of Discourse: The Literature and History of Seventeenth-Century England*, ed. Kevin Sharpe and Steven N. Zwicker (Berkeley: University of California Press, 1987), 204–29; Joan S. Bennett, *Reviving Liberty: Radical Christian Humanism in Milton's Great Poems* (Cambridge, MA: Harvard University Press, 1989); David Quint, *Epic and Empire: Politics and Generic Form from Virgil to Milton* (Princeton, NJ: Princeton University Press, 1993), 268–308, 325–40; Achinstein, *Milton and the Revolutionary Reader*, 177–223; Norbrook, *Writing the English Republic*, 433–95; Barbara Kiefer Lewalski, "*Paradise Lost* and Milton's Politics," *Milton Studies* 38 (2000): 141–68; and John Coffey, "Pacifist, Quietist, or Patient Militant? John Milton and the Restoration," *Milton Studies* 42 (2002): 149–74.

[88] Cf. *The Reason of Church-Government* (January/February 1642), in *CPW*, I 816–17, with Conversation held on 1 April 1827, in Johann Peter Eckermann, *Gespräche mit Goethe in den letzten jahren seines lebens* (Jena: E. Diederichs, 1905), II 298–99. See Barbara Kiefer Lewalski, "Milton and the Hartlib Circle: Educational Projects and Epic *Paideia*," in *Literary Milton: Text, Pretext, Context*, ed. Diana Treviño Benet and Michael Lieb (Pittsburgh, PA: Duquesne University Press, 1994), 202–19.

[89] See Marshall Grossman, "Milton and the Rhetoric of Prophecy," in *The Cambridge Companion to Milton*, 167–81.

And leprous sin will melt from earthly mould,
And Hell it self will pass away,
And leave her dolorous mansions to the peering.

Yea Truth, and Justice then
Will down return to men,
    Orb'd in a Rain-bow; and like glories wearing
Mercy will sit between
Thron'd in Celestial sheen,
    With radiant feet the tissued clouds down stearing,
And Heav'n at some Festivall,
Will open wide the Gates of her high Palace Hall.[90]

There is no reason to suppose that Milton thought so dramatic a transformation within his capacity or that of any man. But there can be little doubt that he wrote *Paradise Lost, Paradise Regained,* and *Samson Agonistes,* at least in part, to instruct his readers in the moral and intellectual virtues required for self-government – "to mend our corrupt and faulty education," as he put it in *The Readie and Easie Way to Establish a Free Commonwealth,* in such a fashion as "to make the people fittest to chuse, and the chosen fittest to govern."[91] When he had first entered the lists, Milton had announced it as his aim to leave "something so written to aftertimes, as they should not willingly let it die," and he had recognized even then what all readers since have acknowledged – that he was far abler as "a Poet soaring in the high regions of the fancies with his garland and singing robes about him" than when "sitting here below in the cool element of prose," wherein "knowing my self inferior to my self, led by the genial powers of nature to another task, I have the use, as I may account it, but of my left hand."[92]

   It is not difficult to discover the didactic purpose informing the magnificent poems that Milton fashioned late in life with his right hand. When, in his *Defense of the English People,* he remarks in passing on the propensity for "poets to frame for the best of their characters" speeches reflecting "an outlook approximating their own (*sensum ferè suum*),"[93] he tips us off regarding a practice that he will himself adopt. It would, for example, be easy for readers of *Paradise Lost* to take at face value Satan's depiction of himself as a "Patron of liberty" in rebellion against "the Tyranny of Heav'n" were the angel Gabriel not so quick in unmasking Milton's villain as a "sly hypocrite" who "once fawn'd, and cring'd, and servilly ador'd/Heav'ns awful Monarch" and who now acts "in hope/To dispossess him, and . . . reigne" in his stead.[94]

---

[90] See "On the Morning of Christ's Nativity: The Hymn" 12.117–15.148 (25 December 1629), in *CW,* I:1 1–11 (at 6–7).

[91] *The Readie and Easie Way to Establish a Free Commonwealth,* second edition (1–10 April 1660), in *CPW,* VII 443.

[92] Consider the program laid out by Milton in *The Reason of Church-Government* (January/February 1642), in *CPW,* I 804–23 (esp. 808, 810).

[93] *Pro Populo Anglicano Defensio* (24 February 1651) V: see *CW,* VII 326–37. For a recent translation of the pertinent chapter, see *A Defence of the People of England* (24 February 1651) V, tr. Donald C. Mackenzie, in *CPW,* IV:1 446.

[94] *Paradise Lost* 1.124, 4.957–61, in *CW,* II:1 12, 140.

As Gabriel's testimony suggests, Milton's Satan is not a virtuous republican: he is a Machiavel – endowed with a taste for transgression and a liking for moral and political anarchy, and he is the very model of a "new prince": morally dexterous in the extreme, willing, when it suits the occasion, to assume any posture and deploy any argument that will promote the attainment of his ambition.[95] When he makes apology for tempting Eve and for destroying the "harmless innocence" of mankind's first parents, he resorts to the language of "necessitie,/the Tyrants plea," made familiar by Machiavelli and respectable by the advocates of raison d'état. In accord with "public reason just," Satan argues that he has no choice – that "Honour and Empire with revenge enlarg'd,/By conquering this new World, compels me now/To do what else though damnd I should abhorre."[96] Milton may deny that "Spirits damn'd/Loose all thir virtue," but he does so only to have his Messiah later clarify which of the virtues they do, in fact, lose, revealing that "by strength" such spirits "measure all," that "of other excellence" they are "Not emulous, nor care who them excells."[97]

We should not then be surprised to discover that for Satan self-government is not an end in itself. Like the republic described in the *Discourses on Livy*, his new regime serves a putatively higher end. In Council, at a time when success hangs in the balance, he encourages his closest allies by confiding in them, revealing that their real goal is not freedom, but conquest and tribute, profit and acquisitions – that they have been found "worthy not of Libertie alone,/Too mean pretense, but what we more affect,/Honour, Dominion, Glorie, and renowne."[98]

In *Paradise Regained*, Satan attempts to lure Christ with the same bait, promising him "fame and glory,...the reward/That sole excites to high attempts the flame/Of most erected Spirits." Here, however, he encounters a check – for, in his youth, as we have already been told, Jesus had aspired to "victorious deeds," which, he says,

> Flam'd in my heart, heroic acts, one while
> To rescue *Israel* from the *Roman* yoke,
> Then to subdue and quell o're all the earth
> Brute violence and proud Tyrannick pow'r,
> Till truth were freed, and equity restor'd.

But, upon reflection at that time, he had "held it more humane, more heavenly first/By winning words to conquer willing hearts,/And make perswasion do the

---

[95] Note Machiavelli, *Il principe* 1, 6–18 (esp. 6 and 13), in *Opere*, 258, 264–84, and see the Preface to Part I, above. On this point, Riebling, "Milton on Machiavelli," 573–97, is of value. *Paradise Lost* could, in fact, be read in light of Miguel E. Vatter, *Between Form and Event: Machiavelli's Theory of Political Freedom* (Dordrecht: Kluwer Academic, 2000).

[96] *Paradise Lost* 4.388–94, in CW, II:1 120.

[97] *Paradise Lost* 2.482–83, 6.820–22, in CW, II:1 55, 207. Satan confirms this charge in praising the "dauntless vertue" of Eve: see *Paradise Lost* 9.692–98, in CW, II:2 285. For further evidence, see *Paradise Lost* 10.354–409, 436–503, in CW, II:2 317–22, and cf. *Paradise Lost* 11.688–99, 712–18 with *Paradise Lost* 11.787–807, in CW, II:2 370–71, 373–74.

[98] *Paradise Lost* 6.420–22, in CW, II:1 193.

work of fear;/At least to try, and teach the erring Soul/Not wilfully mis-doing, but unware/Misled; the stubborn only to subdue."⁹⁹

In response to the invitation subsequently proffered by Satan, the Savior goes one step further, restating the aristocratic critique of empire and glory first laid out by the ancient philosophers. "For what is glory," he asks, "but the blaze of fame,"

> The peoples praise, if always praise unmixt?
> And what the people but a herd confus'd,
> A miscellaneous rabble, who extol
> Things vulgar, & well weigh'd, scarce worth the praise.
> They praise and they admire they know not what;
> And know not whom, but as one leads the other;
> And what delight to be by such extoll'd,
> To live upon thir tongues and be thir talk,
> Of whom to be disprais'd were no small praise?

Nor is Milton's hero friendly to the means by which such glory is ordinarily obtained – for soon thereafter he takes care to add that

> They err who count it glorious to subdue
> By Conquest far and wide, to over-run
> Large Countries, and in field great Battels win,
> Great Cities by assault: what do these Worthies,
> But rob and spoil, burn, slaughter, and enslave
> Peaceable Nations, neighbouring, or remote,
> Made Captive, yet deserving freedom more
> Then those thir Conquerours, who leave behind
> Nothing but ruin wheresoe're they rove,
> And all the flourishing works of peace destroy,
> Then swell with pride, and must be titl'd Gods,
> Great Benefactors of mankind, Deliverers,
> Worship't with Temple, Priest and Sacrifice;
> One is the Son of *Jove*, of *Mars* the other,
> Till Conquerour Death discover them scarce men,
> Rowling in brutish vices, and deform'd,
> Violent or shameful death thir due reward.

If, he adds, "there be in glory aught of good,/It may by means far different be attain'd/Without ambition, war, or violence;/By deeds of peace, by wisdom eminent,/By patience, temperance." And where Satan had urged him to take as his models "the son of *Macedonian Philip*," "young *Scipio*," "young *Pompey*," and "Great *Julius*," Jesus mentions not only "patient *Job*" but, in telling fashion, "Poor *Socrates*," who "By what he taught and suffer'd for so doing,/For truths sake suffering death unjust, lives now/Equal in fame to proudest Conquerours."¹⁰⁰

---

⁹⁹ See *Paradise Regained* 1.215–26, 3.7–42, in CW, II:2 412–13, 442–43.

¹⁰⁰ Cf. *Paradise Regained* 3.31–107, in CW, II:2 443–46, with Arist. *Pol.* 1323a14–1325b32, and see Carnes Lord, *Education and Culture in the Political Thought of Aristotle* (Ithaca, NY: Cornell University Press, 1982), 180–202. Note also *Paradise Lost* 11.689–99, in CW, II:2 370.

Of course, the pitch that Satan makes to Christ is a con – as is the one he makes to his fellow fallen angels in *Paradise Lost*. His aim is neither liberty nor a glory shared but "glorie sole," for we are told in the latter work that his is a "Monarchal pride."[101] If, in his character as a "new prince," the fiend has any obvious English model, it is Oliver Cromwell,[102] whom Milton, in the end, thought a Sulla: invincible on the field of battle, impeccable in the republican principles he mouths, but ambitious for dominion above all else.[103] Many another adherent of the Good Old Cause came to regard the Lord Protector as an "Artificer of fraud ... that practisd falshood under saintly shew/Deep malice to conceale, couch't with revenge."[104]

Satan's most grievous sin is not, then, the mistake made by Milton himself – for, in the most crucial regard, their situations are unlike. Milton rebelled against an unworthy king. Of this he remained supremely confident. He could, therefore, in righteous indignation appropriate the words of his Satan and ask, "Who can in reason then or right assume/Monarchie over such as live by right/His equals, if in power and splendor less,/In freedome equal?"[105] No one could justly reproach him in the Aristotelian manner in which the seraph Abdiel reproaches Satan: that it is not "*Servitude* to serve whom God ordains,/Or Nature; God and Nature bid the same,/When he who rules is worthiest, and excells/Them whom he governs." In soliloquy, when there is no one present to witness his remorse, Satan is forced to concede that his rebellion stemmed from "Pride and worse Ambition" and that "Heav'ns matchless King ... deserved no such return/From me, whom he created what I was." Milton had no such confession to make. On his own behalf, if confronted with such a reproach, he could quite readily point to the Stuart monarchs and in reply deploy Abdiel's own words: "This is servitude,/To serve th'unwise."[106]

---

[101] *Paradise Lost* 2.428, 9.135, in *CW*, II:1 53, II:2 265.

[102] See Worden, *Literature and Politics in Cromwellian England*, 343–47. That Satan stands in as well for the Stuart kings and even, perhaps, for all earthly kings I do not doubt: see Christopher Hill, *Milton and the English Revolution* (London: Faber and Faber, 1977), 341–448; Stevie Davies, *Images of Kingship in Paradise Lost: Milton's Politics and Christian Liberty* (Columbia: University of Missouri Press, 1983); Bennett, *Reviving Liberty*, 33–58; and Quint, *Epic and Empire*, 268–81. I would only insist that the reference to Cromwell is far less oblique. Satan even displays Cromwell's penchant for bursting into tears while speaking in public: see *Paradise Lost* 1.619–21, in *CW*, II:1 30. In this connection, see Scott, *Commonwealth Principles*, 318–20.

[103] Such would appear to be the implication of the epigraph, adapted from Juvenal *Sat.* 1.15–16, which Milton added to the second edition of *The Readie and Easie Way to Establish a Free Commonwealth* (1–10 April 1660), in *CPW*, VII 405: see Armitage, "John Milton: Poet against Empire," 213.

[104] *Paradise Lost* 4.121–23, in *CW*, II:1 110. Among those inclined to discern in Cromwell Machiavelli's "new prince" were Marchamont Nedham, Andrew Marvell, and Edmund Waller: see Worden, *Literature and Politics in Cromwellian England*, 86–102, who cites the evidence and the pertinent secondary literature.

[105] *Paradise Lost* 5.794–97, in *CW*, II:1 172.

[106] Consider *Paradise Lost* 6.175–81 in light of 4.32–57, in *CW*, II:1 107–8, 184, and see Arist. *Pol.* 1283b20–84b33. Cf. Michael Bryson, "'His Tyranny Who Reigns': The Biblical Roots of Divine Kingship and Milton's Rejection of 'Heav'n's King,'" *Milton Studies* 43 (2004): 111–44, who misses Milton's point.

Pietas in Patriam

In Milton's judgment, his own error was, in fact, a sign of his nobility. In a sonnet composed in 1655 and addressed to a friend, he pronounced himself "content though blind," aware that he had lost his eyes "overply'd/In libertyes defence, my noble task."[107] After the Restoration, to be sure, he would complain to an acquaintance that "devotion to the fatherland (*Pietas in Patriam*)" had "bewitched me with her lovely name," and he would concede that, in the end, she had "almost, so might I say, deprived me of that same fatherland (*expatriavit*)."[108] In *Paradise Lost*, he would describe himself as having "fall'n on evil dayes,/On evil dayes, though falln'n, and evil tongues;/In darkness, and with dangers compast round,/And solitude." But, in the very same passage, he would defiantly insist that his "voice" was "unchang'd/To hoarce or mute."[109]

When the author of *Paradist Lost* had God praise Abdiel,

> who single hast maintaind
> Against revolted multitudes the Cause
> Of Truth, in word mightier then they in Armes;
> And for the testimonie of Truth hast born
> Universal reproach, far worse to beare
> Then violence,

he was, as readers have long recognized, almost certainly reflecting on his own conduct in time of loneliness and duress. And the poet presumably again had himself in mind when he celebrated in his own voice "the Seraph *Abdiel* faithful found,/Among the faithless, faithful only hee;/Among innumerable false, unmovd,/Unshak'n, unseduc'd, unterrifi'd," adding, "His Loyaltie he kept, his Love, his Zeale;/Nor number, nor example with him wrought/To swerve from truth, or change his constant mind/Though single."[110] No one can doubt Milton's commitment to constancy.

If Milton bore any responsibility for his own sad plight, it was, he supposed, because of the generous confidence that he had reposed in the virtues of his compatriots.[111] In *Paradise Regained*, when Satan once again tempts Christ, urging him to liberate the Romans from their imperial yoke, the Son of God demurs, reiterating one last time Sallust's famous explanation for Rome's rise and her decline.

> That people victor once, now vile and base,
> Deservedly made vassal, who once just,

---

[107] "Sonnet XXII" (1655), in CW, I:1 68. On the same theme, see *Pro Populo Anglicano Defensio Secunda* (30 May 1654), in CW, VIII 66–77. For a recent translation of the description Milton provides, see *A Second Defence of the English People* (30 May 1654), tr. Helen North, in CPW, IV:1 587–92.

[108] Letter from John Milton to Peter Heimbach, Councillor to the Elector of Brandenburg, on 15 August 1666, in CW, XII 112–15. For a recent translation, see Letter from John Milton to Peter Heimbach, Councillor to the Elector of Brandenburg, on 15 August 1666, tr. Robert W. Ayers, in CPW, VIII 3–4.

[109] *Paradise Lost* 7.24–28, in CW, II:1 212.

[110] *Paradise Lost* 5.896–903, 6.30–35, in CW, II:1 176, 179.

[111] There is as well a hint of the autobiographical in the description of Enoch that Milton attributes to the archangel Michael: see *Paradise Lost* 11.660–73, 689–711, in CW, II:2 369–71.

> Frugal, and mild, and temperate, conquer'd well,
> But govern ill the Nations under yoke,
> Peeling thir Provinces, exhausted all
> By lust and rapine; first ambitious grown
> Of triumph that insulting vanity;
> Then cruel, by thir sports to blood enur'd
> Of fighting beasts, and men to beasts expos'd,
> Luxurious by thir wealth, and greedier still,
> And from the daily Scene effeminate.

"What wise and valiant man," he concludes, "would seek to free/These thus degenerate, by themselves enslav'd,/Or could of inward slaves make outward free?"[112]

Tyranny

For "the Tyrant" himself, Milton was willing to make "no excuse."[113] In *Paradise Lost*, when the archangel Michael describes Nimrod's "Empire tyrannous," he depicts that mighty hunter as a man "Of proud ambitious heart, who not content/With fair equalitie, fraternal state,/Will arrogate Dominion undeserv'd/Over his breathren, and quite dispossess/Concord and law of Nature from the Earth," and, in a passage evocative of Milton's attitude regarding the arguments advanced by James I and his descendants, Michael indicates that Nimrod will do so either "in despite of Heavn'n,/Or from Heav'n claiming second Sovrantie/And from Rebellion shall derive his name,/Though of Rebellion others he accuse."[114] Adam then responds by articulating what one of the book's earliest known readers immediately recognized as the author's "old Principle" and soon thereafter denounced as among "the great faults in his Paradyse Lost." Adam's statement was, in fact, as this reader noted, a recapitulation of the "plea for our Original right" first advanced in *The Tenure of Kings and Magistrates*,[115] for in it Adam describes Nimrod as "to himself assuming/Authoritie usurpt, from God not giv'n," and he justifies his denial that any of his own descendants can claim from heaven "second Sovrantie" by insisting that God "gave us onely over Beast, Fish, Fowl/Dominion absolute; that right we hold/By his donation; but Man over men/He made not Lord; such title to himself/Reserving, human left from human free."[116]

---

[112] Cf. *Paradise Regained* 4.44–153 (esp. 132–45), in CW, II:2 460–64, with Sallust *Cat.* 5.9–13.5.

[113] *Paradise Lost* 12.96, in CW, II:2 382.

[114] *Paradise Lost* 12.6–62 (esp. 24–37), in CW, II:2 379–81.

[115] The early reader was John Beale, an active member of the Royal Society who admired Milton's poetic gift almost as much as he detested his political prose: see Evelyn Collection, Christ Church College, Oxford, MS letters 68, f. 1ᵛ (18 November 1668), 93, f. 1vᵛ (18 December 1669), and 108, f. 2ᵛ (24 December 1670), as cited in Maltzahn, "Laureate, Republican, Calvinist: An Early Response to Milton and *Paradise Lost* (1667)," 181–98 (esp. 189–90). In this connection, see also William Poole, "Two Early Readers of Milton: John Beale and Abraham Hill," *Milton Quarterly* 38:2 (May 2004): 76–99.

[116] *Paradise Lost* 12.64–71, in CW, II:2 381. Note also *Paradise Lost* 11.342–48, in CW, II:2 357–58, where Milton has the archangel Michael interpret original sin in a manner that rules out the patriarchalism of Sir Robert Filmer by making it clear that Adam, when fallen, no longer has any authority to pass on.

If Milton justifies tyranny, nonetheless, it is by having Michael explain that since Adam's fall from grace and

> original lapse, true Libertie
> Is lost, which alwayes with right Reason dwells
> Twinn'd, and from her hath no dividual being:
> Reason in man obscur'd, or not obeyd,
> Immediately inordinate desires
> And upstart Passions catch the Government
> From Reason, and to servitude reduce
> Man till then free. Therefore since hee permits
> Within himself unworthie Powers to reign
> Over free Reason, God in Judgement just
> Subjects him from without to violent Lords;
> Who oft as undeservedly enthrall
> His outward freedom.

Sometimes, the archangel then adds, "Nations will decline so low/From vertue, which is reason, that no wrong,/But Justice, and some fatal curse annext/Deprives them of thir outward libertie,/Thir inward lost."[117]

In *Samson Agonistes*, Milton returns to this theme one last time,[118] sounding it in a fashion that must have had particular significance for erstwhile adherents of the Good Old Cause. "But what more oft in Nations grown corrupt," the poem's protagonist asks,

> And by thir vices brought to servitude,
> Then to love Bondage more then Liberty,
> Bondage with ease then strenuous liberty;
> And to despise, or envy, or suspect
> Whom God hath of his special favour rais'd
> As thir Deliverer; if he aught begin,
> How frequent to desert him, and at last
> To heap ingratitude on worthiest deeds?

When he wrote these lines, Milton was surely thinking of his own fate and of the far worse fate meted out to so many of his regicide friends,[119] and he was admonishing his compatriots in much the same manner as he had in the past. If he ever composed an epitaph for England's failed republican experiment, this is it.[120]

---

[117] *Paradise Lost* 12.79–101, in CW, II:2 381–82.

[118] For the late date of the play's composition, see Mary Ann Radzinowicz, *Toward "Samson Agonistes": The Growth of Milton's Mind* (Princeton, NJ: Princeton University Press, 1978), 387–407.

[119] In this connection, see Howard Nenner, "The Trial of the Regicides: Retribution and Treason in 1660," in *Politics and the Political Imagination in Later Stuart Britain*, ed. Howard Nenner (Rochester, NY: University of Rochester Press, 1997), 21–42.

[120] Consider *Samson Agonistes* 268–76, in CW, I:2 346, in light of Blair Worden, "Milton, *Samson Agonistes*, and the Restoration," in *Culture and Society in the Stuart Restoration: Literature, Drama, History*, ed. Gerald MacLean (Cambridge, UK: Cambridge University Press, 1995), 111–36, and *Literature and Politics in Cromwellian England*, 358–83. See also Radzinowicz, *Toward "Samson Agonistes"*, 111–79 (esp. 167–79).

Providence and Prudence

The fact that the English republic had come to a bad end did not in Milton inspire resignation and despair. Nor did it induce him to embrace a blind and reckless audacity. Between the two, in the manner of Aristotle, he charted what Machiavelli had more than once denounced as "a middle course (*via del mezzo*)."[121] In a notorious passage in *The Prince*, the latter had asserted that if one reflects on the variability of fortune, human obstinacy, and the inability of men to adjust their modes of proceeding to the temper of the times, one must conclude that "it is better to be impetuous than cautious (*respettivo*), for fortune is a lady, and it is necessary, if one wishes to hold her down, to beat her and strike her. And one sees that she allows herself to be vanquished more by these than by those who coldly proceed. And, therefore, as a lady, she is always friendly to the young because they are less cautious (*respettivi*), more ferocious, and command her with greater audacity."[122] Elsewhere in both *The Prince* and his *Discourses on Livy*, he had contended that the great obstacle to human success is man's inability to be "entirely bad."[123] But Milton was not persuaded. Where, like the Satan of *Paradise Lost*, the Florentine had taught his disciples to regard every event, whether advantageous or calamitous, as an *occasione* boldly to be seized,[124] Milton preached that one must patiently await the opportunities afforded by nature and nature's God.[125]

---

[121] See Niccolò Machiavelli, *Del modo di trattare i popoli della Valdichiana ribellati, Discorsi* 1.6, 26–27, 2.23, 3.2–3, 21, 40.2, and *AG* 3.155–60 (at 159), in *Opere*, 13–16, 84–87, 109–10, 179–81, 197–99, 226–28, 249, 342–43.

[122] See Machiavelli, *Il principe* 25, in *Opere*, 295–96. Machiavelli had been thinking about this question for some time: see *Capitolo di Fortuna* (1506), Letter to Giovan Battista Soderini, 13–21 September 1506, and Exchange of Letters with Francesco Vettori on 13, 15, 18, and 30 March; 9, 16, 19, 21, and 29 April; 20, 26, and 27 June; 12 July; 4, 5, 10, 20, 25, and 26 August; 23 November; and 10, 19, and 24 December 1513; 5 and 18 January; 4, 9, and 25 February, February–March; 16 April; 16 May; 10 June; 27 July; 3 August; and 3, 4, 10, 15, 20, and 30 December 1514; and 16 and 31 January 1515, in Machiavelli, *Opere*, 976–79, 1082–83, 1128–92. And he continued to do so: see Niccolò Machiavelli, *Clizia* 4.1, in *Opere*, 904. That Machiavelli rejects the notion that *phrónēsis* is adequate as a guide is perfectly clear; that he thereby takes a postmodern turn seems improbable: cf., however, John M. Najemy, *Between Friends: Discourses of Power and the Desire in the Machiavelli-Vettori Letters of 1513–1515* (Princeton, NJ: Princeton University Press, 1993), and Vatter, *Between Form and Event*, passim (esp. 131–215).

[123] Consider Machiavelli, *Discorsi* 1.26–27, 41, in light of *Il principe* 15–18, in *Opere*, 109–10, 125–26, 280–84.

[124] With rare exceptions, when *occasione* is used to describe an opportunity to be seized, it is associated with a coup d'état on the part of a prince; with the founding of a polity by one alone; with political manipulation on the part of a prince, a magistrate, or a ruling order; or with a conquest: consider its appearance in Machiavelli, *Il principe* 7, 11, 20, 26, and in *Discorsi* 1.9–10, 13.1, 14, 16.5, 27, 40–41, 47.2, 49.2, 50, 59, 2.Pref.3, 9, 17.1, 19.2, 20, 22.1, 23.2, 27.1, 29, 3.2–3, 5, 6.20, 15.1, 44.1, in *Opere*, 90–93, 96–98, 100–101, 109–10, 123–26, 129–32, 142–43, 145–46, 158–59, 168–69, 174–75, 178–80, 186, 188–90, 197–200, 210–11, 221, 251, 265–69, 274, 289–91, 296–98, in light of the term's *locus classicus* in *Il principe* 6, in *Opere*, 264–65. Note, in this connection, Machiavelli, *Discorsi* 1.3.1, 6.2, in *Opere*, 81, 85.

[125] Cf. David Norbrook, "Republican Occasions in *Paradise Regained* and *Samson Agonistes*," *Milton Studies* 42 (2002): 122–48, who errs not only in supposing the republican Machiavelli a civic humanist but also in presuming that pre-Machiavellian thought was somehow oblivious to the need to take advantage of the favorable conjunctures that present themselves, and who

In *Samson Agonistes*, as in *Paradise Regained*, which he published together as an ensemble in 1671, Milton counsels neither slavish acquiescence nor imprudent defiance but long-suffering in the face of adversity and a resort to prudence when opportunity presents itself. Milton's Jesus models himself on Job and Socrates, as we have seen, and not on Alexander, Scipio, Pompey, and Caesar. He awaits his time – aware that he will suffer scourging, wear a crown of thorns, and undergo crucifixion – and in the end he forges victory from the trappings of defeat: as does Samson, blinded and chained, in the Temple of Dagon.

With this last event in mind, Milton reminds his despondent compatriots "how comely it is and how reviving/To the Spirits of just men long opprest!"

> When God into the hands of thir deliverer
> Puts invincible might
> To quell the mighty of the Earth, th'oppressour,
> The brute and boist'rous force of violent men
> Hardy and industrious to support
> Tyrannic power, but raging to pursue
> The righteous and all such as honour Truth;
> He all thir Ammunition
> And feats of War defeats
> With plain Heroic magnitude of mind
> And celestial vigour arm'd,
> Thir Armories and Magazins contemns,
> Renders them useless, while
> With winged expedition
> Swift as the lightning glance he executes
> His errand on the wicked, who surpris'd
> Lose thir defence distracted and amaz'd.

But at the same time Milton takes inordinate pains to remind his subjugated brethren that an occasion proper for heroic deeds is something providential and that "patience is more oft the exercise/Of Saints, the trial of thir fortitude,/Making them each his own Deliverer,/And Victor over all/That tyrannie or fortune can inflict."[126]

It is, nonetheless, tempting to suppose that Milton aspired to be numbered among the heroes "Whom Patience finally must crown"[127] and that he had in mind his own prospective achievements as a poet, an educator, and statesmen when he called upon his readers to reflect on the deeds of great Samson:

> straining with all his nerves he bow'd,
> As with the force of winds and waters pent,
> When Mountains tremble, those two massie Pillars
> With horrible convulsion to and fro,
> He tugg'd, he shook, till down they came and drew

---

ends up eliding what are postures quite radically opposed, with Coffey, "Pacifist, Quietist, or Patient Militant?" 149–74, who quite rightly insists that Milton's emphasis falls on patience.

[126] *Samson Agonistes* 1268–91, in CW, I:2 382–83.

[127] *Samson Agonistes* 1295–96, in CW, I:2 383.

> The whole roof after them, with burst of thunder
> Upon the heads of all who sate beneath,
> Lords, Ladies, Captains, Councellors, or Priests,
> Their choice nobility and flower, not only
> Of this but each *Philistian* City round
> Met from all parts to solemnize this Feast.[128]

We do not know whether, in general, Milton thought the pen mightier than the sword, but that he had considerable respect for the power of his own rhetorical gifts as a poet there can be no doubt.[129] At the very least, he is reassuring his former associates that all is not as it seems: that the Restoration had not brought to an end the Good Old Cause. In all likelihood, he still aspired to play a leading role in bringing down on those who had built it and sustained it a polity that he regarded as a grand edifice of tyranny, superstition, and oppression.

In any case, one thing is clear. From the moment that he first entered the lists with his attacks on episcopacy until the very end, John Milton presented himself to the public as a classical republican. In none of what he wrote for publication is there the slightest sign that he found anything of value in Machiavelli that was not already present in the classical authors whom he so esteemed. In fact, like Sir Henry Vane, the English statesman whom he seems most to have admired,[130] like his old companion in studies Colonel Robert Overton,[131] and like those

---

[128] *Samson Agonistes* 1640–56, in CW, I:2 395–96.

[129] For the vision that sustained his efforts throughout, see *The Reason of Church-Government* (January/February 1642), in *CPW*, I 804–23.

[130] The sonnets that Milton penned in praise of Fairfax in August 1648 and of Cromwell in May 1652 quickly shift from eulogy to admonition, while the one addressed to Vane in July of the latter year is a panegyric throughout: Cf. "Sonnet XV" (August 1648?) and "Sonnet XVI" (May 1652), with "Sonnet XVII" (January–July 1652), in CW, I:1 64–66. As Worden, "John Milton and Oliver Cromwell," 250–52, points out, Milton never had reason to regret his admiration for Vane. For a detailed account of the latter's political career, see Violet A. Rowe, *Sir Henry Vane the Younger: A Study in Political and Administrative History* (London: Athlone Press, 1970). Vane's public political posture closely resembled Milton's own: see Margaret Judson, *The Political Thought of Sir Henry Vane the Younger* (Philadelphia: University of Pennsylvania Press, 1969); John H. F. Hughes, "The Commonwealthmen Divided: Edmund Ludlowe, Sir Henry Vane and the Good Old Cause, 1653–1659," *The Seventeenth Century* 5:1 (Spring 1990): 55–70; and David Parnham, *Sir Henry Vane, Theologian: A Study in Seventeenth-Century Religious and Political Discourse* (Madison, NJ: Fairleigh Dickinson Press, 1997); "Reconfiguring Mercy and Justice: Sir Henry Vane on Adam, the 'Natural Man,' and the Politics of the Conscience," *Journal of Religion* 79:1 (January 1999): 56–85; and "Politics Spun Out of Theology and Prophecy: Sir Henry Vane on the Spiritual Environment of Public Power," *History of Political Thought* 22:1 (Spring 2001): 53–83, as well as Scott, *Commonwealth Principles*, 159–62, 188–89, 280–81, 296–98, 304–5 (with 51–53, 57–58, 88, 105, 140, 217–18, 271).

[131] Consider *Pro Populo Anglicano Defensio Secunda* (30 May 1654), in CW, VIII 232–35, in light of Blair Worden, "Classical Republicanism and the Puritan Revolution," in *History and Imagination: Essays in Honour of H. R. Trevor-Roper*, ed. Hugh Lloyd-Jones, Valerie Pearl, and Blair Worden (London: Duckworth, 1981), 182–200 (at 191 with n. 40). For a recent translation of the pertinent passage, see *A Second Defence of the English People* (30 May 1654), tr. Helen North, in *CPW*, IV:1 676. It is especially telling that Overton looked with favor on the Parliament of Saints: see J. Frank McGregor, "Robert Overton (c. 1609–c. 1672)," in *Biographical Dictionary of British Radicals in the Seventeenth Century*, ed. Richard L. Greaves and Robert Zaller (Brighton, UK: Harvester Press, 1982–1984), II 279–81; Barbara

other gentlemen from among the godly republicans who retained and displayed a deep appreciation for the merits of classical antiquity, Milton seems to have had much more in common with Aristotelians of the Christian epoch, such as Richard Hooker, Marsilius of Padua, Dante Alighieri, and Thomas Aquinas.[132] In only one regard can one say that Milton made common cause with the disciples of the crafty Florentine, and it is this crucial issue that we must now address.

Taft, "'They that pursew perfaction on earth . . .': The Political Progress of Robert Overton," in *Soldiers, Writers and Statesmen of the English Revolution*, 286–303; and Worden, *Literature and Politics in Cromwellian England*, 326–34. Note also David Norbrook, "'This Blushinge Tribute of a Borrowed Muse': Robert Overton and his Overturning of the Poetic Canon," *English Manuscript Studies, 1100–1700*, ed. Peter Beal and Jeremy Griffiths 4 (1993): 220–66.

[132] For the link between Milton and Hooker, see Bennett, *Reviving Liberty*, passim.

4

The Liberation of Captive Minds

From the detailed catalogue of the arguments presented in Niccolò Machiavelli's *Discourses on Livy* that John Milton drew up late in 1651 and early in 1652, there is one glaring omission. The Englishman attended not at all to the Florentine's critique of priestcraft. This can hardly be due to a lack of interest in the subject on his part. We know, in fact, that no subject was nearer and dearer to Milton's heart. Priestcraft was the principal theme of the pamphlets that poured forth from his pen in 1641 and 1642,[1] and, as a concern, it was no less evident twenty-five years later in the very last book of his *Paradise Lost*, where it is featured as the preeminent predilection of sinful man in the Christian epoch that began with Christ's sacrifice on the cross.[2]

Like Machiavelli, Milton was trained in classical rhetoric. He had read and taken to heart what Aristotle, Cicero, and Quintilian had had to say. He generally understood his immediate audience very well, and for sound rhetorical reasons he always couched his argument initially with an eye to what he took to be their abiding concerns. For this reason, in his early pamphlets, he addressed the question of ecclesiastical polity first and foremost on the basis of an appeal to the sanction of Scripture and, then, by means of an extended meditation on the history of the Christian church. Milton's procedure in this regard cannot, however, hide the fact that the heart of the argument that he advanced in *Of Reformation Touching Church-Discipline in England*, in *Of Prelatical Episcopacy*, in *Animadversions upon the Remonstrants Defence Against Smectymnuus*, in *The Reason of Church-Governement*, and in *An Apology Against a Pamphlet* was an application to episcopalianism in Protestant lands of Machiavelli's analysis of the cultural hegemony of the ecclesiastical principality, and a restatement of the critique that the Florentine had directed against the "ambitious idleness" of the Roman Catholic clergy. Nor can Milton's modus operandi conceal that what he had to say in this regard was grounded in a partial appropriation and restatement of his predecessor's contention that the Christian church had

---

[1] See *Of Reformation* (May 1641), *Of Prelatical Episcopacy* (June/July 1641), and *Animadversions upon the Remonstrants Defence Against Smectymnuus* (July 1641), in *CPW*, I 576–77, 650, 676–77. Milton was evidently proud of his intervention in public affairs at this time: see *Pro Populo Anglicano Defensio Secunda* (30 May 1654), in *CW*, VIII 126–35. For a recent translation of the description of his early endeavors that Milton provides, see *A Second Defence of the English People* (30 May 1654), tr. Helen North, in *CPW*, IV:1 621–26.

[2] See *Paradise Lost* 12.502–51, in *CW*, II:2 396–98.

"rendered the world weak and given it in prey to wicked men."[3] It may be difficult to conceive of John Milton repeating the line that Christopher Marlowe puts in the mouth of his *Machevill*: "I count Religion but a childish Toy." But in his enthusiasm, as we shall soon see, Milton really does come quite close to uttering the very next line: I "hold there is no sinne but Ignorance."[4]

A Corporation of Impostors

In his anti-episcopacy tracts, Milton nowhere cites Machiavelli himself, but, like the Florentine,[5] he does make effective use of Lucretius' analysis of the power of religious fear,[6] and, tellingly, before long he will even recommend *De rerum natura* as a text appropriate for the instruction of the young.[7] Moreover, in the first of these early pamphlets, Milton twice refers to a letter written by "the great and learned *Padre Paolo*," whom he soon thereafter identifies as "the great Venetian Antagonist of the *Pope*."[8]

As state theologian of Venice at the time of the papal interdict in 1606, Paolo Sarpi had achieved renown among Protestants and *politiques* throughout Europe by defending the absolute sovereignty of the state against the jurisdictional claims of the pope.[9] Moreover, in 1619, this politically astute Servite friar had secured for himself even greater fame upon the publication of his controversial *History of the Council of Trent*. "[T]he great unmasker of the *Trentine* Councel,"[10] as Milton called him, was no less important for the English pamphleteer than was Lucretius, and the analysis underpinning Sarpi's narrative dovetailed neatly with the critique of religion articulated by Epicurus in the works presented in Diogenes Laertius' *Lives of the Eminent Philosophers* and forcefully restated by Lucretius in *De rerum natura* – copies of which Sarpi owned and had no doubt carefully perused.[11]

Early in the 1640s, Milton read (or, more likely, reread, this time with very great care) Sarpi's great masterpiece, copying into his Commonplace Book some

---

3 See Chapter 2, this volume.

4 Christopher Marlow, *The Jew of Malta* Prologue 5–15, in *The Complete Works of Christopher Marlow*, ed. Fredson Bowers (Cambridge, UK: Cambridge University Press, 1973), I 263.

5 See Chapter 2, this volume.

6 See Lucr. 1.62–158, 2.1–61, 3.1–93, 830–1094, 4.1–25, 5.1194–1240.

7 See *Of Education* (June 1644), in *CPW*, II 394–96, and consider *Areopagitica* (November 1644), in *CPW*, II 498, in which Milton indicates that he is aware of the reason why some think *De rerum natura* a work worthy to be banned.

8 See Milton, *Of Reformation* (May 1641), in *CPW*, I 581, 595.

9 See David Wootton, *Paolo Sarpi: Between Renaissance and Enlightenment* (Cambridge, UK: Cambridge University Press, 1983), 45–76. Note also William J. Bouwsma, *Venice and the Defense of Republican Liberty: Renaissance Values in the Age of the Counter Reformation* (Berkeley: University of California Press, 1968), and "Venice and the Political Education of Europe," in *Renaissance Venice*, ed. J. R. Hale (London: Faber & Faber, 1973), 445–66.

10 See Milton, *Areopagitica* (November 1644), in *CPW*, II 501.

11 See Gian Ludovico Masetti Zannini, "Libri di fra Paolo Sarpi, e notizie di altre biblioteche dei Servi (1599–1600)," *Studi storici dell'ordine dei Servi di Maria* 20 (1970): 174–202, esp. 193 (no. 67) and 198 (no. 215).

thirteen passages pertinent to his concerns,[12] and it is clear that he also then consulted Sarpi's *History of the Inquisition*, which was published in the original Italian in 1638 and translated into English for publication the next year by the son of Machiavelli's great admirer Alberico Gentili.[13] The considerable degree to which Milton's diatribes against episcopacy closely track Machiavelli's critique of priestcraft no doubt owes something to the former's close familiarity with *De rerum natura*. But, in its more particular treatment of ecclesiastical history, Milton's argument appears to be derivative from Sarpi's Machiavellian analysis of the Roman Catholic Church as a conspiracy concocted for the purpose of exploiting the natural superstition of ordinary men in such a fashion as to extract resources and secure clerical domination.[14]

In keeping with the analysis articulated by the Servite friar, Milton starts out by discussing, in a fashion strikingly reminiscent of Lucretius, the "Servile, and thral-like feare" that purportedly grips "the superstitious man" – who, "being scarr'd...by the pangs and gripes of a boyling conscience, all in a pudder shuffles up to himselfe such a *God*, and such a *worship* as is most agreeable to remedy his feare." In the first of his tracts, it is to this unreasoning fear and to its canny exploitation by "the late legerdemain of the Papists" that the Englishman traces "the black and settled Night of *Ignorance* and *Antichristian Tyranny*" that had purportedly engulfed Europe prior to the Reformation.[15]

To the extent that England has been behindhand in reformation, Milton then contends, it is due to the quasi-papist ecclesiastical polity of the English church. Bishops he refers to as "a Tyrannicall crew and Corporation of Impostors." Of the prelates associated with the Church of England, he writes, "See what gentle, and benigne Fathers they have beene to our liberty." And then, by way of explanation, he observes that England's bishops practice an exceedingly lucrative "trade," for "by the same Alchymy that the *Pope* uses," they "extract heaps of *gold*, and *silver* out of the drossie *Bullion* of the Peoples sinnes."

---

[12] See "Milton's Commonplace Book," in CW, XVIII 149, 151, 154–55, 165, 180, 190, 213–14. For a somewhat better English translation and extensive notes, see "Milton's Commonplace Book," tr. Ruth Mohl, in CPW, I 396–98, 402, 406–7, 424, 451, 467, 500–501. For the period in which the pertinent passages were transcribed, see James Holly Hanford, "The Chronology of Milton's Private Studies," *Publications of the Modern Language Association of America* 36:2 (June 1921): 251–314 (at 267–71). Milton draws on Sarpi's *History of the Council of Trent* in *The Doctrine and Discipline of Divorce* (1 August 1643), in *Areopagitica* (November 1644), and in *Tetrachordon* (4 March 1645), in CPW, II 300–301, 500–503, 510–11, 517, 638 (with the attendant notes).

[13] Consider Paolo Sarpi, *Historia della sacra Inquisitione* (Serravale: Fabio Albicocco, 1638), and *History of the Inquisition*, tr. Robert Gentilis (London: Humphrey Mosley, 1639), in light of *Areopagitica* (November 1644), in CPW, II 492, 503, 529 (with the attendant notes).

[14] Consider Pietro Soave Polano, *Historia del Concilio Tridentino* (London: Giovanni Billio, 1619), and Sarpi, *Historia della sacra Inquisitione*, in light of Wootton, *Paolo Sarpi*, passim (esp. 104–17, 124–8). The pseudonym on the title page of the former work is an anagram for Paolo Sarpi Veneto.

[15] See *Of Reformation* (May 1641), in CPW, I 522, 524, 553, In this connection, see also *Animadversions upon the Remonstrants Defence Against Smectymnuus* (July 1641), and *The Reason of Church-Government* (January/February 1642), in CPW, I 702–3, 727–28, 849.

With considerable justice, moreover, these prelates fear "that the quick-sighted *Protestants* eye[,] clear'd in great part from the mist of Superstition, may at one time or other looke with a good judgement into these their deceitfull Pedleries," and so, Milton explains, to obviate the danger, they set out "to gaine as many associats of guiltines as they can, and to infect the temporall Magistrate with the like lawlesse though not sacrosacrilegious extortion."

To this end, England's prelates "ingage themselves to preach, and perswade an assertion for truth the most false, and to this *Monarchy* the most pernicious and destructive that could bee chosen." "What," Milton asks, could be "more banefull to *Monarchy* then a Popular Commotion, for the dissolution of *Monarchy* slides aptest into a *Democraty*; and what stirs the Englishmen, as our wisest writers have observ'd, sooner to rebellion, then violent and heavy hands upon their goods and purses?"

Yet these devout *Prelates*, spight of our great Charter, and the soules of our Progenitors that wrested their liberties out of the *Norman* gripe with their dearest blood and highest prowesse, for these many years have not ceas't in their Pulpits wrinching, and spraining the *text*, to set at nought and trample under foot all the most sacred, and life blood Lawes, Statutes, and Acts of *Parliament* that are the holy Cov'nant of Union, and Marriage betweene the King and his Realme, by proscribing, and confiscating from us all the right we have to our owne bodies, goods and liberties.

According to Milton, the ultimate aim of clergymen so situated is "to thrust the Laitie under the despoticall rule of the *Monarch*, that they themselves might confine the *Monarch* to a kind of Pupillage under their *Hierarchy*."[16] To English liberty, clergymen of this sort will never be fathers gentle and benign.

In *The Reason of Church-Government*, Milton restates this argument with even greater vehemence. If you force "the Angell of the Gospell ... to expresse his irresistible power by a doctrine of carnall might, as Prelaty is," he warns, the angel will employ that "fleshly strength which ye put into his hands to subdue your spirits by a servile and blind superstition, and that againe shall hold such dominion over your captive minds, as returning with an insatiat greedinesse and force upon your worldly wealth and power wherewith to deck and magnifie her self, and her false worships, she shall spoil and havock your estates, disturbe your ease, diminish your honour, inthraul your liberty under the swelling mood of a proud Clergy." Moreover, he then adds, when the prelates and their priestly followers "have glutted their ingratefull bodies, at least if it be possible that those open sepulchers should ever be glutted, and when they have stufft their Idolish temples with the wastefull pillage of your estates, ... [t]hat they may want nothing to make them true merchants of Babylon, as they have done to your souls, they will sell your bodies, your wives, your children, your liberties, your Parlaments, all these things, and if there be ought else dearer then these, they will sell [it] at an out-cry in their Pulpits to the arbitrary and illegall dispose

---

[16] See *Of Reformation* (May 1641), in *CPW*, I 537, 592–93, 595. In this connection see also *Of Reformation* (May 1641), *Animadversions upon the Remonstrants Defence Against Smectymnuus* (July 1641), and *The Reason of Church-Government* (January/February 1642), in *CPW*, I 610–11, 662–64, 702–3, 718–21, 727–28, 730–31, 782–83, 792–93.

of any one that may hereafter be call'd a King, whose mind shall serve him to listen to their bargain."[17]

The Fescu of an *Imprimatur*

In the beginning, Milton was prepared to embrace presbyterianism as an alternative to episcopacy, and in this spirit he denounced as "hinderers of *Reformation*" those whom he termed "Libertines" – by which he meant men such as George Digby, a member of Parliament who regarded presbyterian "Discipline" as "intolerable," arguing that "for one Bishop now in a Dioces we should then have a Pope in every Parish." "It is not any Discipline that they could live under, it is the corruption, and remisnes of Discipline that they seek," Milton thundered in response. "Episcopacy duly executed, yea the Turkish, and Jewish rigor against whoring, and drinking; the dear, and tender Discipline of a Father; the sociable, and loving reproof of a Brother; the bosome admonition of a Friend is a *Presbytery*, and a Consistory to them."[18] It was not very long, however, before Milton found himself forced to acknowledge with regard to the ecclesiastical polity sought by the presbyterians of Scotland and their English allies that "this is not to put down Prelaty, this is but to chop an Episcopacy, this is but to translate the Palace *Metropolitan* from one kind of dominion into another,"[19] and soon thereafter he began to make common cause with men who really were libertines, as we shall eventually have occasion to observe.[20]

From the outset, Milton had insisted that "the Evangelical precept forbids Churchmen to intermeddle with worldly imployments." As he put it, "the Churchmans office is only to teach men the Christian Faith, to exhort all, to incourage the good, to admonish the bad, privately the lesse offender, publickly the scandalous and stubborn; to censure, and separate from the communion of *Christs* flock, the contagious, and incorrigible, to receive with joy, and fatherly compassion the penitent." Milton was never willing to sanction the magistrate using his authority to reinforce ministerial exhortation. There is, he insisted at the outset, "no necessity, nor indeed possibility of linking the one with the other in a speciall conformation."[21] Moreover, he thought that "nothing is more sweet to man" than "the liberty of speaking," and early on he objected to episcopacy on the grounds that under "your Monkish prohibitions, and expurgatorious indexes, your gags and snaffles, your proud *Imprimaturs*," speaking was "girded, straight lac't almost to a broken-winded tizzick." Not

---

[17] See *The Reason of Church-Government* (January/February 1642), in *CPW*, I 850–61 (esp. 850–51).

[18] See *Of Reformation* (May 1641), in *CPW*, I 570, 605, where Milton is responding to a speech Digby delivered on 9 February 1641. In this connection, see also *The Reason of Church-Government* (January/February 1642), in *CPW*, I 750–56.

[19] See *Areopagitica* (November 1644), in *CPW*, II 541.

[20] See Chapter 6, this volume.

[21] See Milton, *Of Reformation* (May 1641), in *CPW*, I 575–76. See also *Of Reformation* (May 1641), *Animadversions upon the Remonstrants Defence Against Smectymnuus* (July 1641), and *The Reason of Church-Government* (January/February 1642), in *CPW*, I 553–54, 716, 761–66, 831–50.

long thereafter, he meekly suggested to Parliament that "a more free permission of writing at sometimes might be profitable, in such a question especially wherein the Magistrates are not fully resolv'd; and both sides have equall liberty to write, as now they have."[22]

By November 1644, when he published *Areopagitica*, Milton had shed his meekness and was prepared to take a principled stand against prior restraint of the press, asking with great audacity, "What advantage is it to be a man over it is to be a boy at school, if we have only scapt the ferular, to come under the fescu of an *Imprimatur?*" It was by way of explanation that he then added,

He who is not trusted with his own actions, his drift not being known to be evil, and standing to the hazard of law and penalty, has no great argument to think himself reputed in the Commonwealth wherin he was born, for other then a fool or a foreiner. When a man writes to the world, he summons up all his reason and deliberation to assist him; he searches, meditats, is industrious, and likely consults and conferrs with his judicious friends; after all which done he takes himself to be inform'd in what he writes, as well as any that writ before him; if in this the most consummat act of his fidelity and ripenesse, no years, no industry, no former proof of his abilities can bring him to that state of maturity, as not to be still mistrusted and suspected, unlesse he carry all his considerat diligence, all his midnight watchings, and expence of *Palladian* oyl, to the hasty view of an unleasur'd licencer, perhaps much his younger, perhaps far his inferiour in judgement, perhaps one who never knew the labour of book-writing, and if he be not repulst, or slighted, must appear in Print like a punie with his guardian, and his censors hand on the back of his title to be his bayl and surety, that he is no idiot, or seducer, it cannot be but a dishonor and derogation to the author, to the book, to the privilege and dignity of Learning.[23]

Of course, Milton did not deny "that it is of greatest concernment in the Church and Commonwealth, to have a vigilant eye how Bookes demeane themselves, as well as men; and thereafter to confine, imprison and do sharpest justice on them as malefactors." Even then, this aspiring poet was very far from thinking books "absolutely dead things." He insisted, instead, that they "doe contain a potencie of life in them to be as active as that soule was whose progeny they are," and he was prepared to suppose that "they do preserve as in a violl the purest efficacie and extraction of that living intellect that bred them." "I know," he wrote,

they are as lively, and as vigorously productive, as those fabulous Dragons teeth; and being sown up and down, may chance to spring up armed men. And yet on the other hand unless warinesse be us'd, as good almost kill a Man as kill a good Book; who kills a man kills a reasonable creature, Gods Image; but hee who destroyes a good Booke, kills reason it selfe, kills the Image of God, as it were in the eye.

---

[22] See *Animadversions upon the Remonstrants Defence* (July 1641), and *An Apology Against a Pamphlet* (April 1642), in *CPW*, I 669, 907. Much that is to come is foreshadowed in *The Reason of Church-Government* (January/February 1642), in *CPW*, I 783–84, 794–800, 820.

[23] See *Areopagitica* (November 1644), in *CPW*, II 531–32. For the character of the parliamentary licensing regime against which Milton was protesting, see Jason T. Peacey, *Politicians and Pamphleteers: Propaganda during the English Civil Wars and Interregnum* (Aldershot, UK: Ashgate, 2004), passim (esp. 132–62).

"Many a man," he concluded, "lives a burden to the Earth; but a good Booke is the pretious life-blood of a master spirit, imbalm'd and treasur'd up on purpose to a life beyond life."[24]

Philosophic Freedom

Milton's fear was that licensing and censorship would contribute "primely to the discouragement of all learning, and the stop of Truth." He worried that it would result in "disexercising and blunting our abilities in what we know already." But this was not his first concern, for he was also a devotee of what he tellingly called "*Philosophic* freedom."[25] Thanks to Tommaso Campanella and Galileo Galilei, this was, even then, a loaded phrase.

In 1615, as the controversy concerning the heliocentric theory of Copernicus was coming to a head, Galileo addressed a letter to the Grand Duchess Christina in which he objected to the obstacles that served "to block the road to free philosophizing concerning the things of the world and of nature (*precluder la strada al libero filosofare circa le cose del mondo, e della natura*)." Though unpublished prior to 1636, the letter circulated in manuscript and had an impact.[26] The following year, at some point not long before 5 March 1616, in a futile effort to head off a condemnation of Copernican theory by the Congregation of the Holy Office at Rome,[27] Campanella submitted a report to Bonifacio Cardinal Caetani in which he included an eloquent and compelling defense of Galileo and argued for a comprehensive *libertas philosophandi*. Six years thereafter, when Tobias Adami published the work in Frankfurt, the grounds on which Campanella had based his appeal became widely known.[28] It was under this

---

[24] See *Areopagitica* (November 1644), in *CPW*, II 492–93.

[25] See *Areopagitica* (November 1644), in *CPW*, II 491–92, 537.

[26] See Letter to Christina of Lorraine, grand duchess of Tuscany, in 1615, in Galileo Galilei, *Le Opere di Galileo Galilei*, ed. Antonio Favaro and Isidoro del Lungo (Florence: Typografia di G. Barbèra, 1890–1909), V 309–48 (at 320–21). For a translation, see *Discoveries and Opinions of Galileo*, ed. and tr. Stillman Drake (New York: Doubleday Anchor Books, 1957), 175–216 (at 187). Note, in this connection, Luigi Guerrini, "'Con fatiche veramente atlantiche': Il primato della scienza nella *Lettera a Cristina di Lorena*," *Bruniana & Campelliana* 9:1 (2003): 61–81.

[27] See Salvatore Femiano, "Introduzione," in Tommaso Campanella, *Apologia per Galileo*, ed. Salvatore Femiano (Milan: Marzorati, 1971), 15–30 (at 21–30). Cf. Antonio Corsano, "Campanella e Galileo," *Giornale critico della filosofia italiana* 44:3 (July–September 1965): 313–32 (esp. 318–19), and see Bernadino M. Bonansea, "Campanella's Defense of Galileo," in *Reinterpreting Galileo*, ed. William A. Wallace, *Studies in Philosophy and the History of Philosophy*, ed. William A. Wallace (Washington, DC: Catholic University of America Press, 1986), XV 205–39.

[28] See Tommaso Campanella, *Apologia pro Galileo*, ed. Tobias Adami (Frankfurt: Godfried Tambach, 1622), 11–32 (esp. 27, where he deploys the crucial phrase). For an overview, see Luigi Firpo, "Campanella e Galileo," *Atti della Accademia della Scienza di Torinto, Classe di Scienze Morali* 103 (1969): 49–69. More recently, see John M. Headley, "Campanella on Freedom of Thought: The Case of the Cropped Pericope," *Bruniana & Campanelliana* 2:1–2 (1996): 165–77, and *Tommaso Campanella and the Transformation of the World* (Princeton, NJ: Princeton University Press, 1997), 80–81, 96–98, 145–79, who suspects that, prior to composing his letter to the grand duchess, Galileo had received from Campanella a missive in which he outlined the argument subsequently presented in *Apologia pro Galileo*. For a brief discussion of the previous history of the notion, see the as-yet-unpublished seminar paper by Ian W. F. Maclean, "Galen's

banner, after Galileo was himself condemned by the Inquisition in 1633, that the clarion call issued by the two was taken up in France and elsewhere by erudite libertines and proponents of the new science – most notably, by Galileo's friend and agent Elie Diodati,[29] a Protestant from a prominent family that had fled Lucca in Italy, who was in Paris a member of the *Tétrade* alongside Pierre Gassendi, François de La Mothe le Vayer, and Gabriel Naudé.[30]

Milton can hardly have been unaware of the significance of the phrase that he appropriated and in English deployed.[31] After all, in 1638 and 1639, he had been abroad, and there is reason to suppose that in Paris he had made contact with Diodati, who was a second cousin once removed of his oldest and dearest friend, Charles Diodati. This would help explain how Milton subsequently gained access to Hugo Grotius in Paris, to Galileo Galilei in his place of confinement outside Florence, and to literary circles within the latter town. It dovetails neatly with his subsequent sojourn in Geneva at the home of his friend's uncle, Jean Diodati,[32] and it may even have occasioned his initial reading of Paolo Sarpi's *History of the Council of Trent* and his *History of the Inquisition*, for with the controversial Servite friar, the Diodati were quite closely linked.

Jean Diodati had become acquainted with Sarpi and with his secretary, chief intellectual ally, and future biographer, Fulgenzio Micanzio, when he visited Venice in 1608, in the wake of the Interdict, hoping to bring that polity over

---

De optimo mode docendi and *Ars parva* in the Sixteenth Century: Anti-Skepticism, Rational Medicine and the *libertas philosophandi*," Paper Delivered at the Second Workshop of Team Two, "Skepticism in Medieval and Renaissance Thought," Uppsala, Sweden, 7–9 May 2005, which its author generously allowed me to peruse.

[29] See Stéphane Garcia, *Elie Diodati et Galilée: Naissance d'un réseau scientifique dans l'Europe du XVIIe siècle* (Florence: L. S. Olschki, 2004), 229–363 (esp. 327–63), along with Armand Beaulieu, "Les Réactions des savants français au début du XVIIe siècle devant l'heliocentrisme de Galilée," in *Novità celesti e crisi del sapere*, ed. Paolo Gulluzzi (Florence: Giunti Barbèra, 1984), 373–82; Lisa T. Sarasohn, "French Reactions to the Condemnation of Galileo, 1632–1642," *Catholic Historical Review* 74:1 (January 1988): 34–54; and Michel-Pierre Lerner, "La Réception de la condamnation de Galilée en France au XVIIe siècle," in *Largo campo di filosofare. Eurosymposium Galileo 2001*, ed. José Luis Montesinos Sirera and Carlos Solís Santos (La Orotava: Fundación Canaria Orotava de Historia de la Ciencia, 2001), 513–47. Later, the call for a *libertas philosophandi* was restated by Descartes, Spinoza, and Hume, among others: see Michael A. Stewart, "*Libertas philosophandi*: From Natural to Speculative Philosophy," *Australian Journal of Politics and History* 40: Special Issue (1994): 29–46.

[30] See Garcia, *Elie Diodati et Galilée*, 217–27. This connection may help explain the character of Diodati's response. See Pierre Charron, *De la sagesse*, ed. Barbara de Negroni (Paris: Fayard, 1986), 25–43 (esp. 35–43), where one can find the preface both as published in 1601 and as revised for the 1604 edition, and [François de La Mothe le Vayer], *Dialogues faits à l'imitation des anciens* (Paris: Fayard, 1988), 11–16, which appeared in 1630 and 1631, and consider Nicola Badaloni, "Libertinismo e scienza negli anni di Galilei e Campanella," in *Ricerche su letteratura libertina e letteratura clandestina nel Seicento*, ed. Tullio Gregory et al. (Florence: La Nuova Italia, 1981), 213–29.

[31] See Robert B. Sutton, "The Phrase *Libertas Philosophandi*," *Journal of the History of Ideas* 14:2 (April 1953): 310–16.

[32] Note Donald Clayton Dorian, *The English Diodatis* (New Brunswick, NJ: Rutgers University Press, 1950), 97–181 (esp. 168–73, with 282 n. 59), and William Riley Parker, *Milton: A Biography* (Oxford, UK: Clarendon Press, 1968), I 15, 21, 29–31, 44, 56, 59–61, 67–71, 79, 101, 103, 150, 152–53, 155–57, 174; then, see Garcia, *Elie Diodati et Galilée*, 46–47, 121–22.

permanently to the Protestant side; and though his mission had proven abortive, the three men had come to a good understanding. Later, when Micanzio complained that the original edition of Sarpi's *History of the Council of Trent* published in London had been altered and improperly introduced by its editors there, it was Jean Diodati who produced a satisfactory and accurate French translation and who then arranged for the publication in Geneva of a corrected Italian edition faithful to what Sarpi had actually written. He it was also who arranged for the posthumous publication of Sarpi's *History of the Interdict* in 1624, and there is reason to suspect that he played a crucial role in securing publication of Sarpi's *History of the Inquisition* in Italian in 1638, while Milton was on the continent. Elie Diodati was the figure who took responsibility at each turn for the diffusion of Sarpi's work among the *literati,* and he may have played a role in prying loose from the Venetian authorities Sarpi's report on the Inquisition, for we know that he visited the serene republic in 1636. There is even reason to think that the two relatives of Milton's childhood friend played a role in arranging the English translation of that work published in 1639, for the uncle of Robert Gentili, the book's translator, was married to a first cousin of Elie Diodati; and soon after the publication in London of Sarpi's book, this same Roberto Gentili rendered into English the biblical commentaries of none other than Jean Diodati.[33] Although Milton's sojourn abroad was brief, from an educational perspective, it could hardly have been better timed, for he could not have chosen for himself companions who had devoted more attention to reflecting on the problem posed by what came to be known as priestcraft.

On the impressionable young Englishman, the experience had, as one might expect, a profound and lasting effect. During his travels, as Milton reports in *Areopagitica,* he had visited "Countries," such as France and Italy, subject to a rigorous licensing regime. "I can," he eagerly adds, "recount what I have seen and heard ... where this kind of inquisition tyrannizes." When he had "sat among their lerned men," he had "bin counted happy to be born in such a place of *Philosophic* freedom, as they suppos'd England was," and in Italy he had heard learned men of this sort "bemoan the servil condition into which lerning amongst them was brought." It was licensing and censorship, he was told, it was a denial of *libertas philosophandi,* "which had dampt the glory of Italian wits," for "nothing had bin there writt'n now these many years but flattery and fustian."[34]

Milton's concern was heightened by his recognition that a great transformation was in his time already underway. It is not fortuitous that in *Areopagitica* he twice cites Sir Francis Bacon. Nor is it an accident that therein he not only touches on the fate meted out to Galileo but proudly alludes to his own encounter with that great proponent of Copernican astronomy and mathematical physics, who is, surely not by accident, the only seventeenth-century figure

[33] See Garcia, *Elie Diodati et Galilée,* 59–83.
[34] See *Areopagitica* (November 1644), in *CPW,* II 537–38. In this connection, note Milton's description of his sojourn in Italy in *Pro Populo Anglicano Defensio Secunda* (30 May 1654), in *CW,* VIII 120–27. For a recent translation, see *A Second Defence of the English People* (30 May 1654), tr. Helen North, in *CPW,* IV:1 614–20.

whom he will subsequently mention by name in *Paradise Lost*.[35] Although the
principal focus of Milton's early rhetoric was religion, by 1644 – if not, in fact,
from the very start – he had a great deal more in mind than man's salvation
in the hereafter. He had read Bacon's *New Atlantis*,[36] and he was not among
those who supposed that "we are to pitch our tent here, and have attain'd the
utmost prospect of reformation." In fact, by that year, if not well before, he
had come to regard the Reformation begun by Luther and Calvin as radically
inadequate, as defective and incomplete. He looked forward, as he cryptically
put it, "ev'n to the reforming of Reformation it self," and he worried that the
worst consequence of a prior restraint of the press would be a "hindring and
cropping [of] the discovery that might bee yet further made both in religious
and civill Wisdome."[37]

The Theologico-Political Dilemma

There may have been more to Milton's call for a "reforming of Reformation
it self" than immediately meets the eye. Elie Diodati's friend Gabriel Naudé,
who knew Italy well, is said to have described the peninsula that Milton visited .
in 1638 as "a land of imposture (*fourberie*) and superstition." It is "filled," he
reportedly claimed, not just with priests, monks, and the laymen under their
sway, but with "freethinkers (*libertins*) and atheists and people who believe
nothing" at all.[38]

Some historians regard this report as spurious and think its contents incredible.[39] Some insist that, if it has any foundation, it is solely in the heated imaginations of early seventeenth-century French religious apologists, such as *Père*
François Garasse and *Père* Marin Mersenne.[40] The incredulity of historians

---

[35] See *Areopagitica* (November 1644), in *CPW*, II 534, 538, 542, and note *Paradise Lost* 5.262, in
   CW, II:1 153. The significance of this last passage has provoked considerable discussion: for one
   recent attempt to come to grips with it, see Maura Brady, "Galileo in Action: The 'Telescope'
   in *Paradise Lost*," *Milton Studies* 44 (2005): 129–52, who cites the pertinent bibliography.

[36] See *An Apology Against a Pamphlet* (April 1642), in *CPW*, I 881.

[37] See *Areopagitica* (November 1644), in *CPW*, II 548–50 (esp. 549), 553.

[38] See *Naudæana*, 46–47, 104–5, in *Naudæana et Patiniana, ou Singularitez Remarquables, prises
   des Conversations de Mess. Naudé et Patin*, second edition (Amsterdam: François vander Plaats,
   1703), which should be read in light of René Pintard, *Le Mothe le Vayer – Gassendi – Guy Patin:
   Études de bibliographie et di critique suivies de textes inédit de Guy Patin* (Paris: Boivin et Cie,
   [1943]), 47–61. For further evidence, see *Naudæana*, 8, 15–16, 30–33. In this connection, see
   Giorgio Spini, *Ricerca dei libertini: La teoria dell'impostura delle religioni nel Seicento italia*no,
   second edition (Florence: La Nuova Italia, 1983).

[39] See, to take an especially distinguished example, Paul O. Kristeller, "The Myth of Renaissance Atheism and the French Tradition of Free Thought," *Journal of the History of Philosophy* 6:3 (July 1968): 233–43, and "Between the Italian Renaissance and the French Enlightenment: Gabriel Naudé as an Editor," *Renaissance Quarterly* 32:1 (Spring 1979): 41–72, who,
   in telling fashion, is similarly unwilling to credit the quite similar testimony of Petrarch: see
   Kristeller, "Petrarch's 'Averroists': A Note on the History of Aristotelianism in Venice, Padua,
   and Bologna," *Bibliothèque d'Humanisme et de Renaissance* 14:1 (March 1952): 59–65.

[40] See Louise Godard de Donville, *Le Libertin des origines à 1665: Un Produit des apologètes*
   (Paris: Papers on French Seventeenth-Century Literature, 1989), and "L'Invention du 'libertin'
   en 1623 et ses conséquences sur la lecture des textes," *Libertinage et philosophie au XVIIe siècle*
   6 (2002): 7–18. To their list of mildly deranged apologists, the critics so intent on dismissing
   the worries of Garasse and Mersenne would presumably be quick to add Gabriel du Préau,

in this regard, their resolute unwillingness to give credence to contemporary suspicions, tells us rather more about the historicist prejudices of our own day than about Europe in the sixteenth and seventeenth centuries. The presumption that in any given age all men must think alike – and that in an age of faith there can be no unbelievers – does not stand up to scrutiny.[41] In the medieval Islamic world, there were atheists, we know.[42] In Italy, as we have seen, Machiavelli was justly regarded as an unbeliever by those who knew him best,[43] and Paolo Sarpi's notebooks confirm the suspicion, widespread in his time, that the author of *The History of the Council of Trent* regarded not just Roman Catholicism, but all religion, as imposture. They show, moreover, that he gradually came to doubt the social and political utility of religion altogether and that he eventually concluded that Christianity in particular is fundamentally incompatible with political life (*contraria al viver civile*) – and they justify the presumption that his political and literary activity was aimed neither at Roman Catholic reform nor at promoting Protestantism per se, but at fomenting sectarian divisions for the purpose of weakening and ultimately eliminating Christianity as a political force.[44]

Des faux Prophetes; seducteurs et hypochrites (Paris: Jacques Macé, 1564), and Filippo Fabri, *Adversus impios atheos: disputationes quatuor philosophicae* (Venice: M. Ginammi, 1627). On the latter, see Antonino Poppi, "Un teologo di fronte alla cultura libertina del Rinascimento italiano: l'*Adversus impios atheos* di Filipp Fabri," *Quaderni per la storia dell'Università di Padova* 4 (1971):103–18. More generally, see Tullio Gregory, "Apologeti e libertini," *Giornale critico della filosofia italiana* 79:1 (January–April 2000): 1–35.

[41] Cf. Lucien Paul Victor Febvre, *Le Problème de l'incroyance au XVIᵉ siècle: La Religion de Rabelais* (Paris: Albin Michel, 1947), with Febvre, *Origène et Des Périers, ou l'énigme du Cymbalum Mundi* (Paris: Droz, 1942), and "Dolet, Propagator of the Gospel," in Febvre, *A New Kind of History and Other Essays*, ed. Peter Burke, tr. Keith Folca (New York: Harper & Row, 1973), 108–59, and Malcolm C. Smith, "A Sixteenth-Century Anti-Theist (on the *Cymbalum Mundi*)," *Bibliothèque d'Humanisme de Renaissance* 53:3 (October 1991): 593–618; then, see David Wootton, "Unbelief in Early Modern Europe," *History Workshop* 20 (Autumn 1985): 82–100, and "Lucien Febvre and the Problem of Unbelief in the Early Modern Period," *Journal of Modern History* 60:4 (December 1988): 695–730. In this connection, see Wootton, "The Fear of God in Early Modern Political Theory," in *Historical Papers 1983*, ed. Canadian Historical Association (Ottawa 1983), 56–80.

[42] Note Friedrich Niewöhner, "Are the Founders of Religions Impostors?" in *Maimonides and Philosophy: Papers Presented at the Sixth Jerusalem Philosophical Encounter, May 1985*, ed. Shlomo Pines and Yirmiyahu Yovel (Dordrecht: Martinus Nijhoff, 1986), 233–45, and see Sarah Stroumsa, *Freethinkers of Medieval Islam: Ibn al-Râwândî, Abû Bakr al-Râzî and Their Impact on Islamic Thought* (Leiden: Brill, 1999); and Dominique Urvoy, "La Démystification de la religion dans les textes attribués à Ibn Al-Muqaff," in *Atheismus im Mittelalter und in der Renaissance*, ed. Friedrich Niewöhner and Olaf Pluta (Wiesbaden: Harrassowitz Verlag, 1999), 85–94.

[43] See Chapter 1, this volume.

[44] Cf. Paolo Sarpi, *Pensieri filosofici e scientific* 380, 403–5 with 406–7, 413–14, 423, and consider Sarpi, *Pensieri sulla religione*, passim (esp. 13–43), in Sarpi, *Pensieri naturali, metafisici et matematici*, ed. Luisa Cozzi and Libero Sosio (Milan: Riccard Ricciardi, 1996), 289, 306–9, 314–15, 320, 643–67. Then, see Wootton, *Paolo Sarpi*, passim, and Vittorio Frajese, "Sarpi e la tradizione scettica," *Studi storici* 29:4 (October–December 1988): 1029–50, "Sarpi interprete del *De la Saggesse* de Pierre Charron: I *Pensieri sulla religione*," *Studi Veneziani* 20 (1990): 59–85, and *Sarpi scettico: Stato e chiesa a Venezia tra Cinque e Seicento* (Bologna: Il Mulino, 1994), as well as Alberto Tenenti, "Libertinismo e etica politica in Paolo Sarpi," *Studi Veneziani* 38 (1999): 67–77.

In Italy, Machiavelli and Sarpi were no doubt the odd men out, but they can hardly have been unique. That there were others, that they were tolerably numerous, and that in an age of fierce religious persecution, when the Inquisition was especially active and alert,[45] they thought it prudent to practice dissimulation – of this Giulio Cesare Vanini and Tommaso Campanella were no less fully persuaded than were the apologists Garasse and Mersenne.[46] Moreover, the same conviction was held by the as-yet-unidentified, exceptionally well-read Parisian author who, in the late 1650s, espoused atheism in the widely circulated clandestine tract *Theophrastus redivivus*.[47] The fact that the terms *atheist* and *libertine* first appeared in Latin in the 1530s, and then gradually found their way into the vernacular languages of Europe, and the fact that the term *deist* followed suit some two decades thereafter – all of this suggests that something novel was afoot.[48] In later years, the marquis de Condorcet summed up what had been in sixteenth- and seventeenth-century Europe the common sense of the matter when he remarked, "For a long time, there existed in Europe, and especially in Italy, a class of men who rejected all superstitions, were indifferent to every form of worship, submitted themselves to reason alone, and regarded all religions as the inventions of man – which one might mock in secret but which prudence or policy required one to appear to respect."[49] We can be confident that he was better informed about what was then the recent past than we are now.

---

[45] With regard to the situation in Italy at this time, see Antonio Rotondò, "La censura ecclesiastica e la cultura," in *Storia d'Italia*, ed. Romano Ruggiero and Corrado Vivanti (Turin: Giulio Einaudi, 1972–), V:2 1397–1492, and Luigi Firpo, "Filosofia italiana e Controriforma," *Rivista di filosofia* 41:2 (April–June 1950): 150–73, 41:4 (October–December 1950): 390–401, 42:1 (January–March 1951): 30–47, along with Firpo, "Correzioni d'autore coatte," in *Studi e problemi di critica testuale* (Bologna: Commissione per i testi di lingua, 1961), 143–57. This dimension of Milton's trip to Italy escaped the attention of his most important biographer: see Parker, *Milton: A Biography*, I 169–82.

[46] The argument presented by Henri Busson, *Les Sources et le développement du rationalisme dans la littérature française de la renaissance (1533–1601)* (Paris: Letouzey & Ané, 1922), is confirmed by Tullio Gregory, *Theophrastus redivivus: Erudizione e ateismo nel Seicento* (Naples: A. Morano, 1979), 15–17, n. 10.

[47] Consider *Theophrastus redivivus*, ed. Guido Canziani and Gianni Paganini (Florence: La Nuova Italia, 1981), in light of the analysis by Gregory, *Theophrastus redivivus*, passim. Had he paid more attention to this document and to what its existence demonstrates with regard to the subterranean intellectual currents operative in Paris in the 1650s, Jonathan I. Israel, *Radical Enlightenment: Philosophy and the Making of Modernity 1650–1750* (Oxford, UK: Oxford University Press, 2001), would not have attributed to Spinoza the influence that he did.

[48] See Henri Busson, "Les Noms des incrédules au XVIIe siècle," *Bibliothèque d'Humanisme et de Renaissance* 16:3 (September 1954): 273–83; Gerhard Schneider, *Der Libertin: Zur Geistes- und Sozialgeschichte des Bürgertums im 16. und 17. Jahrhundert* (Stuttgart: J. B. Metzler, 1970), 35–44; Jean-Claude Margolin, "Rèflexions sur l'emploi du terme *libertin* au XVIe siècle," in *Aspects du libertinisme au XVIe siècle* (Paris: J. Vrin, 1974), 1–33; and Concetta Bianca, "Per la storia del termine *atheus* nel Cinquecento: Fonti e traduzione greco-latine," *Studi filosofici* 3 (1980): 71–104.

[49] Cf. Marquis de Condorcet, *Esquisse d'un tableau historique du progrès de l'esprit humain*, ed. O. H. Prior and Yvon Belaval (Paris: J. Vrin, 1970), 127 with ibid., 51–58, 81–82, 105–6, and see Don Cameron Allen, *Doubt's Boundless Sea: Skepticism and Faith in the Renaissance* (Baltimore, MD: Johns Hopkins University Press, 1964), 28–74.

Naudé's teacher at Padua, the renowned Aristotelian Cesare Cremonini,[50] appears to have been a member of the class described by Condorcet. "This Cremonini was a grand figure," Naudé reportedly claimed, "with a mind lively and capable of everything." Above all, he was

a man educated in the ways of the world (*déniaisé*) and cured from foolishness (*gueri de sot*), who knew the truth perfectly well, though in Italy no one dare speak it. All the professors in that country, but particularly those in Padua, are men familiar with the ways of the world (*gens déniaisez*). All the more for being recent arrivals at the pinnacle of science, they want to be free from the vulgar errors of the ages. . . . In Italy, Cremonini hid his game shrewdly: he possessed not a shred of piety but he wished to be thought pious nonetheless (*nihil habebat pietatis et tamen pius haberi volebat*). One of his maxims was: within, as you please; out of doors, as custom dictates (*intus ut libet, foris ut moris est*).[51]

Cremonini seems to have been typical of Italy's Latin Averroists, who had always been for the most part a cautious lot in no way eager to disabuse their unphilosophical neighbors of the salutary prejudices and superstitions they so fondly embraced.[52] Elsewhere, it is even reported that Cremonini refused to have any but the most pious of Christians as servants in his household. "If they

[50] See Maria Assunta del Torre, *Studi su Cesare Cremonini: Cosmologia e logica nel tardo aristotelismo padovano* (Padova: Antenore, 1968), and *Cesare Cremonini: Aspetti del pensiero e scritti*, ed. Ezio Riondato e Antoniono Poppi (Padua: Accademia Galileiana di scienze, lettere ed arti, 2000).

[51] See *Naudæana*, 53–57. Naudé, who purportedly spent three months in Cremonini's company, is best known for his Machiavellian treatise *Considérations politiques sur les coups d'état* (1639): see Friedrich Meinecke, *Machiavellism: The Doctrine of Raison d'Etat and Its Place in Modern History*, tr. Douglas Scott (London: Routledge & Kegan Paul, 1957), 196–204, and Peter S. Donaldson, *Machiavelli and Mystery of State* (Cambridge, UK: Cambridge University Press, 1988), 111–85. Cf. David Wootton, "From Fortune to Feedback: Contingency and the Birth of Modern Political Science," in *Political Contingency: Studying the Unexpected, the Accidental, and the Unforeseen*, ed. Ian Shapiro and Sonu Bedi (New York: New York University Press, 2007), 21–53 (esp. 46–49). For his importance in France as a transmitter of Italian libertine thought, see René Pintard, *Le Libertinage érudit dans la première moitié du XVIIᵉ siècle*, second edition (Geneva: Slatkine, 1983), esp. 156–78, 206–14, 245–70, 304–11, 367–69, 381–82, 390–91, 415–16, 442–76, 540–75. The maxim attributed to Cremonini quickly became a libertine motto: *Theophrastus redivivus*, I 35.

[52] Pietro Pomponazzi (1462–1525), is a case in point: note Pomponazzi, *Tractatus de immortalitate animae* (Bologna: n.p., 1516), which is conveniently reprinted in facsimile along with an English translation in Pomponazzi, *Tractatus de immortalitate animae*, tr. William Henry Hay II (Haverford, PA: Haverford College, 1938), i–xxxv, where one should read xxxiii–xxxv in light of xxiv–xxvii, xxix, xxxii–xxxiii. A revised version of Hay's translation can be found in *The Renaissance Philosophy of Man*, ed. Ernst Cassirer, Paul Oskar Kristeller, and John Hermann Randall, Jr. (Chicago: University of Chicago Press, 1948), 280–381, in which one should read 377–81 in light of 350–57, 363–65, and 373–75 before considering Martin Pine, "Pomponazzi and the Problem of 'Double Truth,'" *Journal of the History of Ideas* 29:2 (April 1968): 163–76. Petrarch was shocked by the lack of piety privately evidenced by the disciples of Aristotle and Averroës whom he encountered in the mid-fourteenth century: consider Petrarch, *On His Own Ignorance and That of Many Others* (1368), in *The Renaissance Philosophy of Man*, 47–133 (esp. 65–120), in light of Letter to Boccaccio on 28 August 1364, in ibid., 140–41, and see Letters to Giovanni de'Dondi dell'Orologio on 17 November 1370 and to Luigi Marsili in 1370, in ibid., 142–43. At that time, Bologna, rather than Padua, seems to have been the Italian university most closely associated with Averroist thought: see Kristeller, "Petrarch's 'Averroists,'" 59–65.

believed in God no more than I do," he is said to have explained, "I would not be safe in my own home."[53]

One reason the description of Cremonini attributed to Naudé should be judged plausible is that it accords quite well with what we know of the posture adopted by Averroës and his predecessors among those called in Arabic the *falāsifa*.[54] At Padua, Cremonini can hardly have escaped familiarity with this strain of thought. The passages from Averroës' commentaries on Aristotle's *Physics* and *Metaphysics* that served as the basis for this outlook were among the sources on which Pietro Pomponazzi lectured in his classes at the University of Bologna in 1514. Moreover, he discussed them in such a manner as to bring home to his students their full meaning,[55] and he did so, we must suppose, not just that year but on other occasions as well, from the time of his *Auseinandersetzung* with Averroës when he taught in Padua at the turn of the century until his death in 1525. And though Pomponazzi exercised caution in what he wrote for clandestine circulation in manuscript and possible posthumous publication,[56] and even greater caution in that which he himself ushered into print,[57] in these works also his outlook is clear to those with eyes to see.[58]

[53] See [Phillipe Louis Joly], *Remarques critiques sur le dictionnaire de Bayle* (Dijon: François Desventes, 1748–1752), I 289.

[54] See Chapter 2, this volume.

[55] See Bruno Nardi, "Filosofia e religione," *Giornale critico della filosofia italiana* 30:3 (July–September 1951): 363–81, which is reprinted in Nardi, *Studi su Pietro Pomponazzi* (Florence: Felice Le Monnier, 1965), 122–48.

[56] See Pietro Pomponazzi, *Libri quinque de fato, de libero arbitrio, et de praedestinatione*, ed. Richard Lemay (Lugano: Thesauri Mundi, 1957), 75–77, 89–91, 152–67, 193–98, 202, 205–6, 208–9, 223–24, 262, 274, 407, 450–54, and Pomponazzi, *De naturalium effectuum causis, sive de incantionibus* (1515–20) 4–5, 10, 12, in Pomponazzi, *Opera*, ed. Guglielmo Gratarolus (Basel: Henricpetrina, 1567), 38–68 (at 53–54, 65–67), 110–208 (esp., 146–47, 200–208), 219–97 (esp., 282–97), which is also available in a reliable French translation: see Pietro Pomponazzi, *Les Causes des merveilles de la nature, ou, Les Enchantements*, tr. Henri Busson (Paris: Rieder, 1930), 131–49 (at 142, 148–49), 172–217 (esp. 191–93, 213–17), 222–63 (esp. 250–63). In this connection, see Henri Busson, "Introduction," in ibid., 9–105, who shows just how extensively Giulio Cesare Vanini plagiarized from the work; Giancarlo Zanier, *Ricerche sulla diffusione e fortuna del "De incantionibus" di Pietro Pomponazzi* (Florence: La Nuova Italia, 1975), who discusses the manuscript's circulation more generally; and Eugenio Garin, *Astrology in the Renaissance: The Zodiac of Life*, tr. Carolyn Jackson, June Allen, and Clare Robertson (London: Arkana, 1990), 96–105 (with the attendant notes).

[57] Consider the fourteenth chapter of Pomponazzi, *Tractatus de immortalitate animae* xxiv–xxxiii (where one should pay special attention to xxiv–xxvii, xxix, xxxii–xxxiii), in light of the disclaimers in the fifteenth and final chapter (ibid xxxiii–xxxv), which can both be found in English translation in *The Renaissance Philosophy of Man*, 350–77 (where one should pay special attention to 350–57, 363–65, 373–75) and 377–81; then, see Bruno Nardi, "Il preteso desiderio naturale dell'immortalità," *Giornale critico della filosofia italiana* 34:3 (July–September 1955): 385–403, which is reprinted in Nardi, *Studi su Pietro Pomponazzi*, 247–68, and note Pietro Pomponazzi, *Apologiae libri tres* (1518) I.3, III.3–4, and *Defensorium autoris* (1519) 42, 55–56, 85, in Pomponazzi, *Tractatus acutissimi, utillimi et mere peripatetici* (Venice: Octavianus Scotus, 1525), 61vb, 73vb–75ra, 88va, 92va–93rb, 108rb.

[58] Note Lynn Thorndike, *A History of Magic and Experimental Science* (New York: Columbia University Press, 1923–1958), V 94–110 (esp. 98–99, 107–9); Giovanni di Napoli, "Libertà e fato in Pietro Pomponazzi," in *Studi in onore di Antonio Corsano* (Manduria: Lacaita, 1970), 175–220, which is reprinted in di Napoli, *Studi sul Rinascimento* (Naples: Giannini, 1973),

Moreover, in his Averroism, Pomponazzi was by no means alone.[59] The great publishing project begun in the 1470s by the Averroists at the University of Padua had reached its completion a century later, and the works of Aristotle and the commentaries of Averroës were easily accessible. By the late sixteenth century, Averroism had become the common property of speculative men.

One consequence is that in this period the distinctive political vocabulary and the theologico-political doctrines deployed by the *falāsifa* are frequently to be found. Writing in the 1550s, for example, Girolamo Cardano was perfectly capable of adopting a neutral stance when comparing from a moral and political perspective what he tellingly identified as the law (*lex*) of the idolaters with the various and distinct *leges* promulgated by the Jews, the Christians, and the Muslims,[60] and he was similarly prepared to treat the generation and dissolution of such a *lex* as a natural phenomenon that a student of nature's progress could readily predict.[61] Writing thirty years thereafter, Giordano Bruno took for granted the Averroist presumption that religion exists to provide for the moral indoctrination of "peoples boorish, uncouth, and unrefined (*rozzi populi*)," while rational demonstration is reserved for the few "capable of contemplation (*gli contemplativi*)."[62] After being told that the truth "profits the

85–159; and Franco Graiff, "I prodigi e l'astrologia nei commenti di Pietro Pomponazzi al *De caelo*, alla *Meteora* e al *De generatione*," *Medioevo* 2 (1976): 331–61, and see Martin L. Pine, *Pietro Pomponazzi: Radical Philosopher of the Renaissance* (Padua: Antenore, 1986), and "Pietro Pomponazzi's Attack on Religion and the Problem of the *De fato*," in *Atheismus im Mittelalter und in der Renaissance*, 145–72, along with Wim van Dooren, "Pomponazzi and Averroes," in ibid., 309–18.

[59] See Tullio Gregory, "Aristotelismo e libertinismo," *Giornale critico della filosofia italiana* 61:2 (May–August 1982): 153–67, which is reprinted in *Aristotelismo veneto e scienza moderna*, ed. Eugenio Garin (Padua: Antenore, 1983), I 279–95, and translated in Gregory, *Genèse de la raison classique: De Charron à Descartes*, tr. Marilène Raiola (Paris: Presses Universitaires de France, 2000), 63–80, and Nicholas Davidson, "Unbelief and Atheists in Italy, 1500–1700," in *Atheism from the Reformation to the Enlightenment*, ed. Michael Hunter and David Wootton (Oxford, UK: Oxford University Press, 1992), 55–85; and see Spini, *Ricerca dei Libertini*, 7–25.

[60] See Girolamo Cardano *De subtilitate libri XII* (Paris: Jacob Dupuys, 1551), 212ʳ–214ʳ. For a French translation, see Girolamo Cardano, *De la subtilité* (Paris: Guillaume le Noir, 1556), 242ᵛ–243ʳ. Note also Girolamo Cardano, *De sapientia libri quinque* (Nuremberg: J. Petreius, 1544), 127–28.

[61] See Girolamo Cardano, *Claudii Ptolemai Pelsiensis libri quattuor: De astrorum iudiciis* II Praef., in Cardano, *Opera omnia*, ed. Charles Spon (Lyons: Ioannis Antonii Huguetan and Marci Antonii Ravaud, 1663), V 220–21.

[62] See Giordano Bruno, *De l'infinito, universo e mundi* (1584) I, in Bruno, *Opere italiane*, second edition, ed. Giovanni Gentile (Bari: Gius, Laterza & Figli, 1925–1927), I 287–306 (esp. 301–302). See also Bruno, *Spaccio de la bestia trionfante* (1583) II, in ibid., II 85–94 (esp. 90). In this connection, see Spini, *Ricerca dei libertini*, 57–82; Rita Sturlese, " 'Averroè quantumque arabo et ignorante di lingua greca . . .': Note sull'Averroismo di Giordano Bruno," in *Averroismus im Mittelalter und in der Renaissance*, 319–50 (esp. 332–37); and the recent work by Miguel Angel Granada: "Maquiavelo y Giordano Bruno: Religión civil y crítica del cristianismo," *Bruniana & Campanelliana* 4:2 (1998): 343–68; "*Esser spogliato dall'umana perfezione e giustizia*: Nueva evidencia de la presencia de Averroes en la obra y en el proceso de Giordano Bruno," *Bruniana & Campanelliana* 5:2 (1999): 305–31; "*Venghino a farsi una sanguisuga*: Nota a un pasaje suprimido de la versión definitiva de la *Cena de le ceneri*," *Bruniana & Campanelliana* 8:1 (2002): 265–76; "*Per fuggir biasmo, o per giovar altrui*: El elogio del nolano en la *Cena de le ceneri* y una posible polémica con San Agustín y Dante," *Bruniana & Campanelliana* 8:2 (2002):

contemplative" and not "the vulgar" and that, in consequence, "the divine books (*le divini libri*)" leave "demonstration and speculation concerning the things of nature" to "philosophy" and operate "through the laws to ordain practices" consistent with "moral conduct," one of his characters echoes Averroës' shocking suggestion that only "the wise and generous spirits" capable of contemplation "are truly men." As for the "laws," he explains, they have as their "end not so much a quest for the truth of things and speculation as goodness in customs, the advantage of the community, the persuasion of the people, and conduct favorable to human conversation, the maintenance of peace, and the growth of the commonwealth."[63]

The starting point for Paolo Sarpi's philosophical ruminations on the subject of religion in the late sixteenth and early seventeenth centuries was the same Averroist understanding. The Venetian friar owned an edition of the Arab philosopher's commentaries on Aristotle, in which his *Incoherence of the Incoherence* was also to be found,[64] and he had evidently studied Averroës with care. In his notebooks he puzzled over the multitude's incapacity for science and its dependence on the imagination, he pondered whether religion can serve alongside politics as a species of political medicine, and he considered the ineradicable tension between *philosophia* and *lex* or, as he appropriately termed it, *tora*.[65] In similar fashion, the relationship between *lex* and *ratio* was one of the central themes addressed by the renegade Carmelite Giulio Cesare Vanini in the books he published in 1615 and 1616.[66] Such was also the focus adopted by the author of *Theophrastus redivivus* in the mid-seventeenth century.[67] And, as this last

---

333–73; *Giordano Bruno: Universo infinito, unión con Dios, perfección del hombre* (Barcelona: Herder, 2002); and *La Reivindicación de la filosofía en Giordano Bruno* (Barcelona: Herder, 2005).

[63] See Giordano Bruno, *La cena de le ceneri* (1584) IV, ed. Giovanni Aquilecchia (Turin: Giulio Einaudi, 1955), 182–88.

[64] See Zannini, "Libri di fra Paolo," 197 (no. 179).

[65] Ponder Paolo Sarpi *Pensieri filosofici e scientifici* nos. 380, 403–9, 412–14, 420, 422–23, 468, 470–71, 504, 506, in that order, which is the order in which his thinking unfolded, and consider Sarpi's later *Pensieri medico-morali* and *Pensieri sulla religione*, all in Sarpi, *Pensieri naturali, metafisici et matematici*, 289, 306–11, 314–16, 318–20, 352–54, 371, 603–32, 643–67, in light of Wootton, *Paolo Sarpi*, 13–43. Sarpi's use of the term *tora* in these ruminations suggests the likelihood that, like Thomas Aquinas and many another Scholastic, he had read Maimonides' *Guide of the Perplexed* in a Latin translation: see Wolfgang Kluxen, "Literargeschichtliches zum lateinischen Moses Maimonides," *Recherches de théologie ancienne et médiévale* 21 (1954): 23–50.

[66] See Franco Bozzi, "La *ratio* e le *leges* in Giulio Cesare Vanini," *Il pensiero politico* 8:3 (1975): 299–321, and Jean-Pierre Cavaillé, *Dis/simulations: Jules-César Vanini, François La Mothe le Vayer, Gabriel Naudé, Louis Machon et Torquatto Accetto: Religion, morale et politique au XVIIe siècle* (Paris: Champion, 2002), 39–140.

[67] See Gianni Paganini, "*Legislatores* et *impostores*: Le *Theophrastus redivivus* et la thèse de l'imposture des religions à la moitié du XVIIᵉ siècle," in *Sources antiques de l'irréligion moderne: Le Relais italien, XVIᵉ–XVIIᵉ siècles*, ed. Jean-Pierre Cavaillé and Didier Foucault (Toulouse: Presses Universitaires du Mirail, 2001), 181–218. Note also Paganini, "L'Anthropologie naturaliste d'un esprit fort: Thèmes et problèmes pomponaciens dans le *Theophrastus redivivus*," *XVIIᵉ siècle* 37:4 (October–December 1985): 349–77, and Guido Canziani, "Une Encyclopédie naturaliste de la Renaissance devant la critique libertine du XVIIᵉ siècle: Le *Theofrastus redivivus* lecteur de Cardan," *XVIIᵉ siècle* 37:4 (October–December 1985): 279–406.

example suggests, in Milton's day, Latin Averroists were by no means to be found in Italy alone.

That Milton also was familiar with the lineaments of the Averroist argument goes without saying. He was, after all, the best-read Englishman of his generation, and in England he was second to none in his admiration of Aristotle. It is, of course, possible that he regarded Averroës with contempt, that he never perused his commentaries and never read through *The Incoherence of the Incoherence*, but it is unlikely. Moreover, even if he saw no reason to delve into Averroës' works and did not bother, there is evidence that he did work his way through another, no less influential presentation of the theologico-political doctrine of the *falāsifa*, for in his published works he displays an intimate familiarity with the Latin translation of Maimonides' *Guide of the Perplexed* produced and published by Johann Buxtorf of Basel in 1629,[68] and for guidance in constructing an interpretation of the Jewish Bible, he turned to Maimonides' disciple Gersonides,[69] who was responsible for writing the first supercommentaries on Averroës and who inspired his students to imitate his example in this regard.[70]

The Tyranny of Custom

The principal source for the propagation of Averroist doctrine in the France that Milton visited in 1638 appears to have been Pierre Charron.[71] In the preface to

---

[68] Consider *The Doctrine and Discipline of Divorce* (1 August 1643), in *CPW*, II 257, and *Pro Populo Anglicano Defensio* (24 February 1651) II, in *CW*, VII 102–3, in light of Kluxen, "Literargeschichtliches zum lateinischen Moses Maimonides," 23–50. For a recent translation of the latter passage, see *A Defence of the People of England* (24 February 1651) II, tr. Donald C. Mackenzie, in *CPW*, IV:1 354. For a brief discussion of the influence exercised by Maimonides in the Latin West, see Chapter 2, note 52, this volume.

[69] See Harris Francis Fletcher, *Milton's Rabbinical Readings* (Urbana: University of Illinois Press, 1930), 38–40, 55–56, 65–67, 93–96, 102–3, 108, 111–12, 129–40, 144–46, 165, 263–64, 291, 308, 311.

[70] See Ruth Glasner, "Levi ben Gershom and the Study of Ibn Rushd in the Fourteenth Century," *Jewish Quarterly Review* 86:1–2 (July 1995): 51–90. Note also Glasner, "The Early Stages in the Evolution of Gersonides' *Wars of the Lord*," *Jewish Quarterly Review* 87:1–2 (July 1996): 1–46, and Charles H. Manekin, "Conservative Tendencies in Gersonides' Religious Philosophy," in *The Cambridge Companion to Medieval Jewish Philosophy*, ed. Daniel H. Frank and Oliver Leaman (Cambridge, UK: Cambridge University Press, 2003), 304–42.

[71] See Tullio Gregory, *Etica e religione nella critica libertina* (Naples: Guida, 1986), 71–109, which is reprinted in translation as "Pierre Charron's 'Scandalous Book,'" in *Atheism from the Reformation to the Enlightenment*, 87–109. Note also Tullio Gregory, "La sagezza scettica di Pierre Charron," *De homine* 21 (1967): 163–82. These two essays are now available in a French translation: see Gregory, *Genèse de la raison classique*, 113–56. See also Gianni Paganini, "Sages, spirituels, esprits forts: Filosofia dell'*esprit* e tiplogia umana nell'opera di Pierre Charron," in *La sagezza moderna: Temi e problemi dell'opera di Pierre Charron*, ed. Vittorio Dini and Domenico Taranto (Naples: Edizione Scientifiche Italiane, 1987), 113–56. Cf. Jean Daniel Charron, *The "Wisdom" of Pierre Charron: An Original and Orthodox Code of Morality* (Chapel Hill: University of North Carolina Press, 1960), and Richard Henry Popkin, *The History of Scepticism: From Savonarola to Bayle* (New York: Oxford University Press, 2003), 57–61, who, as one would expect, treats Charron as a fideist, with Renée Kogel, *Pierre Charron* (Geneva: Librairie Droz, 1972), 77–104, who shows that one does not have to be in any way suspicious to recognize that something is amiss.

the second, expurgated edition of his book *Of Wisdom*, which was published
in Paris in 1604, shortly after his death, he drew a sharp distinction between the
philosophical few and the unenlightened multitude, and he did so in the time-
honored fashion of Plato and the Arab *falāsifa*, juxtaposing those whom he
termed *les esprits forts*, "men of strong mind" distinguished by a noble capacity
to face up to the truth and manage it, with those whom he called *les esprits
foibles*, "men mentally weak," foolish, and likely to be profoundly damaged
by exposure to true science. Moreover, within the latter category – in a manner
fully sanctioned by Plato, Averroës, and Pomponazzi, as we shall soon see –
the French thinker went on to distinguish two kinds of men: "the better part
of the common sort," who are by nature and temperament weak, incapable,
shallow, and prone to "sottishness," and a second, much smaller class, distinct
in some respects from "the common, prophane, and popular sort," which is
naturally hot, ardent, audacious, and prone to "folly." Charron was not much
interested in the first group: they are, he observed in a later chapter, "born
to obey, serve, and be led," and about them there is little more to be said. It
is the second group, which corresponds with the class of auxiliaries in Plato's
Republic, instruction that he found intriguing – and not simply or even primarily
because its members could "more easily be corrected by instruction (*discipline*)
than the first."[72]

The members of Charron's second class have this in common with Plato's
auxiliaries: they are spirited, and they are incapable of philosophy. In Plato's
initial analysis, two facts stand out: such men are indispensable for the defense
of the political community, and they are, at the same time, a great threat to its
welfare. Unless they can somehow be made public spirited, they will abuse the
position of privilege conferred on them by their superior capacity to wield force.
In consequence, apart from the first book, which serves as an introduction,[73]
the early books of Plato's *Republic* have as their focus not so much the education of the auxiliaries as their thoroughgoing indoctrination in civic virtue, and
they appear to be designed in part to bring home to the reader of the dialogue
just how intractable this difficulty is. Moreover, by the end of Plato's elaborate
account of the education of this class, when the time comes for him to distinguish the auxiliaries as a species of sheepdogs from the true guardians, who are
the shepherds of his city, two things become clear: that the intellectual openness
required of the latter is profoundly at odds with the obstinacy in adhering to
sanctioned opinion that distinguishes the former, and that, in being called upon
to give up family, property, and high civic office, the former are being asked to
sacrifice for the good of the whole the only goods within their reach.[74]

[72] Consider Pierre Charron, *De la sagesse*, ed. Barbara de Negroni (Paris: Fayard, 1986), 25–43
(esp. 35–40), in light of Jean de la Bruyère, *Les Caractères*, in la Bruyère, *Oeuvres complètes*,
ed. Julien Benda (Paris: Bibliothèque de la Pléiade, 1957), 450.

[73] See Pl. *Resp.* 2.357a.

[74] See Pl. *Resp.* 2.372b17–7.541b10, with special attention to the peculiar twists and turns taken
by Socrates' account at 2.374b1–76d6 and 3.410a5–5.480a8, and with an eye to the distinction
Socrates eventually draws between lovers of learning and lovers of wisdom, to that which he
draws between auxiliaries and true guardians, and to the psychological foundations for these
distinctions.

Thanks to the availability in Latin of the epitome of Plato's *Republic* that appears at the beginning of Plato's *Timaeus*, and thanks as well to the wide circulation afforded Calcidius' Latin commentary on the latter work, Plato's political sociology and the political psychology on which it was built were well known in the late Middle Ages and the early Renaissance throughout the Latin West.[75] Averroës' account was, however, far less well known. The Arab philosopher had studied the pertinent books of Plato's *Republic* with very great care,[76] and he had paid close attention as well to Alfarabi's *Book of Letters* and to the treatment therein of religion and its attendant arts, jurisprudence and theology, in relation to the logical arts, among which the author of that work included not only philosophic demonstration and dialectic, but rhetoric and even poetry.[77] Toward the end of his life, Averroës adopted Plato's political sociology and reconfigured it, precisely as Alfarabi had done – for the purpose of making sense of the peculiar difficulties that arise in modern societies distinguished from their pagan predecessors by the cultural hegemony of a monotheism grounded in prophetic revelation. In *The Book of the Decisive Treatise Determining the Connection Between Law and Wisdom* and in its sequel, *Uncovering of the Sign Posts of the Proofs Concerning the Beliefs of the Religious Community*, the Cordoban deployed this tripartite division of humanity with an eye to clarifying what it was that had occasioned "the turbulence of the dialectical theologians" and what it was that accounted for the sectarian divisions that, in his day, to an increasing degree beset Islam. Averroës' main aim was to bring home to men of intelligence, who might otherwise be attracted by the attack launched against the *falāsifa* by al-Ghazāli, the degree to which Islam would be prone to sectarian strife and self-destruction if it were left entirely to its own devices, given over to the jurists and the dialectical theologians, and deprived of supervision by philosophers concerned solely with the community's this-worldly welfare.

---

[75] Note Pl. *Tim.* 17b5–19b2, and see Paul Edward Dutton, *Illustre civitatis et populi exemplum*: Plato's *Timaeus* and the "Transmission from Calcidius to the End of the Twelfth Century of a Tripartite Scheme of Society," *Mediaeval Studies* 45 (1983): 79–119. In this connection, note also Paul Edward Dutton, "Material Remains of the Study of *The Timaeus* in the Late Middle Ages," in *L'Enseignement de la philosophie au XIIIe siècle: Autour du "Guide de l'étudiant" du ms. Ripoli 109*, ed. Claude Lafleur and Joanne Carrier (Turnhout: Brepols, 1997), 203–30, along with Gian Carlo Garfagnini, "Platone 'teologo' e politico: Il sogno di uno stato 'divino,'" *Rinascimento* n. s. 42 (2002): 3–30, and James Hankins, "The Study of *The Timaeus* in Early Renaissance Italy" and "Pierleone da Spoleto on Plato's Psychogony (Glosses on *The Timaeus* in Barb. Lat. 21)," in *Humanism and Platonism in the Italian Renaissance* (Rome: Edizioni di Storia e Letteratura, 2003–4) II *Platonism*, 93–154.

[76] Consider *Averroes on Plato's Republic* 25.10–79.23 in light of Muhsin S. Mahdi, "Alfarabi et Averroès: Remarques sur le commentaire d'Averroès sur la *République* de Platon," in *Multiple Averroès*, ed. Jean Jolivet (Paris: Les Belles Lettres, 1978), 91–101; Charles E. Butterworth, *Philosophy, Ethics, and Virtuous Rule: A Study of Averroes' Commentary on Plato's Republic* (Cairo: American University in Cairo Press, 1986); and Rémi Brague, "Averroès et la *République*," in *Images de Platon et lectures de ses œuvres: Les Interprétations de Platon à travers les siècles*, ed. Ada Neschke-Hentschke (Louvain-la-neuve: Peeters, 1997), 99–114.

[77] See *Alfarabi's Book of Letters (Kitāb al-Hurūf)*, ed. Muhsin Mahdi (Beirut: Dār al-Mashriq, 1970) §§ 108–57, in *Medieval Islamic Philosophical Writings*, ed. and tr. Muhammad Ali Khalidi (Cambridge, UK: Cambridge University Press, 2005), 1–27.

To this end, Averroës abandoned Plato's focus on the city's need for spirited men in time of war, and he attended to the role that such men tended to play within Islam. To this same end, he followed Alfarabi in articulating a political sociology grounded on the distinction between men suited to demonstration, men suited to dialectic, and men responsive to rhetoric and poetry alone, intimating that grave danger arose chiefly when spirited men – suited to arguing dialectically, from uncertain premises to conclusions less certain still – seized control, squabbled over matters incapable of a resolution that can give rise to consensus, and mixed the various modes of reasoning in works designed to rally to one faction or another men able to assimilate and genuinely understand rhetoric and poetry alone.[78] To grasp what this analysis entailed, one need only attend to the peculiar treatment given Aristotle's *Rhetoric* and *Poetics* by the *falāsifa*.

In discussing the former work, Alfarabi, Avicenna, and Averroës had considerably less to say concerning the close relationship that it posited between rhetoric and public deliberation than one might initially expect, and in discussing the latter, they paid very little attention to its theatrical focus. This shift in emphasis cannot have been due to gross ignorance on their part: they could read as well as anyone else, and they were sensitive to the glaring defects present in the translation of *The Poetics* that had reached them. In assessing their treatment of this part of the Aristotelian corpus, one should keep in mind the fact that they lived in a world largely bereft of public deliberation, a world from which the theater was absent as well. Accordingly, with an eye to what they took to be needs peculiar to societies based on prophecy and revelation, the *falāsifa* treated both of Aristotle's works with an eye to what then loomed large – religion's propagation by means of scriptural poetry to a multitude wholly reliant on the

---

[78] Note the distinction among demonstration, dialectics, and rhetoric and the parallel distinction between those responsive to each that provides the skeleton on which Averroës hangs his argument in *The Book of the Decisive Treatise Determining the Connection between Law and Wisdom* passim (esp., 26–60), in Averroës, *The Decisive Treatise and Epistle Dedicatory*, ed. and tr. Charles E. Butterworth (Provo, UT: Brigham Young University Press, 2001), 1–36 (esp. 18–33), and that provides the foundation for what he has to say in *Uncovering of the Sign Posts of the Proofs Concerning the Beliefs of the Religious Community* 150.5–154.15, 157.6–159.9, 162.3–9, 165.13–167.14, 173.14–174.2, 178.10–180.19, 182.3–185.2, 193.1–194.17, 240.1– 241.4, 249.8–251.14, which will soon be available in careful translation by Charles E. Butterworth; for the time being, one must rely on *Faith and Reason in Islam: Averroes' Exposition of Religious Arguments*, tr. Ibrahim Y. Najjar (Oxford, UK: One World, 2001), 33–38, 41–43, 47, 51–53, 59–60, 64–66, 68–71, 78–80, 121–22, 129–31. For the *editio princeps* of both works and a translation into German, see *Philosophie und Theologie von Averroes*, tr. Marcus Joseph Müller (Munich: G. Franz, 1859–1875). On these works, see Muhsin S. Mahdi, "Averroës on Divine Law and Human Wisdom," in *Ancients and Moderns: Essays on the Tradition of Political Philosophy in Honor of Leo Strauss*, ed. Joseph Cropsey (New York: Basic Books, 1964), 114–31, and "Remarks on Averroes' Decisive Treatise," in *Islamic Theology and Philosophy: Studies in Honor of George F. Hourani*, ed. Michael E. Marmura (Albany: State University of New York Press, 1983), 188–202, 305–8, along with Charles E. Butterworth, "Averroës: Politics and Opinion," *The American Political Science Review* 66:3 (September 1972): 894–901, and "The Source that Nourishes: Averroes's Decisive Determination," *Arabic Sciences and Philosophy* 5:1 (March 1995): 93–119, and Richard C. Taylor, "'Truth Does Not Contradict Truth': Averroes and the Unity of Truth," *Topoi* 19:2 (March 2000): 3–16.

imagination for its understanding of the universe and man's place in it, and the use of rhetoric and dialectic for the defense of religious doctrine in sermons and books of theology. This focus, nowhere more fully articulated than in *The Book of Letters*, explains why Alfarabi and his successors followed the school of Alexandria and the Arab philosopher Al-Kindi in treating Aristotle's *Rhetoric* and his *Poetics* as parts of his *Organon*,[79] for their intention was not simply to suggest that rhetoric and poetry exhibit a logic all their own and to explore its character.[80] Above all else, they wanted to highlight the logical shortcomings of dialectic, rhetoric, and poetry when compared with rational demonstration, to establish thereby philosophy's claim to superintendence over religion, to suggest

[79] Note Richard Walzer, "Zur traditionsgeschichte der Aristotelischen *Poetik*," *Studi italiani di filologia classica* n. s. 11 (1934): 5–14, which is reprinted in Walzer, *Greek into Arabic: Essays on Islamic Philosophy* (Oxford, UK: B. Cassirer, 1962), 129–36, and cf. Dimitri Gutas, "On Translating Averroes' Commentaries," *Journal of the American Oriental Society* 110:1 (January–March 1990): 92–101, who is inclined to suppose that the *falāsifa* were slavishly following the school of Alexandria, with Charles E. Butterworth, "Translation and Philosophy: The Case of Averroes' Commentaries," *International Journal of Middle East Studies* 26:1 (February 1994): 16–35, who credits them with philosophical and political discernment and suggests that they made a fully conscious choice, and note Maroun Aouad and Marwan Rashed, "Commentateurs 'satisfaisants' et 'non satisfaisants' de la *Rhétorique* selon Averroès," in *Averroes and the Aristotelian Tradition: Sources, Constitution and Reception of the Philosophy of Ibn Rushd (1126–1198)*, ed. Gerhard Endress and Jan A. Aertsen (Leiden: Brill, 1999), 83–124.

[80] Note Deborah L. Black, *Logic and Aristotle's Rhetoric and Poetics in Medieval Arab Philosophy* (Leiden: Brill, 1990), and consider the various contributions by Maroun Aouad – "Les Fondements de la *Rhétorique* d'Aristote reconsidérés par Fārābī, ou le concept de point de vue immédiat et commun," *Arabic Sciences and Philosophy* 2:1 (March 1992): 133–80; "Définition du concept de loué selon le point de vue immédiat dans la *Rhétorique du Šifā*," in *Perspectives arabes et médiévales sur la tradition scientifique et philosophie grecque*, ed. Ahmad Hasnawi, Abdelali Elamrani-Jamal, and Maroun Aouad (Leuven–Paris: Peeters, 1997), 409–51; "Les Fondements de la *Rhétorique* d'Aristote reconsidérés par Averroès dans *L'Abrégé de la rhétorique*, ou le développement du concept de 'point de vue immédiat,'" in *Peripatetic Rhetoric after Aristotle*, ed. William W. Fortenbaugh and David C. Mirhady (New Brunswick, NJ: Transaction, 1994), 261–313; and "Définition par Averroès du concept de 'point de vue immédiat' dans le *Commentaire moyen de la Rhétorique*," *Bulletin d'études orientales* 48 (1996): 115–30, in light of Charles E. Butterworth, "Opinion, point de vue, croyance et supposition," in *Perspectives arabes et médiévales sur la tradition scientifique et philosophie grecque*, 453–64. Note also Maroun Aouad and Gregor Schoeler, "Le Syllogisme poétique selon al-Fārābī: Un Syllogisme incorrect de la deuxième figure," *Arabic Sciences and Philosophy* 12:2 (September 2002): 185–96. The crucial passages on which the *falāsifa* based their claim regarding the logical status of rhetoric and poetry are Arist. *An. Post.* 71b17–34, *Top.* 100a25–101a24, *Soph. El.* 165a38–b11, and *Rh.* 1354a1–11. In this connection, note Myles F. Burnyeat, "Enthymeme: Aristotle on the Logic of Persuasion," in *Aristotle's Rhetoric: Philosophical Essays*, ed. David J. Furley and Alexander Nehamas (Princeton, NJ: Princeton University Press, 1994), 3–55, and Jacques Brunschwig, "Rhétorique et dialectique: Rhétorique et topiques," in ibid., 57–96, which, revised and abridged, are reprinted as Burnyeat, "Enthymeme: Aristotle on the Rationality of Rhetoric," in *Essays on Aristotle's Rhetoric*, ed. Amélie Oksenberg Rorty (Berkeley: University of California, 1996), 88–115, and as Brunschwig, "Aristotle's Rhetoric as a 'Counterpoint' to Dialectic," in ibid., 34–55. It says much about the state of the philosophy profession today that in neither volume is there any mention of the extensive commentary on the subjects they treat that is to be found in Alfarabi, Avicenna, and Averroës: see Steven Harvey, "Conspicuous by His Absence: Averroes' Place Today as an Interpreter of Aristotle," in *Averroes and the Aristotelian Tradition*, 32–49.

the manner in which the three defective logical arts might nonetheless properly be used by a philosophical practitioner of *kalām* or a philosophical lawgiver acting in the guise of a prophet, to protect philosophy from religious assault, and to provide for the this-worldly welfare of the community by way of various species of reasoning that the multitude would find persuasive even when the premises from which the reasoning began, the arguments articulated thereon, or the images projected were misleading or demonstrably false.[81]

In the twelfth and thirteenth centuries, some of the pertinent works were translated into Latin, but, as far as we can tell,[82] the most revealing texts were

---

[81] In this connection, note William F. Boggess, "Alfarabi and the *Rhetoric*: The Cave Revisited," *Phronesis* 15:1 (1970): 86–90, and Muhsin Mahdi, "Science, Philosophy, and Religion in Alfarabi's *Enumeration of the Sciences*," in *The Cultural Context of Medieval Learning*, ed. John Emery Murdoch and Edith Dudley Sylla (Dordrecht: Reidel, 1975), 113–147, and see Charles E. Butterworth, "The Rhetorician and his Relationship to the Community," in *Islamic Theology and Philosophy*, 111–36, 297–98. Then, see Averroës, *Three Short Commentaries on Aristotle's Topics, Rhetoric, and Poetics*, ed. and tr. Charles E. Butterworth (Albany: State University of New York Press, 1977), 43–84, which should be read in light of Charles E. Butterworth, "Introduction," in ibid., 1–41; Averroës, *Middle Commentary on Aristotle's Poetics*, tr. Charles E. Butterworth (Princeton, NJ: Princeton University Press, 1986), 59–142, which should be read in light of Charles E. Butterworth, "Introduction" in ibid., 1–49; and Averroës, *Commentaire moyen à la Rhétorique d'Aristote*, ed. and tr. Maroun Aouad (Paris: J. Vrin, 2002), II: *Édition et traduction*, which should be read in conjunction with Michael Blaustein, "The Scope and Methods of Rhetoric in Averroes' *Middle Commentary on Aristotle's Rhetoric*," in *The Political Aspects of Islamic Philosophy: Essays in Honor of Muhsin S. Mahdi*, ed. Charles E. Butterworth (Cambridge, MA: Harvard University Press, 1992), 262–303; with Charles E. Butterworth, "Averroes' Platonization of Aristotle's *Art of Rhetoric*," in *La Rhétorique d'Aristote: Traditions et commentaires de l'Antiquité au XVIIᵉ siècle*, ed. Gilbert Dahan and Irène Rosier-Catach (Paris: J. Vrin, 1998), 227–40; and with Maroun Aouad, "Le Fil directeur," in Averroës, *Commentaire moyen à la Rhétorique d'Aristote* I: *Introduction générale*, 51–126. Much can also be learned from commentary provided by Aouad in Averroës, *Commentaire moyen à la Rhétorique d'Aristote* III: *Commentaire du commentaire*, passim. In this connection, note Charles E. Butterworth, "Comment Averroès lit les *Topiques* d'Aristote," in *Penser avec Aristote*, ed. Mohammed Allal Sinaceur (Toulouse: Erès, 1991), 701–23, and consider the brief but telling remarks of Alexander Altmann, "*Ars rhetorica* as Reflected in Some Jewish Figures of the Italian Renaissance," in *Essential Papers on Jewish Culture in Renaissance and Baroque Italy*, ed. David B. Ruderman (New York: New York University Press, 1992), 63–84 (at 63–67). Consider Al-Fārābī, *Deux ouvrages inédits sur la Rhétorique*, ed. Jacques Langhade and Mario Grignaschi (Beirut: Dar El-Machreq, 1971), in light of William F. Boggess, "Hermannus Alemannus's Rhetorical Translations," *Viator* 2 (1971): 227–50, and note Maroun Aouad, "La Doctrine rhétorique d'Ibn Riḍwān et la *Didascalia in Rhetoricam Aristotelis ex glosa Alpharabii*," *Arabic Sciences and Philosophy* 7:2 (September 1997): 163–245, 8:1 (March 1998), 131–60, and "Le Texte arabe du chapitre sur la *Rhétorique* d'Ibn Riḍwān et ses correspondants dan la *Didascalia in Rhetoricam Aristotelis et glosa Alpharabii*: Fragments du *Grand Commentaire à la Rhétorique* d'al-Fārābī," in *La Rhétorique d'Aristote*, 169–225. Note also Dominique Mallet, "*Kalām* et dialectique dans le commentaire des *Topiques* d'Alfarabi," *Bulletin d'études orientales* 48 (1996): 165–82.

[82] It is highly likely, however, that a great deal was revealed in works, such as Alfarabi's commentary on Aristotle's *Nicomachean Ethics*, which were translated into Latin and consulted in the late Middle Ages but have either not survived or not yet been found: see D. Salmon, "The Mediaeval Latin Translations of Alfarabi's Works," *The New Scholasticism* 13 (1939): 245–61, and note Shlomo Pines, "La Philosophie dans l'économie du genre humain selon Averroès: Une Réponse à al-Farabi?" in *Multiple Averroès*, 189–207 (at 202–5), which is reprinted in *The Collected Works of Shlomo Pines* (Jerusalem: Magnes Press, 1979–1997), III: *Studies in the History of Arabic*

not. Alfarabi's *Book of Letters* and Averroës' *Decisive Treatise* – the two surviving works in which one finds clearly spelled out the political intention underpinning the decision to treat rhetoric and poetry as logical arts – appear to have
been unavailable. One consequence was that, when writers in the Latin West
followed their Arab predecessors in treating *The Rhetoric* and *The Poetics* as
part of Aristotle's *Organon*, they tended to confine themselves to an elaboration
of the logic of rhetorical argument and poetic representation.[83]

There were, however, exceptions to this rule, for in the works of Averroës that
were translated into Latin there are passages presupposing the political sociology that he borrowed from Alfarabi's *Book of Letters*, and in some quarters
these passages were noticed. For example, in his long commentary on Aristotle's *De anima*, Averroës takes some care to specify the role that intellect can
play in shaping the conduct of man and the role that imagination does play in
determining the behavior of animals.[84] Then, he pauses to remark that human
beings who fall short intellectually because of natural defects and fail to achieve
the natural end of men can only equivocally be called men, and he immediately
adds that some are held back because of habituation (*consuetudo*).[85] Again,
in his commentary on the last section of the second book of Aristotle's *Metaphysics*, immediately after discussing the manner in which *consuetudo*, when
formed by religious law, can be an obstacle to philosophy,[86] Averroës pauses to
consider "what happens to men with regard to the sciences as a consequence of
the diversity of nature and as a consequence of a paucity of instruction in logic."
In this context he distinguishes those who "seek a thoroughgoing examination
(*perscrutatio maxima*)" of every question and are "by nature philosophers"
from four other groups.

There are those, he tells us, who pursue demonstration but only on the
model of mathematics, and they turn out to have difficulty in understanding
nature, which does not fully conform. There are those who rely only on "the
testimony of the multitude (*testimonium multorum*)" and who "cannot make
their way through probabilistic arguments and demonstrations (*pertransire ser-
mones probabiles, et demonstrationes*)." These refuse to credit conclusions
unsupported by fame, and it is apparently among their number that we find
"the *mutakallimūn* (*loquentes*), who deny that it is impossible that something

Philosophy, ed. Sarah Strouma, 357–75 (at 369–73), and Jeanine Quillet, "L'Aristotélisme de
Marsile de Padoue et ses rapports avec l'Averroïsme," *Medioevo* 5 (1979): 81–142.

[83] See Deborah L. Black, "Traditions and Transformations in the Medieval Approach to Rhetoric
and Related Linguistic Arts," in *L'Enseignement de la philosophie au XIIIe siècle*, 233–54, who
takes the part for the whole.

[84] See Averroës, Comments II.152–62, III.1–39, 48–57 on Aristotle's *De anima* 427b6–432a14,
433a5–434a15, in *Averrois Cordubensis commentarium magnum in Aristotelis De anima libros*,
ed. F. Stuart Crawford (Cambridge, MA: Medieval Academy of America, 1953), 361–507, 515–
30.

[85] See Averroës, Comment III.36 on Aristotle's *De anima* 431b16–19, in *Averrois Cordubensis
commentarium magnum in Aristotelis De anima libros*, 479–502 (esp. 495), which should be
read in light of Comment II.162 on Aristotle's *De anima* 429a2–9, in ibid., 377–78.

[86] See Comment II.14 on Aristotle's *Metaphysics* II.3 (995a1–6), in *Aristotelis Stagiritae omnia
quae extant opera . . . Averrois Cordubensis in ea opera omnes qui ad nos pervenere commentarii*
(Venice: Giunta, 1550–1552), VIII 17ra, and note the discussion in Chapter 2, this volume.

emerge from nothing (*negabant impossibile esse aliquid de nihilo*)." There are those, moreover, who rely on "the testimony of a composer of verse (*testimonium versificatoris*)." These are men in whom, as a consequence of a natural defect (*per naturam*), "the imaginative faculty is dominant over the cogitative faculty (*virtus imaginativa dominat super virtute cogitativa*)," and they are seen "not to believe in demonstrations unless the imagination provides them with an escort (*concomitetor eas*)." These are to be distinguished, he then adds, from the fourth group – "those who find it impossible to learn either because of sloth or feebleness (*segnities*), or because they are infected by error." These, because they cannot lay hold of and comprehend precision in argument, "are irritated (*contristantur*)" by it and dismiss precision in philosophical disputation as a species of impudence indistinguishable in character from the bold and shameless precision that merchants display when counting out coins.[87]

These passages seem to have been read and assimilated by the nameless author of a prologue to an otherwise lost Latin commentary, composed in the mid-1270s, which survives in manuscript in the Bibliothèque Nationale in Paris. In it, we are told that there are three kinds of men: *triplex est genus hominis*. "Some are informed (*informati*) hardly or not at all by the excellences (*virtutes*)" necessary if one is to have "an elevated intellect," for, he says, mentioning *De anima*, "they possess an intellect immersed in fantasy and imagination," and they "are said to be human brutes (*homines brutales*)." There are others, he adds, who possess these "excellences in sufficiency, and such men are contemplatives and very good." To speak of these two groups as human, he notes in passing, is to speak, "as the Commentator remarks, equivocally." There is also, he then adds, a third group who "are informed not by these excellences but rather by errors opposed to these excellences and by vices opposed to morals, which are contracted by habituation to that which is bad (*consuetudo ad malum*)."[88]

In *Middle Commentary on Aristotle's Topics* there is another passage, in which Averroës begins by suggesting that there are "something like (*circa*) three species of men" and then goes on to contrast "the man of demonstration (*vir demonstrativus*)" not only with "the man of dialectic (*vir dialecticus*)" but with those who "are by nature (*naturaliter*) sophists." When confronted with "two things that are opposed," those who are "wise" prefer "the better one," he explains. "Those who are by nature dialectical" regard "the good and the bad as equal," while the men devoted to the sophistic art "choose the worse."[89] This passage, to which John of Jandun alludes in the *Exposition on the Third Book of De Anima* that he penned toward the end of the first quarter of the

---

[87] See Comments II.15–16 on *Aristotle's Metaphysics II.3 (995a6–20), in Aristotelis Stagiritae omnia quae extant opera...Averrois Cordubensis in ea opera omnes qui ad nos pervenere commentarii*, VIII 17rb–va.

[88] Consider Constantino Marmo, "Anonymi Philosophia 'Sicut dicitur ab Aristotile': A Parisian Prologue to Porphyry," *Cahiers de l'Institut du Moyen-Âge Grec et Latin* 61 (1991): 140–46 (at 143), in light of Arist. *De an.* 429a2–9.

[89] See Comment VIII.4 on Aristotle's *Topics* VIII.10–14 (161a1–164b8), in *Aristotelis Stagiritae omnia quae extant opera...Averrois Cordubensis in ea opera omnes qui ad nos pervenere commentarii*, I 320ra–vb.

fourteenth century, he appears to have read in conjunction with the passages from Averroës cited earlier – for, in his work, which survives in manuscript in the Vatican library, he brings the two analyses together, suggesting a quadripartite division of humanity – with the philosophers at the top; with the common sort (*volgares*), country folk (*rustici*), merchants, craftsmen, jurists, and others "who do not use any faculties other than sensation and the imagination" at the bottom; and with mathematicians and students of natural science in between.[90] Other examples could no doubt be cited: John of Jandun's writings were well known in Averroist circles.[91]

It was not, however, until the early sixteenth century – or, at least, so it appears – that anyone displayed a full understanding of the argument presented by Alfarabi in his *Book of Letters* and redeployed by Averroës in his *Decisive Treatise*. So far as anyone today is aware, neither of these works was ever translated into Latin, but the latter and its sequel, *Uncovering of the Sign Posts of the Proofs Concerning the Beliefs of the Religious Community*, were translated into Hebrew in the late thirteenth or early fourteenth century, and in that version they circulated widely and were read. We can clearly trace their influence in the writings of figures as disparate as Samuel ibn Tibbon, Shem Tob ibn Falaquera, Yedaiah Bedersi, and Elijah del Medigo,[92] and, perhaps as an accidental by-product of conversations that grew out of del Medigo's intense interest in Averroës' analysis and its pertinence for understanding the doctrinal divisions plaguing the Jewish community late in the fifteenth century,[93]

[90] See MS. Vat. lat. 760, 99vb–100ra, which is quoted at length in Alexander Murray, *Reason and Society in the Middle Ages* (Oxford, UK: Clarendon Press, 1985), 267–70 (with particular reference to 469–70, nn. 22–23).

[91] See, for example, Nicoletto Vernia, *Quaestio an medicina nobilior atque praestantior sit iure civili* (March 1482), in *La disputa della arti nel Quattrocento*, ed. Eugenio Garin (Florence Vallecchi, 1947), 111–23 (esp. 112–15, 119–23), who takes up the arguments that John of Jandun had deployed against the jurists.

[92] See Norman Golb, "The Hebrew Translation of Averroes' *Fasl al-Maqāl*," *Proceedings of the American Academy for Jewish Research* 25 (1956): 91–113, 26 (1957): 41–64, and note Georges Vajda, "An Analysis of the *Ma'amar yiqqawu ha-Mayim* by Samuel b. Judah Ibn Tibbon," *Journal of Jewish Studies* 10:3–4 (1959): 137–49, and Steven Harvey, *Falaquera's Epistle of the Debate: An Introduction to Jewish Philosophy* (Cambridge, MA: Harvard University Press, 1987). Four copies of the Hebrew translation of Averroës' *Decisive Treatise* survive – two in Leiden, one in Oxford, and one in Paris.

[93] The depth of del Medigo's interest in what could be learned from Averroës concerning the quarrels of his co-religionists is evident in a treatise that he finished on 31 December 1490: see M. David Geffen, "Faith and Reason in Elijah del Medigo's *Beḥinat ha-Dat* and the Philosophic Background of the Work" (Ph.D. dissertation, Columbia University, 1970), who provides a rough English translation of the expurgated version of this work published in 1629 and discusses it in detail, and Geffen, "Insights into the Life and Thought of Elijah del Medigo, Based upon His Published and Unpublished Works," *Proceedings of the American Academy for Jewish Research* 41–42 (1973–74): 69–86; Alfred L. Ivry, "Remnants of Jewish Averroism in the Renaissance," in *Jewish Thought in the Sixteenth Century*, ed. Bernard Dov Cooperman (Cambridge, MA: Harvard University Press, 1983), 243–65 (esp. 250–61), and Seymour Feldman, "The End and Aftereffects of Medieval Jewish Philosophy," in *The Cambridge Companion to Medieval Jewish Philosophy*, 414–45 (esp. 416–20). In this connection, see also Adolf Hübsch, "Elia Delmedigos *Bechinat ha-Dath* und Ibn Roschd's *Façl ul-maqâl*," *Monatsschrift für Geschichte und Wissenschaft des Judentums* 31 (1882): 555–63, 32 (1883): 28–46, and Julius Guttman, "Elias del

the tripartite taxonomy of humanity outlined in *The Decisive Treatise* and in its sequel eventually found its way into the literature produced by the Latin Averroists as well.[94]

Pietro Pomponazzi is a case in point.[95] In Padua, where he studied and taught in the 1480s and early 1490s, he is likely to have become acquainted with del Medigo, and through him he may have had direct or indirect access to the lineaments of the argument presented by the Arab philosopher in his *Decisive Treatise*.[96] In his *Tract on the Immortality of the Soul*, Pomponazzi not only adopted the analysis of human types articulated in Averroës' work; he extended it in a fashion indicating that he fully understood the logic underlying the Arab philosopher's argument. In keeping with Averroës' intention, he substituted for his tripartite scheme a quadripartite taxonomy, singling out for discussion not only the men of demonstration, who are attracted, he says, to a virtuous life by its nobility alone; the dialecticians, who are sensitive to arguments appealing to praise and blame; and those responsive solely to rhetoric and the prospect of

Medigos Verhältnis zu Averroës in seinem *Bechinat ha-Dat*," in *Jewish Studies in Memory of Israel Abrahams* (New York: Press of the Jewish Institute of Religion, 1927), 192–208. Note also Kalman P. Bland, "Elijah del Medigo, Unicity of the Intellect, and Immortality of the Soul," *Proceedings of the American Academy for Jewish Research* 61 (1995): 1–22, who suggests on del Medigo's part a theologico-political agenda. The unexpurgated version of del Medigo's tract has now been published in a critical edition: see *Sefer Behinat ha-dat of Elijah Del-Medigo*, ed. Jacob Joshua Ross (Tel Aviv: Chaim Rosenberg School of Jewish Studies, 1984).

94 In the late fifteenth century and in the sixteenth century, the linguistic divide was by no means unbridgeable: see Charles S. F. Burnett, "The Second Revelation of Arabic Philosophy and Science: 1492–1562," in *Islam and the Italian Renaissance*, ed. Charles S. F. Burnett and Anna Contadini (London: Warburg Institute, 1999), 185–98, and "The Two Faces of Averroes in the Renaissance," in *Al-Ufq al-kawni li-fikr Ibn Rushd*, ed. Muhammad Al-Misbahi (Marrakesh: Al Jam'iyah al-Falsafiyah al-Maghribiyah, 2001), 87–94. In this connection, note Giuliano Tamani, "I libri ebraici di Pico della Mirandola," in *Giovanni Pico della Mirandola: Convegno internazionale di studi nel cinquecentesimo anniversario della morte, 1494–1994*, ed. Gian Carlo Garfagnini (Florence: L. S. Olschki, 1997), II 491–530 (esp. 510–15), and see Mauro Zonta, "Due note sulle fonti ebraiche di Giovanni Pico e Giordano Bruno," *Rinascimento* n. s. 40 (2000): 143–53. In later years, Judah ben Isaac Abravanel, who was well known as the author Leone Ebreo, and Jacob Mantino, who translated much of Averroës into Latin, may have played a similar role as an intermediaries: see Shlomo Pines, "Medieval Doctrines in Renaissance Garb? Some Jewish and Arabic Sources of Leone Ebreo's Doctrines," in *Jewish Thought in the Sixteenth Century*, 365–98, which is reprinted in *The Collected Works of Shlomo Pines* V: *Studies in the History of Jewish Thought*, ed. Warren Zev Harvey and Moshe Idel, 626–59; Mauro Zonta, "The Relationship of European Jewish Philosophy to Islamic and Christian Philosophers in the Late Middle Ages," *Jewish Studites Quarterly* 7:2 (2000): 127–40 (at 139–40); and Feldman, "The End and Aftereffects of Medieval Jewish Philosophy," 420–24. Then, see David Kaufmann, "Jacob Mantino: Une page de l'histoire de la Renaissance," *Revue des études juives* 27:53 (July–September 1893): 30–60, 27:54 (October–December 1893): 207–38.

95 See Luca Bianchi, "Filosofi, uomini e bruti: Note per la storia di un'antropologia 'averroista,'" *Rinascimento* n. s. 32 (1992): 185–201, which is reprinted in Bianchi, *Studi sull'aristotelismo del Rinascimento* (Padua: Il Poligrafo, 2003) 41–61, along with Bianchi, "Pomponazzi politicamente corretto? La disuguaglianza fra gli uomini nel *Tractatus de immortalitate animae*," in ibid., 63–99.

96 In this connection, note Wim van Dooren, "Ibn Rušd's Attitude towards Authority," in *Perspectives arabes et médiévales sur la tradition scientifique et philosophique grecque*, 623–33 (at 632), who draws attention to a passage in *De incantionibus* in which Pomponazzi ascribes to Averroës a claim that is advanced by the Arab philosopher in the *Decisive Treatise* and there alone.

earthly reward and punishment, but also the "greater part of mankind," who can, he asserted, be moved by poetry – with its promise of reward and its threat of punishment in the hereafter – and by it alone.[97]

There were others after Pomponazzi who appear to have been familiar with the Averroist argument. In *De subtilitate*, for example, Girolamo Cardano echoes Averroës in suggesting that there are three kinds of men, and he characterizes them in a fashion suggesting on his part a reworking of the Arab philosopher's political sociology. Some, he argues, are a divine character and neither deceive nor are deceived. Others there are of a human character who deceive and are not deceived. And then there are the brutes, who do not deceive but are deceived. But the majority fall into a class intermediate between the human and the brutal, for they both deceive and are deceived.[98]

The first, however, to make a polemical use of the argument laid out in *The Decisive Treatise* appears to have been Pierre Charron, who modeled *De la sagesse* on Cardano's *De sapientia*.[99] In his master work, he followed Averroës quite closely, especially his application of Platonic political psychology to the case of the dialectical theologians and his defense of the *falāsifa* against the attack mounted by al-Ghazāli. When members of Charron's second class, those naturally hot, ardent, audacious, and prone to "folly," are denied "cultivation and instruction" or are given a species that eventuates in "a clash with and sworn prejudice against certain opinions," their minds take on, he observed, "a strong coloring," which renders them incapable of further learning. At the same time, they become puffed up, presumptuous, and bold, and they sometimes "take up arms to sustain and defend opinions" that they have all too quickly settled upon. It is against this class of bigots that Charron proposed in his book to "make open war." But, apart from calling them "pedants," he did not otherwise identify the enemy – except by saying that the sort of man he has in mind is immoderate, opinionated, partisan, and prejudiced; that he is arrogantly and boldly resistant to the wise man; and that he not only attacks the sage, "speaking with resolution and in a magisterial manner," but pursues him "with a fixed (*certaine*) and intestine hatred," intent on censuring, decrying, and condemning one whom he sees as a rival. Only later did Charron specify that these men "subject themselves to the opinions and municipal laws of the place wherein they find themselves from the very moment that they are hatched," that they are enslaved "not only by observance and usage . . . but also heart and soul, and that they think that what one believes in their village has the real

---

[97] See the fourteenth chapter of Pomponazzi, *Tractatus de immortalitate animae* xxiv–xxxiii (at xxix), which can be found in English translation in *The Renaissance Philosophy of Man*, 350–77 (at 363–65).

[98] See Cardano, *De subtilitate libri XII*, 211ʳ. For a French translation, see Cardano, *De la subtilité*, 241ʳ. Elsewhere, in *De sapientia*, Cardano toys with the notion that there are three sources of proof – reason (*ratio*), authority (*auctoritas*), and experience (*experientia*) – contending that the first satisfies the wise, that the second is sufficient for the people, and that the third has force with everyone: see Cardano, *De sapientia libri quinque*, 29–30. Later, in this work, he will assert that there are three kinds of men – princes, those who serve, and those who live in a free city: see ibid., 130.

[99] On the relationship between the two works, note the comment attributed to Gabriel Naudé in *Naudæana*, 17, and see Giuliano Procacci, "Machiavelli e Cardano," in Procacci, *Studi sulla fortuna del Machiavelli* (Rome: Instituto Storico Italiano, 1965), 77–106 (at 100–1).

touch of truth...and is the only or, at least, the best rule for living well." It
was then that he also remarked on the fact that the men in this class "make all
of the noise and produce all of the disputes in the world" and observed that
"the chief and most cunning" in their number actually "govern the world" in
which we live.[100]

It is only when one comes to grips with Charron's suggestion that, in his
day, men of this temperament tend to belong to the school of Aristotle;[101] it is
only when one ruminates on the full implications of his furious diatribe against
the tyranny exercised over the human mind by custom;[102] it is only when one
reconsiders in this light the significance of his contention that all religions have
in them that which is an affront to common sense, of his observation that religious allegiance is in practice a matter of municipal law, and of his assertion that
we become Christians, Jews, and Muslims before we know that we are men;[103]
it is only when one digests his repeated, ostentatious disclaimers that he does
not intend the fierce criticism he aims at dogmatism to apply in any way to the
Christian religion and when one notices that, on such occasions, this passionate
proponent of intellectual liberty tends to cite from the Vulgate the injunction
from Saint Paul deployed against the philosophers in 1277 by Bishop Etienne
Tempier that Christians should subject judgment to authority, "making captive
the intellect out of a reverence for Christ (*captivantes intellectum ad obsequium
Christi*)"[104] – it is only then that the attentive reader begins to suspect that the
most important members of the despised class on which this celebrated cler-
gyman declared war were in his day those among his fellow Christians who
were at the same time well educated and supremely devout. These suspicions
become certainties when one takes note of two facts: that, at the very beginning
of his book, Charron classes himself among the philosophers, and that later he
indicates that philosophers tend to be unbelievers, even atheists, and are no less
virtuous for being such.[105]

This last claim should not in itself give one pause, but it is accompanied
by another argument that should, for this second argument is contrary to the
Averroist stance that serves as Charron's starting point. In his book, Charron
is ostentatiously conservative in the Averroist fashion, insisting that a wise
man will conform outwardly, in both word and deed, to the expectations of
the society in which he lives,[106] but it is striking that he nowhere endorses,
as Averroës does,[107] Aristotle's claim that man is a political animal and his
contention that politics is needed as a supplement to ethics for the promotion
of moral virtue. Moreover, at least with regard to words, Charron ignores his
own advice. He acknowledges that, in the past, philosophers such as Heraclitus

---

[100] Consider Charron, *De la sagesse*, 25–43 (esp. 35–40), in conjunction with ibid., 291–93, 335–38, 369–71, 388–89, 401–5.

[101] See Charron *De la sagesse*, 291–92, 401–5.

[102] See Charron *De la sagesse*, 485–501.

[103] See Charron *De la sagesse*, 449–52.

[104] Note Charron, *De la sagesse*, 370–73, 385–415, and then consider ibid., 385–415, 445–67 (esp. 388, 450), in light of the material cited in Chapter 2, note 73, this volume.

[105] See Charron *De la sagesse*, 39, 462–64

[106] See Charron, *De la sagesse*, 489–507.

[107] See Chapter 2, this volume.

and Democritus tended to speak in a manner jocular or deliberately obscure, and he describes their procedure in a manner intended to bring to mind the essays of his deceased friend Michel de Montaigne:

> They speak in a low voice, with their mouths half open; they disguise their language; they mix and stuff their propositions to make them pass quite smoothly among a great many others and make use of so much artifice that these propositions are hardly noticed. They do not speak in a terse fashion, distinctly, clearly, with an air of certitude, but do so ambiguously like oracles.

That he will himself do the same, however, Charron firmly denies. "I come after and fall below them," he concedes, "but I speak in good faith, clearly and distinctly, that which I think and believe."[108] And he is very nearly as good as his word, for if he finds it necessary, for fear of the censor, to write in the very manner that he ascribes to men like Heraclitus and Democritus, he nonetheless does so, in contrast to his predecessors among the Latin Averroists, in such a fashion as to be quite easily understood. Even more to the point, he does so in the vernacular, appealing – as Machiavelli had done early and Montaigne late in the sixteenth century – to a broad public, inclusive of a great many who were literate but not fully at home in the specialized language employed by the Catholic Church and generally used by the learned men of the age.

Moreover, in the clearest possible language, as near as possible to the center of his chief work's central book, Charron openly challenges the Averroist contention that religion – and, in particular, belief in an afterlife where virtue is rewarded and vice punished – is in any way supportive of moral virtue. There, after pointing to the use of religious fear for the purpose of political manipulation, he laments the "execrable crimes" that "the zeal for religion has produced," and there, without mentioning his source, he quotes two notorious lines illustrating Lucretius' denunciation of religion as an inspiration for monstrous deeds. "Beware," he writes, "of one who is an honest man out of scruple and because of a religious bridle, and esteem him hardly at all." Beware of "the man who has religion without honesty (*preud'homie*)." Charron is not willing to say that the latter is "more wicked... than one who has neither" religion nor honesty. But he does regard him as "much more dangerous." Such a man, he explains, "having no taste, no image, or conception of *preud'homie* except with regard to religion and in its service, and thinking that being a good man is nothing other than taking care to advance and promote his own religion, believes that everything – whether it be treason, perfidy, sedition, rebellion, or any other offense, whatever it might be – is not only lawful and permitted, excused (*colorée*) by zeal and a care for religion." He also believes that such conduct is "praiseworthy, meritorious, and grounds for canonization, if it serves the progress and advancement of religion and the overthrow of its adversaries."[109]

---

[108] See Charron, *De la sagesse*, 370–71.

[109] Note Lucr. 1.80–101, and see Charron, *De la sagesse*, 445–66 (esp. 452–56, 462–65). Cf. Alfarabi, *Plato's Laws* Introduction 1–3, in *Medieval Political Philosophy*, ed. Ralph Lerner and Muhsin Mahdi (Glencoe, IL: Free Press, 1963), 83–85.

If Charron broke with the Averroist consensus, if he followed Machiavelli in abandoning the cause of moral virtue and in applying to Christianity Lucretius' savage critique of all religion, he evidently had his reasons. In contrast with Pomponazzi, but like Montaigne, he had witnessed the wars of religion, those in his native France.[110] He was no doubt well-informed concerning those that had preceded them in Germany, and he had the sense to recognize that there might well be more such wars to come. In his book, he said no more than that which Montaigne had intimated,[111] and fairly often he said what he said using Montaigne's own words.[112] He was merely voicing what every *politique* took for granted. But actually saying such things out loud – "in a terse fashion, distinctly, clearly, with an air of certitude" – nonetheless mattered, for the publication of Charron's book appears to have marked a sea change in European thought.

That its influence was profound there can hardly be doubt. In the period stretching from 1601 to 1634, the book was reprinted in one form or another some twenty-four times.[113] It first appeared in English in 1608, and it was reprinted in 1612, 1615, 1620, 1630, and 1640. There is reason to believe that *Of Wisdom* was no less important than *De rerum natura* in helping Sarpi to make the transition from an Averroism deeply indebted to Pomponazzi to an outright hostility to religion itself,[114] and we know that Elie Diodati and his friends in the *Tétrade* were devotees of Charron.[115] The odds are good, given the work's publication history, that today we see no more than the tip of what was then a very large iceberg. Though now forgotten, *De la sagesse* was read by virtually all educated men throughout much of Europe.

The Logic of Popular Enlightenment

Whether Milton was also a devotee remains unclear – for though he was certainly familiar with the theologico-political doctrine of the *falāsifa* and though he drew on Gersonides for his interpretation of what he treated as the Old Testament, it is by no means certain that he ever read *De la sagese*. Given,

---

[110] Little is known concerning Charron's life, but that he witnessed the excesses to which these wars gave rise is perfectly clear: for a brief but nonetheless revealing biography, see Kogel, *Pierre Charron*, 15–24.

[111] See David Lewis Schaefer, *The Political Philosophy of Montaigne* (Ithaca, NY: Cornell University Press, 1990).

[112] Cf. Jean D. Charron, "Did Charron Plagiarize Montaigne?" *French Review* 34:4 (February 1961): 344–51 with Floyd Gray, "Reflections on Charron's Debt to Montaigne," *French Review* 35:4 (February 1962): 377–82, and see Françoise Kaye, *Charron et Montaigne: Du Plagiat à l'originalité* (Ottawa: Éditions de l'Université d'Ottawa, 1982).

[113] See Kogel, *Pierre Charron*, 47. By 1672, it had been reprinted twelve times more: see ibid., 13.

[114] See Wootton, *Paolo Sarpi*, 24–28, and Frajese, "Sarpi interprete del *De la sagesse* de Pierre Charron: I *Pensieri sulla religione*," 59–85.

[115] For a brief summary of the evidence, see Kogel, *Pierre Charron*, 157–61, which should be read in conjunction with Tullio Gregory, "Il libertinismo erudito," in Gregory, *Etica e religione nella critica libertina*, 11–70, which is reprinted in slightly abbreviated form as Gregory, "'Libertinage Erudit' in Seventeenth-Century France and Italy: The Critique of Ethics and Religion," *British Journal for the History of Philosophy* 6:3 (October 1998): 323–49.

however, the widespread interest that the book inspired in the years in which he devoted himself to his studies, and given the depth of his own concern with the subject on which it focused, it is hard to imagine that he passed it by and resolutely directed his gaze elsewhere – especially since Charron's work seems to have shaped the reaction of learned men in both France and Italy to the condemnation visited on Galileo by the Roman Catholic Church shortly before the English poet's continental tour.

There are, moreover, occasions in the early 1640s in which Milton resorts to language highly reminiscent of that deployed by Charron. He, too, is concerned, as we have seen, with the manner in which Christianity can be configured in such a fashion as to produce "captive minds." In one of his anti-episcopacy tracts, he even warns that in modern times "tyranny" has acquired a "second life," that it has come to be "an ambiguous monster," which must be "slaine in two shapes," given that it is "guarded with superstition which hath no small power to captivate the minds of men otherwise most wise."[116]

Moreover, there is evidence that Milton carefully pondered the power of *consuetudo*. He begins one of the tracts that he wrote in defense of divorce with the suggestion that if one were to ask "who of all Teachers and Maisters that have ever taught, hath drawn the most Disciples after him, both in Religion, and in manners, it might bee not untruly answer'd, Custome," and he goes on thereafter to restate Charron's complaint – that custom

proving but of bad nourishment in the concoction, as it was heedlesse in the devouring, puffs up unhealthily, a certaine big face of pretended learning, mistaken among credulous men, for the wholesome habit of soundnesse and good constitution; but is indeed no other, then that swoln visage of counterfeit knowledge and literature, which not onely in private marrs our education, but also in publick is the common climer into every chaire, where either Religion is preach't, or Law reported: filling each estate of life and profession, with abject and servil principles; depressing the high and Heaven-born spirit of Man, farre beneath the condition wherein either God created him, or sin hath sunke him.

"Error," he thunders, "supports Custome, Custome count'nances Error. And these two betweene them would persecute and chase away all truth and solid wisdome out of humane life," making it "their chiefe designe to envie and cry-down the industry of free reasoning, under the terms of humor, and innovation."[117]

But if Milton had ever seriously entertained the conviction – intimated by Plato, voiced by Averroës, Maimonides, Pomponazzi, and Bruno, and taken as a starting point for further rumination by Charron and Sarpi – that the great mass of men are invincibly ignorant and in need of indoctrination by way of religion, by the time of his return from Italy and France, he was inclined to the view that, in modern circumstances, the establishment of a regime of tutelage is inconsistent with philosophic freedom, even for the few. This caused him to attempt to unleash the radical potential inherent in the Protestant doctrine of

[116] See *An Apology Against a Pamphlet* (April 1642), in *CPW*, I 924.
[117] See *The Doctrine and Discipline of Divorce* (1 August 1643), in *CPW*, II 222–24.

the priesthood of all believers,[118] and it induced him to adopt something like the position subsequently articulated by Thomas Hobbes, who would argue that "in order that it might prosper, philosophy ought to be free and subject to coercion neither by fear nor by shame," and who would therefore urge, as we shall eventually see, that "the multitude (*vulgus*) be gradually enlightened (*eruditur*)."[119]

In the face of the obstacles, Milton was astonishingly sanguine – some would say, naive. He did not fear that, in the clash of opinions, falsehood would win out. "[T]hough all the windes of doctrin were let loose to play upon the earth," he wrote, "so Truth be in the field, we do injuriously by licencing and prohibiting to misdoubt her strength. Let her and Falshood grapple; who ever knew Truth put to the wors, in a free and open encounter. Her confuting is the best and surest suppressing." To "a discreet and judicious reader," he explained, "bad books" are, in fact, a boon: they "serve in many respects to discover, to confute, to forewarn, and to illustrate."[120] Moreover, he insisted, "[h]e that can apprehend and consider vice with all her baits and seeming pleasures, and yet abstain, and yet distinguish, and yet prefer that which is truly better, he is the true warfaring Christian." It was in this context that he penned these famous words:

I cannot praise a fugitive and cloister'd Vertue, unexercis'd & unbreath'd, that never sallies out and sees her adversary, but slinks out of the race, where that immortall garland is to be run for, not without dust and heat. Assuredly we bring not innocence into the world, we bring impurity much rather: that which purifies us is triall, and triall is by what is contrary. That vertue therefore which is but a youngling in the contemplation of evill, and knows not the utmost that vice promises to her followers, and rejects it, is but a blank vertue, not a pure; her whiteness is but an excrementall whiteness. . . . Since therefore the knowledge and survay of vice is in this world so necessary to the constituting of human vertue, and the scanning of error to the confirmation of truth, how can we more safely, and with lesse danger scout into the regions of sin and falsity then by reading all manner of tractats, and hearing all manner of reason?

"[T]his," Milton argues, "is the benefit which may be had of books promiscuously read."[121] After all, when God gave man "reason, he gave him freedom to choose, for reason is but choosing"; and though He commands us "to temperance, justice, continence, yet [He] powrs out before us ev'n to a profusenes all desirable things, and gives us minds that can wander beyond all limit and satiety." "Why," he demands, "should we then affect a rigor contrary to the manner of God and of nature, by abridging or scanting those means, which books freely permitted are, both to the triall of vertue, and the exercise of truth?"[122]

---

118 Milton's rhetorical posture in this regard is especially visible in *A Treatise of Civil Power in Ecclesiastical Causes* (16 February 1659), in *CPW*, VII 239–72.

119 Note Thomas Hobbes, *Lux mathematica* Ep. Ded., in *LW*, V 92, and *De homine* XIV.13, in *LW*, II 128–29.

120 See *Areopagitica* (November 1644), in *CPW*, II 512–13, 561.

121 See *Areopagitica* (November 1644), in *CPW*, II 514–17.

122 See *Areopagitica* (November 1644), in *CPW*, II 527–28.

Old Priest Writ Large

How anyone as intent on the liberation of the multitude from clerical tutelage as was Milton could ever have imagined presbyterianism consistent with the division of responsibilities between minister and magistrate that he quite rightly regarded as its prerequisite is a genuine mystery. That before long he felt compelled to redirect against the English presbyterians and their Scottish allies the ire that he had once reserved for the Roman Catholic Church and English episcopacy is certainly no wonder. In *Areopagitica*, he began by denying that what he had written was "the disburdning of a particular fancie," and he asserted that he had spoken for "all those who had prepar'd their minds and studies above the vulgar pitch to advance truth in others, and from others to entertain it." Then, he reported what he characterized as "the generall murmur." If it come again "to inquisitioning," he wrote, and to "licencing," if "we are so timorous of our selvs, and so suspicious of all men, as to fear each book, and the shaking of every leaf, before we know what the contents are, if some who but of late were little better then silenc't from preaching, shall come now to silence us from reading, except what they please, it cannot be guest what is intended by some but a second tyranny over learning: and [this] will soon put it out of controversie that Bishops and Presbyters are the same to us both name and thing."[123]

Two years or so thereafter, what he had once described as "the general murmur" had become for Milton a fixed conviction, and in fury he posed the following question:

> Because you have thrown of your Prelate Lord,
> And with stiff Vowes renounc'd his Liturgie
> To seise the widdow'd whore Pluralitie
> From them whose sin ye envi'd, not abhor'd,
> Dare ye for this adjure the Civill Sword
> To force our Consciences that Christ set free,
> And ride us with a classic Hierarchy?

And with Paolo Sarpi's great history in mind, he then warned, "But we do hope to find out all your tricks,/Your plots and packing wors then those of *Trent*,/That so the Parliament/May with their wholsom and preventive Shears/Clip your Phylacteries, though bauk your Ears/And succour our just Fears/When they shall read this clearly in your charge/*New Presbyter* is but *Old Priest* writ Large."[124] By this time, Milton was ready to denounce as disguised popery the religious settlement in nearly every corner of Protestant Europe – though, even in his fury, he was not prepared to suggest as a punishment proper to its exponents the gruesome penalty exacted under Charles I on the English presbyterian leader William Prynne.

From the Machiavellian analysis of the logic of priestcraft that he limned in *Of Reformation Touching Church-Discipline*, and from the conclusion, which

---

[123] See *Areopagitica* (November 1644), in *CPW*, II 539.
[124] See "On the New Forcers of Conscience under the Long Parliament" (August 1646?), in *CW*, I:1 71.

he soon thereafter reached, that disestablishment and full religious liberty for Protestant Christians is the only plausible antidote, Milton never budged. Some months after the battle of Worcester, not long after his secretaries ceased copying passages from Machiavelli's *Discourses on Livy* into his Commonplace Book, at a time when John Owen, former chaplain of the New Model Army, and other proponents of congregationalism on the Massachusetts model were pressing on the Rump an Erastian church settlement, Milton addressed a sonnet to Oliver Cromwell that ended with the following lines: "And Dunbarr feild resounds thy praises loud/And Worsters laureat wreath; yet much remaines/To conquer still; peace hath her victories/No less renownd then warr, new foes aries/Threatning to bind our soules with secular chaines:/Helpe us to save free Conscience from the paw/Of hireling wolves whose Gospell is their maw."[125]

If, in the end, Milton came to think the Rump no better than the Long Parliament, it was not solely because of the ignorance and corruption that its members displayed. It was even more because in 1652, at the instigation of Owen and his colleagues, the Council of State had suppressed *The Racovian Catechism*, which Milton in the course of his duties had licensed for publication, and because in February of that year a parliamentary committee had raked him over the coals for sanctioning the printing of that Socinian tract and had seen to it that the authority to license books and periodicals was placed in the hands of someone less friendly to the *libertas philosophandi.*[126] By the same token, if, eventually, Milton came to despise and loathe the Lord General victorious at Dunbar and Worcester, it was not solely because the latter had betrayed the republican cause. It was also because, in 1654, as Lord Protector, Cromwell had issued two ordinances implementing Owen's plan, establishing thereby a national church supported by a tithe enforceable at law, imposing upon its otherwise independent congregations a regime of centralized magisterial supervision, and providing for a qualified toleration of "gathered" churches outside the state system.[127] In Milton's opinion, this amounted to the institution of "a state-tyranie over the church" and even to a species of "civil papacie." The Lord Protector had become, he implied, "no less antichrist in this main point of antichristianism" and "no less a pope...than he at *Rome.*" In his considered judgment, "they who force, though professing to be protestants, deserve as little to be tolerated themselves" as the Roman Catholics, "being no less guiltie of poperie in the most popish point."[128]

The Practice of *Kalām*

Milton's revolutionary zeal and his commitment to popular enlightenment and an ethos of intellectual progress sit uneasily alongside his profound admiration

[125] See "Sonnet XVI" (May 1652), in *CW,* I:1 65.

[126] See Blair Worden, *Literature and Politics in Cromwellian England: John Milton, Andrew Marvell, Marchamont Nedham* (Oxford: Oxford University Press, 2007), 241–49.

[127] See Blair Worden, "Toleration and the Cromwellian Protectorate," *Studies in Church History* 21 (1984): 199–233, and Jeffrey R. Collins, "The Church Settlement of Oliver Cromwell," *History* 87:1 (January 2002): 18–40.

[128] See Milton, *A Treatise of Civil Power in Ecclesiastical Causes* (16 February 1659), in *CPW,* VII 239–72 (esp. 244, 252, 254).

for Plato and Aristotle and his genuine adherence to the tenets of classical republicanism. Neither of the Greek philosophers thought popular enlightenment possible or the attempt to achieve it desirable, and Aristotle regarded even the notion of rewarding inventors as suspect on the grounds that promoting innovation of any kind was likely to erode the respect and awe that underpinned the habit of abiding by the law.[129] Thereby, the peripatetic echoed the outlook inculcated by the classical city with its thoroughgoing emphasis on the authority of civic tradition as embodied in the ancient constitution (*patríos politeía*) and ancestral custom (*mos maiorum*).[130] In embracing classical republicanism with its commitment to the notion that, even under the best of circumstances, moral and political reason need the reinforcement of tradition, and in calling at the same time for an extension of the *libertas philosophandi* to the public at large, Milton seems to have been attempting to square the circle.

The same can be said with regard to Milton's Christology. In *Paradise Regained*, for example, he depicts Jesus Christ as having self-consciously modeled himself not only on Job, who learned in the course of his sufferings that wisdom is "fear of the Lord" and that all attempts to penetrate the secrets of God's creation are an affront to the Lord,[131] but on the intellectual seeker Socrates as well.[132] This is a juxtaposition that should give one pause, for between the two ways of seeing the world there is an unbridgeable chasm.

William Blake no doubt erred in suggesting that Milton was "of the Devils party without knowing it," and Percy Bysshe Shelley may have been wrong when he contended that *Paradise Lost* "contains within itself a philosophical refutation of that system, of which, by a strange and natural antithesis, it has been a chief popular support."[133] But neither was a fool. In reading, as in writing, poetry, they knew what they were about, and, in the case at hand, both were persuaded that something was very much awry. John Milton was either profoundly confused and at loggerheads with himself, as Blake contended. Or, like Marsilius of Padua, on whose political thinking he certainly drew, the author of *Areopagitica*, *Paradise Lost*, *Paradise Regained*, and *Samson Agonistes* was an Averroist of sorts, attempting to come to grips with the cultural hegemony of a revealed religion that he judged not only ill suited in its inherited form to the purpose of promoting secular ends such as moral virtue, domestic harmony,

[129] Consider Arist. *Pol.* 1268a6–11, 1268b22–1269a27, in light of *Eth. Nic.* 1094a26–b11.

[130] See Paul A. Rahe, *Republics Ancient and Modern: Classical Republicanism and the American Revolution* (Chapel Hill: University of North Carolina Press, 1992), 105–35.

[131] See Job 28:12–28, 38:1–39:30, and note Prov. 9:10. These passages help explain why Spinoza could later depict the Jews as loathing philosophy: see Benedict de Spinoza, *Tractatus theologico-politicus* XI.24, in *Spinoza opera*, ed. Carl Gebhardt (Heidelberg: C. Winters Universitätsbuchhandlung, 1925), III 158, with Leo Strauss, "Introduction," *Persecution and the Art of Writing* (Glencoe, IL: Free Press, 1952), 7–21 (at 20–21).

[132] Cf. *Paradise Regained* 3.31–107, in CW, II:2 443–46, with Arist. *Pol.* 1323a14–1325b32, and see Carnes Lord, *Education and Culture in the Political Thought of Aristotle* (Ithaca, NY: Cornell University Press, 1982), 180–202. Note also *Paradise Lost* 11.689–99, in CW, II:2 370.

[133] See William Blake, "The Marriage of Heaven and Hell," in *The Complete Poetry and Prose of William Blake*, ed. David V. Erdman, newly rev. ed. (Berkeley: University of California Press, 1982), 33–44 (at 34–35), and Percy Bysshe Shelley, "A Defence of Poetry," in *The Complete Works of Percy Bysshe Shelley*, ed. Roger Ingpen and Walter E. Peck (New York: C. Scribner's Sons, 1926–1930), VII 109–40 (at 129–31).

and devotion to the common good but incompatible with the well-being of philosophy as well. This would help explain why the only passage in Machiavelli's *Discourses on Livy* dealing with religion that Milton singled out for further consideration was the Florentine's contention that no one is accorded greater honor than the founder of a religion.[134]

If Milton really was an Averroist of sorts, the author of *Paradise Lost* was neither a devout Christian nor a genuine Socinian nor even, as some have supposed, a believing Arian. He was a thoroughgoing and highly circumspect infidel instead. He was a philosophical poet on the model of Vergil and Dante.[135] He was an enlightened practitioner of *kalām*, who penned *De doctrina Christiana* not as a statement of his private creed but as the outline for a Christianity shorn, insofar as possible, of doctrines philosophically unsound and politically dangerous. If this hypothesis is true, Milton may well have regarded himself as a prophet on the lines envisaged by Alfarabi, the Arab *falāsifa*, and Maimonides. He was a man possessed of uncanny capacity to charm and persuade those wholly reliant upon the imagination for their understanding of the world, as he well knew, and in the poetry he composed late in the 1650s and thereafter, he appears to have been intent on deploying his remarkable rhetorical gifts in verse for the purpose of reshaping in a politic fashion the superstition dominant in his own time. If this hypothesis is true, if there really is more to Milton's commitment to "the reforming of Reformation it self" than immediately meets the eye, one would then cite his commitment to philosophy and the profound anticlericalism to which this gave rise if one were called upon to explain how a man seemingly so pious could have chosen as his "particular friend" and "crony" a figure as notorious for libertinism as was Marchamont Nedham[136] – the remarkable publicist to whose achievements as a popularizer and adaptor of Machiavellian political science we now must turn.

---

[134] See "Milton's Commonplace Book," in *CW*, XVIII 197–98. For a somewhat better English translation and extensive notes, see "Milton's Commonplace Book," tr. Ruth Mohl, in *CPW*, I 475–76.

[135] See Eve Adler, *Vergil's Empire: Political Thought in the Aeneid* (Lanham, MD: Rowman and Littlefield, 2003), and Ernest L. Fortin, *Dissent and Philosophy in the Middle Ages: Dante and His Precursors*, tr. Marc A. LePain (Lanham, MD: Lexington Books, 2002).

[136] See Anthony à Wood, "From *Fasti Oxonienses* or *Annals* of the University of Oxford" (1691), and Edward Phillips, *The Life of Mr. John Milton* (1694), in *The Early Lives of Milton*, ed. Helen Darbishire (London: Constable & Co., 1932), 44, 74. For useful, if occasionally exaggerated, accounts of the ties linking the two, see Blair Worden, "Milton and Marchamont Nedham," in *Milton and Republicanism*, ed. David Armitage, Armand Himy, and Quentin Skinner (Cambridge, UK: Cambridge University Press, 1995), 156–80, and *Literature and Politics in Cromwellian England*, esp. 14–53, 154–357, 386–98; Joad Raymond, "The Cracking of the Republican Spokes," *Prose Studies* 19:3 (December 1996): 255–74; and Nicholas von Maltzahn, "From Pillar to Post: Milton and the Attack on Republican Humanism at the Restoration," in *Soldiers, Writers and Statesmen of the English Revolution*, ed. Ian Gentles, John Morrill, and Blair Worden (Cambridge, UK: Cambridge University Press, 1998), 265–83 (at 281–83).

PART III

MACHIAVELLIAN REPUBLICANISM ANGLICIZED

Preface

Marchamont Nedham was a journalist, one of the very first and most distinguished members of a breed in his day entirely new to the world.[1] He was born in August 1620 at Burford in Gloucestershire into a genteel family of modest means. He studied at All Souls College at a time when that now venerable institution actually had students,[2] and he took his bachelor of arts from the University of Oxford in 1637. That year or the next, he accepted a position as an usher at Merchant Taylor's School in London, and in 1640 he successfully sought better remunerated employment as an underclerk at Gray's Inn. Three years thereafter, as internecine strife tore England apart and effective censorship fell into abeyance, Marchamont Nedham discovered his true métier. He was, then, barely twenty-three years in age.

Nedham was an entertainer of sorts and a time-server – "a jack of all sides," as one contemporary critic put it, "transcendently gifted in opprobrious and treasonable Droll."[3] In the course of a long and checkered career – stretching from early in the English Civil War in 1643 to a time shortly before his death in 1678, when the Exclusion Crisis was just getting underway – he displayed a political and moral flexibility and a lust for lucre exceeded only by his talent.[4]

---

[1] In this connection, see Joseph Frank, *The Beginnings of the English Newspaper, 1620–1660* (Cambridge, MA: Harvard University Press, 1961), and Joad Raymond, *The Invention of the Newspaper: English Newsbooks, 1641–1649* (Oxford, UK: Clarendon Press, 1996). Note also *Making the News: An Anthology of the Newsbooks of Revolutionary England, 1641–1660*, ed. Joad Raymond (New York: St. Martin's Press, 1993), and Jason T. Peacey, *Politicians and Pamphleteers: Propaganda during the English Civil Wars and Interregnum* (Aldershot, UK: Ashgate, 2004); "'The counterfeit silly curr': Money, Politics, and the Forging of Royalist Newspapers during the English Civil War," *Huntington Library Quarterly* 67:1 (March 2004): 27–57; and "The Management of Civil War Newspapers: *Auteurs*, Entrepreneurs, and Editorial Control," *The Seventeenth Century* 21:1 (Spring 2006): 99–127.

[2] I am indebted to Simon Green, sub-warden and historian of All Souls College, Oxford, who confirmed that All Souls College really did have students in its early years.

[3] See James Heath, *A Brief Chronicle of the Late Intestine War*, the second impression greatly enlarged (London: n.p., 1663), 492.

[4] For the details, see Joseph Frank, *Cromwell's Press Agent: A Critical Biography of Marchamont Nedham, 1620–1678* (Lanham, MD: University Press of America, 1980). For a more penetrating analysis of what Nedham was up to, see Blair Worden, "'Wit in a Roundhead': The Dilemma of Marchamont Nedham," in *Political Culture and Cultural Politics in Early Modern England: Essays Presented to David Underdown*, ed. Susan D. Amussen and Mark A. Kishlansky

He began as a fierce defender of the parliamentary cause, switched in 1647 to the side of the king[5] – and then, some nine months after his royal patron's demise, while on the lam from Newgate Jail, he wrote to offer his services to the presiding officer of the regicide court.[6]

Nedham's was not a costive muse. In the course of his career, he published more than thirty-four pamphlets and books.[7] In addition, he composed most of the copy that appeared in the Roundhead newsbook *Mercurius Britanicus* and eventually took over its management, then edited the Cavalier newsbook *Mercurius Pragmaticus*; then (for a brief time under license from John Milton), he edited the newsbook *Mercurius Politicus* – in turn for the Rump, for the Nominated Parliament, for the Protectorate, and for the Rump twice again, celebrating the coups d'état that overthrew each and, in the end, even hailing the return of the king. On the eve of the Restoration, after publishing a brief but bitter satire warning the Roundheads of vengeance to come,[8] he prudently withdrew into exile. But soon he managed to purchase for himself a personal pardon and almost immediately took up his pen to write for the new king;

(Manchester, UK: Manchester University Press, 1995), 301–37; "Milton and Marchamont Nedham," in *Milton and Republicanism*, ed. David Armitage, Armand Himy, and Quentin Skinner (Cambridge, UK: Cambridge University Press, 1995), 156–80; "Marchamont Nedham and the Beginnings of English Republicanism, 1649–1656," in *Republicanism, Liberty, and Commercial Society, 1649–1776*, ed. David Wootton (Stanford, CA: Stanford University Press, 1994), 45–81; and *Literature and Politics in Cromwellian England: John Milton, Andrew Marvell, and Marchamont Nedham* (Oxford, UK: Oxford University Press, 2007), 14–357, 388–98, along with Joad Raymond "The Cracking of the Republican Spokes," *Prose Studies* 19:3 (December 1996): 255–74, and " 'A Mercury with a Winged Conscience': Marchamont Nedham, Monopoly and Censorship," *Media History* 4:1 (June 1998): 7–18; Jonathan Scott, *Commonwealth Principles: Republican Writing of the English Revolution* (Cambridge, UK: Cambridge University Press, 2004), 136–40, 156–58, 220–21, 241–47, 256–59, 266–68, 274–75, 283–84; and Jason T. Peacey, "The Struggle for *Mercurius Britanicus*: Factional Politics and the Parliamentarian Press, 1643–1646," *The Huntington Library Quarterly* 68:3 (September 2005): 517–43, and "The Management of Civil War Newspapers," 99–127. Note also *Making the News*, 332–79, and Peacey, *Politicians and Pamphleteers*, passim. I have profited also from Perez Zagorin, *A History of Political Thought in the English Revolution* (London: Routledge and Paul, 1954), 121–27; Philip A. Knachel, "Introduction," in Nedham, CCES, ix–xlii; and Vickie B. Sullivan, *Machiavelli, Hobbes, and the Formation of a Liberal Republicanism in England* (New York: Cambridge University Press, 2004), 113–43.

5 Nedham served the royalists not only as a propagandist but also as a spy: see Jason T. Peacey, "Marchamont Nedham and the Lawrans Letters," *Bodleian Library Record* 17 (2000): 24–35.

6 See Letters from Marchamont Nedham to Henry Oxinden, 8 and 19 November 1649, in *The Oxinden and Peyton Letters, 1642–1670*, ed. Dorothy Gardiner (London: Sheldon Press, 1937), 160–61; and for the terms of the deal, see Anthony à Wood, *Athenæ Oxonienses* (London, F. C. & J. Rivington: 1813–20), III 1180–90 (at 1181).

7 See Frank, *Cromwell's Press Agent*, 196–99, whose list is undoubtedly incomplete.

8 See [Marchamont Nedham], *Newes from Brussels, In a Letter from a Neer Attendant on His Maiesties Person. To a Person of Honour Here, Which Casually Became thus Publique* (London: Livewell Chapman, 1660), which is conveniently reprinted in *Somers Tracts*: see *A Collection of Scarce and Valuable Tracts*, second edition revised and augmented, ed. Sir Walter Scott (London: T. Cadell and W. Davies, 1809–1815), VII 390–92. The appearance of this pamphlet attracted the attention of the royalists abroad and of the erstwhile Roundheads making arrangements for the Restoration at home: see "Report of Miles Barton to Edward Hyde," 30 March 1660, in *Calendar of the Clarendon State Papers*, ed. H. O. Coxe et al. (Oxford, UK: Clarendon Press, 1872–1970), IV 628–29. Raymond, "The Cracking of the Republican Spoke," 255–74 (esp. 258–62), gives a good account of what Nedham was trying to do.

and, while many of his erstwhile associates suffered execution, imprisonment, or exile, he ended his days writing pamphlets for Charles II, the earl of Danby, and their Tory allies against the Exclusion Whigs and their leader, the first earl of Shaftesbury, whom Nedham had the effrontery to denounce not just as "*a man of . . . dapper Conscience, and dexterity, that can dance through a Hoop; or that can be a Tambler through Parties, or a small Teazer of Religions, and Tonzer of Factions,*" but also as "*a Pettifogger of Politicks*" ever ready "*to shift Principles like Shirts*; and *quit an unlucky Side in a fright at the noise of a New Prevailing Party,*" and even as "a *Will-with-a-Wisp, that uses to lead Men out of the way; then leaves them at last in a Ditch and Darkness, and nimbly retreats for Self-security.*"[9]

No darker pot ever insulted a kettle. As should by now be clear, Nedham was himself a man of dapper conscience and dexterity; he had a well-earned reputation for shifting principles like shirts; and he was certainly a Will-with-a-Wisp, possessed of what one contemporary described as "a dextrous faculty of creeping into the breech of every rising Power."[10] What he lacked in integrity, this louche and inky wretch made up for in audacity. The vigor of the language that he deployed in his denunciation of Shaftesbury, his light touch therein, and the vividness of the metaphors he found apt suggest on his part a certain grudging admiration for the man – the appreciation of one virtuoso for a bravura performance on the part of another.

Nedham's own virtuosity as a flack invited on the part of his critics similar flights of fancy. On the eve of the Restoration, an opponent described him as "a Mercury with a winged conscience, the Skip-Jack of all fortunes, that like a Shittle-cock drive him which way you will, falls still with the Cork end forwards."[11] In a satirical pamphlet published early in 1660, the editor of *Mercurius Politicus* is represented as taking leave of his regicide associates with the following words: "for now [that] the *scæne's* alter'd, *I* must go change my habit; if ever the times turn, [however,] you shall find me as faithful as *I* was before."[12] Another critic predicted at that time that Nedham would soon be writing for the Cavaliers. "He is like a Catt," he wrote, "that (throw him which way you will) still light[s] on his feet."[13]

---

[9] See [Marchamont Nedham], *A Pacquet of Advices and Animadversions, Sent from London to the Men of Shaftesbury* (London: [s.n.], 1676), 2, 30, which was written in response to the first earl of Shaftesbury's *Letter from a Person of Quality to his Friend in the Country* (1675), reprinted in *The Works of John Locke* (London: T. Tegg, W. Sharpe and Son, 1823), X 200–246. Nedham's reply is thought to have been exceedingly effective: see K. H. D. Haley, *The First Earl of Shaftesbury* (Oxford, UK: Clarendon Press, 1968), 414–15.

[10] See *Fanatique Queries, Propos'd to the Present Assertors of the Good Old Cause* (London: Printed for Praise-God-Barebones, the Rumps Leather–seller, 1660), 4.

[11] [Samuel Butler], *The Character of the Rump* (London: [s.n.], 1660), 3.

[12] See *The Private Debates, Conferences and Resolutions, Of the Late Rump* (London: [s.n.], 1660), 30, as cited by Raymond, "The Cracking of the Republican Spokes," 258.

[13] See *A Word for All: Or, The Rumps Funeral Sermon: Held forth by Mr. Feak to a Conventicle of Fanatiques at Bedlam upon the Last Dissolution of the Half Quarter Parliament* (London: [s.n.], 1660), 24 – where the pagination is deliberately confused, this being the fourth of the pamphlet's six pages, none of which are properly numbered. See Raymond, "The Cracking of the Republican Spokes," 257–58, who cites this passage and argues for assigning the pamphlet to Samuel Butler.

If this particular journalist did, in fact, land right-side up and light on his feet at every toss and turn, if he was almost always in someone's pay, it was because, at every stage in the set of struggles that defined his age, his was the indispensable pen. No one in his generation knew how to sway English public opinion more effectively than he. Marchamont Nedham could not only sow the whirlwind, but, as we shall soon see, he could ride the storm.

5

Marchamont Nedham and the Regicide Republic

The opinions of ordinary people matter. They have always mattered, even when dormant, and they always will. From time immemorial, the presumptions of ordinary folk have provided the underpinning for political regimes. In Nedham's day, however, popular opinion mattered as it had mattered at no time subsequent to the demise of the Roman Republic, for it had been thoroughly aroused from its torpor, and the people had been apprised of their power and instructed in its legitimacy. Thanks to movable type, the populace of England had become what it had never been in the past: a *public* – a wakeful community authorized to judge.[1] The birth of the periodical press served to confirm and sustain a transformation that had for the most part already transpired.

To the Great Rebellion, the printing press was even more essential than it had been to the Reformation. The surviving English pamphlet literature of the period stretching from 1628 to 1660 is greater than that of the American and

---

[1] See Joseph Frank, *The Beginnings of the English Newspaper, 1620–1660* (Cambridge, MA: Harvard University Press, 1961), and Joad Raymond, *The Invention of the Newspaper: English Newsbooks, 1641–1649* (Oxford, UK: Clarendon Press, 1996). For the political and social setting within which the newsletter and, then, the newspaper first emerged, see Richard Cust, "News and Politics in Early Seventeenth-Century England," *Past & Present* 112 (August 1986): 60–90; and, then, Dagmar Friest, *Governed by Opinion: Politics, Religion and the Dynamics of Communication in Stuart London, 1637–45* (London: Tauris Academic Studies, 1997), and Jason T. Peacey, *Politicians and Pamphleteers: Propaganda during the English Civil Wars and Interregnum* (Aldershot, UK: Ashgate, 2004), and "The Management of Civil War Newspapers: *Auteurs*, Entrepreneurs, and Editorial Control," *The Seventeenth Century* 21:1 (Spring 2006): 99–127. In this regard, early Stuart England anticipated eighteenth-century France in nearly every regard: cf. Keith Michael Baker, "Politics and Public Opinion under the Old Regime: Some Reflections," in *Press and Politics in Pre-Revolutionary France*, eds. Jack R. Censer and Jeremy D. Popkin, (Berkeley: University of California Press, 1987), 204–46, which is revised, expanded, and reprinted as Baker, "Public Opinion as a Political Invention," in his *Inventing the French Revolution* (Cambridge, UK: Cambridge University Press, 1990), 167–99, along with Mona Ozouf, "L'Opinion public," in *The French Revolution and the Creation of Modern Political Culture*, ed. Keith Michael Baker et al. (Oxford, UK: Pergamon Press, 1987–1994) I: *The Political Culture of the Old Regime*, 419–34; Arlette Farge, *Subversive Words: Public Opinion in Eighteenth-Century France*, tr. Rosemary Morris (University Park: Penn State University Press, 1995); and James Van Horn Melton, *The Rise of the Public in Enlightenment Europe* (Cambridge, UK: Cambridge University Press, 2001). For further discussion, see Paul A. Rahe, *Soft Despotism, Democracy's Drift* (New Haven, CT: Yale University Press, 2008), forthcoming.

French revolutions put together.[2] The weekly newsbook was an offspring of the pamphlet, distinguished from the diurnals that had been issued on occasion in the quite recent past by its character as a periodical. As such, it presupposed on the part of the people not only a right to be informed concerning matters of public policy but a continuing and unending desire to know.

This new literary form made its debut on 29 November 1641, in the wake of the Irish rebellion, just two days before Parliament presented the Grand Remonstrance to a startled and distraught king. Its inventor John Thomas was an entrepreneurial young bookseller and printer of pamphlets, closely associated with John Pym, who sought to answer what, at this critical juncture, Pym and his associates in Parliament evidently took to be a felt need – by reporting to the people the deliberations that had given rise to the remonstrance, by promising to them subsequent reports at regular intervals, and by extending to them thereby an unprecedented invitation, asking that they in their wisdom adjudicate the bitter dispute between Parliament and the king.[3]

The fact that John Thomas prospered, that imitators quite soon entered the market, and that a royal court notoriously reluctant to compromise its inherent authority by flattering the public with a direct appeal for support nonetheless found it necessary to sponsor Cavalier newsbooks to respond to the Roundhead onslaught speaks volumes about the newsbook's significance. Each of these weeklies sought to rally those sympathetic to its faction, to inform and encourage them, and to provide them with the arguments necessary to sustain the cause. Each sought to persuade the uncommitted and dishearten the opposition. Each sought as well to reshape and direct opinion and to prepare the public for shifts in policy already then contemplated or at a distance foreseen. Along the way, even the royalist pamphleteers and newsbook editors contributed powerfully, if unwittingly, to a process of democratization by which a much larger public was invited to join the political nation – and, in the event, did so as well.[4]

The Middle Ground

The Cavaliers, who had good reason to regret this development, were especially sensitive to its consequences. Looking back in mid-December 1648, some

---

[2] For an extended meditation on the transformation then taking place, see Adrian Johns, *The Nature of the Book: Print and Knowledge in the Making* (Chicago: University of Chicago Press, 1998).

[3] See Raymond, *The Invention of the Newspaper*, 80–126; note "The Grand Remonstrance, with the Petition Accompanying It," 1 December 1641, in *CDPR*, 202–32; and, for an extract from the first newsbook, see *The Heads of Severall Proceedings in this Present Parliament* 1 (22–29 November 1641), in *Making the News: An Anthology of the Newsbooks of Revolutionary England, 1641–1660*, ed. Joad Raymond (New York: St. Martin's Press, 1993), 33–34. Foreshadowing such reports of parliamentary debates was the publication of speeches made in the House of Commons: see Alan D. T. Cromartie, "The Printing of Parliamentary Speeches, November 1640–July 1642," *Historical Journal* 33:1 (March 1990): 23–44.

[4] See Raymond, *The Invention of the Newspaper*, 20–79, 184–268. Once Charles I realized the necessity for propaganda, the royalist effort became formidable: see Peter W. Thomas, *Sir John Berkenhead, 1617–1679: A Royalist Career in Politics and Polemics* (Oxford, UK: Clarendon Press, 1969), 28–126.

seven weeks before the execution of Charles I, the editor of *Mercurius Impartialis* attributed "the ruines both of King and people" to "the Pulpit and the Presse." It was "from thence," he argued, that "his Majesties Subjects [have] beene Poysoned with Principles of Heresie, Schisme, Faction, Sedition, Blasphemy, Apostacie, Rebellion, Treason, Sacriledge, Murther, Rapine, Robbery, and all [the other] enormous Crimes, and detestable Villanies, with which this Kingdome hath of later times swarmed."[5]

Thomas Hobbes to the contrary notwithstanding, the press was arguably more of a force in this period than the pulpit itself.[6] As the unknown author of the third century of Traiano Boccalini's celebrated *News Bulletins from Parnassus* seems to have foreseen, the invention of movable type offered a new species of clerk, the man of letters, an opportunity to pass judgment on the princes of Europe and an occasion in which to invite his readers to do so as well. It promised to liberate the classically trained humanist from mere service to power and to transform him into what we now call "the public intellectual." Boccalini, by reviving satire in the manner of Lucian, had shown with droll humor, of the very sort that Marchamont Nedham would imitate, just how this might most effectively be done.[7] In making censors of the learned and judges of ordinary readers, as they both recognized, the public prints promised emancipation to all.[8]

This did not escape the notice of contemporary witnesses. As one newsbook writer observed on the eve of the execution of the king, there was a real difference between the English in Queen Elizabeth's day and those in his own time.

---

[5] *Mercurius Impartialis* 1 (12 December 1648), as cited in Raymond, *The Invention of the Newspaper*, 186.

[6] See Raymond, *The Invention of the Newspaper*, 290–95.

[7] See Traiano Boccalini, *De' ragguagli di Parnaso* (1612–17) 3.27, in *Ragguagli di Parnaso e scritti minori*, ed. Luigi Firpo (Bari: Gius, Laterza, & Figli, 1948), III 82–98. This particular passage, which Girolamo Briani is thought to have written shortly after Boccalini's death in 1613, was sufficiently well known in England that, in 1645, it inspired imitation: note George Wither, *The Great Assises Holden in Parnassus by Apollo and His Assessors* (London: Edward Husbands, 1645), which was reprinted for the Luttrell Society by Basil Blackwell in 1948, and see William F. Marquardt, "The First English Translators of Trajano Boccalini's *Ragguagli di Parnaso*: A Study of Literary Relationships," *Huntington Library Quarterly* 15:1 (November 1951): 1–19; then, consider Joad Raymond, "*The Great Assises Holden in Parnassus*: The Reputation and Reality of Seventeenth-Century Newsbooks," *Studies in Newspaper and Periodical History: 1994 Annual*, ed. Michael Harris and Tom O'Malley (Westport, CT: Greenwood Press, 1996), 3–17, and *The Invention of the Newspaper*, 210–21, along with Peacey, "The Management of Civil War Newspapers," 99–127.

[8] Whether this promise was ever likely to be redeemed was debated from the very start: see Ben Jonson, *The Staple of News*, ed. Anthony Parr (Manchester, UK: Manchester University Press, 1988), which anticipates in almost every regard the critique of the project of popular enlightenment more fully articulated by Jean-Jacques Rousseau, *Discours sur les sciences et les arts* (1751), ed. Jean Starobinski, in *Oeuvres complètes de Jean-Jacques Rousseau*, ed. Bernard Gagnebin and Marcel Raymond (Paris: Bibliothèque de le Pléiade, 1959–1995), III 1–30, and subsequently recast in neo-Marxist terms by Jürgen Habermas, *Strukturwandel der Öffentlichkeit: Untersuchungen zu einer Kategorie der bürgerlichen Gesellschaft* (Neuwied: Hermann Luchterhand Verlag, 1962), 158–270, which is now available as Habermas, *The Structural Transformation of the Public Sphere: An Inquiry into a Category of Bourgeois Society*, tr. Thomas Burger (Cambridge, MA: MIT Press, 1989), 141–250.

The former had been "rather guided by the tradition of their Fathers, than by acting principles in reason and knowledge. But to the contrary in these our dayes, the meanest sort of people are not only able to write, &c. but to argue and discourse on matters of highest concernment; and thereupon do desire, that such things which are most remarkable, may be truly committed to writing, and made publique."[9] As this observation suggests, it was printing, even more than the pulpit, that conjured back into existence and opened up once again for the first time since the time of Cicero the space that the ancient Greeks had termed *tò méson* – "the middle ground" – and the Romans, *res publica*.[10] It was this public space and its potential for fostering popular enlightenment that John Milton had set out to defend in November 1644 when he published his attack on the licensing of the press in *Areopagitica*.[11]

More than three decades after the first appearance of the newsbook, the poet Andrew Marvell, who had for a time under the Protectorate assisted Milton in the performance of his duties as Secretary of Foreign Tongues,[12] could easily imagine a "young Priest" of the High Anglican persuasion "inclined to sacrifice to the Genius of the Age; yea, though his Conscience were the Offering," deploying the pulpit so hated by Hobbes against "the Press" envisaged as a "*villanous* Engine . . . invented much about the same time with the Reformation, that hath done more mischief to the Discipline of our Church, than all the Doctrine can make amends for." It would be characteristic of so "malapert" a "Chaplain," he supposed, that he should regard "*Printing*" as a disturber of "the Peace of Mankind" and lament "that Lead, when moulded into Bullets,

---

[9] See Daniel Border, in *The Perfect Weekly Account* 45 (17–28 January 1649): 357, as cited in David Norbrook, *Writing the English Republic: Poetry, Rhetoric and Politics, 1627–1660* (Cambridge, UK: Cambridge University Press, 1999), 200.

[10] Consider Joad Raymond, "The Newspaper, Public Opinion, and the Public Sphere in the Seventeenth Century," in *News, Newspapers, and Society in Early Modern Britain*, ed. Joad Raymond (London: Frank Cass, 1999), 109–40, in light of Hannah Arendt, *The Human Condition* (Chicago: University of Chicago Press, 1958), and that work's sequel, Habermas, *The Structural Transformation of the Public Sphere*, which first appeared in German in 1962; then, see Paul A. Rahe, "The Primacy of Politics in Classical Greece," *American Historical Review* 89:2 (April 1984): 265–93; *Republics Ancient and Modern: Classical Republicanism and the American Revolution* (Chapel Hill: University of North Carolina Press, 1992), 15–444 (esp. 28–44); and Chapter 1, this volume.

[11] Consider *Areopagitica* (November 1644), in *CPW*, II 486–570, in light of Rahe, "The Primacy of Politics in Ancient Greece," 265–93, *Republics Ancient and Modern*, 15–444 (esp. 28–54), and the discussion of Aristotle and Cicero in Chapter 1, this volume. Cf. David Norbrook, "*Areopagitica*, Censorship, and the Early Modern Public Sphere," in *The Administration of Aesthetics: Censorship, Political Criticism, and the Public Sphere*, ed. Richard Burt (Minneapolis: University of Minnesota Press, 1994), 3–33, and *Writing the English Republic*, 118–39, which, though useful, nonetheless errs on two counts – in presupposing the accuracy of J. G. A. Pocock's Arendtian account of civic humanism, and in attributing to Milton a notion of "communicative rationality" similar to that espoused by Hannah Arendt's disciple Jürgen Habermas rather than an understanding of moral and political rationality along Aristotelian lines. Cf. also Donald L. Guss, "Enlightenment as Process: Milton and Habermas," *PMLA* 106:5 (October 1991): 1156–69.

[12] Regarding Marvell's trajectory in this period and his relationship with both Milton and Nedham, see Blair Worden, *Literature and Politics in Cromwellian England: John Milton, Andrew Marvell, Marchamont Nedham* (Oxford: Oxford University Press, 2007), esp. 14–30, 54–153.

is not so mortal as when founded into Letters" – all the while thinking to himself,

> " 'Twas an happy time when all Learning was in Manuscript, and some little Offi-
> cer ... did keep the Keys of the Library. When the Clergy needed no more knowledg
> then to read the Liturgy, and the Laity no more Clerkship than to save them from Hang-
> ing. ... There have been wayes found out to banish Ministers, to fine not only the People,
> but even the Grounds and Fields where they assembled in Conventicles: But no Art yet
> could prevent these seditious meetings of Letters. Two or three brawny Fellows in a
> Corner, with meer Ink and Elbow-grease, do more harm than an *hundred Systematical
> Divines* with their *sweaty Preaching.*"[13]

Marvell's satire was exceedingly apt. A decade before, at the time of the Restoration, the royalist penman Roger L'Estrange had in all seriousness made precisely
the same point, observing that "it has been made a Question long agoe, whether
more mischief then advantage were not occasion'd to the Christian world by
the Invention of Typography."

The Very Model of a Modern Sophist

That L'Estrange articulated this argument in a pamphlet demanding that none
other than Marchamont Nedham be indicted for treason should come as no
surprise. It only stands to reason. For, after all, Nedham was a true pioneer.
He was the first intellectual journalist, the very model of a modern sophist, the
harbinger of much that was to come; and, by 1660, his name had come to be
synonymous with the press. This man of many masks, who had passed himself off as *Mercurius Britanicus*, then as *Mercurius Pragmaticus*, and finally as
Mercurius Politicus, was, as L'Estrange readily conceded, "the *Golia[t]h* of the
Philistines," and his "pen was in comparison of others like a Weavers beam." It
is, L'Estrange added, "incredible what influence" his weekly newsbooks "had
upon numbers of inconsidering persons." Nedham had "with so much malice
calumniated his Sovereign, so scurrilously abused the Nobility, so impudently
blasphemed the Church, and so industriously poysoned the people with dangerous principles" that, had "the Devil himself (the Father of Lies)" held this
particular journalist's "office, he could not have exceeded him."[14]

As seems only fitting, this same diabolical colossus it was who first deployed
in the public prints Niccolò Machiavelli's reflections on the rise and fall of
republics, doing so in a systematic effort to sort out the practical exigencies of
England's republican experiment. Nedham had, in fact, never been averse to the
Florentine, and from quite early on he had brazenly championed raison d'état
as preached by the duc de Rohan, arguing that it is material interest, not justice,

---

[13] See Andrew Marvell, *The Rehearsal Transpros'd* (1672), in *The Rehearsal Transpros'd and The
Rehearsal Transpros'd: The Second Part*, ed. D. I. B. Smith (Oxford, UK: Clarendon Press, 1971),
4–5.

[14] See [Roger L'Estrange], *A Rope for Pol, or, A Hue and Cry after Marchemont Nedham* (London,
[s.n.]: 1660) Advertisement to the Reader. Cf. Anthony à Wood, *Athenæ Oxonienses* (London,
F. C.& J. Rivington: 1813–20), III 1182, who plagiarizes his own description of Nedham from
L'Estrange.

honor, or religion, that makes the world go round.[15] In *The Case of the Kingdom Stated, According to the Proper Interests of the Severall Parties Ingaged*, the first tract that Nedham wrote in any way sympathetic to the royalist cause, he first cited this renowned Huguenot grandee, then analyzed in cold-blooded terms the interests of England's various contending parties, and ultimately advised patience on the part of the king, arguing that Charles could profit from the quarrel then emerging between the presbyterians and independents if he tarried until the moment when "his onely *Interest* will be, to *close* with that *Party* which gives most *hope* of *Indulgence* to his *Prerogative*, & greatest probability of *favor* to his *Friends*." The policy of divide and rule is, he explained, "what *Machiavell* sets downe as a sure *Principle* towards the purchase of *Empire*."[16]

Of course, when the rhetorical situation required it, Nedham could pass himself off as a believing Christian and frequently did so, and he was perfectly capable of speaking in the familiar accents of moral rectitude, denouncing one side or the other for an addiction to hypocrisy, blasphemy, and vice.[17] But nearly as often, especially when the opportunity for candor presented itself, he displayed an outright contempt for high-mindedness of virtually every kind. "Interest," he insisted, "is the true *Zenith* of every State and Person, according to which they may certainly be understood, though cloathed never so much with the most specious disguise of Religion, Justice and Necessity: And Actions are the effects of Interests, from whom they proceed, and to whom they tend naturally as the stone doth downward."[18]

[15] In this connection, see Felix Raab, *The English Face of Machiavelli: A Changing Interpretation, 1500–1700* (London: Routledge & Kegan Paul, 1964), 159–63, 228–30, and J. A. W. Gunn, *Politics and the Public Interest in the Seventeenth Century* (London: Routledge & Kegan Paul, 1969), 33–35, 43–44, 52. Note also, Blair Worden, "'Wit in a Roundhead': The Dilemma of Marchamont Nedham," in *Political Culture and Cultural Politics in Early Modern England: Essays Presented to David Underdown*, ed. Susan D. Amussen and Mark A. Kishlansky (Manchester, UK: Manchester University Press, 1995), 301–37 (esp. 317–19), and *Literature and Politics in Cromwellian England*, 14–30. For Nedham's most elaborate statement along these lines, see Marchamont Nedham, *Interest Will not Lie* (London: Tho. Newcomb, 1659).

[16] See M[archamont] N[edham], *The Case of the Kingdom Stated, According to the Proper Interests of the Severall Parties Ingaged*, second edition (London: [s.n.], 1647), passim (esp. sig. A2v, 1).

[17] See, for example, *MP* 14 (5–12 September 1650): 209; 15 (12–19 September 1650): 260; 17 (26 September–3 October 1650): 279; 18 (3–10 October 1650): 306; 54 (12–19 June 1651): 863–65; 66 (4–11 September 1651): 1045–47 (where the pagination is confused); 67 (11–18 September 1651): 1061–63. Note also *MP* 2 (13–20 June 1650): 17–18; 3 (20–27 June 1650): 33–34, 40, 43; 4 (27 June–4 July 1650): 56–57; 5 (4–11 July 1650): 70–72; 6 (11–18 July 1650): 84; 7 (18–25 July 1650): 107–8; 8 (25 July–1 August 1650): 113–15, 126–27; 10 (8–15 August 1650): 146–47; 13 (29 August–5 September 1650): 193–95, 201; 15 (12–19 September 1650): 259; 17 (26 September–3 October 1650): 291; 50 (15–22 May 1651): 802–4 (esp. 804); 55 (19–26 June 1651): 879–82; 56 (26 June–3 July 1651): 885–87; 57 (3–10 July 1651): 903; 60 (24–31 July 1651): 949–51. Nedham's tone in these passages, when he pretends to a piety he does not share, is nearly always much more subdued than that to be found in dispatches authored by religious enthusiasts: see, for example, *MP* 20 (17–24 October 1650): 326–28, 333–35; 22 (31 October–7 November 1650): 368–69; 28 (12–19 December 1650): 461–63; 66 (4–11 September 1651): 1051–55.

[18] See A Friend to this Commonwealth [Marchamont Nedham], *The Case Stated between England and the United Provinces, in this Present Juncture* (London: Thomas Newcomb, 1652), 23.

Nedham's skepticism in matters religious and moral, his propensity for scoffing, and his fascination with Machiavelli may, in fact, be the key to understanding his astonishing trajectory. He was venal and mercenary but not lacking in courage. In that unstable age, he accommodated every twist and turn in the course of events without betraying the slightest sign of any discomfort or shame, and he served each and every one of his masters with vigor and panache, displaying a gift for invective and a literary virtuosity that made him one of the minor wonders of the age. It was almost as if moral and political dexterity was for Nedham a matter of principle. He seems to have taken to heart his friend Henry Oxinden's contention that, to survive in the world, one must practice "the art of dissimulation" and not be "startled" or "troubled chameleon-like, as the necessity of occasion serves, to turn into all shapes" since even "the most constant men must be content to change their resolutions according to the alterations of time."[19]

Chameleon-like Nedham certainly was, and he was shameless as well. Some would have called him reptilian, and many thought him louche. But servile and fawning – this he was never. He may have been pliant, accommodating, and all too ready to please; he earned the obloquy to which he was exposed. But if he was quite often bent, Nedham never once bowed. He was a bruised reed that did not break. On two occasions, Nedham was imprisoned for what he had written, and he repeatedly tested the limits of what his employers could tolerate. In 1660, when he joined John Milton in futile resistance to the rising royalist tide, he consciously courted the noose. Think of him what you will: Marchamont Nedham was anything but risk averse.

Moreover, when he stuck out his neck, this gifted scrivener was not just chasing cheap thrills. He seems invariably to have been pursuing a political agenda all his own. There need be no doubt that he preferred republican government to hereditary monarchy and religious toleration within an exceedingly loose Erastian establishment organized along congregationalist lines to the species of enforced uniformity and discipline sought variously by episcopalian royalists and presbyterian divines. But Marchamont Nedham's preferences, serious for him though they clearly were, can never have been more than a secondary consideration, for he was first and foremost a practical man – always willing to settle for the best that he thought he could get, never disposed to a bootless sacrifice of self, and perfectly ready to argue that, in adversity, it is one's God-given duty to turn one's coat,[20] which, of course, more than once he dutifully did.

---

[19] British Library, Additional MS. 28,001 (Oxinden papers), fos. 117, 118v, as cited by Worden, "'Wit in a Roundhead,'" 304. One can get a sense of flavor of the friendship between the two from reading their correspondence with one another and with those who know them: see Letters Signed and Unsigned from Marchamont Nedham to Henry Oxinden on 2 October 1648, 29 January 1649, 8 and 19 November 1649, and 21 June 1655; Letters from James Thompson to Henry Oxinden on 19 and 25 January 1649; Letter from Henry to Katherine Oxinden on 6 November 1651; Letter from Phineas Andrews to Henry Oxinden on 1 March 1655; Letter from Henry Oxinden to Marchamont Nedham on 30 June 1655; and Letter from Henry Oxinden to his Wife on 27 November 1655, in *The Oxinden and Peyton Letters*, 142–43, 146–50, 160–61, 166–69 (at 168–69), 197–202, 206–8 (at 208).

[20] See *MP* 66 (4–11 September 1651): 1045 (which is mistakenly numbered 1055).

Turncoat

At no point prior to the Restoration was there greater doubt as to Marchamont Nedham's capacity to ride the storm that he had done so much to stir up than there was in the autumn of 1649. Nedham had continued to function in his guise as *Mercurius Pragmaticus* for some months after the execution of the king by simply switching his allegiance to the legitimate heir, Charles, once prince of Wales, now pretender to the throne. On 15 June, however, the Council of State ordered his arrest, and in due course Nedham was apprehended and dispatched to Newgate Jail for an extended stay.[21] Later, he made his escape. But his subsequent experience as "a pilgrim about the Country" was less than satisfactory, as he explained in a letter to Oxinden dated 8 November.

"The Truth in good earnest," he confessed, "is, I am much distressed every way." At this point, Nedham was secreted in London, daring "not so much as [to] peep abroad to converse with any," and "constrained to associate with Rats, old Bookes, and Cobwebs, in the suburbs of Hell, where I hope nobody will imagine to find mee except my one only friend." In the course of his pilgrimage, Nedham seems to have lost everything but his sense of humor: "Nay," he remarked to Oxinden,

did you but see my Clothes, you would suppose them plunder'd from half a dozen Factions, or beg'd for God's sake in as many severall Nations; and this habit I rant in, partly out of necessity, partly on purpose to obscure myself; whereto my Perewig likewise very much contributes, being red, and so lookes like a Cap-case drop't from some well-complexion'd sinner that had been executed at Tiburn, beg'd by the Colledge for an Anatomie, and after converted at the 'Pothecarie's into Mummie.

He needed money and asked for five pounds, but, as always, he had a "designe ... to preserve" his "Peace upon rationall Terms," and almost immediately thereafter he appears to have put his plan into effect.[22]

Soon after Nedham penned this missive to Henry Oxinden, he managed to get a message through to his old friend John Bradshaw of Gray's Inn, presiding officer of the regicide court and Lord President of the Rump's Council of State, and another to his old neighbor in Burford William Lenthall, speaker of the Long Parliament and now of the Rump. On 14 November, these two worthies joined together to secure for the former editor of the royalist news-book *Mercurius Pragmaticus* a pardon and a release from the threat of renewed confinement in Newgate Jail.[23]

Thereafter, Nedham found himself in much the same rhetorical situation as the Rump's new Secretary for Foreign Tongues. Like John Milton, whose

---

[21] See Entry 15 June 1649, in *Calendar of State Papers, Domestic Series, 1649–1660*, ed. Mary Anne Everett Green (London: Longman, 1875–1876), I 537 (1649–50), and consider Wood, *Athenæ Oxonienses*, III 1181.

[22] See Letters from Marchamont Nedham to Henry Oxinden, 8 and 19 November 1649, in *The Oxinden and Peyton Letters*, 160–61.

[23] See Entry under 14 November 1649, in *Calendar of State Papers, Domestic Series, 1649–1660*, I 554 (1649–50), and consider Wood, *Athenæ Oxonienses*, III 1181, in light of Letter from Marchamont Nedham to Henry Oxinden, 19 November 1649, in *The Oxinden and Peyton Letters*, 161, which mentions Bradshaw alone.

"crony" and "particular friend" he was already or quite soon became,[24] Nedham confronted an unenviable task, well suited to his formidable skills – for in return for his freedom he had agreed to come to the defense of a profoundly unpopular, thoroughly unrepresentative, political regime produced by a military coup. To make matters worse, this was a regime that exercised authority in the name of the people of England and purported to speak on their behalf.[25]

Engagement

John Milton's defense of the English commonwealth was characteristically high-minded. He began with an appeal to Providence, first observing that "whenever it pleases His mind most wise," God "is wont to hurl down haughty and unbridled kings who exalt themselves above the measure of mankind," and then adding that "He often overturns them altogether along with their whole house." In the particular case under consideration, he insisted,

It was by His manifest inclination and divine power (*numen*) that we were suddenly alert to the security and liberty which we had so nearly lost. Him we followed as our Leader, venerating the divine footprints here and there impressed. The path on which we embarked was by no means imperceptible (*obscuram*): it was evident (*illustrem*) – revealed by His portents and laid open to us.

"There," he reassured his readers, there, on the side of the commonwealth's detractors, "stand guile, deceit, ignorance, and barbarism, while here with us are to be found light, truth, reason, and the learning and doctrine of all the finest epochs."[26]

In a fashion no less characteristic,[27] Marchamont Nedham opted for an entirely opposite course, eschewing high-mindedness when he published his

---

[24] See Anthony à Wood, "From *Fasti Oxonienses* or *Annals* of the University of Oxford" (1691), and Edward Phillips, *The Life of Mr. John Milton* (1694), in *The Early Lives of Milton*, ed. Helen Darbishire (London: Constable & Co., 1932), 44, 74. Note also Blair Worden, "Milton and Marchamont Nedham," in *Milton and Republicanism*, ed. David Armitage, Armand Himy, and Quentin Skinner (Cambridge, UK: Cambridge University Press, 1995), 156–80, and *Literature and Politics in Cromwellian England*, 31–53, 154–357, 386–98, and Joad Raymond, "The Cracking of the Republican Spokes," *Prose Studies* 19:3 (December 1996): 255–74. As Worden's account makes clear, the two may have met in the early 1640s when, on occasion, Milton participated in the gaudies held at Gray's Inn. It is also worth noting that some five days after Nedham's arrest the Council of State directed Milton to familiarize himself with what Nedham had written for *Mercurius Pragmaticus*: see Entries under 18 and 23 June 1649, in *Calendar of State Papers, Domestic Series, 1649–1660*, I 537–38 (1649–50).

[25] Note "Commons' Resolution," 4 January 1649, in *The Stuart Constitution, 1603–1688: Documents and Commentary*, ed. John P. Kenyon (Cambridge, UK: Cambridge University Press, 1966), 324, and see David Underdown, *Pride's Purge: Politics in the Puritan Revolution* (Oxford, UK: Clarendon Press, 1971), 7–256, and Sarah Barber, *Regicide and Republicanism: Politics and Ethics in the English Revolution* (Edinburgh, UK: Edinburgh University Press, 1998), 121–201.

[26] *Pro Populo Anglicano Defensio* (24 February 1651) V, in *CW*, VII 4–6, 12. For a recent translation of the pertinent passages, see *A Defence of the People of England* (24 February 1651) V, tr. Donald C. Mackenzie, in *CPW*, IV:1 305, 307.

[27] See Worden, *Literature and Politics in Cromwellian England*, 218–40 (esp. 222–35), 347–54, who accurately portrays the disparity between Milton's republicanism and that of Marchamont Nedham while failing to recognize just how closely it echoes the disparity between the republicanism of Aristotle and Cicero and that of Machiavelli.

defense of the republic. Such was, as I have already noted, his general inclination, but, in the circumstances, he had very little choice. For some time, as we have seen, he had been the chief apologist for the royalist cause, and everyone knew it. It says much about Nedham's skill that he turned all of this to advantage when the occasion presented itself. Where Milton, writing for the most part in Latin, sought to rally to the Commonwealth's banner classically educated gentlemen already sympathetic to the republican cause and to propagate within Christendom more generally a principled defense,[28] Nedham addressed himself in English to those among his compatriots who were in a moral predicament not unlike the one that he had so easily and nonchalantly managed to surmount in November 1649.

For reasons that are perfectly understandable, the Rump had from the outset been deeply, even obsessively concerned with the question of loyalty.[29] As early as 22 February 1649, less than a month after the execution of Charles I, it had voted to require members of its Council of State to swear an oath that they would "adhere to this present Parliament, in the maintenance and defence of the public liberty and freedom of this nation ... and in the maintenance and defence of their resolutions concerning the settling of the government of this nation for the future in way of a Republic, without King or House of Lords."[30] In the face of Leveller agitation within the army, a loyalty oath was imposed ad hoc on the soldiers of various regiments the following spring and summer; and in early September, the Rump voted to extract such an oath from members of the London council and from the mayors and officers of the various boroughs and corporations throughout the land. Then, on 11 October, it decided to require, as a condition of holding their positions of privilege, that a great variety of figures take what came to be called "the Engagement." All members of Parliament and the Council of State had to promise that they would be "true and faithful to the Commonwealth of England, as it is now established, without a King or House of Lords" – as did all judges, employees, and officers of the Commonwealth; all soldiers and sailors; all sheriffs and borough employees; all clergymen holding a benefice and participant in the Assembly of Divines; all of the masters, fellows, schoolmasters, and scholars of the colleges of Eton, Winchester, and Westminster; and all of the heads of house, dons, and degree candidates at the universities of Oxford and Cambridge.[31] And finally, on 2 January 1650, the

---

[28] His success abroad, which was considerable, is testimony to the manner in which republican sympathies were inspired everywhere in Europe by the classical education accorded its leading men: see Leo Miller, "In Defence of Milton's *Pro Populo Anglicano Defensio*," *Renaissance Studies* 4:3 (September 1990): 300–328.

[29] On the Engagement and its significance, see Barber, *Regicide and Republicanism*, 174–201.

[30] Consider "Engagement Taken by the Members of the Council of State," 22 February 1649, in *CDPR*, 384, in light of Sarah Barber, "The Engagement for the Council of State and the Establishment of the Commonwealth Government," *Historical Research* 63:150 (February 1990): 44–57. The Commonwealth of England is called both "a *Republique*" and "*A Free State*" in "A Declaration of the Parliament of England, Expressing the Grounds of Their Late Proceedings, and of Setling the Present Government in the Way of A Free State," 22 March 1649, in *The Struggle for Sovereignty: Seventeenth-Century English Political Tracts*, ed. Joyce Lee Malcolm (Indianapolis, IN: Liberty Press, 1999), I 369–90 (at 380–84).

[31] See entries under 11–12 October 1649, in *Calendar of States Papers, Domestic Series, 1649–1660*, I 336, 338–39 (1649–50).

Rump took the ultimate step, stipulating that, by 20 February, all male citizens eighteen years of age and older subscribe to the Engagement,[32] denying to those who refused to pledge allegiance to the new regime not just office and emolument but the right to undertake or defend themselves against an action in court.[33]

The imposition of the Engagement occasioned a crisis of conscience not only on the part of Cavaliers, who had taken an oath of allegiance to the king, but also on the part of those Roundheads who, in subscribing to the Solemn League and Covenant in and after 25 September 1643, had sworn "to preserve and defend the...person and authority" of the king, testifying that they had "no thoughts or intentions to diminish His Majesty's just power and greatness."[34] In consequence, a spirited debate erupted as to the propriety of these former Cavaliers and Roundheads taking the Engagement.[35] Nedham was himself a former royalist, and he had been induced, as he so delicately put it, to "reflect with an impartial eye upon the affairs of this new government." As such, he was perfectly situated to make the case that in the circumstances it was right, just, and appropriate that former adherents of the king take the Engagement. Lest his readers forget that he was the celebrated author of *The Case of the Kingdom Stated*, Nedham entitled his new pamphlet *The Case of the Commonwealth of England Stated* and modeled its title page on that of the earlier work.[36]

The Conscientious Pretender

In *The Case of the Commonwealth of England Stated*, Nedham addressed his argument to "those two parties whereof the world consists, viz., the conscientious man and the worldling"; and while careful to identify himself with the former, he intimated that the latter made up the majority, "the greater part of the world being led more by appetites of convenience, and commodity than the dictates of conscience." His opponent – whom he described as "our

---

[32] "Engagement to be Taken by All Men of the Age of Eighteen," 2 January 1650, in *CDPR*, 391.

[33] For its eventual repeat, see *MP* 178 (3–10 November 1653): 2850–52.

[34] For the text of the latter, see "Solemn League and Covenant," 25 September 1643, in *CDPR*, 267–71. On the substance, see Edward Vallance, "'An Holy and Sacramental Paction': Federal Thought and the Solemn League and Covenant in England," *English Historical Review* 116:465 (February 2001): 50–75.

[35] See John M. Wallace, "The Literature of the Engagement Controversy, 1649–1652: An Annotated List of Pamphlets," *Bulletin of the New York Public Library* 68:6 (June 1964): 385–405. Much has been written on this subject: see Perez Zagorin, *A History of Political Thought in the English Revolution* (London: Routledge and Paul, 1954), 62–70, 121–31; Quentin Skinner, "History and Ideology in the English Revolution," *Historical Journal* 8:2 (1965): 151–78; John M. Wallace, *Destiny His Choice: The Loyalism of Andrew Marvell* (Cambridge, UK: Cambridge University Press, 1968), 43–68; Glenn Burgess, "Usurpation, Obligation and Obedience in the Thought of the Engagement Controversy," *Historical Journal* 29:3 (September 1986): 515–36; Barber, *Regicide and Republicanism*, 182–95; and Edward Vallance, "Oaths, Casuistry, and Equivocation: Anglican Responses to the Engagement Controversy," *Historical Journal* 44:1 (March 2001): 59–77. See also Margaret A. Judson, *From Tradition to Political Reality: A Study of the Ideas Set Forth in Support of the Commonwealth Government in England, 1649–1653* (Hamden, CT: Archon Books, 1980).

[36] See Nedham, *CCES*, 3, and Joseph Frank, *Cromwell's Press Agent: A Critical Biography of Marchamont Nedham, 1620–1678* (Lanham, MD: University Press of America, 1980), 76.

modern Pharisee, the conscientious pretender and principal disturber of the public peace" – was a practitioner of the nefarious arts that James Harrington would later term "Priest-craft."[37] Nedham's task was to drive a wedge between the genuinely "conscientious man" and this "conscientious pretender" and to reconcile the former with "the worldling": first, by persuading him that circumstances had released him from the obligations attendant on his oath; then, by slyly and seductively debunking conscientiousness in general; and, finally, by convincing all concerned that it was in their interest and in that of their country that they pledge allegiance to the government in place.[38]

To this end, where Milton had given voice to Puritan triumphalism, Nedham embraced a species of fatalism, citing the writers of classical antiquity and the Scriptures promiscuously, as they served his turn; obfuscating in a Machiavellian manner the difference between divine Providence and the turns and twists of blind fate; demonstrating by example after example that "the best established and mightiest governments of the world have been but temporary"; and arguing that, in contemporary England, "the corruption of the old form hath proved the generation of another which is already settled in a way visible and most substantial before all the world; so that 'tis not to be doubted but, in despite of opposition, it will have a season of continuance as others have had according to the proportion of time allotted by Divine Providence." In the end, he warned the various and divided adherents of the Stuart house, "we shall find it but labor in vain, that we have but fortified castles in the air against fatal necessity to maintain a fantasy of pretended loyalty; the consequence whereof will be that at length in cool blood we may have leisure to consider how foolishly we have hazarded our lives and fortunes and sacrificed the lives of others with the common good and peace of the nation for the satisfying of an opinionated humor."[39]

To those, in the grips of such an opinionated humor, who objected on high moral grounds that the rule of the Rump was founded solely upon force, Nedham replied that all governments, from the time of Nimrod on, were based on "the power of the sword," and he then surveyed the history of the world from ancient times, with particular attention paid to the experience of his own compatriots, to establish that it was ever so. "Whosoever therefore shall refuse submission to an established government upon pretense of conscience in regard to former allegiances, oaths, and covenants, or upon supposition that it is by the sword unlawfully erected," he concluded, "deserves none but the character of peevish, and a man obstinate against the reason and custom of the whole world. Let his pretense be what it will, resistance, in the eye of the law of nations, is treason."[40]

[37] Consider James Harrington, *Pian Piano or, Intercourse between H. Ferne, D^r. in Divinity and J. Harrington, Esq. Upon Occasion of the Doctors Censure of the Common-wealth of Oceana* (London: Nath. Brook, 1656), 8, 60, in light of Mark Goldie, "The Civil Religion of James Harrington," in *The Languages of Political Theory in Early-Modern Europe*, ed. Anthony Pagden (Cambridge, UK: Cambridge University Press, 1987), 197–222.

[38] Nedham, *CCES*, 4.

[39] Nedham, *CCES*, 7–14. Cf. Machivelli, *Il principe* 25, in *Opere*, 295–96.

[40] Nedham, *CCES*, 15–29.

Then, Nedham proceeded to show that the arguments advanced by many of the royalists in the 1640s militated against resistance on their part in the 1650s. "If," he observed, citing Hugo Grotius and other comparable authorities, "at any time it seem good to the wise disposer of states and kingdoms (who puts down one and sets up another) to permit the expulsion of such as were formerly in possession and admit others in their places, it cannot in reason be expected that those which refuse obedience to their authority should receive the benefit of protection." Conquest, he avers, settles the question of right, as it always has, and oaths of allegiance are rendered null and void, as both Seneca and the Anglican divine Robert Sanderson concede, when those to whom they were made have forfeited the title to rule. It is then incumbent on subjects, as Saint Paul argued in the thirteenth chapter of Romans, to submit to those established in power and "not to presume to dispute how they came by their power." "This course," he insists, "is most agreeable to the sense of all expositors, the practice of all times, and the voice even of natural reason, since the opening of a gap to question supreme powers and touch the tender eye of their authority would let out all into confusion, tumult following tumult, like billow upon billow, till the world were overwhelmed with a sea of miseries and distractions."[41]

When, in the very week that his own Engagement tract first appeared, a supporter of the Commonwealth published under the title *De corpore politico or The Elements of Law* a manuscript that Thomas Hobbes had first circulated among the king's supporters in the wake of the Short Parliament,[42] Nedham could hardly contain his delight. To the second edition of *The Case of the Commonwealth Stated*, which was available for purchase by 4 July 1650, he gleefully added an appendix demonstrating the manner in which the arguments of this notorious royalist concerning the reciprocal relationship between protection and obedience accorded with his own.[43]

---

[41] Nedham, *CCES*, 30–50.

[42] On this work, see Quentin Skinner, "Conquest and Consent: Thomas Hobbes and the Engagement Controversy," in *The Interregnum: The Quest for Settlement, 1646–1660*, ed. G. E. Aylmer (Hamden, CT: Archon Books, 1972), 79–98 (esp. 95). Note also Skinner, "The Ideological Context of Hobbes's Political Thought," *Historical Journal* 9:3 (1966): 286–317. These two essays are revised and reprinted in Quentin Skinner, *Visions of Politics* (Cambridge, UK: Cambridge University Press, 2002) III: *Hobbes and Civil Science*, 264–307.

[43] Cf. Nedham, *CCES*, 129–39 (esp. 135–39), with Thomas Hobbes, *De corpore politico or The Elements of Law, Moral & Politick* (London: J. Martin and J. Ridley, 1650), which is reprinted in *EW*, IV 77–228. Hobbes's book appeared at about the same time as the first edition of Nedham's work. For the second edition's date of publication, see *MP* 4 (27 June–4 July 1650): 64, and note J. Milton French, "Milton, Needham, and *Mercurius Politicus*," *Studies in Philology* 33 (1936): 236–52 (at 240–41). For the circulation of Hobbes's manuscript in and after April and May 1640, consider John Aubrey, *'Brief Lives,' Chiefly of Contemporaries, Set Down by John Aubrey, between the Years 1669 & 1696*, ed. Andrew Clark (Oxford, UK: Clarendon Press, 1898), I 333–34, in light of B. D. Greenslade, "Clarendon and Hobbes's *Elements of Law*," *Notes and Queries* n. s. 4:4 (April 1957): 150. In this connection, see also Martin Dzelzainis, "Edward Hyde and Thomas Hobbes's *Elements of Law, Natural and Politic*," *Historical Journal* 32:2 (June 1989): 303–17. For the circumstances of its publication ca. 4 May 1650, see Ferdinand Tönnies, "The Editor's Preface," in Hobbes, *Elements of Law*, v–xi. The Tönnies edition, which first appeared in 1889, was based on a close study of the surviving manuscripts then available

Opinionated Humors Dispelled

In the second part of his book, Nedham argued "the utility and benefit of a sub-mission," demonstrating "the great improbability" that the "Royalists, Scots, Presbyterians, Levellers" standing "in opposition to the present government" should ever effect "their designs"; noting "the grand inconveniences which must needs follow . . . to the prejudice of the whole nation" should any of them succeed therein; and, then, pointing out, almost as an afterthought, "the excellency of a free state or commonwealth as it is now established in England, and what happiness we may reap thereby."[44]

He began with the royalists and considered the prospects of each dissident group in turn. That those in exile, who had lost their estates and who adhered "to the Prince out of necessity," had an interest in overturning the English commonwealth Nedham readily acknowledged. He denied, however, that any advantage would accrue to those still in England who adhered to the Stuart champion "out of humor" alone. If the royalist cause were to succeed, they would "be but masters of what they have already." If it miscarried, as was highly likely, they would be guilty of their own ruin.[45] There was, he demonstrated, virtually no possibility that the royalists would receive any help from abroad: the rulers in Spain, Portugal, France, Denmark, Sweden, the Holy Roman Empire, and Holland had other fish to fry; mercenary forces would be ineffective; and there were no grounds for supposing that Scotland or Ireland could provide effective aid. The royalists could nowhere find soldiers able to face the New Model Army – "one of the most generous, best-accomplished, and most victorious armies in Christendom." In any case, he added, in England, "it is not likely that the gentry, men of estates, will stir in any considerable number to hazard their possessions, being yet scarce warm in them, after a purchase made upon dear rates of composition"; and if they did, he added, their uprising would "be snapped and nipped in the bud, the militia being so well-settled and a party ready in arms in every county."[46]

Moreover, Nedham insisted, there could be "no medium of reconcilement betwixt our present governors and the son of the late King." All are agreed that "if ever he come into possession, it must be by conquest and the power of the sword." The consequence would be tyranny, as had always been the case in England's past.

Machiavel speaks very aptly, that a nation which hath cast off the yoke of tyranny or kingship . . . and newly obtained their liberty, must look to have all those for enemies that were familiars and retainers to the king or tyrant. Who, having lost their preferments, will never rest but seek all occasions to re-establish themselves upon the ruins of liberty and to aspire again unto a tyranny; that exercising an arbitrary power, they may take more sharp revenge against all those that dare but pretend unto liberty.

and is superior to the version published in 1650 and reprinted by Molesworth. A critical edition
   is anticipated.
44 Nedham, *CCES*, 51.
45 Nedham, *CCES*, 53–54.
46 Nedham, *CCES*, 54–60.

In such circumstances, Nedham added, it would be folly to expect an "act of oblivion." One would, moreover, be "extremely deceived," as Machiavelli also warns, to think "by new courtesies to take out of their minds the remembrance of old injuries." Parliaments would be few, taxes would be high, and the king would be bound to reward those who had aided his return – whether they be "foreign desperadoes," ambitious "Scots," or "English grandees." "All mistaken Royalists, as well as others, who live now under the protection of the present government," he concluded, "are concerned out of necessity and in respect to their own well-being and benefit to wish well thereunto rather than prosecute the private interest of a single family and of a few fugitives, its dependents, to the hazard of their own families, with the peace and happiness of their native country."[47]

In addressing the Scots and the English presbyterians, Nedham made much the same argument, but here he also tipped his hand in a manner suggesting that his real purpose was to rally the royalists to the new order and isolate the presbyterians. This last had long been his goal. In writing *The Case of the Kingdom Stated*, he had denounced "*Uniformity-mongers*" as "the only Enemies of a *State*" and argued that "to rob the *Soul* of its Freedom," as they proposed, "must needs cause a *Colick* (with inflammation) in the bowels of a *Kingdom*," and he made the same point in almost precisely the same terms in his *Case of the Commonwealth of England Stated*, qualifying his commitment to religious freedom only in conceding that it is appropriate that the magistrate root out "those wild pretenders that profess manifest libertinism and blasphemy."[48]

Of the Scots, Nedham writes in defending the Commonwealth, "I am sorry I must waste paper upon this nation." Their aim is "encroachment . . . upon the English nation." In the religious sphere, they "urged their own discipline as the only pattern to reform the church by" so that "their pharisaical priests" could dominate "the consciences" of the English. In politics, they sought to insinuate "themselves into places of honor, profit, and power." Their purpose has always been to subordinate Parliament to the Kirk, and their religion is little more than "a sacred hunger after gold."[49]

Nedham's brief treatment of the Scots was a prelude to a no less vituperative, but nonetheless cogent, assault on their principal allies the English presbyterians, to whom he attributed all of the vices that Machiavelli had ascribed to the species of Christianity predominant in his own time. Presbyterianism, Nedham observed, has "contracted so many adulterations of worldly interest that it hath lost the beauty which it once appeared to have and serves every sophister as a cloak to cover his ambitious design." The form of ecclesiastical polity that John Calvin had introduced in Geneva for prudential reasons

---

[47] Nedham, *CCES*, 61–70. Cf. Machiavelli, *Il principe* 5 and *Discorsi* 1.16, in *Opere*, 99–101, 263–64.

[48] Cf. Nedham, *The Case of the Kingdom Stated*, 10 (where the page number should be 8), and *Mercurius Pragmaticus* 29 (10–17 October 1648), reprinted in *Making the News*, 356–57, with *CCES*, 123–25. See also Marchamont Nedham, *Independencie No Schisme* (London: Robert White, 1646). As a royalist editor, Nedham continued this diatribe against the presbyterians: see Frank, *Cromwell's Press Agent*, 45–65.

[49] Nedham, *CCES*, 71–86.

England's presbyterians had come to treat as "the necessity and universality of a divine right" though they were "as little able as the bishops to show their pedigree from the Apostles." Nedham lamented that "so many knowing men and of able parts should prove so degenerous as to prostitute themselves and the majesty of the nation to serve the ambitious ends of a few priests." In his judgment, the course which the presbyterians proposed was "destructive to every man's interest of conscience and liberty" and would eventuate in "an intolerable tyranny over magistrates and people." This "mad discipline" would not only eliminate the bishops and clip "the wings of regality." It would, he warned, "intrench also upon the lawyers, curb the gentry in their own lordships by a strange way of parochial tyranny, and bring all people into the condition of mere galley slaves while the blind priests sit at the stern and their hackney dependants, the elders, hold an oar in every boat." The key to understanding what lay at the heart of presbyterianism was "the popish trick taken up by the presbyterian priests in drawing all secular affairs 'within the compass of their spiritual jurisdiction.'" In claiming the right to judge "scandalous sins," they extended their reach to "every action of human life. So that all the people besides their favorites, from the counselor to the beggar, must at every turn stoop like asses to be ridden by them and their arbitrary assemblies." Presbyterian discipline is, Nedham firmly insisted, indistinguishable from that exercised by "the Church of Rome." Wherever there is "a jurisdiction in the church...distinct from the civil," it will prove impossible to keep "church discipline within its limits."[50]

Nedham's chapter on the Levellers serves as an introduction to his brief argument for the virtues of the government already in place. It is the only chapter in which he echoes Milton's endorsement of the classical principle of differential moral and political rationality, and he ends it on a suitably aristocratic note by quoting Horace on his hatred for the vulgar crowd. The error of the Levellers is, Nedham suggests, prudential. Their outlook is incompatible with the lasting settlement they seek. They have "disseminated such strange principles of pretended freedom among the common sort of soldier and people that it became evident to all the world they sought not liberty but licentiousness." They have espoused "a democratic or popular form that puts the whole multitude into an equal exercise of the supreme authority, under pretense of maintaining liberty" without reflecting on the fact that such a polity "is in the judgment of all statesmen the greatest enemy of liberty." If given authority, Nedham explains, the "rude multitude" would not only "satisfy their natural appetites of covetousness and revenge upon the honorable and wealthy." The many are "so brutish," he insists, so entirely "void of reason," that they would resort to "an unbridled violence in all their actions"; and "to make way for that their liberty,...a most dissolute licentiousness or a license to do even what they list," they would trample "down all respects of things sacred and civil." If instituted, Nedham contends, the polity of the Levellers would plunder the rich, give power to the ignorant, mistreat the virtuous, and succumb to

[50] Cf. Nedham, *CCES*, 87–95, with Machiavelli, *Discorsi* 2.2.2, in *Opere*, 149–50.

demagoguery. The "discontents, emulations, and tumults" to which it would give rise would eventually engender "regal tyranny." The only form of government capable of preserving his compatriots from "tyranny" and "confusion," the only one likely "to promote the peace, wealth, and honor of the English nation," is a "free state" of the very sort established by the Rump – in which "men are permitted the freedom of their souls and consciences in the profession of religion" and virtue is given scope.[51]

Although Nedham makes what he represents as a powerful and compelling case on behalf of the new regime, he is nonetheless forced to admit that his compatriots "lightly...prize this invaluable jewel of liberty which hath cost the Commonwealth so much blood and treasure"; that they trample "the precious pearl under their feet like swine so that the Parliament meet now with as many difficulties to preserve, as ever they had to purchase it"; and that England's free state would be doomed had the Commonwealth "not a party of its own throughout the nation, men of valor and virtue, free from those corruptions of excess and riot, and sensible of liberty." To understand why his compatriots are "so degenerous in spirit as to vassalize themselves and neglect the maintenance of their liberty," to explain the "general corruption and depravation of manners" that besets his country, Nedham suggests that one turn to the chapters in "the Florentine's subtile discourses upon Livy," in which Machiavelli "compares such as have been educated under a monarchy or tyranny to those beasts which have been caged or cooped up all their lives in a den where they seem to live in as much pleasure as other beasts that are abroad, and if they be let loose, yet they will return in again because they know not how to value or use their liberty."[52]

In the sequel to his *Case of the Commonwealth of England Stated*, Nedham would set himself the formidable task, almost wholly neglected by those who had at first rallied to the Rump,[53] of taking just such a nation, "bred up and instructed in the brutish principles of monarchy," and teaching its members

---

[51] Nedham, *CCES*, 96–111. See Hor. *Carm.* 3.1.1. Cf. Nedham in his guise as a royalist reporting on Pride's Purge: *Mercurius Pragmaticus* 36–37 (5–12 December 1648), reprinted in *Making the News*, 359–69 (esp. 359–60). During his short stint as a royalist propagandist, Nedham had castigated the Levellers in similar terms: see Frank, *Cromwell's Press Agent*, 45–65.

[52] Cf. Nedham, *CCES*, 111–28 (esp. 111–12, 114), with Machiaveli, *Discorsi* 1.16–18, in *Opere*, 99–104. In *MP* 69 (25 September–2 October): 1093–95 (at 1093), which serves as a preface to the series of editorials that he later republished as *The Excellencie of a Free State*, Nedham used the last few sentences of the passage quoted, cutting only the reference to Machiavelli. For the "party" loyal to the Commonwealth, see David Underdown, "'Honest' Radicals in the Counties, 1642–49," in *Puritans and Revolutionaries: Essays in Seventeenth-Century History Presented to Christopher Hill*, ed. Donald Pennington and Keith Thomas (Oxford, UK: Clarendon Press, 1978), 186–205.

[53] As Judson, *From Tradition to Political Reality*, passim (esp. 10–11), points out, in the critical period stretching from February 1649 to September 1651, virtually no one, apart from John Milton, mounted a principled defense of republican government as such. For an exception to the rule, see "A Declaration of the Parliament of England, Expressing the Grounds of Their Late Proceedings, and of Setling the Present Government in the Way of A Free State," 22 March 1649, in *The Struggle for Sovereignty*, I 380–84.

"to be true commonwealth's-men, and zealous against monarchic-interest, in all its appearances and incroachments whatsoever."[54] To make sense of the particular manner in which he in due course pursued this aim, we will have to examine in some detail the convoluted political history of the regicide regime and the role Nedham played in the first eight years of its turbulent existence.

[54] See Nedham, *EFS*, 46–47.

6

Servant of the Rump

Marchamont Nedham published *The Case of the Commonwealth of England Stated* in early May 1650. Two weeks later, on 24 May, the Council of State voted to pay him £50 "as a gift for service already done" and to confer on him a pension of £100 "whereby he may subsist while endeavouring to serve the Commonwealth; this to be done for one year, by way of probation."[1] Nedham was not behindhand in seeking to justify this handsome salary and to guarantee its continuance.[2]

On 8 June, he presented to the Council of State a prospectus for a weekly newsbook, "Comprizing the Sūm of all Intelligence wth. the Affaires and Designes now on foot, in the three Naçons, of England, Ireland and Scotland," to be written "in defence of the Comonwealth, and for Informaçon of the People." He proposed calling it *Mercurius Politicus* "because the present Goūnm[t] is verā πολιτεία as it is opposed to the despotick forme," and he argued that, if the journal was "to vndeceive the People," it had to to be "written in a Jocular way" lest it "never bee cryed vp." It was, therefore, "to sayle in a middle way, between the Scylla and Charybdis of Scurrility and prophanes," it being Nedham's presumption that "those truths w[ch]. the Multitude regard not in a serious dresse, being represented in pleasing popular Aires, make Musick to y[e]. Comon sence, and charme the Phantsie; w[ch]. ever swayes the Scepter in Vulgar Judgem[tp]; much more then Reason."[3]

Five days later, Nedham brought out the new journal's first issue, taking from Horace's *Ars poetica* his motto "to turn the serious into play," and asking his readers,

Why Should not the *Common-wealth* have a *Fool*, as well as the *King* had? 'Tis a point of *State*, and if the old *Court*-humors should return in this new Form, 'twere the ready Road to Preferment, and a *Ladies* Chamber. But you'll say, I am out of fashion because

[1] Entry under 24 May 1650, in *Calendar of State Papers, Domestic Series, 1649–1660*, ed. Mary Anne Everett Green (London: Longman, 1875–1876), II 174 (1650).
[2] In this endeavor, to judge by the records that survive, he appears to have been successful: see Entries under 11 May, 19 June, 21 September, and 29 December 1654; 20 March, 17 April, 24 May, 30 November, and 20 December 1655; 29 February and 30 May 1656; 29 September 1657; 25 February and 4 October 1658, in *Calendar of State Papers, Domestic Series, 1649–1660*, VII 447, 449, 455, 458 (1654); VIII 127, 604 (1655); IX 585, 588 (1655–56); X 591–92 (1656–57); XI 556–57 (1657–58); XII 584 (1658–59).
[3] See "Prospectus for *Mercurius Politicus*," 8 June 1650, in *The Life Records of John Milton*, ed. J. Milton French (New Brunswick, NJ: Rutgers University Press, 1949–1958), II 310–312.

I make neither *Rimes* nor *Faces*, for *Fidlers* pay, like the *Royal Mercuries*; Yet you shall know I have authority enough to create a fashion of my own, and make all the world to follow the humor.[4]

In this time of ever more rigorous and effective censorship,[5] *Mercurius Politicus* quickly established its authority and became the most influential English journal. It was, as Nedham contended quite early on, "the only *State-Almanack*, to tell what [the] *Weather* is in the *Commonwealth*, and every mans Conscience."[6] Editing this weekly and, in due course, its sister publication *The Publick Intelligencer* would constitute Nedham's principal employment for nearly ten years.[7]

Marchamont Nedham worked for the Commonwealth, but he was by no means its drudge. By instinct he was an agitator, and in keeping with the partisan origins of the newsbook he ordinarily acted in concert with factions or ginger groups inside Parliament and with political insurgents without. During the first civil war, when he wrote for *Mercurius Britanicus* under a license from the Lord General, he consistently lent his support to the army and to those in Parliament intent on achieving a decisive victory in their war against the king; and, in matters of ecclesiastical polity, when the issue eventually forced itself on the attention of all, he fiercely backed the independents against their presbyterian opponents – less out of sectarian sympathy, as we have seen, than for the purpose of promoting civil liberty.[8]

In pursuing the agenda of the radicals, Nedham could be exceptionally bold. Quite early on, he denounced Queen Henrietta Maria, Prince Rupert, and Prince Maurice in the most vituperative of terms; and in December 1643 he even hinted that, in all his actions, Charles I had taken as his model Machiavelli's new prince. In 1645, he stepped up his assaults on the king, intimating that his replacement would be a fine thing.[9] When, in July and early August of that year, he took advantage of the army's seizure of a treasure trove of incriminating royal correspondence and its subsequent publication to raise a *"Hue and Cry"* after the errant monarch; to describe him as *"a wilfull King, which hath gone astray these foure yeares from his Parliament, with a guilty Conscience, bloody Hands, a*

---

[4] *MP* 1 (6–13 June 1650): 1.

[5] See William M. Clyde, *The Struggle for the Freedom of the Press: From Caxton to Cromwell* (London: Oxford University Press, 1934), 162–292; Frederick Seaton Siebert, *Freedom of the Press in England, 1476–1776: The Rise and Decline of Government Controls* (Urbana, IL: University of Illinois Press, 1952), 219–33; and Jason T. Peacey, *Politicians and Pamphleteers: Propaganda during the English Civil Wars and Interregnum* (Aldershot, UK: Ashgate, 2004), passim (esp. 132–202).

[6] See *MP* 5 (4–11 July 1650): 69.

[7] See Joseph Frank, *Cromwell's Press Agent: A Critical Biography of Marchamont Nedham, 1620–1678* (Lanham, MD: University Press of America, 1980), 87–123.

[8] See Frank, *Cromwell's Press Agent*, 18–23, and Jason T. Peacey, "The Struggle for *Mercurius Britanicus*: Factional Politics and the Parliamentarian Press, 1643–1646," *Huntington Library Quarterly* 68:3 (September 2005): 517–43, and "The Management of Civil War Newspapers: *Auteurs*, Entrepreneurs, and Editorial Control," *The Seventeenth Century* 21:1 (Spring 2006): 99–127.

[9] See Frank, *Cromwell's Press Agent*, 23–25, and Blair Worden, "'Wit in a Roundhead': The Dilemma of Marchamont Nedham," in *Political Culture and Cultural Politics in Early Modern England: Essays Presented to David Underdown*, ed. Susan D. Amussen and Mark A. Kishlansky (Manchester, UK: Manchester University Press, 1995), 301–37 (at 314–16).

Heart full of broken Vowes and Protestations"; and to hint that execution was the only "remedy" appropriate "for such obstinacie,"[10] the House of Lords took umbrage and jailed his printer and licenser.[11] This setback did not prevent Nedham from contending in May 1646, when the first civil war had come to an end, that Charles was a tyrant nor did it inhibit him from intimating that Parliament should exact retribution from him, as well as from his advisors, for all the innocent blood that they had spilled.[12] Although this astonishing outburst resulted in Nedham's arrest, in his being silenced, and in the suppression of *Mercurius Britanicus*, there can be no doubt that his denunciations did much to dispel the attitude of deference that Englishmen had always accorded their king and to prepare public opinion for the regicide to come.[13]

After taking the Engagement and publishing his tract in its defense, Nedham used *Mercurius Politicus* to promote the program of his patron John Bradshaw and of Bradshaw's principal allies in the Rump Thomas Chaloner and Henry Marten,[14] and he did all that he could to solidify the uneasy alliance within that assembly linking Chaloner and Marten with the godly republicans, such as Sir Henry Vane, who regarded the Roundhead victories at Naseby, Dunbar, Worcester, and elsewhere as a sign that the establishment of the republic was a part of God's plan for England. Thus, where some thought it prudent to play down the regicide and appeal for support to a public broader than the few who could stomach that dread deed, Nedham bolstered these two sets of radicals in their audacity by celebrating the event, by insisting that a repudiation of monarchy be the cornerstone of the new regime, and by encouraging on the Commonwealth's part an ambitious foreign policy aimed not just at promoting Protestantism but at spreading the revolution to a continent that seemed, in the wake of the Reformation, the Wars of Religion in France, and the Thirty Years' War in Germany, to be poised on the edge of a republican transformation comparable to the one that England had herself undergone.[15]

[10] See *Mercurius Britanicus* 90 (14–21 July 1645): 809–16, 91 (21–28 July 1645): 817–24, and 92 (28 July–4 August 1645): 825–32, which are conveniently reprinted in *Making the News: An Anthology of the Newsbooks of Revolutionary England, 1641–1660*, ed. Joad Raymond (New York: St. Martin's Press, 1993), 339–49. Nedham's suggestion that the king had blood on his hands should be read, as, he knew perfectly well, it would be read by his contemporaries, in light of Gen. 9:6 and Num. 35:33. For the significance of Nedham's contention, see Patricia Crawford, "Charles Stuart, That Man of Blood," *Journal of British Studies* 16:2 (Spring 1977): 41–61.

[11] See Frank, *Cromwell's Press Agent*, 26–27.

[12] See *Mercurius Britanicus* 129 (4–11 May 1646): 1103–10 and 130 (11–18 May 1646): 1111–18. The second of these is conveniently reprinted in *Making the News*, 349–50.

[13] Consider Frank, *Cromwell's Press Agent*, 28–30, and Worden "'Wit in a Roundhead,'" 305–16, in light of Crawford, "Charles Stuart, That Man of Blood," 41–61. For the manner in which the press, on both sides, contributed to the polarization that took place in the course of the first civil war, see Peter W. Thomas, *Sir John Berkenhead, 1617–1679: A Royalist Career in Politics and Polemics* (Oxford, UK: Clarendon Press, 1969), 75–98.

[14] Marten and Chaloner, who had been the recognized leaders of an anti-monarchical, republican ginger group within the House of Commons since 1646, were catapulted into a leading position by Pride's Purge: see Sarah Barber, *Regicide and Republicanism: Politics and Ethics in the English Revolution* (Edinburgh, UK: Edinburgh University Press, 1998), 1–239.

[15] See Blair Worden, *The Rump Parliament, 1648–1653* (Cambridge, UK: Cambridge University Press, 1974), 174, 251–61; "Classical Republicanism and the Puritan Revolution," in *History*

Nedham encouraged his early readers to savor just "how sweet the Air of a *Commonwealth* is beyond that of a *Monarchy*," and he insisted that "the late *Charls* died a *Martyr*" not for justice and religion, as the Cavaliers claimed, but "for Tyranny and Treason." When he had occasion to report that the Genoese had squelched a plot aimed at overthrowing their republic, Nedham remarked that "there cannot be a greater *Crime*, than an endeavour to overthrow the Government of a *Free-State* or *Common-wealth*." When the opportunity presented itself for mentioning the jurist who had read out the verdict in condemnation of the king, he insisted that his benefactor John "*Bradshaw*" possessed "a name that shall live with Honor in our *English* Histories." He would later single out "that heroick and most *Noble Act of Justice*, in judging and executing the *late King*" as "an Act agreeing with the law of God, . . . consonant to the laws of men, and the practice of all wel-ordered States & Kingdoms," and he promised to make this "evident ere long (among many other particulars) in a set *Treatise*, by a cloud of *Instances*, derived from the scope of *holy Writ*, the very principles of *right Reason*, *Law* and *Example*." The regicide was, he contended, "the *Basis* whereon the *Common-wealth* is founded," and he insisted that, if ever the English free state was to "be completed, it must be by honouring and intrusting those noble Instruments and Hands, who laid the Foundation, or now help with open hearts to carry on the *Building*."[16]

For "the *Mummery* of *Royalty*" whereby "every one bends the Knee, blesses, and adores the *Idol*" Nedham evidenced nothing but contempt.[17] In the manner of his beloved Machiavel,[18] he refused to acknowledge a distinction between kingship and tyranny.[19] "Tarquin" was a surname that he reserved for Charles, the exiled pretender, and for his younger brother James, the duke of York,[20]

---

and Imagination: Essays in Honour of H. R. Trevor-Roper, ed. Hugh Lloyd-Jones, Valerie Pearl, and Blair Worden (London: Duckworth, 1981), 182–200 (esp. 195–200); and "Milton and Marchamont Nedham," in *Milton and Republicanism*, ed. David Armitage, Armand Himy, and Quentin Skinner (Cambridge, UK: Cambridge University Press, 1995), 156–80 (at 161–66), as well as Sarah Barber, *A Revolutionary Rogue: Henry Marten and the English Republic* (Phoenix Mill: Sutton, 2000), 36 (which should be read with 184, n. 75). See also Worden, "'Wit in a Roundhead,'" 326–27; "Marchamont Nedham and the Beginnings of English Republicanism, 1649–1656," in *Republicanism, Liberty, and Commercial Society, 1649–1776*, ed. David Wootton (Stanford, CA: Stanford University Press, 1994), 45–81 (at 62–63, 71–74); and *Literature and Politics in Cromwellian England: John Milton, Andrew Marvell, Marchamont Nedham* (Oxford, UK: Oxford University Press, 2007), 174–240, where Milton, who follows the same line, is the focus and Nedham is brought in for comparative purposes.

16 See *MP* 5 (4–11 July 1650): 65; 7 (18–25 July 1650): 101; 8 (25 July–1 August 1650): 123–24; 49 (8–15 May 1651): 784; 67 (11–18 September 1651): 1062. Note also *MP* 16 (19–26 September 1650): 275. Nedham can operate also by way of indirection: see *MP* 32 (9–16 January 1651): 522–23, 526–27, 533; 33 (16–23 January 1651): 549; 43 (27 March–3 April 1651): 695–97; 50 (15–22 May 1651): 802–4.

17 See *MP* 9 (1–8 August 1650): 131.

18 Note Nedham, *CCES*, 62.

19 See, for example, *MP* 52 (29 May–5 June 1651): 831–33; 53 (5–12 June 1651): 847–49 (where 848 and 849 are misnumbered); 64 (21–28 August 1651): 1013–16; 65 (28 August–4 September 1651): 1029–32.

20 See, for example, *MP* 2 (13–20 June 1650): 17; 3 (20–27 June 1650): 40, 45, 48; 4 (27 June–4 July 1650): 49, 55–56, 58, 63–64; 5 (4–11 July 1650): 65–66, 79–80; 6 (11–18 July 1650): 81, 87–88, 95; 7 (18–25 July 1650): 101; 8 (25 July–1 August 1650): 113, 115, 127–28; 9 (1–8 August

for they were the surviving members of what he regarded as a *"Tyrannick Family."*[21] As we should then expect, Nedham thought it perfectly appropriate that, at the Old Exchange, the statue of their father Charles I be beheaded, then removed, and replaced with an inscription reading, *"Exit Tyrannus, Regum ultimus, Anno Libertatis Angliæ restitutæ primo, Annoq; Dom. 1648. Januarii. 30."*[22]

From the start, *Mercurius Politicus* devoted considerable space to news of events abroad. Its perspective was, however, resolutely English and republican throughout. In the third issue of *Mercurius Politicus*, for example, Nedham described the *Frondeurs* as "the *French Roundheads*."[23] The *"honest party"* in the Parlement of Paris, he reported some weeks later, had "at length" begun "to vote with an *English* spirit, for the suppressing of *Delinquents*, and all oppressors of the people."[24] If they were to succeed, it was incumbent on them to "take example…from the heroick *Parliament* of *England*."[25] The French, he exulted elsewhere, are "resolved to be *Monkified* no longer with *Chains* at their heels, and *Collars* about their Necks." Now, "truly, it is high time the *French Tooth Drawers*…learn of our *English*…to draw all the Teeth of that *Monster*, that gripes the Princes of *the Blood*, as well as the People."[26] Nedham found much to celebrate in the fact that "the poor Beast of *Prerogative*.…goes now upon its *last legs* in France."[27]

Nedham was even more attentive to the struggle taking place within the United Provinces between the House of Orange, which was closely tied by kinship and marriage to the Stuart house,[28] and the republican forces dominant

---

1650): 129, 131, 144; 10 (8–15 August 1650): 159; 11 (15–22 August 1650): 161, 174; 12 (22–29 August 1650): 179–80, 187; 14 (5–12 September 1650): 209, 211; 15 (12–19 September 1650): 259; 16 (19–26 September 1650): 274; 17 (26 September–3 October 1650): 290; 20 (17–24 October 1650): 336, 340; 26 (28 November–5 December 1650): 435; 27 (5–12 December 1650): 440; 52 (29 May–5 June 1651): 832; 62 (7–14 August 1651): 983; 63 (14–21 August 1651): 999; 65 (28 August–4 September 1651): 1040; 66 (4–11 September 1651): 1047 (where the pagination is confused); 67 (11–18 September 1651): 1063; 73 (23–30 October 1651): 1165.

[21] See *MP* 39 (27 February–6 March 1651): 624 and 50 (15–22 May 1651): 799–801. See also *MP* 51 (22–29 May 1651): 815–17; 52 (29 May–5 June 1651): 831–33.

[22] See *MP* 11 (15–22 August 1650): 162. Note *MP* 28 (12–19 December 1650): 464.

[23] See *MP* 3 (20–27 June 1650): 36. Nedham followed events in France closely: see *MP* 1 (6–13 June 1650): 10–12; 3 (20–27 June 1650): 35–37; 4 (27 June–4 July 1650): 53- 55; 5 (4–11 July 1650): 73–78; 6 (11–18 July 1650): 86–91, 95; 7 (18–25 July 1650): 104–7; 8 (25 July–1 August 1650): 118–23; 10 (8–15 August 1650): 149–57, 159; 11 (15–22 August 1650): 170–73; 17 (26 September–3 October 1650): 292; 20 (17–24 October 1650): 340; 23 (7–14 November 1650): 381. The analogy was not entirely lost on the French: see Philip A. Knachel, *England and the Fronde: The Impact of the English Civil War and Revolution on France* (Ithaca, NY: Cornell University Press, 1967), and Nannerl Keohane, *Philosophy and the State: The Renaissance to the Enlightenment* (Princeton, NJ: Princeton University Press, 1980), 213–37.

[24] See *MP* 10 (8–15 August 1650): 147.

[25] See *MP* 11 (15–22 August 1650): 172.

[26] See *MP* 4 (27 June–4 July 1650): 61–62.

[27] See *MP* 10 (8–15 August 1650): 156. See, however, *MP* 40 (6–13 March 1651): 650–51. Then, note *MP* 42 (20–27 March 1651): 683.

[28] In this connection, see Simon Groenveld, "The House of Orange and the House of Stuart, 1639–1650: A Revision," *The Historical Journal* 34:4 (December 1991): 955–72.

in Amsterdam and elsewhere.[29] "The *Storm* that began in *England*," he predicted in the very first issue of his gazette, "having taken its course by *France*,
is like to end in the *Low-Countries*."[30] He encouraged his readers to think
republicanism the wave of the future; and while recounting the travails that the
young Louis XIV had suffered in the course of the civil disorders then gripping
France, Nedham celebrated the fact that theirs was "an Age for Kings to run
the *Wildgoose-chase*, to hold life and Soul together."[31]

Nedham was by no means peculiar in entertaining such hopes. As we have
seen, Milton regarded himself as a propagator of republican revolution throughout Christendom.[32] The Venetian ambassador to Spain reported back to the
doge and the Senate of the Serene Republic concerning the Spanish king's irri-
tation at the English upon learning that their admiral Robert Blake had had
the effrontery to remark in the public square at Cadiz that "with the example afforded by London all kingdoms will annihilate tyranny and become
republics," that "England had done so already; France was following in her
wake; and as the natural gravity of the Spaniards rendered them somewhat
slower in their operations, he gave them ten years for the revolution in their
country." "After his victory in Scotland [at the battle of Dunbar]," this ambassador added, "Cromuel" is said to have written "to the parliament that through
that success they might consider the affairs of the interior safe, and that for the

---

[29] See *MP* 1 (6–13 June 1650): 16; 8 (25 July–1 August 1650): 127; 9 (1–8 August 1650): 136–41;
10 (8–15 August 1650): 160; 11 (15–22 August 1650): 167–68; 15 (12–19 September 1650):
253–55; 18 (3–10 October 1650): 307; 20 (17–24 October 1650): 336–40; 22 (31 October– 7
November 1650): 371; 28 (12–19 December 1650): 461; 57 (3–10 July 1651): 908–9; 95 (25
March–1 April 1652): 1498, 1502; 110 (8–15 July 1652): 1731; 112 (22–29 July 1652): 1763–
67; 117 (26 August–2 September 1652): 1835; 118 (2–9 September 1652): 1858–61; 119 (9–16
September 1652): 1875–76; 122 (30 September–7 October 1652): 1922–23, 1925 (misnumbered
as 1952) – 26; 123 (7–14 October 1652): 1938; 125 (21–28 October): 1968; 127 (4–11 November
1652): 2004; 128 (11–18 November 1652): 2012–16; 129 (18–25 November 1652): 2027–32,
2035–36; 136 (6–13 January 1653): 2159; 138 (27 January–3 February 1653): 2206–7; 139 (3–10
February 1653): 2121–22; 140 (10–17 February 1653): 2238; 152 (5–12 May 1653): 2425; 154
(19–26 May 1653): 2467; 155, which is misnumbered as 153, (26 May–2 June 1653): 2483–85;
159 (23–30 June 1653): 2544–45; 161 (7–14 July 1653): 2571–75, 2578; 162 (14–21 July 1653):
2594; 164 (28 July–4 August 1653): 2622–23; 165 (4–11 August 1653): 2642–43; 166 (11–18
August 1653): 2655–59; 167 (18–25 August 1653): 2682–83; 168 (25 August–1 September 1653):
2688–89; 170 (8–15 September 1653): 2720–22, 2731; 171 (15–22 September 1653): 2748–49;
173 (29 September–6 October 1653): 2780–81; 181 (24 November–2 December 1653): 3002;
184 (16–22 December 1653): 3051–52; 192 (9–16 February 1654): 3277; 203 (27 April–4 May
1654): 3457–60; 204 (4–11 May 1654); 3362 (which is misnumbered)–66; 214 (13–20 July 1654):
3626 (which is misnumbered) – 27; 215 (20–27 July 1654): 3647–48; 216 (27 July–3 August
1654): 3665; 218 (10–17 August 1654): 3693; 219 (17–24 August 1654): 3713–15; 220 (24–31
August 1654): 3727–29; 221 (31 August–7 September 1654): 3757–59; 224 (21–28 September
1654): 3785, 3792–93. In the editorials that would eventually reappear in his *Excellencie of a
Free State*, Nedham frequently adverted to the defects of Dutch policy with regard to the House
of Orange: see *MP* 101 (6–13 May 1652): 1587–88; 102 (13–20 May 1652): 1595; 103 (20–27
May 1652): 1612–13; 106 (10–17 June 1652): 1660–61. In this connection, see Herbert Rowen,
John de Witt, Grand Pensionary of Holland, 1625–1672 (Princeton, NJ: Princeton University
Press, 1978), 25–43.

[30] See *MP* 1 (6–13 June 1650): 16.

[31] See *MP* 4 (27 June–4 July 1650): 54.

[32] See Chapter Three, this volume.

future they must think of helping other nations to throw off the yoke, and to consolidate their own government by establishing republican neighbours."[33]

When the Prince of Orange, son-in-law of Charles I and stalwart supporter of the Stuart cause, unexpectedly died of smallpox in the fall of 1650 and the United Provinces opted to leave the office of stadholder and that of captain-general vacant,[34] Nedham encouraged the hopes entertained by the Bradshaw-Chaloner-Marten connection and their godly republican associates for a firm alliance with the United Provinces or even a political union.[35] When these hopes were dashed in the face of the Dutch expectation that Cromwell's forces in Scotland were doomed to fall prey to the pretender and his army of Scots,[36] and the two republican factions in Parliament joined together once again after the battle of Worcester to pass the Navigation Act on 9 October 1651 as a means for punishing their recalcitrant, back-sliding Dutch brethren, *Mercurius Politicus* carefully prepared its readers for the possibility of war.[37] Then, when

[33] See Report of Pietro Basadonna, Venetian Ambassador to Spain, to the Doge and Senate, 8 February 1651, in *Calendar of State Papers and Manuscripts relating to English Affairs: Existing in the Archives and Collections of Venice, and in Other Libraries of Northern Italy*, ed. Rawdon Brown et al. (London: Longman Green, 1864–1947), XXVIII 169–70 (1647–52).

[34] Nedham followed these events on an almost daily basis: see *MP* 23 (7–14 November 1650): 374–75, 380, 382–84, 387; 24 (14–21 November 1650): 392–93, 397–400, 406; 26 (28 November–5 December 1650): 427, 433; 27 (5–12 December 1650): 451–52; 28 (12–19 December 1650): 459; 29 (19–26 December 1650): 476; 37 (13–20 February 1651): 604; 38 (20–27 February 1651): 616–17; 39 (27 February–6 March 1651): 636; 41 (13–20 March 1651): 669–70; 42 (20–27 March 1651): 679. See Rowen, *John de Witt*, 43–56.

[35] For the first inklings of this possibility, see *MP* 27 (5–12 December 1650): 447–48. Nedham's hopes are made explicit in *MP* 31 (2–9 January 1651): 512. See, then, *MP* 32 (9–16 January 1651): 533–34; 33 (16–23 January 1651): 540, 545–46, 549; 35 (30 January–6 February 1651): 577–78; 38 (20–27 February 1651): 616; 41 (13–20 March 1651): 670. Such a union was England's goal throughout: see *MP* 184 (16–22 December 1653): 3051–52; 188 (12–19 January 1654): 3200–01.

[36] One can trace the rise and fall of English hopes in this regard in the frequent dispatches from the United Provinces that Nedham prints during the negotiations then taking place at the Hague: see *MP* 43 (27 March–3 April 1651): 695–97, 700; 44 (3–10 April 1651): 709, 713–17; 45 (10–17 April 1651): 722, 724–26, 728–29, 732–34; 46 (17–24 April 1651): 745–47, 749; 47 (24 April–1 May 1651): 759–61, 764–66; 48 (1–8 May 1651): 776–79; 49 (8–15 May 1651): 792–93; 50 (15–22 May 1651): 808–10; 51 (22–29 May 1651): 827–29; 52 (29 May–5 June 1651): 834–35, 842–43; 53 (5–12 June 1651): 857–58; 54 (12–19 June 1651): 870–72; 55 (19–26 June 1651): 882–83 (where the pagination should be 892–93); 56 (26 June–3 July 1651): 897–98; 57 (3–10 July 1651): 908–9. For a jocio-serious analysis of the failure of England's embassy: see *MP* 57 (3–10 July 1651): 913–14. For the drift of events in the United Provinces after the English embassy returned home, see *MP* 58 (10–17 July 1651): 928–29; 59 (17–24 July 1651): 939, 943–46; 60 (24–31 July 1651): 959–60; 67 (11–18 September 1651): 1067–68; 69 (25 September–2 October 1651): 1099–1103; 70 (2–9 October 1651): 1117–18; 71 (9–16 October 1651): 1134–35; 72 (16–23 October 1651): 1144–49; 73 (23–30 October): 1162, 1165–67; 74 (30 October–6 November 1651): 1184–86. The jocio-serious tone of some of the dispatches supposedly sent from Leiden suggests that their author was Nedham himself. For a discussion of Nedham's attitude with respect to foreign policy in this period and that of Andrew Marvell, see Worden, *Literature and Politics in Cromwellian England*, 116–33.

[37] See, for example, *MP* 71 (9–16 October 1651): 1128–29. The act appears to have had its intended effect: see *MP* 74 (30 October–6 November 1651): 1184–86; 76 (13–20 November 1651): 1210–11; 78 (27 November–4 December 1651): 1250–51; 81 (18–25 December 1651): 1295; 82 (25 December 1651–1 January 1652): 1315–16; 87 (29 January–5 February 1652): 1386–87 (the second

an unprovoked attack by an Orangist Dutch admiral on an English fleet put
an end to diplomacy and gave rise to armed conflict between the two Protestant republics the following year,[38] the newsbook gave the war its unstinting support,[39] and its editor published a pamphlet in defense of the English

set of pages so numbered); 89 (12–19 February 1652): 1422; 90 (19–26 February 1652): 1434–
36; 91 (26 February–4 March 1652): 1449, 1451–52; 92 (4–11 March 1652): 1468–69, 1471–72;
94 (18–25 March 1652): 1481, 1488; 95 (25 March–1 April 1652): 1504; 97 (8–15 April 1652):
1536. Well before the death of the prince of Orange, Nedham had intimated that the well-being of
"the *Hollanders* . . . in respect to the maintainance of the *Trade*, & *Authority* of the *Provinces*"
depended upon "an *Amity*" being "confirmed betweene the two Republicks of *England* and
Holland." See *MP* 15 (12–19 September 1650): 253.

[38] One cannot make sense of the Rump's initial overture to the Dutch, of the Navigation Act
and the first Anglo-Dutch War, and of the Protectorate's eventual abandonment of the Rump's
foreign policy in this regard without attending closely to the revolutionary élan uniting the two
republican factions dominant in the Rump and, then, examining the less radical outlook that
Oliver Cromwell adopted after his sobering experience with the Nominated Parliament: cf. J.
E. Farnell, "The Navigation Act of 1651, The First Dutch War and the London Merchant Community," *Economic History Review*, second ser., 16 (1963–64): 439–54; Charles Wilson, *Profit
and Power: A Study of England and the Dutch Wars* (London: Longmans, Green, 1957), 25–89;
Robert Brenner, "The Civil War Politics of London's Merchant Community," *Past & Present* 58
(February 1973): 53–107, and *Merchants and Revolution: Commercial Change, Political Conflict, and London's Overseas Traders, 1550–1653* (Princeton, NJ: Princeton University Press,
1993), 494–637 (esp. 577–637); and Simon Groenveld, "The English Civil Wars as a Cause of
the First Anglo-Dutch War, 1640–1652," *The Historical Journal* 30:3 (September 1987): 541–66,
with Steven C. A. Pincus, *Protestantism and Patriotism: Ideologies and the Making of English
Foreign Policy, 1650–1688* (Cambridge, UK: Cambridge University Press, 1996), 11–191.

[39] See *MP* 103 (20–27 May 1652): 1620–24; 105 (3–10 June 1652): 1645; 106 (10–17 June
1652):1661–64; 108 (24 June–1 July 1652): 1690–94; 109 (1–8 July 1652): 1711–16; 110
(8–15 July 1652): 1731; 111, which is misnumbered as 112, (15–22 July 1652): 1741–43; 112
(22–29 July 1652): 1749, 1763–67; 114 (5–12 August 1652): 1790–93; 116 (19–26
August 1652): 1824–25; 117 (26 August–2 September): 1835, 1840–44; 118 (2–9 September
1652): 1858–61; 119 (9–16 September 1652): 1875–77; 121 (23–30 September 1652): 1898–99,
1907–11; 122 (30 September–7 October 1652): 1923–24; 123 (7–14 October 1652): 1943–44;
125 (21–28 October 1652): 1968, 1972–73; 126 (28 October–4 November 1652): 1987–91; 127
(4–11 November 1652): 1996–98, 2003–4, 2007–8; 128 (11–18 November 1652): 2012–18; 129
(18–25 November 1652): 2027–32, 2035–36, 2038–40; 130 (25 November–2 December 1652):
2053–55 (which deserves particular attention); 131 (2–9 December 1652): 2064–66; 132 (9–16
December 1652): 2080–82, 2085–87; 133 (16–23 December 1652): 2089–91, 2096–2104; 134
(23–30 December 1652): 2106–12, 2115–19; 135 (30 December 1652–6 January 1653): 2142–43;
the first 136 (6–13 January 1653): 2156–59; the second 136 (13–20 January 1653): 2166–75; 137
(20–27 January 1653): 2181, 2191–92; 138 (27 January–3 February 1653): 2206–7; 139 (3–10
February 1653): 2210, 2116–18, 2121–24; 140 (10–17 February 1653): 2230–32, 2238; 141
(17–24 February 1653): 2249–54, 2258–60; 142 (24 February–3 March 1653): 2261–63, 2265–
66, 2273–75; 143 (3–10 March 1653): 2281–90; 144 (10–17 March 1653): 2296–97, 2301–02,
2305–7; 145 (17–24 March 1653): 2321–22; 146 (24–31 March 1653): 2332–34, 2338–39; 147
(31 March–7 April 1653): 2353–55; 148 (7–14 April 1653): 2369–70; 149 (14–21 April 1653):
2384–87; 151 (28 April–5 May 1653): 2411–13; 155 (which is misnumbered as 153) (26 May–2
June 1653): 2483–85; 156 (2–9 June 1653): 2496–98; 157 (9–16 June 1653): 2511–14; 158 (16–23
June 1653): 2530–32 (where all of the pages are misnumbered); 159 (23–30 June 1653): 2542–
45; 160 (30 June–7 July 1653): 2560–63; 162 (14–21 July 1653): 2594; 163 (21–28 July 1653):
2608–10; 164 (28 July–4 August 1653): 2621–23, 2626–28; 165 (4–11 August 1653): 2638–39,
2642–44; 166 (11–18 August 1653): 2645–49, 2655–59; 167 (18–25 August 1653): 2682–83;
170 (8–15 September 1653): 2720–22, 2730; 173 (29 September–6 October 1653):2780–81; 178
(3–10 November 1653): 2856–57; 185 (22–29 December 1653): 3145, 3150; 186 (29 December

cause.[40] Moreover, with Bradshaw's encouragement and aid, Nedham translated into the vernacular *Mare Clausum seu Dominium Maris* – John Selden's classic defense of England's claim to dominion over the narrow seas against the arguments of the Dutch and their protagonist Hugo Grotius for a universal freedom of the seas. To this he added material specifying the pertinence of the book's argument to the dispute then underway.[41]

A Libertine Alliance

Nedham must have found his alliance with the Bradshaw-Chaloner-Marten connection congenial. He was on the best of terms with John Bradshaw, whom he had apparently known in his youth before the civil wars when the latter was a lawyer and he a clerk at Gray's Inn. At Bradshaw's table, we are told, he frequently took his meals,[42] and in Bradshaw's will, he would in due course be remembered alongside the poet and propagandist John Milton, whose friendship they shared.[43] The poet and the publicist would similarly be remembered in the will of Sir Peter Wentworth, a member of the Long Parliament and close friend of Henry Marten, who had been a central figure in Marten's anti-monarchical faction in the 1640s and who, though he had absented himself during the trial of the king, rallied to the Rump after the royal blood had been shed.[44]

1653–5 January 1654): 3170; 188 (5–12 January 1654): 3200–3201; 192 (9–16 February 1654): 3277–78; 193, misnumbered 93, (16–23 February 1654): 3294; 194 (23 February–2 March 1654): 3308–9; 195 (2–9 March 1654): 3325; 198 (23–30 March 1654): 3371–72.

[40] See A Friend to this Commonwealth [Marchamont Nedham], *The Case Stated between England and the United Provinces, in this Present Juncture* (London: Thomas Newcomb, 1652), passim.

[41] Consider John Selden, *Of the Dominion; or, Ownership of the Sea* (1635), ed. and tr. Marchamont Nedham (London: William Du-gard, 1652) sig. A2v, in light of John Selden, *Mare Clausum; The Right and Dominion of the Sea* (1635), ed. James Howell (London: Andrew Kembe and Edward Thomas, 1663) Advertisement, and see Anthony à Wood, *Athenæ Oxonienses* (London, F. C. & J. Rivington: 1813–20), III 1188. According to the advertisement which appeared in *MP* 130 (25 November–2 December 1652): 2056, the book was "printed and published by appointment of the Councell of State." That body subsequently rewarded Nedham for his efforts as translator: see Entry under 10 February 1653, in *Calendar of State Papers, Domestic Series, 1649–1660*, V 486 (1652–53).

[42] See [John Cleveland], *The Character of MP* (London: [s.n.], 1650), 7–8.

[43] See "Codicil to John Bradshaw's Will," 10 September 1655, and "Will of John Bradshaw," 16 December 1659, in French, *The Life Records of John Milton*, IV 47, 287. Note William Riley Parker, *Milton: A Biography* (Oxford, UK: Clarendon Press, 1968), I 540 (with II 1071, n. 104), and Worden, *Literature and Politics in Cromwellian England*, 45–47, 95, 102, 116, 130, 158, 195–200, 205, 245, 256–57, 269, 276, 294, 306, 349, 399, 404.

[44] Consider French, *The Life Records of John Milton*, V 64, in light of Esther S. Cope, "Sir Peter Wentworth (1592–1675)," in *Biographical Dictionary of British Radicals in the Seventeenth Century*, ed. Richard L. Greaves and Robert Zaller (Brighton, UK: Harvester Press, 1982–1984), III 300–301. See also J. H. Hexter, *The Reign of King Pym* (Cambridge, MA: Harvard University Press, 1941), 48–152 (esp. 56–57, 60, 70, 119); David Underdown, *Pride's Purge: Politics in the Puritan Revolution* (Oxford, UK: Clarendon Press, 1971), 106–256 (esp. 126, 137, 188, 217, 219, 241), and Worden, *The Rump Parliament*, 33–60, 86–102, 211–36, 317–41 (esp. 34, 44, 94, 222, 336, 340).

Nedham had long been favorable to Marten as well.[45] The two were kindred
spirits – impish, irreverent, and witty to a fault. Nedham was not in a position
to come to Marten's defense when, on 16 August 1643, the republican firebrand
made the tactical error of remarking that "it were better one family should be
destroyed than many" while defending a Puritan divine who, in his private
papers, had speculated that it might eventually prove necessary to root out
the king and the royal line, and John Pym seized on this as an opportunity to
have his troublesome colleague expelled from the House of Commons.[46] At this
point, Nedham may still have been employed as an underclerk at Gray's Inn,
though his tenure there would quite soon come to an end. But when Marten
was restored to his seat on 6 January 1646, *Mercurius Britanicus* did turn aside
to warmly welcome him back;[47] and, in the time of turmoil that followed,
both men flirted with the Levellers without ever formally joining their ranks.[48]
Given what we know of these two, we can be confident that Nedham would
have been amused had he heard the story, as he presumably did, that, when
called upon to examine the king's possessions, Marten had dressed his friend
the radical poet George Wither in the robes and crown reserved for the royal
investiture so that the latter could, "with a thousand Apish and Ridiculous
actions," expose "those Sacred Ornaments to contempt and laughter." In the
circumstances, *Mercurius Pragmaticus* would no doubt have erupted in horror
and disgust, but *Mercurius Britanicus* and *Mercurius Politicus* would have been
tempted to boast, as Marten is said to have done, "*That there will be no further
use of these Toys and Trifles.*"[49]

---

[45] For an overview of Marten's quite colorful career, see C. M. Williams, "The Anatomy of a Radical
Gentleman: Henry Marten," in *Puritans and Revolutionaries: Essays in Seventeenth-Century
History Presented to Christopher Hill*, ed. Donald Pennington and Keith Thomas (Oxford, UK:
Clarendon Press, 1978), 118–38. For a more detailed, if less focused account, see Barber, *A
Revolutionary Rogue*, passim. See also Barber, *Regicide and Republicanism*, 1–201, and David
Norbrook, *Writing the English Republic: Poetry, Rhetoric and Politics, 1627–1660* (Cambridge,
UK: Cambridge University Press, 1999), 93–101.

[46] See C. M. Williams, "Extremist Tactics in the Long Parliament, 1642–1643," *Historical Studies*
15:57 (October 1971): 136–50.

[47] *Mercurius Britanicus* 113 (5–12 January 1646): 1000.

[48] See Barber, *Regicide and Republicanism*, 11–120 (esp. 40–65, 81–86), and *Revolutionary Rogue*,
14–15, 18–22, 29–31, 35–36; then, consider Frank, *Cromwell's Press Agent*, 20–21, 28; Worden,
"'Wit in a Roundhead,'" 320–21; Joad Raymond, *The Invention of the Newspaper: English
Newsbooks, 1641–1649* (Oxford, UK: Clarendon Press, 1996), 186–87; and Jonathan Scott,
Commonwealth Principles: Republican Writing of the English Revolution (Cambridge, UK:
Cambridge University Press, 2004), 82–84, 137, 241–47.

[49] See Peter Heylyn, *Aërius Redivivus, or the History of the Presbyterians*, second edition (London: Wilkinson, 1672), 452. Note also Roger Manley, *The History of the Rebellions in England,
Scotland and Ireland* (London: L. Meredith and T. Newborough, 1691), 68, who repeats the
story. Both are quoted at length in Paul Bunyan Anderson, "George Wither and the 'Regalia,'"
Philological Quarterly 14:4 (October 1935): 366–68, who connects the putative event to George
Wither's appointment to the commission for disposing of the late king's goods on 10 October
1650. It is, of course, conceivable that this took place in June 1643 when the pertinent room in
Westminster Abbey was searched by Marten and Sir Henry Mildmay, as Williams, "Extremist
Tactics in the Long Parliament," 141, suggests – but Wither's involvement and Marten's remark
better fit the later date. Wither was a satirist and poet who supported Parliament in the civil
wars and later wrote panegyrics concerning the Rump: note Robert Zaller, "George Wither

Nedham had much in common also with Marten's associate Chaloner; with their friend Thomas May, poet and official historiographer of the Long Parliament and the Rump; with the former Leveller John Wildman, Marten's agent, confidant, and nephew by marriage; and with Henry Neville, whom Chaloner, Marten, and Algernon Sidney had recruited to the Rump in October 1649. These men were as notorious for their libertinism, their wit, and irreverence as was the editor of *Mercurius Politicus*;[50] and they were despised for their scandalous comportment and their irreligious demeanor by godly republicans as various as Oliver Cromwell and Sir Henry Vane.[51]

Marten was "as far from a Puritane as light from darknesse," John Aubrey reports.[52] "All that he moved for was upon Roman and Greek principles," adds Gilbert Burnet. "He never entered into matters of religion, but on design to laugh both at them and at all morality; for he was both an impious and vicious man"; and even "in his imprisonment" after the Restoration, "he delivered himself up unto vice and blasphemy."[53] What remains of Marten's unpublished writing suggests a firm commitment to republicanism, a keen interest in the thinking of both Machiavelli and Hobbes, a predilection for polygamy, and an all-encompassing religious skepticism on his part.[54]

Thomas Chaloner and Thomas May were cut from the same cloth. The former was, we are told by Anthony à Wood, "as far from [being] a puritan

(1588–1667)," in *Biographical Dictionary of British Radicals in the Seventeenth Century*, III 335–37, and see David Norbrook, "Levelling Poetry: George Wither and the English Revolution, 1642–1649," *English Literary Renaissance* 21:2 (Spring 1991): 217–56 (esp. 217–19); "'Safest in Storms': George Wither in the 1650s," in *Heart of the Heartless World: Essays in Cultural Resistance in Memory of Margot Heinemann*, ed. David Margolies and Maroula Joannou (London: Pluto Press, 1995), 19–32, and *Writing the English Republic*, 2, 86–92, 140–58, 228–42, 351–57, who casts doubts on the pertinent anecdote.

[50] See Worden, *The Rump Parliament*, 36–37, 72–73, 260–61; "Classical Republicanism and the Puritan Revolution," 195; and "'Wit in a Roundhead,'" passim (esp. 326–27).

[51] See Bulstrode Whitelocke, *Memorials of the English Affairs from the Beginning of the Reign of Charles the First to the Happy Restoration of King Charles the Second* (Oxford, UK: Oxford University Press, 1853), IV 5, and *The Diary of Bulstrode Whitelocke, 1605–1675*, ed. Ruth Spalding (Oxford, UK: Oxford University Press, 1990), 286; consider the Letter from William Rowe to Oliver Cromwell on 28 December 1650, in *Original Letters and Papers of State: Addressed to Oliver Cromwell; Concerning the Affairs of Great Britain*, ed. John Nickolls (London: William Bowyer, 1743), 43–44, disparaging "Tom Chaloner, Harry Nevill and those witts," and reporting on Vane's dissatisfaction with an individual whom he suspected of "clubb[ing] it with Tom Chaloner, Tom May (when living) and that gangue."

[52] See *ABL*, 266.

[53] See Gilbert Burnet, *The History of My Own Time*, ed. Osmund Airy (Oxford, UK: Clarendon Press, 1897–1900), I 282–83. Marten was a drinker, an adulterer, and privately a proponent of polygamy. Whether he was a whoremonger as well is contested: cf. Barber, *A Revolutionary Rogue*, 141–66, with Jason McElligott, "The Politics of Sexual Libel: Royalist Propaganda in the 1640s," *Huntington Library Quarterly* 67:1 (March 2004): 75–99 (esp. 82–87). All that is certain is that his personal behavior invited disparagement on these grounds: see Susan Wiseman, "'Adam, the Father of all Flesh': Porno-Political Rhetoric and Political Theory in and after the English Civil War," *Prose Studies* 14:3 (December 1991): 134–57 (at 139–44), and note "Letter from London," 20 April 1653, in *Calendar of the Clarendon State Papers*, ed. H. O. Coxe et al. (Oxford, UK: Clarendon Press, 1872–1970), II 200.

[54] See Barber, *A Revolutionary Rogue*, 47–89.

or a presbyterian as the east is from the west; for he was a boon companion, was of Harry Marten's gang, was of the natural religion, and loved to enjoy the comfortable importances of this life, without any thought of laying up for a wet day, which at his last he wanted." The latter, who translated and extended Lucan's *Pharsalia* and who was wont to draw comparisons between revolutionary England and republican Rome, this distinguished antiquarian describes as "a debauchee ad omnia," who "entertained ill principles as to religion, spoke often very slightingly of the *Holy Trinity*, [and] kept beastly and atheistical company, of whom Tho. Chaloner the regicide was one."[55]

Much the same can be said for John Wildman and Henry Neville. In December 1648, when the Council of Officers met at Whitehall to consider the Levellers' second *Agreement of the People*, Wildman made an open display of religious agnosticism when he rose to deny emphatically that magistrates should be accorded any role in policing conscience.[56] Many years later, John Toland was told that in conversation concerning "the many sects of Religion in the world" Wildman and Anthony Ashley Cooper, first earl of Shaftesbury,

came to this conclusion at last; that notwithstanding those infinite divisions caus'd by the interest of the Priests and the ignorance of the People, All Wise Men Are of the Same Religion: whereupon a Lady in the room, who seem'd to mind her needle more than their Discourse, demanded with some concern what that Religion was? to whom the Lord Shaftesbury strait reply'd, Madam, wise men never tell. And indeed, considering how dangerous it is made to tell the truth, tis difficult to know when any man declares his real sentiment of things.[57]

Neville was even more inclined than Wildman to flaunt his impiety, savoring, as he did, its capacity to shock. On one occasion, in 1648 or 1649, he reportedly remarked that "nothing could be said for the Scripture which could not be said for the Alcoran."[58] Ten years after Wildman's display of skepticism, Neville would be charged with "atheism and blasphemy" by a fellow member

---

[55] See Wood, *Athenæ Oxonienses*, III 531–33, 809–10, who is drawing on *ABL*, 158, 269, and consider "Notes on Report of Sir Allan Broderick to Edward Hyde," 24 June 1659, in *Calendar of the Clarendon State Papers*, IV 249. Note, in this connection, "Tom May's Death," in *The Complete Works of Andrew Marvell*, ed. Alexander B. Grosart (New York: AMS Press, 1966), I 237–40, and see David Norbrook, "Lucan, Thomas May, and the Emergence of a Republican Literary Culture," in *Culture and Politics in Early Stuart England*, ed. Kevin Sharpe and Peter Lake (Stanford, CA: Stanford University Press, 1993), 45–66, and *Writing the English Republic*, 23–65, 225–28, 271–80, and Raymond, *The Invention of the Newspaper*, 284–90.

[56] See "Council of Officers at Whitehall," 14 December 1648, in *The Clarke Papers: Selections from the Papers of William Clarke*, ed. C. H. Firth (London: Camden Society, 1891–1901), II 120–21, which is reprinted in *Puritanism and Liberty: Being the Army Debates (1647–9) from the Clarke Manuscripts with Supplementary Documents*, ed. A. S. P. Woodhouse (London: J. M. Dent and Sons, 1938), 125–69 (at 160–61), and in *The Levellers in the English Revolution*, ed. G. E. Aylmer (Ithaca, NY: Cornell University Press, 1975), 139–41.

[57] See John Toland, "Clidophorous, or Of the Esoteric and Exoteric Philosophy," in Toland, *Tetradymus* (London: J. Brotherton and W. Meadows, 1720), 94–95.

[58] See "Notes on Report from Sir Arthur Slingsby to Edward Hyde," 25 February 1659, in *Calendar of the Clarendon State Papers*, IV 152. For one aspect of Neville's subsequent career, see Nicholas von Maltzahn, "Henry Neville and the Art of the Possible: A Republican *Letter Sent to General Monk* (1660)," *The Seventeenth Century* 7:1 (Spring, 1992): 41–52.

of Richard Cromwell's Parliament when he was overheard remarking – in the presence of three clergymen, no less – that "he was more affected by reading Cicero than the Bible." At the time, it was thought revealing that his defenders were less inclined to deny the charge than to argue for its dismissal on procedural grounds.[59]

There can be little doubt as to Neville's hostility to organized religion. In a dialogue that he penned later in his life, his spokesman would aver that he "could wish there had never been any" clergy at all.[60] The letter purportedly written by Machiavelli on April Fool's Day some ten years after his own death that Neville forged for inclusion in the preface to his translation of the Florentine's works includes a lengthy diatribe against the Roman Catholic clergy that is obviously applicable to the priests and prelates of other sects.[61] In the course of denouncing the "insatiable Ambition and Avarice" of the "Bishops of *Rome*" and the depredations of their "*Janizaries*," Neville's Machiavelli denounced the clergy as "the Causers of all the Solicisms and Immoralities in Government, and of all the Impieties and Abominations in Religion, and by consequence of all the Disorder, Villany, and Corruption we suffer under in this detestable Age."[62] In the dialogue Neville published five years thereafter, his spokesman restated this argument in some detail.[63]

Of the entire group with whom Nedham was associated, one could say what the Anglican divine Gilbert Burnet later wrote of Marten, Wildman, Sidney, and Neville: that they "pretended to little or no religion, and acted only upon the principles of civil liberty."[64] If, when Henry Marten denounced "*all* [the]

[59] Consider the entry under 16 February 1658/1659, in *Diary of Thomas Burton, Esq., Member in the Parliaments of Oliver and Richard Cromwell from 1656 to 1659*, ed. John Towill Rutt (London: Henry Colburn, 1828), III 296–305, in light of the Letter from M. de Bordeaux to Cardinal Mazarin on 27 February 1659, in François Pierre Guillaume Guizot, *Histoire du protectorat de Richard Cromwell et du rétablissement des Stuart (1658–1660)*, second edition (Paris: Didier, 1856), I 309–14 (at 311), and see "Notes on Report of John Barwick to Edward Hyde," 16 February 1659, and "Notes on Report of Sir Arthur Slingsby to Edward Hyde," 25 February 1649, in *Calendar of the Clarendon State Papers*, IV 150, 152.

[60] See Henry Neville, *Plato Redivivus* (1681), in *Two English Republican Tracts*, ed. Caroline Robbins (London: Cambridge University Press, 1969), 115.

[61] For a useful discussion, see Vickie B. Sullivan, *Machiavelli, Hobbes, and the Formation of a Liberal Republicanism in England* (New York: Cambridge University Press, 2004), 173–98, who nonetheless fails to see that, despite his disclaimers, the argument advanced by Neville's Machiavelli applies to Anglicanism and to most of the other Protestant sects.

[62] See *The Works of the Famous Nicholas Machiavel, Citizen and Secretary of Florence* (London: John Starkey, 1675) sig. (***) r – sig. (***2) r.

[63] See *Plato Redivivus*, 115–19.

[64] See Burnet, *The History of My Own Time*, I 120. See also "Notes on Report of John Cooper to Edward Hyde," 17 March 1659, and "Notes on Report of John, baron Mordaunt of Reigate, viscount Mordaunt of Avalon, to Edward Hyde," 6 June 1659, in *Calendar of the Clarendon State Papers*, IV 161, 222, where we are told that that Henry Neville is "an Atheist and Commonwealth's man" and, then, that "H. Nevill is of no religion" at all. On Sidney, whom scholars tend to think a religious man, cf. Blair Worden, "The Commonwealth Kidney of Algernon Sidney," *Journal of British Studies* 24:1 (January 1985): 1–40; Jonathan Scott, *Algernon Sidney and the English Republic, 1623–1677* (Cambridge, UK: Cambridge University Press, 1988), and *Algernon Sidney and the Restoration Crisis, 1677–1683* (Cambridge, UK: Cambridge University Press, 1991); and J. G. A. Pocock, "England's Cato: The Virtues and Fortunes of Algernon

210   *Machiavellian Republicanism Anglicized*

King craft...and Court-craft in the world," he included in his denunciation *"Clergy craft"* as well, it was because, like most of the highly educated in their day, he and his closest allies were familiar with Lucretius, with Machiavelli, and with Paolo Sarpi's now forgotten *History of the Council of Trent*, which had fleshed out in detail for all to digest the logic underpinning Machiavelli's contention that, by playing on the fears generated by the natural human propensity for superstition, Christianity had "rendered the world weak" and had "given it in prey to wicked men." Their self-chosen task, pursued with great vigor by *Mercurius Britanicus* and *Mercurius Politicus*, was to expose to the disdain of the larger world the various techniques, closely akin to witchcraft, by which cunning kings, courtiers, and clergymen had established and sustained, in Catholic and Protestant lands alike, a dominion that Sir Francis Bacon had once obliquely praised Machiavelli for depicting as both *"tyrannical and unjust."*[65]

It is, therefore, in no way surprising that, in the very first issue of *Mercurius Politicus*, Nedham should denounce the royalists and their presbyterian allies as *"Priest ridden,"* and that he should subsequently argue that "for the carrying on" of their "traiterous *Designe"* the latter "have farr out-stript the *Jesuit*, both in *Practise and Project."* It makes sense that he should contend that his contemporaries, for all of their sophistication, "may be still at the same pass" as their *"Fore-Fathers"* since the *"new Clergie* are still the same *Idol*, only a little disguised with a new dress of *Mummery,"* and it is perfectly fitting that he should similarly depict "the vanity of admiring *Kings*, [of] placing Them

---

Sidney," *Historical Journal* 37:4 (December 1994): 915–35, with Sullivan, *Machiavelli, Hobbes, and the Formation of a Liberal Republicanism in England*, 199–226.

[65] Consider [Henry Marten], *Corrector of the Answerer of the Speech without Doores* (Edinburgh, UK: Evan Tyler, 1646), 7, in light of Pietro Soave Polano [which is an anagram for Paolo Sarpi Veneto], *A Historie of the Councel of Trent*, tr. Nathanael Brent (London: Robert Barker and John Bill, 1620); note Machiavelli, *Discorsi* 2.2.2, in *Opere*, 149–50, which is cited at length in Chapter Two, this volume, and see Bacon, "Of Goodness and Goodness of Nature," *Essayes or Counsels, Civill and Morall*, ed. Michael Kiernan, XIII, in *OFB*, XV 38–41. Sarpi's book has an interesting history. It was smuggled out of Venice in 1618 by the English ambassador in a series of discrete parcels. In London, with support from James I, Sir Francis Bacon, and the archbishop of Canterbury, it was edited by Marc'Antonio de Dominis, the renegade Catholic archbishop of Split, published in the original Italian, and then translated into virtually every European language for circulation throughout Western Christendom. The Anglicans who sponsored its publication and the Protestants on the continent who embraced it seem not to have recognized at the time that its acid analysis of what came to be called priestcraft could and would soon be turned against them. See Francis A. Yates, "Paolo Sarpi's 'History of the Council of Trent,'" *Journal of the Warburg and Courtauld Institute* 7 (1944): 123–43; Gaetano Cozzi, "Fra Paolo Sarpi, l'anglicanesimo e la *Historia del Concilio Tridentino*," *Rivista storica italiana* 68:4 (December 1956): 556–619; and Noel Malcolm, *De Dominis, 1560–1624: Venetian, Anglican, Ecumenist, and Relapsed Heretic* (London: Strickland & Scott Academic, 1984), 35–60. For an overview, see Peter Burke, "The Great Unmasker: Paolo Sarpi, 1552–1623," *History Today* 15:6 (June 1965): 426–32, and David Wootton, *Paolo Sarpi: Between Renaissance and Enlightenment* (Cambridge, UK: Cambridge University Press, 1983). See also, and Vittorio Frajese, "Sarpi e la tradizione scettica," *Studi storici* 29:4 (October–December 1988): 1029–50, "Sarpi interprete del *De la sagesse* de Pierre Charron: I *Pensieri sulla religione*," *Studi Veneziani* 29 (1990): 59–85, and *Sarpi scettico: Stato e chiesa a Venezia tra Cinque e Seicento* (Bologna: Il Mulino, 1994), as well as Alberto Tenenti, "Libertinismo e etica politica in Paolo Sarpi," *Studi Veneziani* 38 (1999): 67–77.

in a lofty seat of *Impunity*, like *Gods*," as a species of "*Idolatry*" grounded in a "*Superstition*" inculcated by the "*antiquated Cheats of the Clergy.*" By eliminating ecclesiastical jurisdiction altogether and by rigorously subordinating the church to a republican state, Nedham hoped to strip from "the *mystery of Tyranny*" all the "gaudy Robes, and gay Appearances" conferred upon it by "*ancient Christian Policie.*"[66]

To grasp fully what such a reform entailed, one must attend carefully to the third issue of the English commonwealth's semi-official gazette, wherein its editor makes a passing, but highly revealing observation to the effect that "*Churchmen* of all Religions and Nations are of the same humor, to imbroile the world up to the ears in Blood rather than part with one Tit[t]le of that Power and Profit, which may serve to satisfie the avarice and Ambition of their Interest and order."[67] In the 1640s and 1650s, when Marchamont Nedham and his sponsors threw their weight behind the independents – echoing Milton's as yet unpublished claim that "*New Presbyter* is but *Old Priest* writ Large," insisting on a radical interpretation of the Protestant doctrine of the priesthood of all believers, and contending that "*with God there is no respect of Persons*"[68] – they harbored intentions regarding the Christian religion far more subversive than their godly republican allies ever imagined.[69]

---

[66] See *MP* 1 (6–13 June 1650): 4; 55 (19–26 June 1651): 879–82; 56 (26 June–3 July 1651): 885–87; 58 (10–17 July 1651): 917–18; and 99 (22–29 April 1652): 1553–56. For a systematic statement of Nedham's critique of presbyterianism, see *MP* 114 (5–12 August 1652): 1785–89.

[67] See *MP* 3 (20–27 June 1650): 46. Then, ponder the extensive evidence for there being an intimate link between anticlericalism and English republicanism: *MP* 2 (13–20 June 1650): 17–18; 3 (20–27 June 1650): 33–34, 40, 43; 4 (27 June–4 July 1650): 56–57, 62; 5 (4–11 July 1650): 70–72; 6 (11–18 July 1650): 84; 7 (18–25 July 1650): 107–8; 8 (25 July–1 August 1650): 113–15, 126–27; 10 (8–15 August 1650): 146–47; 13 (29 August–5 September 1650): 193–95, 201; 15 (12–19 September 1650): 259; 17 (26 September–3 October 1650): 291; 50 (15–22 May 1651): 813–14; 54 (12–19 June 1651): 863–65; 60 (24–31 July 1651): 949–51; 61 (31 July–7 August 1651): 965–67 (where the pagination is confused); 63 (14–21 August 1651): 997–99; 67 (11–18 September 1651): 1061–63; 99 (22–29 April 1652): 1553–56. Needless to say, it is by no means fortuitous that, in this context, Nedham makes pointed reference to the Council of Trent: *MP* 5 (4–11 July 1650): 72.

[68] Note *MP* 58 (10–17 July 1651): 918, and see Milton, "On the New Forcers of Conscience under the Long Parliament" (August 1646?), in *CW*, I:1 71, which should be read in conjunction with *Areopagitica* (November 1644), in *CPW*, II 537–42. Although inclined to an exceedingly latitudinarian Erastianism, Nedham preferred religious liberty along the lines envisaged by Milton to the species of Erastianism promoted by independents, such as John Owen, who were no less prone to zeal than their presbyterian opponents: see Worden, *Literature and Politics in Cromwellian England*, 249–54.

[69] To a remarkable degree, the evidence for the outlook of this group of men has escaped the notice of those scholars who have searched for evidence of religious skepticism in this period: see G. E. Aylmer, "Unbelief in Seventeenth-Century England," in *Puritans and Revolutionaries: Essays in Seventeenth-Century History*, ed. Donald Pennington and Keith Thomas (Oxford, UK: Clarendon Press, 1978), 22–46, and Christopher Hill, "Freethinking and Libertinism: The Legacy of the English Revolution," in *The Margins of Orthodoxy: Heterodox Writing and Cultural Response, 1660–1750*, ed. Roger D. Lund (Cambridge, UK: Cambridge University Press, 1996), 54–70. Unfortunately, Michael Hunter, "The Problem of 'Atheism' in Early Modern England," *Transactions of the Royal Historical Society* 5th ser., 35 (1985): 135–57, limits his purview to the period before the English Civil War.

Mercurius Politicus

For almost a year, starting in late September 1650, some weeks after the Round-head victory over the Scots at Dunbar, Nedham reprinted in *Mercurius Politicus* excerpts from *The Case of the Commonwealth of England Stated*.[70] Then, soon after the New Model Army's decisive victory at the battle of Worcester on 3 September 1651 had put paid to royalist hopes, brought an end to the emergency, and opened up the possibility that there would soon be a general constitutional settlement, Nedham reversed this procedure, gradually elaborating in newsbook editorials published in the period stretching from 9 October 1651 to 12 August 1652 much of the argument that would make up the book that he promised his readers he would eventually publish: *The Excellencie of a Free State*.[71]

In excerpting his tract in support of the Engagement, Nedham made only minor revisions – but he did omit three-quarters of the work, dropping the scholarly apparatus and many of the historical examples, eliminating altogether the chapters on fate and on the Levellers, rearranging what remained, and altering a word or phrase from time to time. He also took care to excise positive references to Machiavelli and to add passages disparaging the Florentine; and, though he once again quoted extensively from Hobbes's discussion of the connection between protection and obedience, he failed to give the royalist author the attribution he deserved.[72]

For the most part, these changes were probably dictated by the character of the audience for which *Mercurius Politicus* was at first intended.[73] The scholarly apparatus and historical examples would have been of little interest to most of the Commonwealth's Puritan supporters. In general, they regarded Machiavelli and Hobbes as suspect, and they were far more likely to attribute

---

[70] For a list of the passages reprinted, see either J. Milton French, "Milton, Needham, and *Mercurius Politicus*," *Studies in Philology* 33 (1936): 236–52 (at 239–42), and Elmer A. Beller, "Milton and *Mercurius Politicus*," *Huntington Library Quarterly* 5:4 (July 1942): 479–87 (at 480), or Frank, *Cromwell's Press Agent*, 182–84.

[71] See Frank, *Cromwell's Press Agent*, 93–101. For Nedham's promise, see *MP* 97 (8–15 April 1652): 1525–26. For a list of the editorials that he recycled, see either French, "Milton, Needham, and *Mercurius Politicus*," 242–44, and H. Sylvia Anthony, "*Mercurius Politicus* under Milton," *Journal of the History of Ideas* 27:4 (October 1966): 593–609, or Frank, *Cromwell's Press Agent*, 183–85. In *The Excellencie of a Free State*, Nedham drew on only three editorials published prior to the battle of Worcester: see *MP* 36 (6–13 February 1651): 575–76; 37 (13–20 February 1651): 591–93; and 64 (21–28 August 1651): 1013–16. Note also *MP* 68 (18–25 September 1651): 1077–79.

[72] See *MP* 31 (2–9 January 1651): 503–4; 32 (2–16 January 1651): 519–20; 33 (16–23 January 1651): 535–36; 34 (23–30 January 1651): 551–52. Charles I's Protestant Dutch champion Salmasius received the treatment meted out to Hobbes: see *MP* 27 (5–12 December 1650): 439–40; 28 (12–19 December 1650): 455–57; 29 (19–26 December 1650): 471–73

[73] There is speculation that John Milton, Nedham's licenser from 17 March 1651 to 22 January 1652, played a role in shaping the revisions. This is possible, but it unnecessarily complicates the story. An operator like Nedham had to be acutely sensitive to the proclivities of his audience and would quite naturally make revisions in light of his changing perception of the rhetorical situation. Cf. Anthony, "*Mercurius Politicus* under Milton," 593–609, with Parker, *Milton*, II 948–49.

the establishment of the republic to divine Providence than to the accidents of fate.[74]

For suppressing his critique of the Levellers, however, Nedham seems to have had reasons all his own. In the mid and late 1640s, he had been on the best of terms with John Lilburne. In January 1645, he had contributed a laudatory preface, signed M. N., to Lilburne's *An Answer to Nine Arguments*.[75] In 1646, the two are thought to have co-authored at least one pamphlet, *Vox Plebis*, if not more;[76] and, as we have had opportunity to observe, Nedham had occasionally made common cause with the Levellers.[77] By the time that his Engagement tract appeared, the Leveller mutinies had been put down, and Leveller opposition had ceased to pose a threat to the new regime.[78] In the months that followed, moreover, their critique of the Rump began to ring increasingly true.

Nedham's *Case of the Commonwealth of England Stated* had been a job application: in it, as one would expect, he was willing to give his prospective employers every benefit of the doubt. In only one passage did he appear to be agitating for action on the part of the Rump, and even there his concern may have been evident only in retrospect. "How much safer, then," he wrote in the course of criticizing the Levellers, "must it needs be for the people of this nation, to leave the succession of representatives and the form of a council in the future, with the time and manner of their constitution and rules for election, to be ordered by the wisdom and discretion of Parliament than after the humor of some obscure persons whose knowledge and interest in the public matters is no whit comparable to theirs and therefore not to be valued in competition with them for the ordering of such affairs as so highly concern the good and peace of the public."[79]

In this particular, as the Levellers had repeatedly warned, it turned out to be considerably less safe to trust in the wisdom and discretion of the Rump than Nedham had led his readers to expect. The members of this assembly recognized perfectly well that upon which everyone else was agreed: that the

---

[74] See Frank, *Cromwell's Press Agent*, 90–92. Pertinent to a consideration of the last of my three points is Blair Worden, "Oliver Cromwell and the Sin of Achan," in *History, Society and the Churches: Essays in Honour of Owen Chadwick*, ed. Derek Beales and Geoffrey Best (Cambridge, UK: Cambridge University Press, 1985), 125–45. For further discussion along similar lines, see Worden, "Providence and Politics in Cromwellian England," *Past & Present* 109 (November 1985): 55–99.

[75] See [John Lilburne], *An Answer to Nine Arguments* (London: [s.n.], 1645).

[76] Cf. *Vox Plebis, or, The Peoples Out-Cry against Oppression, Injustice, and Tyranny* (London: [s.n.], 1646), 1–3 and 60–68, which reflect Nedham's peculiar preoccupations, with the rest of the pamphlet, which echoes Lilburne's characteristic concerns, and then see Worden, "'Wit in a Roundhead,'" 320–21, along with Scott, *Commonwealth Principles*, 82–84, 115, 137, 220, 241–47.

[77] For the details, see Frank, *Cromwell's Press Agent*, 20–21, 28; Worden, "'Wit in a Roundhead,'" 320–21; Raymond, *The Invention of the Newspaper*, 186–87; and Scott, *Commonwealth Principles*, 82–84, 241–47. In this connection, see Jason T. Peacey, "John Lilburne and the Long Parliament," *The Historical Journal* 43:3 (September 2000): 625–45

[78] See Underdown, *Pride's Purge*, 261, 267–68, and Worden, *The Rump Parliament*, 186–236 (esp. 186–202, 213–21).

[79] Nedham, CCES, 106.

Long Parliament's sitting had gone on too long. The army's Council of Officers had reminded them of this fact in no uncertain terms on 20 January 1649
when they presented to them a revised version of the Leveller's second *Agreement of the People*, calling for a dissolution by the end of April, demanding
reapportionment, a reformed franchise, and provision for biennial elections.[80]
Two months later, when the Rump voted to abolish the monarchy, its members responded pointedly to the army's challenge by resolving also to "put a
period to the sitting of this present Parliament, and dissolve the same so soon
as may possibly stand with the safety of the people that hath betrusted them,
and with what is absolutely necessary for the preserving and upholding the
Government now settled in the way of a Commonwealth," and they promised
at the same time to "carefully provide for the certain choosing, meeting, and
sitting of the next and future representatives, with such other circumstances of
freedom in choice and equality in distribution of members to be elected thereunto, as shall most conduce to the lasting freedom and good of this Commonwealth."[81]

The Rump found it relatively easy to work out a design for reapportionment;
and, once its members took up the subject in earnest, they moved with some
alacrity to reform the franchise.[82] But they were understandably reluctant and
slow to make provision for fresh elections – for they had every reason to suspect
that, even if known royalists were excluded from the electorate and the list of
parliamentary candidates, genuinely free elections would result in their own
repudiation and replacement and eventuate in a restoration of the monarchy.
And so they persistently toyed with the unsatisfactory expedient of holding
closely regulated and managed by-elections, instead – aiming solely thereby at
the recruitment of new members to fill the seats left empty by death, resignation,
withdrawal, and seclusion.[83] With the passage of time, the Leveller critique
gained in plausibility.

Nowhere, to be sure, did Nedham ever explicitly criticize the government
of the day. His was, after all, a mercenary pen; and ostensibly he was, at any
given moment, fully at the disposal of the powers then in place. Yet one can
hardly read the highly didactic editorials that he published in *Mercurius Politicus* during the year following the battle of Worcester without recognizing that

[80] Cf. "The Agreement of the People," 15 January 1649, in *CDPR*, 359–71 (esp. 359–64), and
in *Leveller Manifestoes of the Puritan Revolution*, ed. Don M. Wolfe (New York: Humanities
Press, 1967), 331–54 (esp. 337–42), with "Foundations of Freedom: Or an Agreement of the
People," 15 December 1648, in *Puritanism and Liberty*, 355–67, and in *Leveller Manifestoes of
the Puritan Revolution*, 293–303; then, see Barbara Taft, "The Council of Officers' *Agreement
of the People*, 1648/9," *Historical Journal* 28:1 (March 1985): 169–85.

[81] "The Act Abolishing the Office of King," 17 March 1649, in *CDPR*, 384–87 (at 386–87).

[82] See Vernon F. Snow, "Parliamentary Reapportionment Proposals in the Puritan Revolution,"
English Historical Review 74:292 (July 1959): 409–42, and Worden, *The Rump Parliament*,
139–60.

[83] For the details, see Worden, *The Rump Parliament*, 1–262 (esp. 161–262), and Austyn H. Woolrych, *Commonwealth to Protectorate* (Oxford, UK: Clarendon Press, 1982), 1–67. For the
species of recruitment practiced prior to Pride's Purge, see David Underdown, "Party Management in the Recruiter Elections, 1645–1648," *English Historical Review* 83:327 (April 1968):
235–64.

their author was conducting a political campaign aimed at what Milton would later dismiss as "the conceit of successive Parlaments."[84]

It is in no way surprising that Nedham lent a hand when, in the wake of the battle of Worcester, Oliver Cromwell returned from the army to Westminster and launched a campaign, with at least a semblance of support from Neville, Chaloner, and Marten, to persuade the Rump to pass a constitutional settlement guaranteeing frequent elections and successive Parliaments.[85] There is even reason to suspect that Nedham was, by then, itching to enter the fray, for he appears to have had a version of his *Excellencie of a Free State* ready in draft when the critical occasion presented itself;[86] and, on the very day in which Parliament finished electing the committee tasked with drawing up the bill for a new representative, he launched his campaign by repeating a pointed remark already made in *The Case of the Commonwealth of England Stated* – the significance of which Cromwell and his colleagues in the Rump could hardly mistake: "It is," Nedham began, "a noble saying, though *Machiavel's*; *Not he that placeth a vertuous government in his own Hands, or family, but he that establisheth a free and lasting Form, for the peoples constant security, is most to be commended.*"[87]

The Impasse

Unfortunately, for new elections, the time only seemed to be ripe. The victory at Worcester in early September 1651 had, in fact, done nothing to alter the crucial circumstance hobbling the regicide republic – for at no time after the execution of Charles Stuart on 30 January 1649 was there any likelihood that a parliament freely elected on any practicable franchise would sustain the Commonwealth of England, as it was then established, "without a King or House of Lords."

As we have seen, the members of the Rump understood this quite early on: it was for this reason that they kept coming back to the idea of recruiting new members to fill their ranks. In the end, desperate, though he was, to find an expedient for broadening the new regime's base of support, Oliver Cromwell

---

[84] See *The Readie & Easie Way to Establish a Free Commonwealth*, First Edition (February 1660), in CPW, VII 369.

[85] Note Worden, *The Rump Parliament*, 265–316 (esp. 265–67), and Woolrych, *Commonwealth to Protectorate*, 25–67 (esp. 26–27), where we learn that Neville, Chaloner, and Marten were elected on 24–25 September 1651 to the committee tasked with drawing up the bill for a new representative, and see Worden, "Milton and Marchamont Nedham," 166–74, and "Marchamont Nedham and the Beginnings of English Republicanism," 60–74.

[86] See Anthony, "*Mercurius Politicus* under Milton," 596, 600–04, and Worden, "Marchamont Nedham and the Beginnings of English Republicanism," 418, n. 37, who draws attention to the fact that Nedham's close friend and long-time collaborator, John Hall, must have had a draft of *The Excellencie of a Free State* ready to hand when he wrote *The Grounds & Reasons of Monarchy Considered* (London: [s.n.], 1650). The version printed in *The Oceana and Other Works of James Harrington*, ed. John Toland (London: T. Becket, T. Cadell, and T. Evans, 1771), 1–30, has been tinkered with by Toland. Hall had been hired early on by the Council of State to write pamphlets on the commonwealth's behalf: see Entry under 14 May 1649, in *Calendar of State Papers, Domestic Series, 1649–1660*, I 139 (1649–50).

[87] Cf. *MP* 68 (18–25 September 1651): 1077 with Nedham, *CCES*, 118, and see Machiavelli, *Discorsi* 1.9–10, in *Opere*, 90–93.

came to understood this as well: it was for this reason chiefly that he intervened on 20 April 1653 to oust the Rump. In the discussions that he been
carrying on with the Council of Officers from October 1652 on, he had hit
on what, in his mood of increasing frustration and despair, he took to be an
expedient. His plan he revealed to a handful of his parliamentary colleagues
the evening of 19 April 1653, when he suggested that a handpicked council of
"known persons, men fearing God, and of approved integrity" could perhaps
accomplish what the Rump had failed to achieve and, by carrying out "a just
and righteous reformation," appease their disaffected compatriots, make them
"forget Monarchy," and persuade them of "their true interest in the election of
successive Parliaments."[88]

To the bill for a new representative – then, finally, under sustained pressure
from the army, taking shape in the Rump – Cromwell raised two objections.
On the one hand, he treated as highly suspicious the Rump's unprecedented
plan to delay its dissolution until after the elections and to adjudicate those
elections itself, thereby making those of its members seeking reelection judges
in their own cause; and he expressed fear, perhaps with some reason, that the
members of the Rump aimed in this fashion "to make use" of the bill for
a new representative "to recruit the House with persons of the same spirit
and temper, thereby to perpetuate their own sitting." On the other hand, he
appears to have been firmly persuaded that they would fail in this supposed
scheme and that presbyterians, neuters, and others profoundly hostile to the
regicides and their republic would ultimately gain sway. When the Rump sought
to forestall the Lord General's alternative plan by abruptly passing the bill for a
new representative the morning after his alternative had first in private conclave
been broached, Oliver Cromwell erupted in fury, doffed his velvet gloves, and
revealed the iron fist hitherto concealed within.[89]

[88] Consider "Declaration by the Lord General and the Council on the Dissolution of the Long
Parliament," 22 April 1653, in *CDPR*, 400–04 (esp. 402–3), in light of Whitelocke, *Memorials
of the English Affairs*, IV 4–6, and *The Diary of Bulstrode Whitelocke*, 285–87, and *The Memoirs
of Edmund Ludlow, Lieutenant-General of the Horse in the Army of the Commonwealth of
England, 1625–1672*, ed. C. H. Firth (Oxford, UK: Clarendon Press, 1894), I 349–51, and
see Worden, *The Rump Parliament*, 317–84 (esp. 333–35), and Woolrych, *Commonwealth to
Protectorate*, 24–67 (esp. 50–53, 62–65). Ludlow's memoirs, which we have for the years prior
to 1660 only in a version edited, abbreviated, and thoroughly rewritten by John Toland in such
a manner as to tone down or even eliminate the author's apocalyptic religiosity and make him
seem like a late-seventeenth-century Country Whig, remain valuable as a source nonetheless.
But they do need to be used by historians with discretion and care – especially where religion
and matters pertinent to the preoccupations of Country Whigs at the time of the standing-army
controversy are under discussion; and one needs to keep in mind that, where the memoirs seem
to confirm our other sources, Ludlow or Toland may simply be paraphrasing those same sources.
For a thorough discussion, see Blair Worden, "Introduction," in Edmund Ludlow, *A Voyce from
the Watch Tower, Part Five: 1660–1662*, ed. A. B. Worden, Camden Fourth Series, Volume 21
(London: The Royal Historical Society, 1978), 1–80. See also Worden, *Roundhead Reputations:
The English Civil Wars and the Passions of Posterity* (London: Allen Lane, 2001), 21–121.
[89] First, consider the defensive tone of, the equivocal language deployed in, and the inconsis-
tencies evident in Cromwell's repeated apologies for his intervention: see "Declaration by the
Lord General and the Council on the Dissolution of the Long Parliament," 22 April 1653, in
CDPR, 400–04 (esp. 401); along with "Speech to the Nominated Parliament," 4 July 1653; "His
Highnesse the Lord Protector's Speech to the Parliament in the Painted Chamber," 12 September 1654; and "Speech to the Committee," 21 April 1657, in *WrSOC*, III 52–66 (esp. 54–60),

Quietly and respectfully, we are told, he entered the chamber. He took his seat and listened for a time to the debate, and then rose to speak. At first he seemed calm. He even praised the Rump. But, then, he suddenly reversed course and charged its members with injustice and self-dealing; and, impulsive as always, Cromwell gave way to a towering rage; poured forth his fury on Bulstrode Whitelocke, Henry Marten, Sir Peter Wentworth, Thomas Chaloner, Henry Neville, Sir Arthur Haselrig, and his old friend Sir Henry Vane; and had his soldiers put an end to their sitting forthwith. "I will put an end to your prating," he said. "You are no Parliament. I say, you are no Parliament."[90]

Seven weeks thereafter, Cromwell put his bold plan into effect. Acting ostensibly on behalf of the Council of Officers, in his capacity as Lord General, he summoned to the so-called Nominated Parliament "divers persons fearing God, and of approved fidelity and honesty."[91] The result was not at all what he had anticipated. Profound divisions emerged almost immediately after this assembly's first meeting on 4 July 1653, pitting the religious radicals in its membership – above all, the Fifth Monarchists, who, in anticipation of the Apocalypse, regarded the gathering as a Parliament of Saints called upon to rule by the grace of God – against their less confident brethren, who could neither respect nor stomach their colleagues' claims to divine inspiration; and the

451–62 (esp. 453–54), IV 484–97 (esp. 486–88). Then, read with care the semi-official report that appeared in *Several Proceedings in Parliament* 186 (14–21 April 1653): 2944, which is reprinted in William Cobbett, *Parliamentary History of England, from the Norman Conquest in 1066 to the Year 1803* (London: T. C. Hansard, 1806–1820), III 1381–82, and in WrSOC, II 645–46, and the report that Gilbert Mabbott sent the army on 23 April 1653, in *The Clarke Papers*, III 1–2. Then, cf. C. H. Firth, "Cromwell and the Expulsion of the Long Parliament in 1653," *English Historical Review* 8:31 (July 1893): 526–34, and "The Expulsion of the Long Parliament," *History* n. s. 2 (1917–18): 129–43, 193–206, with Blair Worden, "The Bill for a New Representative: The Dissolution of the Long Parliament, April 1653," *English Historical Review* 86:340 (July 1971): 473–96, and see Worden, *The Rump Parliament*, 139–60, 265–384 (esp. 333–39, 345–63). Cf. Woolrych, *Commonwealth to Protectorate*, 24–102 (esp. 62–67), and note Sarah Barber, "Irish Undercurrents to the Politics of April 1653," *Historical Research* 65 (1992): 315–35, and Sean Kelsey, *Inventing a Republic: The Political Culture of the English Commonwealth, 1649–1653* (Stanford, CA: Stanford University Press, 1997), 151–99. For an overview, see J. S. A. Adamson, "Oliver Cromwell and the Long Parliament," in *Oliver Cromwell and the English Revolution*, ed. John Morrill (London: Longman, 1990), 49–92.

90 See *Journal of the Earl of Leicester*, 20 April 1653, in *Sydney Papers, Consisting of a Journal of the Earl of Leicester, and Original Letters of Algernon Sydney*, ed. R. W. Blencowe (London: John Murray, 1825), 139–41; *The Memoirs of Edmund Ludlow*, I 351–56; Whitelocke, *Memorials of the English Affairs*, IV 5–7, and *The Diary of Bulstrode Whitelocke*, 285–87; "Letter from London," 20 April 1653, in *Calendar of the Clarendon State Papers*, II 200; "Diary of Denis Bond," MS., Dorset Record Office: 20 April 1653; John Streater, *Secret Reasons of State in Reference to the Affairs of These Nations, at the Interruption of this Present Parliament* (London: [s.n.], 1659), 3; and [James Heath], *Flagellum, or, The Life and Death, Birth and Burial of Oliver Cromwel* (London: L. R., 1663), 135; and John Forster, *The Statesmen of the Commonwealth*, ed. J. O. Choules (London: Longman, Brown, Green and Longmans, 1853), V 58–67. Apart from "The Letter from London" sent to Edward Hyde and the diary of Dennis Bond, who was then about to complete his tenure as President of the Council of State, to which Blair Worden, "Harrington's *Oceana*: Origins and Aftermath, 1651–1660," in *Republicanism, Liberty, and Commercial Society*, 111–38 (at 117 n. 18), draws our attention, the evidence is cited in full in WrSOC, II 640–45.

91 See "Summons to a Member of the So-Called Barebones Parliament," 6 June 1653, in *CDPR*, 405.

bitterness that then arose and grew thereafter eventually caused the Nominated Parliament to dissolve in acrimony on 12 December – at which time Cromwell was forced to confess that this brief experiment in godly rule had been a snare and a delusion.[92] The entire episode was, as he later put it, "a story of my own weakness and folly."[93]

Long before this, the regicide regime had reached an impasse. As the months dragged on after the execution of the king, its perpetrators had come to distrust one another. To an increasing degree, those in the Rump had come to regard the New Model Army as a mercenary force inured to meddling in political matters not within its sphere of competence and even to think it a tool ideally suited for use by a grandee ambitious for tyranny, while their counterparts in the army had come to look upon the Rump as an entrenched oligarchy whose members were intent on lining their pockets and perpetuating their rule. Both were right, of course, and both were profoundly wrong – for in the circumstances neither the army nor the Rump could have safely instituted "Parliaments rightly – that is, freely, equally and successively chosen" – of the sort which they and those who had supported Parliament in and after the civil wars against Charles I had always aimed to guarantee.[94] Moreover, given their own history and the many sacrifices that they had made along the path on which they had traveled since the Long Parliament first met on 3 November 1640, neither the army nor the Rump could have taken satisfaction in anything short of this goal.

It is not clear that Marchamont Nedham ever quite fully appreciated the predicament in which he and his fellow republicans found themselves. The editorials written in favor of frequent, successive parliaments, which he published in *Mercurius Politicus* in the months stretching from 9 October 1651 to 12 August 1652, treat this reform program as a panacea and cast aspersions on standing powers of every sort, military and civilian alike.[95] The same can be said for these essays collected and revised to reflect the change in circumstances, which his printer Thomas Brewster registered with the Stationers' Company on 28 November 1655,[96] and which he published as a tract late in June 1656 at what seemed a critical juncture not unlike the one that had putatively presented itself in the wake of the great Roundhead victory.

---

[92] For its rise and fall, see Woolrych, *Commonwealth to Protectorate*, 103–351.

[93] Note "Speech to the Committee," 21 April 1657, in *WrSOC*, IV 484–97 (at 489), and see Woolrych, *Commonwealth to Protectorate*, 103–351.

[94] For the passage quoted, see *A Declaration:, or Representation from His Excellency Sir Thomas Fairfax, and of the Army Under his Command, Humbly Tendered to the Parliament*, St. Albans, 14 June 1647, which is reprinted in *Puritanism and Liberty*, 403–9 (esp. 406–7), and in *The Stuart Constitution, 1603–1688: Documents and Commentary*, ed. John P. Kenyon (Cambridge, UK: Cambridge University Press, 1966), 295–301 (esp. 299–300).

[95] See Worden, "Marchamont Nedham and the Beginnings of English Republicanism," 62–74.

[96] For the date of registration, see *A Transcript of the Registers of the Worshipful Company of Stationers, 1640–1708*, ed. G. E. Briscoe Eyre (London: p.p., 1913–1914), II 20.

7

The Good Old Cause

On 20 April 1653, when Oliver Cromwell ousted the Rump and then intervened to shut down the Council of State as well, Marchamont Nedham's old patron John Bradshaw administered to the Commonwealth's Lord General a verbal slap in the face. "Sir," he said, "we have heard what you did in the House in the morning, and before many hours all England will hear it: but, Sir, you are mistaken to think that the parliament is dissolved; for no power under heaven can dissolve them but themselves; therefore take you notice of that." Similar sentiments were expressed by Sir Arthur Haselrig and Thomas Scot.[1]

Bradshaw, Haselrig, and Scot were not the first to breathe defiance.[2] Nor would they be the last. Parliament had entered the Civil War intent on preserving its prerogatives from encroachment by the king. It was inconceivable that any substantial number of those who so prided themselves on being its members would acquiesce in its dissolution at the hands of one of their own servants. Henry Marten spoke for the great majority of his colleagues when, in an open letter to Cromwell that he prudently refrained from dispatching to the printer, he accused the Lord General of having accomplished that fateful morning "the same thing which the last King and his Father did so long designe." Such was the considered opinion of those preeminent among his colleagues.[3]

---

[1] See *The Memoirs of Edmund Ludlow, Lieutenant-General of the Horse in the Army of the Commonwealth of England, 1625–1672*, ed. C. H. Firth (Oxford, UK: Clarendon Press, 1894), I 357, and Letter from Sir Edward Nicholas to Sir Edward Hyde on 22 May 1653, in *The Nicholas Papers: Correspondence of Sir Edward Nicholas*, ed. George F. Warner (Westminster: The Camden Society, 1886–1920), II 12–13.

[2] Sir Peter Wentworth and Sir Henry Vane spoke up that morning when Cromwell interrupted the sitting of the Rump: see *The Memoirs of Edmund Ludlow*, I 351–55. See also Bulstrode Whitelocke, *Memorials of the English Affairs from the Beginning of the Reign of Charles the First to the Happy Restoration of King Charles the Second* (Oxford, UK: Oxford University Press, 1853), IV 5–7, and *The Diary of Bulstrode Whitelocke, 1605–1675*, ed. Ruth Spalding (Oxford, UK: Oxford University Press, 1990), 285–87; and "Letter from London," 20 April 1653, in *Calendar of the Clarendon State Papers*, ed. H. O. Coxe et al. (Oxford, UK: Clarendon Press, 1872–1970), II 200.

[3] Cf. University of Leeds, Brotherton Collection, Marten Loder MSS vol. 93, ff. 2–4v, 39–40v, which can be found in C. M. Williams, "The Political Career of Henry Marten" (D. Phil. thesis, University of Oxford, 1954), 538–58 (Appendix C, no. 3), as cited in Sarah Barber, *A Revolutionary Rogue: Henry Marten and the English Republic* (Phoenix Mill: Sutton, 2000), 38–39, with Whitelocke, *Memorials of the English Affairs*, IV 6–7, and *The Diary of Bulstrode Whitelocke*, 286–87, and *The Memoirs of Edmund Ludlow*, I 357–58, 386–93, 406–36, II 6–36, 45–92. In this connection, see Blair Worden, *The Rump Parliament, 1648–1653* (Cambridge, UK: Cambridge

In the event, however, it mattered little what Bradshaw, Marten, Sir Peter Wentworth, Thomas Chaloner, Algernon Sidney, and Henry Neville thought of the matter, and the opinions of Haselrig, Scot, and Sir Henry Vane were of no greater significance. In the immediate aftermath of Cromwell's constitutional coup, no one with the power to act paid any appreciable attention when John Wildman outlined in his *Mite to the Treasury, of Consideration in the Common-wealth* what he took to be a workable republican constitutional plan. And the aldermen of London who signed petitions in late May, objecting to what Cromwell had done, demanding a reinstatement of the Rump, and calling for fresh elections were quickly deprived of office.[4] Real control rested with the New Model Army, and the army had had its fill of the Rump.[5] Cromwell's officers heartily welcomed his intervention, as they had that of Colonel Thomas Pride on 6 December 1648, and they were notably sanguine in early June 1653 when the Lord General summoned to the Nominated Parliament "divers persons fearing God, and of approved fidelity and honesty." If Cromwell's connivance in the collapse of this assembly on 12 December of that year and his establishment of the Protectorate four days thereafter seriously disturbed them, they nonetheless remained quiet. Major General Thomas Harrison, a leading member of the Council of Officers who had played a prominent role in selecting the membership of the Nominated Parliament, and a handful of religious radicals associated closely, as he was, with the Fifth Monarchists active in that assembly signaled their displeasure by resigning their commissions, but the rest remained silent.

Within the army, there was one significant exception to this pattern of acquiescence. John Streater was a printer by trade and a soldier by circumstance. He fought at Newbury, was wounded at Edgehill, and may well have done additional service during the second civil war. From 1650 to 1653, he was in Ireland, working at first as a fortifications engineer. There, he rose to become quartermaster general of the Commonwealth forces. In the spring of 1653, as it happens, Streater was on leave in London. In March, as if in anticipation of Cromwell's dismissal of the Rump, he published a tract on the preservation of liberty, urging popular vigilance, citing Roman precedents, and pointedly warning against entrusting any individual with excessive power.[6] In April, he attended some of the meetings, held at the Cockpit in Whitehall, in which Cromwell and his

University Press, 1974), 335–41, 364–65. Cf. Austin H. Woolrych, *Commonwealth to Protectorate* (Oxford, UK: Clarendon Press, 1982), 81–83. For a brief overview of the aftermath, see Sarah Barber, *Regicide and Republicanism: Politics and Ethics in the English Revolution* (Edinburgh, UK: Edinburgh University Press, 1998), 202–39. Consider also the fragmentary open letter that Henry Neville seems to have composed at about the same time: Berkshire Record Office, D/EN/F8/1, which is discussed in some detail in Blair Worden, "Harrington's *Oceana*: Origins and Aftermath, 1651–1660," in *Republicanism, Liberty, and Commercial Society, 1649–1776,* ed. David Wootton (Stanford, CA: Stanford University Press, 1994), 111–38 (at 116–20).

4 Note J[ohn] W[ildman], Well-Wisher to the Publique, *A Mite to the Treasury, of Consideration in the Common-wealth* (London: Thomas Newcomb, 1653), and see Barber, *Regicide and Republicanism,* 202–5.

5 See Whitelocke, *Memorials of the English Affairs,* IV 6, and *Diary of Bulstrode Whitelocke,* 287.

6 See John Streater, *A Glympse of that Jewel, Judicial, Just, Preserving Libertie* (London: Giles Calvert, 1653).

officers searched for a way out of the impasse that they and the Rump faced, and he was present there on 20 April when Cromwell spoke just before and after ousting the Rump. Horrified at what had transpired, Streater penned ten queries on the spot and shared his objections with those of his colleagues who were also in the room. These queries, which circulated thereafter in manuscript, questioned whether Cromwell's intervention was not, in fact, "a preparation to Absoluteness and Tyranny," and they raised the possibility that his officers might be persuaded to reverse course and arrange forthwith to have a new Parliament elected by the people "according to their undeniable Rights." From the army, Streater was soon thereafter discharged.

Being cashiered did not deter this intrepid soldier from following through on the logic of what he had written. Within six weeks, he was arrested; and on 27 August 1653, he was imprisoned on the authority of Cromwell's Nominated Parliament for writing, printing, and publishing a newsbook entitled *The Grand Politick Informer*, in which he criticized entrusting a commonwealth's arms to a single person, examined the means best suited for the prevention of despotism, and surveyed various ways in which power can be wrested from the hands of a tyrant. After he managed by way of legal challenges to secure his release from prison on 11 February 1654, Streater immediately returned to the fray, launching in April and May two short-lived newsbooks which he used as vehicles for exploring in abstract terms the political wisdom, pertinent to the current situation, which was to be found in *The Politics* of Aristotle, in the histories of Livy and Tacitus, and in Suetonius' biography of Julius Caesar. Streater's commentary on these classical texts left little doubt as to his hostility to the Protectorate and his preference that there be frequent parliamentary elections. He even hinted at the legitimacy of tyrannicide.[7] In these months, Streater seems to have been alone. Otherwise, at least in public, almost no one else spoke up.[8] But Streater's reaction to Cromwell's coup d'état was, nonetheless, a harbinger of the turmoil that was to come. It was this turmoil that would occasion Nedham's publication of *The Excellencie of a Free State*.

---

[7] See Adrian Johns, *The Nature of the Book: Print and Knowledge in the Making* (Chicago: University of Chicago Press, 1998), 266–87, and Joad Raymond, "John Streater and *The Grand Politick Informer*," *The Historical Journal* 41:2 (June 1998): 567–74. Note also Nigel Smith, "Popular Republicanism in the 1650s: John Streater's 'Heroick Mechanicks,'" in *Milton and Republicanism*, ed. David Armitage, Armand Himy, and Quentin Skinner (Cambridge, UK: Cambridge University Press, 1995), 137–55, and *Literature and Revolution in England, 1640–1660* (New Haven, CT: Yale University Press, 1994), 196–99, along with Jonathan Scott, *Commonwealth Principles: Republican Writing of the English Revolution* (Cambridge, UK: Cambridge University Press, 2004), 96–97, 116–17, 158–59, 178–81, 221–22, 269–70, 278–79. The biographical information provided by Robert Zaller, "John Streater (fl. 1642–1687)," in *Biographical Dictionary of British Radicals in the Seventeenth Century*, ed. Richard L. Greaves and Robert Zaller (Brighton, UK: Harvester Press, 1982–1984), III 211–12, is corrected and substantially supplemented in Johns, *The Nature of the Book*, 266–323.

[8] Much that was unfriendly to the Protectorate was, of course, privately committed to paper with pen and ink, and even more was no doubt conveyed in speech: see, for example, David Norbrook, "Lucy Hutchinson versus Edmund Waller: An Unpublished Reply to Waller's *A Panegyrick to my Lord Protector*," *The Seventeenth Century* 11:1 (Spring 1996): 61–86, and Lucy Hutchinson, *Order and Disorder*, ed. David Norbrook (Oxford, UK: Blackwell, 2001).

The Republican Revival

When the Nominated Parliament suddenly and unexpectedly voted its own dissolution on 12 December 1653, those within its membership who had concerted this constitutional coup knew that the Council of Officers was ready to act. In the course of the two months preceding, Major General John Lambert had drawn up what came to be called *The Instrument of Government*; and, after making certain adjustments required by Cromwell, he had elicited the Lord General's consent. This instrument was promulgated on 16 December when Cromwell was inaugurated Lord Protector of the Commonwealth of England, Scotland, and Ireland. It specified that the Lord Protector summon Parliament on 3 September 1654, the anniversary of Cromwell's magnificent victories at Dunbar and Worcester.[9] For the first time in fourteen years, there was to be a general election, and it was to be held on the franchise and with the reapportionment worked out earlier by the Rump.[10] By eliciting consent from the people of England, Scotland, and Ireland, Cromwell aimed to legitimate his rule and transform Lambert's *Instrument of Government* into a paramount constitution specifying and thereby limiting the powers of the Lord Protector and of Parliament alike.

It was not until after Parliament had convened on the appointed day that there were any serious signs of unrest. Written into *The Instrument of Government* was a provision specifying that the indentures of election for every member of parliament state that "the persons elected shall not have power to alter the government as it is hereby settled in one single person and a Parliament."[11] This did not prevent the election of a considerable number of individuals unfriendly to the terms of that pledge – among whom were to be found Major John Wildman; such stalwarts of the Rump as John Bradshaw, Sir Arthur Haselrig, Thomas Scot, and Lord Grey of Groby; and two otherwise undistinguished regimental commanders from the New Model Army: Colonel John Okey and Colonel Thomas Saunders. When it became apparent that the new Parliament was disinclined to ratify *The Instrument of Government* as given, the Lord Protector summoned its members to the Painted Chamber on the morning of 12 September 1654; laid out an elaborate defense of his conduct in and after the expulsion of the Rump in April 1653; and specified the four "fundamentals" contained in the proposed Protectorate constitution that he could not brook their changing – that there be government by a single person and Parliament, that Parliaments not make themselves perpetual, that there be liberty of conscience in religion, and that control over the armed forces be shared between the single person and Parliament.[12] Before allowing Parliament to resume its session, he demanded, as a condition of service, that its members subscribe to what came to be called "the Recognition," promising not only "to be true and faithfull to the Lord Protector and the Commonwealth of England, Scotland,

---

[9] See "The Instrument of Government," 16 December 1653, in *CDPR*, 405–17.

[10] For the details, see Woolrych, *Commonwealth to Protectorate*, 343–90.

[11] See "The Instrument of Government," 410.

[12] See "His Highnesse the Lord Protector's Speech to the Parliament in the Painted Chamber," 12 September 1654, in *WrSOC*, III 451–62 (esp. 458–60).

and Ireland" but to comply with "the Tenor of the Indenture" whereby each was "returned to serve in this present Parliament" by refusing their "consent" to any proposal designed "to alter the Government, as it is settled in a single person and a Parliament."[13] Despite the advice proffered to them by John Streater, who urged that they subscribe and then challenge the legality of Cromwell's demand,[14] Wildman, Bradshaw, Haselrig, Scot, Grey, and the two colonels were thereby induced to absent themselves from Parliament, and they were joined in refusing the Recognition by two dozen of their colleagues.[15]

Within days trouble was brewing in the army. By the middle of September 1654, apparently with the approval of John Bradshaw, John Wildman had drafted the *Humble Petition of Several Colonels of the Army*, and he had secured the signatures of Colonel Okey, Colonel Saunders, and Colonel Matthew Alured, younger brother to a member of the Rump.[16] Major Wildman was an experienced agitator, and he knew the disposition of the army very well. His tract *The Case of the Armie Truly Stated* had contributed in no small way to stirring up sentiment in favor of the Levellers' original *Agreement of the People* on the eve of the army's Putney debates in October 1647; he had played a significant role in forging the Levellers' second *Agreement of the People*; and he had been a prominent participant in the discussions that took place before the Council of Officers concerning this proposal in November and December 1648.[17]

The *Humble Petition* was, in its way, a rhetorical masterpiece. It attacked Cromwell's quasi-monarchical status under *The Instrument of Government*, challenging his possession of a limited veto and what amounted in practice to his unchecked rule over a standing army easily made mercenary. It demanded that there be "successive Parliaments" not just "freely and equally chosen by the people" but actually possessed of the supreme power in the land. And in sounding these familiar themes, which it identified with what it termed the "good cause" and "that old cause of liberty against tyranny," it quoted extensively from various petitions drafted for the army between 1647 and 1649 by Cromwell's deceased son-in-law Henry Ireton – including the *Declaration* that

---

[13] For the terms of the Recognition, see WrSOC, III 462–63.

[14] See John Streater, *Secret Reasons of State in Reference to the Affairs of These Nations at the Interruption of this Present Parliament* (London: s.n., 1659), 19–20, and the discussion in Johns, *The Nature of the Book*, 286–87.

[15] See Samuel Rawson Gardiner, *History of the Commonwealth and Protectorate, 1649–1655* (Adelstrop, UK: Windrush Press, 1988–1989), III 167–96.

[16] See Barbara Taft, "*The Humble Petition of Several Colonels of the Army*: Causes, Character, and Results of Military Opposition to Cromwell's Protectorate," *Huntington Library Quarterly* 42:1 (Winter 1978): 15–41.

[17] For a useful, if less than entirely reliable biography of Wildman, see Maurice Ashley, *John Wildman, Plotter and Postmaster: A Study of the English Republican Movement in the Seventeenth Century* (New Haven, CT: Yale University Press, 1947). See also Louis A. Knafla, "Sir John Wildman (1623–1693)," in *Biographical Dictionary of British Radicals in the Seventeenth Century*, III 323–25. In this connection, see [John Wildman], *The Case of the Armie Truly Stated*, 15 October 1647, in *Leveller Manifestoes of the Puritan Revolution*, ed. Don M. Wolfe (New York: Humanities Press, 1967), 198–222. On the Levellers and the debates at Putney, see Austin Woolrych, *Soldiers and Statesmen: The General Council of the Army and Its Debates, 1647–1648* (Oxford, UK: Clarendon Press, 1987).

the army had presented to Parliament on 14 June 1647, the *Remonstrance of His Excellency Thomas Lord Fairfax and of the Generall Councell of Officers Held at St. Albans the 16 of November, 1648*, and the revised version of the Levellers' second *Agreement of the People* that the Council of Officers had presented to the Rump on 20 January 1649.[18]

Had Wildman, Okey, Saunders, Alured, and their allies been allowed freely to circulate the *Humble Petition* among the officers of the army and to collect signatures, there can be no doubt that many would have rallied to what would quite soon be dubbed the "Good Old Cause."[19] As it happened, however, Cromwell's spymaster John Thurloe managed to nip the conspiracy in the bud and confiscate the petition. Alured, who had been making mischief for some time, was cashiered and jailed for a year for mutiny. Okey was tried for treason, acquitted, and then left to his own devices on condition that he surrender his commission; and Saunders was allowed to appear before Cromwell and state the grounds of his discontent on condition that he, too, resign his commission. Others were more severely treated. Lieutenant General Edmund Ludlow, who was caught circulating copies of the colonels' petition and various seditious pamphlets among his fellow officers in Ireland, was imprisoned, and John Milton's friend Major General Robert Overton suffered a similar fate when he was found to be orchestrating dissatisfaction among the army's officers in Scotland. By the time that Major Wildman was finally captured on 10 February 1655 and sentenced to seventeen months of confinement, Cromwell was once again fully in command of the officer corps that he had so often led to victory on the field of the sword.[20]

---

[18] In this connection, see *A Declaration:, or Representation from His Excellency Sir Thomas Fairfax, and of the Army Under his Command, Humbly Tendered to the Parliament, St. Albans, 14 June 1647*, which is reprinted in *Puritanism and Liberty: Being the Army Debates (1647–9) from the Clarke Manuscripts with Supplementary Documents*, ed. A. S. P. Woodhouse (London: J. M. Dent and Sons, 1938), 403–9 and in *The Stuart Constitution, 1603–1688: Documents and Commentary*, ed. John P. Kenyon (Cambridge, UK: Cambridge University Press, 1966), 295–301; and *Remonstrance of His Excellency Thomas Lord Fairfax and of the Generall Councell of Officers Held at St. Albans the 16 of November, 1648*, which is reprinted in *The Parliamentary or Constitutional History of England*, second edition (London: J. and R. Tonson, 1761–1763), XVIII 161–238. Then, consider "The Agreement of the People," 15 January 1649, in *CDPR*, 359–71, and in *Leveller Manifestoes of the Puritan Revolution*, 331–54, in light of Barbara Taft, "The Council of Officers' *Agreement of the People*, 1648/9," *Historical Journal* 28:1 (March 1985): 169–85.

[19] See Barbara Taft, "That Lusty Puss, The Good Old Cause," *History of Political Thought* 5:4 (Winter 1984): 447–64 (esp. 453–56), and Barber, *Regicide and Republicanism*, 202–39.

[20] See Taft, "*The Humble Petition of Several Colonels of the Army*," 15–41. In and after 1656, Ludlow would associate himself with Henry Neville and James Harrington: see John H. Hughes, "The Commonwealthmen Divided: Edmund Ludlowe, Sir Henry Vane and the Good Old Cause, 1653–1659," *The Seventeenth Century* 5:1 (Spring 1990): 55–70. It is telling in Overton's case that he looked with favor on the Nominated Parliament: see J. Frank McGregor, "Robert Overton (c. 1609–c. 1672)," in *Biographical Dictionary of British Radicals in the Seventeenth Century*, II 279–81, and Barbara Taft, "'They that pursew perfaction on earth . . .': The Political Progress of Robert Overton," in *Soldiers, Writers and Statesmen of the English Revolution*, ed. Ian Gentles, John Morrill, and Blair Worden (Cambridge, UK: Cambridge University Press, 1998), 286–303. Note also David Norbrook, "'This Blushinge Tribute of a Borrowed Muse':

By this time, however, the Lord Protector faced difficulties on another front. The purged Protectorate Parliament had met for something like the five months stipulated in *The Instrument of Government*. It had debated the terms of that instrument in fine detail, but it had balked at approving the third and the fourth of Cromwell's "fundamentals" – those stipulating liberty of conscience in religion, and shared control over the armed forces – for its members could stomach neither the sects nor the prospect that Cromwell or a successor would once again unleash the army on Parliament. And so on 22 January 1655 the Lord Protector had angrily declared his Parliament dissolved.[21] Cromwell was no more adept at parliamentary management than James I and Charles I had been.[22]

In the months that followed, the Lord Protector continued to rule as in the recent past, but his polity lacked the legal foundation that he had sought – and when, late in the summer of 1655, news arrived of the failure of Cromwell's "Western design" against the Spanish in Hispaniola, his morale and that of his supporters reached a new low.[23] There had already been a series of royalist risings, and the Lord Protector thought it essential to head off further unrest. In August, the Council of State voted to shut down all the newsbooks apart from *Mercurius Politicus* and its new sister publication *The Publick Intelligencer*, conferring on Marchamont Nedham an effective monopoly in the dissemination and management of news.[24] In the fall, Cromwell divided his realm into eleven military districts headed by major generals tasked not only with providing for public order but with enforcing moral discipline along Puritan lines.[25] Never before had local autonomy been so systematically infringed. Never before

---

Robert Overton and his Overturning of the Poetic Canon," *English Manuscript Studies, 1100–1700*, ed. Peter Beal and Jeremy Griffiths 4 (1993): 220–66.

[21] See "His Highness' Speech to the Parliament in the Painted Chamber at Their Dissolution," 22 January 1655, in *WrSOC*, III 579–93, and Gardiner, *History of the Commonwealth and Protectorate*, III 171–255. See also the various materials collected and analyzed by the editor in *WrSOC*, III 463–579 (esp. 463–79, 482–83, 485–86, 495–504, 509–10, 513–14, 519–20, 523–27, 540–41, 545–49, 555–63, 567–69, 571–79).

[22] See Hugh R. Trevor-Roper, "Oliver Cromwell and His Parliaments," in *The Seventeenth Century: Religion, Reformation, and Social Change* (New York: Harper & Row, 1968), 345–91.

[23] See Karen Ordahl Kupperman, "Errand to the Indies: Puritan Colonization from Providence Island through the Western Design," *William and Mary Quarterly*, third series, 45:1 (January 1988): 70–99, and David Armitage, "the Cromwellian Protectorate and the Languages of Empire," *Historical Journal* 35:3 (September 1992): 531–55. Note, in this connection, Blair Worden, "Oliver Cromwell and the Sin of Achan," in *History, Society and the Churches: Essays in Honour of Owen Chadwick*, ed. Derek Beales and Geoffrey Best (Cambridge, UK: Cambridge University Press, 1985), 135–45.

[24] Note Entry under 28 August 1655, in *Calendar of State Papers, Domestic Series, 1649–1660*, ed. Mary Anne Everett Green (London: Longman, 1875–1876), VIII 300–301 (1655), and see Joad Raymond, "'A Mercury with a Winged Conscience': Marchamont Nedham, Monopoly and Censorship," *Media History* 4:1 (June 1998): 7–18.

[25] See David Watson Rannie, "Cromwell's Major-Generals," *English Historical Review* 10:39 (July 1895): 471–506; Ivan Roots, "Swordsmen and Decimators: Cromwell's Major-Generals," in *The English Civil War and After, 1642–1658*, ed. R. H. Parry (Berkeley: University of California Press, 1970), 78–82; and Christopher Durston, *Cromwell's Major-Generals: Godly Government during the English Revolution* (Manchester, UK: Manchester University Press, 2001). Much can also be learned from the material collected and analyzed by the editor in *WrSOC*, III 594–851

had the local notables in the counties and boroughs been summarily shunted aside. To the putative citizens of the Commonwealth of England, Scotland, and Ireland, it was in this fashion brought home, as never before, that, for all of its pretenses, the Protectorate was a military dictatorship, if not, in fact, a tyranny outright.[26]

Resentment grew, popular confidence declined, and Spain, understandably miffed at the attack on Hispaniola, threatened war. By the spring of 1656, it had become obvious, even to the major generals themselves, that their dominion could neither be financed by the decimation tax on royalist property nor politically sustained in the face of the resentment it had inspired, and they persuaded Cromwell, against his better instincts, that it would be necessary once again to resort to a general election.[27]

Some months before this decision was made, as Cromwell's spymaster John Thurloe subsequently reported to the Lord Protector, a conspiracy had grown up among the Fifth Monarchists unhappy at the dissolution of the Nominated Parliament, and "those, who were all this while behind the curtain, . . . began to thinke, that these men might be made good use of; and in order thereto, the first step must be to reconcile the 5 monarchy and the common wealth partye."[28] It was presumably in this connection that the godly republicans who had served in the Rump joined forces with their less pious counterparts to revive what both parties agreed in denominating the Good Old Cause[29] – with Sir Henry Vane publishing *A Healing Question Propounded and Resolved* in mid-May 1656,[30] and the mysterious R. G. (Richard Goodgroom, Henry Neville, John

---

(esp. 594–602, 606–27, 638–73, 695–98, 703–5, 719–20, 738–40, 746–47, 758–62, 793–97, 826–30, 836–51).

[26] Resentment of the species of central control reimposed by Cromwell at this point did much to persuade the gentry that their own position within the county communities would be unsustainable unless there was a Stuart restoration: see David Underdown, "Settlement in the Counties, 1653–1658," in *The Interregnum: The Quest for Settlement, 1646–1660*, ed. G. E. Aylmer (London: MacMillan, 1972), 165–82.

[27] For an overview of developments, see Gardiner, *History of the Commonwealth and Protectorate*, III 256–346.

[28] See John Thurloe, "A Relation of the Raising of the Fifth-Monarchy-Men" (1657), in *A Collection of the State Papers of John Thurloe*, ed. Thomas Birch (London: Printed for the Executor of F. Gyles, 1742), VI 184–86.

[29] For evidence that Sir Henry Vane and Henry Neville were in cahoots not long after the appearance of *A Healing Question Propounded and Resolved* and *A Copy of a Letter from an Officer of the Army in Ireland to the Protector*, see the Letter from Major General Robert Lilburne to John Thurloe on 9 August 1656, in *A Collection of the State Papers of John Thurloe*, V 296, which reports that, in his bailiwick, there had been "meetings with Sir Henry Vane, Mr. Neville and some of that gang." Sir Arthur Haselrig is mentioned as well. More generally, see Taft, "That Lusty Puss, The Good Old Cause," 447–64. Although this campaign failed to bring down Oliver Cromwell, when renewed shortly after his death, it contributed mightily to Richard Cromwell's fall: see A. H. Woolrych, "The Good Old Cause and the Fall of the Protectorate," *Cambridge Historical Journal* 13:2 (1957): 133–61, and note Ivan Roots, "The Tactics of the Commonwealthsmen in Richard Cromwell's Parliament," in *Puritans and Revolutionaries: Essays in Seventeenth-Century History*, ed. Donald Pennington and Keith Thomas (Oxford, UK: Clarendon Press, 1978), 283–309.

[30] See [Sir Henry Vane], *A Healing Question Propounded and Resolved* (London: Thomas Brewster, 1656), passim (esp. 25), which is conveniently reprinted in John Forster, *The Statesmen of*

Wildman, or someone else who was familiar with the complex constitutional scheme then being worked out by James Harrington) presenting to the world in early June *A Copy of a Letter from an Officer of the Army in Ireland to the Protector, concerning his Changing of the Government.*[31]

According to Thurloe's summary account, those commonwealthmen who were intent on building a broad coalition inclusive of the Fifth Monarchists held a meeting with the leaders of the latter shortly before Vane's book was published, in which the manuscript was read aloud apparently in the hope that it would provide a foundation for the articulation of a common program of reform.[32] Elsewhere, he reports an even more ominous development: that at some point prior to 8 July 1656 the "fifth-monarchy-men" decided to organize their ranks in distinct cells in a manner foreshadowing the methods later adopted by underground revolutionary conspiracies – with the leaders of each cell acquainted with one another and the members of the various cells otherwise unknown to those outside each unit. Henry Ireton's younger brother, Clement, John Lawson, Richard Goodgroom, and John Okey were known to be colluding. Goodgroom sought out Thomas Harrison, and Goodgroom and Okey met with John Bradshaw, who "encouraged them in their discontents" and "told them, that the long parliament, though under a force," was "the supreme authority of England."[33]

the *Commonwealth*, ed. J. O. Choules (London: Longman, Brown, Green and Longmans, 1853), III 361–81 (esp. 380), and in *Somers Tracts*: see *A Collection of Scarce and Valuable Tracts*, second edition, revised and augmented, ed. Sir Walter Scott (London: T. Cadell and W. Davies, 1809–1815), VI 304–15 (esp. 314). On the significance of Vane's pamphlet, cf. Worden, "Oliver Cromwell and the Sin of Achan," 125–45 (esp. 135–41), and Armitage, "The Cromwellian Protectorate and the Languages of Empire," 531–55 (esp. 544–45), with Ruth E. Mayers, "Real and Practicable, Not Imaginary and Notional: Sir Henry Vane, *A Healing Question*, and the Problems of the Protectorate," *Albion* 28:1 (Spring 1996): 37–72, and Scott, *Commonwealth Principles*, 279–81 (with 52–53, 105, 140–41, 217–18).

[31] See R. G., *A Copy of a Letter from an Officer of the Army in Ireland to the Protector, concerning his Changing of the Government* (London: n.p., 1656), passim (esp. 22), which purports to have been written by the officer in question on 24 June 1654, and which was reprinted in facsimile by the Rota at the University of Exeter in 1974. On the pamphlet's authorship, note John Toland, "The Life of James Harrington," in *WoJH*, xv–xvi, and Hughes, "The Commonwealthmen Divided," 67, nn. 18 and 25; then, see J. G. A. Pocock, "Historical Introduction," in *PWoJH*, 6–12. Apart from Goodgroom, Neville, and Wildman, who are the most likely candidates, Edmund Ludlow and John Streater deserve consideration. Blair Worden makes a strong case for taking seriously the letter's supposed date of composition: see "Harrington's *Oceana*," 115–20. See also Scott, *Commonwealth Principles*, 282–83. It is striking that "the good old cause" is mentioned only in the postscript apparently written in 1656 by the letter's putative editor.

[32] See Thurloe, "A Relation of the Raising of the Fifth-Monarchy-Men" (1657), in *A Collection of the State Papers of John Thurloe*, VI 185. The fact that his book was, in effect, a party manifesto helps explain why Sir Henry Vane was called before the Protectorate Council and ultimately jailed: see Letter from John Thurloe to Henry Cromwell, Major-General of the Army of Ireland on 26 August 1656, in ibid., V 349–50. At this time, Vane was also active distributing copies of the pamphlet *England's Remembrancers, or a word in season to all Englishmen about the electing members to the approaching parliament*. See The Examination of Andrew Thornton, Francis Fidling, John Cock, and John Chapman as well as the Letter from Major-General Whalley to Secretary Thurloe, 22–23 August 1656, in ibid., V 342–43.

[33] See "The Effect of the Meeting of the Fifth-Monarchy Men," 8 July 1656, in *A Collection of the State Papers of John Thurloe*, V 197.

It was at this critical juncture, when the Protectorate seemed to be most vulnerable and its opponents, mindful of the fury inspired by the rule of the major generals, were about to take up the cry "noe swordsmen, noe decimator,"[34] that Vane's printer Thomas Brewster launched *The Excellencie of a Free State* – without, however, openly acknowledging the obvious: that the "Well-wisher to Posterity" who authored this spirited contribution to the insurgency then in progress was Cromwell's principal publicist, the well-known editor of the semi-official journals *Mercurius Politicus* and *The Publick Intelligencer*.[35]

Servant of the Protectorate

Throughout the period that began with Cromwell's ouster of the Rump, Nedham had been stalwartly loyal to his employer.[36] Although he had for the most part given up writing editorials in August 1652, probably under duress,[37] in the news reports, the petitions, and the letters that he printed in *Mercurius Politicus* after 20 April 1653, he nonetheless managed to convey a certain distaste for the Rump and relief at the change in government.[38] In the same oblique fashion, he registered respect,[39] then, turning on a dime, displayed a disregard

---

[34] See Letter from Major-General Robert Lilburne to Secretary Thurloe on 9 August 1656, in *A Collection of the State Papers of John Thurloe*, V 296.

[35] On the significance of Nedham's timing, see J. G. A. Pocock, "James Harrington and the Good Old Cause: A Study of the Ideological Context of his Writings," *The Journal of British Studies* 10:1 (November 1970): 30–48 (at 36–39).

[36] See David Norbrook, *Writing the English Republic: Poetry, Rhetoric and Politics, 1627–1660* (Cambridge, UK: Cambridge University Press, 1999), 326–31. Note also Blair Worden, *Literature and Politics in Cromwellian England: John Milton, Andrew Marvell, Marchamont Nedham* (Oxford, UK: Oxford University Press, 2007), 137–53. In this connection, note *MP* 201 (13–20 April 1654): 3428; 204 (4–11 May 1654): 3474–75; 208 (1–8 June 1654): 3535–36, 3539–40; 212 (29 June–6 July 1654): 3599–3602; 213 (6–13 July 1654): 3618–19; 222 (7–14 August 1654): 3761–64 (esp. 3764); 223 (14–21 August 1654): 3773. One might, however, want to reflect on the significance inherent in Nedham's decision to report at length the developments that led to election of Thomas Scot to the first Protectorate Parliament: see *MP* 213 (6–13 July 1654): 3615–18.

[37] See Worden, *Literature and Politics in Cromwellian England*, 249–54.

[38] The overall impression left is that the coup d'état was justified, that the new government is fully in control, that the army is rallying to its standard, and that, while some foreigners were surprised at the event, all are quickly adjusting to the new reality: see *MP* 150 (21–28 April 1653): 2386–91, 2395–96; 151 (28 April–5 May 1653): 2407–8, 2410–11; 152 (5–12 May 1653): 2417–18, 2422–23, 2426–27; 153 (12–19 May 1653): 2433–35, 2448 (which should be 2438); 155, wrongly numbered 153, (26 May–2 June 1653): 2475–78, 2481; 156 (2–9 June 1653): 2489; 157 (9–16 June 1653): 2502–7; 160 (30 June–7 July 1653): 2550–52, 2563–64.

[39] One is left with the impression of an orderly assembly going about its business in an efficient manner: see *MP* 157 (9–16 June 1653): 2506–7; 160 (30 June–7 July 1653): 2563–64; 162 (14–21 July 1653): 2582–87, 2595–96; 163 (21–28 July 1653): 2598–2601; 164 (28 July–4 August 1653): 2614–17, 2619–21, 2625; 165 (4–11 August 1653): 2636–37, 2639–41, 2644; 166 (11–18 August 1653): 2647–49, 2652–53; 168 (25 August–1 September 1653): 2691–98; 169 (1–8 September 1653): 2712–14 (where the pages are correctly numbered but arranged in the wrong order); 170 (8–15 September 1653): 2723–26; 171 (15–22 September 1653): 2739–40, 2746–47; 172 (22–29 September 1653): 2752–53, 2759–62; 173 (29 September–6 October 1653): 2770–78; 174 (6–13 October 1653): 2780–91; 175 (13–20 October 1653): 2797–96 (where the pagination is, indeed, reversed), 2800–02; 176 (20–27 October 1653): 2812–15, 2821, 2826; 177

bordering on disdain for the Nominated Parliament.[40] Later, he welcomed the first Parliament of the Protectorate, celebrated the Lord Protector's attempt to rein it in, and then nonchalantly saw it off.[41] He took particular care in his coverage of the major generals to vindicate that embattled regime.[42]

Within six to seven weeks of the Protectorate's establishment, Nedham also produced an anonymous pamphlet – *A True State of the Case of the Commonwealth of England, Scotland, and Ireland, And the Dominions Thereto Belonging; In Reference to the Late Established Government by a Lord Protector and Parliament* – aimed at reconciling "the Well-affected," especially those in the army and the gathered churches, to the new regime.[43] In it, he denied the charge, advanced by republicans and royalists of all stripes, that, in establishing the rule of a single person and Parliament, "we had turned our backs on our former Principles, and introduced again that very Thing, which was the great bone of contention, (the removal whereof seemed to include the very state of the Quarrel between the late King and the Parliament) and so fought our selves round till we rest upon the old bottom, and in conclusion given judgment against our selves in all the things contended for against the King." And he set out to prove therein that the new government "fully correspond[s] with the primary Ends and Intentions of such as engaged in the late Controversie with the King, upon principles of common Freedom."[44] In this connection, he cited Henry Parker's well-known defense of the Parliamentary cause – *Observations upon Some of his Majesties Late Answers and Expresses* (1642) – and he invoked two of the three army manifestoes that John Wildman would later cite in his

---

(27 October–3 November 1653): 2830–36, 2838, 2842; 178 (3–10 November 1653): 2847–53; 179 (10–17 November 1653): 2864–66, 2870–71; 181 (24 November–2 December 1653): 2892–93, 2899–3000; 182 (2–9 December 1653): 3015–16, 3018; 183 (9–16 December 1653): 3130–35, 3137–38.

[40] Its dissolution and the establishment of the Protectorate are reported in a manner suggesting that nothing untoward has happened at all: see *MP* 183 (9–16 December 1653): 3038 (which is misnumbered as 3138); 184 (16–22 December 1653): 3052–54; 185 (22–29 December 1653): 3139–41, 3152–53; 186 (29 December 1653 – 5 January 1654): 3157–68; 187 (5–12 January 1654): 3173–78; 189 (19–26 January 1654): 3215, misnumbered 3207, – 17; 191 (2–9 February 1654): 3262; 192 (9–16 February 1654): 3265–67, 3270; 193, misnumbered 93, (16–23 February 1654): 3288–89; 194 (23 February–2 March 1654): 3298–99; 195 (2–9 March 1654): 3325; 197 (16–23 March 1654): 3353–56; 198 (23–30 March 1654): 3364–68; 199 (30 March–6 April 1654): 3577–80 (which is misnumbered 3390), 3382–85; 204 (4–11 May 1654): 3467–68; 208 (1–8 June 1654): 3535–36.

[41] Cf. *MP* 209 (8–15 June 1654): 3543–44; 211 (22–29 June 1654): 3585, 3587; 214 (13–20 July 1654): 3632–36; 215 (20–27 July 1654): 3650–51; 216 (27 July – 3 August 1654): 3668; 219 (17–24 August 1654): 3709–10; 221 (31 August – 7 September 1654): 3741–48; 222 (7–14 August 1654): 3752 with *MP* 222 (7–14 August 1654): 3761 64; 223 (14–21 August 1654): 3777–80, and, then, see *MP* 241 (18–25 January 1655): 5082, where, in accord with the Old Style, the date is listed as 18–24 January 1654.

[42] See *MP* 285 (22–29 November 1655): 5781; 287 (5–13 December 1655): 5805, 5811; 293 (17–24 January 1656): 5916; 296 (7–14 February 1656): 5958–59.

[43] See Nedham, *True State*, passim (esp. 3). In London, this work appeared on 8 February 1654 and was advertised in *Mercurius Politicus* the following day: see *MP* 191 (2–9 February 1654): 3262 and *WrSOC*, III 193. It was subsequently reprinted in Leith: see *MP* 198 (23–30 March 1654): 3374. The Rota at the University of Exeter produced a facsimile reprint in 1978.

[44] See Nedham, *True State*, 3.

Humble Petition of Several Colonels of the Army: the *Declaration* presented to
Parliament on 14 June 1647, and the *Remonstrance* issued on 16 November
1648.[45]

In making his case, Nedham briefly revisited the grounds of the controversy
between Parliament and the king. Then, he restated the reasons advanced by
the Army and the Rump in defense of Pride's Purge, and he indicted the Rump
itself as a narrow oligarchy of "unaccountable persons" plotting their own
perpetuation in office. Because the Rump had united "the *Legislative* and *executive Powers* in the same persons," he argued, it was prone to "Corruption
and Tyranny" and apt to "contract an arbitrary distemper in the execution of
Law." Moreover, by governing as well as legislating and by failing to call new
elections, the Rump had "wholly perverted the end of Parliaments; so that the
People being delaied (and so in effect denied) Answers to their Petitions, no dore
being open for the redress of Grievances, nor any hope of easing the People of
their burthens, it was found at length by experience, that a standing Parliament
was it self the greatest Grievance."[46]

Nedham then examined in detail the high hopes of those within the officer
corps who had summoned the Nominated Parliament and the sorry record of
its accomplishments. Among the purportedly God-fearing men "of approved
fidelity" who were invited to participate in its deliberations, he explained, "there
was a Party of men," largely made up of Fifth Monarchists, "who assumed to
themselves only the name of Saints, from which Title they excluded all others that were not of their Judgment and opinion." These men "led off divers
well-meaning Gentlemen of the House along with them, to private Meetings
of their own appointment, upon pretence of seeking the Lord by prayer for
direction," but actually for the purpose of concerting their efforts to dominate
the assembly. It was their purpose "to twist the Spiritual and Civil Interest both
in one," and they insisted that "none ought to be in Authority but Saints by
calling," recurring thereby "to the very Papall and Prelatick principle" that had
occasioned the quarrel between Parliament and the king, and laying "a Foundation ... for imposing upon mens consciences, and [for] severe persecution."
England's painful "experience" with the rule of this self-styled Parliament of
Saints had, he added, taught his compatriots to reject the notion that "*temporal
Power and Authority is and ought to be founded in grace*" on the grounds that
"God works not now in any such extraordinary way, but hath left the world to

---

[45] Cf. Nedham, *True State*, 5, 34, 36, 40–42, with [Henry Parker], *Observations upon Some of
his Majesties Late Answers and Expresses* (London: [s. n.], 1642), which is reprinted in facsimile in *Tracts on Liberty in the Puritan Revolution: 1638–1647*, ed. William Haller (New York:
Columbia University Press, 1933–1934), II 167–213, and is also available in an abbreviated and
modernized form in *Revolutionary Prose of the English Civil War*, ed. Howard Erskine-Hall
and Graham Storey (Cambridge, UK: Cambridge University Press, 1983), 35–63; *A Declaration:, or Representation from His Excellency Sir Thomas Fairfax, and of the Army Under his
Command, Humbly Tendered to the Parliament*, St. Albans, 14 June 1647, which is reprinted
in *Puritanism and Liberty*, 403–9 and in *The Stuart Constitution*, 295–301; and *Remonstrance
of His Excellency Thomas Lord Fairfax and of the Generall Councell of Officers Held at St.
Albans the 16 of November, 1648*, which is reprinted in *The Parliamentary or Constitutional
History of England*, XVIII 161–238.

[46] See Nedham, *True State*, 4–11, 17, 22–25, 36–38.

be ordered by the moral improvement of natural Endowments and Faculties" alone.[47]

Finally, he turned to *The Instrument of Government* itself, insisting that, "though the Commonwealth may now appear with a new face in the outward Form, yet it remains still the same in Substance, and is of a better complexion and constitution then heretofore." Now finally, he claimed, its "Foundation" has been "laid in the People." There were no hereditary offices. The executive and legislative powers were separate and distinct, and both flowed from the community as a whole. It eliminated the possibility of "ever-sitting Parlaments" while guaranteeing "a convenient succession of those Supreme Assemblies." In the short run, it excluded from office "men dis-affected to the true Interest" of the nation, but it made long-term provision for "extinguishing all animosities, and putting into oblivion the memory of all those Feids [sic] and divisions contracted by Civil War." It empowered the Lord Protector with the right to "prevent a razing of those Foundations of Freedom that have been but newly laid" without giving him in addition anything more than the power to delay and force a reconsideration of ordinary legislation that he deemed unwise. It made "a Christian provision for the Liberty of tender Consciences" without giving "to subtile heads and carnal minds" occasion "to display innumerable Parties and Factions under the banner of Religion, spreading abroad most blasphemous Opinions in defiance even of the holy Scriptures, and of God the *Father*, *Son*, and *Spirit*." In short, it guaranteed to the English, the Scots, and the Irish "their Liberty as Christians, and their Rights as Men," and, he added at the end, it could even be said to "have taken in the good of all the three sorts of Government, and bound them all in one." Never before had England been "really Free," Nedham insisted, "not in a way of enjoying its Freedom so fully as now."[48]

The Lord Protector was so pleased with this tract that he drew heavily on its argument when he met with members of the first Protectorate Parliament to demand that they take the Recognition.[49] And, in the speech that he later delivered on the occasion of this Parliament's dissolution, he found occasion publicly to recommend the work itself.[50] It would, therefore, be tempting to take this tract's argument at face value, to suppose that Nedham was a genuine admirer of the Protectorate, and conclude that he was satisfied with the overall turn of events, but this would be an error. In *Mercurius Politicus*, from time to time, he seems to intimate on his own part a certain critical detachment from the regime, and it may be telling that this accomplished stylist composed *A True State of the Case of the Commonwealth* in so bland and banal, so long-winded and dull a fashion that his modern biographer could not believe him its author.[51] Moreover, what this subtle distancing suggests is confirmed by *The*

---

[47] See Nedham, *True State*, 12–21, 25–27.

[48] See Nedham, *True State*, 27–52.

[49] See "His Highnesse the Lord Protector's Speech to the Parliament in the Painted Chamber," 12 September 1654, in *WrSOC*, III 451–462 (esp. 452–60).

[50] See "His Highness' Speech to the Parliament in the Painted Chamber at their Dissolution," 22 January 1655, in *WrSOC*, III 579–93 (at 587–88).

[51] See Joseph Frank, *Cromwell's Press Agent: A Critical Biography of Marchamont Nedham, 1620–1678* (Lanham, MD: University Press of America, 1980), 135–36 n. 83. There can be little doubt

Excellencie of a Free State, which one can hardly read without becoming aware of the depth of Nedham's dismay at all that had transpired since England had been declared a Commonwealth and Free State on 19 May 1649.

The Excellencie of a Free State

In the preface to the latter tract, Nedham announces and then restates the theme that he had so frequently touched on in the first year following the Roundhead victory at Worcester: that "nothing will satisfy for all the blood and treasure that hath been spilt and spent, make England a glorious commonwealth, and stop the mouths of all gainsayers, but a due and orderly succession of the supreme authority in the hands of the people's representatives." Only such a succession can "secure the liberties and freedoms of the people from the incroachments and usurpations of tyranny." Roman history, he adds in his introductory chapter, teaches that the people "never had any real liberty, till they were possessed of the power of calling and dissolving the supreme assemblies, changing governments, enacting and repealing laws, together with a power of chusing and deputing whom they pleased to this work, as often as they should judge expedient for their own well-being, and the good of the public."[52]

Nedham's historical allusions verge on allegory. When he describes Solon as having left "the only pattern of a free-state fit for all the world to follow," when he praises the Athenian lawgiver for placing "the power of legislation, or law-making, in a successive course of people's assemblies," and when he then pointedly adds that the Athenian thereby avoided "kingly tyranny on the one side, and senatical incroachments on the other," he clearly has the tyranny of Cromwell and the encroachments of the Rump in mind. Similar concerns account for his assertion that Gracchus was right to tell his compatriots that it "was a sore affliction from the gods, that they should suffer so much for the ignorance or negligence of their ancestors, who when they drove out kings, forgot to drive out the mysteries and inconveniences of kingly power, which were all reserved within the hands of the senate." Nedham had no more use for a polity in which "all authority was confined within the walls of a standing senate" than did the Levellers. The consequences, he invites his readers to conclude on their own without explicit guidance from him, were precisely the same in contemporary England as they had been long before in early republican Rome: "The senate having got all power into their own hands, in a short time degenerated from their first virtue and institution, to the practice of avarice, riot, and luxury: whereby the love of their country was changed into a study of ambition and faction: so that they fell into divisions among themselves, as well as oppressions over the people; by which divisions, some leading grandees, more

---

as to the pamphlet's authorship: as Worden, *The Rump Parliament*, 362, has shown, in a fashion characteristic of Nedham, who was never wont to waste his words, its author lifted from *MP* 109 (1–8 July 1652): 1705–6 a passage that he redeployed in *True State*, 10. Note also *True State*, 12, 30–32, 36–38, 51, where, in the precise manner of Nedham, the pamphlet's author emphasizes just how important it is that there be "a Succession of Supreme Assemblies."

[52] See Nedham, *EFS*, v, x, xv.

potent then their fellows, took occasion to wipe their noses, and to assume the power into their own hands." What is required in such circumstances, Nedham intimates, is "a tumult," of the precise sort so vehemently praised by Machiavel: one "under the conduct" of a "tribune" such as that "Canuteius" who was responsible for overthrowing the Decemviri.[53]

In similar fashion, Nedham obliquely attacks Oliver Cromwell when he once again identifies as "a noble saying, (though Machiavel's)" the claim: "'Not he that placeth a virtuous government in his own hands, or family; but he that establisheth a free and lasting form, for the people's constant security, is most to be commended.'" Lest his point be missed, Nedham goes on to discuss "the pride of Richard Nevil, the great Earl of Warwick," who "made and unmade kings at his pleasure" – as, his readers need not be reminded, Cromwell had made and unmade parliaments – remarking that, from the "story" of this great magnate's life, "we may very well conclude, how unsafe it is in a new alteration, to trust any man with too great a share of government, or place of trust; for such persons stand ever ready (like that Warwick) upon any occasion of discontent, or of serving their own interests, to betray and alter the government." It concerns "every commonwealth, in such a case, to see and beware that Warwick's Ghost be not conjur'd up again to act a part in some new tragedy."[54]

It would be appropriate to treat Nedham's *Excellencie of a Free State* as his contribution to the revival of the Good Old Cause, for that it certainly was.[55] But Nedham's tract was no mere occasional piece like the brief pamphlets penned by Vane and the mysterious R. G., and his goal in the work was not simply or even primarily polemical. He really was intent, as he had been in 1651 and 1652, on instructing his compatriots in the logic underpinning the modern republic.[56] He really did aim at enlightening his generation, and generations to come, with regard to the conditions prerequisite for the flourishing of a free state – and to this extent he really did succeed: his book was by no means forgotten, as in due course we will have occasion to document.[57]

Nedham's Modern Populism

If, when he recycled sections of his Engagement tract in *Mercurius Politicus*, Marchamont Nedham deliberately suppressed his earlier criticism of the Levellers, it was, one must suspect, not solely or even chiefly because they had ceased to be a threat nor even because he had gradually come to share the misgivings that they had voiced from the outset regarding the intentions of Oliver Cromwell, the Long Parliament, and the Rump. At times, in the 1640s,

---

[53] Nedham, *EFS*, xv–xx.
[54] Cf. Nedham, *EFS*, xxiv–xxviii, with Machiavelli, *Discorsi* 1.9–10, in *Opere*, 90–93.
[55] See Blair Worden, "Marchamont Nedham and the Beginnings of Republicanism, 1649–1656," in *Republicanism, Liberty, and Commercial Society*, 45–81 (at 74–81); and *Literature and Politics in Cromwellian England*, 305–19.
[56] See Vickie B. Sullivan, *Machiavelli, Hobbes, and the Formation of a Liberal Republicanism in England* (New York: Cambridge University Press, 2004), 113–43.
[57] See the Epilogue, this volume.

as we have had occasion to observe,[58] Nedham had been quite friendly to John Lilburne and to the Leveller cause. Such seems, in fact, to have been his inclination whenever he was given free rein,[59] and John Lilburne was evidently aware of Nedham's proclivities, for, in an open letter to Oliver Cromwell penned early in April 1652, while he was living in enforced exile in Holland, Lilburne went out of his way to heap praise on the "notable preambles" to the "*thursday newes-bookes*" then being published by "*Politicus*" in support of republican government and frequent, successive parliaments.[60]

As a pamphleteer, Lilburne was rhetorically shrewd. There is very little in the way of argument to be found in John Wildman's *Humble Petition of Several Colonels of the Army* that was not prefigured four years before in Lilburne's diatribe demanding fresh elections. Like his onetime colleague, Lilburne charged Cromwell with betraying the revolution, and he, too, was ready to fling in the Lord General's face the promises embedded in the various army declarations and remonstrances penned in the 1640s by the latter's recently deceased friend and son-in-law Henry Ireton.[61] As a reader, John Lilburne was no less astute, for he attended closely to what lay between the lines. In the epilogue to *Pro Populo Anglicano Defensio*, in which Milton exhorted the Commonwealthmen to justify the regicide and prove it a worthy act by their own upright behavior, the old Leveller rightly discerned a reproof to the Rump.[62] In the editorials penned by *Mercurius Politicus*, he recognized a warning issued to the Lord General himself.[63]

---

[58] See Chapter Six, this volume.

[59] See, for example, *MP* 157 (9–16 June 1653): 2514–16; 158 (16–23 June 1653): 2525–30, where Nedham does Lilburne the favor of printing the three addresses he sent Cromwell when he seized on the occasion of the latter's ouster of the Rump as an opportunity to return from enforced exile to England. To Lilburne's unsuccessful struggle to have his banishment annulled, he paid close attention: see *MP* 161 (7–14 July 1653): 2580; 162 (14–21 July 1653): 2589–91; 164 (28 July – 4 August 1653): 2625; 165 (4–11 August 1653): 2644; 166 (11–18 August 1653): 2660; 167 (18–25 August 1653): 2672, 2686. He mentioned his imprisonment in the Tower of London on 28 August 1653: see *MP* 168 (25 August–1 September 1653): 2702. But he did not record the old Leveller's conviction on a charge of treason the day before. In due course, he did print an advertisement for the officially sanctioned book arguing Lilburne's guilt: see *MP* 181 (24 November–2 December 1653): 3006.

[60] See John Lilburne, *As You Were, or, The Lord General Cromwel and the Grand Officers of the Armie their Remembrancer* (n.p.: [s.n.], 1652), 29. Whether he had read the criticism directed his way in *MP* 97 (8–15 April 1652): 1536 before he penned these words is unclear.

[61] See Lilburne, *As You Were*, 11–29. Lilburne's propensity in this regard has not escaped notice: see Andrew Sharp, "John Lilburne and the Long Parliament's *Book of Declarations*: A Radical's Exploitation of the Words of Authorities," *History of Political Thought* 9:1 (Spring 1988): 19–44.

[62] Consider *Pro Populo Anglicano Defensio* (24 February 1651) XII, in *CW*, VII 550–55, in light of Lilburne, *As You Were*, 15–16, which is conveniently reprinted in *The Life Records of John Milton*, ed. J. Milton French (New Brunswick, NJ: Rutgers University Press, 1949–1958), III 217–20. For a recent translation of the pertinent passage, see *A Defence of the People of England* (24 February 1651) XII, tr. Donald C. Mackenzie, in *CPW*, IV:1 535–36.

[63] See Lilburne, *As You Were*, 29. Lilburne may have had in mind *MP* 37 (13–20 February 1651): 591–93, wherein Nedham discussed the career of Richard Neville, the earl of Warwick, concluding that it concerns "every new *Commonwealth* . . . to see and beware, that *Warwicks* ghost be not conjured up again, to Act a part in some new *Tragedy*." This preamble, its immediate

Lilburne was right also in expressing confidence in Marchamont Nedham, for nowhere in the newsbook editorials that the old Leveller so admired and nowhere in the volume in which they later reappeared does one find anything comparable to the passages, scattered throughout the chapter in *The Case of the Commonwealth of England Stated* attacking the Levellers, in which, as we have seen, Nedham rang changes on the assertion of differential moral and political rationality that underpinned the ancient Greek and Roman criticism of popular government.[64] Instead, in his "notable preambles" and in *The Excellencie of a Free State*, Nedham explicitly embraces modern populism on the precise terms in which it was first espoused by Niccolò Machiavelli. After remarking that "if liberty is the most precious jewel under the sun, then when it is once in possession, it requires more than an ordinary art and industry to preserve it," he goes on to identify the crucial element in the requisite art by reiterating the Florentine's controversial claim that liberty can be preserved only "by placing the guardianship in the hands of the people."[65]

In this connection, to be sure, Nedham is prepared to quote Cicero on man's capacity to rule, and he argues "that by the light of nature people are taught to be their own carvers and contrivers, in the framing of that government under which they mean to live." In the same context, he asserts that the people are "the only proper judges of the convenience or inconvenience of a government when it is erected, and of the behaviour of governors after they are chosen." He celebrates the fact "that in the people's form, men have liberty to make use of that reason and understanding God hath given them, in chusing of governors, and providing for their safety in government." He even remarks, in a manner suggestive of Aristotle's discussion of man's nature as a political animal, that, where the people are denied this prerogative, the course followed is "destructive to the reason, common interest, and majesty of that noble creature, called man," serving "no other end, but to transform men into beasts."[66] This brief disquisition in praise of man's rational capacities is no more, however, than a passing rhetorical flourish, conferring a certain specious dignity on a populist argument that is otherwise Machiavellian through and through. Like his Florentine mentor, Nedham thought it essential for the success of his modern republican project that it be disguised as a return to classical norms.

Marchamont Nedham nowhere quotes verbatim Machiavelli's claim that it is incumbent on anyone intent on setting up a republic and ordaining its laws to presuppose that "all men are wicked and that they will make use of the malignity of their spirit whenever they are free and have occasion to do so."[67] But he does ground his defense of the guardianship of the people on the Machiavellian assertion that ordinary folk possess a defect in appetite,

---

predecessor, and *MP* 64 (21–28 August 1651): 1013–16 were the only editorials published prior to the battle of Worcester that Nedham chose to include in *The Excellencie of a Free State*.

[64] See Chapter Five, this volume.

[65] Consider Nedham, *EFS*, xiv, 2, 18–19, in light of Machiavelli, *Discorsi* 1.5, in *Opere*, 83–84, and see Chapters Two, and Three, and Six, this volume.

[66] Cf. Nedham, *EFS*, 33–35, with Arist. *Pol.* 1252b27–1253a39, 1278b15–30, 1280a25–1281a10, 1283b42–1284a3.

[67] See Machiavelli, *Discorsi* 1.3.1, in *Opere*, 81.

being "bounded within a more lowly pitch of desire and imagination" than the grandees, and he defends the people against the charge of "inconstancy" in good Machiavellian fashion by insisting that they are far less inconstant than "standing powers," who generally run "into all the extremes of inconstancy, upon every new project, petty humour, and occasion that" seems "favourable for effecting of their by-designs." Nedham does not, however, attribute the constancy of the people to their moral superiority. Here, too, he follows the Florentine. If "in the framing of laws," he writes, the "aim" of the people "was ever at the general good," it is simply and solely because the general good is, in fact, indistinguishable from "their own interest." Such a coincidence of their own self-interest and the good of the whole cannot, however, be attributed to the grandees.[68]

This last fact is of decisive importance and needs to be underlined – if for no other reason than because Nedham's republic differs profoundly from that of Machiavelli in one crucial particular. The Commonwealth of England, Scotland, and Ireland is not a civic republic. It occupies a large territory – an expanse so vast that direct popular rule is simply impossible and that legislative representation must be adopted as an expedient. Within Nedham's republic, the gap that exists between the grandees who govern as both legislators and magistrates and the people who are governed is far greater than that with which Machiavelli concerned himself.

In consequence, "extreme jealousy" is Nedham's political watchword. "The interest of freedom is," he insists, "a virgin that every one seeks to deflour; and like a virgin, it must be kept from any other form, or else (so great is the lust of mankind after dominion) there follows a rape upon the first opportunity." Frequent popular elections and a "due and orderly succession of power and persons" are, in fact, "the only remedy against self-seeking, with all the powerful temptations and charms of self-interest."[69]

Nedham really did think that it was Solon of Athens and not one of Machiavelli's Romans who left "the only pattern of a free-state fit for all the world to follow," for the Athenian lawgiver fully entrusted "the power of legislation, or law-making" to "a successive course of people's assemblies," and he avoided thereby the Roman dilemma: "kingly tyranny on the one side, and senatical incroachments on the other."[70] Every "standing senate" will be, he warns with Roman history in mind, "more studious of their own, than the common good." Indeed, no matter how "good a patriot" a particular individual may be, "yet if his power be prolonged, he will find it hard to keep self from creeping in upon him, and prompting him to some extravagancies for his own private benefit." The only safe reliance is, then, self-interest, for moral virtue is generally a sham and always a weak reed. If a man "be shortly to return to a condition common with the rest of his brethren, self-interest binds him to do nothing but what is

[68] Cf. Nedham, *EFS*, 21–22, 78–80, with Machiavelli, *Discorsi* 1.16.3–5 and 58, which should be read in light of 1.2.3, 44, 54, and 57, in *Opere*, 79–80, 100–1, 126–27, 136, 139–42, and see Chapter Two, this volume.

[69] Consider Nedham, *EFS*, xii–xiii, 8–9, 18–19, 81.

[70] Nedham, *EFS*, xvi–xvii.

just and equal; he himself being to reap the good or evil of what is done, as well as the meanest of the people."[71]

The Spirit of Distrust

Thus, when Nedham sets out to catalogue "the errors of government" and to list the "rules of policy," the spirit of political distrust is his primary theme. If he is willing to condemn popular ingratitude to the benefactors of the commonwealth, he nonetheless takes this as an occasion to remind his readers that "it concerns them, for the public peace and security, not to impose a trust in the hands of any person or persons, further than as they may take it back again at pleasure." Honors, he warns in this context, "change 'men's manners'; accessions, and continuations of power and greatness, expose the mind to temptations: they are sails too big for any bulk of mortality to steer an even course by." A great many "free-states and commonwealths" have,

by trusting their own servants too far, ... been forced, in the end, to receive them for their masters. Nor is it to be wondered at by any, considering that immoderate power soon lets in high and ambitious thoughts; and where they are once admitted, no design [is] so absurd, or contrary to a man's principles, but he rusheth into it, without the least remorse or consideration: for the spirit of ambition is a spirit of giddiness; it foxes men that receive it, and makes them more drunk than the spirit of wine.

"Without question," Nedham concludes, "it highly concerns a people that have redeemed and rescued their liberties out of the hands of tyranny, and are declared a free-state, so to regulate their affairs, that all temptations, and opportunities of ambition, may be removed out of the way: or else there follows a necessity of tumult and civil dissension, the common consequence whereof hath ever been a ruin of the public freedom."[72]

As this suggests, Nedham envisages elections as a salutary alternative to tumults. They are, he intimates, a far better remedy than the one devised by Machiavelli, for they accomplish Machiavelli's end without occasioning genuine disorder. They are, in fact, the perfect substitute for a risky venture that, in Nedham's opinion, should always be a last resort, reserved for those rare occasions when no other expedient will serve. By reining in the magistrates and putting them to the test, by suspending for a brief moment all governance and reminding the rulers and the ruled of the former's subjection to and dependence on the latter, by ritually reenacting government's emergence from the consent of the governed, such elections force at frequent and regular intervals a chastening return to the republic's *principii* – its origins in the primordial fear that dispels every form of inequality and inspires in men of all humors a profound longing for security and well-being.[73]

---

[71] Nedham, *EFS*, 9, 12.

[72] Nedham, *EFS*, 134–35.

[73] After considering Nedham, *EFS*, 64–70, reread *EFS*, 135, and cf. Machiavelli, *Discorsi* 1.1–6, 3.1, 22.3, in *Opere*, 77–87, 195–96, 228–29.

To check temptation and restrain ambition, Nedham advocated a separation of powers as well.[74] Nedham was a close student of Machiavellian statecraft. He acknowledged the Tacitean distinction that the Florentine's admirers drew between "*acta imperii,* and *arcana imperii*: that is, acts of state, and secrets of state," and he asserted that the former properly belong to "the legislative power" while reserving the latter for "the executive part of government" since the *arcana imperii* are "of a nature remote from ordinary apprehensions, and such as necessarily require prudence, time, and experience, to fit men for management." He reluctantly conceded that "much in reason may be said, and must be granted, for the continuation of such trusts in the same hands, as relate to matter of counsel, or administration of justice, more or less, according to their good or ill-behaviour," and he was therefore willing to allow "a prudential continuation of these . . . upon discretion" since, if those exercising the executive power "do amiss, they are easily accountable to the people's assemblies." But he was not willing to countenance a similar "continuation" for the members of Parliament,[75] and he insisted that the legislative and executive functions and those exercising them remain distinct.

Where "the legislative and executive powers of a state" are allowed "to rest in one and the same hands and persons," Nedham warned, "unlimited arbitrary power" is always the result. It is consequent, then, that in keeping "these two powers distinct, following in distinct channels, so that they may never meet in one, save upon some short extraordinary occasion, consists the safety of a state." The "reason" is, Nedham insists, perfectly "evident." Where "the lawmakers (who ever have the supreme power) should be also the constant administrators and dispensers of law and justice, then (by consequence) the people would be left without remedy, in case of injustice, since no appeal can lie under heaven against such as have the supremacy." A combination of these powers is "inconsistent with the very intent and natural import of true policy: which ever supposeth that men in power may be unrighteous." One must always, he adds, presume "the worst."[76]

For similar reasons, Nedham observes, one must constitute "authority" in such a manner "that it shall be rather a burthen than benefit to those that undertake it; and be qualified with such slender advantages of profit or pleasure, that men shall reap little by the enjoyment." Only in this fashion can one guarantee that "none but honest, generous, and public spirits" will "desire to be in authority, and that only for the common good."[77] To achieve this end, Nedham follows Machiavelli in advocating public accusations. "All powers,"

---

[74] In this connection, see M. J. C. Vile, *Constitutionalism and the Separation of Powers,* second edition (Indianapolis, IN: Liberty Fund, 1998).

[75] See Nedham, *EFS,* 60–64. Cf. Tac. *Ann.* 2.36.2 (along with 1.6.6, 2.59.4) and *Hist.* 1.4.2, and see Peter S. Donaldson, *Machiavelli and Mystery of State* (Cambridge, UK: Cambridge University Press, 1988), 111–40. In this connection, note also Malcolm Smuts, "Court-Centred Politics and the Uses of Roman Historians, c. 1590–1630," in *Culture and Politics in Early Stuart England,* ed. Kevin Sharpe and Peter Lake (Stanford, CA: Stanford University Press, 1993), 21–43 (esp. 28–29).

[76] Nedham, *EFS,* 147–54 (esp. 147–49).

[77] Nedham, *EFS,* 3.

he says, must be made "accountable for misdemeanors in government." When "he that ere-while was a governor" is "reduced to the condition of a subject" and "lies open to the force of the laws," he "may with ease be brought to punishment for his offence." Others, then, who "succeed will become the less daring to offend, or to abuse their trust in authority, to an oppression of the people." In the absence of such an institution, Nedham insists, there will be "no security of life and estate, liberty and property." A "liberty of accusation by the people, before their supreme assemblies," he adds, "cuts the very throat of all tyranny; and doth not only root it up when at full growth, but crusheth the cockatrice in the egg, destroys it in the feed, in the principle, and in the very possibilities of its being for ever after."[78]

The capstone of Nedham's edifice was to be the militia. Machiavelli is sometimes depicted as a proponent of arms-bearing citizenship.[79] In fact, the Florentine did praise the Romans for admitting those whom they conquered into *societas* and even for extending to some of them *civitas sine suffragio* and *civitas optimo iure*, and this he did with an eye to their deployment of these *socii* and newly made citizens on the field of the sword.[80] But he never contended that arms-bearing should depend on citizenship or vice versa. In *The Prince* and in his *Discourses on Livy*, he criticized mercenary forces as unreliable; and, in both, he insisted that a prince and a republic alike need their own arms.[81] To this end, in his *Art of War*, he championed the creation of a popular militia – but this was to be drawn not only or even primarily from the citizens of Florence, for the infantry that he had in mind was to be made up almost entirely from the subject population inhabiting the *contado* lying outside that city's walls.[82] "One's own arms," as he explained in *The Prince*, "are those which

---

[78] Cf. Nedham, *EFS*, 42, 72–76, with Machiavelli, *Discorsi* 1.7–8, in *Opere*, 88–90.

[79] The *locus classicus* is J. G. A. Pocock, *The Machiavellian Moment: Florentine Political Thought and the Atlantic Republican Tradition* (Princeton, NJ: Princeton University Press, 1975), 194–218 (esp. 199–203, 208–14), 384–86. See also Pocock, "Historical Introduction," in *PWoJH*, 18–19, 43–44; and Quentin Skinner, *The Foundations of Modern Political Thought I: The Renaissance* (Cambridge, UK: Cambridge University Press, 1978), 173–75. Note, in this connection, Hans Baron, *The Crisis of the Early Italian Renaissance: Civic Humanism and Republican Liberty in an Age of Classicism and Tyranny* (Princeton, NJ: Princeton University Press, 1966), 430–32.

[80] Consider Machiavelli, *Discorsi* 2.3–4, 13.2, 23, in *Opere*, 151–54, 163–64, 179–81, in light of *Discorsi* 3.49.4, in *Opere*, 254. In this connection, see also *Discorsi* 2.21, in *Opere*, 177–78. Machiavelli speaks of the Roman practice of founding colonies on the territory of those conquered with the same concern in mind: consider *Discorsi* 2.6–7, in *Opere*, 155–56, in light of *Discorsi* 2.30.3–4, in *Opere*, 191.

[81] See Machiavelli, *Il principe* 12–13, 20, and *Discorsi* 1.21, 2.10, 12.4, 13.2, 20, 24, 30, 3.31.4, in *Opere*, 105–6, 159–60, 162–64, 176, 181–84, 190–91, 239, 275–78, 289–91, which should be read in light of Machiavelli, *Discorsi* 3.24, in *Opere*, 231.

[82] See Machiavelli, *AG* 1, in *Opere*, 305–13. As I pointed out some time ago, Allan H. Gilbert's English translation of *The Art of War*, in which *ordinanza* is rendered not as "militia," but as "citizen army," is misleading on the crucial point. Note Paul A. Rahe, *Republics Ancient and Modern II: New Modes and Orders in Early Modern Political Thought* (Chapel Hill: University of North Carolina Press, 1994), 324, and cf. Niccolò Machiavelli, *The Art of War*, in Machiavelli, *The Chief Works and Others*, tr. Allan H. Gilbert (Durham, NC: Duke University Press, 1965), II 573–87, with Niccolò Machiavelli, *Art of War*, ed. and tr. Christopher Lynch (Chicago: University of Chicago Press, 2003), 13–26.

are composed either of subjects (*sudditi*) or of citizens or of creatures that are your own (*creati tuoi*)."[83]

Machiavelli's concern throughout was simply that one's military manpower be plentiful and that one's arms be really and truly at one's beck and call. With regard to the bearing of arms, everything that he recommended, whether to a prince or a republic, was instrumental to ensuring the fidelity of a sufficiently large, well-trained armed force. The first modern political theorist to insist, as the ancients had done, that in a republic the citizens must be soldiers and all the soldiers citizens so that citizenship and the bearing of arms should be inextricably linked was Marchamont Nedham, and it is telling that he cites not Machiavelli but Aristotle to bolster his case.[84]

Political participation as such was not Nedham's primary concern. Like Machiavelli, he was simply persuaded that, to be viable, a polity must rely on its own arms. To this observation, however, he added a corollary never explicitly mentioned by the Florentine sage: that "the sword, and sovereignty, ever walk hand in hand." If "the people be continually trained up in the exercise of arms," he contended, and if "the militia [be] lodged only in the people's hands," then "nothing" can "at any time be imposed upon the people, but by their consent; that is, by the consent of themselves; or of such as were by them instrusted." Among the ancient Romans, he explained, "a general exercise of the best part of the people in the use of arms" was universally regarded as "the only bulwark of their liberty: this was reckoned the surest way to preserve it both at home, and abroad; the majesty of the people being secured thereby, as well against domestic affronts from any of their own citizens, as against the foreign invasions of bad neighbours." It was only when "necessity constrained" the Romans "to erect a continued stipendiary soldiery (abroad in foreign parts) either for the holding, or winning of provinces" that "luxury increasing with dominion, the strict rule and discipline of freedom was . . . quitted," and stipendiary "forces were kept up at home" as well. It was then that liberty was lost.[85]

Of course, when Nedham speaks of "the people," he does not have everyone in mind. In his discussion of the militia, when he suggests that the militia be lodged in the people's hands, he indicates that it suffices that it be lodged in the hands of "that part of them, which are most firm to the interest of liberty." Later, when he describes the practice of the ancient Romans in this regard, he with impressive accuracy observes that early on "their arms were never lodged

---

[83] See Machiavelli, *Il principe* 13, in *Opere*, 278.

[84] Consider Nedham, *EFS*, 114–19, in light of Arist. *Pol.* 1297b1–27, and see Paul A. Rahe, *Republics Ancient and Modern: Classical Republicanism and the American Revolution* (Chapel Hill: University of North Carolina Press, 1992), 28–135. One might, of course, cite Leonardo Bruni's *De militia*, but this is, in the first place, a pre-modern text written within a civic humanist framework, prior to the sharp break with classical republicanism that characterizes the thinking of Machiavelli and Nedham, and it espouses the establishment of an order of civic knighthood for the leading citizens of Florence, not a civic militia of the sort that had existed in the thirteenth century. Cf. Charles Calvert Bayley, *War and Society in Renaissance Florence: The De militia of Leonardo Bruni* (Toronto: University of Toronto Press, 1961), with James Hankins, "Civic Knighthood in the Early Renaissance: Leonardo Bruni's *De militia* (ca. 1420)," forthcoming in Hankins, *Leonardo Bruni and Renaissance Republicanism*.

[85] See Nedham, *EFS*, 114–19.

in the hands of any, but such as had an interest in the public; such as were acted by that interest, not drawn only by pay; such as thought themselves well paid, in repelling invaders, that they might with freedom return to their affairs: for, the truth is, so long as Rome acted by the pure principles of a free-state, it used no arms to defend itself, but, such as we call, sufficient men; such, as for the most part were men of estate, masters of families, that took arms (only upon occasion) *pro aris et focis*, for their wives, their children, and their country." In the time immediately following the expulsion of the Tarquins, Nedham pointedly adds with the House of Stuart, as always, in mind, "the militia was lodged and exercised," as it was in his own day, "in the hands of that party, which was firm to the 'interest of freedom.'"[86]

Elsewhere Nedham acknowledges as well that, in the aftermath of a civil war, such as the one in England so recently fought, "there ought to be an especial care had to the composure and complexion" of the public assemblies, "where it is ever to be supposed, there will be many discontented humours a-working, and labouring to insinuate themselves into the body of the people, to undermine the settlement and security of the commonwealth, that by gaining an interest and share with the better sort, in the supreme authority, they may attain those corrupt ends of policy, which were lost by power." For this reason, he excludes from political participation those, such as the royalists, the presbyterians, the malignants, and the neuters, "who have forfeited their rights by delinquency, neutrality, or apostacy, &c. in relation to the divided state of any nation."[87]

Nedham is not even willing to go as far as the Levellers. He begins by conceding the democratic principle: that, in "a commonwealth in its settled and composed state, when all men within it are presumed to be its friends, questionless, a right to chuse and to be chosen, is then to be allowed the people, (without distinction) in as great a latitude, as may stand with right reason and convenience, for managing a matter of so high consequence as their supreme assemblies." But he then goes on to emphasize the role left to "human prudence" in discerning the dictates of "right reason and convenience" and in determining thereby "the latitude ... to be admitted more or less, according to the nature, circumstances, and necessities" of the nation and the times, and he elsewhere specifies that in his own country it would be appropriate to exclude from the ranks of those choosing and chosen "the confused promiscuous body of the people."[88] Moreover, he considers an enforced "equality" in wealth of the sort frequently then attributed to the Levellers to be "irrational and odious," and he prefers that there be established only what he calls "an equability of condition among all the members" of the commonwealth "so that no particular man or men shall be permitted to grow over-great in power; nor any rank of men be allowed above the ordinary standard, to assume unto themselves the

---

[86] See Nedham, *EFS*, 114–16. Nedham's understanding of the logic underlying the fall of the Roman republic was acute: see Claude Nicolet, *The World of the Citizen in Republican Rome*, tr. P. S. Falla (Berkeley: University of California Press, 1980).

[87] Nedham, *EFS*, 38, 56–60, 172–76.

[88] Nedham, *EFS*, 38, 56.

state and title of nobility."[89] In this, as in everything, Marchamont Nedham
was a practitioner of political distrust.

The End of Government

Although hostile to the claims of a titled nobility, Nedham was no more averse
to the spirit of honor, dominion, glory, and renown than was his Florentine
mentor. He delighted in the fact that "in this form of government by the people,
the door of dignity stands open to all (without exception) that ascend thither
by the steps of worth and virtue," and he believed that "the consideration
whereof hath this noble effect in free states, that it edges mens spirits with an
active emulation, and raiseth them to a lofty pitch of design and action." In
this regard, Rome was the exemplar. When it became a free state, the "thoughts
and power" of the people

> began to exceed the bounds of Italy, and aspire towards that prodigious empire. For
> while the road of preferment lay plain to every man, no public work was done, nor any
> conquest made; but every man thought he did and conquered all for himself, as long
> as he remained valiant and virtuous: it was not alliance, nor friendship, nor faction,
> nor riches, that could advance men; but knowledge, valour, and virtuous poverty, was
> preferred above them all.[90]

Honor, dominion, glory, and renown did not, however, constitute Nedham's
primary theme; and, in this important particular, he really did differ from the
author of the *Discourses on Livy*. Marchamont Nedham seems, in fact, to
have been the very first to have recognized and realized the bourgeois potential
inherent in Machiavelli's argument, for he followed through on the logic of
the Florentine's modern populism by grounding the polity exclusively on the
desire of the people for security while subordinating to that desire quite systematically the vain aspirations of the grandees for honor, glory, conquest, and
command.

"The end of all government is (or ought to be)," Nedham wrote, "the good
and ease of the people, in a secure enjoyment of their rights, without pressure and oppression." This he took to be a sufficient justification for popular
government: for "the people" are "most sensible of their own burthens," and
"being once put into a capacity and freedom of acting, are the most likely to
provide remedies for their own relief." After all, they alone "know where the
shoe wrings, what grievances are most heavy, and what future fences they stand
in need of, to shelter them from the injurious assaults of those powers that are
above them."

> It is but reason, they should see that none be interested in the supreme authority, but
> persons of their own election, and such as must in a short time return again into the same
> condition with themselves, to reap the same benefit or burthen, by the laws enacted, that
> befals the rest of the people. Then the issue of such a constitution must needs be this,

[89] Nedham, *EFS*, 39.
[90] Nedham, *EFS*, 14–15.

that no load shall be laid upon any, but what is common to all, and that always by common consent; not to serve the lusts of any, but only to supply the necessities of their country.[91]

In drawing out, elaborating, and extending the prosaic, bourgeois element within Machiavelli's spirited republican teaching, Nedham sought to forge a workable compromise between the modern populism championed by the Florentine and the traditional, English parliamentary concern with the safeguarding of rights, the protection of persons and property, and the redress of grievances.

In one other telling regard, Nedham seems to shy away from Machiavelli's argument. He had long championed raison d'état, as we have seen, and there is no reason to suppose that the future author of *Interest Will Not Lie* had altered his outlook in this regard. But he apparently calculated that it was one thing to persuade the supporters of the Commonwealth to embrace the surface teaching of the *Discourses on Livy* and another to convince them to adopt that of *The Prince*. Not for the first or the last time in his life Nedham opted for obfuscation, insisting that his free state reject "that reason of state which is the statesman's reason, or rather his will and lust, when he admits ambition to be a reason, preferment, power, profit, revenge, and opportunity, to be reason, sufficient to put him upon any design of action that may tend to the present advantage; though contrary to the law of God, or the law of common honesty and nations." In "opposition to this sandy foundation of policy, called 'reason of state,'" he urged in good Puritan fashion "a simple reliance upon God in the vigorous and present actings of all righteousness," and he rejected as "an impiety that ought to be exploded out of all nations, that bear the name of Christians," the "violation of faith, principles, promises, and engagements, upon every turn of time, and advantage."

Of course, immediately after denouncing the time-serving and the chicanery that he had so long and so skillfully practiced himself, Nedham acknowledged the force of the argument, "exprest in Machiavel," that because "the greatest part of the world" is "wicked, unjust, deceitful, full of treachery and circumvention, there is a necessity that those which are downright, and confine themselves to the strict rule of honesty, must ever look to be over-reached by the knavery of others." To be sure, he then treats as "a sad inference, and fit only for the practice of Italy" the Florentine's contention that," because some men are wicked and perfidious, I must be so too"; and he does insist, as is only just, that "the ancient Heathen would have loathed" Machiavelli's argument. But Nedham then suddenly reverses course by slyly adopting the teaching of "that unworthy book of his, entitled 'The Prince,'" and he turns this teaching to the advantage of the distrustful modern populism pioneered by the very same author in his *Discourses on Livy*. To this end, Nedham quotes at considerable length from "that unworthy" tract lest in the future his compatriots fail to recognize what he calls "the old court Gospel," and he warns them against neglecting to keep

[91] Nedham, *EFS*, 11.

watch on "the great ones of the world" who tend, he says, to be quite attached to the "doctrine" preached in *The Prince*. "If the right of laws be the way of men," Nedham observes, and if "force [be that] of beasts and great ones, then it concerns any nation or people to secure themselves, and keep great men from degenerating into beasts, by holding up of law, liberty, privilege, birth-right, elective power, against the ignoble beastly way of powerful domination." If the people are to be proper guardians for their liberty, he concludes, they must be alert to the machinations of those who "sometimes resemble the lion, and sometimes the fox," and they must "cage the lion, and unkennel the fox, and never leave till they have stript the one, and unraised the other."[92]

In pretending to repudiate the mode of thinking that he had always advocated in the past and that he would so soon again deploy in his pamphlet *Interest Will Not Lie*, in feigning a rejection of the Machiavellian critique of morality that served as a foundation for the particular species of republicanism that he himself so ostentatiously embraced, Nedham inadvertently drew attention to the chief obstacle standing in the way of a popular acceptance of the republican teaching of the Florentine. By a strange quirk of fate, the removal of that obstacle was reserved for a figure who seemed in no way at all to sympathize with the republicanism espoused in the *Discourses on Livy* by Nedham's beloved Machiavel. His name was Thomas Hobbes.

[92] Cf. Nedham, *EFS*, 141–47, 163–72, with Machiavelli, *Il principe* 15–18, in *Opere*, 280–84, and see Chapter Two, this volume. See also *MP* 60 (24–31 July 1651): 959; 112 (22–29 July 1652): 1753–55; and 113 (29 July–5 August 1652): 1769–73.

PART IV

THOMAS HOBBES AND THE NEW REPUBLICANISM

Preface

On Good Friday in 1588, the year of the Spanish Armada, Thomas Hobbes was born the younger son of an ill-educated, exceedingly bibulous, and imprudently pugnacious curate then living in the village of Westport just outside the town of Malmesbury in the county of Wiltshire.[1] From the obscurity to which his paternity would otherwise have condemned him, he was rescued by a childless and prosperous paternal uncle, who sent him to grammar school in Westport to study Greek and Latin and thence on to the University of Oxford. Later he was promoted to prominence by the noble Cavendish family, which hired the young scholar as a tutor in the summer of 1608, kept him on as a gentleman servitor after his charge came of age, and introduced him to many of England's leading lights. As Hobbes demonstrated when he translated Thucydides in his prime and Homer's *Iliad* and *Odyssey* in extreme old age, few Englishmen were as thoroughly steeped in the classics. More to the point, few had a better opportunity to drink in the new principles first broached in the sixteenth and early seventeenth centuries, and few were as eager to do so.

When, as a young scholar, Hobbes abandoned Oxford's Magdalen Hall for Hardwick Hall in Derbyshire, he left the world of the old learning for that of the new, and in the process he exchanged a contemplative posture for one of engagement in the affairs of the time. William Lord Cavendish, baron of Hardwick and, from August 1618, first earl of Devonshire, was an active man at court and an acquaintance of Sir Francis Bacon, author of *The Advancement of Learning*.[2] Bacon was a mainstay of the Jacobean regime, and he was destined for high office. He would be named a baron, then a viscount. He would join the Privy Council and become Lord Keeper of the Seal. And, between February 1607 and the spring of 1621 – when he was impeached for bribery by the House

---

[1] The most recent biography, A. P. Martinich, *Hobbes: A Biography* (Cambridge, UK: Cambridge University Press, 1999), is less noteworthy for the astuteness of its author's judgments than for its comprehensive treatment of the evidence. See, for a greater sensitivity to what Hobbes intended, Quentin Skinner, "Introduction: Hobbes's Life in Philosophy," in Skinner, *Visions of Politics* (Cambridge, UK: Cambridge University Press, 2002) III: *Hobbes and Civil Science*, 1–37, and Noel Malcolm, "A Summary Biography of Hobbes," in *Aspects of Hobbes* (Oxford, UK: Clarendon Press, 2002), 1–26.

[2] For a detailed examination of Bacon's master work, see Jerry Weinberger, *Science, Faith, and Politics: Francis Bacon and the Utopian Roots of the Modern Age: A Commentary on Bacon's Advancement of Learning* (Ithaca, NY: Cornell University Press, 1985).

of Commons and convicted by the House of Lords, fined, briefly imprisoned in the Tower of London, and then driven from the court – he would serve James I in turn as Solicitor General, Attorney General, and Lord Chancellor of the realm.[3] Few philosophers have ever risen as high.

Not long after Hobbes's arrival at Hardwick Hall, Lord Cavendish's like-named son and eventual heir established himself as Bacon's devotee. The younger Cavendish's first publication, *A Discourse against Flatterie*, which appeared anonymously in 1611 when he was twenty, was modeled on the ten essays that Bacon had first published in 1597,[4] as were the ten "Essayes," penned at about the same time and dedicated as "this dayes present" to the baron of Hardwick by his "mos[t] observant and dutifull sonne W. Cavendis-she."[5] When, with Hobbes, young Sir William set off for a grand tour of the continent in June 1614 and paused in Venice for the winter with an eye to per-fecting his Italian,[6] he did so by undertaking a translation into that tongue of the second edition of Bacon's essays, first published in 1612.[7]

Toward the end of their stay in Venice, Hobbes's pupil and future patron befriended the Servite friar Fulgenzio Micanzio, who was, as we have already

---

[3] See Lisa Jardine and Alan Stewart, *Hostage to Fortune: The Troubled Life of Francis Bacon* (New York: Hill and Wang, 1999). Note also, in this connection, Nieves Mathews, *Francis Bacon: The History of a Character Assassination* (New Haven, CT: Yale University Press, 1996).

[4] Cf. [Sir William Cavendish], *A Discourse against Flatterie* (London: Walter Burre, 1611), with Sir Francis Bacon, *Essaies*, in *WoFB*, VI 523–34. Given the close ties that developed between Cavendish and Bacon, it is conceivable that, before writing this discourse, young Sir William had seen in manuscript the second edition of Bacon's essays, which was published in 1612: see *WoFB*, VI 537–91.

[5] The manuscript was discovered in the early 1930s at Chatsworth (MS: D3), ancestral seat of the dukes of Devonshire, by Leo Strauss, *The Political Philosophy of Hobbes: Its Basis and Its Genesis* (Chicago: University of Chicago Press, 1952), xii–xiii (esp. n. 1), and is conveniently reprinted by Friedrich Otto Wolf, *Die neue Wissenschaft des Thomas Hobbes: Zu den Grundlagen der Politischen Philosophie der Neuzeit, Mit Hobbes' Essays* (Stuttgart-Bad Cannstatt: Friedrich Frommann Verlag, 1969), 135–67, who errs, we can now be confident, in asserting (ibid., 113–34) what Strauss suspected but was ultimately unwilling to affirm – that Hobbes was himself the author: note Douglas Bush, "Hobbes, William Cavendish, and 'Essayes,'" *Notes and Queries* n.s. 20:5 (May 1973): 162–64, and see Noel B. Reynolds and John L. Hilton, "Thomas Hobbes and the Authorship of the *Horae Subsecivae*," *History of Political Thought* 14:3 (Autumn 1993): 361–80. The ten essays were later revised, expanded, and published along with two additional essays – "Of a Country Life," and "Of Religion": see [Sir William Cavendish], "Observations," in *Horæ Subsecivæ: Observations and Discourses* (London: Edward Blount, 1620), 1–222. From the fact that the ten essays in draft differ from the "Observations" published in *Horæ Subsecivæ* chiefly in being bereft of references reflecting Sir William's travels on the continent, one can infer that they were written beforehand: cf. James Jay Hamilton, "Hobbes's Study and the Hardwick Library," *Journal of the History of Philosophy* 16:4 (October 1978): 445–53 (at 451–52), with Noel Malcolm, "Hobbes, Sandys, and the Virginia Company," *Historical Journal* 24:2 (June 1981): 297–321 (at 320–21), which is reprinted in *Aspects of Hobbes*, 53–79 (at 78), and needs to be adjusted with regard to chronology in light of Malcolm, "Additional Notes," in ibid., 79.

[6] For the precise dates of the tour, see Noel Malcolm, *De Dominis, 1560–1624: Venetian, Anglican, Ecumenist, and Relapsed Heretic* (London: Strickland & Scott Academic, 1984), 120, n. 280, and "Additional Notes," in *Aspects of Hobbes*, 79, who cites the account books of Sir William's father (Chatsworth MS 29: 371, 453), and Linda Levy Peck, "Hobbes on the Grand Tour: Paris, Venice, or London?" *Journal of the History of Ideas* 57:1 (January 1996): 177–83.

[7] See Malcolm, *De Dominis*, 47–52 (with the attendant notes).

observed, the secretary, chief intellectual ally, and future biographer of Paolo Sarpi, the renowned state theologian of Venice.[8] Micanzio he introduced to the writings of Bacon, and in effect he no doubt did so for Sarpi as well.[9] With the first of these two Venetians, Sir William would conduct a correspondence focused on the writings of Bacon, Sarpi's *History of the Council of Trent*, and the religious wars of the day, which would last the rest of his life.[10]

When he returned to Hardwick Hall and learned that Micanzio had attempted in vain to have his workmanlike translation of Bacon's essays published in Venice, the heir to that establishment took up the Servite friar's suggestion that he find a printer for the translation in London. At Micanzio's behest and with his assistance, he approached his correspondent's friend Marc'Antonio de Dominis, the renegade Catholic archbishop of Spalato recently arrived in London as an exile and Anglican convert, and he persuaded him to translate Bacon's Latin book *De sapientia veterum* into Italian. This work, and his own translation of the essays, young Sir William passed on in due course to Bacon's close associate Sir Tobie Matthew, who looked them over, added corrections of his own, penned a dedication to Cosimo II de' Medici, grand duke of Tuscany, and arranged for their publication together in London. In July 1618 or soon thereafter, copies of the volume were shipped to the grand duke in Florence and to Micanzio in Venice, and the latter soon reported that, with the assistance of the grand duke's secretary of state, he had managed to have the translations further corrected and reprinted in Florence, then Venice.[11] In the

---

[8] See Chapter Four, this volume.

[9] Whether Hobbes and his pupil actually met Sarpi is an open question: see Richard Tuck, *Hobbes* (Oxford, UK: Oxford University Press, 1989), 6–11.

[10] Hobbes translated Micanzio's letters from Italian into English, almost certainly with an eye to their circulation, for at least one additional copy was made, and Bacon's chaplain, William Rawley, evidently had access to this correspondence. In fact, he quotes Micanzio at length in the brief "Life of the Honourable Author," which he had printed as a preface to Sir Francis Bacon, *Resuscitatio, or, Bringing into public light several pieces of the works, civil, historical, philosophical, & theological, hitherto sleeping, of the right honourable Francis Bacon*, ed. William Rawley (London: William Lee, 1657), and which is conveniently reprinted in WoFB, I 1–18 (at 15). For the correspondence, see Fulgenzio Micanzio, *Lettere a William Cavendish (1615–1628), nella versione inglese de Thomas Hobbes*, ed. Roberto Ferrini and Enrico de Mas (Rome: Instituto Storico D. S. M., 1987). For an analysis of its significance, see Vittorio Gabrieli, "Bacone, la Riforma e Roma nella Versione Hobbesiana d'un Carteggio di Fulgenzio Micanzio," *English Miscellany* 8 (1957): 195–250. In this connection, see also Enrico de Mas, *Sovranità politica e unità cristiana nel seicento anglo-veneto* (Ravenna: Longo, 1975).

[11] Consider Francis Bacon, *Saggi morali, con un'altro suo trattato Della sapienza degli antichi*, ed. Tobie Matthew (London: John Bill, 1618), in light of the thorough and ingenious reconstruction of events by Malcolm, *De Dominis*, 47–54, and see Francis Bacon, *Saggi morali, et un tratto Della sapienza de gl'antichi*, ed. Andrea Cioli (Venice: Pietro Dusinelli, 1619), and [Francis Bacon], *Saggi morali, et un trattato Della sapienza degl'antichi* (Florence: n. p., 1619). Although in some respects superseded, Arnold Harris Mathew and Annette Calthrop, *The Life of Sir Tobie Matthew, Bacon's Alter Ego* (London: E. Mathews, 1907), remains valuable. De Dominis was not the only renegade Catholic of note to come into close contact with Bacon: see C. F. Senning, "Vanini and the Diplomats, 1612–1614: Religion, Politics, and Defection in the Counter-Reformation Era," *Historical Magazine of the Protestant Episcopal Church* 54:3 (1985): 219–39; Francesco de Paola, *Giulio Cesare Vanini da Taurisano, filosofo europeo* (Fasano: Schena, 1998); *Giulio Cesare Vanini e il libertinismo*, ed. Francesco Paolo Raimondi

meantime, Hobbes's pupil had put Micanzio into direct contact with Bacon himself.[12]

These doings constitute the visible portion of what must have been a much more considerable interchange. By 1619, the earl of Devonshire's son was so well known for his enthusiasm for the Baconian project that in a sermon, dedicated to him and preached in his presence before England's Lord Chancellor at York House in October of that year, he was described as being in league with "that noble Advancement of Learning" personified by his host.[13] That Hobbes's patron was later among the handful of intimate friends remembered in the last will and testament that Bacon dictated in December 1625 should come, then, as no surprise.[14] Nor should it be shocking that Hobbes's subsequent political speculation, which was of profound importance for the evolution of republican political thought, took place within the framework provided by the great project suggested by Bacon – which, in company with his patron, he had himself enthusiastically embraced.

(Galatina: Congedo, 2000); Jean-Pierre Cavaillé, *Dis/simulations: Jules-César Vanini, François La Mothe le Vayer, Gabriel Naudé, Louis Machon et Torquatto Accetto: Religion, morale et politique au XVIIe siècle* (Paris: Champion, 2002), 39–140; and Didier Foucault, *Giulio Cesare Vanini, 1585–1619: Un Philosophe libertin dans l'Europe baroque* (Paris: Champion, 2003).

[12] This correspondence appears to have begun in 1616 (see Letter from Fulgenzio Micanzio to Sir William Cavendish on 31 March 1616, in Micanzio, *Lettere a William Cavendish* III.78–89) and to have continued until shortly before Bacon's death: see Letter from Sir Francis Bacon to Fulgenzio Micanzio, almost certainly written in the autumn of 1625, in *WoFB*, XIV 530–32. In this connection, consider Letters from Fulgenzio Micanzio to William Cavendish on 6 and 13 May and 16 September 1622, in Micanzio, *Lettere a William Cavendish* XXX.160–69, XXXI.146–50, XLI.1–22, in light of Letter from Fulgenzio Micanzio to William Cavendish in 1626, in ibid., LXXI.8–25.

[13] See George Croom Robertson, *Hobbes* (Edinburgh, UK: William Blackwood and Sons, 1901), 19, n. 2.

[14] See "The Last Will of Francis Bacon, Viscount St. Alban," 19 December 1625, in *WoFB*, XIV 539–45 (at 542).

8

Thomas Hobbes's Republican Youth

Thomas Hobbes could not have escaped a connection with Sir Francis Bacon had he wanted to.[1] As we have already seen, he was implicated from the moment he arrived at Hardwick Hall. The presentation copy of the ten "Essayes" deliberately composed on the Baconian model, which young Sir William Cavendish gave to his father, is a fair copy in the handwriting of his tutor,[2] and Hobbes in all likelihood supervised his pupil's composition of *A Discourse against Flatterie* and its publication as well.

We do not know when the Malmesbury philosopher first met Sir Francis Bacon, but the account books of the first earl of Devonshire show Hobbes visiting the Lord Chancellor on his employer's behalf in May 1619 and again in May 1620,[3] and it is most unlikely that this was the first time their paths had crossed. Indeed, it is perfectly possible that their first encounter took place more than a decade before. We know, moreover, that Bacon corrected the Italian translation of his essays before the final version of the London edition was published in 1618,[4] and it is reasonable to suppose that Hobbes, who had in the interim become Sir William's secretary, played a considerable role in the management of this project and even in the work of translation.

In addition, perhaps as a consequence of Micanzio's keen interest in having translated into Latin the third and final edition of Bacon's essays, which was

[1] For a thorough survey of the evidence, see Robin Bunce, "Thomas Hobbes' Relationship with Francis Bacon: An Introduction," *Hobbes Studies* 16 (2003): 41–83.

[2] See John T. Harwood, *The Rhetorics of Thomas Hobbes and Bernard Lamy* (Carbondale: Southern Illinois University Press, 1986), 26–27, n. 31; Peter Beal, *English Literary Manuscripts* (London Mansell, 1987), II 583, and Noel Malcolm, "Robert Payne, the Hobbes Manuscripts, and the 'Short Tract'," in *Aspects of Hobbes* (Oxford, UK: Clarendon Press, 2002), 80–145 (at 142), have confirmed the claim first made by Leo Strauss, *The Political Philosophy of Hobbes: Its Basis and Its Genesis* (Chicago: University of Chicago Press, 1952), xii–xiii (esp. n. 1), and reaffirmed by Friedrich Otto Wolf, *Die neue Wissenschaft des Thomas Hobbes: Zu den Grundlagen der Politischen Philosophie der Neuzeit, Mit Hobbes' Essays* (Stuttgart-Bad Cannstatt: Friedrich Frommann Verlag, 1969), 116. Cf. Arnold A. Rogow, *Thomas Hobbes: Radical in the Service of Reaction* (New York: Norton, 1986), 249–52.

[3] See Noel Malcolm,"A Summary Biography of Hobbes," in *Aspects of Hobbes*, 1–26 (at 6, with n. 22), who cites Chatsworth, MS Hardwick 29: 605, 633.

[4] A copy of the book with Bacon's corrections in the margins was once on the shelves at Hardwick Hall: see Noel Malcolm, *De Dominis, 1560–1624: Venetian, Anglican, Ecumenist, and Relapsed Heretic* (London: Strickland & Scott Academic, 1984), 52.

then in preparation,[5] Hobbes subsequently came to be quite closely associated with their author. As Hobbes later told his good friend John Aubrey, when young Cavendish visited Bacon and his secretary accompanied him, the latter not only joined Bacon's entourage but was the only member of that group with any understanding of what their master was about. Accordingly, Aubrey reports, he "was beloved by his lordship, who was wont to have him walke with him in his delicate groves where he did meditate: and when a notion darted into his mind, Mr Hobbs was presently to write it downe, and his lordship was wont to say that he did it better then any one els about him; for that many times, when he read their notes he scarce understood what they writt, because they understood it not clearly themselves." For the same reason, Aubrey explains, "the Lord Chancellour Bacon loved to converse with" Hobbes and sought his help "in translating severall of his Essayes into Latin, one, I well remember, is that *Of the Greatnes of Cities*: the rest I have forgott."[6]

There is one tolerably clear indication that in these years Hobbes himself fell under Bacon's sway. In 1620, the well-known London bookseller Edmund Blount published a volume entitled *Horæ Subsecivæ: Observations and Discourses*, without, however, specifying the name of its author.[7] Among the "Discourses" contained therein was the *Discourse against Flatterie*, which Sir William Cavendish had published anonymously in 1611, and among the "Observations" were the ten "Essayes" that he had composed for his father under Hobbes's tutelage at about the same time. To these works, which had been revised and expanded, apparently in light of what Cavendish and his tutor had learned on their grand tour, were added two essays, written almost certainly by Cavendish himself, and three discourses composed in a noticeably different

---

5 Cf. Letter from Fulgenzio Micanzio to Sir William Cavendish on a date unspecified, late in 1625 or in 1626, in Fulgenzio Micanzio, *Lettere a William Cavendish (1615–1628), nella versione inglese de Thomas Hobbes*, ed. Roberto Ferrini and Enrico de Mas (Rome: Instituto Storico D. S. M., 1987) LXIX.59–63, with Letter from Sir Francis Bacon to Fulgenzio Micanzio, almost certainly written in the autumn of 1625, in WoFB, XIV 530–32, and see Vittorio Gabrieli, "Bacone, la Riforma e Roma nella Versione Hobbesiana d'un Carteggio di Fulgenzio Micanzio," *English Miscellany* 8 (1957): 195–250 (at 204–5). Micanzio was exceedingly eager to see the new essays that Bacon was composing and the older essays augmented, and in 1622 Bacon sent him a fair copy of six new essays: see Letters from Fulgenzio Micanzio to William Cavendish on 17 June 1616, 6 and 13 May, and 16 September 1622, and in 1626, in ibid., IV.5–19, XXX.160–69, XXXI.146–50, XLI.1–22, LXXI.8–25. Whether the six essays sent had already been translated into Latin or not is unclear. What is clear is that Micanzio translated them into Italian, concocted a seventh essay out of *De dignitate et augmentis scientiarum* 8.1 (which is reprinted in WoFB, I 745–49 and translated at V 31–34), added some material of his own, and managed to get them published in Venice: note Francis Bacon, *Sette saggi morali non più veduti: e tradotti nell'Italiano, contrentaquattro esplicationi d'altretante sentenze di Salomone* (Venice: Girolamo Piuti, 1626), and see Malcolm, *De Dominis*, 120, n. 288. This remarkable tribute to the fallen Lord Chancellor is proof positive that A. P. Martinich, *Hobbes: A Biography* (Cambridge, UK: Cambridge University Press, 1999), 37–40, is wrong in denying that Micanzio was genuinely interested in Bacon's thought. For a thoughtful introduction to this edition of the essays, see Robert K. Faulkner, *Francis Bacon and the Project of Progress* (Lanham, MD: Rowman and Littlefield, 1993), 27–126.

6 John Aubrey, *'Brief Lives,' Chiefly of Contemporaries, Set Down by John Aubrey, between the Years 1669 & 1696*, ed. Andrew Clark (Oxford, UK: Clarendon Press, 1898), I 70, 331.

7 See *Horæ Subsecivæ: Observations and Discourses* (London: Edward Blount, 1620).

style. Wordprint analysis strongly suggests what, in any case, we would otherwise suspect – that these were not the handiwork of Cavendish but were
written, instead, by his secretary.[8] It says a great deal about Hobbes's outlook
at the time that, when he composed "A Discourse of Lawes" for inclusion in
Horæ Subsecivæ, he fleshed out its argument with a series of passages translated without attribution from a Latin manuscript of Bacon's, available to him
at Hardwick Hall, to which the Lord Chancellor had given the title "Aphorisms
on the Greater Law of Nations or the Fountains of Justice and Law."[9]

Bacon's influence was not short lived. More than forty years thereafter,
Samuel Sorbière, the friend and admirer responsible for translating Hobbes's
De cive into French,[10] would go so far as to call that book's author "a survival
from Bacon (*un reste de Bacon*), under whom he wrote in his youth."[11] That
there is something to the claim cannot be gainsaid. Hobbes retained throughout
his life an easy familiarity with the writings of his onetime mentor. He freely
borrowed phrases and ideas from the Lord Chancellor,[12] and on occasion, he

[8] After reading the Preface to Part Four, note 5, this volume, consider *Horæ Subsecivæ* in light
of the evidence presented by Noel B. Reynolds and John L. Hilton, "Thomas Hobbes and
the Authorship of the *Horae Subsecivae*," *History of Political Thought* 14:3 (Autumn 1993):
361–80. Note, however, John C. Fortier, "Hobbes and 'A Discourse of Laws': The Perils of
Wordprint Analysis," *Review of Politics* 59:4 (Fall 1997): 861–87; then, cf. John L. Hilton,
Noel B. Reynolds, and Arlene W. Saxonhouse, "Hobbes and 'A Discourse of Laws': Response to
Fortier," ibid., 889–903, with John C. Fortier, "Last Word," ibid., 905–14, and consider Richard
Tuck, "Hobbes and Tacitus," in *Hobbes and History*, ed. G. A. J. Rogers and Tom Sorrell
(London: Routledge, 2000), 99–111. Although I am by no means persuaded that wordprint
analysis is infallible, I see no reason to doubt the attribution to Hobbes of the three discourses
singled out by Reynolds and Hilton. That *Horæ Subsecivæ* had its origins in the Cavendish
household and that Sir William Cavendish penned the "Observations" and the "Discourse
Against Flattery" published therein is virtually certain. From the style, it is abundantly clear
that the author of the three discourses now attributed to Hobbes was someone other than the
author of the "Observations" and the "Discourse Against Flattery," and the three remaining
discourses are in style and to some degree also in mode of argument strikingly similar to the
later works of Hobbes. These discourses have recently been republished in a critical edition: see
Three Discourses: A Critical Modern Edition of Newly Identified Work of the Young Hobbes,
ed. Noel B. Reynolds and Arlene W. Saxonhouse (Chicago: University of Chicago Press, 1995).

[9] Cf. Francis Bacon, *Aphorismi de jure gentium maiore sive de fontibus justiciae et juris*, in Mark
Neustadt, "The Making of the Instauration: Science, Politics, and Law in the Career of Fran-
cis Bacon" (Ph.D. diss., John Hopkins University, 1987), 239–71, with [Thomas Hobbes], "A
Discourse of Lawes," in *Horæ Subsecivæ*, 505–42, and see Fortier, "Hobbes and 'A Discourse
of Laws': The Perils of Wordprint Analysis," 861–87 (esp. 872–80), and Andrew Huxley, "The
Aphorismi and *A Discourse of Laws*: Bacon, Cavendish, and Hobbes, 1615–20," *Historical
Journal* 47:2 (June 2004): 399–412, who appears to have been unaware of Fortier's prior discovery and who errs in asserting that Bacon's *Aphorismi* have been discussed by no one other
than Daniel R. Coquillette, *Francis Bacon* (Stanford, CA: Stanford University Press, 1992), 237–
44. Had he read more widely, he would have come across both Fortier's article and Faulkner,
Francis Bacon and the Project of Progress, 215–19.

[10] See Thomas Hobbes, *Elemens philosophiques du citoyen: Traicté politique, où les fondemens
de la societé civile sont descouverts*, tr. Samuel Sorbière (Amsterdam: Iean Blaeu, 1649).

[11] See Samuel Sorbière, *Relation d'un voyage en Angleterre, où sont touchées plusieurs choses qui
regardent l'estat des sciences, & de la religion, & autres matières curieuses* (Cologne: Pierre
Michel, 1666), 75. The original edition was published in Paris in 1664.

[12] See François Tricaud, "*Homo homini Deus*, *Homo homini Lupus*: Recherche des sources des
deux formules de Hobbes," in *Hobbes-Forschungen*, ed. Reinhart Koselleck and Roman Schnur

even cited Bacon's work.[13] Moreover, throughout his life, he continued to rec-
ommend that his friends and associates read the work that his patron and
Fulgenzio Micanzio had persuaded Marc'Antonio de Dominis to translate into
Italian – Bacon's *De sapientia veterum*.[14]

Bacon's Project

Hobbes's mentor was a genuine revolutionary. Lord Macaulay would later
describe him as one of the "few imperial spirits" to exercise "the rare prerogative" of giving "to the human mind a direction which it shall retain for ages." If
"the aim of the Platonic philosophy was to exalt man into a god," he explained,
that "of the Baconian philosophy was to provide man with what he requires
while he continues to be man." If the "aim of the Platonic philosophy was to
raise us far above vulgar wants," that "of the Baconian philosophy was to supply our vulgar wants. The former aim was noble; but the latter was attainable."
It was not, he cautioned, "by furnishing philosophers with rules for performing
the inductive process well, but by furnishing them with a motive for performing
it well, that he conferred so vast a benefit on society."[15]

Macaulay's conviction was shared by no less a personage than Immanuel
Kant, who signaled his own adherence to the Baconian project by turning to
the *Great Instauration* for an epigraph with which to adorn the second edition
of his *Critique of Pure Reason* – asking his readers, as Bacon had once asked
his, to regard what he proposed therein not as "an opinion" to be embraced
but as "a project (*opus*)" to be completed, and encouraging them "to hold it as
certain that we have laid foundations not for any particular sect or sentiment
(*placitum*) but for human utility, grandeur, and growth in power (*utilitas et
amplitudo humana*)."[16]

The full significance of the transformation that Bacon initiated is ill appreciated today,[17] and for this Bacon is himself responsible – for he deemed it essential to profess orthodoxy while plotting its demise. Regarding this practice,

(Berlin Duncker & Humblot, 1969), 61–70, and Karl Schuhmann, "Francis Bacon und Hobbes'
Widmungsbrief zu *De cive*," *Zeitschrift für philosophische Forschung* 38:2 (April–June 1984):
165–90, which is reprinted in Karl Schuhmann, *Selected Papers on Renaissance Philosophy and
on Thomas Hobbes*, ed. Piet Steenbakkers and Cees Leijenhorst (Dordrecht: Kluwer Academic,
2004), 1–24.

[13] See Hobbes, *Problemata physica* II, in *LW*, IV 316–17, and *Decameron physiologicum*, in *EW*,
VII 112.

[14] See Letters from François du Verdus to Thomas Hobbes on 20 August 1654, 23 December 1655,
and 3 August 1664, in *CTH*, I 193–98, 216–29, II 621–29.

[15] See Thomas Babington Macaulay, "Lord Bacon," in Macaulay, *Critical, Historical, and Miscel-
laneous Essays* (New York: Hurd & Houghton, 1860), III 336–495 (esp. 458–59, 463–64, 480).
In this connection, see also Laurence Lampert, *Nietzsche and Modern Times: A Study of Bacon,
Descartes, and Nietzsche* (New Haven, CT: Yale, 1993), 15–141.

[16] Cf. Immanuel Kant, *Kritik der reinen Vernunft* (April 1787), in Kant, *Werke in Zehn Bänden*,
ed. Wilhelm Weischedel (Darmstadt: Wissenschaftliche Buchgesellschaft, 1968–1971), III 7, with
Bacon, *Instauratio magna*, ed. Graham Rees and Maria Wakely, Praef., in *OFB*, XI 22–25.

[17] For a partially realized, important, recent attempt to do him justice, see Richard Kennington,
On Modern Origins: Essays in Early Modern Philosophy, ed. Pamela Kraus and Frank Hunt
(Lanham, MD: Lexington Books, 2004).

he was remarkably candid, in a fashion suggesting on his part a thorough familiarity with the Averroist argument.[18] There are, he suggests, two ways of conveying a doctrine to posterity: "the *Exoteric* method" and "the acroamatic or enigmatical method," which was used "among the ancients, and employed with judgment and discretion." It is the latter method that he deems of use. Its "intention," he tells us, seems to have been "by obscurity of delivery to exclude the vulgar (that is the profane vulgar) from the secrets of knowledges, and to admit those only who have either received the interpretation of the enigmas through the hands of the teachers, or have wits of such sharpness and discernment as can pierce the veil."[19] These techniques he did not find off-putting in the slightest. He recognized that his new science defied common sense. Since, as he put it, "true philosophy" cannot "be coaxed from the preconceptions of the intellect," he doubted whether it could "lower itself to the capacities of the multitude (*ad captum vulgi*) except through its utility and works," and so he insisted that "no one of greatly superior intellect" could safely present himself to those "inferior in intelligence" except when "wearing a mask."[20] For his part, therefore, Bacon was quite happy to endorse "the discretion anciently observed . . . of publishing part, and reserving part to a private succession, and of publishing in a manner whereby it shall not be to the capacity nor taste of all, but shall as it were single and adopt his reader." In his estimation, such discretion generally served "both for the avoiding of abuse in the excluded, and the strengthening of affection in the admitted"; and for that reason, it was "not to be laid aside" by those intent on propagating the new scientific philosophy.[21] The devices which "the ancients" had employed "principally in the publication of books" he proposed "to transfer to the method of delivery" overall.[22]

Bacon recommended "that Men in their *Innovations* . . . follow the Example of Time it selfe; which indeed *Innovateth* greatly, but quietly, and by degrees scarce to be perceived."[23] Consequently, with an eye to what he had earlier called "the discretion anciently observed," he was himself, as he tells us in *The Advancement of Learning*, "studious to keepe the Auncient Termes," especially where his "Conception & Notion" might "differ from" what had come before.

[18] See Chapter Two, this volume.

[19] See Bacon, *De dignitate et augmentis scientiarum* 6.2, in WoFB, I 663–65 (translated at IV 449–50). See also Bacon, *The Advancement of Learning*, ed. Michael Kiernan, II.xvii.5, in OFB, IV 124.

[20] See Bacon, *Redargutio philosophiarum*, in WoFB, III 562. Note Bacon *Novum organum*, ed. Graham Rees and Maria Wakely, II Praef., in OFB, XI 56–59.

[21] See Bacon, "Valerius Terminus" 18, in WoFB, III 247–49. Note Bacon, "Valerius Terminus" 11, in WoFB, III 236–37.

[22] See Bacon, *De dignitate et augmentis scientiarum* 6.2, in WoFB, I 663–65 (translated at IV 449–50). See also Bacon, *De interpretatione naturae* Proemium, 12.9, in WoFB, III 520, 786–87, and *Temporis partus masculus* 1 and *Cogitata et visa de interpretatione naturae*, in WoFB, III 528–29, 618–19. Then, note Bacon, *The Advancement of Learning* II.xxiii.47, in OFB, IV 179; consider Bacon, Praef, *De sapientia veterum*, in WoFB, VI 625–28 (translated at 695–99), in light of "Procus Junonis, sive dedecus," *De sapientia veterum* 16, in WoFB, VI 654 (translated at 728), and see "Prometheus, sive status hominis," *De sapientia veterum* 26, in WoFB, VI 668–76 (translated at 745–53), especially the last sentence.

[23] See Francis Bacon, "Of Innovations," *The Essayes or Counsels, Civill and Morall*, ed. Michael Kiernan, XXIV, in OFB, XV 75–76.

In this, he intimates, citing a tag from Tacitus' *Annals*, his model was Augustus Caesar, who carried out "some alteration" in Roman institutions but, "according to the Moderate proceeding in Civill government," retained the old forms and continued to employ the traditional vocabulary for the Roman magistracies. Like the remarkable dynast who buried the Roman Republic and founded the Principate, the author of the *Instauratio magna* and the *Novum organum* was evidently prepared to pretend that a profound change in regime was simply a restoration of the *mos maiorum*.[24]

In Bacon's day, many were fooled; and, of course, in our own, many still are. Denis Diderot and Jean le Rond d'Alembert, who modeled the *Encyclopédie* on Bacon's *Great Instauration*,[25] were among those who saw through the ruse. "While adversaries, poorly instructed or malign in intention, openly made war on philosophy," wrote d'Alembert in the *Preliminary Discourse* to their immense project, "it sought refuge, so to speak, in the works of a few great men – who, without having the dangerous ambition of tearing the blindfolds from the eyes of their contemporaries, prepared from afar, in the shadows and silence, the light (*la lumière*) from which, they supposed, the world would little by little, by insensible degrees secure illumination." Of these "illustrious personages," he then announced, "the immortal Chancellor of England Francis Bacon should be placed at the head."[26]

Bacon achieved the requisite reorientation of philosophy by substituting for the traditional Christian concern with the salvation of souls an aspiration to do charitable works of a more secular sort, which might "in some measure subdue and overcome the necessities and miseries of men" in this world as opposed to the next.[27] What his invention of what is now called the social Gospel involved he spelled out succinctly in *De sapientia veterum*, the work treasured by Micanzio and Hobbes. "Natural philosophy," he wrote, "proposes to itself, as its noblest work of all, nothing less than the restitution and renovation (*instauratio*) of things corruptible, and (what is indeed the same thing in a lower degree) the conservation of bodies in the state in which they

---

[24] What Bacon neglects to cite from Tac. *Ann*. 1.1–5 is at least as important as the three words that he actually quotes: consider Bacon, *The Advancement of Learning* II.vii.2, in *OFB*, IV 80–81, and *De dignitate et augmentis scientiarum* III.4, in *WoFB*, I 548–49 (translated at IV 344–45), in light of Machiavelli, *Discorsi* 1.25, in *Opere*, 108–9. To Augustus, Bacon elsewhere attributes a preeminence quite rare: see Bacon, "Imago civilis Augusti Caesaris," "Nemesis, sive vices rerum," and "Sphinx, sive scientia," *De sapientia veterum* 23, 28, in *WoFB*, VI 339, 662–63, 677–80 (translated at 347, 737–39, 755–58).

[25] See Jean le Rond d'Alembert, "Discours préliminaire des editeurs," and Dénis Diderot, "Encyclopédie," in *Encyclopédie, ou dictionnaire raisonné des sciences, des arts, et des métiers*, ed. Denis Diderot and Jean Le Rond d'Alembert (Paris: Briasson et al., 1751–1757, 1762–1772; Neufchatel: Samuel Faulche & Compagnie, 1765; Amersterdam: Marc-Michel Rey, 1776–1780), I i–liii (esp. xxiv–xv), V 635–48a.

[26] D'Alembert, "Discours préliminaire des editeurs," xxiv.

[27] See Bacon, *Instauratio magna* Distributio operis, in *OFB*, XI 36–37. In this connection, see Timothy H. Paterson, "On the Role of Christianity in the Political Philosophy of Francis Bacon," *Polity* 19:3 (Spring 1987): 419–42, which should be read in conjunction with Paterson, "The Secular Control of Scientific Power in the Political Philosophy of Francis Bacon," *Polity* 21:3 (Spring 1989): 457–80.

are, and the retardation of dissolution and putrefaction."[28] This was the ulti-mate aim of what Bacon call his *Instauratio magna*. As René Descartes recog-nized, the English philosopher's goal was not just "the invention of an infinity of contrivances (*artifices*) that would enable us to enjoy without any effort the fruits of the earth and all the commodities which are to be found there, but chiefly also...the conservation of health, which is without doubt the princi-pal good and the foundation of all the other good things in this life," and it was this that inspired the French philosopher to become Bacon's disciple and to take up his project, refine his method, and propose in his *Discourse on Method* a course of conduct by which men might be made "the masters and possessors of nature."[29] Bacon speaks of himself as "a trumpeter (*buccinator*)" but denies that his "trumpet...summons and excites men in order that they might mutually cut each other to ribbons with contradictions or strive with one another in gladiatorial contest (*prælientur et digladientur*)." It summons them "rather in order that, having made peace among themselves, they might turn with united forces against the Nature of Things (*Natura Rerum*), storm and seize her strongholds and fortified retreats, and extend the confines of human empire (*fines humani imperii*)."[30] After 1630, if not well before, this project would come to be the focus of Hobbes's life as well.

Bacon and Machiavelli

When Bacon first proposed a reorientation of theory in *The Advancement of Learning*, he took great care to acknowledge his greatest debt. The English statesman had no more use for "the Philosophers" who "make imaginary Lawes for imaginary common-wealths" than had Niccolò Machiavelli. Even if one were to concede that they have "made good & fair Exemplars & cop-pies, carieng the draughts and pourtraitures of *Good, Vertue, Duety, Felicity*," he explained, these theorists have clearly failed to show human beings "how to attain these excellent marks, and how to frame and subdue the will of man to become true and conformable to these pursuites." Consequently, he com-plained, "their discourses are as the Stars, which give little light because they are so high."[31] It was in this spirit that he wrote, "we are much beholden to *Macciavell* & others that write what men doe, and not what they ought to do."[32]

---

[28] See Bacon, "Orpheus, sive philosophia," *De sapientia veterum* 11, in WoFB, VI 646–48 (trans-lated at 720–22), which should be read in light of Timothy H. Paterson, "Bacon's Myth of Orpheus: Power as a Goal of Science in *Of the Wisdom of the Ancients*," *Interpretation* 16:3 (May 1989): 427–44.

[29] There is, in fact, excellent reason for supposing that the French philosopher composed the letter himself: see Hiram Caton, "Les Écrits anonymes de Descartes," *Études philosophiques* n. s. 21:4 (October–December 1976): 405–14, and "Descartes' Anonymous Writings: A Recapitulation," *Southern Journal of Philosophy* 20:3 (1982): 299–311. See also Lampert, *Nietzsche and Modern Times*, 145–70.

[30] See Bacon, *De dignitate et augmentis scientiarum* IV.1, in WoFB, I 579–80 (translated at IV 372–73).

[31] See Bacon, *The Advancement of Learning* II.xx.1, xxiii.49, in OFB, IV 133–34, 180.

[32] See Bacon, *The Advancement of Learning* II.xxi.9, in OFB, IV 144, and *De dignitate et augmentis scientiarum* 7.2, in WoFB, I 729 (translated at V 17).

With this statement, Bacon did more than endorse the Florentine's repudiation of the classical and Christian understanding of virtue and his substitution of a view that defined human excellence strictly in terms of its contribution to "security and well-being."[33] With it, he hinted as well that the moral reorientation pioneered by Machiavelli in the fifteenth chapter of *The Prince* was the underpinning of his own proposal that natural science be redirected toward the same ends.[34] Lest his readers fail to recognize the relationship between the Florentine's posture with regard to politics and his own with regard to nature, he added to the expanded Latin edition of his *Advancement of Learning* the following observation: "'Things are preserved from destruction by bringing them back to their first principles,' is a rule in Physics; the same holds good in Politics (as Macchiavelli rightly observed)."[35]

To the same end, Bacon included, as the thirteenth entry in the edition of his essays that Hobbes helped translate into Latin, a remarkable piece entitled "Of Goodnesse *And* Goodnesse of Nature," in which he takes as his authority with regard to that "*Goodnesse*," called "*Humanitie*," which concerns itself with "the affecting of the Weale of men" and putatively "answers to the *Theological Vertue Charitie*," not a churchman but "one of the Doctors of *Italy*," no less a man than "*Nicholas Macciavel*." According to Bacon, this goodness "admits no Excesse, but Errour," and such errors "may be committed." In Italy, he reports by way of illustration, they "have an ungracious Proverb; *Tanto buon che val niente*: So good, that he is good for nothing." It is with regard to just such an error that he turns to Machiavelli for guidance. This man is noteworthy, Bacon tells us, because he "had the confidence to put in writing, almost in plaine Termes, *That the Christian Faith, had given up Good Men in prey, to those, that are Tyrannicall, and unjust*." Bacon does not specify that Machiavelli had objected to Christianity chiefly because it made men "weak" and "effeminate" by causing them "to confer less esteem on the honors of this world" than on beatitude in the world to come. He does not mention that the Florentine writer had attacked Christianity for treating as "the greatest good" qualities such as "humility, lowliness, and the contempt for human things." He leaves it to his readers to discover these facts for themselves by perusing the *Discourses on Livy*. In his essay, he merely urges them to take to heart Machiavelli's critique of the particular error propagated by the Christian faith. "Seeke the Good of other Men," he exhorts his readers, "but be not in bondage, to their Faces or Fancies; For that is but Facilitie, or Softnesse; which taketh an honest Minde Prisoner." Then, to indicate what he means by "Fancies," to combat "Facilitie" and "Softnesse," and to illustrate how a man might be *So good, that he is*

---

[33] See Machiavelli, *Il principe* 15, in *Opere*, 280.

[34] If one fails to take cognizance of this moral reorientation and insists on regarding Machiavelli as a classical republican, one will be deeply confused regarding Bacon as well: see, for example, Markku Peltonen, "Politics and Science: Francis Bacon and the True Greatness of States," *Historical Journal* 35:2 (June 1992): 279–305. For an essay corrective of this tendency, of which Peltonen seems to have been unaware, see Jerry Weinberger, "The Politics of Bacon's *History of Henry the Seventh*," *The Review of Politics* 52:4 (Fall 1990): 553–81.

[35] Cf. Machiavelli, *Discorsi* 3.1, in *Opere*, 195–97, with *De dignitate et augmentis scientiarum* 3.1, in *WoFB*, I 541 (translated at IV 338).

good for nothing," the English philosopher dismisses the clear teaching of the Gospels and elaborates a bizarre scriptural justification for the view that "The Love of our Neighbours" should properly be subordinated to "the Love of our Selves." Then, to bring home the radically novel character of the moral code that he recommends, Bacon contrives to end on an apparently pious but, in fact, exceedingly blasphemous note perfectly consistent with his quest to provide man with a species of secular salvation on earth. "But above all," he writes, if a man blessed with goodness "have *St. Pauls* Perfection, that he would wish to be an *Anathema* from *Christ* for the Salvation of his Brethren, it shewes much of a Divine Nature, and a kinde of Conformity with *Christ* himselfe."[36]

Though thinly disguised, Bacon's point, once suspected, is startlingly clear.[37] But, lest there be doubt, when in the same volume he surveys "The *Causes of Atheisme*," he mentions "lastly, *Learned Times*, specially with Peace and Prosperity: For Troubles and Adversities doe more bow Mens Mindes to *Religion*." The deflation of religion – to which learning, peace, and prosperity would so mightily contribute – would, in turn, undermine the ethos supporting austere virtue and would thereby prepare the way for the humane recognition of human frailty that underpins the Baconian project. Bacon's words deserve careful attention:

They that deny a *God*, destroy Mans nobility: For certainly Man is of Kinne to the Beasts, by his body; And if, he be not of Kinne to *God* by his Spirit, he is a Base and Ignoble Creature. It destroies likewise Magnanimity, and the Raising of Humane Nature: For take an Example of a Dog; and mark what a Generosity, and Courage he will put on, when he findes himselfe maintained, by a Man; who to him is in stead of a *God*, or *Melior Natura*: which courage is manifestly such, as that Creature, without that Confidence, of a better Nature, then his owne, could never attaine. So Man, when he resteth and assureth himselfe, upon divine Protection and Favour, gathereth a Force and Faith; which Humane Nature, in it selfe, could not obtaine. Therefore, as *Atheisme* is in all respects hatefull, so in this, that it depriveth humane Nature, of the Meanes to exalt it selfe above Humane Frailty.

When read in isolation, this passage would appear to be a vigorous condemnation of atheism, but this aspect of its argument is pretense and nothing more. Bacon acknowledges as much when he quotes as "Noble and Divine" Epicurus' notorious dictum – "*Non Deos vulgi negare profanum; sed vulgi Opiniones*

---

[36] Consider "Of Goodness and Goodness of Nature," *The Essayes or Counsels, Civill and Morall* XIII, in *OFB*, XV 38–41, in light of Machiavelli, *Discorsi* 2.2, 3.1 (with an eye to the shift from humility to humanity in 1.41), in *Opere*, 125–26, 148–50, 195–97, and see Exod. 32:30–33, Rom. 9:3, and Harvey C. Mansfield, "Party and Sect in Machiavelli's *Florentine Histories*," in *Machiavelli and the Nature of Political Thought*, ed. Martin Fleisher (Princeton, NJ: Princeton University Press, 1972), 209–66 (at 214, n. 6), which is reprinted in Mansfield, *Machiavelli's Virtue* (Chicago: University of Chicago Press, 1996), 137–75 (at 330, n. 6). It is by no means fortuitous that Bacon chose to make "Of Seditions *And* Troubles" the fifteenth essay in his collection: it corresponds nicely with Machiavelli, *Il principe* 15, in *Opere*, 280.

[37] It has nonetheless escaped the attention of historians writing on atheism in this period: see G. E. Aylmer, "Unbelief in Seventeenth-Century England," in *Puritans and Revolutionaries: Essays in Seventeenth-Century History*, ed. Donald Pennington and Keith Thomas (Oxford, UK: Clarendon Press, 1978), 22–46, and Michael Hunter, "The Problem of 'Atheism' in Early Modern England," *Transactions of the Royal Historical Society*, 5th ser., 35 (1985): 135–57.

Diis applicare profanum": it is not impious to deny the gods of the vulgar; it is impious to apply to the gods the opinions of the vulgar. To see what he has in mind when he speaks of vulgar belief, one need only turn from "Of Atheisme" to the essay immediately following, "Of Superstition."

In it, Bacon reverses course. From Machiavelli, he had learned the literary game of bait and switch, and in his essays he plays it with considerable aplomb. No longer does he assert that he would "rather beleeve all the Fables in the *Legend*, and the *Talmud*, and the *Alcoran*, then that this universall Frame, is without a Minde," as he had at the beginning of the preceding essay. Now he insists that atheism is preferable to all forms of superstition. Precisely because it deprives men of the means for exalting themselves above human frailty, disbelief renders them fearful of death and peaceable in general.

Atheisme leaves a Man to sense; to Philosophy; to Naturall Piety; to Lawes; to Reputation; All which may be Guides to an outward Morall vertue, though *Religion* were not; But *Superstition* dismounts all these, and erecteth an absolute Monarchy, in the Mindes of Men. Therefore *Atheisme* did never perturbe *States*; For it makes Men wary of themselves, as looking no further: And we see the times enclined to *Atheisme* (as the Time of *Augustus Cæsar*) were civil Times. But *Superstition*, hath beene the Confusion of many States, And bringeth in a new *Primum Mobile*, that ravisheth all the Spheares of Government.

To cap things off, Bacon then proceeds to catalogue "The *Causes of Superstition*" and mentions "lastly, Barbarous Times, Especially joyned with Calamities and Disasters." Thus, the circumstances which are mentioned in one essay as the cause of religion are mentioned in the following essay as the cause of superstition, and of course these are the very circumstances which modern science strives to eliminate entirely.[38] When, in the second edition of his essays, Bacon had the temerity to include among the "times enclined to *Atheisme*" not just the age of his own exemplar Augustus Caesar but "our owne times in some Countries,"[39] he presumably had in mind the England of Christopher Marlowe and the France of Pierre Charron, as well as the Italy of Pietro Pomponazzi and Cesare Cremonini, of Girolamo Cardano and Giordano Bruno, of his acquaintance Giulio Cesare Vanini, and of the Venetian state theologian Paolo Sarpi.

If in these two essays Bacon flagrantly and repeatedly contradicts himself, he does so to purpose, for, despite its twists and turns, his argument has a persistent drift. Like Machiavelli, the English statesman was that oxymoron, a political Epicurean. As such, he could conceive of "no cause of war more pious than the overthrow of a tyranny under which the people lies prostrate without spirit or vigour, as if turned to stone by the aspect of Medusa."[40]

---

[38] Cf. Bacon, "Of Atheisme," *The Essayes or Counsels, Civill and Morall* XVI, in *OFB*, XV 51–54, where Bacon cites Epicurus from Diog. Laert. 10.123 as an authority, with Bacon, "Of Superstition," *The Essayes or Counsels, Civill and Morall* XVII, in *OFB*, XV 54–56.

[39] See Bacon, "Of Superstition," *Essaies* 15, in *WoFB*, VI 560–61.

[40] To grasp Bacon's overall strategy, one should read "Perseus, sive bellum," *De sapientia veterum* 7, in *WoFB*, VI 641–43 (translated at 714–17). In this connection, consider Bacon, *Advertisement Touching an Holy Warre*, in *WoFB*, VII 12–36, in light of Jerry Weinberger, "On Bacon's *Advertisement Touching a Holy War*," *Interpretation* 9:2/3 (September 1981): 191–206;

Bacon qualified his endorsement of Machiavelli in a single, vitally important respect. In his *Discourses on Livy*, the Florentine had singled out three sorts of men as particularly worthy of eulogy: first and foremost, the authors and founders of religions; then, those who had established republics or kingdoms; and finally, those commanders of armies who had extended the possessions of their kingdom or country.[41] In his *Novum organum*, which appeared in 1620, Bacon raised the same question and published a similar list but pointedly omitted the authors of the world's religions altogether, and to statesmen he gave short shrift. The high praise that his Florentine predecessor had bestowed on "founders of cities and empires, legislators, saviors of their country from long endured evils, quellers of tyrannies, and the like" Bacon reserved for "the authors of inventions" – men whose discoveries had extended "benefits . . . to the whole race of man." It was, he suggested, both more wholesome and more noble for men to labor "to establish and extend the power and dominion of the human race itself over the universe" than for them to engage in similar exertions merely "to extend the power of their country and its dominion among men."[42] In this fashion, Bacon followed through on the logic of Machiavelli's argument, adjusted his claims, and supplemented his conclusions – first, by reversing the Socratic turn from natural to moral and political philosophy,[43] and then by effecting a transformation of Machiavellian *virtù*, which was to have profound consequences for the thinking of Hobbes. More than any other man, Bacon was responsible for the peculiar subordination of theory to practice that dictated the application of reason (*lógos*) to the mechanical and industrial arts (*téchnai*) and thereby gave birth to modern technological science.[44]

There is no reason to doubt that Hobbes, his patron, and their friends in Venice understood the implications of Bacon's argument with regard to the Christian religion. As we have seen,[45] Sarpi's notebooks confirm the suspicion, widespread in his own day, that he was an atheist, and we can presume that a similar outlook helped spark Micanzio's interest in the Baconian project. It is especially revealing that those in England responsible for producing and

Lampert, *Nietzsche and Modern Times*, 67–115; and Ralph Lerner, "The *Jihad* of St. Alban," *The Review of Politics* 64:1 (Winter 2002): 5–26.

[41] Machiavelli, *Discorsi* 1.10, in *Opere*, 91–93. Cf. Arist. *Pol.* 1253a29–39.

[42] Consider Bacon, *Novum organum* 1.129, in *OFB*, XI 192–97, in light of Richard Kennington, "Bacon's Humanitarian Revision of Machiavelli," in Kennington, *On Modern Origins*, 57–78. See also Bacon, *The Advancement of Learning* I.vii.1, in *OFB*, IV 38, and *De interpretatione naturae* Proemium, in *WoFB*, III 518.

[43] Cf. Bacon, *Novum organum* 1.79 and *The Advancement of Learning* I.v.11, in *OFB*, IV 31–32, XI 124–27, with Cic. *Tusc.* 5.4.10–11, and see Bacon, "Orpheus, sive philosophia," *De sapientia veterum* 11, in *WoFB*, VI 646–48 (translated at 720–22).

[44] For the close connection between Baconian science and the mechanical arts, see Bacon, *Novum organum* 1.98–99, 110, 117, 129, in *OFB*, XI 154–59, 168–69, 174–77, 192–97, and *Cogitata et visa de interpretatione naturae*, in *WoFB*, III 612–17. I have argued in detail elsewhere that Hobbes's political project is best interpreted as an attempt to provide a political setting within which Bacon's scientific project can more effectually be pursued: see Paul A. Rahe, *Republics Ancient and Modern: Classical Republicanism and the American Revolution* (Chapel Hill: University of North Carolina Press, 1992), 233–398.

[45] See Chapter 4, this volume.

publishing the Italian translation of the 1612 edition of Bacon's essays displayed a marked sensitivity with regard to Bacon's treatment of Christianity. It
can hardly be an accident that, where the author of the essays had described
Machiavelli as "one of the doctors of *Italie*," on the first page in the Italian translation published in London he is called "that impious (*quel empio*)
Niccolò Machiavelli."[46] Nor can it be fortuitous that "Of Superstition" was
dropped in its entirety from this Italian translation – for the only other significant omission was that of the lead essay in the 1612 edition: a piece, entitled
"Of Religion," which had caught the attention of the censor in Venice and
had spoiled Micanzio's initial attempt to have young Sir William's translation
published there.

It is not at all difficult to see why, upon reading this particular essay, the censor should have balked. Nor is it hard to understand why Paolo Sarpi's amanu-
ensis should have been so eager that the offending piece be "augmented" by its
author in a later edition rather than "lopped."[47] For, in it, Bacon outdid even
Pierre Charron in bluntly confronting the greatest scandal of the age – the fact
that Christendom was rent by religious "quarrels, and divisions," which "were
evills unknowne to the Heathen." This phenomenon he explained by observing
that, while "the gods of the Heathen were good fellowes," the "true God" was a
"jealous God," and he then quoted from Lucretius' diatribe against religion the
poet's famous lament concerning its capacity to persuade men to commit evil
deeds on the model of Agamemnon's sacrifice of his daughter Iphigenia at Aulis.
Had Lucretius witnessed the sectarian warfare, the massacres, and conspiracies
typifying post-Reformation Europe, Bacon added, he "would have been seven
times more Epicure and Atheist then he was." Finally, with an eye still on the
difference between paganism and Christianity, the English philosopher argued
pointedly that "it is better Religion should deface mens understanding, then
their piety and charitie; retaining reason only but as an *Engine*, and *Charriot
driver* of cruelty, and malice."[48]

The censor in Venice had been especially distressed at something that
Hobbes's patron had apparently added by way of explanation: "That all men
ought to unite their forces & witts for the destruction of that doctrine which
under the pretence of piety teacheth massacres."[49] It may seem surprising that
in England the licenser should have failed to catch Bacon's drift, but if the Solicitor General of the realm – and Bacon identified himself as such on the title page

---

[46] Cf. Bacon, "Della bontá, e bontá di natura," in *Saggi morali*, 1, with Bacon, "Of Goodnesse,
and Goodnes of Nature," *The Essaies* 3, in *WoFB*, VI 545. Where Machiavelli is mentioned in
Bacon, "Of Custome and Education," *The Essaies* 27, in *WoFB*, VI 572–73, there is a reference
to "un certo Autore" in Bacon, "Del costume & educatione," in *Saggi Morali*, 59.

[47] See Letter from Fulgenzio Micanzio to William Cavendish on 12 January 1618, in *Lettere a
William Cavendish* VIII.1–15. In the third edition Bacon complied with Micanzio's request in
such a manner as to make his argument less shocking: cf. Bacon, "Of Religion," *Essaies* 1, in
WoFB, VI 543–44, with Bacon, "Of Unity in Religion," *The Essayes or Counsels, Civill and
Morall* III, in *OFB*, XV 11–16.

[48] Cf. Bacon, *Saggi morali*, passim, with Bacon, "Of Religion" and "Of Superstition," *Essaies* 1
and 15, in *WoFB*, VI 543–44, 560–61, and see Lucr. 1.80–101

[49] See Letter from Fulgenzio Micanzio to William Cavendish on 12 January 1618, in *Lettere a
William Cavendish* VIII.7–13.

of the book – was not entirely above suspicion, he was surely beyond the reach of so minor a functionary.

The Sources of Civil Knowledge

That in their two decades together Hobbes and his young patron pored over the manuscripts penned and the books published by Bacon is certain. The holdings then at Hardwick Hall help to tell the tale. That they read more widely there can also hardly be doubt; and though the evidence is scanty, we can be confident that the works of Niccolò Machiavelli, Francesco Guicciardini, Traiano Boccalini, and Michel de Montaigne, as well as the writings of Jean Bodin, Giovanni Botero, Justus Lipsius, Hugo Grotius, Paolo Sarpi, and Marc'Antonio de Dominis, figured in their ruminations. We are told by Hobbes that, in his youth, Sir William displayed a keen interest in "*History*, and *Civill knowledge*,"[50] and we know that, by the late 1620s, if not, in fact, well before, volumes by the authors mentioned were on the shelves of the library made available for Sir William's use and for that of his secretary – for there survives a catalogue of this library from the period, and it was drawn up by none other than Thomas Hobbes himself.[51]

That Machiavelli played a special role in the self-education of young Sir William and his secretary also seems highly likely. By his choice of words, Hobbes himself implies as much. For, in linking political prudence with historical study, he echoes an observation that Bacon had made with regard to "Civil Knowledge," especially the "wisdome touching Negotiation or Business," and that concerning "government." In "times," such as his own time, that "abound with history," wrote he, "the form of writing which of all others is fittest for this variable argument of negotiation and occasions is that which Machiavel chose wisely and aptly for government; namely, *discourse upon histories or examples*."[52]

That the two young Englishmen should seek to become well informed in precisely this fashion makes, moreover, perfect sense. The Cavendish family was politically prominent, and its horizons were broad. Sir William was elected to the House of Commons in or soon after October 1610,[53] before he was twenty years in age; and, in this capacity, he served in the Addled Parliament from April to June 1614 and again in the Parliaments that sat from January 1621 to February 1622, from February 1624 to March 1625, and from May to

---

[50] Thomas Hobbes, Epistle Dedicatorie, in Thucydides, *Eight Bookes of the Peloponnesian Warre*, tr. Thomas Hobbes (London: Hen. Seile, 1629) sig. A1ᵛ, and reprinted in *EW*, VIII iv.

[51] Consider James Jay Hamilton, "Hobbes's Study and the Hardwick Library," *Journal of the History of Philosophy* 16:4 (October 1978): 445–53, in light of *Thomæ Hobbes Malmesburiensis vita, carmine expressa, authore seipso*, in *LW*, I lxxxv–lxxxviii.

[52] See *The Advancement of Learning* II.xxiii.1–9 (esp. 8–9), in *OFB*, IV 156–63 (esp. 162–63).

[53] See Linda Levy Peck, "Hobbes on the Grand Tour: Paris, Venice, or London?" *Journal of the History of Ideas* 57:1 (January 1996): 177–83 (at 179), who cites a letter sent by Henry Howard, earl of Northampton, to the Bailiffs and Burgesses of Bistoph's Castle, Shropshire, on 21 October 1610, urging Sir William's selection.

August 1625.[54] Moreover, in the early 1620s, he was an active member of the Virginia Company and its offspring, the Somers Islands Company, and Hobbes assisted him in the performance of his duties and was made by his master a member himself.[55] It is revealing that, when the two toured France, Germany, and Italy between June 1614 and October 1615,[56] Sir William and his tutor not only took the trouble of learning French and Italian; they developed an interest in Venetian affairs that they would continue to pursue down to the time of the former's death in 1628. When his patron "read," Hobbes reports, he did so in such a manner "that the Learning he tooke in by study, by iudgement he digested, and converted into Wisdome, and ability to benefit his Countrey."[57]

It was presumably in the congenial environment at Hardwick Hall, conducive as it evidently was to study and reflection, that Hobbes penned the two Machiavellian discourses that were published anonymously in 1620 in *Horæ Subsecivæ* alongside the essays and the "Discourse against Flattery" composed by Sir William and his own Baconian "Discourse of Lawes." In "A Discourse upon the Beginning of Tacitus," the young Hobbes meditated on the final destruction of the Roman Republic and on the establishment of the Roman Principate by Augustus Caesar.[58] In "A Discourse of Rome," he salted a highly

---

54　See Martinich, *Hobbes*, 28–77. As Linda Levy Peck, "Constructing a New Context for Hobbes Studies," in *Politics and the Political Imagination in Later Stuart Britain*, ed. Howard Nenner (Rochester: University of Rochester Press, 1997), 161–79, points out, this means that Cavendish and Hobbes were caught up in the politics of the Jacobean court well before either became involved with the Virginia Company.

55　On 19 June 1622, Hobbes was given a share in the Virginia Company so that he could vote as his patron directed and act on his behalf, which he did: see Malcolm, "Hobbes, Sandys, and the Virginia Company," 297–321, which is reprinted in *Aspects of Hobbes*, 53–79, and Martinich, *Hobbes*, 60–64.

56　For the precise date of their return, see Malcolm, *De Dominis*, 120, n. 280, and "Additional Notes," in *Aspects of Hobbes*, 79, who cites the account books of Sir William's father (Chatsworth MS 29: 371, 453). More generally, see Martinich, *Hobbes*, 29–40.

57　Hobbes, Epistle Dedicatorie, in Thucydides, *Eight Bookes of the Peloponnesian Warre* sig. A1ᵛ, and reprinted in *EW*, VIII iv.

58　See [Thomas Hobbes], "A Discourse upon the Beginning of Tacitus," in *Horæ Subsecivæ*, 223–324. For a context within which to interpret the significance of Hobbes's decision to write on Tacitus, see Alan T. Bradford, "Stuart Absolutism and the 'Utility' of Tacitus," *Huntington Library Quarterly* 46:2 (Spring 1983): 127–55; J. H. M. Salmon, "Stoicism and Roman Example: Seneca and Tacitus in Jacobean England," *Journal of the History of Ideas* 50:2 (April 1989): 199–225; David Womersley, "Sir Henry Savile's Translation of Tacitus and the Political Interpretation of Elizabethan Texts," *Review of English Studies* n. s. 42:167 (August 1991): 313–42; Malcolm Smuts, "Court-Centred Politics and the Uses of Roman Historians, c. 1590–1630," in *Culture and Politics in Early Stuart England*, ed. Kevin Sharpe and Peter Lake (Stanford, CA: Stanford University Press, 1993), 21–43; and Richard Tuck, *Philosophy and Government, 1572–1651* (Cambridge, UK: Cambridge University Press, 1993), 1–119, who fails to appreciate what earlier students of Tacitism and raison d'état understood – this tradition's profound but frequently unspoken debt to Machiavelli: cf. Giuseppe Toffanin, *Machiavelli e il "Tacitismo": La "politica storica" al tempo della Controriforma* (Padua: A. Draghi, 1921); Friedrich Meinecke, *Machiavellism: The Doctrine of Raison d'État and Its Place in Modern History*, tr. Douglas Scott (New Brunswick, NJ: Transaction, 1998), 1–204; George L. Mosse, *The Holy Pretence: A Study in Christianity and Reason of State from William Perkins to John Winthrop* (Oxford, UK: Blackwell, 1957); Rodolfo de Mattei, *Il problema della 'ragion di stato' nell'età della Controriforma* (Milan: Ricciardi, 1979); Peter S. Donaldson, *Machiavelli and Mystery of State* (Cambridge,

conventional travelogue with ruminations on the greatness of pagan Rome and reflections on the foundations of the power exercised by its successor in dominion, the Roman Catholic Church.[59] In both, he took to heart Bacon's observation regarding "the form of writing" best suited for the exposition of the parts of "Civil Knowledge" that deal with negotiation, business, and policy.

In neither work, however, did Hobbes see fit to mention Bacon's mentor Machiavelli by name. Nor did he do so anywhere else – and, in the past, scholars tended in a mechanical fashion to take such an absence of dispositive evidence as conclusive evidence for an absence of influence.[60] But it is preposterous to suppose that a man of Hobbes's erudition and penetration, intimately familiar with the works of Sir Francis Bacon, should ignore an author to whom Bacon had acknowledged that he was much beholden and fail to think through the implications of a critique of conventional morality that Bacon had found so inspiring – and when one rereads Hobbes's political works in light of this presumption, one finds evidence of the Florentine's presence at every critical juncture.[61]

The New Prince

In the case of the two discourses in which Hobbes concerns himself with ancient and modern Rome, his debt to Niccolò Machiavelli is obvious, but in the first of the two he nonetheless appears to have taken his initial cue from Sir Francis Bacon. When Machiavelli composed *The Prince* and first began working on his *Discourses on Livy*, he may have had Suetonius ready to hand,[62] but he appears not to have had access to the first six books of Tacitus' *Annals*.[63] Perhaps in

UK: Cambridge University Press, 1988), 111–40; Peter Burke, "Tacitism, Scepticism and Reason of State," in *The Cambridge History of Political Thought, 1450–1700*, ed. J. H. Burns and Mark Goldie (Cambridge, UK: Cambridge University Press, 1991), 479–98; and Victoria Kahn, *Machiavellian Rhetoric: From the Counter-Reformation to Milton* (Princeton, NJ: Princeton University Press, 1994), 60–165.

[59] See [Thomas Hobbes], "A Discourse of Rome," in *Horæ Subsecivæ*, 325–417 (esp. 330–38, 354–63, 374–78, 389–97, 403–7).

[60] For this nonsequitur, David Wootton, "Thomas Hobbes's Machiavellian Moments," in *The Historical Imagination in Early Modern Britain: History, Rhetoric, and Fiction, 1500–1800*, ed. Donald R. Kelley and David Harris Sacks (Cambridge, UK: Cambridge University Press, 1997), 210–42, quite rightly takes his fellow scholars to task.

[61] This suggests that Hobbes made the transition from philosophy to history and from the old to the new morality under the influence of Machiavelli and Bacon rather than Thucydides and at an earlier time than Strauss, *The Political Philosophy of Hobbes*, 30–128, at first supposed.

[62] The book had been available since the time of Boccaccio and Petrarch; and, albeit without attribution, Machiavelli quotes from Suet. *Iul.* 34 – but not until Machiavelli, *Discorsi* 3.13.2, in *Opere*, 219.

[63] The manuscript was brought to Rome by Pope Leo X in or soon after 1508, and the pertinent books were first published there in 1515: see Robert W. Ulery, Jr., "Cornelius Tacitus," in *Catalogus translationum et commentariorum: Mediaeval and Renaissance Latin Translations and Commentaries*, ed. Paul Oskar Kristeller, F. Edward Cranz, and Virginia Brown (Washington, DC: Catholic University of America Press, 1960–), VI 87–174 (esp. 92–97), VIII 334–35. It is revealing that Machiavelli makes no use of this material until he is well into the third book of his *Discorsi*: cf. Machiavelli, *Discorsi* 3.19–23, in *Opere*, 225–30, with Tac. *Ann.* 3.52–55, and see Leo Strauss, *Thoughts on Machiavelli* (Glencoe, IL: Free Press, 1958), 160–65. He

consequence, he had less to say concerning Augustus Caesar than one might expect. Sir Francis Bacon was differently circumstanced – and, as we have seen, he modeled his own activities as the founder of modern science on those of the statesman depicted in Tacitus' account. For him, as for Hobbes, Augustus Caesar was the supreme example of what the latter, consciously echoing Machiavelli, spoke of as a "new Prince."[64]

Thomas Hobbes was no less impressed with the achievements of Augustus than was his English mentor. But, in his "Discourse upon the Beginning of Tacitus," his focus was more narrowly political than Bacon's had been, and therein he displayed a sympathy for the species of "libertie" peculiar to what he called a "*Commonwealth*" or "*free State*," which would be notably absent three decades thereafter when he published his masterpiece *Leviathan*.[65] Moreover, though he was not averse to investigating how it was that "*Augustus . . . tooke upon him the Monarchy by force*," his real concern was the manner in which Caesar's adopted son "so settled it, as the State could never recover liberty," for it was by "politike provisions" that Augustus distinguished himself from Cinna, Sulla, and the like. They could "have mollified or extinguished the fiercer, allured the gentler sort, prepared the whole State to a future servitude," but they neglected to do so.[66]

Hobbes analyzed the machinations of Augustus in almost precisely the same fashion in which his compatriots would three decades later interpret the conduct of Oliver Cromwell. In his opinion, the Roman grandee understood the republic as Machiavelli envisaged fortune: he regarded it as "feminine," and he was rightly persuaded "that it would yeeld sooner to violence, then flattery."[67] He cannily exploited the fact that in his time the republic no longer possessed what Machiavelli termed "its own arms," and when it "put Armes into" his "hands for" its "defence," Augustus advanced "himselfe" in precisely the fashion that Machiavelli would later recommend to ambitious captains: "by converting" these arms to its "destruction."[68] More to the point, Caesar's heir anticipated Machiavelli in supposing "the love of the people . . . the principall pillar of a new soveraignty" and in recognizing that "the multitude was not stirred to sedition so much, with extraordinarie power, as [with] insolent Titles, which might put

makes use of it as well in his *Florentine Histories*, which were composed in the early 1520s: cf. Machiavelli, *Istorie fiorentine* 2.2, in *Opere*, 659–60, with Tac. *Ann.* 1.79. In this connection, see Kenneth C. Schellhase, "Tacitus in the Political Thought of Machiavelli," *Il pensiero politico* 4:3 (1971): 381–91, and Schellhase, *Tacitus in Renaissance Political Thought* (Chicago: University of Chicago Press, 1976), 3–30 (esp. 12–13), 66–84 (esp. 78–83).

[64] Consider [Hobbes], "A Discourse upon the Beginning of Tacitus," 223–324 (esp. 255, 257), in light of Machiavelli, *Il principe* passim and *Discorsi* 1.25–26, in *Opere*, 108–9, 255–98.

[65] Cf. [Hobbes], "A Discourse upon the Beginning of Tacitus," 235, 237, 261, 304–6, 310, with Hobbes, *Leviathan* II.xxi.

[66] See [Hobbes], "Discourse upon the Beginning of Tacitus," 235.

[67] Consider [Hobbes], "Discourse upon the Beginning of Tacitus," 236–37, in light of Machiavelli, *Il principe* 25 (at the end), in *Opere*, 296.

[68] Consider [Hobbes], "Discourse upon the Beginning of Tacitus," 237–38, in light of Machiavelli, *Il principe* 12–13, 20 and *Discorsi* 1.21, 2.10, 12.4, 13.2, 20, 24, 30, 3.31.4, in *Opere*, 105–6, 159–60, 162–64, 176, 181–84, 190–91, 239, 275–78, 289–91, which should be read in conjunction with Machiavelli, *Discorsi* 3.24, in *Opere*, 231.

them to consider of that power, and of the losse of their libertie." Augustus knew that "a new Prince ought to avoid those names of authoritie, that rubbe upon the Subjects wounds, and bring hatred, and envy, to such as use them," He recognized that "it is not wisedom for one that is to convert a *free State* into a *Monarchy*, to take away all the shew of their libertie at one blowe, and on a suddaine make them feele servitude." Once he had "power over the bodies of the people," he aimed to "obtaine it over their minds, and wils, which" Hobbes regarded as "the noblest and surest command of all other."[69]

Moreover, like Machiavelli, Augustus knew that "it is impossible to please all men" and that "it is therefore best for a new Prince to joyne himselfe to, and obtaine the favour of that part in his State, which is most able to make resistence against him," and this he did, following "the best order that can be, to assure a new soveraignty, *which, is to afford the Souldier money, the People a good market, and all men ease and quietnesse.*"[70] Hobbes regarded him as "a master in the Art of government." Caesar's heir understood "the Art of conforming to times, & places, and persons," which "consisteth much in temperate conversation, and ability upon just cause, to containe and dissemble his passions, and purposes." He managed affairs with such sagacity that by the time he died "[w]hatsoever might have caused a desire of returning to their former libertie, and bred a grudging of the old disease, was now removed" since "[f]ew remained that had seene the ancient Republique," and "there is never in men so strong a desire of things they have not seene, as of those things which they have." If at that time there still existed any "longing" in the Romans of the sort "which might arise ... through relation, and report, they had therein also some satisfaction. For whereas they might have heard of the names of Consuls, Tribunes, Censors, and the like, the same they found also in the present State; though the authoritie of them all, remained onely in *Augustus.*"[71]

Though Hobbes's admiration for Augustus' accomplishments as a new prince knew few bounds, he nonetheless emulated his Florentine mentor in regretting the loss, consequent upon that prince's success, of the "deepe wisedom, great, and extraordinary valour," which "thrive best" in "a *free State,*" where "they are commonly accompanied with ambition, and rewarded with honour."[72] In the same spirit he echoed Tacitus' lament that under a monarchy historians tend to sacrifice truth for the sake of flattery.[73] If at thirty-two years of age Thomas Hobbes was not a thoroughgoing republican on Machiavellian lines, it was presumably because his enthusiasm for ancient Rome was almost purely

---

[69] Consider [Hobbes], "Discourse upon the Beginning of Tacitus," 240–42, 254–55, 261, in light of Machiavelli, *Il principe* 6–9, 20, in *Opere*, 264–72, 289–91, and see Machiavelli, *Discorsi* 1.25, in *Opere*, 108–9.

[70] Consider [Hobbes], "Discourse upon the Beginning of Tacitus," 257–60, in light of Machiavelli, *Il principe* 19, 21, in *Opere*, 284–89, 291–93, and see Machiavelli, *Discorsi* 1.16.3–5, in *Opere*, 100–101.

[71] See [Hobbes], "Discourse upon the Beginning of Tacitus," 297, 304–5, 320.

[72] Cf. [Hobbes], "Discourse upon the Beginning of Tacitus," 306 with Machiavelli, *Discorsi* 1.20, 43, 2.2.3, 3.25, and *Istorie fiorentine* 3.1, in *Opere*, 105, 126, 150–51, 231–32, 690–91.

[73] Cf. Hobbes], "Discourse upon the Beginning of Tacitus," 244–47, with Tac. *Ann.* 1.1.

academic, "a matter," as Sir Philip Sidney had once put it, "more in imagination than practice," appealing solely to "the discoursing sort of men."[74]

Rome Ancient

It should not then be surprising that, like Machiavelli, Hobbes regarded pagan Rome as a marvel. "[I]n this place, and those times," he observed in his "Discourse of Rome," "there were conjoyned all singularities together, best workmen, best wits, best Souldiers, and so in every kinde Superlative."[75] After touring Italy, he wondered how it was that "the inhabitants of so wilde a place could ever come to such a greatnesse," and "from thence proceeded . . . cogitations" much like those found at the end of the first chapter of the first book of Machiavelli's *Discourses on Livy*:

First, that ease and delicacie of life is the bane of noble actions, and wise counsels. A man that is delighted, and whose affections bee taken with the place wherein hee lives, is most commonly unapt, or unwilling to bee drawne to any change, and so consequently unfit for any enterprise, that may either advance his owne honour, or the good of his Country. Any actions that reach farther then their owne private contents, in their estimation bee needlesse and unprofitable Labours. And it hath many times happened, that whilst men live in this Lethargie, that Countries, Cities, their owne fortunes and all, have been lost through their negligence.

Againe, a life of pleasure doth so besot and benumme the sences, and so farre effeminate the spirits of men, that though they bee naturally prone to an active life, yet custome has brought them to such a habit, that they apprehend not any thing farther then the compasse of their owne affections; thinke nothing beyond their present enjoyments.

On the basis of these considerations, Hobbes then adds, "I declined to the contrary, that a place of hardnesse, and a life exercised in actions of valour and not idlenesse, hath ever produced the bravest men, & arrived at the greatest fortune. . . . To prepare a man fit for both [action and direction], nothing so much prevailes as a hard and weary life, such an agitation as will not permit idlenesse, nor the minde to settle too much upon private ends, which being so, could never be aptly applyed for Publique" ends. His contemporaries he encouraged to puzzle over the fact "that a poore and hard life, a desolate, and almost uninhabitable place, brought forth such men, and they performed such actions, as in this age (we are most of us so much degenerate) we can hardly heare of without incredulitie."[76]

Of course, Hobbes was no less aware than Machiavelli that there was more to "the *Romane* Story" than the harshness of the city's immediate environment. After all, in antiquity, there were other peoples, such as the Samnites, who occupied mountain valleys considerably more barren than the fertile plain of Latium, and all such peoples that were within reach eventually succumbed to

74 Sir Philip Sidney, *The Countess of Pembroke's Arcadia* (*The Old Arcadia*), ed. Jean Robertson (Oxford, UK: Clarendon Press, 1973), 320–21.

75 See [Hobbes], "A Discourse of Rome," 357–38.

76 Cf. [Hobbes], "A Discourse of Rome," 330–38, with Machiavelli, *Discorsi* 1.1.4–5, in *Opere*, 77–78.

Rome. Moreover, by dint of conquest, Rome eventually ceased to be poor. The "multitude and riches" of the "Statues, and other Antiquities," that Hobbes had seen in Rome, "do," he observed, "wonderfully argue the magnificence of those times, wherein they have exceeded all that went before, or followed after them; and yet this sumptuousnesse nothing diverted their minds from a generous and active life, but rather instigated them; which now we most commonly finde contrary." In the end, then, the key to Rome's success was not the barrenness of the Italian landscape; it was the set of institutions and practices that turned "sumptuousnesse" into a motive for both action and direction. As Hobbes put it,

the ancient Statues of the *Romanes*, do strangely immortalize their fame; and it is cer-taine that men of those times were infinitely ambitious, to have their memories in this kind, recorded; & such was the benignity of that people, that they willingly yeelded to honour their acts, by publique expression, and in a kind, to Deifie the persons of their worthiest men, wch industry of theirs may bee gathered by the numbers of Statues of *Cicero*, *Seneca*, *Brutus*, *Cassius*, the *Horatii*, and *Curiatii*, *Cato*, and many more, whose vertue, more than their greatnesse, made them famous. Otherwise if I had only seen the Statues of the most powerfull men, and ancient Emperours, I should have thought there had been in those times as great Timeservers, as there be now, where power & authority is more esteemed of, then vertue or valour. Yet I think, if ever men of any place, in any time desired to have their names and actions to continue to Posterity, not knowing any farther immortalitie, these were they, and this one consideration pro-duced better effects of vertue and valour, then Religion, and all other respects doe in our dayes.[77]

Hobbes does not conclude his ruminations in the manner of Machiavelli by tracing the degeneracy of his contemporaries in a straightforward manner to the Christian faith. Instead, he raises the matter obliquely, in the manner of Bacon, by supplementing his discussion of the relative effectiveness of modern religion and of the pagan quest for this-worldly immortality with a response to those who may "drawe ill conclusions from these Antiquities, either tending to *Atheisme*, or *Superstition*." Although ostensibly aimed at deterring them from such temptations, his remarks are, in fact, designed to encourage them to reflect further on the reasons why theirs is a "declining age of the world, where men for learning, and height of wit, come short of those which preceded," and he ends this digression in the manner of Bacon – on an apparently pious but, in fact, blasphemous note – by expressing his surprise "at the strange blindnesse of such, who in this cleere Sun-shine of Christianity, have such a mist before their eyes (imaginary not reall) that they will still turne the image of the *incorruptible God*, into the likenesse of a corruptible man."[78]

---

[77] See [Hobbes], "A Discourse of Rome," 334, 355–58.

[78] Cf. [Hobbes], "A Discourse of Rome," 358–63, with Machiavelli, *Discorsi* 1 Proemio, 2.2.2, 3.1.4, in *Opere*, 76, 149–50, 196–97; see "Of Atheisme" and "Of Superstition," *The Essayes or Counsels, Morall and Civill* XVI–XVII, in *OFB*, XV 51–56; and consider Thomas Hobbes, "Of the Life and History of Thucydides," in Thucydides, *Eight Bookes of the Peloponnesian Warre* a1^v, and reprinted in *EW*, VIII xv.

Rome Modern

Immediately after having intimated with breathtaking audacity that the doctrine of the Incarnation is an example of superstition no less egregious than pagan idolatry, Hobbes turns from ancient to Christian Rome, and after conducting his reader on a hurried tour of that city's seven great churches, he ends his account of "the Religious antiquities, and Reliques of *Rome*" with an extended disquisition on what he calls "the Artifice of these popish traders, that they are faine to sell their commodities" by the "false light" of "miraculous reports . . . , most of them rather fayned then true," and "to set a glosse upon their Religion, by these and such like Illusions." Moreover, in doing so, the Malmesbury philosopher resorts to language reminiscent of Averroism, with its analysis of the power of *consuetudo* and its contention that the common sort of men are mired in the imagination and incapable of following and appreciating the force of rational demonstration.[79] His readers he asks to join him in considering "how easily men are drawne by circumstances, to thinke they embrace certainties, by shadowes to conclude truth, and by outward shew of zeale and Religion, to imbrace impiety."

Such is the flexibility of our nature. . . . [With many, a] false miracle prevailes farther then the written verity, a Monasticall, and severe seeming habit more perswades, then sincerity in life and manners; the representation of an image strikes deeper into their affections, then that way whereby God has made himselfe manifest in the *Scriptures*. So that they are carried away with every winde; so great is their corruption, so stupid their senses, so monstrous their ignorance.

By this you may see, it is no difficult matter to perswade these mens consciences to ones owne fancy, and to serve ones owne turne. Alasse, an outward shew of devotion, and a few good words carries them into admiration, and to imagine that *God* is better pleased with ceremony, then truth, with forme then substance. This trade hath been so long, and this deceit so customary, that many, though otherwise of strong capacities, are blinded with the same ignorance as it were by prescription: but if they would but give themselves leave to review the grounds, upon which they retaine these opinions, and search to the originall from whence they sprung, they would quickly discover the deceit. But if men will beleeve impossibilities, and for no other reason, but because other men doe so, and their Fathers did so before them; I can thinke no otherwise of such, then as of blind men, who are to follow their leaders, and may be somtimes drawn into the ditch.[80]

To this, after briefly remarking on the palaces and gardens, the colleges, churches, and religious houses that dot Rome, Hobbes pauses to analyze "the Policy" that the Church of Rome pursues for the "confirmation, and establishing of their *Religion*," and he does so in a fashion reminiscent of Machiavelli's discussion of the "return to first principles" effected by Saint Francis and Saint Dominic, and no less indebted to the account provided in Bacon's essay "Of Superstition." According to Hobbes, this policy

consists, first, in an outward shew of devotion, with strange expressions of humility, set forth in the poore and austere life of many orders, in their sundry acts of penitence, in their dayly visitation of their Churches, in their outward actions of griefe, and repentance

---

[79] See Chapters 2 and 4, this volume.
[80] See [Hobbes], "A Discourse of Rome," 374–78. Note Matt. 15:14.

at the celebration of *Masse*. Wherein is inserted all possible inventions, to catch mens affections, and to ravish their understanding: as first, the gloriousnesse of their *Altars*, infinit numbers of *images*, *priestly ornaments*, and the divers actions they use in that service; besides the most excellent and exquisite *Musike* of the world, that surprizes our eares. So that whatsoever can be imagined, to expresse either *Solemnitie*, or *Devotion*, is by them used.

In addition, they make use of "their acts of *Charitie*, wherein they exceed, and imagine this a great argument to make the world beleeve the truth, & certainty of their *Religion*," and they deploy "*miracles*, with which they make such a noise, and would have them infallible arguments to uphold their *faith*."[81]

The "last policy" that Hobbes singles out for discussion is "the course of their teaching, and disciplining," as exemplified by the practice of the English College, which forbids its novices to read Protestant tracts until they have been thoroughly indoctrinated in the Catholic faith and then, once "their opinion is prejudicated," exposes them to the alternative. Being "so strongly instructed of one side, and strangely opinionated of the other, hee is a rare man, and receives from *God* a great blessing, that ever findes the true difference. And thus being woven in their nets, they be in a manner destitute of all possibility of recovery."[82]

In the end, however, Hobbes shared Machiavelli's confidence with regard to "the Christian republic (*la republica cristiana*)" that "its ruin or its scourging is near."[83] The "ambitious thoughts, and unsatisfied desires after the wealth and glory of this world" that animated the prelates he regarded as "impertinent"; the "extremity of their pride" he considered "adva[n]tageous against them."

When the People be taught moderation and sobriety, and see excesse and liberty in their teachers, none is so blinde but must see their deceit. When they are instructed in acts of charity, and perswaded to impoverish themselves to enrich a *Priest*, who can shadow their cosenage? When they pronounce Indulgences, and we pay for them; what man can think the *Pope* hath so much interest in *God*, as to make him pardon us, for his profit? When they professe sanctity and strictnesse of life; who will beleeve him, when, after he hath gotten to be a *Bishop* or *Cardinal*, he is found to be as proud, seditious and covetous as the rest? When the *Pope* professeth poverty, and as they say in his procession, when he is elected, being carried publikely to shew himselfe to the world, hurles brasse amongst the people, and uses these words of *Saint Peter, Gold and silver have I none, but that which I have, I give unto thee*, what man perceives not their abusing of the *Scripture*, and mocking of the people? When the Pope, to shew his humility upon the *Maundy Thursday*, washes the feet of the poore, and in the meane time is attended with Cardinals, and Embassadors, some giving him water, some the towell, others holding his traine, himselfe carried into, and out of the roome, as if he were too good to tread on the earth; what man can bee so stupid that discernes not his pride?[84]

---

[81] Consider [Hobbes], "A Discourse of Rome," 389–90, in light of Machiavelli, *Discorsi* 3.1.4, in *Opere*, 196–97, and Bacon, "Of Superstition," *Essaies* 15, in WoFB, VI 560–61.

[82] See [Hobbes], "A Discourse of Rome," 392–94.

[83] See Machiavelli, *Discorsi* 1.12.1, in *Opere*, 95.

[84] See [Hobbes], "A Discourse of Rome," 404–7.

From comments such as these, it is easy to recognize what Hobbes had in common with Fulgenzio Micanzio and with the author of *A History of the Council of Trent*, whom Micanzio so faithfully served. Indeed, when one peruses Hobbes's brief discussion of the papal revenues and reads his contention that "it is quite contrary to the ordinance of *God*, and different from the example of *Christ*, and *his Apostles*," for prelates "to challenge temporall jurisdiction or superiority, when their charge is onely to *instruct*," one is induced to wonder whether Micanzio, or Sarpi himself, had made available to Hobbes and his patron a manuscript copy of the unpublished *Treatise of Matters Beneficiary*, which the latter had penned circa 1609.[85] There is also reason to entertain the possibility that, well before *Horæ Subsecivæ* was dispatched to the printer, Hobbes had perused Sarpi's *Historia del Concilio Tridentino*. The manuscript was smuggled out of Venice to London in the summer of 1618,[86] and, by the following April, Hobbes's patron had seen a copy.[87] Hobbes's discussion of priestcraft certainly suggests that he had absorbed and digested Sarpi's Machiavellian analysis of Roman Catholicism as a long-standing conspiracy aimed at eliciting resources and securing power.[88]

The Fairy Kingdom

This analysis of priestcraft Hobbes never abandoned.[89] Thirty-one years later, when he published *Leviathan*, he took care to explore in depth what he called "The Power of Spirits Invisible." Superstition he traced to the same root as science, arguing that the anxiety that causes the few endowed with strong passions, with judgment, and wit to search out the causes of things induces the pusillanimous and credulous multitude "that make little, or no enquiry into the naturall causes of things . . . to suppose, and feign unto themselves, severall kinds of Powers Invisible; and to stand in awe of their own imaginations; and in time of distresse to invoke them; as also in the time of an expected good successe,

---

[85] Cf. [Hobbes], "A Discourse of Rome," 396, 403–4, with Paolo Sarpi, *Trattato delle materie beneficiare* (Mirandola: n. p., 1676), and *A Treatise of Matters Beneficiary*, tr. W. Denton (London: William Crook, 1680). Although published half a century after Sarpi's death in 1623, the work was finished well before Hobbes and Sir William Cavendish visited Venice: see Wootton, *Paolo Sarpi*, 1–11, 78–93.

[86] For the process by which the work was conveyed in fourteen separate packets from Venice to London in the period stretching from June to September 1618 and then prepared for publication the following year by the archbishop of Spalato, see Frances Yates, "Paolo Sarpi's History of the Council of Trent," *Journal of the Warburg and Courtauld Institutes* 7 (1944): 123–43; Gaetano Cozzi, "Fra Paolo Sarpi, l'Anglicanesimo e la *Historia del Concilio Tridentino*," *Rivista storica italiana* 68:4 (December 1956): 559–619; and Malcolm, *De Dominis*, 55–60 (with the attendant notes).

[87] See Letter from Fulgenzio Micanzio to Sir William Cavendish on 17 April 1619, in Micanzio, *Lettere a William Cavendish* XIII.80–83.

[88] For the work's rhetorical strategy, see Wootton, *Paolo Sarpi*, 104–17.

[89] His fervent dislike of unpleasing priests is evident even in the translations of Homer's *Iliad* and *Odyssey* that he produced at the end of his life: see Paul Davis, "Thomas Hobbes's Translations of Homeric Epic and Anticlericalism in Late Seventeenth Century England," *The Seventeenth Century* 12:2 (Autumn 1997): 231–55.

to give them thanks; making the creatures of their own fancy, their Gods."[90] It was this natural and inescapable propensity that the clergy exploited – and none with greater success than the prelates of the Roman Catholic Church.

That institution Hobbes described as "the *Ghost* of the deceased *Romane Empire*, sitting crowned upon the grave thereof," and near the end of his book he launched into an elaborate and comic but deadly serious comparison between the Papacy and the Kingdom of the Fairies, suggesting that the "Darkenesse, Solitudes, and Graves" inhabited by the latter correspond with the "Obscurity of Doctrine" and the "Monasteries, Churches, and Churchyards" of the former. "The *Ecclesiastiques*," he reports,

take from young men, the use of Reason, by certain Charms compounded of Metaphysiques, and Miracles, and Traditions, and Abused Scripture, whereby they are good for nothing else, but to execute what they command them. The *Fairies* likewise are said to take young Children out of their Cradles, and to change them into Naturall Fools, which Common people do therefore call *Elves*, and are apt to mischief....

When the *Fairies* are displeased with any body, they are said to send their Elves, to pinch them. The *Ecclesiastiques*, when they are displeased with any Civill State, make also their Elves, that is, Superstititous, Enchanted Subjects, to pinch their Princes, by preaching Sedition; or one Prince enchanted with promises, to pinch another.

The *Fairies* marry not; but there be amongst them *Incubi*, that have copulation with flesh and bloud. The *Priests* also marry not....

To this, and such like resemblances between the *Papacy*, and the Kingdome of *Fairies*, may be added this, that as the *Fairies* have no existence, but in the Fancies of ignorant people, rising from the Traditions of old Wives, or old Poets: so the Spirituall Power of the *Pope* (without the bounds of his own Civill Dominion) consisteth onely in the Fear that Seduced people stand in, of their Excommunication; upon hearing of false Miracles, false Traditions, and false Interpretations of the Scripture.

All of this explains, Hobbes continues, why it was so easy for Henry VIII and Queen Elizabeth to conduct an "Exorcisme...to cast them out."

But, in 1651, the Malmesbury philosopher was no longer as sanguine as once he had been. "[W]ho knows," he asked, whether "this Spirit of Rome, now gone out, and walking by Missions through the dry places of China, Japan, and the Indies, that yeeld him little fruit, may not return, or rather an Assembly of Spirits worse than he, enter, and inhabit this clean swept house, and make the End thereof worse than the Beginning? For it is not the Romane Clergy onely, that pretends the Kingdome of God to be of this World, and thereby to have a Power therein, distinct from that of the Civill State." Hobbes had already alluded to the pretensions to independence propagated by the Anglican bishops, and he referred even more emphatically to the ambitions of the presbyterian clergy.[91] The class whom he described as "unpleasing Priests" was to be found, he insisted in the version of *Leviathan* that he eventually published, "not oncly amongst Catholiques, but even in that Church that hath presumed most of Reformation."[92]

---

[90] See Hobbes, *Leviathan* I.xi.23–xii.32, xiv, who cites Stat. *Theb.* 3.657–61.

[91] Hobbes, *Leviathan* IV.xlvii.

[92] See Hobbes, *Leviathan* I.xii.32. In the manuscript version that Hobbes presented to Charles II in November 1651, the last clause is absent and the following appears: "On whom when men by

Hobbes was no less infuriated than was John Milton at "the suppression of True Philosophy, by such men, as neither by lawfull authority, nor sufficient study, are competent Judges of the truth."[93] "In order that it might prosper," he argued, "philosophy ought to be free and subject to coercion neither by fear nor by shame," and to this end, he urged that "the multitude (*vulgus*) be gradually enlightened (*eruditur*)."[94] Consequently, in *Leviathan*, he declared war on the entire "*Confederacy of Deceivers*" who employ "Pious Frauds" on "them that have not much knowledge of naturall causes, and of the nature, and interests of men," and there he did battle with those who take advantage of "the ordinary ignorance, stupidity, and superstition of mankind" in order "*to obtain dominion over men in this present world*."[95] It is in this light that one should consider Hobbes's lengthy discussion of theological questions in the third and fourth parts of *Leviathan*,[96] for, like the author of *Paradise Lost*, the Malmesbury philosopher found it necessary to make of himself an enlightened practitioner of *kalām*.[97]

When one pores over the *juvenilia* of Thomas Hobbes, one can see that he had a great deal in common with John Milton, Marchamont Nedham, and their friends, and in some important regards to the very end of his life he continued to hold opinions closely akin to theirs. Had his thinking with regard to politics more narrowly understood not taken a remarkable turn in the years leading up to the English Civil War, we might today include him as a senior statesmen alongside younger men such as Henry Marten, Thomas Chaloner, Thomas May, John Wildman, Algernon Sidney, Henry Neville, and the like. But, of course, the thinking of Thomas Hobbes did take a turn, and it is to this transformation that we will now turn.

common frailety are Carried to execute their anger, they scare downe not onely Religion, wch they reduce to Private fancy, but also the Civil government that would uphold it, reducing it to the naturall Condition of Private force." See Karl Schuhmann and G. A. J. Rogers, "Introduction to Thomas Hobbes *Leviathan*," in Thomas Hobbes, *Leviathan: A Critical Edition*, ed. G. A. J. Rogers and Karl Schuhmann (Bristol: Thoemmes Continuum, 2003), I 58.

93 Cf. Hobbes, *Decameron physiologicum*, in *EW*, VII 77, with *Leviathan* IV.xlvi.42, and see *Behemoth*, 95–96 and *De cive* II.x.3n.

94 Cf. Hobbes, *Lux mathematica* Ep. Ded, in *LW*, V 92, with *De homine* XIV.13, in *LW*, II 128–29.

95 See Hobbes, *Leviathan* III.xxxvii.7–12, IV.xliv.1–2, xlvii.20.

96 See Hobbes, *Leviathan* III.xxxii–IV.xlv.

97 See Chapters 2 and 4, this volume; consider Richard Tuck, "The Christian Atheism of Thomas Hobbes," in *Atheism from the Reformation to the Enlightenment*, ed. Michael Hunter and David Wootton (Oxford, UK: Clarendon Press, 1992), 111–30, and "The Civil Religion of Thomas Hobbes," in *Political Discourse in Early Modern Britain*, ed. Nicholas Phillipson and Quentin Skinner (Cambridge, UK: Cambridge University Press, 1993), 120–38; and see Jeffrey R. Collins, *The Allegiance of Thomas Hobbes* (Oxford, UK: Oxford University Press, 2005).

9

The Making of a Modern Monarchist

It would be tempting to suppose that in his youth Thomas Hobbes followed Niccolò Machiavelli slavishly, adopting his outlook in every particular. There is, however, no reason to suppose that the English writer ever shared the Florentine's liking for tumults. In his "Discourse upon the Beginning of Tacitus," he displayed his signature distaste for disorder, remarking that "civill warre is the worst thing that can happen to a State."[1] Even more telling, in "A Discourse of Lawes," the third of his three contributions to *Horæ Subsecivæ* and the one most indebted to Sir Francis Bacon, he described anarchy in terms foreshadowing his later description of the state of nature:

If men were not limited within certaine rules, such confusion would follow in government, that the differences of Right & wrong, Just and unlawfull, could never be distinguished; and that would cause such distraction in the people, & give so great an overthrow to conversation, and commerce amongst men, that all right would be perverted by power, and all honestie swayed by greatnesse: so that the equall administration of *Justice*, is the true knot that binds us to unity and peace amongst ourselves, and disperseth all such violent and unlawfull courses, as otherwise libertie would insinuate, preserving every man in his right, and preventing others, who if they thought their actions might passe with impunitie, would not measure their courses, by the rule of *Aequum* and *Iustum*, but by the square of their owne benefit, and affections: & so not being circumscribed within reasonable bounds, their reason becomes invisible; whereas when they finde that Justice has a Predominant power, they are deterred from proceeding in those acts, that otherwise their owne wils, and inclination would give them leave to effect.[2]

Nor are there grounds for supposing that Hobbes ever shared Machiavelli's taste for savagery. As early as 1629, when he published his translation of Thucydides, he deplored the fact that, for the most part, men come *"to the reading of History, with an affection much like that of the* People, *in* Rome, *who came to the spectacle of the* Gladiators, *with more delight to behold their bloud, then their Skill in Fencing."*[3] Moreover, by November 1641, when he penned the dedicatory epistle to *De cive*, Hobbes was prepared to take Cato the Censor's description of

---

[1] See [Thomas Hobbes], "A Discourse upon the Beginning of Tacitus," in *Horæ Subsecivæ: Observations and Discourses* (London: Edward Blount, 1620), 239.

[2] See [Thomas Hobbes], "A Discourse of Lawes," in *Horæ Subsecivæ*, 504–42 (at 507–8).

[3] See Thomas Hobbes, "To the Readers," in Thucydides, *Eight Bookes of the Peloponnesian Warre*, tr. Thomas Hobbes (London: Hen. Seile, 1629) A4[r], and reprinted in *EW*, VIII ix.

kings as "a species of rapacious beasts" and apply it to Machiavelli's beloved Rome.[4] It was not, however, until *Leviathan* that Hobbes directed his ire at Machiavelli himself.

Hobbes's *Kehre*

In what constitutes his most mature effort in political science, the philosopher from Malmesbury was especially blunt in his rejection of classical antiquity. "In these western parts of the world," he observed, "we are made to receive our opinions concerning the institution and rights of commonwealths from *Aristotle, Cicero*, and other men, Greeks and Romans, that living under popular states, derived those rights, not from the principles of nature, but transcribed them into their books out of the practices of their own commonwealths." This propensity he had come to regard as a catastrophe. In *Behemoth*, a dialogue on the English civil wars that he penned in the early years after the Restoration, he would ask, "[W]ho can be a good subject to monarchy, whose principles are taken from the enemies of monarchy, such as were Cicero, Seneca, Cato, and other politicians of Rome, and Aristotle of Athens, who seldom speak of kings but as of wolves and other ravenous beasts?"[5] In *De cive*, which Hobbes published nearly a decade before *Leviathan*, he had included Plato and Plutarch on a list of figures whom he derided as "the maintainers of the Greek and Roman anarchies," and, in *Historia ecclesiastica*, which he composed quite late in his life, he mentions Cicero, Seneca, and even Tacitus among the "thousands [who] have followed" Aristotle in this regard.[6] "[B]y reading of these Greek and Latin authors," he observes in *Leviathan*, "men from their childhood have gotten a habit (under a false show of liberty) of favouring tumults and of licentious controlling the actions of their sovereigns, and again of controlling those controllers, with the effusion of so much blood as I think I may truly say: there was never anything so dearly bought, as these western parts have bought the learning of the Greek and Latin tongues."[7]

One may doubt whether Hobbes was ever a devotee of the political thought of Aristotle and Cicero. Nowhere, not even in his *juvenilia*, does he contend that man is by nature a political animal. Nowhere does he identify as the distinctive human feature man's capacity for reasoned speech (*lógos*) concerning the advantageous, the just, and the good. Nowhere does he endorse

---

[4] Cf. Hobbes, *De cive* Ep. Ded. [1]–[3], with Plut. *Cat. Mai.* 8.

[5] See Hobbes, *Leviathan* II.xxi.8, and Hobbes, *Behemoth*, 158. Note also Hobbes, *Elements of Law* II.viii.10. In this connection, see Karl Schuhmann, "Hobbes and the Political Thought of Plato and Aristotle," in *Politica e diritto in Hobbes*, ed. Giuseppi Sorgi (Milan: A. Giuffrè, 1995), 1–36 (esp. 21–36), reprinted in Karl Schuhmann, *Selected Papers on Renaissance Philosophy and on Thomas Hobbes*, ed. Piet Steenbakkers and Cees Leijenhorst (Dordrecht: Kluwer Academic, 2004), 191–218 (esp. 207–18).

[6] See Hobbes, *De cive* III.xii.3, and Hobbes, *Historia ecclesiastica* 365–84, in *LW*, V 359.

[7] See Hobbes, *Leviathan* II.xxi.8. For an extended meditation on these passages, see Moshe Berent, "Hobbes and the 'Greek Tongues,'" *History of Political Thought* 17:1 (Spring 1996): 36–59, and "*Stasis*, or the Greek Invention of Politics," *History of Political Thought* 19:3 (Autumn 1998): 331–62.

the classical republican doctrine of differential moral and political rationality. Indeed, nowhere in his discussion of the Roman Republic does he emphasize the centrality of political deliberation or remark on the role accorded oratory. Such a stance would have been hard to square with his undoubted admiration for Machiavelli, who was, as we have seen, openly dismissive of the ancient political philosophers, their imaginary republics, their propensity to judge men and events from a moral perspective, and their presumptions concerning the character of human rationality.[8] And it would have put Hobbes no less at odds with his mentor Bacon, who shared Machiavelli's distaste for the classical political philosophers; who classified Aristotle and his pupil Theophrastus, along with the founders of the other philosophical schools, as little better than sophists peddling a "*sapientia . . . professoria*," a wisdom suited to public presentation by a professional teacher, tending to give rise "to disputation, a species exceedingly adverse to inquiry regarding truth"; and who traced the bitter quarrels dividing Christendom in his own day to what he called "pugnacious and thorny philosophy of Aristotle."[9]

Missing from Hobbes's *juvenilia*, however, was the vehemence with which in *De cive*, *Leviathan*, *Behemoth*, and the *Historia ecclesiastica* he rejects the peripatetic and his many disciples. There is, of course, a reason for his newfound polemical edge. Well before April 1640, when the Short Parliament met and Hobbes, at the instigation of the earl of Newcastle, began working in earnest on his *Elements of Law*,[10] his distaste for Aristotle and his heirs had ceased to be a matter merely academic, and by the time that he published *De cive* in a limited edition in April 1642, his worst fears had been realized: civil war had engulfed his native land. Given his presumptions, Hobbes had every reason to be fierce and unrelenting in the case he made against classical republicanism and those who interpreted the interplay between King and Parliament in light of the ruminations of Aristotle and Polybius on the mixed regime. In his judgment, those among his own friends from the circle at Great Tew who had foisted such an interpretation of the English constitution on Charles I, had unwittingly done English kingship untold harm.[11]

In his *Elements of Law*, in *De cive*, and in *Leviathan*, the philosopher of Malmesbury went to the very heart of the matter. To the veneration shown *lógos* in antiquity he paid particular attention, and he explored as well the ethos of vainglory that followed from what he regarded as man's unjustified

---

[8] See Chapters 1 and 2, this volume.

[9] See Francis Bacon, *Novum organum*, ed. Graham Rees and Maria Wakely, 1.71, 89, in *OFB*, XI 112–15, 143–46.

[10] Consider Hobbes, *Elements of Law* Ep. Ded. and *Considerations upon the Reputation of Thomas Hobbes*, in *EW*, IV 414, in light of *ABL*, 230.

[11] Consider Charles I, *XIX. Propositions Made by Both Houses of Parliament, to the Kings Most Excellent Majestie: With His Majesties Answer Thereunto* (York, 1642), in *The Struggle for Sovereignty: Seventeenth-Century English Political Tracts*, ed. Joyce Lee Malcom (Indianapolis, IN: Liberty Fund, 1999), I 145–78, in light of Michael Mendle, *Dangerous Positions: Mixed Government, the Estates of the Realm, and the Making of the Answer to the XIX Propositions* (University: University of Alabama Press, 1985). In this connection, see David L. Smith, *Constitutional Royalism and the Search for Settlement, c. 1640–1649* (Cambridge, UK: Cambridge University Press, 1994).

pride in his capacity for reason and speech. To these, he attributed the prevalence of faction within the ancient republics. To these, he attributed the sectarian disputes that rent Christendom. On these, he blamed the collapse of civility in his own country. Hobbes was persuaded that, in the crucial regard, the possession of *lógos* renders men not more but less political than Aristotle's ants and his bees. Precisely because of their limitations, these dumb animals are incapable of argument and dispute, and they therefore have nothing to fear from sedition. To begin with, he remarked, they are free from all "contestation of honour and preferment," and the "naturall appetite" of such creatures is "conformable" so that "they desire the common good which among them differs not from their private." If they are "voyd of reason" and have "the use of their voyce" solely "to signify their affections to each other," it is an advantage of sorts, for these apparent defects prevent the ants and the bees from finding fault with the administration of the commonwealth, from falling prey to illusion regarding good and evil, and from perceiving injury where there is no real harm. "[T]he tongue of man is," he concluded, "a trumpet of warre, and sedition."[12]

In most regards, the argument that Hobbes in *Leviathan* directed against the admirers of ancient Greece and Rome was a restatement: it recapitulated the grounds for Machiavelli's critique of the classical republican longing for consensus and concord, it recast the savage attack that Bacon had directed against the philosophical underpinnings of Christian theology, and it repeated what Hobbes himself had said in his *Elements of Law* and *De cive*. There was, however, one element in Hobbes's analysis that was genuinely new – his excoriation of those modern admirers of the classical achievement who thought it appropriate that subjects exercise a measure of control over sovereigns, who harbored an affection for political "tumults," and who believed it possible to elicit good government from controls intelligently designed and conflict cunningly channeled. This attack was, moreover, surprising – for, as its author knew, the first and most distinguished of those who favored tumults and judged political bridles desirable and efficacious was none other than Niccolò Machiavelli,[13] and though inclined in England to defend prerogative, to such expedients Sir Francis Bacon had not been himself entirely averse.[14]

---

[12] Cf. Hobbes, *De cive* II.v.5, xii.3, with Arist. *Pol.* 1252b27–1253a39. For earlier and later versions of this discussion, see Hobbes, *Elements of Law* I.xix.5, and *Leviathan* II.xvii.6–12. Since my ultimate focus in this chapter is Hobbes's impact on the English republicans, in quoting *De cive*, I use the slapdash English translation of the otherwise anonymous C. C. (probably, the young poet Charles Cotton), which was published in March 1651 under the title *Philosophicall Rudiments Concerning Government and Society*: see Hobbes, *Philosophicall Rudiments*, which should be read in light of Noel Malcolm, "Charles Cotton, Translator of *De cive*," *Huntington Library Quarterly* 61:2 (2000): 259–87, which is reprinted in Malcolm, *Aspects of Hobbes* (Oxford, UK: Clarendon Press, 2002), 234–58. For a more accurate translation, see Thomas Hobbes, *On the Citizen*, ed. and tr. Richard Tuck and Michael Silverthorne (Cambridge, UK: Cambridge University Press, 1998).

[13] Cf. Hobbes, *Leviathan* II.xxi.8, with Machiavelli, *Discorsi* 1.2–6, 34–35, in Machiavelli, *Opere*, 78–87, 116–18, which should be read in light of Polyb. 6.2.1–58.13.

[14] See Francis Bacon, *The Advancement of Learning*, ed. Michael Kiernan, II.xxii.6 (at the end), in *OFB*, IV 149–50.

Hobbes had the Florentine and his admirers in the Rump Parliament fore-most in mind when, in *Leviathan*, he rejected the very idea that there was such a thing as what he had once with evident admiration termed "a *free State*."[15] As late as May 1640, when he put the finishing touches on his *Elements of Law*, the Malmesbury philosopher had been willing to endorse Aristotle's claim that "*[t]he ground or intention of a democracy, is liberty*" as well as the peripatetic's reliance on the fact that "*men ordinarily say this: that no man can partake of liberty, but only in a popular commonwealth.*"[16] To refute this powerful pre-sumption, to which Aristotle in his day and many another since had appealed, Hobbes in *Leviathan* narrowed the definition of liberty, treating it solely and simply as "the absence of opposition" or "external impediments of motion" in such a fashion as to restrict its application to "*bodies*" and divorce it entirely from questions of political participation. This enabled him to deny that lib-erty is more effectually provided for in a republic, such as Lucca, than in an absolute monarchy, such as he hoped to see established in England. In keep-ing with his aim, Hobbes has nothing at all to say about citizenship. When he speaks of liberty with regard to the political sphere, he speaks solely of "the *liberty of subjects*," which, in republics and monarchies alike, consists solely "in all kinds of actions by the laws praetermitted" wherein "men have the lib-erty of doing what their own reasons shall suggest for the most profitable to themselves." As for the "liberty whereof there is so frequent and honourable mention in the histories and philosophy of the ancient Greeks and Romans, and in the writings and discourse of those that from them have received all their learning in the politics," Hobbes feigns incredulity. He denies that this could possibly be "the liberty of particular men." It makes no sense, he asserts, to suppose that it is anything other than "the liberty of the commonwealth" itself.

Hobbes insists on narrowing the definition of this crucial term because he is persuaded that "it is an easy thing for men to be deceived by the specious name of liberty and . . . mistake that for their private inheritance and birth right, which is the right of the public only." In his opinion, this error has been especially influential in Europe, and it has produced "sedition and change of government" because it is "confirmed by the authority of men in reputation for their writings in this subject."[17] At some point in the three decades separating the composition of his two discourses concerning Rome and that of *Leviathan*, Hobbes's political thinking had evidently taken a genuine turn.

[15] See Chapter 8, this volume.
[16] Cf. Hobbes, *Elements of Law* II.viii.3 with Arist. *Pol.* 1317a40–b17, and see Hobbes, *De cive* II.x.8.
[17] See Hobbes, *Leviathan* II.xxi, which should be read in light of *De cive* II.x.8. On the overall significance of the shift in perspective that takes place in Hobbes's thinking in the years stretching from 1640 to 1651, see Leo Strauss, *The Political Philosophy of Hobbes: Its Basis and Its Genesis* (Chicago: University of Chicago Press, 1952), 59–78. See also Quentin Skinner, "Thomas Hobbes on the Proper Signification of Liberty," *Transactions of the Royal Historical Society* 5th ser., 40 (1990): 121–51, which is reprinted in revised form in Quentin Skinner, *Visions of Politics* (Cambridge, UK: Cambridge University Press, 2002) III: *Hobbes and Civil Science*, 209–37.

Thucydidean Ruminations

It is impossible to date with any precision the first stage in Hobbes's *Kehre*. If the Malmesbury philosopher penned anything extensive on the subject of politics in the twenty years separating the publication of *Horæ Subsecivæ* in 1620 and the circulation of his *Elements of Law* in manuscript in and after May 1640, it has not been unearthed. There is only one brief document that is pertinent – the "Life and History of Thucydides," with which he prefaced the translation of the Greek historian that he published in 1629, shortly after the death of his pupil, patron, employer, and friend, the second earl of Devonshire. In it, Hobbes hazards a series of telling remarks, decidedly unfriendly to republican government, which clearly foreshadow the position that he takes in *Elements of Law* and *De cive*.

To grasp the significance of these remarks, one must be attentive to the degree to which Hobbes revered Thucydides. In *The Advancement of Learning*, Bacon had singled out the Greek historian for praise, arguing that "NAR-RATIONS, or RELATIONS," such as Thucydides' "War of *Peloponnesus*" are generally superior to chronicles "in veritie & sinceritie" because they exhibit "an argument comprehensible within the notice and instructions of the Writer." "RUMINATED HISTORY" – which contains a "scattered" account of "actions . . . thought worthy of memorie, with politique discourse and obser-vation thereupon, not incorporate into the History, but seperately, and as the more principall in their intentio*n*" – he had regarded as something apart, classi-fying it among "Bookes of policie." It is, he insisted, "the true office of History to represent the events themselves, together with the counsels, and to leave the observations, and conclusions thereupon, to the liberty and facultie of every mans judgement."[18] Hobbes agreed.

Thucydides is to history, Hobbes tells prospective readers of his translation, as Homer is to poetry, Aristotle to philosophy, and Demosthenes to eloquence – for "*the* principall *and* proper worke *of History*" is "*to instruct, and enable men, by the knowledge of Actions* past, *to beare themselves prudently in the* present, *and providently towards the* Future," and in this pursuit Thucydides surpasses all others. The Greek historian's successors may insert into their narratives "*very wise discourses*" of the sort admired by Bacon, which "*commend the knowledge of the Writer.*" They may engage in "*subtile coniectures, at the secret aymes, and inward cogitations of such as fall under their Penne,*" and for this also they are perhaps to be praised. But Thucydides is cut from different cloth. He "*is one,*" Hobbes insists, "*who, though he never digresse to reade a Lecture, Morall or Politicall, upon his owne Text, nor enter into mens hearts, further then the actions themselves evidently guide him, is yet accounted the most Politique Historiographer that ever writ.*" The reason for this is clear.

He filled his Narrations with that choice of matter, and ordereth them with that Iudge-ment, and with such perspicuity and efficacy expresseth himselfe, that, as Plutarch *saith, he maketh his Auditor a Spectator. For he setteth his Reader in the Assemblies of the*

---

[18] See Bacon, *The Advancement of Learning* II.ii.5–12, in *OFB*, IV 66–70. Note also Bacon, *De dignitate et augmentis scientiarum* II.vii–x and *Considerations Touching a War with Spain*, in *WoFB*, I 507–14 (translated at IV 304–12), XIV 474.

People, *and in the* Senates, *at their debating; in the* Streets, *at their Seditions; and in the* Field *at their Battels. So that looke how much a man of understanding, might have added to his experience, if he had then lived, a beholder of their proceedings, and familiar with the men, and businesse of the time; so much almost may he profit now, by attentive reading of the same here written.*

In short, by setting exercises of a sort, Thucydides enables his reader to live through events that transpired in a distant age and become practiced in civil prudence. If such a one is properly attentive, Hobbes contends, he "*may from the narrations draw out lessons to himself, and of himselfe be able, to trace the drifts and counsailes of the Actors to their seate,*"[19] which, of course, is precisely what Hobbes himself did.

Hobbes read Thucydides with the same care that Machiavelli had lavished on Lucretius. In his brief biography of the historian, the English philosopher introduces him as a man of noble birth "descended from the *Thracian* Kings." He tells us therein that Thucydides studied rhetoric with Antiphon, and he suggests that he "was sufficiently qualified, to have become a great Demagogue, and of great authority with the *People*." If the Athenian historian evidenced "no desire at all to meddle in the government," Hobbes observes, it was arguably because "in those times it was impossible for any man to give good and profitable counsell for the Common-wealth and not incurre the displeasure of the *People*."

For their opinion was such of their owne power, and of the facility of atchieving whatsoever action they undertooke, that such men onely swayed the Assemblies, and were esteemed wise and good Common-wealthsmen, as did put them upon the most dangerous and desperate enterprizes. Whereas he that gave them temperate, and discreet advice, was thought a Coward, or not to understand, or else to maligne their power. And no marvell; for much prosperity (to which they had now for many yeeres been accustomed) maketh men in love with themselves; and it is hard for any man to love that counsell which maketh him love himselfe the lesse. And it holdeth much more in a Multitude, then in one Man; For a man that reasoneth with himselfe, will not be ashamed to admit of timerous suggestions in his businesse, that he may the stronglyer provide; but in publique deliberations before a Multitude, Feare (which for the most part adviseth well, though it execute not so) seldome or never sheweth it selfe, or is admitted. By this meanes it came to passe amongst the *Athenians*, who thought they were able to doe any thing, that wicked men and flatterers drave them headlong into those actions that were to ruine them; and the good men either durst not oppose, or if they did, undid themselves.

If, then, Thucydides "forbore to come into the Assemblies, and propounded to himselfe, a private life as farre as the eminency of so wealthy a person, and the writing of the History he had undertaken, would permit," his aim was "that he might not be either of them that committed, or of them that suffered evill." Moreover, with respect to "his opinion touching the government of the State, it is manifest that he least of all liked the *Democracy*."

And upon divers occasions, hee noteth the emulation and content of the Demagogues, for reputation, and glory of wit; with their crossing of each others counsels to the dammage of the Publique; the inconstancy of Resolutions, caused by the diversity of ends, and

[19] See Thomas Hobbes, "To the Readers," in Thucydides, *Eight Bookes of the Peloponnesian Warre* sig. A3, and reprinted in *EW*, VIII vii–viii.

power of Rhetorique in the Orators; and the desperate actions undertaken upon the flattering advice of such as desired to attaine, or to hold what they had attained of authority and sway amongst the common people. Nor doth it appeare that he magnifieth any where the authority of the *Few*; amongst whom he saith every one desireth to be chiefe, and they that are undervalued, beare it with lesse patience then in a *Democracy*; whereupon sedition followeth, and dissolution of the government. Hee prayseth the government of *Athens*, when it was mixt of the *Few* and the *Many*; but more he commendeth it, both when *Pisistratus* raigned (saving that it was an usurped power) and when in the beginning of this Warre, it was *Democraticall* in name, but in effect *Monarchicall* under *Pericles*. So that it seemeth that as he was of Regall descent, so he best approved of the *Regall Government*.[20]

Such were among the lessons that Hobbes extracted from his reading of the narration provided by the Greek historian.

For these seemingly tendentious claims as a proper reading of Thucydides, there is more foundation than one might suppose. In truth, however, they reveal even more about Hobbes's preoccupations. Indeed, when read in light of his *juvenilia*, they suggest that at some point in the 1620s – in response, one must suspect, to the impeachment of Sir Francis Bacon, in reaction to the assassination of the duke of Buckingham, and in dismay at the parliamentary struggles that eventuated in the Petition of Right – the Malmesbury philosopher turned to Thucydides, savoring him in the original Greek, and, under his influence, abandoned the Tacitism of his youth, gave up his infatuation with Machiavelli's Rome, and began thinking along the lines later evident in his *Elements of Law*, in *De cive*, and in *Leviathan*.

The publication of his translation of Thucydides was, as Hobbes later acknowledged,[21] a deliberate political act – carried out in the hope that his contemporaries might take warning from the Greek historian's account of the manner in which political competition and the attendant oratory designed to stir up the passions of the public had fostered "sedition" at Athens and elsewhere in Greece and had in nearly every case produced what Hobbes pointedly identified as a "dissolution of the government."[22] With regard to the absence within Thucydides of "[d]igressions for instructions cause, and other such open conveyances of Precepts (which is the Philosophers part)," the English philosopher was sanguine. In his judgment, Thucydides had "so cleerly set before mens eyes, the wayes and events, of good and evill counsels, that the Narration it selfe doth secretly instruct the Reader, and more effectually then possibly can

---

[20] Cf. Hobbes, "Of the Life and History of Thucydides," in Thucydides, *Eight Bookes of the Peloponnesian Warre* sig. a1ʳ–a2ʳ, and reprinted in *EW*, VIII xiii–xvii, with Thuc. 2.65.9, 6.54.5–6, 8.97.2.

[21] See *Thomæ Hobbes Malmesburiensis vita, authore seipso*, in *LW*, I xiv.

[22] In this connection, cf. Arnold A. Rogow, *Thomas Hobbes: Radical in the Service of Reaction* (New York: W. W. Norton, 1986), 78–91, who thinks the analogy with his own times intimated by Hobbes ridiculous, with Jonathan Scott, "The Peace of Silence: Thucydides and the English Civil War," in *The Certainty of Doubt: Tributes to Peter Munz*, ed. Miles Fairburn and W. H. Oliver (Wellington: Victoria University Press, 1996), 90–116, revised, abbreviated, and reprinted in *Hobbes and History*, ed. G. A. J. Rogers and Tom Sorrell (London: Routledge, 2000), 112–36, who quite rightly regards Hobbes as perspicacious.

be done by Precept."[23] To reinforce the lesson Hobbes commissioned from the engraver Thomas Cecill a frontispiece juxtaposing Sparta, King Archidamus, and a ruler consulting with a small council of the city's elegantly dressed "best men (*aristoi*)" with Athens, Pericles, and a demagogue addressing the *hoi polloi*, many of them clothed in rags.[24] The Malmesbury philosopher was no doubt pleased when his translation was reprinted in 1634 and again in 1648 and 1676, for it was from Thucydides that he appears first to have learned to think of the human tongue as "a trumpet of warre, and sedition," and he evidently expected subsequent readers to follow in his wake. As a source of civil knowledge, in Hobbes's estimation, the Greek historian far surpassed the Florentine sage.[25]

It is easy to see why an admirer of Machiavelli and Bacon would be attracted to Thucydides. The three had much in common. To begin with, in the face of *Fortuna*, none of them espoused resignation, a resort to prayer, and a reliance upon Providence. Hobbes, drawing on the pithy biography penned by the Byzantine scholar Marcellinus, dwells on his report that Thucydides studied with Anaxagoras, "whose opinions, being of a straine above the apprehension of the vulgar, procured him the estimation of an *Atheist*, which name they bestowed upon all men that thought not as they did, of their ridiculous Religion," and he goes out of his way to suggest that Thucydides resembled his mentor. It would not be "much to be regarded," he insists, if Thucydides "were

---

[23] Note Thomas Hobbes, "Of the Life and History of Thucydides," in Thucydides, *Eight Bookes of the Peloponnesian Warre* sig. a3ʳ, and reprinted in *EW*, VIII xxii, and see Strauss, *The Political Philosophy of Hobbes*, 79–107.

[24] On Cecill, see Margery Corbett and Ronald Lightbown, *The Comely Frontispiece: The Emblematic Title-Page in England, 1550–1660* (London: Routledge and Kegan Paul, 1979), 185.

[25] The literature charting Hobbes's debt to Thucydides is considerable and quite thoughtful: note Strauss, *The Political Philosophy of Hobbes*, 33–34, 44–45, 59–60, 64–68, 74–76, 79–81, 108–12 (esp. 108–12), and see Richard Schlatter, "Thomas Hobbes and Thucydides," *Journal of the History of Ideas* 6:3 (June 1945): 350–62, and "Introduction," *Hobbes's Thucydides* (New Brunswick, NJ: Rutgers University Press, 1975), xi–xxviii; Peter Pouncey, *The Necessities of War: A Study of Thucydidean Pessimism* (New York: Columbia University Press, 1980), 151–57; George Klosko and Daryl Rice, "Thucydides' and Hobbes's State of Nature,' *History of Political Thought* 6:3 (Winter 1985): 405–9; Clifford W. Brown, "Thucydides, Hobbes, and the Derivation of Anarchy," *History of Political Thought* 8:1 (Spring 1987): 33–62, and "Thucydides, Hobbes and the Linear Causal Perspective," *History of Political Thought* 10:2 (Summer 1989): 215–56; Clifford Orwin, "Stasis and Plague: Thucydides on the Dissolution of Society," *Journal of Politics* 50:4 (November 1988): 831–47; and Gabriella Slomp, "Hobbes, Thucydides and the Three Greatest Things," *History of Political Thought* 11:4 (Winter 1990): 565–86, and *Thomas Hobbes and the Political Philosophy of Glory* (London: Macmillan, 2000), 51–83; and Peter J. Ahrensdorf, "The Fear of Death and the Longing for Immortality: Hobbes and Thucydides on Human Nature and the Problem of Anarchy," *American Political Science Review* 94:3 (September 2000): 579–93. Thucydides figures also in Quentin Skinner, "Thomas Hobbes: Rhetoric and the Construction of Morality," *Proceedings of the British Academy* 76 (1991): 1–61, and in Skinner, "Thomas Hobbes and the Renaissance *Studia humanitatis*," in *Writing and Political Engagement in Seventeenth-Century History*, ed. Derek Hirst and Richard Strier (Cambridge, UK: Cambridge University Press, 2000), 69–88, which are revised and reprinted in Skinner, *Hobbes and Civil Science*, 38–65, 87–141, as well as in Skinner, *Reason and Rhetoric in the Philosophy of Hobbes* (Cambridge, UK: Cambridge University Press, 1996), 161–80, 229–30, 234–35, 238–39, 242–49, 282–83, 340, 362 – but in this body of work he is given less prominence than is perhaps his due.

by some reputed an *Atheist* to[o]. For though he were none, yet it is not improbable, but by the light of naturall reason, he might see enough in the Religion of these Heathen, to make him thinke it vaine, and superstitious." This, he adds, may have been "enough to make him an *Atheist*, in the opinion of the People," but the treatment of religion in his history suggests that he was "on the one side not superstitious, on the other side, not an *Atheist*."[26] Hobbes's choice of language in this passage is telling, and by now it should be familiar. In regard to religion, he thereby intimates, the posture proper to a politic historiographer is the skepticism and irony adopted by Machiavelli, recommended by Bacon in his essays, and exemplified by Charron in *Of Wisdom* and by Hobbes himself in his "Discourse of Rome."[27]

There were other similarities no less enticing to a man like Hobbes. Machiavelli, Bacon, and Thucydides were students of power politics. All three thought in terms of efficient linear causality. As a consequence, the threesome all became historians, for they regarded human nature as constant and unchanging and looked on past developments as a tolerably good guide to future events.[28] Tough minded and unsentimental they were in the extreme.

Thucydides differed from Machiavelli and Bacon in but one particular. He brought to the subject on which they all focused certain peculiarities evident also in Hobbes's *juvenilia*: an acute sensitivity to the fragility of civil society, a tragic awareness that anarchy always impends, a conviction of the moral order's dependence upon political order, and a pronounced preference for peace and domestic tranquillity. If, in the manner of Heraclitus and Democritus, Thucydides regarded motion as somehow prior to rest, he was inclined to prefer rest, nonetheless; and he recoiled in horror from that in which Machiavelli would later revel. His history is best read – as Hobbes appears to have read it – as a critique of what came to be called *Realpolitik*, carried out from within.[29]

While reading Thucydides and struggling to find words in which to render his far-from-simple Greek, Hobbes had come face-to-face with the abyss. In these years, he witnessed his own country's fecklessness in the wars against Spain and France and traced its defeats to the struggle taking place between Parliament and King. He watched aghast as the leading figures in Parliament pilloried the ministers of James I and cornered his hapless successor, Charles I, and he no doubt had Buckingham in mind when he wrote, with regard to the banishment of Thucydides himself, "For where affaires succeed amisse,

[26] Consider Hobbes, "Of the Life and History of Thucydides," in Thucydides, *Eight Bookes of the Peloponnesian Warre* sig. a1ᵛ, and reprinted in *EW* xiii–xv, in light of Strauss, *The Political Philosophy of Hobbes*, 74–76. Cf. Schlatter, "Introduction," xxvii.

[27] See Chapters 4 and 8, this volume.

[28] Cf. Thuc. 1.22.4 and 3.82.2, with Machiavelli, *Discorsi* 1.Pref., 3.43, in *Opere*, 76, 250, and consider Bacon's discussion of "the Architecture of Fortune" in *The Advancement of Learning* II.xxiii.1–50, in *OFB*, IV 156–81.

[29] See Paul A. Rahe, "Thucydides' Critique of Realpolitik," *Security Studies* 5:2 (Winter 1995): 105–41, which is reprinted in *Roots of Realism: Philosophical and Historical Dimensions*, ed. Benjamin Frankel (London: Frank Cass, 1996), 105–41. Cf. Brown, "Thucydides, Hobbes and the Linear Causal Perspective," 215–56 (esp. 225–31), who attributes to Thucydides the proto-Machiavellian thesis consistently advanced by the Athenians, against which he is, in fact, leveling a critique.

though there want neither providence, nor courage in the Conduction, yet with those that iudge onely upon events, the way to calumny is always open, and *Envy*, in the likenesse of *Zeale* to the Publique good, easily findeth credit for an accusation."[30]

In Thucydides, at this time, Hobbes read of Pericles, a man gifted with "fore-sight," who had exercised in Athens a sway justifying the claim that in his day the city was "in name a State *Democraticall*, but in fact, *A government of the principall Man*." Then, he learned that, after the death of this great statesman, his compatriots had acted "contrary in all" to the good advice he had proffered and that "in such other things besides, as seemed not to concerne the Warre" with Sparta, they "managed the State, according to their private ambition and covetousnesse, pernitiously both for themselves, and their Confederates." And with Thucydides, Hobbes traced Athens' failings to the fact that those who came to be dominant in the city after Pericles' death, "being more equall amongst themselves, and affecting every one to be the chiefe, applyed themselves to the people, and let goe the care of the Common-wealth." Moreover, as the English-man eventually discovered, during and after the Sicilian expedition, "through private quarrels about, who should beare the greatest sway with the people," these popular leaders "both abated the vigour of the Armie, and then also first troubled the State at home with division."[31] Thucydides wrote the book, but every word quoted here was penned by his translator, Thomas Hobbes.

Dissolution of Government

Thucydides had much to teach Hobbes concerning the dissolution of govern-ment, and there can be no doubt that the English philosopher was an atten-tive pupil. As scholars have noticed,[32] Hobbes's famous account of the state of nature is to a considerable degree derivative from the description of early Greece with which Thucydides begins his history. "[A]t first," Hobbes's Thucydides writes regarding what was an age of migrations, "there were often removals, every one easily leaving the place of his abode, to the violence alwayes of some greater number." In consequence, he adds,

Trafficke was not, nor mutuall entercourse, but with feare, neither by Sea nor Land; and every man so husbanded the ground, as but barely to live upon it, without any stocke of Riches; and planted nothing, (because it was uncertaine when another should invade them, and carry all away, especially, not having the defence of Walls); but made account to be Masters in any place, of such necessary sustenance, as might serve them from day to day, they made little difficulty to change their habitations. And for this cause, they were of no ability at all, eyther for greatnesse of Cities, or other provision.

"In such condition," Hobbes tells us in *Leviathan*, "there is no place for Indus-try; because the fruit thereof is uncertain; and consequently no Culture of the

---

[30] See Hobbes, "Of the Life and History of Thucydides," in Thucydides, *Eight Bookes of the Peloponnesian Warre* sig. a2ʳ, and reprinted in *English Writings* xix.

[31] See Thuc. 2.65, as translated by Hobbes, in Thucydides, *Eight Bookes of the Peloponnesian Warre*, 115–17, and reprinted in *EW*, VIII 219–22.

[32] See Klosko and Rice, "Thucydides and Hobbes's State of Nature," 405–9.

Earth; no Navigation, nor use of the commodities that may be imported by Sea; no commodious Building." If his account is distinguished from that of Thucydides, it is chiefly with regard to the Baconian character of the first five of the following items that he adds to this litany of woes: "no Instruments of moving, and removing such things as require much force; no Knowledge of the face of the Earth; no account of time; no Arts; no Letters; no Society; and which is worst of all, continuall feare, and danger of violent death; And the life of man, solitary, poore, nasty, brutish, and short."[33] Hobbes was able to grasp the degree to which domestic tranquility is essential for the progress of science without having read the now famous letter in which Bacon compared himself with "the miller of Huntingdon, that was wont to pray for peace amongst the willows; for while the winds blew, the wind-mills wrought, and the water-mill was less customed," for the Malmesbury philosopher was no less aware than his mentor that "controversies of religion" and other sources of civil strife "must hinder the advancement of sciences."[34]

As scholars have also noticed,[35] Hobbes is indebted to Thucydides for his political psychology. That this should be the case is no way be surprising. In *The Advancement of Learning*, Bacon had charged Aristotle with neglecting "the perturbations & distempers of the affections." Although the peripatetic had "written divers volumes of Ethiques," he had left untouched what Bacon considered "the principall subject thereof." Only in his *Rhetoric* did Aristotle take up the affections, and then "but colaterally, & in a second degree, (*as they may be mooved by speech*)," though he "handleth them well for the quantity." If one really wants to study this subject, Bacon insists, one must look not just at Aristotle's *Rhetoric*: one must turn also to "the poets and writers of Histories [who] are the best Doctors of this knowledge." From them, one can learn,

How affections are kindled and incyted: and how pacified and refrained; and how againe Conteyned from Act, & furder degree: how they disclose themselves, how they work, how they varye, how they gather and fortifie, how they are inwrapped one within another, and howe they doe fighte and encounter one with another, and other the like particularityes: Amongst the which this last is of speciall use in Morall and Civile matters: howe I say to sett affection againste affection, and to Master one by another, even as wee use to hunt beast with beaste, and flye byrde with birde, which otherwise percase wee coulde not so easily recover: upon which foundation is erected that excellent use of *Præmium* and *pœna*. whereby Civile states Consist, implying the predominante affections of *feare* and *hope*, for the suppressing and brideling the rest.[36]

What Bacon calls "the affections" forms a subject to which Hobbes was exceedingly attentive, and in this sphere, as in so many others, he followed his

---

[33] Cf. Thuc. 1.2.1–2, as translated by Hobbes, in Thucydides, *Eight Bookes of the Peloponnesian Warre*, 2, and reprinted in *EW*, VIII 2, with Hobbes, *Leviathan* I.xiii.9.

[34] Consider Letter to Sir Tobie Matthew on 10 October 1609, in *WoFB*, XI 137–38, in light of Bacon, *De dignitate et augmentis scientiarum* VIII.3 (at the end), in *WoFB*, I 827–28 (translated at V 109–10).

[35] See Schlatter, "Introduction," xxi–xxii; Brown, "Thucydides, Hobbes, and the Derivation of Anarchy," 33–62; and Slomp, "Hobbes, Thucydides and the Three Greatest Things," 566–86, especially the last.

[36] See Bacon, *The Advancement of Learning* II.xxii.6, in *OFB*, IV 149–50.

mentor's lead. In the early 1630s, he composed in Latin an epitome of Aristotle's *Rhetoric*, which was soon thereafter translated into English and published anonymously.[37] Aristotle Hobbes described to his friend John Aubrey as "the worst Teacher that ever was, the worst Politician and Ethick – a Countreyfellow that could live in the World would be as good: but his *Rhetorique*" he nonetheless singled out as "rare,"[38] and he later drew on Aristotle's *Rhetoric* for the account of laughter that he provided in his *Elements of Law* and *Leviathan* as well as for the analysis of the passions that he limned in those two works and in *De homine*.[39] But the debt that he owed Thucydides was greater still.

In antiquity, Dionysius of Halicarnassus had charged Thucydides with obscurity. This charge Hobbes deemed unjust. Only rarely, he insisted, was Thucydides difficult to decipher – and never so "in the Narrations of things done, nor in the descriptions of places, or of battels." Of course, when the historian contemplated "those humane passions, which either dissembled or not commonly discoursed of, doe yet carry the greatest sway with men, in their publique conversation," he had no choice. Nor had he any in depicting "the Characters of mens humours and manners, and [in] applying them to affaires of consequence." If, Hobbes remarked, "one cannot penetrate into" such passions, humors, and manners "without much meditation, we are not to expect a man should understand them at the first speaking," and in any case, when one is dealing with such matters, it is "impossible not to be obscure to ordinary capacities, in what words soever a man deliver his mind." Thus, if "*Thucydides* in his Orations, or in the Description of a Sedition, or other thing of that kind, be not easily understood," it is by "those onely that cannot penetrate into the nature of such things."[40]

Hobbes evidenced few, if any, doubts regarding his own penetration, and when he succeeded in reaching what he judged the heart of the matter, he was tenacious in holding on to what he had learned. In the middle of the first book of his history, Thucydides provided Hobbes with an account of a public debate that he never forgot. According to Thucydides' report, when challenged

---

[37] Cf. *A Briefe of the Art of Rhetorique, Containing in Substance All that Aristotle Hath Written in His Three Bookes of that Subject* (London: Andrew Crook, 1637), which is reprinted in *The Rhetorics of Thomas Hobbes and Bernard Lamy*, ed. John T. Harwood (Carbondale: Southern Illinois University Press, 1986), 33–128, with MSS Chatsworth MS. D.1, pp. 1–143; note Harwood's introduction, in *The Rhetorics of Thomas Hobbes and Bernard Lamy*, 1–32; and note Karl Schuhmann and G. A. J. Rogers, "Introduction to Thomas Hobbes *Leviathan*," in Thomas Hobbes, *Leviathan: A Critical Edition*, ed. G. A. J. Rogers and Karl Schuhmann (Bristol: Thoemmes Continuum, 2003), I 77. As Schuhmann and Rogers indicate, there are reasons to doubt that Hobbes was responsible for the English translation, which will be spelled out in detail before long.

[38] See *ABL*, 237. Note, in this connection, Hobbes, *Leviathan* IV.xlvi.11.

[39] See Strauss, *The Political Philosophy of Hobbes*, 35–42, and Quentin Skinner, "Why Laughing Mattered in the Renaissance," *History of Political Thought* 22:3 (Autumn 2001): 418–47, which is revised, expanded, and reprinted in Skinner, *Hobbes and Civil Science*, 142–76.

[40] See Hobbes, "Of the Life and History of Thucydides," in Thucydides, *Eight Bookes of the Peloponnesian Warre* sig. a4ᵛ–b1ʳ, and reprinted in *EW*, VIII xxix–xxx.

by Corinthian ambassadors at an assembly held at Sparta,[41] the Athenians who happened to be present defended their establishment of an empire by claiming that they had been "*forced*" to do so "*out of the nature of the thing it selfe; as chiefly for feare, next for honour, and lastly for profit.*" More than three decades after publishing his translation, Hobbes traced to the same three motives the aggressive spirit that gives rise to the war of all against all in the state of nature. "[I]n the nature of man," as he put it, there are "three principall causes of quarrell. First, Competition; Secondly, Diffidence; Thirdly, Glory. The first, maketh men invade for Gain; the second, for Safety; and the third, for Reputation." The enterprising spirit that the Corinthians had attributed to the Athenians Hobbes attributes to all mankind.[42]

That the motives to which the Athenians trace their own conduct play a considerable role in Thucydides' own account of the descent into anarchy Hobbes undoubtedly noticed as well. In the middle of the second book of his history, the Greek historian pauses to describe and analyze a plague that struck Athens early in the Peloponnesian War, killing perhaps as much as one-third of the city's population, subverting civic morale, and spawning lawlessness.[43] Thucydides' depiction of its psychological, moral, and political consequences is justly famous, and Hobbes does a remarkable job in rendering his Greek into English. The plague was, as he puts it, a "sickenesse which farre surmounted all expression of words, and . . . exceeded humane nature, in the cruelty wherwith it handled each one." Particular suffering was reserved for the country folk who had moved into Athens for protection against the Spartan attackers, for they had no houses in the town. Many lived in what Hobbes calls "stifling boothes" so that "the mortality was now without all forme; and dying men lay tumbling one upon another in the streetes, and men halfe dead, about every Conduit through desire of water." The temple precincts, where many "dwelt in Tents, were all full of the dead that died within them."

[F]or oppressed with the violence of the Calamitie, and not knowing what to doe, men grew carelesse both of holy, and profane things alike. And the Lawes which they formerly used touching Funerals, were all now broken; every one burying where hee could finde roome. And many for want of things necessary, after so many deathes before, were forced to become impudent in the Funerals of their friends. For when one had made a Funeral Pile, another getting before him, would throw on his dead, and give it fire. And when one was in burning, another would come, and having cast thereon him whom he carried, goe his way againe. And the great licentiousnesse, which also in other kindes was used in the Citie, began at first from this disease. For that which a man before would dissemble; and not acknowledge to be done for voluptousnesse, he durst now doe freely, seeing before his eyes such quicke revolution, of the rich dying, and men worth nothing, inheriting their estates; insomuch as they iustified a speedy fruition of their goods, even for their pleasure; as men that thought they held their lives

---

[41] See Thuc. 1.70, as translated by Hobbes, in Thucydides, *Eight Bookes of the Peloponnesian Warre*, 36–39, and reprinted in *EW*, VIII 74–76.

[42] Cf. Thuc. 1.75, as translated by Hobbes, in Thucydides, *Eight Bookes of the Peloponnesian Warre*, 41, and reprinted in *EW*, VIII 78, with Hobbes, *Leviathan* I.xiii.6–8.

[43] See Orwin, "Stasis and Plague: Thucydides on the Dissolution of Society," 831–47, whose discussion of both the plague and the revolution at Corcyra deserves careful attention.

but by the day. As for paines, no man was forward in any action of honour, to take any, because they thought it uncertaine whether they should dye or not, before they atchieved it. But what any man knew to bee delightfull, and to bee profitable to pleasure, that was made both profitable and honourable. Neither the feare of the Gods, nor Lawes of men, awed any man. Not the former, because they concluded it was alike to worship or not worship, from seeing that alike they all perished: nor the latter, because no man expected that lives would last, till he received punishment of his crimes by iudgement. But they thought there was now over their heads, some farre greater Iudgement decreed against them; before which fell, they thought to enioy some little part of their lives.[44]

As Thucydides' narrative makes clear, fear and the desire for honor are more than simply motives for quarrel. In ordinary, civilized circumstances, when reinforced by the hopes and expectations to which peace and prosperity give rise, they are the mainstays of political and social order.

In similar fashion, Hobbes must have puzzled over Thucydides' description of the "quarrels" that had arisen elsewhere within Greece "betweene the Patrons of the Commons, that sought to bring in the *Athenians*, and the *Few*, that desired to bring in the *Lacedaemonians*." While working on his translation, he cannot have escaped observing the "many and heynous things" that had "happened in" Athens and in the other cities as a consequence of the "Sedition" that arose. And like Thucydides, he knew that the events that had transpired in Hellas so long ago were by no means unique: "they have beene before, and shall be ever, as long as humane nature is the same." It was with his own country in mind that Hobbes brooded over the Greek historian's vivid description of the revolutions to which Corcyra and later many of the other cities within Hellas had been subject in the course of the war, noting the manner in which the conspirators learned "what had beene done in" other cities and "farre exceeded the same in newnesse of conceipt, both for the art of assailing, and for the strangenesse of their revenges."

But what appears most to have preoccupied the future author of *Leviathan* was Thucydides' vivid description of the manner in which, under the pressure of events in the various cities, language lost its purchase on reality, and moral anarchy ensued. "[I]n peace and prosperity," he observes, "aswell Cities as private men, are better minded because they bee not plunged into necessity of doing any thing against their will; but War taking away the affluence of daily necessaries, is a most violent Master, & conformeth most mens passions to the present occasion." As a consequence of this reorientation of the passions, Thucydides ominously adds, "The received value of names imposed for signification of things, was changed into arbitrary," and

inconsiderate boldnesse, was counted true-hearted manlinesse; provident deliberation, a hansome feare; modesty, the cloake of cowardice; to be wise in every thing, to be lazie in every thing. A furious suddennesse was reputed a point of valour. To re-advise for the better security, was held for a faire pretext of tergiversation. Hee that was fierce, was alwayes trusty; and hee that contraried such a one, was suspected. Hee that did

---

[44] See Thuc. 2.47–53 (esp. 50, 52–53), as translated by Hobbes, in Thucydides, *Eight Bookes of the Peloponnesian Warre*, 106–10, and reprinted in *EW*, VIII 201–9 (esp. 205, 207–9).

insidiate, if it tooke, was a wise man; but hee that could smell out a Trap laid, a more
dangerous man then hee: But hee that had beene so provident, as not to neede to doe
the one or the other, was said to bee a dissolver of society, and one that stood in feare
of his adversary. In briefe, he that could outstrip another in the doing of an evill act,
or that could perswade another thereto, that never meant it, was commended. To bee
kinne to another, was not to be so neere as to be of his society, because these were
ready to undertake any thing, and not to dispute it. For these Societies were not made
upon prescribed Lawes of profit, but for rapine, contrary to the Lawes established. And
as for mutuall trust amongst them, it was confirmed not so much by divine Law, as
by the communicatio[n] of guilt. And what was well advised of their adversaries, they
received with an eye to their actions, to see whether they were too strong for them,
or not, and not ingenuously. To be revenged was in more request, then never to have
received iniurie. And for Oathes (when any were) of reconcilement, being administred
in the present for necessity, were of force to such as had otherwise no power: but upon
opportunity, he that first durst, thought his revenge sweeter by the trust, then if he had
taken the open way. For they did not onely put to account the safenesse of that course,
but having circumvented their Adversary by fraud, assumed to themselves withall, a
masterie in point of wit. And dishonest men for the most part are sooner called able,
then simple men honest. And men are ashamed of this title, but take a pride in the
other.

Here again political psychology came into play – for, according to Thucydides,
"[t]he cause of all this" was "*desire of rule*, out of *Avarice* and *Ambition*, and
the zeale of contention from those two proceeding."

For such as were of authority in the Cities, both of the one and the other Faction,
preferring under decent titles, one the *politicall equality of the multitude*, the other the
moderate *Aristocratie*, though in words they seemed to be servants of the Publique, they
made it *in effect* but the Prize of their contention. And striving by whatsoever meanes
to overcome, both ventured on most horrible outrages, and prosecuted their revenges
still further, without any regard of Iustice, or the publike good, but limiting them, each
Faction, by their owne appetite: and stood ready, whether by uniust sentence, or with
their owne hands, when they should get power, to satisfie their present spight. So that
neither side made account to have any thing the sooner done for Religion [of an Oath,]
but hee was most commended, that could passe a businesse against the haire with a faire
Oration. The neutrals of the Citie were destroyed by both Factions; partly because they
would not side with them, and partly for envie that they should so escape.

In the end, the consequences were almost too horrible for contemplation, for
"wickednesse [was] on foot in every kind, throughout all *Greece*, by the occasion of their sedition."

Sincerity (whereof there is much in a generous nature) was laughed downe. And it was
farre the best course, to stand diffidently against each other, with their thoughts in
battell array, which no speech was so powerfull, nor Oath terrible enough to disband.
And being all of them, the more they considered, the more desperate of assurance, they
rather contrived how to avoid a mischiefe, then were able to rely on any mans faith.
And for the most part, such as had the least wit, had the best successe; for both their
owne defect, and the subtilty of their adversaries, putting them into a great feare to
be overcome in words, or at least in pre-insidiation, by their enemies great craft, they
therefore went roundly to worke with them, with deedes. Whereas the other, not caring

though they were perceived, and thinking they needed not to take by force, what they might doe by plot, were thereby unprovided, and so the more easily slaine.[45]

On this passage and on everything that had occasioned the pattern of events described, Hobbes had by 1629, in his capacity as a translator, ruminated at length – and he wanted his fellow Englishmen to do so as well lest they suffer the like. The man who went into exile shortly after the Long Parliament began its sitting in November 1640, and who later boasted of having been "the first of all that fled,"[46] had seen storm clouds forming on the horizon eleven years before.

By the time he reached the age of forty, Hobbes had turned his back on the republican yearnings of his youth, and on modern and strictly prudential grounds – with no reference to divine right, historical contract, or the dictates of the common law – he had embraced monarchy as the form of government most conducive to silencing "the trumpet of warre and sedition,"[47] and to promoting domestic tranquillity thereby. He could imagine, to be sure, the establishment of a tongue-tied republic on the Venetian model, in which the people in their collective capacity played no role in deliberation but committed "the handling of state affairs to a few," and he was prepared to concede that, in such a fashion, one can avoid civil disorder even in a democracy if the people "bestow the power of deliberating . . . either on one, or some very few, being content with the nomination of Magistrates, and publique Ministers, that is to say, with the authority without the ministration."[48] But these remarks were an aside, for he did not think it especially likely that, outside Venice, such a polity would ever come into existence, and in his overall outlook he would never again reverse course. Instead, he would extend to the *respublica Christiana* the critique of republican contentiousness that he had developed in the course of translating Thucydides, and when the English Civil War did, indeed, as he had long feared, break out, he would most vehemently blame disputatious divines.

It was, to be sure, one thing to identify the disease and another to find a remedy. Thucydides had helped Hobbes immeasurably with the former task, and the Malmesbury philosopher had no doubt found instructive and stimulating the observation advanced by the Mytilenians at Olympia that "*the equality of mutuall feare, is the onely band of faith in Leagues*" and the Athenians' assertion in the Melian Dialogue that "*in humane disputation, iustice is then only agreed on, when the necessity is equall.*"[49] Moreover, Thucydides' contention that, under Pericles, when Athens was well governed, there was a democracy in name and a monarchy in fact had apparently pointed Hobbes in the direction that he was to go.[50] To finish the journey, however, and to learn how to

---

[45] See Thuc. 3.82–83, as translated by Hobbes, in Thucydides, *Eight Bookes of the Peloponnesian Warre*, 187–90, and reprinted in *EW*, VIII 347–51.

[46] See Thomas Hobbes, "Considerations upon the Reputation of Thomas Hobbes," in *EW*, IV 413–40 (at 414).

[47] See Hobbes, *De cive* II.v.5.

[48] See Hobbes, *Elements of Law* II.v.8 and *De cive* II.x.15.

[49] See Thuc. 3.11.2 and 5.89, as translated by Hobbes, in Thucydides, *Eight Bookes of the Peloponnesian Warre*, 150, 341, and reprinted in *EW*, VIII 278, IX 99.

[50] See Thuc. 2.65.9.

frame his argument, he had to confront and digest the thinking of Lucretius and the Epicureans, and he then had to rethink and recast their doctrine in light of Machiavelli's powerful critique of its moral psychology, Bacon's wholesale repudiation of classical ontology, and Galileo's systematic application of mathematics to a universe envisaged in the Epicurean manner as nothing but matter in motion.

The Very Model of a Modern Moralist

We do not know when Thomas Hobbes first read *De rerum natura*. For understandable reasons, the authorities who designed the curricula for England's grammar schools and for the University of Oxford chose not to include on either syllabus a poem quite rightly regarded as a fount of atheism,[1] and in his various autobiographical works, Hobbes is silent on the subject.[2] In consequence, Lucretius is rarely mentioned in the secondary literature on Hobbes's political thought[3] – although there is evidence that his influence on the Malmesbury

[1] For a brief overview, see J.-P. Pittion, "Lucrèce et l'épicurisme en Angleterre: Époque Tudor et jacobéenne," in *Présence de Lucrèce*, ed. Rémy Poignault (Tours: Centre de Recherches A. Piganiol, 1999), 299–311. In antiquity, Epicurus was regarded as a thinly disguised atheist: see Cic. *Nat. D.* 1.44.123, 3.1.3.

[2] See *Thomæ Hobbes Malmesburiensis vita, authore seipso*, and *Thomæ Hobbes Malmesburiensis vita, carmine express, authore seipso*, in *LW*, I xiii–xxi, lxxxv–xcix, which should be read in light of François Tricaud, "Éclaircissements sur les six premières biographies de Hobbes," *Archives de philosophie* 48:2 (April–June 1985): 277–86.

[3] His name can be found in the indices of none of the following works: Leo Strauss, *The Political Philosophy of Hobbes: Its Basis and Its Genesis* (Chicago: University of Chicago Press, 1952); C. B. Macpherson, *The Political Theory of Possessive Individualism* (Oxford, UK: Clarendon Press, 1962); Johann P. Sommerville, *Thomas Hobbes: Political Ideas in Historical Context* (New York: St. Martin's Press, 1992); Quentin Skinner, *Reason and Rhetoric in the Philosophy of Hobbes* (Cambridge, UK: Cambridge University Press, 1996); A. P. Martinich, *Hobbes: A Biography* (Cambridge, UK: Cambridge University Press, 1999); Quentin Skinner, *Visions of Politics, III: Hobbes and Civil Science* (Cambridge, UK: Cambridge University Press, 2002); Noel Malcolm, *Aspects of Hobbes* (Oxford, UK: Clarendon Press, 2002); and Vickie B. Sullivan, *Machiavelli, Hobbes, and the Formation of a Liberal Republicanism in England* (New York: Cambridge, University Press, 2004). There is, however, a useful discussion of Hobbes and Lucretius in James H. Nichols, Jr., *Epicurean Political Philosophy: The De rerum natura of Lucretius* (Ithaca, NY: Cornell University Press, 1976), and in recent years scholars interested in early modern Epicureanism have begun to explore Hobbes's debt to that tradition: cf. Arrigo Pacchi, "Hobbes e l'epicureismo," *Rivista di storia della filosofia* 33:1 (January–March 1978): 54–71, with Olivier Bloch, "Gassendi et la théorie politique de Hobbes," in *Thomas Hobbes: Philosophie première, théorie de la science et politique*, ed. Yves Charles Zarka and Jean Bernhardt (Paris: Vrin, 1990), 339–46, and with Gianni Paganini, "Hobbes, Gassendi, and the Tradition of Political Epicureanism," in *Der Garten und die Moderne: Epikureische Moral und Politik vom Humanismus bis zur Aufklärung* (Stuttgart-Bad Canstatt: Friedrich Frommann Verlag, 2004), 113–37, which should be read in conjunction with Gianni Paganini, "Hobbes, Gassendi, e la psicologia del meccanicismo," in *Hobbes Oggi*, ed. Arrigo Pacchi (Milan: Franco Angeli Editore, 1990), 351–445, and Gianni Paganini, "Hobbes, Gassendi et le *De cive*," in *Materia actuosa: Antiquité, âge classique, lumières: Mélanges en l'honneur d'Olivier Bloch*, ed. Miguel Benitez, Antony McKenna, Gianni Paganini, and Jean Salem (Paris: Champion, 2000), 183–206. Scholars interested chiefly

philosopher was considerable. He was, after all, one of the handful of authors
whom Hobbes himself actually deigned to mention.[4] Moreover, the English
philosopher's physics, as he readily acknowledged, owed a great deal to the
Epicurean account espoused by the Roman poet,[5] and the charge that he was
an Epicurean was frequently leveled against Hobbes by contemporary critics.[6] By the eighteenth century, one could, in fact, speak of "an epicurean or a
Hobbist" as if there was no difference, and no less an authority than David
Hume did so.[7]

It is tolerably likely that Hobbes read *De rerum natura* on the sly during
his years at Magdalen Hall. He arrived at Oxford in the wake of an Aristotelian revival,[8] and in his day the university statutes not only specified that
students study with extreme care the works of Aristotle dealing with physics,
metaphysics, psychology, rhetoric, morals, and politics.[9] They also forbade the
assignment of authors inclined to "sterile and empty disputations dissenting
from the ancient and true philosophy" of the peripatetic.[10] Hobbes quickly
discovered that he had little use for Aristotelian logic and physics: he tells us
that he preferred to spend his time in bookshops, perusing travelers' accounts
of exploration overseas, poring over maps of the earth and depictions of the

in Hobbes himself are beginning to take note: see, for example, Bernd Ludwig, *Die Wiederentdeckung des Epikureischen Naturrechts: Zu Thomas Hobbes' philosophischer Entwicklung von
De cive zum Leviathan im Pariser Exil, 1640–1651* (Frankfurt am Main: V. Klostermann, 1998),
and Patricia Springborg, "Hobbes and Epicurean Religion," in *Der Garten und die Moderne*,
161–244, and "Hobbes's Theory of Civil Religion," in *Pluralismo e religione civile: Una prospet-
tiva storica e filosofica*, ed. Gianni Paganini and Edoardo Tortarolo (Milan: Bruno Monadori,
2004), 59–94.

[4] See, for example, Thomas Hobbes, "The Answer of Mr. Hobbes to Sir William Davenant's
Preface before Gondibert," in *EW*, IV 444–45, where Hobbes denies that Lucretius should be
considered a poet and lists him, instead, among the "natural philosophers."

[5] See Thomas Hobbes, *De corpore* IV.xxvi.3, xxviii.8, in *LW*, I 339–42, 387, and *Concerning
Body* IV.xxvi.3, xxviii.8, in *EW*, I 415–19, 476. Note also Hobbes, *Dialogus physicus de naturis
aeris*, in *LW*, IV 233–96 (at 277, 283), which is translated by Simon Schaffer in Steven Shapin
and Simon Schaffer, *Leviathan and the Air–Pump: Hobbes, Boyle, and the Experimental Life*
(Princeton, NJ: Princeton University Press, 1985), 345–91. This material should be read in light
of Letters Exchanged with Samuel Sorbière on 23 January and 6 February 1657, in *CTH*, I
433–38, 442–46.

[6] See Charles Trawick Harrison, "The Ancient Atomists and English Literature of the Seventeenth
Century," *Harvard Studies in Classical Philology* 45 (1934): 1–79, who documents but does not
credit the charges.

[7] See David Hume, *An Enquiry Concerning the Principles of Morals* App. II.249, in *Enquiries
Concerning the Human Understanding and Concerning the Principles of Morals*, second edition,
ed. L. A. Selby-Bigge (Oxford, UK: Clarendon Press, 1972), 296–97.

[8] See Charles. B. Schmitt, *John Case and Aristotelianism in Renaissance England* (Kingston:
McGill–Queen's University Press, 1983), 13–76. For an overview, see Charles. B. Schmitt, "Philosophy and Science in Sixteenth-Century Universities," in *The Cultural Context of Medieval
Learning*, ed. John Emery Murdoch and Edith Dudley Sylla (Dordrecht: D. Reidel, 1975), 485–
530.

[9] For the list of books prescribed at the time of the general reform of the universities in 1564
and 1565, see *Statuta antiqua universitatis oxoniensis*, ed. Strickland Gibson (Oxford, UK:
Clarendon Press, 1931), 389–90.

[10] The statutes enacted on 12 March 1586 are especially revealing: *Statuta antiqua universitatis
oxoniensis*, 437.

heavens, and letting his imagination run riot.[11] In developing a marked distaste for Aristotle, Hobbes was by no means alone: in the universities of the early Jacobean period, there were instructors with a lively interest in the sciences, who were perfectly capable of raising objections to the dogma then regnant,[12] and there were humanists who held Scholastic logic in contempt: in fact, one such delivered a diatribe on the subject in Magdalen Hall during Hobbes's sojourn there.[13] Moreover, in Hobbes's day, many a young humanist – moved by an interest in astronomy and science, theology, or ethics and politics; blessed with an inquiring spirit and a skeptical temper; and spurred on by dissatisfaction with the philosophical doctrine taught in the texts officially prescribed – quietly sought enlightenment in the company of Lucretius.[14] In the eyes of spirited young men, there never is anything quite as tantalizing as forbidden fruit.

If, however, Lucretius was not among the authors whom Hobbes worked his way through while at Magdalen Hall, the latter presumably did so during the two decades he spent as tutor, then secretary to Sir William Cavendish at Hardwick Hall. The circumstances in which he lived were, to say the least, conducive to the development of such an interest; and especially after his return along with Cavendish from their extended sojourn in Italy, he was well disposed. By this time, Hobbes tells us, his ability in Greek and Latin had deteriorated. Moreover, he had become extremely sensitive to the fact that the philosophy and logic in which he had become proficient at Magdalen Hall was judged "a mockery by sagacious men." And so, Hobbes reports, putting aside as "vain this logic and philosophy, he decided to devote whatever empty time he had to the Greek and Latin tongues, and, upon returning to England, he turned diligently to historians and poets," such as Valerius Flaccus, Vergil, Homer, Euripides, Sophocles, Plautus, Aristophanes, and, of course, Thucydides.[15]

The Epicurean Persuasion

Preeminent among the "sagacious men" of Hobbes's acquaintance in these years who regarded the Aristotelian philosophy and logic taught at Oxford as a "mockery" was Sir Francis Bacon, who much preferred Democritus, Epicurus,

---

[11] Consider *Thomæ Hobbes vita, authore seipso*, and *Thomæ Hobbes Malmesburiensis vita, carmine expressa, authore seipso*, in *LW*, I xiii, lxxxvi–lxxxvii, in light of *ABL*, 229, and see Martinich, *Hobbes*, 8–18.

[12] This was especially true in mathematics, which was accorded autonomy, and in astronomy, where the influence of Copernicus was felt: see Mordechai Feingold, *The Mathematicians' Apprenticeship: Science, Universities and Society in England 1560–1640* (Cambridge, UK: Cambridge University Press, 1984).

[13] Consider British Library MS Harl. 6460, fols. iv, 2r, in light of Noel Malcolm's brief discussion in "A Summary Biography of Hobbes," in *Aspects of Hobbes*, 5.

[14] For a lively and instructive account of what it was like for such a young man to attend a grammar school, then a university, in this age, see David Riggs, *The World of Christopher Marlowe* (New York: Henry Holt, 2004), 25–126.

[15] Consider *Thomæ Hobbes Malmesburiensis vita, authore seipso*, and *Thomæ Hobbes Malmesburiensis vita, carmine expressa, authore seipso*, in *LW*, I xiii–xiv, lxxxviii, in light of *ABL*, 229.

and Lucretius.[16] Bacon could, of course, be coy. In *The Advancement of Learning* and again in the lead essay of the third and final edition of his *Essays*, a piece entitled "Of Truth," he quoted at length the opening lines of the second book of *De rerum natura*:

It is a view of delight,... to stand or walke upon the shoare side, and to see a Shippe tossed with tempest upon the sea; or to bee in a fortified Tower, and to see two Battailes ioyne uppon a plaine. But it is a pleasure incomparable, for the minde of man to bee settled, landed, and fortified in the certaintie of truth; and from thence to descrie and behould the errours, perturbations, labours, and wanderings up and downe of other men.

In both cases, he left it to his more discerning readers to decipher the significance of the reference by tracing the passage to its original context, in which it appears as a celebration of the superior satisfactions possessed by those who renounce religion and repudiate teleology, refuse all trust in Providence, acknowledge to themselves that there is no life after death, and absent themselves from the cares of public life.[17]

Bacon could also be remarkably blunt. His admiration for Lucretius he advertised by citing him by name in the very first paragraph of the second edition of his essays. The Roman poet's notorious sally linking religion with crime he set off in such a fashion as to make it serve almost as an epigraph to a volume otherwise unadorned, and he followed up immediately with a meditation on death in which, without citing the Roman poet, he recast much of the argument of *De rerum natura* with an eye to Christianity's hegemony, noting that "Men feare death, as Children feare to goe in the darke," observing that "naturall feare" in both "is encreased with tales," remarking on the "mixture of vanitie, and of superstition" present in "religious meditations" on death, and illustrating from "the *Friers* Bookes of Mortification" the techniques which the clergy deploy to heighten and play on this fear. Lest he be misunderstood, in the volume's fourteenth essay, Bacon cited as an authority with regard to the propriety of religious doctrine none other than Epicurus himself.[18]

Bacon's admiration for the Epicurean tradition was by no means restricted to its posture regarding religion. From quite early on, this proponent of the scientific project was inclined to take as a fruitful starting point for his new physics an atomism derived from, if not quite identical to, the theory espoused by Democritus, Epicurus, and Lucretius. Hobbes – who knew *De sapientia veterum* well, greatly admired the book, and recommended it to others – can hardly have failed to meditate on Bacon's discussion of the atomist hypothesis in "Cupid, or the Atom."[19]

---

[16] See Charles Trawick Harrison, "Bacon, Hobbes, Boyle, and the Ancient Atomists," *Harvard Studies and Notes in Philology and Literature* 15 (1933): 191–218 (esp. 192–200).

[17] Cf. Bacon, *The Advancement of Learning*, ed. Michael Kiernan, I.viii.5, whence comes the translation, and Bacon, "Of Truth," *The Essayes or Counsels, Civill and Morall*, ed. Michael Kiernan, I, in *OFB*, IV 52, XV 7–9, with Lucr. 2.1–61.

[18] Consider Bacon, "Of Religion," "Of Death," and "Of Atheisme," *Essaies* 1–2, 14, in *WoFB*, VI 543–45, 559–60, in light of Lucr. 1.62–158, 2.1–61, 3.1–93, 830–1094, 4.1–25, 5.1194–1240.

[19] See Bacon, "Cupido, sive Atomus," *De sapientia veterum* XVII, in *WoFB*, VI 654–57 (translated at 729–31).

In 1620, the year in which *Horæ Subsecivæ* was published, Bacon brought out his *Instauratio magna* and his *Novum organum*. Given the strength of the Lord Chancellor's authority, it is inconceivable that Hobbes ignored the latter work's denunciation of Plato, Aristotle, and the founders and leaders of the various philosophical schools, and it is hard to believe that he failed to reflect on the praise it conferred on Empedocles, Anaxagoras, Leucippus, Democritus, Parmenides, Heraclitus, Xenophanes, and Philolaus.[20] Nor can Hobbes have missed Bacon's contention in his *Novum organum* and again in *De dignitate et augmentis scientiarum* that "the school of Democritus" – with its propensity to dismiss "Final Causes" as unintelligible, to eliminate "God and Mind from the production (*fabrica*) of things," to derive "the structure of the universe from the infinite preparations (*praelusiones*) and essays of nature (which they called Fate or Fortune)," and "to dissect nature" into its constituent parts – had "penetrated more deeply into nature than the other schools."[21] He can hardly have overlooked Bacon's statement that "nothing in nature is more true" than the notorious Epicurean denial that anything ever comes of or is reduced to nothing, and he must have noticed as well his mentor's explicit endorsement of Democritus' claim that, while matter is eternal, the particular world in which we live is not.[22] Moreover, there is good reason to think that Hobbes took to heart Bacon's exhortation that "matter," rather than "forms," which are purportedly nothing but "figments (*commenta*) of the human mind," should "be the focus of consideration" along with matter's "configurations (*schematismi*) and alterations in configuration (*meta-schematismi*), and pure action, and the law of action or motion."[23] For when the second earl of Devonshire died and Hobbes found that his time was more his own, he turned to the questions Bacon had raised, and he adopted as his working hypothesis the central doctrine of the creed espoused by Democritus, Epicurus, and Lucretius: the supposition that the universe is constituted by matter in motion and nothing else.

In this endeavor, Hobbes received encouragement and support from his deceased patron's cousins Sir Charles Cavendish and William, earl of Newcastle, and through them he came into contact with a host of like-minded men, who were also inclined to entertain as an hypothesis the Epicurean conviction that all sensation is somehow reducible to touch, that secondary qualities are illusory, and that extension alone is real.[24] In the 1630s, Hobbes became friendly with Newcastle's chaplain Robert Payne, a gifted mathematician and a devotee

---

[20] See Bacon, *Novum organum*, ed. Graham Rees and Maria Wakely, 1.63, 71, 77, in *OFB*, XI 98–101, 112–15, 120–23. In this connection, see Richard Kennington, "Bacon's Critique of Ancient Philosophy in *New Organon* 1," in Kennington, *On Modern Origins: Essays in Early Modern Philosophy*, ed. Pamela Kraus and Frank Hunt (Lanham, MD: Lexington Books, 2004), 17–32.

[21] See Bacon, *Novum organum* 1.51, in *OFB*, XI 88–89, and *De dignitate et augmentis scientiarum* 3.4, in *WoFB*, I 569–70 (translated at IV 363–64).

[22] See Bacon, *Novum organum* 1.48, 2.40, in *OFB*, XI 84–87, 350–51, and Bacon, *De principiis atque originibus secundum fabulas Cupidinis et Cœli*, in *WoFB*, II 110 (translated at V 491).

[23] See Bacon, *Novum organum* 1.51, in *OFB*, XI 88–89.

[24] See Stephen Clucas, "The Atomism of the Cavendish Circle: A Reappraisal," *The Seventeenth Century* 9:2 (Autumn 1994): 247–73.

of the new science.[25] While conducting the third earl of Devonshire on a tour
of the continent, he managed to secure an interview with Galileo Galilei in Florence, and then, while in Paris, he met and became closely associated with *Père*
Marin Mersenne, a close friend of René Descartes, whose cell at the Convent
of the Annunciation served as a forum for philosophical and scientific speculation and as a clearing-house for news of scientific discoveries from all over
Europe.[26] In the period stretching from Hobbes's withdrawal from England in
November 1640 to Mersenne's death on 1 September 1648, the Malmesbury
philosopher was to while away many an hour in the Minim friar's cell. There,
among others, he would meet *Père* Pierre Gassendi, the best-known Epicurean
of the age, and the two would come to be joined in what Sir Charles Cavendish
described as "a greate friendship."[27]

It would be difficult to exaggerate the importance for Hobbes of his connection with these two French priests. Both proved eager to promote his political
doctrine, and the two were unstinting in the praise they lavished on his new
civil science. It was their letters of recommendation that enabled the Malmesbury philosopher to secure a publisher in Amsterdam for the second edition
of *De cive*, and these, when added as a preface to the book, gave it a cachet
on the continent that it might not otherwise have obtained. For Mersenne,
Hobbes was "that incomparable man" and *De cive* "that outstanding work."
He termed his English friend's tome "a great literary treasure." Because it presented a "noble philosophy, no less clearly demonstrated than the Elements of
Euclid," that would cause the reader to "renounce . . . all the triflings" of the
skeptics and make him "confess a dogmatic doctrine based on the firmest of
footings," it should be considered a "golden book, augmented and adorned
with jewels." Gassendi spoke similarly of "the excellent Hobbes." He could
think of no "writer who examines an argument more deeply than" his friend,
and he knew "no one who in his philosophical work is more free from prejudice." As for *De cive*, though the French priest prudently distanced himself
from its highly unorthodox treatment of the Christian religion, he nonetheless
described it as "truly uncommon, and worthy of being handled by all who
are sensible of higher things." In Paris, he remarked, when the book was first
published, "so few copies of the book were printed, that they produced rather
than satisfied a thirst for it." If Hobbes's agent in this matter, Samuel Sorbière,
to whom their letters were formally addressed, should bring other writings

[25] See Mordechai Feingold, "A Friend of Hobbes and an Early Translator of Galileo: Robert Payne
of Oxford," in *The Light of Nature: Essays in the History and Philosophy of Science Presented
to A. C. Crombie*, ed. J. D. North and J. J. Roche (Dordrecht: Martinus Nihjoff, 1985), 265–80,
and Noel Malcolm, "Robert Payne, the Hobbes Manuscripts, and the 'Short Tract,'" in *Aspects
of Hobbes*, 80–145.

[26] See Harcourt Brown, *Scientific Organizations in Seventeenth Century France (1620–1680)*
(Baltimore, MD: Williams and Wilkins, 1934), 31–63, and Armand Beaulieu, *Mersenne: Le
Grand Minime* (Brussells: Fondation Nicolas-Claude Fabri de Peiresc, 1995), 173–324.

[27] See Letter from Sir Charles Cavendish to John Pell in December 1644, in *A Collection of Letters
Illustrative of the Progress of Science in England from the Reign of Queen Elizabeth to that of
Charles the Second*, ed. James Orchard Halliwell (London: Historical Society of Science, 1841),
86–87.

by Hobbes "to light," Gassendi continued, he would "have bestowed a great blessing on the whole nation of those who take philosophy seriously."[28]

The role that the two priests played in promoting Hobbes's writings needs emphasis. But in no way did it exhaust their contribution to his well-being in the 1640s. Even more important was the vibrant intellectual world to which they introduced their English friend.

Erudite Libertines

In the brief biography published by a member of his order some months after his death, Marin Mersenne is depicted as a devout and zealous Catholic.[29] On this question, few in the scholarly world have been inclined to harbor doubts. There is, nonetheless, good reason to suspect that the friar whom Hobbes befriended in Paris was a cleric of a more worldly sort – eager, above all else, to ease the advance of the new science and, to this end, intent on grounding it in a radical skepticism that ruled out its advancing any metaphysical claims likely to bring it directly into conflict with the Catholic faith,[30] and resolved on recasting scholastic philosophy in such a fashion as to make Christianity more receptive to the grand project proposed by Sir Francis Bacon in *The Advancement of Learning*.[31]

Of course, in his younger days, as a polemicist intent on displaying his hostility to the purveyors of irreligion, Marin Mersenne had seemed exceedingly zealous. On one infamous occasion, he had even lamented that in Paris there were fifty thousand atheists.[32] Even then, however, the Minim friar was given to defending the faith against the atheists, deists, and libertines of the age in a suspect manner, which seems to have been deliberately contrived in such a fashion as to give his opponents' arguments a wider circulation than they would otherwise have had. In the course of mounting an attack on *The Quatrains of the Deist*, for example, he made what had been a clandestine work, available in manuscript to very few, easily accessible to the general public for the first

---

[28] For these events and the two letters in the original Latin and in an English translation, see Editor's Introduction, and Letters to Samuel Sorbière from Mersenne and Gassendi on 25 and 28 April 1646, in Hobbes, *De cive*, 5–13, 85–86, 297–98. See also Letters Exchanged between Mersenne and Sorbière on 21 March and 15 April 1647, in *De cive*, 310 (with n. 2), 312.

[29] See Hilarion de Coste, *La Vie du R. P. Marin Mersenne: Theologien, philosophe et mathematicien de l'Ordre des Peres Minime* (Paris: Sébastien and Gabriel Cramoisy, 1649), which is reprinted in *Les Correspondants de Peiresc*, ed. Philippe Tamizey de Larroque (Geneva: Slatkine, 1972), II 436–97.

[30] See Robert Lenoble, *Mersenne, ou la naissance du mécanisme* (Paris: Vrin, 1943).

[31] One should consider the evidence presented by Peter Dear, *Mersenne and the Learning of the Schools* (Ithaca, NY: Cornell University Press, 1988), in light of the obfuscatory procedure followed and recommended by Sir Francis Bacon: consider *De dignitate et augmentis scientiarum* 3.4, in *WoFB*, I 548–49 (translated at IV 344–45), and *The Advancement of Learning* II.vii.2, in *OFB*, IV 80–81, in light of Tac. *Ann.* 1.1–5.

[32] Consider the unexpurgated version of Marin Mersenne, *Quæstiones celeberrimæ in Genesim* (Paris: Sébastien Cramoisy, 1623) cols. 669–74 (esp. 671), in light of Lenoble, *Mersenne*, xii–xiii, 168–99 (esp. 171–75), 599–600, who charts the derision that Mersenne's remark later elicited from Pierre Bayle, Voltaire, and one contributor to the *Encyclopédie*.

time.[33] His adoption of this modus operandi is rendered all the more suspect by two facts: a senior colleague in the Minim order had expressly warned him that such a procedure was likely to be counterproductive in precisely this fashion,[34] and among the accusations he had quite rightly leveled at Giulio Cesare Vanini in an earlier work was the claim that this renegade Carmelite monk, so recently burned at the stake in Toulouse, had cannily propagated atheism under the cover of subjecting it to assault.[35] With regard to rhetorical indirection, it can hardly be argued that Marin Mersenne was hopelessly naive.

Later, Mersenne altered his deportment with regard to the heterodox. By this time, the Minim friar had come to be closely associated with Nicolas-Claude Fabri de Peiresc, a wealthy antiquary, an early and important patron and practitioner of science, and a *politique* with a noteworthy gift for forming friendships and sustaining them by way of correspondence.[36] In 1602 – shortly before the Papal Interdict was imposed on Venice and Paolo Sarpi, as the state theologian and champion of the Serene Republic, achieved European-wide fame – the young Peiresc had been introduced to the Servite friar, and he had quickly become an ardent admirer. Seventeen years later, in 1619, when he was sent a copy of *The History of the Council of Trent* hot off the presses, he greedily devoured it, and in a frank letter written to an English correspondent he betrayed the depths of his anticlericalism, his Erastianism, and his skepticism with regard to religious dogma by heaping praise on the book, regretting only

---

[33] See Marin Mersenne, *De l'Impiété des déistes, athées et libertins de ce temps* (Paris: Pierre Bilaine, 1624). It may not be fortuitous in the slightest that Mersenne bears so large a responsibility for the shift in apologetic procedure that rendered Christianity vulnerable to modern atheism by conceding that the battle must be fought and decided on the ground provided by philosophy: see Michael J. Buckley, S. J., *At the Origins of Modern Atheism* (New Haven, CT: Yale University Press, 1987), and Alan Charles Kors, *Atheism in France, 1650–1729: I. The Orthodox Sources of Disbelief* (Princeton, NJ: Princeton University Press, 1990), whose books should be read in light of the criticism directed at their contention that it was this shift in apologetic practice that, in fact, produced modern atheism: see Winfried Schröder, *Ursprünge des Atheismus: Untersuchungen Zur Metaphysik- und Religionskritik des 17. und 18. Jahrhunderts* (Stuttgart-Bad Cannstatt: Fromman-Holzboog, 1998), and Gianni Paganini, "*Legislatores* et *impostores*: Le *Theophrastus redivivus* et la thèse de l'imposture des religions à la moitié du XVIIᵉ siècle," in *Sources antiques de l'irréligion moderne: Le Relais italien, XVIᵉ–XVIIᵉ siècles*, ed. Jean-Pierre Cavaillé and Didier Foucault (Toulouse: Presses Universitaires du Mirail, 2001), 181–218.

[34] See Renatus Thuillier, *Diarium patrum et sororum ordinis minimorum provinciae Franciae sive Parisiensis qui religiose abierunt ab anno 1506 ad annum 1700* (Paris: Petrus Giffart, 1709), II 90–113 (at 95–96).

[35] Consider Mersenne, *Quæstiones celeberrimæ in Genesim* cols. 15–674 (esp. 278–674), in light of Lenoble, *Mersenne*, 175–81, and see William L. Hine, "Mersenne and Vanini," *Renaissance Quarterly* 29:1 (Spring 1976): 52–65; Francesco Paolo Raimondi, "Vanini et Mersenne," *Kairos* 12 (1998): 181–253; and Nicholas S. Davidson, "'Le Plus beau et le plus meschant esprit que ie aye cogneu': Science and Religion in the Writings of Giulio Cesare Vanini, 1585–1619," in *Heterodoxy in Early Modern Science and Religion*, ed. John Brooke and Ian Maclean (Oxford, UK: Oxford University Press, 2005), 59–79.

[36] See Hiram Caton, *The Politics of Progress: The Origins and Development of the Commercial Republic, 1600–1835* (Gainesville: University of Florida Press, 1988), 76–81; Lisa T. Sarasohn, "Nicolas-Claude Fabri de Peiresc and the Patronage of the New Science in the Seventeenth Century," *Isis* 84:1 (March 1993): 70–90; and Peter N. Miller, *Peiresc's Europe: Learning and Virtue in the Seventeenth Century* (New Haven, CT: Yale University Press, 2000).

that those in London responsible for editing and presenting that incendiary work had done so in a manner likely to deny it the audience it deserved in Catholic Europe.[37] In the same spirit, fifteen years later, in 1634 and 1635, Peiresc, and others of like mind whom he recruited for the purpose, put pressure on Mersenne to cease his polemics and desist – and the Minim friar complied with their instructions, abandoning apologetics once and for all.[38]

This transformation in Mersenne's conduct, which coincided with a growing interest in science on his part, and with his decision to embrace the mechanics and astronomy of Galileo Galilei,[39] was, in fact, quite radical. Within a year or two of coming under pressure from Peiresc, this onetime scourge of atheists, libertines, and deists was actually prepared to help translate into proper French and to arrange for the clandestine publication in Paris of *De veritate* – a book recently added to the *Index librorum prohibitorum*, which had been composed some years before by Edward, Lord Herbert of Cherbury, the father of English Deism. Mersenne's only proviso was that his role in the enterprise remain secret.[40]

[37] See Letter to William Camden on 15 July 1619, in *Lettres de Peiresc*, ed. Philippe Tamizey de Larroque (Paris: Imprimerie Nationale, 1888–1898), VII 799–803 (at 801–2). Note also Letter to Jacques Dupuy on 29 January 1625, in ibid., I 55–58 (at 55). In this connection, see Cecilia Rizzi, *Peiresc e l'Italia* (Turin: Giappichelli, 1965), 167–84, and Miller, *Peiresc's Europe*, 85–90.

[38] Consider Letters from Nicolas-Claude Fabri de Peiresc on 18 June 1634 and on 5 May and 3 July 1635, in *Correspondance du P. Marin Mersenne, religieux minime*, ed. Paul Tannery and Cornélis de Waard (Paris: Beauchesne, 1932–1988), IV 175–83 (at 181–82), V 162–74 (at 165–67), 274–78 (at 276–78), in light of Beaulieu, *Mersenne*, 56–62, and see Letter from Nicolas-Claude Fabri de Peiresc to Jacques Dupuy on 11 July 1634, in *Correspondance du P. Marin Mersenne*, IV 237–38.

[39] See Beaulieu, *Mersenne*, 107–17, and Daniel Garber, "On the Frontlines of the Scientific Revolution: How Mersenne Learned to Love Galileo," *Perspectives on Science* 12:2 (Summer 2004): 135–63.

[40] Consider Edward, Lord Herbert of Cherbury, *De la Verité entant quelle est distincte de la reuelation, du vray-semblable, du possible & du faux* ([Paris]: s.n., 1639), in light of Letters Exchanged with Edward, Lord Herbert of Cherbury, in 1636, in May–June and early October 1637, and on 7 August 1639, in *Correspondance du P. Marin Mersenne*, VI 353–67, VIII 275–78 (esp. the material quoted on 278), and see Mario M. Rossi, *Alle fonti del deismo e del materialismo moderni* (Florence: La Nuova Italia, 1942), 30–89 (esp. 39–47), and Lenoble, *Mersenne*, 561–63. In the previous century, Christian apologists had spoken with horror of the circulation of an atheist tract that purported to unmask Moses, Jesus, and Mohammed as "the three impostors." Just over three decades after Mersenne's death, Christian Kortholt, a theologian from Kiel, appropriated the tract's title and applied it to Spinoza and to the French priest's friends and close intellectual associates Lord Herbert and Hobbes: see *De tribus impostoribus magnis liber* (Kiel: Joachim Reumann, 1680). Eventually, such a treatise was composed: see Abraham Anderson, *The Treatise of the Three Impostors and the Problem of Enlightenment: A New Translation of the Traité des trois imposteurs (1777 Edition)* (Lanham, MD: Rowman & Littlefield, 1997). In this connection, see Silvia Berti, "The First Edition of the *Traité des trois imposteurs* and its Debt to Spinoza's *Ethics*," in *Atheism from the Reformation to the Enlightenment*, ed. Michael Hunter and David Wootton (Oxford, UK: Oxford University Press, 1992), 183–220, and *Heterodoxy, Spinozism, and Free Thought in Early-Eighteenth Century Europe: Studies on the Traité des trois imposteurs*, ed. Silvia Berti, Françoise Charles-Daubert, and Richard H. Popkin (Dordrecht: Kluwer Academic, 1996), which should be read in conjunction with the material cited in Chapter 2, notes 69 and 80, and Chapte 4, note 42, this volume.

As time passed, Mersenne became bolder. In 1646, as we have seen, he promoted the republication of Hobbes's *De cive*, and when Samuel Sorbière published his letter of commendation at the head of that book, as was evidently the plan, the Minim friar simply pretended to take it amiss. Even more to the point, in 1648, six months before he died, he came to the defense of the Socinians then suffering persecution in Poland. When he upbraided a correspondent from Gdansk with regard to the failure of the congregations in Poland to embrace this tribe of anti-Trinitarians, the man referred him to "the rationale for extirpating atheists" that the French priest had himself published in 1623.[41]

The remarkable depth and scope of the latitudinarianism that Mersenne evidenced as he grew older eventually attracted notice and gave occasion for comment. In his later years, when someone alluded in passing to the Minim friar's hyperbolic claim regarding the number of atheists in Paris, a wag is said to have responded that the old priest's circle of friends was, indeed, quite large. Even if the story is apocryphal, as may well be the case,[42] it is nonetheless apt. For when the old priest died, a friend wrote to the director of the academy at Breda to report the event and remarked, "You are well aware that he did not believe all his religion, . . . that he was of the sort well pleased to have the church service done, and that he dared not recite his Breviary often for fear of spoiling his good Latin."[43]

Pierre Gassendi seems to have been cut from similar cloth. Like Mersenne, he advocated a voluntarist theology rooted in nominalism and a radical epistemological skepticism designed to obviate metaphysical disputes between theologians and students of natural science.[44] He differed from his friend in only one particular. Not even in his youth did he add his voice to that of those attacking the atheists, deists, and libertines of the day. In fact, in 1624, when Mersenne and *Père* François Garasse were busy attacking Pierre Charron, Gassendi announced his profound admiration for and indebtedness to the author of *De la sagesse*.[45] Later, when his friend and patron Peiresc launched a campaign aimed at persuading Mersenne that his polemical posture was impolitic in the extreme, Gassendi quite readily joined in.[46] Moreover, in his work on Epicurus,

---

[41] Cf. Letters to André Rivet and Jan Höwelcke (Hevelius) on 1 March 1648, in *Correspondance du P. Marin Mersenne*, XVI 133–41 (at 134–36, 138, 141), with Letter from Jan Höwelcke (Hevelius) on 24 April 1648, in ibid., XVI 265–71 (at 268), who cites Mersenne, *Quæstiones celeberrimæ in Genesim* cols. 1829–34. In this connection, see Lenoble, *Mersenne*, 558–60, 564–74, and Beaulieu, *Mersenne*, 305–8.

[42] I have not been able to trace the story told by Caton, *The Politics of Progress*, 78, to a seventeenth-century source.

[43] See Letter from André Pineau to the Pasteur Rivet on 11 September 1648 (Leiden University Manuscripts B.P.L. IV, 286 f. 60), in Brown, *Scientific Organizations in Seventeenth Century France*, 36, n. 8. It is in this light that one should contemplate the possibility that Armand Beaulieu, "Un Moine à l'esprit libre," in *Révolution scientifique et libertinage*, ed. Alain Mothu (Turnhout: Brepols, 2000), 35–47, fails to consider.

[44] See Margaret J. Osler, "Providence and Divine Will in Gassendi's Views on Scientific Knowledge," *Journal of the History of Ideas* 44:4 (October 1983): 549–60.

[45] See Renée Kogel, *Pierre Charron* (Geneva: Librarie Droz, 1972), 142–61.

[46] See Letter from Nicolas-Claude Fabri de Peiresc to Jacques Dupuy on 11 July 1634, in *Correspondance du P. Marin Mersenne*, IV 237–38.

Gassendi pursued the rhetorical strategy that Vanini and Mersenne had previously employed. Epicurus' argument he laid out in fine detail and with great precision. On its behalf he displayed not only interest but enthusiasm. Only when he had made a powerful case for Epicurus did he prudently and piously distance himself from a teaching that was obviously contrary to the doctrine of the church that he putatively served.[47] He was also, through much of his life, quite closely associated not only with Elie Diodati, the great admirer of Galileo Galilei and Paolo Sarpi,[48] but also with François de La Mothe le Vayer, and Gabriel Naudé,[49] men subsequently notorious for embracing the radical skepticism championed by Pierre Charron, and widely then suspected of infidelity[50] –

---

[47] See René Pintard, *Le Libertinage érudit dans la première moitié du XVIIe siècle*, second edition (Geneva: Slatkine, 1983), passim (esp. 127–208, 297–302, 326–48, 382–87, 403–18, 424–29, 477–504); John Stephenson Spink, *French Free-Thought from Gassendi to Voltaire* (London: Athlone Press, 1960), 3–168 (esp. 14–17, 85–168); Olivier René Bloch, *La Philosophie de Gassendi: Nominalisme, matérialisme, et métaphysique* (The Hague: Martinus Nijhoff, 1971), esp. 105–6, 112–20, 361–69, 455–57, 474–81, 492–9; and Caton, *The Politics of Progress*, 76–81 (esp. 78, n. 20). For an attempt to square the circle, cf. Margaret J. Osler, "Providence and Divine Will in Gassendi's Views on Scientific Knowledge," 549–60, and "When Did Pierre Gassendi Become a Libertine?" in *Heterodoxy in Early Modern Science and Religion*, 169–92. See also Alberto Tenenti, "La polemica sulla religione di Epicuro nella prima metà del Seicento," *Studi storici* 1:2 (January–March 1960): 227–43, which is reprinted in Tenenti, *Credenze, ideologie, libertinismi: Tra Medioevo ed età modernai* (Bologna: Il Mulino, 1978), 287–306; Tullio Gregory, *Scetticismo ed empirismo: Studi su Gassendi* (Bari: Laterza, 1961), along with Gregory, "Pierre Gassendi dans le quatrième centenaire de son naissance," *Archives internationales d'histoire des sciences* 42:129 (December 1992): 203–26, which is reprinted in Gregory, *Genèse de la raison classique: De Charron à Descartes*, tr. Marilène Raiola (Paris: Presses Universitaires de France, 2000), 157–89. See René Pintard, "Les Problèmes de l'histoire du libertinage," *XVIIe siècle* 32:2 (April–June 1980): 131–61 (esp. 143–46), and note Jean Wirth, "Libertins et Epicuriens: Aspects de irréligion au XVIIe siècle," *Bibliothèque d'Humanisme et de Renaissance* 39:3 (September 1977): 601–27; and Jean-Charles Darmon, "Philosophie épicurienne et littérature au XVIIe siècle: Retour sur quelques problèmes de méthode symptomatiques," *Libertinage et philosophie au XVIIe siècle* 4 (2000): 11–38. One recent attempt to come to grips with this slippery figure sidesteps the question of infidelity: see Lynn Sumida Joy, *Gassendi the Atomist: Advocate of History in an Age of Science* (Cambridge, UK: Cambridge University Press, 1987). Another takes at face value his pretence to piety: see Lisa T. Sarasohn, *Gassendi's Ethics: Freedom in a Mechanistic Universe* (Ithaca, NY: Cornell University Press, 1996).

[48] See Chapter 4, this volume.

[49] For a brief discussion of this foursome, see Stéphane Garcia, *Elie Diodati et Galilée: Naissance d'un réseau scientifique dans l'Europe du XVIIe siècle* (Florence: L. S. Olschki, 2004), 217–27.

[50] The *locus classicus* is Pintard, *Le Libertinage érudit dans la première moitié du XVIIe siècle*, which should be read in its entirety. Note also Spink, *French Free-Thought from Gassendi to Voltaire*, 3–168; consider *Theophrastus redivivus*, ed. Guido Canzani and Gianni Paganini (Florence: La Nuova Italia, 1981), in conjunction with Tullio Gregory, *Theophrastus redivivus: Erudizione e ateismo nel Seicento* (Naples: Morano, 1979); and see Gregory, "Il libertinismo della prima metà del Seicento," and Ornella Pompeo Faracovi, "L'antropologia della religione nel libertinismo francese del Seicento," in *Ricerche su letteratura libertina e letteratura clandestina nel Seicento*, ed. Tullio Gregory et al. (Florence: La Nuova Italia, 1981), 3–47, 119–42, along with Gregory, "Aristotelismo e libertinismo," *Giornale critico della filosofia italiana* 61:2 (May–August 1982): 153–67, and Gregory, "Il libertinismo erudito," in Gregory, *Etica e religione nella critica libertina* (Naples: Guida, 1986), 11–70, which is reprinted in slightly abbreviated form as Gregory, "'Libertinage Erudit' in Seventeenth-Century France and Italy: The Critique of Ethics and Religion," *British Journal for the History of Philosophy* 6:3 (October 1998): 323–49. See also Chapter 2, note 155, and Chapter 4, note 30, this volume. All three of Gregory's essays

and they, too, sometimes joined in the gatherings at Mersenne's cell.[51]

The skeptical philosopher embraced by the *Tétrade* – as Gassendi and his friends called themselves – deserves attention. For their hero Charron was, as we have seen, an Averroist of sorts, who drew a sharp distinction between the philosophical few and the superstitious multitude, between those whom he termed *les esprits forts*, "men of strong mind" distinguished by a noble capacity to face up to the truth and manage it, and those whom he called *les esprits foibles*, "men mentally weak," foolish, and likely to be damaged by exposure to true science. To his admirers, he advised conformity in public for the sake of the well-being of the body politic, free-thinking in private, and a prudent discretion overall.[52] There is ample evidence to suggest that they took his point.

La Mothe le Vayer is an obvious example.[53] In 1630, he published in Paris a volume entitled *Four Dialogues Composed in Imitation of the Ancients*; two or three years later, he added a second volume entitled *Five Dialogues*, indicating by way of the subtitle that they, too, were composed along the same lines. Both purported to be the work of one Orasius Tubero. Both were supposed to have been printed in Frankfurt a quarter of a century before, in 1604 and 1606,

---

are now available in a French translation: see Gregory, *Genèse de la raison classique*, 11–112. Cf. Richard Henry Popkin, *The History of Scepticism: From Savonarola to Bayle* (New York: Oxford University Press, 2003), 80–98, who is inclined to take at face value the claims of the *libertins érudits* to be faithful Christians, with Gianni Paganini, "Haupttendenzen der clandestinen Philosophie," in *Grundriss der Geschichte der Philosophie: Die Philosophie des 17. Jahrhunderts*, revised edition, ed. Friedrich Uebergweg and Jean-Pierre Schobinger (Basel: Schwabe, 1998–), I:1 121–95; David Wootton, "New Histories of Atheism," in *Atheism from the Reformation to the Enlightenment*, 13–53; Gianluca Mori, "L'Athée et le masquee: XVIIᵉ-XVIIIe siècle," *Libertinage et philosophie au XVIIᵉ siècle* 5 (2001): 171–87; and Jean-Pierre Cavaillé, *Dis/simulations: Jules-César Vanini, François La Mothe le Vayer, Gabriel Naudé, Louis Machon et Torquatto Accetto: Religion, morale et politique au XVIIᵉ siècle* (Paris: Champion, 2002), which should all be read in light of Leo Strauss, "Persecution and the Art of Writing," in Strauss, *Persecution and the Art of Writings* (Glencoe, IL: Free Press, 1952), 22–37, and "On a Forgotten Kind of Writing," in Strauss, *What Is Political Philosophy?* (Glencoe, IL: Free Press, 1959), 221–32; Perez Zagorin, *Ways of Lying: Dissimulation, Persecution, and Conformity in Early Modern Europe* (Cambridge, MA: Harvard University Press, 1990), 289–330 (esp. 305–6, 318–28); and Paul A. Rahe, *Republics Ancient and Modern: Classical Republicanism and the American Revolution* (Chapel Hill: University of North Carolina Press, 1992), 233–48.

[51] In this connection, see Nicola Badaloni, "Libertinismo e scienza negli anni di Galilei e Campanella," in *Ricerche su letteratura libertina e letteratura clandestina nel Seicento*, 213–29.

[52] See Chapter 4, this volume.

[53] See Gianni Paganini, "*Pyrrhonisme tout pur* ou *circoncis*? La Dynamique du scepticisme chez La Mothe le Vayer," *Libertinage et philosophie au XVIIᵉ siècle* 2 (1997): 7–31, and Jean-Michel Gros, "Le Masque du 'scepticisme chrétien' chez La Mothe le Vayer," *Libertinage et philosophie au XVIIᵉ siècle* 5 (2001): 83–98; note Sophie Gouverneur, "La Mothe le Vayer et l'entretien de soi," *Libertinage et philosophie au XVIIᵉ siècle* 5 (2001): 99–115, and "La Mothe le Vayer et la politique, ou l'usage libertin du scepticisme antique," *Libertinage et philosophie au XVIIᵉ siècle* 7 (2003): 189–201, and Emmanuel Bury, "Écriture libertine et sources doxographiques: Le Cas La Mothe le Vayer," *Libertinage et philosophie au XVIIᵉ siècle* 6 (2002): 19–36; and see Nicole Gengoux, "Place et function de l'épicurisme dans *Les Dialogues faits à l'imitation des Anciens* de La Mothe le Vayer," *Libertinage et philosophie au XVIIᵉ siècle* 7 (2003): 141–87, as well as Cavaillé, *Dis/simulations*, 141–97.

respectively, by Jean Sarius. In both, under pseudonyms more or less transparent even today, La Mothe le Vayer depicted his friends in the *Tétrade* and others of a similar cast of mind with whom he was accustomed to converse.[54] As a glance at the volumes should make clear, he had reason for caution.

In the authorial letter that serves as the first volume's preface, La Mothe le Vayer sounds an ominous note, celebrating what he calls "the liberty of my style, which despises every constraint, and the license of my thoughts, which are purely natural," and observing that, in the environment in which he lives, these constitute a species of "contraband merchandise, which should not be exposed to the public." Although he proudly disdains seeking for his "philosophical discourses asylum and protection" from a noble patron graced with influence and power, he readily admits that "the force of truth and the authority of reason" may ultimately prove an insufficient safeguard. And so, quoting a well-known line from Epicurus concerning the manner in which the enlightened can provide for one another a theater in which to perform, he urges on his ideal reader "silence, or at least secrecy with regard to our particular conferences." His dialogues are composed, he warns, in such a manner as to be "more fit to lie in obscurity in a friend's study than to suffer embarrassment and the glare of publicity in the full light of day (*à souffrir l'éclat et le plein jour d'une publique lumiere*)." He has no interest in public applause. For the opinions of "a foolish multitude" and for "a century ignorant and perverse" he thinks nothing more appropriate than mockery and contempt. "Let us enjoy," he concludes, "the real and solid contentments of our private get-togethers."

In keeping with the paradox that he has chosen to publish reflections that, he insists, must remain private, La Mothe le Vayer is coy throughout. That he could "justify in religious terms" a moral code that is "purely natural (*purement Physiques*)" he does not doubt. But from doing so he piously refrains, observing that his addressee knows full well the degree to which he has made a "submission" of his "intellect (*esprit*) with regard to matters divine," which he "leaves off treating," so he avers, "out of respect for those who have a right to touch the ark and approach the sanctuary." He nonetheless insists that his reader reflect "on the errors, follies (*sottises*), and the impudence (*impertinences*)" characterizing "the opinions of the vulgar," among whom he includes "the knight, the man of the robe, and the peasant in equal measure." He enjoins this reader to ruminate also "on the tyrannical authority" dominant in "the time" in which they live, on "the customs" that these opinions and this authority "have established," and "on the invincible obstinacy (*l'opiniastreté invincible*) with which" these customs "are blindly sustained."[55]

Lest his readers fail to see that one cannot search out and correctly identify "the tyrannical authority" dominant in the age, and that one cannot discover the source of "the errors, follies, and impudence" exhibited by "the vulgar," without, in fact, touching "the ark" and approaching "the sanctuary," La Mothe le

---

[54] See René Pintard, *La Mothe le Vayer – Gassendi – Guy Patin: Études de bibliographie et de critique suivies de textes inédit de Guy Patin* (Paris: Boivin et Cⁱᵉ Éditeurs, [1943]), 5–31.

[55] See [François La Mothe le Vayer], *Dialogues faits à l'imitation des anciens*, ed. André Pessel (Paris: Fayard, 1988), 11–16.

Vayer eventually takes up the question of "divinity."[56] This he does in a properly secluded place, deep within the second of his two volumes, in a dialogue
that serves, appropriately, as a prelude to a discussion of *l'opiniastreté* deeply
indebted to the critique of *consuetudo* with which Averroës ends his commentary on the second book of Aristotle's *Metaphysics*.[57] There, sandwiched in
between an extensive discussion larded with conventionally pious pronounce-
ments and another of similar character in which he paraphrases Pierre Charron's
repeated restatement of Saint Paul's assertion that one should render the intellect a captive out of reverence for Christ,[58] La Mothe le Vayer conceals a survey
of the thinking of Averroës, Epicurus, Lucretius, and the like, presenting their
arguments in detail so that his reader can consider whether "all our devotions,
all our cults, our prayers and sermons are things vain and ridiculous, invented
by those who wish to profit from their introduction, and confirmed thereafter by
blind, popular custom." And after conceding that these practices may, in fact,
be sustained as well by "those of the greatest foresight (*des plus clairvoyans*),
who judge this fiction very useful for repressing those who are most vicious,"
he nonetheless asserts that, under the influence of "a zeal devoid of discretion," these devotions, cults, prayers, and sermons "have often worked to opposite effect" in such a fashion as to justify Lucretius' well-known accusation –
that "religion has given birth to deeds impious and criminal."[59] Moreover,
in a subsequent passage, he pauses to survey "the immense and prodigious
number of human religions," and he compares them with Ptolemaic astronomy with its cycles and epicycles, arguing that these religions are rationaliza-
tions designed "to make sense of (*expliquer*) the phenomena" constituted by
"the mores, actions, and thoughts of poor mortals." Should a new Copernicus
appear, he suggests, a man prepared to make better sense of the moral world
than the Ptolemies who have founded and reshaped the existing religions, this
genius would meet fierce resistance, for "within this infinity of religions there
is hardly anyone who does not believe that he possesses the true religion and
hardly anyone who refrains from condemning all the others." If truth be told,
he adds, there is hardly anyone of a religious disposition who is averse to
"battling for altars and hearths (*pro aris et focis*) to the last drop of his own
blood."[60]

Eventually, La Mothe le Vayer turns to Charron and sums up his own observations by quoting from *De la sagesse* the notorious quip that "all religions
are foreign (*estranges*) and shocking (*horribles*) to common sense," and in this

---

56 See [La Mothe le Vayer], *Dialogues faits à l'imitation des anciens*, 303–52.
57 Consider [La Mothe le Vayer], *Dialogues faits à l'imitation des anciens*, 353–86 (esp. 358),
    in light of Comments II.14–16 on Aristotle's *Metaphysics* II.3 (995a1–20), in *Aristotelis Sta-
    giritae omnia quae extant opera... Averrois Cordubensis in ea opera omnes qui ad nos per-
    venere commentarii* (Venice: Giunta, 1550–1552), VIII 17ra–va, and see Chapters 2 and 4, this
    volume.
58 After reviewing Chapter 4, this volume, see [La Mothe le Vayer], *Dialogues faits à l'imitation
    des anciens*, 303–13, 347–53 (esp. 348).
59 See [La Mothe le Vayer], *Dialogues faits à l'imitation des anciens*, 329.
60 See [La Mothe le Vayer], *Dialogues faits à l'imitation des anciens*, 330–31.

context he also quotes at length a no less remarkable passage from Sir Francis Bacon's essay "Of Superstition":

Atheism leaves to man sense, philosophy, natural piety, laws, reputation, and everything that may be a guide to virtue, but superstition destroys all these things and erects an absolute monarchy in the minds of men. This is why atheism never troubled states, but only makes men exercise foresight with regard to themselves, as looking no further. And I see that the times inclined to atheism, such as the time of Augustus Caesar and our own time in some countries, have been civil times, while superstition has been the confusion of many states and brings in novelty with regard to the *primum mobile*, which ravishes all the other spheres of government.[61]

It should come, then, as no surprise that, in 1649, when the author of these dialogues was appointed preceptor of the duc d'Anjou, one of his friends should in amazement remark that the future king's brother was to be educated by a man "suspected of the intellectual vice that had formed the basis of the attack directed at Diagoras and Protagoras" in classical antiquity.[62]

The individual who hazarded this observation was in a position to know the truth. Guy Patin was a learned medical doctor and a libertine in his own right. He knew the members of the Tétrade well; and, in 1647, when Thomas Hobbes fell seriously ill, he was the physician called in. From another of his letters, we get a sense of the secretive atmosphere in which Charron's disciples operated, and it illustrates the delight that these erudite libertines took in intellectual transgression. Moreover, in echoing a crucial phrase from the dedicatory letter that served as a preface to the first volume of La Mothe le Vayer's dialogues, it points to the role played by coded language in the intellectual exchanges of Charron's heirs.

Patin had been invited to join Gassendi and their "intimate friend" Naudé, whom he elsewhere describes as a thoroughgoing unbeliever, in what he describes as a "*débauche*" less bibulous than "philosophical," which was slated to take place one Sunday at Naudé's country retreat in Gentilly. "Since all three of us," he observed, "have been cured of bugaboos (*de loup-garou*) and delivered from the evil of scruples, which is the tyrant of consciences, we will perhaps go very near the sanctuary." A year before, when he had attended a similar gathering at the same venue, "there were," he reported, "no witnesses at all, nor should there have been any: we spoke very freely about everything without anyone being by it scandalized."[63]

---

[61] Note Sir Francis Bacon, "Of Superstition," *Essaies* 15, in *WoFB*, VI 560–61, and see [La Mothe le Vayer], *Dialogues faits à l'imitation des anciens*, 339. Where the latter diverges from the former, I have followed La Mothe le Vayer. In this connection, see Marta Fattori, "La diffusione di Francis Bacon nel libertinismo francese," *Rivista di storia della filosofia* 57:2 (April–June 2003): 225–42.

[62] See Letter to André Falconet on 13 July 1649, in *Lettres de Gui Patin*, ed. J. H. Reveillé-Parise (Paris: J.-B. Baillière, 1846), II 523–24.

[63] See Letter to André Falconet on 27 August 1648, in *Lettres de Gui Patin*, II 507–9 (at 508), which should be interpreted in light of Patin's description of Naudé in Letter to Charles Spon in October 1662, in ibid., II 477–85 (at 478–79), and note the manner in which Patin echoes the cryptic language employed by La Mothe le Vayer in the dedicatory letter to the set of dialogues

From another letter, written some years later by Samuel Sorbière, we get confirmation of what we can divine from La Mothe le Vayer's dialogues concerning the Epicurean ethos of such gatherings. Sorbière had attended a get-together at the house of Charles du Bosc along with other known associates of Gassendi and Mersenne, such as Thomas de Martel, Abraham du Prat, and La Mothe le Vayer himself. Although focused "for the most part" on Hobbes, and on "matters philosophical," including the physics of Epicurus as well as that of Hobbes, it was anything but a somber, solemn event. "I sprinkled about learning in abundance," he reports, "and threw in the salt of wit, and it was not without laughter that we stirred up the guests (*convivium*), although also not without a profound meditation on matters quite difficult. But you know our symposiarch, and you know how boisterous and impudent a scoffer I am." Then, by way of explanation, he alludes in coded language to Epicurus' advice that, while engaging in philosophy, his followers should mock the stupidity of the multitude, the absurd idealism of the Platonists, and their own proclivity to take themselves too seriously. "Nothing," he writes, "is more conducive to the good health of the body and to contentment (*Euthymia*) than wise laughter and well-tempered mirth in the company of our more intimate friends."[64]

It is impossible to believe that Lucretius, his atomist physics, his account of sensation, his critique of religion, and his hypothetical history of the origins and evolution of human society never figured in the conversations that took place among those who gathered at Mersenne's cell. Hobbes was not just aware of Gassendi's work on the life of Epicurus.[65] By October 1644, thanks to the friendship that had grown up, he had read in manuscript both that work and what there was of Gassendi's *Animadversions on the Tenth Book of Diogenes Laertius Concerning the Life, Morals, and Sentiments of Epicurus*, and he reported to his friends in England that Gassendi's work "is big as Aristotle's philosphie, but much truer and excellent Latin."[66] Nor was Gassendi's work on Epicureanism for Hobbes a subject of fleeting concern. After his return home,

that he published in 1630: see [La Mothe le Vayer], *Dialogues faits à l'imitation des anciens*, 14. Consider in this context the observations subsequently attributed to Naudé and Patin: see *Naudæana*, 8, 15–16, 30–33, 46–47, 53–57, 104–5, and *Patiniana, ou les bons mots de Mr. Patin*, 6–7, 22–23, 40–42, 51–53, 73, 88–90, 107–8, 117–18, in *Naudæana et Patiniana, ou Singularitez Remarquables, prises des Conversations de Mess. Naudé et Patin*, second edition (Amsterdam: François vander Plaats, 1703), which should be read in light of Pintard, *Le Mothe le Vayer – Gassendi – Guy Patin*, 47–61. On Naudé himself, see Lorenzo Bianchi, *Rinascimento e libertinismo: Studi su Gabriel Naudé* (Naples: Bibliopolis, 1996), and Isabelle Moreau, "Gabriel Naudé, un apologie de la prudence en matière de lecture," *Libertinage et philosophie au XVIIᵉ siècle* 6 (2002): 7–17, as well as Cavaillé, *Dis/simulations*, 198–265.

[64] Consider Letter from Samuel Sorbière to Thomas Hobbes in 2 February 1657, in *CTH*, I 433–37 (at 433), in light of Epicurus, *Sententiae Vaticanae* XLI, in *Epicurus: The Extant Remains*, ed. Cyril Bailey (Oxford, UK: Clarendon Press, 1926), 112, and Pers. 1.12; see Jean Salem, *Tel un Dieu parmi les hommes: l'Éthique d'Épicure* (Paris: J. Vrin, 1989), 140–41, 167–74; and consider Springborg, "Hobbes and Epicurean Religion," 178–79. On Sorbière, see Sophie Gouverneur, "Samuel Sorbière, ou la réhabilitation libertine des passions," *Libertinage et philosophie au XVIIᵉ siècle* 4 (2000): 183–97.

[65] See Letter from Samuel Sorbière to Thomas Hobbes on 19 August 1647, in *CTH*, I 161–62.

[66] See Letter from Sir Charles Cavendish to John Pell on 10 October 1644, in *A Collection of Letters Illustrative of the Progress of Science*, 85.

he displayed a keen interest in laying his hands on the three volumes that his friend had published in 1649.[67]

From a letter Sorbière wrote to Hobbes in July 1645, we get an inkling of what it was, apart from his physics, that sparked the latter's interest in Epicurus and animated the gatherings at the Convent of the Annunciation attended by Hobbes, Gassendi, Sorbière, and the *libertins érudits* – for, in this letter, without attribution and without any indication that he is appropriating another's words, Sorbière applies to his addressee a series of poetic lines that Lucretius had penned in praise of Epicurus' self-emancipation from the madness attendant on religion.[68] Six years later, when in *Leviathan* Hobbes described the propensity of the pusillanimous and credulous multitude "that make little, or no enquiry into the naturall causes of things . . . to suppose, and feign unto themselves, severall kinds of Powers Invisible; and to stand in awe of their own imaginations; and in time of distresse to invoke them; as also in the time of an expected good successe, to give them thanks; making the creatures of their own fancy, their Gods," he confirmed the justice of Sorbière's words of praise by restating with a new polemical edge the critique of religious fear limned in *De rerum natura*.[69]

Thus, if the printer who pirated Hobbes' *Behemoth* in 1679 under the title *The History of the Civil Wars of England From the Year 1640, to 1660* did not find in the manuscript from which he worked the lines drawn from Lucretius' diatribe against religion that appear on the title page of the editions he published,[70] he clearly knew what he was about when he supplied them himself. When Hobbes penned "An Historical Narration Concerning Heresy, and the Punishment Thereof," he chose as its epigraph four lines from *De rerum natura* evocative of the power of religious fear.[71] Moreover, when John Aubrey asked Edmund Waller to pen a few verses concerning their old friend, the latter declined because "he was afrayd of the Churchmen: that, what was chiefly to be taken notice of in his Elogie was that [Hobbes], being but *one*, and a private Person, pulled-downe all their Churches, dispelled the mists of Ignorance, and layd-open their Priest–craft."[72]

---

[67] See Letters from François du Verdus and Thomas de Martel to Thomas Hobbes on 4 and 20 August and 5 September 1654, in *CTH*, I 186–203.

[68] See Letter from Samuel Sorbière to Thomas Hobbes on 11 July 1645, in *CTH*, I 121–23 (esp. 123, n. 2). The manner in which Sorbière chose to end his life is also quite revealing: see Lorenzo Bianchi, "Sorbière's Scepticism: Between Naturalism and Absolutism," in *The Return of Scepticism: From Hobbes and Descartes to Bayle*, ed. Gianni Paganini (Dordrecht: Kluwer Academic, 2003), 267–82 (esp. 269–70).

[69] Cf. Hobbes, *Leviathan* I.xi.23–xii.32, xiv, who cites Stat. *Theb.* 3.657–61, with Lucr. 1.62–158, 2.1–61, 3.1–93, 830–1094, 4.1–25, 5.1194–1240; note Lucr. 5.972–81, 1161–93; and see Pierre-François Moreau, "La Crainte a engendré les dieux," *Libertinage et philosophie au XVIIᵉ siècle* 4 (2000): 147–53.

[70] Consider the initial epigraph on the title page of T. H., *The History of the Civil Wars of England From the Year 1640, to 1660* ([London]: s.n., 1679), in light of Letter from Thomas Hobbes to John Aubrey on 18 August 1679, in *CTH*, II 772–73 (esp. 773, n. 4). Cf. Thomas Hobbes, *Behemoth, or An Epitome of the Civil Wars of England, From 1640, to 1660* (London: s.n., 1679), which lacks epigraphs altogether.

[71] Cf. Thomas Hobbes, "An Historical Narration Concerning Heresy, and the Punishment Thereof," in *EW*, IV 385, with Lucr. 2.54–57.

[72] See *ABL*, 235.

Political Epicureanism

There was another element within the Epicurean creed that was of use to Hobbes. The Malmesbury philosopher was familiar with the account of the origins of civil society initially presented in Aristotle's *Politics* and subsequently refined in Cicero's rhetorical works.[73] But this account he found unsatisfactory, for it was grounded on the presumption that human beings have the potential to be morally and politically rational. It acknowledged, as we have seen, that civil society comes into being on the basis of a calculation of advantage, but it asserted that the political community is thereafter sustained as well by the direct application of *lógos* to questions of justice and the common good[74] – and from Hobbes's perspective, as we have also seen, this last assertion constitutes a fallacy fatal to rational government and conducive to dispute, demagoguery, and endemic disorder.

Epicurus and his followers offered Hobbes an alternative account – consistent with his conviction that the universe is constituted by matter in motion, divorced from every notion of providence natural or divine, and utterly free from teleology – which treated the emergence of civil society as a natural process: a predictable development grounded in the need for defense against wild animals and hostile men, driven by discoveries made possible and even inevitable by accident in the course of infinite time, and accomplished by the working of instrumental reason alone.[75] This account, which derived justice and morality from a calculation of material self-interest, could be found fully elaborated in the fifth book of Lucretius' *De rerum natura*.[76] It could be pieced together from the Epicurean maxims presented at the end of the tenth book of Diogenes Laertius' *Lives of the Eminent Philosophers*.[77] It was laid out in a work penned by Hermarchus, Epicurus' close friend and successor as scholarch, from which a crucial passage was excerpted and preserved in Porphyry's *De abstinentia*.[78] And, of course, Pierre Gassendi had collected and dealt with all of these sources in the great compendium of Epicurean lore that he allowed Hobbes to read in draft.[79] That Hobbes had more than once wrestled with the Epicurean account there can be no doubt.

---

[73] In this connection, see Chapter 1, this volume.

[74] See Chapter 1, this volume.

[75] See Robert Philippson, "Die Rechtsphilosophie der Epikureer," *Archiv für Philosophie, Erste Abteilung: Archiv für Geschichte der Philosophie* 23:3, n. f. 16:3 (April 1910): 289–337, and Victor Goldschmidt, *La Doctrine d'Épicure et le droit* (Paris: J. Vrin, 1977). Note also Carnes Lord, "Aristotle's Anthropology," in *Essays on the Foundations of Aristotelian Political Science* (Berkeley: University of California Press, 1991), 49–73. In this connection, see also Diod. 1.8.1–9 (which should be read with 1.13–16, 43, 90, 2.38.2–6), a writer whom Hobbes read and admired: see Hobbes, *Behemoth*, 91–94, and *Decameron physiologicum*, in *EW*, VII 73–74.

[76] See Lucr. 5.783–1457.

[77] See Diog. Laert. 10.150–54.

[78] Consider Porph. *Abst.* 1.7–12, which was first printed in Greek and in a Latin translation in Italy in the mid-sixteenth century and which was subsequently printed in a French translation in Paris in 1622, in light of Paul A. Vander Waerdt, "Hermarchus and the Epicurean Genealogy of Morals," *Transactions of the American Philological Association* 118 (1988): 87–106.

[79] In this connection, note Ludwig, *Die Wiederentdeckung des Epikureischen Naturrechts*, especially 401–54, who draws attention to the Epicurean origins of the arguments deployed in the thirteenth chapter of Hobbes's *Leviathan*, and see Paganini, "Hobbes, Gassendi and the

Of course, it would be an error to treat Hobbes – or, for that matter, Bacon – as a mere adherent of the Epicurean school. Everything that these men borrowed they digested, recast, and put to use in a novel fashion. They were, to mention only their most important divergence from Epicurean orthodoxy, no more enamored of the quest for tranquility of soul (*ataraxía*) than had been Niccolò Machiavelli, and they therefore rejected the argument for a withdrawal from public life. Like the Florentine, they were inclined to suppose that rest is an illusion and that "the things of men" are as much "in motion" as the physical universe, and, like him, they made no exception for the privileged few. They, too, were persuaded that "the human appetites" are "insatiable"; that "by nature" human beings "desire everything" while "by fortune they are allowed to secure little"; and that since "nature has created men in such a fashion" that they are "able to desire everything" but not "to secure everything," their "desire is always greater than the power of acquisition (*la potenza dello acquistare*)."[80]

In this spirit, Bacon explicitly repudiated Epicurean *ataraxía* and embraced, in its place, "the felicity" that lies in what he called "continuance and proceeding." In men and in other "creatures," he found "two several appetites..., the one to preserve and continue themselves," and the other "to dilate or multiply themselves." To the latter, which he deemed "the worthier," he gave "priority" and "pre-eminence" – partly in recognition of the fact that "our estate" is "mortal and exposed to fortune," and partly because "this Active Good is upheld by the affection which is natural in man towards [the] variety and proceeding" evident in "the enterprises, pursuits, and purposes of life ... whereof men are sensible with pleasure in their inceptions, progressions, recoils, reintegrations, approaches, and attainings to their ends." In endorsing man's yearning for "power, glory, amplification, continuance," Bacon condemned as "pusillanimous and lacking in confidence (*pusilli cujusdam animi et diffidentis*)" those among the ancients who conceived of philosophy as "a discipline or preparation to die." Men are not on earth, he insisted, to be mere "lookers on." Their "felicity" is to be found "in much desiring and much enjoying" rather than "in an equal and constant peace of mind." In consequence, he expressly condemned "the school of Epicurus" for pronouncing "felicity to be nothing other than tranquillity and serenity of soul freed and emptied of perturbation," and he censured those among "the most ancient and venerated philosophers, who too easily withdrew from civil affairs in order to shake off indignities and perturbations and live rather, so they thought, uninjured and inviolable."[81]

Tradition of Political Epicureanism," 113–37, who traces Epicurean influence in the annotations added to the second edition of *De cive*, which was published in 1647.

[80] Note Machiavelli, *Discorsi* 1.6.4, 37.1, 2 Procemio 2–3, 3, in *Opere*, 86–87, 119, 145, and see Machiavelli, *Discorsi* 3.2, in *Opere*, 197–98.

[81] Cf. Bacon, *The Advancement of Learning* I.viii.6, II.xvii.2, xx.8–9, xxi.1–5, in *OFB*, IV 52–53, 122–23, 137–42, and *De dignitate et augmentis scientiarum* 7.1–2, in *WoFB*, I 713–31 (translated at V 3–19), with Pl. *Grg.* 491a–494e, *Phd.* 67e, and *Leg.* 8.828c–d, and see *Novum organum* 1.88, in *OFB*, XI 140–43. In this connection, see Jeffrey Barnouw, "Active Experience vs. Wish-Fulfilment in Francis Bacon's Moral Psychology of Science," *Philosophical Forum* 9:1 (Fall 1979): 78–99.

With this analysis, Hobbes was fully in sympathy, and he placed particular emphasis on its epistemological consequences. To begin with, he expressly rejected the classical and Christian view that there is a "*Summum Bonum*" capable of satisfying man as man, and he echoed Bacon's denial that "Felicity" is "the repose of a mind satisfied." It is, instead, Hobbes insisted, "a continuall progresse of the desire, from one object to another." Moreover, because desire is incoherent and men are insatiable, he continued, they "conceive the same things differently," and "the same man, in divers times, differs from himselfe." Although the true nature of what human beings contemplate may be the same, he then added, "the diversity of our reception of it, in respect of different constitutions of body, and prejudices of opinion gives everything a tincture of our different passions." More often than not, then, the words used by an individual tell us more regarding "the nature, disposition, and interest of the speaker" than they do concerning the subject that he is talking about. Thus, what one man calls wisdom another man thinks of as fear, and what one describes as cruelty another terms justice; indeed, what a man calls prodigality on one occasion, he may later consider magnanimity; and what he thinks of today as gravity he may regard as stupidity tomorrow. As a consequence of the "*inconstant* signification" of the moral terms that men employ, Hobbes concluded, "such names can never be true grounds of any ratiocination," and they can hardly provide a foundation for political harmony.[82] In short, Thucydides' famous description of the descent into moral anarchy occasioned by the revolutions at Corcyra and elsewhere in Greece – in which "[t]he received value of names imposed for signification of things, was changed into arbitrary" – is not, as the Greek historian supposed, an account of an abnormal situation in which men are driven to extremities: it is an accurate depiction of the fundamental human condition.

It is from this moral chaos that Hobbes seeks to elicit order. Because there is no *summum bonum*, because man is insatiable and human felicity is a haphazard progress of desire from one more or less whimsically selected object to another, he longs first and foremost not for any particular end, but rather for the means "to assure for ever, the way of his future desire." In short, he experiences a "perpetuall and restlesse desire of Power after power,"[83] and only this can give to human reason consistent direction and make of a man's "Trayne *of Imaginations*" or "Thoughts" something other than a "wild ranging of the mind." As the Wiltshire philosopher puts it, "From Desire, ariseth the Thought of some means we have seen produce the like of that which we ayme at; and from the thought of that, the thought of means to that mean; and so continually, till we come to some beginning within our own power." In short, "the Thoughts, are to the Desires, as Scouts, and Spies to range abroad, and find the way to the things Desired."[84]

[82] See Hobbes, *Leviathan* Introduction, I.iv.24, ix.1, xv.40–41. See also Hobbes, *Elements of Law* I.v.1–14, vii.3, 6–7; and Hobbes, *De homine* XI.11–15, in *LW*, II 100–103.

[83] See Hobbes, *Leviathan* I.xi.1–2.

[84] See Hobbes, *Leviathan* I.i–iii (esp. iii.3–5), viii.14–16. In this connection, see Jeffrey Barnouw, "Hobbes's Causal Account of Sensation," *Journal of the History of Philosophy* 18:2 (April 1980): 115–30.

Hobbes divides what he calls the "Trayn of regulated Thoughts" into two species. The first type of coherent thinking takes place

> when of an effect imagined, wee seek the causes, or means that produce it: and this is common to Man and Beast. The other is, when imagining any thing whatsoever, wee seek all the possible effects, that can by it be produced; that is to say, we imagine what we can do with it, when wee have it. Of which I have not at any time seen any signe, but in man onely; for this is a curiosity hardly incident to the nature of any living creature that has no other Passion but sensuall, such as are hunger, thirst, lust, and anger. In summe, the Discourse of the Mind, when it is governed by designe, is nothing but *Seeking*, or the faculty of Invention, which the Latines call *Sagacitas*, and *Solertia*; a hunting out of the causes, of some effect, present or past; or of the effects, of some present or past cause.[85]

In consequence, if man surpasses the animals, he does so, as Bacon has already intimated by way of his criticism of Machiavelli, not as *homo politicus* but as *homo faber*. He is by nature an inventor, a hunter of causes and effects, a fashioner of tools, and he alone is driven by what Hobbes calls "a Lust of the mind" to investigate the consequences of particular actions.[86]

All of this has consequences. To begin with, it rules out all ontology, even the metaphysical atomism espoused by Democritus, Epicurus, and Lucretius,[87] for it is to the vain pursuit of formal principles by the ancient philosophers that, first, Bacon and, then, Hobbes trace natural philosophy's fruitlessness in antiquity. In their disparate and feuding schools, as Hobbes puts it, natural philosophy was always "rather a Dream than Science."[88] What is left to man is not, then, the discovery of first principles enabling him to grasp nature as a whole, for he is not by nature contemplative, and instrumental reason is the only tool that he has for understanding. What is left to man is the methodical deployment of instrumental reason in forming hypotheses and in testing by way of experiment their predictive power with regard to the phenomenal world, for they are to be judged not as ultimately right or wrong but solely with regard to their fruitfulness in enabling human beings to master the world constituted by their own sensations.

Bacon and Hobbes were in agreement that human beings lack direct access to the world about them, that their commonsense understanding of the world as a congeries of natural kinds is scientifically unsound as well as misleading, and

---

[85] See Hobbes, *Leviathan* I.iii.5.

[86] See Hobbes, *Leviathan* I.vi. 35. See also *Leviathan* I.v.6, xii. 2–4 , IV.xlvi.1–2. One should read Hobbes, *Elements of Law* I.iii.1–v.4 in light of I.ix.18. In one place, the preeminent twentieth-century student of the subject identifies this claim as "the simple leading thought of Hobbes' teaching about man"; in another, he speaks of it as "the nerve of Hobbes' argument." One should read Leo Strauss, "On the Basis of Hobbes's Political Philosophy," in *What Is Political Philosophy?*, 170–96 (esp. 176, n. 2), in light of Strauss, *Hobbes' politische Wissenschaft* (Neuwied am Rhein: Luchterhand, 1965), 8, and *Natural Right and History* (Chicago: University of Chicago Press, 1974), vii.

[87] In this connection, see Richard Kennington, "Bacon's Ontology," in *On Modern Origins*, 33–56, and Gianni Paganini, "Hobbes among Ancient and Modern Sceptics: Phenomena and Bodies," in *The Return of Scepticism*, 3–35.

[88] See Hobbes, *Leviathan* IV.xlvi.11.

that the only things that they can genuinely know are the trains of reasoning that they have fabricated themselves. All other knowledge, even if practically effective, they regarded as hypothetical and ontologically unsure.[89] The two English philosophers differed from one another, however, in two particulars.

In 1630, while conducting one of his pupils on the grand tour, Hobbes came across a copy of Euclid open to the Pythagorean theorem and was for the first time powerfully struck by the certainty achieved in geometrical reasoning. According to John Aubrey, the Malmesbury philosopher

> was 40 yeares old before he looked on Geometry; which happened accidentally. Being in a Gentleman's Library, Euclid's Elements lay open and 'twas the 47 *El. libri I.* He read the Proposition. *By G___,* sayd he (he would now and then sweare an emphaticall Oath by way of emphasis) *this is impossible!* So he reads the Demonstration of it, which referred him back to such a Proposition; which proposition he read. That referred him back to another, which he also read. *Et sic deinceps* that at last he was demonstratively convinced of that trueth. This made him in love with Geometry.
>
> I have heard Mr Hobbes say that he was wont to draw lines on his thigh and on the sheetes, abed, and also multiply and divide.[90]

In the aftermath, in much the same manner as Mersenne, Gassendi, and Descartes, he adopted – not as a metaphysical conviction but as a working hypothesis – Galileo's assertion that the "universe" is a "book . . . written in the language of mathematics,"[91] and he came to think that civil science could be established in the same fashion and with the same certainty as geometry – by a train of reasoning securely rooted in premises of our own fashioning. In both regards, Hobbes moved beyond Bacon.

Hobbes's Critique of Machiavelli

At some point in the 1630s, Hobbes set out to articulate a novel philosophical system, consisting of a mathematical physics, a mechanistic account of human psychology, and a science of politics consistent with this physics and this psychology. It took the Malmesbury philosopher something like a quarter of a century to finish the project, but early on – perhaps at the very outset – he was fully prepared to lay out the political doctrine that formed its ultimate conclusion. The odds are, in fact, good that in April 1640, when the earl of Newcastle urged him to spell out on paper the doctrine that he had broached in conversation, Hobbes had already written much of what came to be called *The Elements of Law, Natural and Politic,* for parts of the manuscript that

---

[89] In this connection, see Antonio Pérez-Ramos, *Francis Bacon's Idea of Science and the Maker's Knowledge Tradition* (Oxford, UK: Clarendon Press, 1988).

[90] See *ABL,* 230.

[91] See Galileo Galilei, *The Assayer* (1623), in *Discoveries and Opinions of Galileo,* tr. Stillman Drake (Garden City, NY: Doubleday, 1957), 237–38, which should be read in conjunction with Galileo's discussion of primary and secondary qualities in ibid., 273–79. Note also Pietro Redondi, *Galileo Heretic,* tr. Raymond Rosenthal (Princeton, NJ: Princeton University Press, 1987), esp. 9–27, 51–67, 203–332.

Hobbes presented to the earl on 9 May 1640 are highly polished, and parts show evidence of considerable haste.[92]

Hobbes's friend Sir Kenelm Digby had sent him a copy of Descartes' *Discourse on Method* in early October 1637, almost immediately upon its publication,[93] and Hobbes had read the work with care.[94] As an anti-metaphysical materialist monist, he had little use for the metaphysical dualism that Descartes espoused in that work and elaborated more fully in his *Meditations*, and he doubted that Descartes really believed in all of what he had written. But for the French philosopher's work in geometry Hobbes had considerable admiration,[95] and he shared Descartes' conviction that a proper physics could only be elaborated by way of mathematics. The two philosophers owed a common debt to Sir Francis Bacon and Galileo Galilei, and it may have been Descartes' example in the *Discourse on Method* that inspired Hobbes's adoption of introspection as a means – both for sidestepping the subjective character of all experience grounded in sensation, and for attaining to certain knowledge of the sort achieved in mathematics.[96] It is by no means fortuitous that, upon reading *De*

---

[92] Consider BL Harl. MS 4235 in light of Deborah Baumgold, "The Composition of Hobbes's *Elements of Law*," *History of Political Thought* 25:1 (Spring 2004): 16–43.

[93] See Letter from Sir Kenelm Digby on 4 October 1637 in *CTH*, I 51.

[94] See Frithiof Brandt, *Hobbes's Mechanical Conception of Nature* (Copenhagen: Levin & Munksgaard, 1928), 93–99, 137–42; Jean Bernhardt, "La Polémique de Hobbes contre la *Dioptrique* de Descartes dans le *Tractatus Opticus II* (1644)," *Revue internationale de philosophie* 33:129 (1979): 432–42; and Yves Charles Zarka, "La Matière et la représentation: Hobbes lecteur de *La Dioptrique* de Descartes," in *Problématique et réception du Discours de la méthode et des Essais*, ed. Henry Méchoulan (Paris: Vrin, 1988), 81–98.

[95] See *ABL*, 185, 237.

[96] For the manner in which the work done by Descartes and Hobbes on the optical foundations of vision shaped not only their understanding of matter as extension but also their understanding of human nature as a form of subjectivity, consider Hiram Caton, *The Origin of Subjectivity: An Essay on Descartes* (New Haven, CT: Yale University Press, 1973), and "On the Basis of Hobbes's Political Philosophy," *Political Studies* 22:4 (December 1974): 414–31, in light of Alan E. Shapiro, "Kinematic Optics: A Study of the Wave Theory of Light in the Seventeenth Century," *Archive for History of the Exact Sciences* 11:2/3 (1973): 134–266; note Malcolm, "Robert Payne, the Hobbes Manuscripts, and the 'Short Tract'," 80–145, and Timothy Raylor, "Hobbes, Payne, and *A Short Tract on First Principles*," *Historical Journal* 44:1 (March 2001): 29–38; and then see Richard Tuck, "Optics and Sceptics: The Philosophical Foundations of Hobbes's Political Thought," in *Conscience and Casuistry in Early Modern Europe*, ed. Edmund Leites (Cambridge, UK: Cambridge University Press, 1988), 235–63, and "Hobbes and Descartes," in *Perspectives on Thomas Hobbes*, ed. G. A. J. Rogers and Alan Ryan (Oxford, UK: Clarendon Press, 1988), 11–41, who correctly notes the link between modern Pyrrhonism and Machiavellian politics – without, however, indicating an awareness of the profound debt that Montaigne and his successors owe to Machiavelli's critique of moral reason: see David Lewis Schaefer, *The Political Philosophy of Montaigne* (Ithaca, NY: Cornell University Press, 1990), and Rahe, *Republics Ancient and Modern*, 260–74. Tuck's treatment of Grotius in relation to Hobbes, both in the first of the two works cited earlier and elsewhere, leaves much to be desired: see Rahe, *Republics Ancient and Modern*, 368–69 (with nn. 15–18); Perez Zagorin, "Hobbes without Grotius," *History of Political Thought* 21:1 (Spring 2000): 16–40; and Johann Sommerville, "Selden, Grotius, and the Seventeenth-Century Intellectual Revolution in Moral and Political Theory," in *Rhetoric and Law in Early Modern Europe*, ed. Victoria Kahn and Lorna Hutson (New Haven, CT: Yale University Press, 2002), 318–44. In general, Tuck overstates the depth of Hobbes's worries about skepticism: see Popkin, *The History of Scepticism*, 189–207.

cive when it was first published in 1642, Samuel Sorbière immediately jumped
to the conclusion that it had been written by René Descartes.[97] There really
was a kinship between the French philosopher and his English rival.

In the epistle dedicatory to his *Elements of Law*, Hobbes begins with the
epistemological question, arguing that there are "two kinds of learning, mathematical and dogmatical." The first is, he contends, "free from controversies and
dispute, because it consisteth in comparing figures and motion only; in which
things truth and the interest of men oppose not each other." In the second, however, "there is nothing not disputable, because it compareth men and meddleth
with their right and profit; in which, as oft as reason is against a man, so oft will
a man be against reason." It is, he intimates, because reason is enslaved to the
passions "that they that have written of justice and policy in general" are partisan and "do all invade each other, and themselves with contradiction." If, then,
one wishes "to reduce this doctrine to the rules and infallibility of reason," one
must abandon the pretense that men are in a straightforward manner capable
of moral reasoning, one must ground one's argument on the assumption that
human reason is strictly instrumental, and one must "put such principles down
for a foundation, as passion not mistrusting, may not seek to displace." In this
fashion, as Hobbes purports to demonstrate in the remainder of this book,
in *De cive*, and again in *Leviathan*, that what had always seemed "dogmatical" and subject to controversy and dispute can be rendered "mathematical"
and proven true beyond any shadow of doubt.[98] All that one has to do to lay
secure foundations for this argument is "to put men in mind of what they know
already, or may know by their own experience." All that one has to do, if one is

---

[97] When confronted, Descartes denied that he was the book's author and added that "he would
never publish anything on Morals." See Letter from Samuel Sorbière to Thomas de Martel
on 1 February 1643, in Hobbes, *De cive*, 300. In this connection, see Strauss, *The Political
Philosophy of Hobbes*, 44–58. Hobbes discreetly acknowledges his debt by echoing the ironic
suggestion with which Descartes begins his *Discourse on Method*; both men are prepared to
argue from the fact that every man is content with his allotment of good sense and political
wisdom to the conclusion that all men must possess these qualities in equal portions: cf. Hobbes,
Leviathan I.xiii.1–3, with Descartes, *Discours de la méthode* 1, in René Descartes, *Oeuvres et
lettres*, ed. André Bridoux (Paris: Bibliothèque de la Pléiade, 1953), 126. In a letter written to
an unnamed Jesuit priest soon after Hobbes's book appeared, Descartes rightly identifies the
individual who composed the third set of objections to his *Meditations* as the author of *De
cive*. Naturally enough, given the profession of his correspondent, Descartes takes the occasion
piously to repudiate Hobbes's "maxims" as "very bad and very dangerous." Far more revealing
of his actual opinion is the fact that he does not hesitate to remark that his English critic is
"much more skillful (*habile*) in morals than in metaphysics and in physics." Descartes found
it quite remarkable that Hobbes's book had escaped censorship. See René Descartes, *Oeuvres
de Descartes*, ed. Charles Adam and Paul Tannery (Paris: J. Vrin, 1964–1974), 67. Sorbière
reported to Martel in the letter cited earlier that, after reading *De cive*, the French philosopher
remarked that "whoever be the [book's] Father, he is certainly not to the vulgar taste." For the
strained relations between Hobbes and Descartes, see John Laird, *Hobbes* (London: E. Benn,
1934), 48–52, and Miriam Reik, *The Golden Lands of Thomas Hobbes* (Detroit, MI: Wayne
State University Press, 1977), 76–80. When Sorbière traveled to Amsterdam to seek a publisher
for the second edition of *De cive*, Hobbes warned him not to let Descartes know the purpose
of his visit lest the French philosopher try to prevent publication: see Letter from Hobbes to
Sorbière on 16 May 1646, in Hobbes, *De cive*, 300–301.

[98] See Hobbes, *Elements of Law* Ep. Ded.

intent on uncovering the principles from which to derive political science, is to ground one's argument in premises yielded by introspection. "[I]t is impossible to rectify" the pertinent errors, Hobbes explained, "without beginning anew from the very first grounds of all our knowledge, sense." There is no point in reading "books." Instead, one must read "over orderly one's own conceptions: in which meaning," he adds, "I take *nosce teipsum* [know thyself] for a precept worthy the reputation it hath gotten."[99]

Such was the procedure that Hobbes followed in all three of the books in which he presented his political doctrine. If they varied somewhat in form and content, it was in part because Hobbes only gradually found his way to a proper formulation of his doctrine, and in part because, in that time of revolution, the rhetorical occasion and the character and disposition of his audience was in rapid flux.[100] The substance of what Hobbes had to say – the epistemological premises, the central argument regarding the unfolding of human self-consciousness, and his conclusion as to the construction of polity and morality – was the same throughout, and all three books took as their principle task a supplanting of the Aristotelian understanding of morality and politics that had long underpinned political practice in the Christian West.

It was only in *Leviathan*, however, which was for the most part finished some four months before the battle of Dunbar on 3 September 1650,[101] that Hobbes attacked Machiavelli as well – for it was not until the establishment of the English republic in the wake of the trial and execution of Charles I in January 1649 that Hobbes became aware that, in refuting Aristotle, he had done only half of what circumstances required. That there was a modern argument for republicanism, no less hostile to Aristotelian political science than was his own civil science, he had, of course, known from the start. That in his homeland this argument and Machiavelli's more general attempt to make political turmoil and usurpation seem attractive had in his absence acquired considerable purchase he only gradually came to be aware. Prior to 30 January 1649, as we have already had occasion to observe,[102] Machiavelli's republican teaching had generally been regarded as a curiosity.

Hobbes had drafted his *Elements of Law* in English to provide Newcastle and his fellow royalists with a secular argument with which to defend Thomas Wentworth, earl of Strafford; William Laud, archbishop of Canterbury; and others who had served Charles I during the era of personal rule. He had written *De cive* in Latin to establish his reputation as a philosopher among the learned and to make a more fully elaborated version of his new civil science available to students of politics and jurisprudence throughout a Europe no less torn by

---

[99] See Hobbes, *Elements of Law* 1.1.2, 5.14.

[100] For the constantly changing setting within which these works were composed, see Johann Sommerville, "Lofty Science and Local Politics," in *The Cambridge Companion to Hobbes*, ed. Tom Sorell (Cambridge, UK: Cambridge University Press, 1996), 246–73, and Karl Schuhmann, *Hobbes, Une Chronique: Cheminement de sa pensée et de sa vie* (Paris: J. Vrin, 1998), 60–126.

[101] See Letter from Robert Payne to Gilbert Sheldon on 13 May 1650, in "Illustrations of the State of the Church During the Great Rebellion," *The Theologian and Ecclesiastic* 6 (1848): 161–75 (at 172).

[102] See the Prologue, this volume.

religious and civil strife than was his own native land. *Leviathan* was something else again. From a partisan perspective, it was a masterpiece of obfuscation.

In certain important respects, the political posture adopted by Hobbes in *Leviathan* was consistent with that evident in his earlier work. The book was overtly royalist, as one would expect. It was openly sympathetic to England's martyred king, and it was designed to be of service should Charles, the erstwhile prince of Wales, actually manage, with the help of the Scots, to overturn the Rump and establish by force his right to the English throne. At the same time, however, as partisans on both sides of the great political divide almost immediately realized, *Leviathan* was also cleverly crafted in such a manner as to reinforce the Rump's quest for a settlement, should the New Model Army emerge victorious, and it was no less well-suited to counsel and support the Commonwealth's Lord General should Oliver Cromwell justify the expectations of his critics among the royalists, the presbyterians, and the Levellers and become a "new prince" on the Machiavellian model by following the well-worn path once taken by that Caesar Augustus whose accomplishments the young Hobbes had celebrated in his "Discourse upon the Beginning of Tacitus." It was aimed at making it easy for Hobbes to return home; it was argued in a fashion likely to appeal to freethinkers and Erastians in both political camps; and, for understandable reasons, it was not to the taste of those who favored episcopacy, presbyterianism, or separatism.[103] Like John Milton's *Tenure of Kings and Magistrates*, his *Eikonoklastēs*, and his *Defense of the English People*, and like the editorials that Marchamont Nedham penned for *Mercurius Politicus* in the aftermath of the battle of Worcester, *Leviathan* seized on the political opening provided by the great upheavals in and after 1648 and 1649 to articulate in uncompromising terms a novel, revolutionary understanding of the foundations and purpose of government and ecclesiastical polity that his compatriots would hitherto have found not just shocking but objectionable and offensive in the extreme.

In such a fashion, the unsung hero of Hobbes's two early discourses on Rome became the unsung villain of *Leviathan*. In the early chapters of the latter work, Hobbes confronted Machiavelli's shocking suggestion that fidelity, treachery, and the other "qualities which are held to be good" or which "appear" to be vices are not intrinsic qualities of soul but postures, which one needs to assess, assume, and advertise solely with an eye to "one's own security and well-being." Such a presupposition Hobbes regarded not merely as monstrous; he thought it in the case of ordinary men demonstrably false.

The profound significance of the critique of morality initiated in the fifteenth chapter of *The Prince* Hobbes readily acknowledged, but he did so in a typically backhanded way. This he accomplished by the simple expedient of devoting the

---

[103] Cf. Johann P. Sommerville, "Hobbes, Behemoth, Church-State Relations, and Political Obligation," *Filozofski vestnik* 24:2 (2003): 205–22, and "Hobbes and Independency," *Rivista di storia della filosofia* 59:1 (January–March 2004): 155–73, with Jeffrey R. Collins, *The Allegiance of Thomas Hobbes* (Oxford, UK: Oxford University Press, 2005), 115–270, and "Silencing Thomas Hobbes: The Presbyterians and Leviathan," in *The Cambridge Companion to Hobbes's Leviathan*, ed. Patricia Springborg (Cambridge, UK: Cambridge University Press, 2007), 478–99.

like-numbered chapter of his book to moral virtue's defense. He knew perfectly well why it was that in his own day "successfull wickednesse" had "obtained the name of Vertue," and so he singled out for attack an unidentified, but easily recognizable "Foole" who had "sayd," not only "in his heart" but "with his tongue" as well that "there is no such thing as Justice," contending that "every mans conservation, and contentment, being committed to his own care, there could be no reason, why every man might not do what he thought conduced thereunto: and therefore also [that] to make, or not make; keep, or not keep, Covenants, was not against Reason, when it conduced to ones benefit."[104] Careful readers at the time had little difficulty in figuring out just which fool Hobbes had in mind.[105]

Of course, the Malmesbury philosopher was by no means alone in challenging Machiavelli's teaching concerning morality. In rejecting it, he had ample and highly respectable company. His peculiarity – that which made him the very model of a modern moralist – was that he grounded his critique of the Florentine's conclusions on the very arguments that the latter had himself advanced. If Hobbes came to be called "the Monster of Malmesbury," it was because he hewed to "the effectual truth of the matter" no less closely than the Florentine thought to have given to the devil his moniker "Old Nick."

Hobbes's argument takes the form of an exploration of the consequences inherent in accepting Machiavelli's famous assertion that a legislator must "presuppose all men evil (*rei*)" and presume that they will make use of "the malignity" hidden in their hearts at the first "free opportunity."[106] This premise Hobbes justifies by means of a phenomenology of mind. He begins with sensation, its unreliability, and the physiological grounds for doubting whether we can ever know with any precision what lies behind and occasions our perceptions. Then he turns to the natural play of the human imagination in order to bring home to his readers the dependence of all coherence of thought on desire and to establish man's fundamental character as *homo faber* – as an inventor, a hunter of causes and effects, a fashioner of tools driven by "a Lust of the mind" to investigate the consequences of particular actions.[107]

This claim has profound political implications, for the lust of mind which distinguishes Hobbesian man from the beasts is not the idle curiosity of the contemplative: like the longing for riches and honor, this lust "may be reduced to . . . Desire of Power." In fact, because human consciousness is above all else the awareness of consequences, man quite naturally conceives of himself first and foremost as the cause of future effects, as a creature endowed with power. For him, "all conception of future, is conception of power able to produce something." In short, his subjectivity is itself constituted by a "perpetuall solicitude of the time to come . . . So that man, which looks too far before him, in

---

104 Note Psalms 14:1, 53:1; cf. Hobbes, *Leviathan* I.xv.4, with Machiavelli, *Il principe* 15–18, in
   Opere, 280–84, and see Chapter 1, this volume.
105 See, for example, *JHO*, 12–14, 29–30, 34–35.
106 Machiavelli, *Discorsi* 1.3.1, in *Opere*, 81.
107 See Hobbes, *Leviathan* I.vi.35, which should be read in conjunction with *Leviathan* I.v.6–7,
   xii.15, IV.xlvi.1–2. One should also read Hobbes, *Elements of Law* I.iii.1–v.4 in light of I.ix.18.

the care of future time, hath his heart all the day long, gnawed on by feare of death, poverty, or other calamity; and has no repose, nor pause of his anxiety, but in sleep."[108]

It is this anxiety that renders men wicked and produces the malignity hidden in the human heart, for it induces every man to attempt "to assure for ever, the way of his future desire," and this produces a "perpetuall and restlesse desire of Power after power." The resulting quest for power eventually brings the individual face to face with his fellow human beings. Inevitably, given the incapacity of unassisted *lógos* to provide a foundation for community, he treats these men, like everything else he encounters, simply as instruments for dominating nature; and, just as inevitably, they treat him in precisely the same fashion. Thereby, men discover that "the power of one man resisteth and hindereth the effects of the power of another"; and, in the end, they also come to recognize the preeminent political truth: that "power simply is no more, but the excess of the power of one above that of another."[109]

The dawning of this recognition transforms "the life of man" – which ceases to be oriented by ordinary, bodily desire. Under its influence, human life becomes "a race" with "no other goal, nor other garland, but being foremost." Thus, for man, "Joy consisteth in comparing himselfe with other men," and he "can relish nothing but what is eminent." For him, "felicity" has no close connection with bodily need; it is a species of progressive conquest in which each individual strives "continually to out-go the next before." In practice, then, all the passions of man can be reduced to feelings of *relative* power and powerlessness. Vanity attains mastery as we maniacally struggle to sustain "the imagination or conception of our own power, above the power of him that contendeth with us." In the process, since "every man looketh that his companion should value him, at the same rate he sets upon himselfe," men squabble, come to blows, and then kill one another not only or even primarily because their material interests clash but "for trifles, as a word, a smile, a different opinion, and any other signe of undervalue." As Hobbes sums it all up, "Men from their very birth, and naturally, scramble for every thing they covet, and would have all the world, if they could, to fear and obey them."[110]

It is this set of conclusions that justifies the conviction, originally inspired by Hobbes's reading of and rumination on Thucydides, that political order is artificial and quite fragile. It would not matter that human beings are fundamentally equal – "that the weakest has strength enough to kill the strongest, either by secret machination, or by confederacy with others," and that men are quite rightly disinclined to concede that others are wiser than they – were they not also predisposed to quarrel over gain, safety, preeminence, and glory.

---

[108] Hobbes, *Leviathan* I.viii.13–16, xi.1–3, xii.1–7, and *Elements of Law* I.viii.3. See *Elements of Law* I.ix.18. In this regard, Hobbesian and Cartesian introspection are indistinguishable: see Annette Baier, "The Idea of the True God in Descartes," in *Essays on Descartes' Meditations*, ed. Amélie Oksenberg Rorty (Berkeley: University of California Press, 1986), 359–87.

[109] See Hobbes, *Leviathan* I.xi.1–3, and *Elements of Law* I.viii.4.

[110] See Hobbes, *Elements of Law* I.ix.1–21 (esp. 1 and 21), *De cive* I.i.5, 12, *Leviathan* I.xiii.4–7, II.xvii.6–12, *Decameron physiologicum* in *EW*, VII 73. See also *Elements of Law* I.vii.7, ix.19, xvi.11, II.viii.3, *De cive* III.xv.13, *De homine* XI.11–15, in *LW*, II 100–103.

But both equal and quarrelsome men certainly are; and, according to Hobbes, their natural condition is, in consequence, war: "where every man is Enemy to every man." Man's natural inclinations are, in fact, an obstacle to the Baconian project, for in the state of nature

> there is no place for Industry; because the fruit thereof is uncertain; and consequently no Culture of the Earth; no Navigation, nor use of the commodities that may be imported by Sea; no commodious Building; no Instruments of moving, and removing such things as require much force; no Knowledge of the face of the Earth; no account of time; no Arts; no Letters; no Society; and which is worst of all, continuall feare, and danger of violent death; And the life of man, solitary, poore, nasty, brutish, and short.

Hobbes is perfectly willing to concede that in man's natural condition "the notions of Right and Wrong, Justice and Injustice . . . have no place." As he puts it, "Force, and Fraud, are in warre the two Cardinall vertues." Moreover, he recognizes that Machiavelli's account nicely describes the situation of the sovereign, who remains within the state of nature. If he disagrees with the author of *The Prince*, it is only in his adoption of the perspective of ordinary men unlikely to become princes; in his insistence that, in constructing a polity, a legislator must rely on "the Passions that encline men to Peace," such as "Feare of Death; Desire of such things as are necessary to commodious living; and a Hope by their Industry to obtain them"; and in his belief that the war of all against all need not persist.[111] At this point, he restates the Epicurean account of the manner in which civil society emerged on the basis of the calculations of endangered men, recasting it in light of what he had gleaned from the speech of Thucydides' Mytilenians at Olympia and from a passing observation voiced by Thucydides' Athenians in the course of the Melian dialogue as these remarks concerning the foundations for justice in international affairs could be reapplied to the manner in which equality can provide a foundation for justice between men who are in no way by nature friends.[112]

On the crucial question, Hobbes argues that – if Machiavelli was indeed right in asserting that "security and well-being" are the end of human life and the standard by which virtue and vice are to be defined – it is a dictate of reason that ordinary men trade submission for protection and not breach faith,[113] for, except in the case of those extraordinarily situated, the "successfull wicked-nesse" promoted by the Florentine is an oxymoron. In elaborating the logical consequences of this argument, Hobbes establishes the principle of absolute sovereignty and restores the traditional virtues – "*Justice, Gratitude, Modesty, Equity, Mercy,* & the rest of the Laws of Nature*" – to something like their

---

[111] Hobbes, *Leviathan* I.xiii.

[112] See Chapter 9, this volume.

[113] In context, as Hobbes clearly understood, his argument was bound to be taken as an apology on his part for taking the Engagement: see Quentin Skinner, "The Ideological Context of Hobbes's Political Thought," *Historical Journal* 9:3 (1966): 286–317, and "Conquest and Consent: Thomas Hobbes and the Engagement Controversy," in *The Interregnum: The Quest for Settlement, 1646–1660*, ed. G. E. Aylmer (Hamden, CT: Archon Books, 1972), 79–98, revised and reprinted in *Hobbes and Civil Science*, 264–307, as well as Collins, *The Political Allegiance of Thomas Hobbes*, 115–206. Cf. Glenn Burgess, "Contexts for the Writing and Publication of Hobbes's *Leviathan*," *History of Political Thought* 11:4 (Winter 1990): 675–702.

traditional place. In the process, however, he acknowledges the Machiavellian foundations of this restored morality: "These dictates of Reason, men use to call by the name of Lawes; but improperly: for they are but Conclusions, or Theoremes concerning what conduceth to the conservation and defense of themselves."[114]

It was by means of this critical appropriation of the least palatable element within Machiavelli's argument that a notorious English royalist removed the last, seemingly insuperable obstacle that stood, as we have seen,[115] in the way of there being a dramatic increase of interest in his Florentine opponent's argument on behalf of republican rule. In the process, moreover, Hobbes contributed significantly to that natural evolution of Machiavellian thinking by which a teaching originally oriented toward honor, glory, conquest, and command came to be subordinated to the prosaic, bourgeois concerns of the many, "infinite in number," who "desire liberty" solely "in order to live securely," and thereby came to be reined in and confined by the preoccupations of a multitude who embrace freedom solely for the purpose of "being able to possess one's things freely without any suspicion, not having grounds for doubting the honor of women and of children, not fearing for oneself."[116]

The first to recognize the potential significance for republicanism of Thomas Hobbes's adaptation of Machiavelli's critique of moral virtue was, as we shall soon see, a bookish member of a gentry family long established in Northamptonshire and Lincolnshire named James Harrington.[117] He would not be the last. In January 1652, *Mercurius Politicus* had reported with evident delight the fact that the author of *Leviathan* had been expelled from the royal court at Saint–Germain-en-Laye at the insistence of what it termed the "corrupt *Clergy–Interest*" for having propagated in that book "Principles of Atheism and grosse Impiety . . . such as were prejudicial to the Church."[118] Five years later, in an editorial purportedly dispatched from Utopia, that journal would not only identify the turncoat royalist along with Thomas White, John Hall, James Harrington, and "that wondrous wise Republican called *Mercurius Politicus*" as "wits of the Commonwealth, that have so long run a wool-gathering after Government." Tellingly, it would also speak of him as a member of the "jolly Crew of the Inhabitants of the Island of *Oceana*."[119]

---

[114] Hobbes, *Leviathan* I.xiv–xv (esp. xv.40–41).

[115] See Chapter 7, this volume.

[116] Note Machiavelli, *Discorsi* 1.16.3–5, in *Opere*, 100–101, and see Chapter 2, this volume.

[117] For Harrington's family background, see Ian Grimble, *The Harrington Family* (London: J. Cape, 1957).

[118] See *MP* 84 (8–15 January 1652): 1344.

[119] See *MP* 352 (5–12 March 1657): 7641–44 (esp. 7644).

The Hobbesian Republicanism of James Harrington

As a landed gentleman and a private scholar, James Harrington was everything that Marchamont Nedham and Thomas Hobbes were not. Like John Milton, he possessed a competence. He was independent in spirit as well, and his pen was always his own. Since he was never a hireling, he could always speak his mind. Prior to the autumn of 1656, it would have been easy to take him for a royalist. He was not a member of Parliament before or after Pride's Purge, and he made his first undoubted appearance on the public stage when he was appointed gentleman of the bedchamber to Charles I in the time of latter's captivity, less than two years before the Stuart monarch's execution. That he came to be personally favorable to the captive monarch there can be no doubt. He left the king's company only when barred from further attendance by the commissioners in charge, who thought him too partial to Charles.[1]

We are told two stories concerning the genesis of James Harrington's most famous work. According to John Toland, Harrington fell prey to melancholy after the death of the king; found consolation in pursuing his studies, especially as they pertained to the causes of the English monarchy's demise; and then began to write.[2] Harrington reportedly offered another explanation when he was imprisoned after the Restoration and closely questioned by Lord Lauderdale and his associates, one suggesting that his decision to write a book for publication was occasioned by the discussions that took place within the army in October 1654 when the *Humble Petition of Several Colonels of the Army* was first circulated by John Wildman and his associates within the officer corps.[3]

---

[1] For a brief summary of what the surviving sources have to say, see J. G. A. Pocock, "Historical Introduction," in *PWoJH*, 1–5.

[2] See John Toland, "The Life of James Harrington," in *WoJH*, xiv. Note also, in this connection, *ABL*, 208, and Anthony à Wood, *Athenæ Oxonienses* (London, F. C. & J. Rivington: 1813–20), III 1115–17, 1119, who confirm at least part of Toland's tale.

[3] See Pocock, "Historical Introduction," 6–14, who points to the fact that, in his dedicatory epistle, Harrington describes his book as "but a rough draught," adding that he had "not yet been two yers about it" when it first came out in October or November 1656, and who then identifies Harrington's murmuring officers with the signatories of *The Humble Petition of Several Colonels of the Army*, which appeared in October 1654; and consider Barbara Taft, "The Humble Petition of Several Colonels of the Army: Causes, Character, and Results of Military Opposition to Cromwell's Protectorate," *Huntington Library Quarterly* 42:1 (Winter 1978): 15–41, and "That Lusty Puss, The Good Old Cause," *History of Political Thought* 5:4 (Winter 1984): 447–64.

When Oliver Cromwell had "started up the throne," Harrington is said to have told his examiners, the "officers" of the newly created Lord Protector

(as pretending to be for a commonwealth) kept a murmuring, at which he told them he knew not what they meant, nor themselves; but let any of them shew him what they meant by a commonwealth (or that there was any such thing) they should see that he sought not himself: the Lord knew he sought not himself, but to make good the cause. Upon this som sober men came to me and told me, if any man in *England* could shew what a commonwealth was, it was my self. Upon this persuasion I wrote.[4]

These two accounts are by no means incompatible, for the testimony attributed to Harrington presupposes that his having studied the pertinent issues in depth was already well known to the "sober men" in question when they first approached him in the hope that he could make it clear precisely "what a commonwealth was." According to John Aubrey, who may have been in a position to know, the man who first encouraged Harrington to turn his hand to writing on politics was Henry Neville – whom we know to have been associated with Thomas Chaloner, Henry Marten, and Algernon Sidney during his tenure in the Rump. Thomas Hobbes, who had a keen nose for sniffing out the truth, reportedly suspected that Neville was, in fact, his collaborator in this literary enterprise.[5]

Be this as it may, just under two years after the appearance of the *Humble Petition*; some three to four months after the critical juncture in which Sir Henry Vane published *A Healing Question Propounded and Resolved*, the mysterious R. G. published *A Copy of a Letter from an Officer of the Army in Ireland to the Protector, concerning his Changing of the Government*, and Marcha- mont Nedham brought out *The Excellencie of a Free State*; and precisely two days after the opening of the second Protectorate Parliament on 17 September 1656 – Livewell Chapman entered on the Stationers' Register a book by James Harrington that he intended to publish. *The Commonwealth of Oceana* was presumably available for purchase just under seven weeks later when it was advertised in the 29 October–6 November issue of *Mercurius Politicus*.[6]

In assessing Harrington's contribution to the debates of the time, one must always keep in mind his polemical intent. In his *magnum opus*, he spins an elaborate tale regarding a fictitious Lord Archon, who occupies a position in Oceana, Marpesi, and Panopea indistinguishable from that held by the existing Lord Protector of England, Scotland, and Ireland, and who seizes upon his own elevation as an occasion for summoning a constitutional convention tasked

---

[4] Cf. *The Examination of James Harrington* (1662–77), in *WoJH*, xxx, with *JHO*, 125–26, where Harrington deploys Cromwell's phrase in mocking the Lord Protector. Note Andrew Sharp, "The Manuscript Versions of Harrington's *Oceana*," *Historical Journal* 16:2 (June 1973): 227–39, who persuasively argues that the manuscripts of *Oceana* that do survive are copies of an abbreviated version constructed in or after the 1670s for the purpose of attacking the notion that the king needed a standing army and not, as might seem to be the case, copies of an early draft written by Harrington prior to Charles I's execution on 30 January 1649.

[5] See *ABL*, 208. Note also Wood, *Athenæ Oxonienses*, III 1119.

[6] See S. B. Liljegren, "Introduction," in *JHO*, xi; and, regarding the context, consider David Armitage, "The Cromwellian Protectorate and the Languages of Empire," *Historical Journal* 35:3 (September 1992): 531–55 (esp. 548–53), and Chapter 7, this volume.

with the establishment of a genuine and viable republic in the lands that he rules. If Harrington did not, in fact, publish the work in the sincere hope that Oliver Cromwell and the officers of his New Model Army would imitate in Britain what this Lord Archon was said to have accomplished in Oceana, as was arguably the case,[7] he certainly did so for the purpose of discrediting them for their failure to impose a proper constitutional order when their great victory at the battle of Worcester in early September 1651 had brought the emergency to an end and left the principal supporters of the Commonwealth free to contemplate a general settlement of affairs.[8]

The *Archives of Ancient Prudence*

The books and pamphlets which poured forth at a furious rate from James Harrington's pen in the years between the fall of 1656 and the end of 1659 are quite easily misunderstood. In them, he presents himself as a determined opponent of what he calls "modern prudence." He has, he tells us, ransacked "the *Archives of ancient prudence*" in search of evidence and arguments with which "to vindicate the reason of popular government,"[9] and he takes every available opportunity to advertise the admiration that he harbors for ancient Sparta, Athens, and Rome. In his eagerness to adorn his own project with the authority of antiquity, he virtually wraps himself in a toga. One can hardly fault scholars for jumping to the conclusion that, at heart, the man was a classical republican.[10]

---

[7] See Jonathan Scott, *Commonwealth Principles: Republican Writing of the English Revolution* (Cambridge, UK: Cambridge University Press, 2004), 284–93, who makes a powerful case in favor of the view that the book really was addressed to Cromwell.

[8] This is the view proposed by Pocock, "Historical Introduction," 6–42, and defended with vigor and panache by Blair Worden, "James Harrington and *The Commonwealth of Oceana*, 1656," and "Harrington's *Oceana*: Origins and Aftermath, 1651–1660," in *Republicanism, Liberty, and Commercial Society, 1649–1776*, ed. David Wootton (Stanford, CA: Stanford University Press, 1994), 82–138; and *Literature and Politics in Cromwellian England: John Milton, Andrew Marvell, Marchamont Nedham* (Oxford, UK: Oxford University Press, 2007), 105–15.

[9] See JHO, 59, and Harrington, *The Prerogative of Popular Government* (1658), Ep. Ded., in *PWoJH*, 390.

[10] It is especially easy to fall prey to this error if one presumes Machiavelli a classical republican or civic humanist: see Zera S. Fink, *The Classical Republicans: An Essay in the Recovery of a Pattern of Thought in Seventeenth-Century England*, second edition (Evanston, IL: Northwestern University Press, 1962), 52–89; J. G. A. Pocock: "Civic Humanism and its Role in Anglo – American Thought" and "Machiavelli, Harrington and English Political Ideologies in the Eighteenth Century," in *Politics, Language and Time* (New York: Atheneum, 1973), 80–147; *The Machiavellian Moment: Florentine Political Thought and the Atlantic Republican Tradition* (Princeton, NJ: Princeton University Press, 1975), 383–400; "Historical Introduction," 1–152 (esp. 15–76), and "Introduction," in James Harrington, *The Commonwealth of Oceana and a System of Politics*, ed. J. G. A. Pocock (Cambridge, UK: Cambridge University Press, 1992), vii–xxiv; Worden, "James Harrington and *The Commonwealth of Oceana*," and "Harrington's *Oceana*," 82–138; Arihiro Fukuda, *Sovereignty and the Sword: Harrington, Hobbes, and Mixed Government in the English Civil Wars* (Oxford, UK: Clarendon Press, 1997); and Steve Pincus, "Neither Machiavellian Moment nor Possessive Individualism: Commercial Society and the Defenders of the English Commonwealth," *American Historical Review* 103:3 (June 1998): 705–36. Note also J. G. A. Pocock, "James Harrington and the Good Old Cause: A Study of the Ideological Content of His Writings," *Journal of British Studies* 10:1 (November 1970): 30–48.

Like Machiavelli and Marchamont Nedham, Harrington actively courted such a misreading himself.[11]

In *The Commonwealth of Oceana* and in his other writings, Harrington consistently used the distinction between ancient and modern prudence as a way of juxtaposing the arguments from expediency that had traditionally been deployed in favor of purely popular government with those used to defend a regulated monarchy composed of king, lords, and commons.[12] As a consequence, like Nedham and Hobbes, he found it expedient to paper over the chasm separating Machiavelli from Thucydides, Xenophon, Isocrates, Plato, Aristotle, Polybius, Cicero, Livy, Tacitus, Plutarch, and the like; and, in similar fashion, he refused to acknowledge the degree to which contemporary defenders of England's mixed monarchy had rested their case almost entirely on Polybius' analysis and defense of the mixed regime.[13] Like Machiavelli, he wanted to

[11] Doubts have been cast on the classical character of Harrington's thought by the following: John A. Wettergreen, "Note on the Intention of James Harrington's Political Art," *Interpretation* 2:1 (Summer 1971): 64–78, and "James Harrington's Liberal Republicanism," *Polity* 20:4 (Summer 1988): 665–87; Kathleen Toth, "Interpretation in Political Theory: The Case of Harrington," *Review of Politics* 37:3 (July 1975): 317–39 (at 322–39); Jeffrey Barnouw, "American Independence – Revolution of the Republican Ideal: A Response to Pocock's Construction of 'The Atlantic Republican Tradition,'" *The American Revolution and Eighteenth-Century Culture: Essays from the 1976 Bicentennial Conference of the American Society for Eighteenth-Century Studies*, ed. Paul J. Korshin (New York: AMS Press, 1986), 31–73 (at 53–66); Paul A. Rahe, *Republics Ancient and Modern: Classical Republicanism and the American Revolution* (Chapel Hill: University of North Carolina Press, 1992), 408–26; Jonathan Scott, "The Rapture of Motion: James Harrington's Republicanism," in *Political Discourse in Early Modern Britain*, ed. Nicholas Phillipson and Quentin Skinner (Cambridge, UK: Cambridge University Press, 1993), 139–63; Gary Remer, "James Harrington's New Deliberative Rhetoric: Reflections of an Anticlassical Republican," *History of Political Thought* 16:4 (Winter 1995): 532–57; and Vickie B. Sullivan, *Machiavelli, Hobbes, and the Formation of a Liberal Republicanism in England* (New York: Cambridge University Press, 2004), 144–73. I have profited as well from H. F. Russell Smith, *Harrington and his Oceana: A Study of a 17th Century Utopia and Its Influence in America* (Cambridge, UK: Cambridge University Press, 1914); Charles Blitzer, *An Immortal Commonwealth: The Political Thought of James Harrington* (New Haven, CT: Yale University Press, 1960); C. B. Macpherson, *The Political Theory of Possessive Individualism: Hobbes to Locke* (Oxford, UK: Clarendon Press, 1962), 160–93; J. A. W. Gunn, *Politics and the Public Interest in the Seventeenth Century* (London: Routledge & Kegan Paul, 1969), 109–52; J. C. Davis, *Utopia and the Ideal Society: A Study of English Utopian Writing, 1516–1700* (Cambridge, UK: Cambridge University Press, 1981), 206–76; Scott, *Commonwealth Principles*, 11–15, 23–25, 28–33, 53–54, 56, 59, 63, 84, 92–96, 141–46, 155, 161–67, 181–84, 195–96, 204–7, 222–24, 284–96, 301, 304–8, 310, 318, 329, 350–51; and from the works listed in note 10, this chapter. What follows is an adaptation of what I published in 1992 in the chapter cited in this note.

[12] See Harrington, *The Prerogative of Popular Government* (1658), in *WoJH*, 221. Note Harrington's attribution of modernity to ancient Egypt: see *The Prerogative of Popular Government* (1658), in *WoJH*, 253.

[13] Cf. *His Majesty's Answer to the Nineteen Propositions of Both Houses of Parliament*, 18 June 1642, in *The Stuart Constitution, 1603–1688: Documents and Commentary*, ed. J. P. Kenyon (Cambridge, UK: Cambridge University Press, 1966), 21–23, with Polybius 6.3.5–10.14. For the determinative influence exercised by the document cited, see Corinne Comstock Weston, *English Constitutional Theory and the House of Lords, 1556–1832* (New York: Columbia University Press, 1965). See also Corinne Comstock Weston and Janelle Renfrow Greenberg, *Subjects and Sovereigns: The Grand Controversy over Legal Sovereignty in Stuart England* (Cambridge, UK: Cambridge University Press, 1981), and Michael J. Mendle, *Dangerous Positions: Mixed*

acquire for his modern republican project the authority of classical Greece and Rome, and to this end he was perfectly willing to engage in subterfuge.

The classical elements within Harrington's discussion are many and obtrusive,[14] but they are, in fact, peripheral to his overall scheme. Thus, for example, though he often cites Aristotle in support of his argument,[15] the English republican never once alludes to the crucial passage – singled out repeatedly for attack by his chosen antagonist Thomas Hobbes – in which the peripatetic articulates the premise which serves as the foundation for classical republicanism: that man is by nature a political animal endowed with a capacity for *lógos* enabling him to distinguish and make clear to others what is advantageous, just, and good.[16] Nor does he echo any of the passages asserting the primacy of politics that one finds scattered through the other ancient writers he cites.[17] James Harrington is, in fact, a modern populist on the Machiavellian model. Like Nedham and Hobbes, he rejects the classical principle of differential moral and political rationality; and like the former, he explicitly endorses the notion that the multitude is wiser and more constant than any prince can ever be, and he even quotes Machiavelli to this effect. The "reason or interest" of an aristocracy "when they are all together . . . is," he contends, "but that of a party." That of "the people taken apart" may be "but so many private interests," but, when "you take them together, they are the publick interest."[18]

The one thing that Harrington does do in the classical vein is to challenge his contemporaries to rise to the occasion. "If we have any thing of Piety or of prudence," he writes in his *Commonwealth of Oceana*, "let us raise our selves out of the mire of private interest, unto the contemplation of Virtue, and put an hand unto the removal of *this Evil from under the Sun*; this evil against which no

---

Government, the Estates of the Realm, and the Making of the Answer to the XIX Propositions (University: University of Alabama Press, 1985).

[14] See Blitzer, *An Immortal Commonwealth*, 283–93, and Eric Nelson, *The Greek Tradition in Republican Thought* (Cambridge, UK: Cambridge University Press, 2004), 87–126 (esp. 114–21).

[15] See *JHO*, 10, 12–13, 17, 21, 29, 57, 87, 90–91, 123, 136, 142, and Harrington, *The Prerogative of Popular Government* (1658), *The Art of Lawgiving* (1659), *Valerius and Publicola* (1659), *Pian Piano* (1657), *The Stumbling-Block of Disobedience and Rebellion* (1658), *A Letter unto Mr. Stubs* (1660), *Politicaster* (1659), and *A Sufficient Answer to Mr. Stubb* (1660), in *WoJH*, 219, 224–25, 232, 271–72, 275, 281–84, 319, 324, 338, 342, 366, 381, 405, 464, 528, 535–37, 539, 543, 548, 552, 554, 561, 585.

[16] Cf. Hobbes, *Philosophicall Rudiments* II.vi.9, with Arist. *Pol.* 1252b27–1253a39, and see Hobbes, *Leviathan* I.v.2–4. Consider Hobbes, *Elements of Law*, II.i.10, *Philosophicall Rudiments* Pref. [8], II.xii.1, *Leviathan* IV.xlvi.11, 31–32, and then see *Elements of Law* II.x.8, *Philosophicall Rudiments* II.vi.13, III.xvii.12, and Thomas Hobbes, *A Dialogue between a Philosopher and a Student of the Common Laws of England*, ed. Joseph Cropsey (Chicago: University of Chicago Press, 1971), 67. Note Sheldon Wolin, *Politics and Vision: Continuity and Innovation in Western Political Thought*, second edition (Princeton, NJ: Princeton University Press, 2004), 214–56.

[17] See Paul A. Rahe, "The Primacy of Politics in Classical Greece," *American Historical Review* 89:2 (April 1984): 265–93, and *Republics Ancient and Modern*, 28–54.

[18] Cf. *JHO*, 141–42 and the epigraph to *The Prerogative of Popular Government* (1658), in *WoJH*, 213, with Machiavelli, *Discorsi* 1.58, in *Opere*, 140–42, and see Chapters 2, 3, 7, and 9, this volume.

Government that is not secured, can be good; this evill from which the Government that is secure, must be perfect."[19] Apart, however, from acknowledging that establishing such a regime may require public spiritedness on the part of the founders, he is almost entirely silent on the subject of virtue; and in the course of his argument, as we shall soon see, he makes it abundantly clear that the perfection belonging to a government that is genuinely secure presupposes a reliance on the distribution of property and on private interest and precludes any dependence on the personal qualities of the citizens. James Harrington was like Thomas Hobbes in this regard as well, for the two were Platonists of a peculiarly modern sort – convinced that institutional arrangements can achieve what education can never guarantee: the coincidence of wisdom and virtue with political rule.[20]

Regime Typology

Harrington's silence with regard to the principal themes of ancient republican politics is not an oversight. Like Machiavelli, Milton, Nedham, and Hobbes, he was steeped in the classics; and when it suits his turn, he is more than prepared to borrow an argument from Thucydides, Plato, Aristotle, Cicero, and the like. But the "ancient prudence" that really interests him is neither the teaching concerning moral virtue laid out by Aristotle in his *Nicomachean Ethics*, modified, and passed on to the modern West by Cicero and the Stoics nor the doctrine of regime (*politeía*) found in the writings of the ancient political scientists and historians. It is, rather, the institutional teaching articulated by the ancients' "learned Disciple *Machiavill*" – whom he variously terms "the onely Polititian of later Ages," "the sole retreiver of this *ancient Prudence*," "the greatest Artist in the modern World," "the Prince of Polititians," and the "incomparable Patron of the people."[21] Moreover, if truth be told, James Harrington owes far, far less to the many thinkers of classical antiquity than to their great scourge Thomas Hobbes – whom he judges in most things, apart from his monarchist bias, "the best writer, at this day, in the world." If he "oppos'd the politics of Mr. Hobbs," he readily confesses, it was merely "to shew him what he taught me."[22] Accordingly, though Harrington elects "to follow the Ancients" in some respects, he nevertheless intends, as he openly admits, "[t]o go mine own way."[23]

In finding his own path, as his critic Matthew Wren charged at the time, Harrington maintains an even closer "correspondence" with the author of *Leviathan* than he admits and "does silently swallow down such Notions as Mr.

---

[19] *JHO*, 20–21.
[20] Consider *JHO*, 20, 34, in light of Hobbes, *Leviathan* II.xxxi.41, and see *JHO*, 29–30, 53–54, 56, 84–85, 104, 119–20. Cf. Nelson, *The Greek Tradition in Republican Thought*, 87–126, who misapprehends the character of Harrington's Platonism, with Scott, *Commonwealth Principles*, 181–84.
[21] *JHO*, 13, 30, 118, 135.
[22] Harrington, *The Prerogative of Popular Government* (1658), in *WoJH*, 241.
[23] *JHO*, 14.

Hobs hath chewed for him."[24] If he nowhere explicitly addresses the question of first principles, the end and purpose of government, and the foundations of morality, if, in contrast with Nedham, he makes no attempt to distance himself from Machiavelli's critique of the moral tradition, it is because he tacitly accepts Hobbes's brilliant redeployment of that critique to provide morality and politics with a new foundation.[25]

What Harrington means by asserting that he intends "[t]o go mine own way, and yet to follow the Ancients" is nowhere more evident than in his typology of regimes. At first glance, he seems intent on resurrecting a distinction asserted by Plato, Aristotle, and Polybius, tacitly abandoned by Machiavelli, and openly repudiated by Hobbes: that between monarchy and tyranny, between aristocracy and oligarchy, and between well-ordered popular government and the regime variously called democracy, anarchy, or mob rule. In resurrecting this scheme of classification, however, Harrington follows not its ancient proponents but their modern critics, for he jettisons the moral argument that had made the classical distinction intelligible in the first place, and he nowhere acknowledges that the distribution of offices and honors (*táxis tōn archōn*) within a given community determines the education (*paideía*) that shapes the character of its citizens and defines it as a regime.[26] If he seems to restore the traditional typology, it is because he retains the familiar names to camouflage what is, in fact, a new typology grounded on a material and institutional rather than a moral and educational foundation. Harrington does for the political science of the ancients what Hobbes had done for their moral teaching.

In the original conception, monarchy, aristocracy, and the well-ordered popular regime had been the lawful rule of the one, the wealthy few, and the impoverished many over willing subjects in the interest of those ruled, while tyranny, oligarchy, and the disorderly popular regime had been the lawless rule

---

[24] See Matthew Wren, *Considerations on Mr. Harrington's Common-wealth of Oceana: Restrained to the First Part of the Preliminaries* (London: Samuel Gellibrand, 1657), 41.

[25] See Chapter 10, this volume.

[26] Though much may separate Plato from Aristotle, on this fundamental point they were agreed: to understand the ancient Greek *pólis*, one must be willing to entertain two propositions – that the political regime (*politeía*), rather than economic or environmental conditions, is the chief determinant of what one acute, ancient observer (Schol. Pl. *Laws* 1.625b) called "the one way of life of a whole *pólis*," and that education in the broadest and most comprehensive sense (*paideía*) is more important than anything else in deciding the character of the regime: note the prominence of this theme in Pl. *Resp.* 2.376c–4.445a, 6.487b–497a, 7.518b–541b, 8.548a–b, 554a–b, 559b–c, 10.600a–608b, and *Laws* 1.641b–2.674c, 3.693d–701b, 4.722b–9.880e, 11.920a–12.962e. In one passage of *The Politics* (1263b36–37), Aristotle suggests that it is the provision of a common education (*paideía*) – and nothing else – that turns a multitude (*plēthos*) into a unit and constitutes it as a *pólis*; in another (1276a8–1276b15), he indicates that it is the regime (*politeía*) which defines the *pólis* as such. Though apparently in contradiction, the two statements are in fact equivalent. It is not fortuitous that Polybius' celebrated discussion of the Roman *politeía* is, in fact, a discussion of the *paideía* accorded the ruling element (*políteuma*) at Rome: 6.19–58. Precisely the same observation can be made regarding Xenophon's account of the Persian *politeía*: Xen. *Cyr.* 1.2.15. Also see Xen. *Por.* 1.1; Pl. *Resp.* 8.544d–e, *Laws* 4.711c–712a; Isoc. 2.31, 3.37, 7.14; Cic. *Resp.* 1.31.47, 5.3.5–5.7 (with *Laws* 1.4.14–6.19, 3.1.2). In this connection, see Leo Strauss, *Natural Right and History* (Chicago: University of Chicago Press, 1974), 135–38.

of each of the same three elements over unwilling subjects solely in the interest of the rulers themselves. Each of the correct regimes was deemed to exhibit and foster its own peculiar virtue, but – given human weakness – it was thought also to evidence a pronounced tendency to degenerate into its generic opposite. The mixed regime, as outlined by Polybius, was designed to combine the virtues of the various correct regimes while checking their propensity for corruption.[27] This is the species of political analysis that Machiavelli and Hobbes abandoned, and they did so on the supposition that it is naive to think that the dominant element within any polity would ever rule in anyone's interest other than its own.[28]

Harrington shared the conviction of Machiavelli and Hobbes that human desire is insatiate and that reason is therefore enslaved to the passions. With regard to the Malmesbury philosopher's "treatises of human nature, and of liberty and necessity," he wrote, "they are the greatest of new lights, and those which I have follow'd, and shall follow."[29] Consequently, he joined the Florentine sage and the English philosopher in concluding that self-interested rule is what the former had dubbed "the effectual truth of the matter." He reiterates Machiavelli's contention that "*it is the duty of a* Legislator *to presume all men to be wicked.*"[30] He quotes with approval Hobbes's dictum that "*as often as reason is against a man, so often will a man be against reason.*" Moreover, he concedes that, in practice, "*reason is nothing but interest*"; and he concludes that "there be divers *interests*, and so divers *reasons.*"[31] In short, Harrington

---

[27] Cf. Polyb. 6.3.5–10.14 with Pl. *Pol.* 291d–303b, *Laws* 3.689e–702d, 4.712c–715d, 8.832b–d; Arist. *Eth. Nic.* 1160a31–1161b10, *Pol.* 1278b30–1280a5, 1295a7–24, *Rh.* 1365b21–1366a22, and see Pl. *Laws* 6.756e–758a, Arist. *Pol.* 1281b22–38 (esp. 28–31), 1295a25–1297a12 (esp. 1296b14–16), 1297b1–27, 1329a2–17, 1332b12–41. Note, in this connection, Pind. *Pyth.* 2.86–88, Hdt. 3.80–83, and Thuc. 8.97.2. In Harrington's day, the pertinent passages of Cicero's *Republic* (1.20.33–2.44.70, 3.13.23, 25.37–35.48) were as yet undiscovered. Note the shift of emphasis in Marsilius of Padua, *Defensor pacis* I.viii.2–3, ix.5. Cf. Thomas Aquinas *De regimine principum* I.1–3, *Summa theologiae* IaIIae q.95 a.4, q.105 a.1, IIaIIae q.42 a.2, in *Aquinas: Selected Political Writings*, ed. A. P. D'Entrèves and tr. J. G. Dawson (Oxford, UK: Basil Blackwell, 1948), 2–19, 148–51, 130–33, 160–61.

[28] See Machiavelli, *Discorsi* 1.2–8, in *Opere*, 78–90 (which should be read in light of Harvey C. Mansfield, *Machiavelli's New Modes and Orders: A Study of the Discourses on Livy* [Ithaca, NY: Cornell University Press, 1979], 32–62), and Hobbes, *Elements of Law* II.i.3, *Philosophicall Rudiments* II.vii.1–17, x.2, *Leviathan* II.xix.1–2. For the most part, Machiavelli is content to juxtapose republics with principalities: *Il principe* 1, in *Opere*, 258. But he makes it clear that, in the end, even this distinction is illusory: cf. *Discorsi* 1.20 with *Il principe* 9, in *Opere*, 105, 271–72. See Mansfield, "Machiavelli and the Modern Executive," in *Understanding the Political Spirit: Philosophical Investigations from Socrates to Nietzsche*, ed. Catherine H. Zuckert (New Haven, CT: Yale University Press, 1988), 88–110 (esp. 97–102).

[29] Cf. Machiavelli, *Discorsi* 1.5, 37, 2 Proemio, in *Opere*, 83–84, 119, 145–46, with Hobbes, *Leviathan* I.viii.13–16, xi.1–34, xii.1–7, and see Harrington, *The Prerogative of Popular Government* (1658), in *WoJH*, 241. For the treatises that Harrington so admired, see *EW*, IV 1–76, 229–78. In the treatise on human nature, which forms the first part of his *Elements of Law Natural and Politic*, Hobbes articulates the political psychology that provides the foundation for the overall argument presented first in *The Elements of Law*, then in *De cive*, and finally in *Leviathan*.

[30] Cf. *JHO*, 152, with *JHO*, 155, and see Machiavelli, *Discorsi* 1.3.1 with *Il principe* 15, in *Opere*, 81, 280.

[31] Cf. *JHO*, 22, with Hobbes, *Elements of Law* Ep. Ded., *Human Nature* Ep. Ded., in *EW*, IV xiii, and *Leviathan* I.xi.21. In this connection, see *Elements of Law* I.iv.1–x.11, xii.1–xiv.14,

accepts Machiavelli's critique of moral reason and the moral imagination.[32] If he never asserts that man is by nature a political animal, if he never explores the manner in which the ordering of public offices and honors constitutes a species of civic moral education, it is because he has tacitly joined Hobbes in rejecting as practically untenable Aristotle's conviction that man's capacity for moral virtue and his facility for *lógos* or reasoned speech makes it possible for him to ascend from a calculation of his own immediate, material advantage to a concern with what is truly just and good. As he puts it in dismissing the thinking of John Milton and that of the self-styled "saints" who advocate godly rule, "*Give us good men and they will make us good Lawes* is the *Maxime* of a *Demagogue*, and (through the alteration which is commonly perceivable in men, when they have power to work their own wills) exceedingly *fallible.*"

In place of this hoary dictum, Harrington embraces the thoroughly modern principles of "the greatest Artist in the modern World." And so he suggests that "*give us good orders, and they will make us good men* is the *Maxime* of a *Legislator* and the most *infallible* in the *Politickes.*" Thus, in the English republican's estimation, "the perfection of Government lyeth upon such a libration in the frame of it, that no man or men, in or under it, can have the interest; or having the interest, can have the power to disturb it with sedition." While at Rome, he remarks, he once saw a pageant

which represented a kitchen, with all the proper utensils in use and action. The cooks were all cats and kitlings, set in such frames, so try'd and so ordered, that the poor creatures could make no motion to get loose, but the same caused one to turn the spit, another to baste the meat, a third to scim the pot and a fourth to make green-sauce. If the frame of your commonwealth be no such, as causeth everyone to perform his certain function as necessarily as this did the cat to make green-sauce, it is not right.

Harrington's ultimate purpose is precisely that of Hobbes: to "put such principles down for a foundation, as passion, not mistrusting, may not seek to displace."[33] The "superstructures" of the well-ordered commonwealth are intended to be substitutes for the moral and political virtue that no man can be supposed to possess.[34] In a regime such as Oceana, which pursues what

Philosophicall Rudiments I.ii.1, *Leviathan* I.iv.24–v.5, vi.6–7, 49–59, viii.13–16, xv.40–41, II.xix.3–4. Note also *JHO*, 12, 217, and Harrington, *The Prerogative of Popular Government* (1658), *A System of Politics* (ca. 1661), *Politicaster* (1659), and *A Discourse upon this Saying...* (1659), in *WoJH*, 224–25, 241, 477–78, 553, 570–72.

[32] Consider Machiavelli, *Discorsi* 1.6, 2 Proemio in light of *Il principe* 15, in *Opere*, 84–87 (esp. 86–87), 144–46 (esp. 145), 280, and see Paul A. Rahe, "Situating Machiavelli," in *Renaissance Civic Humanism: Reappraisals and Reflections*, ed. James Hankins (Cambridge, UK: Cambridge University Press, 2000), 270–308, along with Chapter 1, this volume.

[33] Cf. *JHO*, 30–32, 56, 185, and Harrington, *The Prerogative of Popular Government* (1658), *The Art of Lawgiving* (1659), *A System of Politics* (ca. 1661), *Political Aphorisms* (1659), and *A Discourse upon this Saying...* (1659), in *WoJH*, 242–46, 403–4, 468–69, 483, 567–74 (esp. 573–74), with Hobbes, *Elements of Law* Ep. Ded., and *Human Nature* Ep. Ded, in *EW*, IV xiii, and see Machiavelli, *Discorsi* 1.4, in *Opere*, 82–83. The passages cited are hard to reconcile with Harrington's contention that "in the politics there is nothing mechanic, or like it." See *The Prerogative of Popular Government* (1658), in *WoJH*, 247.

[34] *JHO*, 32–33, and Harrington, *The Prerogative of Popular Government* (1658), *A System of Politics* (ca. 1661), and *A Discourse Showing...* (1659), in *WoJH*, 271–72, 469, 579.

Machiavelli had pointedly termed "the common benefit of each" by fitting "privat to public" and "even public to privat utility," no one, says Harrington, not even a "*nobleman*," need "*own a shame for preferring his own interest before that of a whole nation.*"[35]

In presenting his new typology of regimes, Harrington stresses the central importance of a single institution: the distribution of land. To institute a monarchy, an aristocracy, or a democracy, he contends, a legislator "must either frame the Government unto the foundation, or the foundation unto the Government." Thus, a legislator can set up a workable monarchy only "[i]f one man be sole Landlord of a territory, or overballance the people, for example, three parts in four." He can effectively establish the aristocratic rule embodied in the "mixed *Monarchy*" favored by proponents of "the *Gothick* ballance" only if "the Few or a Nobility, or a Nobility with the Clergy be Landlords or overballance the people unto like proportion." And he can institute a stable commonwealth only "[i]f the whole people be Landlords, or hold the lands so divided among them, that no one man, or number of men, within the compass of the *Few* or *Aristocracy*, overballance them."

Harrington takes it for granted that it is impossible for a government to maintain an adequate standing army on the basis of its tax revenues alone. He therefore believes that whoever controls a nation's farms and feeds its militia can, if he wishes, control that militia. And he concludes that whoever is able in this fashion to control the militia will be forced eventually, in defense of his own interests, to seize control of the government as well. Thus, where a legislator frames "the Government not according unto the ballance," its rule will be inherently unstable and therefore "not natural but violent." Consequently, Harrington concludes, "if it be at the devotion of a *Prince*, it is *Tyranny*; if at the devotion of the *Few*, *Oligarchy*; or if in the power of the *People*, *Anarchy*: each of which confusions, the ballance standing otherwise, is but of short continuance; because against the nature of the ballance, which not destroyed, destroyeth that which opposeth it." By distinguishing between correct and incorrect regimes in this fashion, Harrington indicates his acceptance of Hobbes' contention that one must judge political arrangements solely with regard to "the difference of Convenience, or Aptitude to produce the Peace, and Security of the people."[36]

It is on this basis that Harrington defends republicanism. He denies that an aristocracy is capable of ruling on its own; and for "the Gothic balance" and the feudal system on which it is grounded, he has little use. The mixed regime is a half-way house between monarchy and republic; and, as Hobbes had already pointed out, it is inherently unstable as such. This "*Master-piece of Moderne Prudence* hath beene cry'd up to the *Skyes*, as the only invention, whereby at once to maintain the soveraignty of a *Prince*, and the liberty of the *people*,"

---

[35] Cf. Harrington, *The Prerogative of Popular Government* (1658), in WoJH, 277–78, with Machiavelli, *Discorsi* I Proemio, in *Opere*, 76.

[36] Consider *JHO*, 14–15, in light of Hobbes, *Leviathan* II.xxix.3–4. Note Harrington, *The Prerogative of Popular Government* (1658), in WoJH, 226–32. Those "black maxims, set down by som politicians, particularly MACHIAVEL in his *prince*" have their natural home where there is "CORRUPTION in government," i.e., in "anarchy, oligarchy, or tyranny." See Harrington, *A System of Politics* (ca. 1661), in WoJH, 482.

Harrington writes, but the history of Europe proves that, even where mixed monarchy accords with "the ballance" of property, "it hath been no other than a wrestling match" between the nobility and their king.[37] In his judgment, the real contest of regimes is between absolute monarchy, as exemplified by the Ottoman Empire, and the species of republicanism he defends himself. The former is grounded on the sultan's ownership of the land and his ability to assign allotments to individual timariots in return for their service; and to it, the English republican is prepared to concede a great deal. But he hastens to add that the Ottoman regime has one, apparently insuperable defect: absolute monarchy requires, for its own defense, a praetorian guard. More often than not, the Ottoman sultan is the creature of the janissaries who serve him in that capacity; and even when this is not the case, they "have frequent interest and perpetual power to raise *sedition*, and to tear the *Magistrate*, even the *Prince* himself, in pieces." It is the burden of Harrington's argument to show that republicanism can be purged of comparable defects.[38]

To this end, he advanced two arguments. The first was comparatively simple to make. Against those, such as Machiavelli, who draw attention to the civil disorders occasioned at Rome by disputes over the distribution of land, he asserts that, in England, where the "wrestling match" between the monarch and the nobility has resulted in there being a relatively egalitarian distribution of such property, it would be easy and painless to establish and maintain the requisite "ballance." One need only pass and enforce an agrarian law restricting dowries, setting a limit to the amount of land one can acquire, and denying those possessed of property greatly in excess of that limit the right to leave a disproportionate amount to any one child.[39]

The second argument was more complex. Against those, such as Hobbes, who point to the inherent contentiousness of republican politics, Harrington articulates new modes and orders designed to achieve within a republican framework what the author of *Leviathan* believed could best be accomplished in an absolute monarchy: the containment, reduction, and virtual elimination of politics itself. In making the attempt, he could console himself that he had intellectual support from no less an authority than Thomas Hobbes – as we shall soon see.

A Republic Tongue-Ty'd

Like Hobbes, Harrington was acutely aware that political "ambition" can easily undermine the stability of a republican regime. When he cites Aristotle's contention that the best democracy is predominantly agricultural, he emphasizes that "such an one" is "the most obstinate assertresse of her liberty, and the

---

[37] Cf. *JHO* 47–48 with Hobbes, *Elements of Law* II.i.15–17, *Philosophicall Rudiments* II.vii.4, *Leviathan* II.xix, pp. 240–41; and note Harrington, *The Art of Lawgiving* (1659) and *A System of Politics* (ca. 1661), in *WoJH* 368–69, 481.

[38] *JHO*, 31–32, 40–41, and Harrington, *The Prerogative of Popular Government* (1658), and *The Art of Lawgiving* (1659), in *WoJH*, 248–49, 368.

[39] *JHO*, 9–10, 15–16, 47–56, 85–99. In this connection, see Harrington, *The Prerogative of Popular Government* (1658), and *The Art of Lawgiving* (1659), in *WoJH*, 242–48, 269–81, 367.

least subject unto innovation or turbulency." This is the balance that he wants to achieve. But he recognizes that commonwealths, such as Athens, where "the City life hath had the stronger influence," have, in fact, "seldome or never been quiet, but at the best are found to have injured their own businesse by overdoing it." Apart from communities much like Venice, where the bulk of the populace was in his day excluded from power, "a Common-wealth consisting but of one City, would doubtlesse be stormy, in regard that ambition would be every mans trade."[40]

If, like Hobbes, Harrington looked askance at city life, it was largely because, again like Hobbes, he greatly feared public debate.[41] "Consider," he exhorted his readers, "how we have been tossed with every wind of Doctrine, lost by the glib tongues of your Demagogs and Grandees in our Havens." Like Hobbes, he had read Thucydides, and he had studied the history of the ancient republics. When he reviewed all that can take place in the political sphere, he could think of "nothing more dangerous" than "debate in a crowd," for "such sport is debate in a Popular Assembly as ... was the destruction of Athens." A commonwealth "where the People is talkative in their political capacity" will inevitably be "carried away by Vain-glorious Men" and "Swim down the sink." It is not, then, surprising that Harrington chose to adapt to the needs of a commonwealth situated on a large territory the one set of republican regulations that had earned the full approval of that form of government's most severe and exacting critic. Like the philosopher of Malmesbury, he found in the modes and orders employed by the Serene Republic of Venice an antidote for "the overflowing and boundless passions" of the "multitude."[42]

"The tongue of man is," Thomas Hobbes once observed, "a trumpet of warre and sedition." To silence that trumpet, Harrington makes of his Oceana a republic "tongue-ty'd." Except behind closed doors, within the narrow confines of its Senate and the various councils drawn from the members of that body, debate and discussion are strictly forbidden. When a law has been promulgated and is soon to be voted on in Oceana's more popular house, the magistrates are to see to it *"that there be no laying of heads together; Conventicles, or Canvassing to carry on, or to oppose any thing."* To the same end, the deputies elected to the lower house are required to take an oath that *"they will neither introduce, cause, nor to their power suffer debate to be introduced into any popular Assembly of this Government, but to their utmost be ayding and assisting to seize and deliver any Person or Persons in that way offending and striking at the*

---

40 Cf. *JHO*, 10, 169, with Arist. *Pol.* 1292b25–30, 1318b6–1319a39.

41 Consider Hobbes, "The Answer of Mr. Hobbes to Sir William Davenant's Preface Before Gondibert," in *EW*, IV 443–44, in light of *Elements of Law* II.ii.5, v.3–8. See *Philosophicall Rudiments* II.x.6–7, 11, *Leviathan* II.xix.5–8. See also Thomas Hobbes, "Of the Life and History of Thucydides," in Thucydides, *Eight Bookes of the Peloponnesian Warre*, tr. Thomas Hobbes (London: Hen. Seile, 1629), a1ᵛ–a2ʳ, and reprinted in *EW*, VIII xv–xviii.

42 Cf. *JHO*, 123–29 (esp. 125–28), with Hobbes, *Elements of Law* II.v.8, *Philosophicall Rudiments* II.x.15, and see Harrington, *A Discourse upon this Saying* ... (1659), in *WoJH*, 573–74. Later, he added, "debate in the people makes anarchy." See Harrington, *The Prerogative of Popular Government* (1658), in *WoJH*, 286. See also *The Art of Lawgiving* (1659), and *A Discourse upon this Saying* ... (1659), in *WoJH*, 418, 570.

Root of this Commonwealth unto the Councill of War." It would be an error
to underestimate the importance that Harrington attached to the prohibition of
canvassing and public debate. To render political maneuvering ineffective, the
fundamental orders of Oceana dictate the use of the secret ballot in legislative
assemblies. To deter discussion, they solemnly stipulate that, if "*any Person or
Persons shall goe about to introduce Debate, into any Popular assembly*" of the
commonwealth "*or otherwise to alter the present Government, or strike at the
root of it,*" the Council of War "*shall apprehend, or cause to be apprehended,
seized, imprisoned; and examine, arraigne, acquit, or condemne, and cause to
be executed any such Person, or Persons, of their proper Power and Authority,
and without appeale.*"[43] With Harrington, for the first time, in a definitive way,
popular consent has replaced public deliberation as the fundamental principle
of republican politics.[44]

The suppression of public discussion and public voting was one way in which
the author of *Oceana* sought through republican orders to eliminate the "middle
ground" that had been the central feature of self-government in ancient times.[45]
There were others as well. Thus, for example, Harrington thought it necessary
to bar from his legislative assemblies the entire profession of lawyers with
"their incurable run upon their own narrow bias," "their perpetuall invectives
against *Machiavill*," and their propensity, as "Tradesmen," for a "knitting of
Nets" when there should be a "making of Lawes."

Harrington was similarly suspicious of divines, who were "neither to be
allow'd Synods nor Assemblies" nor to be "suffred to meddle with affaires of
State,"[46] for from Hobbes he had learned what Pierre Charron had revealed to
the *libertins érudits*: that the marriage between Athens and Jerusalem arranged
by the early doctors of the Christian church had allowed the bitter politics of
the ancient Greek *ekklēsía* to survive within the *respublica Christiana*, and that
when unleashed from the pulpit, no less than when exercised in the assembly, the
"tongue of man" can be "a trumpet of warre and sedition."[47] This worried him
less than it did his infamous countryman, for he deemed it impossible "that mens
animosityes should over ballance their Interest, for any [great] time," and he
was therefore persuaded that a "sound and steddy" government that "taketh in
all *interests*" could easily eliminate "the animosity" and the "triviall" divisions
to which "parties that are *Spiritual*" so often give rise.[48] Nonetheless, like John
Milton and Marchamont Nedham, he regarded civil liberty and the liberty

---

[43] Consider *JHO*, 80, 99–102, 109, 115–17, 127–28, 142, and Harrington, *The Art of Lawgiving*
(1659), *Political Aphorisms* (1659), and *Brief Directions* (1658), in *WoJH*, 417–19, 487–88,
503, in light of Hobbes, *Philosophicall Rudiments* II.v.5. In this connection, note *JHO*, 99–105.

[44] *JHO*, 142–44, 205–6, and Harrington, *The Prerogative of Popular Government* (1658), in
WoJH, 277.

[45] See Rahe, "The Primacy of Politics in Classical Greece," 265–93, and Chapter 1, this volume.

[46] Note *JHO*, 118, and consider *JHO*, 172–74, in light of 163–64.

[47] See Hobbes, *Dialogue*, 122–32 (esp. 123–26); "An Historical Narration Concerning Heresy and
the Punishment Thereof," in *EW*, IV 387–408. See also *Elements of Law* II.vii.9; *Concerning
Body* Ep. Ded., in *EW*, I ix–xi; *Leviathan* IV.xliv.2, xlvi–xlvii; *Behemoth*, 8–20; and Samuel I.
Mintz, "Hobbes on the Law of Heresy: A New Manuscript," *Journal of the History of Ideas*
29:3 (July 1968): 409–14.

[48] *JHO*, 55–56, 209, 217.

of conscience as inseparable, and so he took considerable care to defuse the situation and eliminate every occasion for the exercise of what he was the first to dub "Priest-craft." To this end, he advocated an Erastian church settlement similar to the ecclesiastical polity imagined by Thomas Hobbes and to the one imposed by Oliver Cromwell.[49] In Oceana, he excluded ministers of the Gospel from holding public office, established a modicum of religious freedom for all Christian sects not owing allegiance to a foreign power, and provided for strict civilian control of the established church – chiefly, by authorizing the local parish congregation to select its own parson but also by empowering the Senate's council of religion to supervise the activities of the nation's clergy. Mindful of the manner in which his contemporaries had been "tossed with every wind of Doctrine," Harrington sought to bridle the "glib tongues" of the nation's priests. "If you know not how to rule your Clergy," his Lord Archon warns, "you will most certainly be like a man that cannot rule his Wife," having "neither quiet at home, nor honour abroad."[50]

The English republican was no less fully persuaded than Hobbes that "the soverain power" within a state must be "entire and absolute."[51] But while he considered the full concentration of power "necessary," he thought it *"a formidable creature"* as well, and he compared it with *"the Powder, which (as you are Soldiers) is at once your safety and danger."*[52] Consequently, he tried to suppress or at least contain the ambition for office, for power, and for political glory. To this end, he introduced two institutions: rotation, and what he called "the Venetian ballot." Rotation ensures that all who govern are governed in turn: members of parliament serve for three years and are ineligible for that office for three years thereafter; other officials must similarly vacate any magistracy they have held for a period equal to, if not double the length of their term in office.

The Venetian ballot has a number of provisions. To begin with, it guarantees that all of the magistrates owe their status to the people: the freeholders of the parish over thirty years of age elect parish officials at an assembly held each year; deputies whom they select from among their number gather annually to choose the justices of the peace and the other magistrates of the district, the tribal officeholders, and the tribe's representatives to parliament. Moreover, since the ballot is in every case secret and therefore private, Oceana's citizens, their deputies, and their representatives in Parliament can ignore the contentious questions of justice and the transcendent good and vote their own interests without regard to fear or shame. Finally, the arrangements effectively preclude campaigning for office and thereby contribute further to the suppression of the

---

[49] In this connection, see Jeffrey R. Collins, *The Allegiance of Thomas Hobbes* (Oxford, UK: Oxford University Press, 2005), 115–270 (esp. 185–91).

[50] *JHO*, 37–38, 69–70, 109–10, 125, 169–73, and Harrington, *A System of Politics* (ca. 1661), *Political Aphorisms* (1659), *Pian Piano* (1657), and *A Discourse upon this Saying...* (1659), in *WoJH*, 474–76, 484, 519, 530, 572–74.

[51] Cf. Harrington, *The Art of Lawgiving* (1659), in *WoJH*, 404, with Hobbes, *Leviathan* II.xviii. Note Harrington, *A System of Politics* (ca. 1661), in *WoJH*, 478–79.

[52] *JHO*, 84–85. Note his distrust of the *libido dominandi* so evident in the few. See Harrington, *A System of Politics* (ca. 1661), in *WoJH*, 469.

public deliberation that had been the very soul of classical politics: as in Venice, an individual is chosen by lot and authorized to nominate candidates for the position soon to be vacant, and no one of these can be elected who has not been approved by a majority of those present and eligible to vote.[53]

Rotation and the Venetian ballot enable the citizens of Oceana to ignore public opinion, to consult their interests in private, and to select reasonably able men for high office. Most important of all, they prevent the emergence of a narrow political class and give minimal scope to the great longing "to be first and superior to all others" that had crippled the mythical Achaean army of Homer's *Iliad* and plagued the tumultuous *póleis* of ancient Greece.[54]

Harrington's distrust of man's love for preeminence carries over into every sphere. There is, for example, no indication that Oceana is to be, like the Greek *pólis* and the Roman *civitas*, a repository of memory. The fundamental orders of Harrington's new republic are remarkably detailed, but they make no provision for remembering in verse or for honoring in eulogies delivered at public or familial funeral rites the able men who have served in Oceana's councils and demonstrated prowess in her defense on the battlefield.[55]

Harrington's silence in this regard is by no means fortuitous. Even *Oceana*'s legislator is required to subordinate his own behavior to the suppression of ambition. Harrington recognized that, if he was to persuade a man such as Cromwell to establish a republic, he had to supply him with a motive for doing so and show him that he had a tangible interest in abandoning the power that had fallen to him as a consequence of the Civil War. As he readily concedes, glory is the only plausible motive in such an instance; and so he does everything he can to clothe his Lord Archon in godlike splendor.[56]

But he saw with equal perspicacity that the example set by Oceana's founding father in pursuing glory might well fire the ambitions of the commonwealth's ablest citizens; and so he stipulated that, after publishing his orders and setting the commonwealth in motion, the Lord Archon should retire from office and seek solitude at his country estate so that "no manner of Food might be left unto ambition." Even if recalled to office and given emergency powers and the command of a standing army, the lawgiver of Oceana can be said to have contrived affairs so that "the minds of men were firme in the opinion, that he could be no seeker of himselfe, in the way of earthly Pompe and Glory."[57]

The element of subterfuge evident in Harrington's account of the Lord Archon's comportment finds an echo in his discussion of the procedures

[53] *JHO*, 33, 66–68, 71–82, 99–108, and Harrington, *The Prerogative of Popular Government* (1658), *The Art of Lawgiving* (1659), and *Brief Directions* (1658), in *WoJH*, 282–300, 369–70, 419, 504.

[54] For an Aristotelian analysis of one aspect of the problem that Harrington sought to address, see Bernard Yack, "Community and Conflict in Aristotle's Political Philosophy," *Review of Politics* 47:1 (January 1985): 92–112, and *The Problems of a Political Animal: Community, Justice, and Conflict in Aristotelian Political Thought* (Berkeley: University of California Press, 1993).

[55] For the import of these practices in antiquity, see Rahe, "The Primacy of Politics in Classical Greece," 265–93, and *Republics Ancient and Modern*, 28–54.

[56] Note *JHO*, 58–59, and see *JHO*, 207–26.

[57] *JHO*, 208, 216. Note, in this connection, *JHO*, 204.

followed by the Council of Legislators appointed to advise the man on his promulgation of the laws. At the Council's first meeting, a subcommittee of Prytans was selected by lot to sit "in the great hall of *Pantheon*" and listen to suggestions brought forward by individual members of the general public; it was equipped with a guard of two or three hundred men "lest the heat of the dispute might break the peace"; and its members were instructed to report "such *Propositions* or *Occurrences* as they thought fit" to the Council of Legislators meeting in private. According to Harrington, this was done for two reasons: to give the Council of Legislators the "necessary solitude" and yet enable them to be "acquainted from time to time with the pulse of the people"; and to make "the *people* (who were neither *safely* to be *admitted* unto, nor *conveniently* to be *excluded* from the framing of their *Common-wealth*) verily believe when it came forth, that it was no other than that, whereof they themselves had been the makers."[58] Harrington appears to have been persuaded that, in fashioning a commonwealth meant to be "the most obstinate assertresse of her liberty, and the least subject unto innovation or turbulency," one must take great care to instill in the citizens two convictions: that consent is the sole source of political legitimacy, and that the community's constitution is, in fact, a product of that consent.[59]

A Common-wealth for Encrease

Like Marchamont Nedham, Harrington was too much a Machiavellian to want to eliminate altogether every element of "emulation" and the love of "glory."[60] Nor did he think it possible. In discussing the need for public education and extensive military training and service, he remarked, "A man is a Spirit raised up by the Magick of Nature; if she doe not stand safe and so that she may set him to some good and usefull work, he spets fire, and blowes up Castles; for where there is life, there must be motion or work and the work of idlenesse is mischiefe, . . . But the work of industry is health."[61] *Oceana* was designed to channel this energy away from the political arena into what its author calls "industry." It was intended to be, like Machiavelli's Rome, "a *Common-wealth for encrease*"[62] – but in more ways than the Florentine had had in mind. For Harrington thought its institutions and circumstances as well suited for the promotion of labor and ingenuity as for the conduct of war, and he thereby contributed his mite to the smooth and easy transformation by which a spirited doctrine oriented toward honor, glory, conquest, and command came to be compatible with more prosaic, bourgeois concerns.

This last point needs emphasis. James Harrington was familiar with the thinking of Sir Francis Bacon, and he was no less indebted to the Lord

---

[58] *JHO*, 60–61.
[59] In this connection, see *JHO*, 205–6.
[60] Note *JHO*, 30, 175.
[61] *JHO*, 161–67.
[62] *JHO*, 11, 133–35, 186–98, 221–24, and Harrington, *The Prerogative of Popular Government* (1658), in *WoJH*, 280.

Chancellor than was Hobbes. He had pored over the Bacon's *Essays or Counsels Civill and Moral*; he had perused with some care his other works; and he was much impressed with their author's observation that, where the wealth is widely distributed and entrusted "to those hands, where there is likely to be the greatest sparing and increase," states are well equipped with good soldiers and easily able to meet the expenses of war.[63] He was himself persuaded that, where the territory has been divided among the people and "their industry is not obstructed," their "revenue ... is twofold to that of the nobility," and he was therefore pleased that it would no longer be disputed whether the political community "might not destroy fishes to plant men." He made much of the fact that, as a consequence of Oceana's agrarian law, the rich could "neither oppress the people, nor exclude their industry or merit from attaining to the like estate, power, or honor," and he rejoiced that "a man from the lowest state" might raise himself up by his industry and render "himself capable of all preferments and honors" in the government of Oceana. Like Bacon, Harrington interpreted the curse "*In the sweat of they face shalt thou eat they bread*" as a charter for man's labor, and he therefore equated God's donation of the earth to man with "a kind of selling it for INDUSTRY." He even asserted that it is "inequal" that "the riches of a commonwealth should not go according to the difference of mens industry." In his judgment, the "ballance of justice" requires "having due regard unto the different industry, of different men."[64]

Like Bacon, Harrington was also acutely aware of the example afforded by the Dutch republic. He made much of the United Provinces' victory in the war of independence against monarchical Spain.[65] He noted that "the *Hollander*" has "for industry no equal" and that he "sweat[s] more gold than the *Spaniard* digs."[66] And he contended that, if his plan was adopted, Oceana would be in a position to outdo the Dutch in every sphere. Because Harrington's commonwealth was to be a unitary state rather than a loose federation, it would be comparatively free from the disunion that dogged the United Provinces;[67] and because it would be an agrarian polity equipped with a gentry who had the leisure to study political affairs and who possessed land, which gave them a stake in their country's defense, it would be better administered than the "mechanick" commonwealth of the Dutch. "Mechanicks," Harrington explained, "till they have first feather'd their nests ... are so busied in their private concernments, that they have neither leisure to study the publick, nor

[63] Cf. *JHO*, 9–10, with Bacon, "Of the True Greatness of the Kingdom of Britain," in *WoFB*, VII 47–64 (esp. 60–61). Note also Harrington, *The Art of Lawgiving* (1659), in *WoJH*, 428.

[64] See *JHO*, 187, and Harrington, *The Prerogative of Popular Government* (1658), and *The Art of Lawgiving* (1659), in *WoJH*, 242–43, 246–47, 279, 419; then, consider Harrington, *The Art of Lawgiving* (1659), in *JHO*, 363, in light of Gen.1:28–30, 3:17–19 and *Psalm* 115:16, and see Bacon, *Novum organum*, ed. Graham Rees and Maria Wakely, II.52, in *OFB*, XI 446–47. Cf. *JHO*, 88 with 94–95.

[65] Harrington, *The Prerogative of Popular Government* (1658), in *WoJH*, 257–59, 265.

[66] Cf. *JHO*, 189, with Bacon, "Of Seditions *And* Troubles," *The Essayes or Counsels, Civill and Morall*, ed. Michael Kiernan, XV, in *OFB*, XV 47.

[67] *JHO*, 122, 124, 188–89, and Harrington, *The Art of Lawgiving* (1659), and *Political Aphorisms* (1659), in *WoJH*, 435, 485.

are safely to be trusted with it," since "a man is not faithfully imbarqued in this kind of ship, if he have no share in the freight."[68]

Even in the sphere of "*Manufactures* and *Merchandize*," where "the *Hollander* hath gotten the start of us," Harrington expected Oceana rapidly to catch up. In "the long-run," he asserted,

it will be found that a People Working upon a Forraign Commodity, doth but farm the Manufacture, and that it is entailed upon them only, where the growth of it is native: As also that it is one thing to have the Carriage of other mens Goods, and another for a man to bring his own unto the best market. Wherefore Nature having provided encouragement for these Arts in this nation above others, where [the] people growing, they of necessity must also increase, it cannot but establish them upon a far more sure and effectual foundation than that of the *Hollanders*.

Harrington's agrarian preference in no way prevented him from recognizing that "Industry" is "the nerve of a Commonwealth."[69]

Harrington's contemporaries recognized this. One critic actually complained that Oceana's agrarian law would drive covetous and ambitious men into trade and thereby cause London to grow like Amsterdam. This bothered Harrington not a whit. "[T]he more mouths there be in a city," he explained, "the more meat of necessity must be vented by the country, and so there will be more corn, more cattel and better markets" – which will strengthen the polity by "breeding more laborers, more husbandmen and richer farmers." Indeed, he added, if "[t]he country" grows "more populous, and better stock'd with cattel," there will be more "manure for the land," and it must then "proportionably increase in fruitfulness." "Hence it is," he concluded, "that ... in *Holland* there is scarce a puddle undrain'd, nor a bank of sand cast up by the sea, that is not cover'd with earth, and made fruitful by the people."[70]

It is not fortuitous that Oceana is slated to have a Council of Trade. Nor is it an accident that, in dubbing that deliberative body "*the* Vena Porta *of this Nation*," Harrington should appropriate Bacon's description of the country's merchants.[71] Though framed as an agrarian and martial commonwealth and intended to remain such, Oceana is also to be a decidedly commercial republic, emancipating the acquisitive passions and encouraging the "industry" of warriors, farmers, manufacturers, and traders alike. In James Harrington's hands, the citizen soldier so lionized by the ancient Romans and Greeks becomes a figure thoroughly bourgeois – pursuing his "trade" chiefly for the sake of the profits it brings. In sum, the English republican's "commonwealth for increase" is as Baconian as it is Machiavellian. In it, there will be an outlet for every species of "industry" so that, if "the merchant has his returns in silk or canvas, the soldier will have his return in land."[72]

---

[68] *JHO*, 119. Note Harrington, *The Prerogative of Popular Government* (1658), in *WoJH*, 227.

[69] *JHO*, 169.

[70] Harrington, *The Prerogative of Popular Government* (1658), in *WoJH*, 278–80.

[71] Cf. *JHO*, 110, with Bacon, *History of the Reign of King Henry VII*, in *WoFB*, VI 172, and "Of Empire," *The Essayes or Counsels, Civill and Morall* XIX, in *OFB*, XV 62.

[72] Harrington, *The Prerogative of Popular Government* (1658), in *WoJH*, 280.

An Immortal Commonwealth

To refute Machiavelli's claim that "it is impossible to order a perpetual republic" and to disprove Hobbes's contention that civil disorder is endemic within such regimes, Harrington sought to construct an *"immortal Commonwealth"* utterly free from every *"internall cause of Commotion."* To achieve this, he had to do more than restrict public debate, rein in the lawyers, frustrate priestcraft, quell political ambition, and emancipate economic self-interest.[73] He was, in fact, caught in a quandary. He thought it preposterous to suppose that the fear of death or even the fear of God would reconcile ordinary men with severe oppression. In one passage, he wrote, "A People when they are reduced unto misery and despair, become their own Polititians." In another, he added, "Take the bread out of the peoples mouthes, as did the *Roman Patricians*, and you are sure enough of a war."[74] In short, the only way to prevent the civil strife synonymous with the people's eruption into the political arena is to safeguard their interests. That is, however, inordinately difficult to accomplish: Harrington doubted that a monarchy or oligarchy would ever be solicitous of the interests of ordinary men, and he was painfully aware that the people can never effectively function as "their own polititians." They may be able to "feel," he writes, but they "cannot see."[75]

Where Machiavelli had distinguished between "princes" driven by the desire for dominion and the lust for more, and "the people" fearful of being dominated and intent on retaining what they have,[76] and Hobbes had intimated the like,[77] their English disciple spoke of "the natural aristocracy" and "the natural democracy." Like Hobbes, he identified the former with those among the wealthy who are the most learned, and he appears to have taken it for granted that their superior intelligence derives from the overriding passion for power, riches, knowledge, and honor instilled in them by nature and their upbringing.[78] Harrington was persuaded that initiative in government invariably falls to members of this "natural aristocracy" and that, if allowed to do so, those who have seized or been entrusted with the initiative will inevitably betray the public trust. "[A] man doth not look upon *reason* as it is *right* or *wrong* in it

---

[73] After considering Machiavelli, *Discorsi* 3.17, in *Opere*, 223, which should be read with an eye to *Discorsi* 3.1.3, 22.3, in *Opere*, 195–96, 228–29, and the material collected in Chapter 9, this volume, see *JHO*, 61, 84, 135.

[74] *JHO*, 138, 156. See also *JHO*, 129–33, and Harrington, *The Prerogative of Popular Government* (1658), in *WoJH*, 242–43.

[75] See *JHO*, 118, and Harrington, *The Art of Lawgiving* (1659), and *A System of Politics* (ca. 1661), in *WoJH*, 404, 483, 489.

[76] Cf. Machiavelli, *Discorsi* 1.5, 37, 2 Proemio, with *Il principe* Ep. Ded., 9, in *Opere*, 83–84, 119, 145–46, 257, 271–72.

[77] See Hobbes, *Elements of Law* I.xiv.3, *Philosophicall Rudiments* I.i.4, and *Leviathan* I.xiii.2–5, with "The Answer of Mr. Hobbes to Sir William Davenant's Preface Before Gondibert," in *EW*, IV 443–44, and *Leviathan* II.xxx.6, 14.

[78] Consider *JHO*, 23–25, 117–24 (esp. 119, 123), 145–46, 174–75 and Harrington, *The Prerogative of Popular Government* (1658), in *WoJH*, 215, 236–38, in light of Hobbes, *Leviathan* I.viii.13–16. See *Behemoth*, 159–60. Note that, while men may be more or less equal in their capacity to kill one another and with respect to what they call wisdom, they are by no means equal in their capacity for science: *Leviathan* I.xiii.2. See also *Elements of Law* I.x.1–5.

self," he insisted, "but as it makes for him or against him." Consequently, he added,

> unlesse you can shew such *orders* of a *Government*, as like those of *God* in *nature* shall be able to constrain this or that *creature* to shake off that *inclination* which is more peculiar unto it, and take up that which regards the *common good* or *interest*; all this is to no more end, then to perswade every man in a *popular Government*, not to carve himself of that which he desires most, but to be mannerly at the publick Table, and give the best from himself unto decency and the *common interest*.[79]

Harrington's subsequent fame stems largely from the fact that he was the first proponent of self-government to construct elaborate republican orders independent of the fundamental premise of classical republicanism that one can inculcate civic virtue and public-spiritedness through education. Mindful of what Machiavelli had called "the effectual truth of the matter," he sought to devise institutions which would not just compensate for the defects arising from man's troublesome faculty of speech but actually elicit pursuit of what Machiavelli had pointedly termed "the common benefit of each" from man's natural, ineradicable, and utterly selfish "*inclination . . .* to carve himself of that which he desires most." It was with this in mind that he considered the Florentine's controversial account of the contribution made to her greatness by the struggle between the Senate and the people of republican Rome.

Where the ancients had been obsessed with communal solidarity,[80] Harrington's Florentine mentor was fascinated by political conflict. He reveled in it, and he found virtue in the very party and class divisions that the ancients and their subsequent admirers regarded as the supreme political malady. In his *Discourses on Livy*, as we have seen,[81] he made the unprecedented assertion that it was the institutionalization of just such a conflict that accounted for the greatness of Rome and its superiority to Sparta and the other ancient polities. There are circumstances, he implied, in which certain types of political struggle can be rendered if not quite compatible with stability, then conducive to vitality and long-term prosperity, for the right sort of intestine strife gives rise to the dikes, embankments, and canals of *virtù* that enable a polity to withstand fortune's flood. Harrington thought that he could improve on the man's argument. "There is not a more noble, or usefull question in the Politicks," he wrote, "then that which is started by *Machiavil*, Whether means were to be found whereby the Enmity that was between the Senate and the people of *Rome* might have been removed."[82]

Harrington's strategy for eliminating this enmity was disarmingly simple, and it was designed to cope with the fact that in a republic established on an extended territory the gap between those who govern and those who are governed tends to be far greater than it was in Machiavelli's Florence. Even "*girles*,"

---

[79] *JHO*, 23.
[80] See Rahe, *Republics Ancient and Modern*, 55–135.
[81] See Chapters 1, 2, 3, and 5, this volume.
[82] Cf. Machiavelli, *Discorsi* 1.2–8, in *Opere*, 78–90, with *Il principe* 25, in *Opere*, 295–96; read Chapter 1, note 116, this volume; and see *JHO*, 133–39.

he remarked, know how to guarantee equity in situations where interests are opposed. "For example, two of them have a cake yet undivided, which was given between them, that each of them therefore may have that which is due: Divide, sayes one unto the other, and I will choose; or let me divide, and you shall choose: if this be but once agreed upon, it is enough: for the divident, dividing unequally loses, in regard that the other takes the better half; wherefore she divides equally, and so both have right." In much the same fashion, Harrington contended, "the whole *Mystery* of a *Common-wealth* . . . lyes only in *dividing and choosing*." One need only assign the right of "*debate*" to "the natural aristocracy" while reserving the right to determine the "result" to "the natural democracy."[83]

To finesse the opposition of interests separating the many from the few, Harrington proposed the establishment of a bicameral parliament elected by the people by means of the Venetian ballot, with one house drawn exclusively from the well-to-do and the other predominantly from those with lesser means. Given the natural propensity of mankind to defer to their betters, the handful of men elected to the Senate would inevitably be representative of the nation's "natural aristocracy" – the only group endowed with the education and the leisure for reflection that is prerequisite to political prudence. If allowed to rule on their own, these men would undoubtedly rule in their own interest. There were, however, ways to prevent them from abusing their trust. Harrington was persuaded that "*the many cannot be otherwise represented in a state of liberty, than by so many, and so qualify'd, as may within the compass of that number and nature imbrace the interest of the whole people.*" But he did not doubt that it was possible, in an agrarian commonwealth, to constitute a sizable assembly, elected from constituencies more or less equally populous, "such as can imbibe or contract no other interest than that only of the whole people." To render a Senate drawn from the nation's "natural aristocracy" useful to that commonwealth, one need only empower such a popular assembly with the right to reject or accept by secret ballot whatever this Senate proposes. For, if checked in this fashion, an aristocratic house composed of temporary officeholders would have reason to present no measures but those which, in its wisdom, it deemed best suited to the long-term, public good.[84] Oceana's "natural aristocracy" is to be a modern aristocracy of service; in contrast with the martial aristocracies and urban patriciates of the classical and medieval periods, it is never to rule of right and in its own name.

In all of this, there is evident a popular bias that might, at first glance, seem incompatible with impartial rule. The "natural aristocracy" is not only checked by the many; it is elected by and, in a sense, submerged in the many.[85] If Oceana

[83] *JHO*, 23–25, 115–17, 142–44, and Harrington, *The Prerogative of Popular Government* (1658), in *WoJH*, 235–38.

[84] See *JHO*, 80–81, 115–26, 142–44, and Harrington, *The Prerogative of Popular Government* (1658), *The Art of Lawgiving* (1659), *Political Aphorisms* (1659), and *A Discourse upon this Saying* . . . (1659), in *WoJH*, 215, 236–38, 246–47, 403, 418–19, 487, 570.

[85] See Harrington, *The Prerogative of Popular Government* (1658), in *WoJH*, 243.

eludes the dangers thought by the ancients to be attendant on purely popular government, it is chiefly because "the natural democracy" is instinctively impartial – at least, when liberated from priestcraft, cured of the ambition to which public debate gives rise, and encouraged by the secrecy of the ballot to ignore questions of principle and deliberate in private concerning material interest. In reaching this conclusion, Harrington would appear once again to have had Athens in mind. By ancient standards, that city possessed a remarkably tolerant regime. In fact, it was so tolerant that, in the eyes of the ancient philosophers, democracy hardly qualified as a regime at all. According to one figure in Thucydides, Athens provided "to all an unregulated power over the conduct of life." Democracy confers on the citizens, so Aristotle claims, "the license to do whatever one wants." Plato compared it with "a many-colored cloak decorated in every hue" because it was "decorated with every disposition" and afforded a welcome "to all sorts of human beings."[86]

To Harrington, unconcerned as he was with the fostering of civic virtue, it mattered little that the ancients thought democracy deficient in the ethos of reverence and friendship required by republican government. He was, in fact, heartened by the prosaic aspirations and narrow, paltry concerns that guide democratic man: after all, as Aristotle had observed, the only thing that ordinary farming people ask is that they not be robbed or prevented from earning their own way. Where such men advocate a redistribution of property, it is solely because they have been denied scope for their own industry: "Men that have equall possessions," Harrington notes, "and the same security of their estates and of their liberties that you have, have the same cause with you to defend." Moreover, given the bright prospects for agricultural improvement, where property is secure and widely distributed, no one willing to work need be in want. This last point needs particular emphasis, for it explains why "the whole spirit of the people, even as to matter of government" is summed up for Harrington in the fact that, even when offended, ordinary human beings are inclined to shrug their shoulders and mutter, "*What care I for him? I can live without him.*"[87] It is the general indifference of most men and the willingness of those not in desperate straits to mind their own business and to live and let live that makes possible a nonpartisan, impartial "*Empire of Lawes* and not of *Men*" indistinguishable from "the interest" and therefore the "will" of the people as a whole.[88]

[86] Thuc. 7.69.2; Arist. *Pol.* 1310a28–34, 1317b10–14; Pl. *Resp.* 8.557a–558a. See, in context, Thuc. 2.37.2; Arist. *Pol.* 1280a5, 1281a6, 1291b34–35; *Rh.* 1366a4. See also R. G. Mulgan, "Aristotle and the Democratic Conception of Freedom," *Auckland Classical Essays Presented to E. M. Blaiklock*, ed. B. F. Harris (Oxford, UK: Oxford University Press, 1970), 95–111.

[87] See JHO, 55, 156, and Harrington, *The Prerogative of Popular Government* (1658), *A System of Politics* (ca. 1661), and *A Parallel of the Spirit of the People* (1659), in WoJH, 246–47, 471, 580, and cf. Arist. *Pol.* 1280a7–1287b35 (esp. 1281a11–38), 1318a11–26 (esp. 17–26) with 1292b25–30, 1297b6–8, 1318b6–1319a39, and see 1295a25–1296b1.

[88] See JHO, 12, 21–23, 29, 34, 59, 141–42, and Harrington, *The Prerogative of Popular Government* (1658), *The Art of Lawgiving* (1659), *A System of Politics* (ca. 1661), *The Stumbling-Block of Disobedience and Rebellion* (1658), *Politicaster* (1659), and *A Discourse upon this Saying...* (1659), in WoJH, 224–26, 241–44, 362, 418–19, 469, 539, 553, 570–72.

The Empire of the World

James Harrington shared Marchamont Nedham's conviction that Machiavelli had not gone far enough and that the ancients had been right when they presumed that in a republic the citizens must be soldiers and all the soldiers citizens so that citizenship and the bearing of arms should be inextricably linked.[89] In arguing for such a policy, however, he was no more concerned with encouraging political participation as such than Nedham had been. Like Machiavelli, both were persuaded that, to be viable, a polity must rely on its own arms, and both were convinced as well that the sword and sovereignty go hand in hand. In Harrington's judgment, moreover, a republic prudently administered as an empire of laws, not of men – if equipped with a well-trained citizen militia – would be steady at home and formidable abroad. He was even willing to believe that, by employing the techniques of Roman statecraft, Oceana would be able to give "law unto the Sea," seize "the Empire of the World," and spread free institutions everywhere. The English republican was evidently among those who thought the execution of Charles I and the establishment of the free state a harbinger of world revolution, and he looked forward to the event with considerable relish.[90]

In forecasting the epic struggle to come, Harrington was mindful of the religious sensibilities of the audience to which his book was immediately addressed, for he knew that "[i]t hath been a Maxime with Legislators, not to give Checks unto the present Superstition, but to make the best use of it, as that which is alwayes the most powerfull with the People."[91] Not surprisingly, then, he took considerable care, in much the same fashion as Hobbes had in *Leviathan*,[92] to find biblical sanction for his new modes and orders.[93] When he prophesied that Oceana might achieve "the Empire of the World," he was prepared to describe it as "a Magistrate of God unto mankinde, for the vindication of common right, and the law of Nature," and he was not above suggesting that the series of accidents which had produced a balance of property in England favorable to republicanism was a consequence of divine providence.[94] But it would be a mistake to think that he ever seriously supposed that the prospects of his republic depended at all on divine grace. His argument is, in fact, an example of enlightened *kalām*: it is specifically aimed at demonstrating the extraordinary scope open to the natural prudence of man.[95]

---

[89] Consider *JHO*, 158–98, and see Chapter 5, this volume.

[90] *JHO*, 11, 187–98.

[91] *JHO*, 207.

[92] See Hobbes, *Leviathan* III.xxxii–xliii.

[93] See *JHO*, 28, 187–98, and Harrington, *The Prerogative of Popular Government* (1658), *The Art of Lawgiving* (1659), and *Piano Piano* (1657), in *WoJH*, 239–41, 303–57, 361, 372–401, 517–33.

[94] In general, the balance of property is attributed to providence: *JHO*, 187, and Harrington, *The Art of Lawgiving* (1659), and *The Stumbling-Block of Disobedience and Rebellion* (1658), in *WoJH*, 362, 364, 539.

[95] Cf. Pocock, "Historical Introduction," 70–99, and Mark Goldie, "The Civil Religion of James Harrington," in *The Languages of Political Theory in Early-Modern Europe*, ed. Anthony Pagden (Cambridge, UK: Cambridge University Press, 1987), 197–222, with J. C. Davis, "Pocock's

Harrington's contemporaries were not fooled by his appeal to providence: like the other admirers of Machiavelli's republican teaching known to them, he was a wit notorious for his irreverence and impiety. He lived in an age in which "wit and gallantry" were thought to be synonymous with "atheism,"[96] and by ostentatiously embracing the former, he opened himself up to the latter charge.[97] The presbyterian divine Richard Baxter even thought Harrington and his particular friend Henry Neville pagans of a sort. They "seeme by the contrivance," he wrote, "to be of the old religion, I meane that of old Rome, though something as if they were Christians be intersperst."[98] For this suspicion, which was widely shared, Baxter had excellent grounds, as we have seen.[99] It was not long before Baxter penned these words that Neville was overheard remarking in the presence of three clergymen that, as reading, he preferred Cicero to the Bible,[100] and men at the time recalled his having remarked some ten years before that "nothing could be said for the Scripture which could not be said for the Alcoran."[101] When contemporaries, such as the Anglican divine Gilbert Burnet, subsequently listed Harrington and Neville, along with Henry Marten, John Wildman, and Algernon Sidney, among "those who pretended to little or no religion, and acted only upon the principles of civil liberty,"[102] they were no doubt much closer to the truth than Baxter had been. Though they sometimes acted in concert, there was an immense chasm separating godly

Harrington: Grace, Nature and Art in the Classical Republicanism of James Harrington," *Historical Journal* 24:3 (September 1981): 683–97, and see Blitzer, *An Immortal Commonwealth*, 165–72, 278–83, and Gary Remer, "After Machiavelli and Hobbes: James Harrington's Commonwealth of Israel," *Hebraic Political Studies* 1 (Summer 2006): 440–61. As Pocock ("Historical Introduction," 17) recognizes, the only alternative to his own view is to suppose Harrington's bold project a self-consciously impious assertion of man's complete mastery of affairs.

[96] Consider the statements of Sir George McKenzie, Bishop Stillingfleet, and Joseph Glanville cited in Preserved Smith, *A History of Modern Culture* (Gloucester, MA: Peter Smith, 1957), I 400–401.

[97] See *JHO*, 220–21.

[98] (DWL) *Baxter Treatises*, xxii, f.69, as cited by William M. Lamont, *Richard Baxter and the Millennium* (London: Croom Helm, 1979), 189, who notes that the passage was prudently omitted from *Reliquiae Baxterianae: or, Mr. Richard Baxter's Narrative of the Most Memorable Passages of his Life and Times*, ed. Matthew Sylvester (London: T. Parkhurst, J. Robinson, J. Lawrence, and J. Dunton, 1696), I 118. Pocock, "Introduction," xxiii (esp. n. 52), is quite right in supposing that Lamont errs in thinking that Baxter had Roman Catholicism in mind.

[99] See Chapter 6, this volume.

[100] Consider the entry under 16 February 1658/1659, in *Diary of Thomas Burton, Esq., Member in the Parliaments of Oliver and Richard Cromwell from 1656 to 1659*, ed. John Towill Rutt (London: Henry Colburn, 1828), III 296–305, in light of the Letter from M. de Bordeaux to Cardinal Mazarin on 27 February 1659, in François Pierre Guillaume Guizot, *Histoire du protectorat de Richard Cromwell et du rétablissement des Stuart (1658–1660)*, second edition (Paris: Didier, 1856), I 309–14 (at 311).

[101] See "Notes on Report from Sir Arthur Slingsby to Edward Hyde," 25 February 1659, in *Calendar of the Clarendon State Papers*, ed. H. O. Coxe et al. (Oxford, UK: Clarendon Press, 1872–1970), IV 152.

[102] See Gilbert Burnet, *The History of My Own Time*, ed. Osmund Airy (Oxford, UK: Clarendon Press 1897–1900), I 120. In Wildman's case, there is concrete evidence confirming Burnet's claim: see *The Clarke Papers: Selections from the Papers of William Clarke*, ed. C. H. Firth (London: Camden Society, 1891–1901), II 120–21. On his quite colorful career, see Maurice Ashley, *John Wildman, Plotter and Postmaster: A Study of the English Republican Movement in the Seventeenth Century* (New Haven, CT: Yale University Press, 1947).

republicans, such as Sir Henry Vane, Edmund Ludlow, and Robert Overton, from their secular counterparts – the disciples of Machiavel.[103]

Of course, Harrington, though bold, is not as impudent as Machiavelli. Nowhere does he intimate that God and fortune are two words for the same thing. Nowhere does he repeat the Florentine's contention that fortune is a woman and can therefore be held down, if thrashed and struck hard. Nowhere does he compare her with a river that is sometimes tempestuous and capable of sweeping all before it and sometimes quiet so that one can make provision against its turbulence and regulate its flow by building dikes, embankments, and canals. Nowhere does he even cite the penultimate chapter of *The Prince*. But we can rest assured that this enthusiastic admirer of "the onely Polititian of later Ages" has read and assimilated the pertinent passages of that remarkable book, for the "superstructures" that he is so eager to construct are an attempt to improve on the ancient public works analyzed so brilliantly by the Florentine sage.

Where Machiavelli had insisted on the necessity for a frequent return to first principles, Harrington contends that "a Common-wealth that is rightly instituted" will never require such a "reduction unto her principles." Thus, if the English republican desires above all else "to be familiarly understood," it is because he shares Hobbes' conviction that "the whole mystery of government rightly instituted" is "as demonstrable and certain" and can be made "as obvious and facile, even to vulgar apprehensions, as the meanest of vulgar arts." It is on this premise that he echoes the philosopher of Malmesbury's bold claim that political "architecture" can accomplish what Plato deemed impossible and, by reconciling philosophy with power, render a commonwealth with regard to "internal causes...as immortal, or longlived, as the World."[104]

---

[103] To get a sense of the gap, one should compare the description of Sir Henry Vane to which Edmund Ludlow subscribed with that provided by Algernon Sidney: cf. Ludlow, *A Voyce from the Watch Tower: Part Five: 1660–1662*, ed. A. B. Worden (London: Royal Historical Society, 1978), 310–15, with "The Character of Sir Henry Vane by Algernon Sidney," in Violet Anne Rowe, *Sir Henry Vane the Younger: A Study in Political and Administrative History* (London: Athlone Press, 1970), 275–83. In the latter, Vane's piety is clothed in garb more civic than Christian. On Ludlow and Overton, see R. Howell, "Edmund Ludlow (c. 1617–1692)," and J. Frank McGregor, "Robert Overton (c. 1609–c. 1672)," in *Biographical Dictionary of British Radicals in the Seventeenth Century*, ed. Richard L. Greaves and Robert Zaller (Brighton, UK: Harvester Press, 1982–1984), II 204–5, 279–81, which should be read in conjuction with the section of Ludlow's memoirs edited by Blair Worden and cited in this note; with Worden, *Roundhead Reputations: The English Civil Wars and the Passions of Posterity* (London: Allen Lane, 2001), 21–121; with John H. F. Hughes, "The Commonwealthmen Divided: Edmund Ludlowe, Sir Henry Vane and the Good Old Cause, 1653–1659," *The Seventeenth Century* 5:1 (Spring 1990): 55–70; and with Barbara Taft, "'They that pursew perfaction on earth...': The Political Progress of Robert Overton," in *Soldiers, Writers and Statesmen of the English Revolution*, ed. Ian Gentles, John Morrill, and Blair Worden (Cambridge, UK: Cambridge University Press, 1998), 286–303. Note also David Norbrook, "'This Blushinge Tribute of a Borrowed Muse': Robert Overton and his Overturning of the Poetic Canon," *English Manuscript Studies, 1100–1700*, ed. Peter Beal and Jeremy Griffiths 4 (1993): 220–66. As the trajectories of Vane, Ludlow, and Overton make clear, the godly republicans were, nonetheless, quite often at odds.

[104] Note Machiavelli, *Discorsi* 3.1, 3, 49 and *Il principe* 25, in *Opere*, 195–99, 253–54, 295–96, and cf. *JHO*, 20–21, 34–35, 185–90, 207; Harrington, *Valerius and Publicola* (1659), in *WoJH*, 445; and *An Essay upon Two of Virgil's Eclogues and Two Books of his Aeneis* (1658), in *PWoJH*, 580–81, with Hobbes, *De homine* X.5, in *LW*, II 93–94, and Hobbes, *Six Lessons*

Harrington was perfectly cognizant of the impious character of this extravagant assertion concerning the power and scope of human prudence; and, in one crucial passage, he even draws attention to the fact. In concluding *The Commonwealth of Oceana*, he cites an inscription which, he says, was engraved on the eastern side of the pedestal supporting the equestrian statute set up in the piazza of the Pantheon in the Lord Archon's honor. The last two lines describe the man as one "*Who, setting the Kingdomes of the* Earth *at Liberty, Tooke the Kingdome of the* Heav'ns *by Violence.*" In *The Advancement of Learning*, Bacon had promised men of gigantine ambition "the true *Theomachy.*" Under his Promethean leadership, he asserted, Englishmen can become Titans with the power to seize Olympus and establish what the great statesman of science had once revealingly called "the Kingdom *of Man.*" Harrington asserted the like.[105]

It is not difficult to see why James Harrington should join Machiavelli, Bacon, and Hobbes in thinking of himself as a new Columbus.[106] All four had devoted themselves to charting a new continent in thought. Though not of the same stature as the others, Harrington was, in fact, the first to apply the institutional analysis of politics pioneered by Machiavelli and the new political science of Hobbes to the task of constructing a viable, modern, constitutional republican order. If his audacious plan for an "immortal commonwealth" exercised considerable influence on later practitioners of what Harrington called "political architecture,"[107] it was no doubt largely because of the ingenious manner in which Oceana employed modern representative institutions to substitute the indirect, morally indifferent, and therefore impartial rule of a detached and distant government firmly based on popular consent and shrewdly administered by the nation's "natural aristocracy" for the direct, morally concerned, and therefore partisan rule that had characterized all previously existing polities – monarchies and republics alike.[108]

to the Professors of the Mathematics Ep. Ded., in *EW*, VII 184, and see *Leviathan* II.xxix.1–2, xxx.5, xxxi.41, with Pl. *Resp.* 5.473d.

[105] Cf. *JHO*, 225–26 with *Novum organum* II.Title, in *OFB*, XI 200–201, and *The Advancement of Learning* II.xxi.1, in *OFB*, IV 139–40, in *WoFB*, I 157, III 424–25. In this spirit, Harrington hints at the possibility that "our Religion" may not be "any thing else but a vain boast, scratching and defacing humane nature or reason." See *JHO*, 198.

[106] Cf. *JHO*, 197, and Harrington, *The Prerogative of Popular Government* (1658), in *WoJH*, 219, with Machiavelli, *Discorsi* I Proemio, in *Opere*, 76; Bacon, *Novum organum* I.92, in *OFB*, XI 148–51; and *The Complete Works in Verse and Prose of Abraham Cowley*, ed. Alexander B. Grosart (New York: AMS Press, 1967), II 19.

[107] Harrington, *The Art of Lawgiving* (1659), in *WoJH*, 367. In one passage, he speaks of "political anatomy": *The Art of Lawgiving* (1659), in *WoJH*, 402–3.

[108] Harrington should be read in light of Harvey C. Mansfield, "Modern and Medieval Representation," in *Representation*, ed. J. R. Pennock and G. Chapman, *Nomos* 11 (1968): 55–82, and "Hobbes and the Science of Indirect Government," *American Political Science Review* 65:1 (March 1971): 97–110.

Epilogue

After the Fall

Oliver Cromwell died on 3 September 1658. In one respect, his passing was exceedingly well timed: like the calling of the first Protectorate Parliament, it coincided with the anniversary of his astonishing victories at Dunbar and Worcester. In all other regards, however, the Lord Protector's departure from the world could not have been less opportune. To his son Richard, whom on his deathbed he had nominated as his successor, to the Council of State, to his erstwhile comrades in the New Model Army, and to all who had thrown in their lot with the English Commonwealth he left a terrible mess.[1]

Earlier there had been, so many think, a way out. Had Cromwell turned his back on his own past, we are sometimes told – had he purged the officer corps of the New Model Army, removed from active service all those inclined to think that their sacrifices and God-given victories on the field of the sword sanctioned military interference in the political realm, and then reconfigured the army as a professional force, as Thomas Hobbes upon his return to England no doubt hoped he would[2] – he could have accepted the crown offered him by the Second Protectorate Parliament in 1657, and then he might have achieved the settlement that in the event eluded him. By this expedient, he might even have given his hapless elder son a fighting chance. Englishmen could much more easily stomach a new dynasty than a new regime. After all, they had done so on more than one occasion in the past.

This is, of course, a counter-factual argument, and, as such, it is subject to challenge, but it has considerable force, nonetheless, and it may, in substance, be correct. Events did not, however, take such a course. Oliver Cromwell had proven to be quite flexible, and he had frequently bowed to necessity, but, despite the suspicions directed his way, he was not a Machiavel. When he told his "murmuring soldiers" that he "sought not himself," that he sought only "to

---

[1] For the tangled course of events, see C. H. Firth, *The Last Years of the Protectorate, 1656–1658* (New York: Russell & Russell, 1964), and Godfrey Davies, *The Restoration of Charles II, 1658–1660* (San Marino, CA: Huntington Library, 1955). See also Austin H. Woolrych, "The Good Old Cause and the Fall of the Protectorate," *Cambridge Historical Journal* 13:2 (1957): 133–61, and "Historical Introduction (1659–1660)," in *CPW*, VII 1–228; and Ronald Hutton, *The Restoration: A Political and Religious History of England and Wales, 1659–1667* (Oxford, UK: Clarendon Press, 1985), 3–123. For a brief summary account, see Austin Woolrych, *Britain in Revolution, 1625–1660* (Oxford, UK: Oxford University Press, 2002), 707–79.

[2] See Jeffrey R. Collins, *The Allegiance of Thomas Hobbes* (Oxford, UK: Oxford University Press, 2005).

make good the cause," he spoke the truth. Though capable of decisive action, he was not the man to turn his back on his friends, and he balked at the prospect of becoming king. Such an achievement would have been for him the ultimate humiliation.

So Cromwell left it to his son, his counselors, his officers, and to those otherwise active in Protectorate politics to sort things out themselves, and this, of course, they could not do. In theory, Richard Cromwell had the initiative, but he lacked the requisite moral authority. He had not fought in the civil wars, he was deficient in *gravitas*, he did not possess his father's genius – and in the shadows there was no one else capable of seizing the occasion. When the original Lord Protector passed from the scene, he left behind an empty stage.

Moreover, though the officers of the New Model Army pledged their allegiance to their former commander's son, they did so in such a way as to indicate their adherence as well to what they termed – ominously, in language coined in 1656 by the elder Cromwell's enemies – "that good old Cause." Moreover, they did not hesitate to remind the son that his father had "reckoned the choicest Saints his chiefest Worthies." Nor were they reluctant to admonish the new Lord Protector to keep up the army "under the Command of such Officers as are of honest and godly Principles." In the same spirit, they also urged that "Vacancies" in his "Council, and other Places of Public Trust, be, from Time to Time, supplied and filled up with Men of known Godliness and sober Principles," and they petitioned for a reformation of manners and for the ejection from their livings of "scandalous, ignorant, and insufficient Ministers."[3]

In short, at the very outset of Richard Cromwell's reign, the handwriting was already on the wall. Even at this point, it was utterly predictable that, when the new Lord Protector summoned his first Parliament, Sir Henry Vane, Sir Arthur Haselrig, Thomas Scot, Richard Salwey, Edmund Ludlow, and their former colleagues in the Rump Parliament would sense his weakness, once again rally their forces, and seek allies among the Fifth Monarchists, as they had in 1656; and it was only to be expected that, in the absence of a principled argument on behalf of the Protectorate, the mid-level officers in the army should drift in their direction. They had revered Oliver Cromwell as a soldier and as a man, and to him they had been loyal, but they had never been fully comfortable with the monarchical direction that affairs had taken after the dissolution of the Nominated Parliament.

Nor should it seem odd that Lieutenant General Charles Fleetwood, Richard Cromwell's lukewarm brother-in-law; Major General John Desborough, who was married to Oliver Cromwell's sister; and the other army grandees who formed the so-called Wallingford House Party should fail to bring their junior colleagues to heel. They were prepared to acquiesce in the wishes of their one-time commander, but they felt no particular attachment to the man they called, among themselves, "the young gentleman." Moreover, in standing back and

---

[3] The document is reprinted in *The Parliamentary or Constitutional History of England: From the Earliest Times to the Restoration of Charles II*, second edition (London: J. and R. Tonson et al., 1761–1763), XXI 232–37 (esp. 233–35). For a discussion of its significance, see Davies *The Restoration of Charles II*, 8–10.

in letting developments within the army unfold, they were merely acting in the manner that Oliver Cromwell and Henry Ireton had marked out for them ten years before. The son they treated in the offhand and mildly disrespectful manner in which his father had once treated the Long Parliament. Their guiding passion was indifference tinged, perhaps, with envy, not antipathy. On 23 November 1658, when John Milton, Marchamont Nedham, Andrew Marvell, and John Dryden met at Somerset House in the Strand to walk alongside one another to Westminster Abbey in the funeral march staged by the Protectorate in Oliver Cromwell's honor,[4] they must have wondered just how long his successor would last. Others, less astute than they, did so, we can be sure.

In the event, Richard Cromwell's tenure was brief. For understandable reasons, his Parliament agitated for civilian control of the military. For reasons no less comprehensible, his officers were unwilling to acquiesce in anything of the sort. And, in April 1659, what the presbyterian leader William Prynne accurately described as a "confederated *Triumvirat* of *Republicans, Sectaries,* and *Souldiers*" forced the Lord Protector to dissolve Parliament and, without adequately pondering the consequences, brought the Protectorate to a close.[5] Then – to the delight of Vane, Haselrig, Scot, Ludlow, and the like, and to the satisfaction of Nedham and Milton as well[6] – the army recalled the Rump. The "Good Old Cause" had been given a second chance.

A second chance it had, indeed, been given – but not a second wind. When the surviving Rumpers gathered at Westminster on 6 May, they found themselves face-to-face with the constitutional dilemmas that they had been unable to resolve in the first four years following the execution of Charles I. Although they gave themselves only a year to work out the details, although they underlined their resolve by voting to schedule their own dissolution at the end of that term, as the weeks passed, everyone could see that they had made little, if any, headway in framing a settlement. They had never enjoyed a consensus in this matter, and it did not help that, in their earlier sitting, they had squandered the limited good will that in certain quarters they had once enjoyed. They were regarded with hatred and contempt by the nation, and their awareness of this fact contributed in no small measure to their paralysis. They were right back where they had been in April 1653. They were pledged to hold free elections that would seal their doom.

Mindful of the difficulties that the Rumpers faced and even more mindful of its own interests, the army at the outset pressed for the establishment of a second house modeled on the one that had come into existence under the Protectorate.

---

[4] See "Authorized to Have Mourning for Cromwell's Funeral," 7 September 1658, and "Participates in Funeral Procession of Cromwell," 23 November 1658, in *The Life Records of John Milton*, ed. J. Milton French (New Brunswick, NJ: Rutgers University Press, 1949–1958), IV 235–36, 244–45.

[5] See William Prynne, *The Republicans and Others' Spurious Good Old Cause, Briefly and Truly Anatomized* (S. l.: s.n., 1659), 1.

[6] If the two collaborated in writing the anonymous tract *A Publick Plea Opposed to a Private Proposal*, as Blair Worden suspects, they were quick to rally to the new regime: see Worden, *Literature and Politics in Cromwellian England: John Milton, Andrew Marvell, Marchamont Nedham* (Oxford, UK: Oxford University Press, 2007), 42–44, 326–57.

In the weeks that followed Richard Cromwell's fall, James Harrington published pamphlet after pamphlet, defending the scheme outlined within *Oceana*, and within the House, his old friend Henry Neville pressed the argument. That Harrington's thinking had an impact is suggested by the fact that, in May, Sir Henry Vane thought it appropriate to respond by way of an open letter addressed to Harrington himself, in which he defended the notion that, in the Commonwealth, there should, indeed, be a second house, but one more like that which the army officers had in mind. From his perspective, the fundamental problem was posed by "the depraved, corrupted, and self-interested will of man," which prevents "the People, being once left to its own free motion," from espousing "their true publick interest." In the Scriptures, he had read that *"it is not in man to order his own steps."* Even "at his best," he contended, fallen man "stands in need of the ballancing and ruling motion of Gods Spirit to keep him stedfast." What is required in the current circumstances, he argued, is a "Ruling Senate" or "Council of Elders," and it should be elected either by the saints – "such as are free born, in respect of their holy and righteous principles, flowing from the birth of the Spirit of God in them" – or by the New Model Army – those "who, by their tryed good affection and faithfulness to common right and publick freedome, have deserved to be trusted with the keeping or bearing their own Armes in the publick defence."[7] Against such proposals, Sir Arthur Haselrig, the most influential member of the House, was no less steadfast than in the past. In consequence, the Rump once again began discussing the idea of extending its term and of filling by carefully managed recruitment the seats in the Long Parliament once occupied by those purged on 6 December 1648 by Colonel Thomas Pride.

The Rump compounded its folly in this regard by forgetting that it was, as it always had been, a creature of the army. Haltingly, ineffectually, and fatally, it initiated a program to remodel the army and the militia. Oliver Cromwell could no doubt have accomplished something of the sort, but the Rump could not. It had no mandate whatsoever. It lacked the moral authority necessary to cow the officer corps. Its maneuvers were futile and served only to antagonize its erstwhile allies. And so, in mid-October 1659, not five months after it had recalled the Rump, the army intervened, as it had so frequently in the previous twelve years, and it sent the members of that body packing a second time.

Chaos followed. Within the army there was no consensus of any sort, and those with the initiative – John Lambert and the erstwhile members of the Wallingford House Party – had not the slightest idea what to do next. For a time, the Rump's Council of State continued to meet. Then, an ad hoc Committee of Safety was formed. Constitutional proposals were floated, and, at Miles Coffee House in the New Palace Yard, James Harrington and Henry Neville began holding meetings of what they called the Rota – with luminaries such as the earl of Dorset, Samuel Pepys, John Aubrey, Andrew Marvell, William Petty, and the former Levellers John Wildman and Maximilien Petty in attendance for a

---

7 [Sir Henry Vane], *A Needful Corrective or Ballance in Popular Government, Expressed in a Letter to James Harrington, Esquire, Upon Occasion of a Late Treatise of His, and Published as Seasonable in the Present Juncture of Affaires* (S. I.: s. n., 1659), passim (esp. 6–10).

discussion of and balloting on the elements in the scheme laid out in the pages of *Oceana*. In the weeks that followed, Major General George Monck demanded that the Rump be recalled and purged his army in Scotland of elements on which he could not rely; the army in Ireland and the fleet rallied in support of his demands; supporters of the Rump managed to seize Portsmouth; Thomas Lord Fairfax, once Lord General of the New Model Army, quietly indicated to Monck that he and his neighbors in Yorkshire could be relied on; and slowly, inexorably, the authority of John Lambert and that of the Wallingford House Party dissolved. By 26 December, the Rump was in session once again.

But this time it lacked a shield capable of protecting it from public pressure, and when Monck began on 1 January 1660 a slow march from Scotland to London that had at times something of the quality of a progress, the Rump acquiesced in what it could not prevent. Moreover, when, in February, after a brief sojourn in London, Monck and a small body of troops suddenly descended on Westminster, with the secluded members of the Long Parliament in tow, the Rumpers watched helplessly, in amazement and dismay, as the men ousted in Pride's Purge appointed a new Council of State, installed Monck as commander-in-chief, made arrangements for elections on the old franchise in the old districts, and voted the immediate dissolution of the Long Parliament. By then, it was obvious to everyone that Charles Stuart would return from exile and be crowned Charles II.

Had the Restoration been an unmitigated success, it is conceivable that the thinking of Milton, Nedham, and Harrington, if not also Hobbes, would now be regarded as an historical oddity, as yet another example of reflection devoid of practical consequence. But, of course, the Restoration was anything but an unmitigated success. Within seven years, as James Harrington had predicted in conversations with his friends,[8] the Cavalier Parliament found itself at odds with the king, and the news that James, the duke of York, heir apparent to the throne, had converted to Catholicism heightened the renewed suspicion, already felt in certain quarters, that English liberty was once again imperiled. The crisis that ensued led in turn to renewed constitutional speculation – on the part of Henry Neville, Algernon Sidney, and John Wildman, who reemerged; on the part of Anthony Ashley Cooper, first earl of Shaftesbury, a member of the Nominated Parliament and of Cromwell's original Council of State, whose time had come; on the part of Milton's onetime assistant Andrew Marvell; and on the part of Thomas Hobbes's discreet admirer, John Locke, and a host of others who had come of age in the interim. Moreover, those who engaged in the pamphlet wars associated with what came to be called the Exclusion Crisis appropriated and reworked the arguments advanced by the republicans of the 1650s.[9]

By the time of the Glorious Revolution, the old republican principles – recast by the Whigs in defense of constitutional monarchy in one or another form – had

---

[8] See *ABL*, 209.

[9] See Paul A. Rahe, *Republics Ancient and Modern: Classical Republicanism and the American Revolution* (Chapel Hill: University of North Carolina Press, 1992), 426–29, 445–520, and Vickie B. Sullivan, *Machiavelli, Hobbes, and the Formation of a Liberal Republicanism in England* (New York: Cambridge University Press, 2004), 174–226.

acquired a modicum of respectability. At the time of the standing army controversy at the very end of the seventeenth century and during the period in which
Robert Walpole served as Prime Minister, leading Tories resorted to them. One
cannot make sense of *The Independent Whig* and of *Cato's Letters*, one cannot
fully comprehend the writing of Lord Bolingbroke, one cannot really understand the essays of David Hume and Montesquieu's *Spirit of Laws*, one cannot
adequately appreciate *The Federalist* or, for that matter, the writings of the
Antifederalists without situating them with regard to the republican speculation pioneered by Milton, Nedham, and Harrington and to Hobbes's attempt
to lay a new foundation for morality and politics more generally. The thinking
articulated in these eighteenth-century works is a series of variations on themes
that first became familiar in the 1650s.[10]

Moreover, the works of Milton, Nedham, Hobbes, and Harrington were
reprinted, and in the eighteenth century they were read and ruminated on. There
is, to be sure, no point in attempting to document the influence of Hobbes here.
His importance for Locke, Baruch Spinoza, Bernard Mandeville, the authors
of *Cato's Letters*, and Jean-Jacques Rousseau is obvious, and it would, in fact,
be well nigh impossible to construct a plausible history of political thought in
the seventeenth and eighteenth centuries in which he was not accorded preeminence.[11]

The importance of Milton, Nedham, and Harrington is, however, less fully
appreciated. Of course, scholars do tend to be aware that, by the early eighteenth century, *Paradise Lost* was recognized as a classic. What is less well
known is that, in 1698, John Toland republished in three volumes many of the
prose works written by Milton in both English and Latin, along with a brief
biography of their author;[12] that, in 1738, a revised and expanded edition was
published by Thomas Birch;[13] and that, in 1753, the latter brought forth yet
another edition with further revisions and additions.[14] Even less well known
is the fact that, in 1788, *Areopagitica* was translated into French, and by no
less a luminary than Honoré-Gabriel de Riquetti, comte de Mirabeau;[15] that

---

[10] This story has been told in part: see Rahe, *Republics Ancient and Modern*, 429–44, 521–782;
Sullivan, *Machiavelli, Hobbes, and the Formation of a Liberal Republicanism in England*, 227–
57; and *Machiavelli's Liberal Republican Legacy*, ed. Paul A. Rahe (New York: Cambridge
University Press, 2006), 58–278.

[11] Cf. Jonathan I. Israel, *Radical Enlightenment: Philosophy and the Making of Modernity 1650–
1750* (Oxford, UK: Oxford University Press, 2001), who tried to do so, with Noel Malcolm,
"Hobbes and the European Republic of Letters," in Malcolm, *Aspects of Hobbes* (Oxford, UK:
Clarendon Press, 2002), 457–545.

[12] See John Milton, *A Complete Collection of the Historical, Political, and Miscellaneous Works
of John Milton. To Which Is Prefix'd the Life of the Author*, [ed. John Toland] (Amsterdam:
s.n., 1698). The actual place of publication was London.

[13] See John Milton, *A Complete Collection of the Historical, Political, and Miscellaneous Works
of John Milton: With an Account of the Life and Writings of the Author*, ed. Thomas Birch
(London: A. Millar, 1738).

[14] See John Milton, *The Works of John Milton, Historical, Political, and Miscellaneous: To Which
Is Prefixed, An Account of his Life and Writings*, second edition enlarged, ed. Thomas Birch
(London: A. Millar et al., 1753).

[15] See John Milton, *Sur la Liberté de la presse, imité de l'anglois, de Milton*, tr. Honoré-Gabriel de
Riquetti, comte de Mirabeau (London, s.n., 1788).

the following year this same figure was responsible for the publication of an abridged translation of Milton's republican tract *Pro Populo Anglicano Defensio*;[16] and that in French this incendiary work was reprinted in 1791 and again in 1792.[17]

Marchamont Nedham John Toland ignored, but this did not mean that *Mercurius Politicus* was forgotten. *The Excellencie of a Free State* was eventually reprinted in London in 1767 at the instigation of the dissenting minister Richard Baron.[18] Soon thereafter, it was translated into French by Charles Geneviève Louis Auguste André Timothée, chevalier d'Eon de Beaumont, a former French diplomat then residing as an exile in London, a military hero, spy, republican sympathizer, and admirer of John Wilkes, who managed in the second half of his life to pass himself off as a woman and to persuade the entire world that in his younger days he had for more than thirty years masqueraded successfully as a man. By this notorious figure the translation was published in Amsterdam in 1774.[19] Then, as the crisis that had developed within England's colonies in North America became increasingly grave and began to stir in some quarters a renewed interest in republican forms, the edition of Baron and the translation of d'Eon de Beaumont were made available to the colonists by Thomas Hollis,[20] and in the New World Nedham's book was not just read.

[16] See John Milton, *Théorie de la royauté, d'après la doctrine de Milton: Doctrine de Milton sur la royauté, d'après l'ouvrage intitulé: Défense du peuple anglais*, tr. Jean-Baptiste Salaville (Paris: s.n., 1789). The preliminary dissertation on Milton and his works is by Honoré-Gabriel de Riquetti, comte de Mirabeau.

[17] See John Milton, *Théorie de la royauté d'après les principes de Milton: Avec sa Défense du peuple, par Mirabeau* (s.l., s.n., 1791), and John Milton, *Défense du peuple anglais, Sur le jugement et la condamnation de Charles premier, roi d'Angleterre / Par Milton, Ouvrage propre à éclairer sur la circonstance actuelle où se trouve la France. Réimprimé aux frais des administrateurs du département de la Drôme* (Valence: s.n., 1792).

[18] See Nedham, *EFS*. Note Leslie Stephen, rev. Philip Carter, "Baron, Richard (*d.* 1766)," in *Oxford Dictionary of National Biography* (Oxford, UK: Oxford University Press, 2004), which errs in stipulating a publication date of 1757.

[19] Consider Marchamont Nedham, *De l'Excellence d'un état libre*, tr. Charles Geneviève Louis Auguste André Timothée, chevalier d'Eon de Beaumont, in d'Eon de Beaumont, *Les loisirs du chevalier d'Eon de Beaumont* (Amsterdam: [s.n.], 1774), VI 137–399, in light of the attitudes betrayed in d'Eon de Beaumont, "Discours préliminaire," in ibid., I 7–36 (esp. 20–21). On his career and conduct, see Gary Kates, "The Transgendered World of the Chevalier/Chevalière d'Eon," *Journal of Modern History* 67:3 (September 1995): 558–94; Kates, *Monsieur d'Eon Is a Woman: A Tale of Political Intrigue and Sexual Masquerade* (New York: Basic Books, 1995); and Anna Clark, "The chevalier d'Eon and Wilkes: Masculinity and Politics in the Eighteenth Century," *Eighteenth-Century Studies* 32:1 (Autumn 1998): 19–48.

[20] See Caroline Robbins, *The Eighteenth-Century Commonwealthman: Studies in the Transmission, Development and Circumstance of English Liberal Thought from the Restoration of Charles II until the War with the Thirteen Colonies* (Cambridge, MA: Harvard University Press, 1961), 48–50, 259–70. In this connection, see also Caroline Robbins, "The Strenuous Whig, Thomas Hollis of Lincoln's Inn," *William and Mary Quarterly*, third series, 7:3 (July 1950): 406–53, "Library of Liberty – Assembled for Harvard College by Thomas Hollis of Lincoln's Inn," *Harvard Library Bulletin* 5:1 (Winter 1951): 5–23, 5:2 (Spring 1951), 185–96; and "Thomas Hollis in his Dorsetshire Retirement," *Harvard Library Bulletin* 23:4 (October 1975): 411–28, all reprinted in *Absolute Liberty: A Selection from the Articles and Papers of Caroline Robbins*, ed. Barbara Taft (Hamden, CT: Archon Books, 1982), 168–246, as well as P. D. Marshall, "Thomas Hollis (1720–74): The Bibliophile as Libertarian," *Bulletin of the*

It was excerpted at length, analyzed, criticized, and propagated by John Adams in the third volume of his *Defense of the Constitutions of Government of the United States of America*.[21] Finally, at the height of the French Revolution, *The Excellencie of a Free State* was once again translated into French – this time by Théophile Mandar, a leading figure in the Cordeliers Club – and in 1790 it was published in Paris in a heavily annotated edition, replete with a lengthy preface by the translator, extensive citations, and even appendices drawn from Niccolò Machiavelli, Bishop Bossuet, the baron de Montesquieu, the abbé de Mably, Jean-Jacques Rousseau, and other, lesser lights.[22] In this form, it was read and praised by no less a worthy than Marie Jean Antoine Nicolas Caritat, marquis de Condorcet.[23]

If anything, Harrington fared even better. In 1700, Toland republished *Oceana* and an almost complete collection of the pamphlets penned by Harrington.[24] An expanded edition was published in 1737, some years after Toland's death;[25] and the latter was reprinted in 1747, 1758, and 1771. The republican political architecture that Harrington devised was fundamental for the radical Whigs; and, when David Hume penned his "Idea of a Perfect Commonwealth," he took *Oceana* as his starting point.[26] Harrington's impact on American thinking in the late colonial period was also considerable, and, as one would expect, his republican argument was discussed in detail in the late 1780s by John Adams in his *Defence of the Constitutions of Government of the United States of America*.[27]

Nor was Harrington's influence restricted to the English-speaking world. In *The Spirit of Laws*, Montesquieu paid close attention to his constitutional scheme.[28] Jean-Jacques Rutledge, a native of Dunkirk of mixed French and Irish

   John Rylands University Library of Manchester 66:2 (Spring 1984): 246–63, and W. H. Bond, *Thomas Hollis of Lincoln's Inn: A Whig and his Books* (Cambridge, UK: Cambridge University Press, 1990). I have not been able to confirm Robbins's claim that in English the book was reprinted in Amsterdam in 1774.

[21] See John Adams, *A Defense of the Constitutions of Government of the United States of America* (1787–88) III.5–7, in *The Works of John Adams*, ed. Charles Francis Adams (Boston: Charles C. Little and James Brown, 1850–1856), VI 3–216.

[22] Consider Marchamont Nedham, *De la Souveraineté du peuple, et de l'excellence d'un état libre*, tr. Théophile Mandar (Paris: Chez Lavillette, 1790), in light of Rachel Hammersley, *French Revolutionaries and English Republicans: The Cordeliers Club, 1790–1794* (Woodbridge, UK: Boydell Press, 2005), 9–82.

[23] See Marie Jean Antoine Nicolas Caritat, marquis de Condorcet, *Esquisse d'un tableau historique des progrès de l'esprit humain* (Paris: Flammarion, 1988), 199–200.

[24] See James Harrington, *The Oceana of James Harrington, and his Other Works; Collected, Methodiz'd, and Review'd, With an Exact Account of his Life Prefix'd*, ed. John Toland (London: n.p., 1700).

[25] See James Harrington, *The Oceana and Other Works of James Harrington Esq; Collected, Methodiz'd, and Review'd, with an Exact Account of his Life Prefix'd, by John Toland. To Which Is Added, an Appendix, Containing All the Politcal Tracts Wrote by this Author, Omitted in Mr. Toland's Edition* (London: A. Millar, 1737).

[26] See David Hume, "Idea of Perfect Commonwealth," in Hume, *Essays Moral, Political, and Literary*, revised edition, ed. Eugene F. Miller (Indianapolis, IN: Liberty Fund, 1985), 512–29.

[27] See Adams, *A Defense of the Constitutions of Government of the United States of America* (1787–88) I.5.4, in *The Works John Adams*, IV 427–34.

[28] See Rahe, *Republics Ancient and Modern*, 440–44.

ancestry, became interested in Harrington in the 1780s, and in and after 1785, he went to considerable trouble to inform the French concerning the Englishman's arguments and life. In consequence, when the Revolution broke out, the radical democrats of the Cordeliers Club were already familiar with the Englishman's republican schemes and gave them close attention.[29] Moreover, in part because of Rutledge's success in promoting an interest in Harrington's ideas, his *Political Aphorisms* appeared in French in 1794,[30] and a volume in that language – containing *Oceana*, *Political Aphorisms*, a considerable selection from among Harrington's other pamphlets, and Toland's life of the author – was published in Paris in 1795.[31]

All of this suggests that, if one's goal is to make sense of the evolution of Whig thought, to sort out the character of the American Revolution, or even to think through the logic underpinning the great revolution that took place in France in the late 1780s and the 1790s, one would do well to begin with a survey of the astonishing wave of political speculation that took place in the 1640s and the 1650s in the course of the English revolution. And if one's aim is to make sense of the revival of republicanism in modern times, one should pay special attention, as we have here, to the manner in which John Milton, Marchamont Nedham, Thomas Hobbes, and James Harrington came to grips with the great revolution in political thought initiated in Florence more than a century before their time by the sage thought to have given the devil his moniker "Old Nick."

---

[29] See Hammersley, *French Revolutionaries and English Republicans*, 83–158.

[30] See James Harrington, *Aphorismes politiques de J. Harrington: Traduits de l'anglais, précédés d'une notice sur la vie et les ouvrages de l'auteur*, tr. Noël Aubin (Paris: Didot Jeune, 1794).

[31] See James Harrington, *Oeuvres politiques de Jacques Harrington: Contentant la république d'Océana, les aphorismes, & les autres traités du même auteur; précédées de l'histoire de sa vie, écrite par Jean Toland. Ouvrage traduit de l'anglois*, tr. Pierre François Henry (Paris: Chez Leclerc, 1795).

Index

357

Printed in Great Britain
by Amazon